John Wayne Was Here

John Wayne Was Here

The Film Locations and Favorite Places of an American Icon

ROLAND SCHAEFLI

Foreword by CHRIS MITCHUM

McFarland & Company, Inc., Publishers
Jefferson, North Carolina

Library of Congress Cataloguing-in-Publication Data

Names: Schaefli, Roland, 1968– author. | Mitchum, Christopher, 1943– writer of foreword.
Title: John Wayne was here : the film locations and favorite places of an American icon /
Roland Schaefli ; foreword by Chris Mitchum.
Description: Jefferson, North Carolina : McFarland & Company, Inc., Publishers, 2021 |
Includes bibliographical references and index.
Identifiers: LCCN 2021012752 | ISBN 9781476680064 (paperback : acid free paper) ∞
ISBN 9781476641270 (ebook)
Subjects: LCSH: Wayne, John, 1907-1979—Homes and haunts. | Wayne, John, 1907-1979—Travel. |
Motion picture actors and actresses—United States—Biography. | Motion picture locations.
Classification: LCC PN2287.W454 S33 2021 | DDC 791.4302/8092 [B]—dc23
LC record available at https://lccn.loc.gov/2021012752

British Library cataloguing data are available

ISBN (print) 978-1-4766-8006-4
ISBN (ebook) 978-1-4766-4127-0

On the cover: inset John Wayne in The Searchers, 1956 (Warner Bros./Photofest);
background John Ford Point in Monument Valley,
film location of The Searchers (Shutterstock/MisterStock)

Printed in the United States of America

McFarland & Company, Inc., Publishers
Box 611, Jefferson, North Carolina 28640
www.mcfarlandpub.com

Table of Contents

Foreword
by Chris Mitchum

Duke loved shooting on location. He loved Mexico. Put the two together and he bought a large parcel of land just outside of Durango, Mexico, where he built an entire western town, a house on top of a hill and whatever else was needed for a particular film. A beautiful piece of property with a river running through it, complete with waterfall.

I shot three Westerns with Duke: *Chisum*, *Rio Lobo* and *Big Jake*. Two of them, *Chisum* and *Big Jake*, were shot at Duke's in Durango. Actors and crew stayed at the Campo Mexico Courts. Top stars usually rented a house. On *Chisum*, I rented a house with Ron Soble and Bill Bryant. None of us were top stars. Durango was a tough town then. Most men carried a gun. I never went to sleep without hearing gunfire first. Locations create a lot of great stories.

Rio Lobo started out in Cuernavaca, Mexico. There we shot the opening scene of the derailment and robbery of a train. Howard Hawks would have me come to his hotel after work to have a couple of gin fizzes with him. From there, we went to Rio Rico, Arizona, and shot around that area. I had dinner with Duke at his 26 Bar Hereford Ranch in Eagar, Arizona. We finished shooting in Tucson using the Western street at Old Tucson.

On my first picture with Duke, *Chisum*, he invited me to his house for dinner. Richard Boone, Andy Prine and a host of others were there. After dinner, we sat having drinks, and the conversation, as usually happens with film people, led to the film industry. Someone brought up the name of an agent whom I did not know. It seemed that everyone in the room disliked him—vehemently. Ben Johnson had been quiet the entire conversation. Someone asked, "Ben, what did you think of him?" Ben, who I never heard say an unkind word about anyone, thought for a moment. "He's the most unnecessary son of a bitch I've ever met," he said.

It got to be about one a.m., and we had a six a.m. call. Duke said, "Let's go down to the Tropicana and see the girlie show." Well, when Duke invites, you go. We arrived there and tables were set up in front, next to the stage. Three bottles of Johnnie Walker Scotch were on the table. A bunch of pissed-off–looking Mexicans, all with guns, glared at us; they had been moved away from the front for the "Gringos." We sat and enjoyed the show. The lead dancer was Lolita, with sequins glued to her eyelids. I won't tell you what happened the rest of the evening, only to say I got home at 5 a.m., just in time to shower, shave and go to work. Duke looked like he'd had ten hours of sleep. Stars of yesteryear were a different breed.

I love my memories of location shoots. I'm sure you will love the magic of it all as you turn the pages and Roland shares the stories.

Chris Mitchum.

Chris Mitchum appeared in more than 60 films in 14 countries. Robert Mitchum's son, he started his film career when he appeared in three films with John Wayne. He has worked for several philanthropic organizations and has been a fundraiser for a number of charities.

Preface

"Desert's still the same"

"Look at it. It was once a wilderness. Now it's a garden." —Hallie (Vera Miles) to
Ranse (James Stewart) before the fadeout of *The Man Who Shot Liberty Valance*

Hallie understood. After they buried the mythical western hero, the tamed wilderness turned into a garden. The same is true for the filming sites of these classics. In a constantly changing world, movie locations fade away or become gardens in private backyards. The purpose of this book is to help the John Wayne pilgrim find the tracks.

John Wayne Was Here is not meant to be another meditation on his filmography. It's a biography of sorts, though.

Riding deep into Mexico: Chris Mitchum with saddle partners John and Patrick Wayne. Dog "Laddie" received the "Picture Animal Top Star of the Year" award for *Big Jake* (author's collection).

2

It tells Wayne's story through the locations where he spent most of his adult life. All his ex-wives knew: To him, the time in between two movies was just waiting to go to the next set. He always answered to the siren call of the film location. Now his followers feel the urge in a similar way: They want to go where he went, visit the same places, see the same sights. As you read this account, you may be astonished at how fond of traveling Wayne was. He had something in common with the man who beat Davy Crockett in the election: "Fella sure got around," as his character wisecracked in *The Alamo*. Wayne truly was a world traveler. This is the first attempt to name the locations of his films, the places he frequented as a private person, and provide directions to anyone wishing to make the pilgrimage. It might please the Duke to know that his loyal fans are walking in his footsteps.

"You lookin' for a sign again?"

The frontier is closed, the west is gone. But the same craving for an idealized version of it stays with us. The ultimate star of outdoor dramas has adequately filled that need. He is doing it to this day. If you take this trail beyond, you'll learn what it feels like to walk on Deb's Meadow in Colorado, where Rooster shot it out with the Ned Pepper Gang.

How it feels, after coming thousands of miles to Ireland, to cross that little bridge to Sean Thornton's home place White O'Morn. To stand in awe of the natural wonders at the Ngorongoro Crater where Sean Mercer charged the rhino. A movie location is a physical place where the real and the unreal mingle. Sometimes one might perceive that a place looks smaller in real life than on the big screen. Very often, it is surprising how a location that seems to be in the middle of nowhere in the movie is quite close to a road. But mostly, location hunters feel lucky to have found it at all. Because the dream-makers did not intend for the movie fans to follow their route. They covered their tracks well. In some ways, they're like a Nawyecky Comanche of whom Ethan Edwards said, "Like a man says he's goin' one place when he means to go just the reverse."

Back in the heyday of the Western, they didn't keep records about who had shot what and where. When Budd Boetticher scouted locations in the well-used red hills of Lone Pine, he hitchhiked a long time until he came upon a spot he was sure had never been filmed before. Then he found Raoul Walsh's mark: Walsh had beat him to this location by 25 years. And when John Wayne got enthusiastic about shooting *The War Wagon* in Los Organos, he was

On the Hawaiian set of *Big Jim McLain*: His most frequent traveling companion was this director's chair, given to him by John Ford. As a producer, John Wayne made sure his fellow actors had a chair ready to relax on location (author's collection).

How he loved his coffee on location: taking a break on the old RKO Ranch in Encino while the next setup for *Tall in the Saddle* is prepared (author's collection).

totally ignorant of the fact that the same Raoul Walsh had found this Durango location ten years back.

"Shall We Gather at the River?"

Working on a movie set is "certainly not what people expect it to be," Wayne himself declared. Looking at the actual locations helps us to understand his often-repeated remark, "I don't act—I react." How to react when there's nothing to react to? Lt. Col. Vandervoort dramatically reacts to the sight of his slaughtered men when he is actually staring at a blank wall in a Paris studio. Sean Mercer smilingly observes the bath of the baby elephants—while in reality, on the African location, he is looking the other way. And after John T. Chance hollers on the Western street of Old Tucson,

"Stumpy, I'm coming in," he'll enter the sheriff's office on Stage 4 in Burbank.

Some of the places are gone forever or unrecognizable. Even one of cinema history's most photographed locations, once named the Garden of the Gods, had to yield to civilization. Still, some things never change. Wayne said that himself, when he accompanied John Ford to Monument Valley in 1971, their last time together, for a CBS documentary: "The valley hadn't changed. It never does. But we had." We take Andy Devine's word for it, the gospel truth from *The Man Who Shot Liberty Valance*: "The desert's still the same."

With the help of this trail guide, you'll find 'em in the end. So, saddle up, we're burnin' daylight. Without further ado, *John Wayne Was Here* is now yours. But remember Tom Dunson's warning: "There'll be no quittin' along the way."

If confined to work on the studio set, Wayne would sometimes act like a lion in a cage. Note the clapperboard with the working title "Bull by the Tail." This rare production shot of *Rio Bravo* (with John Russell) also reveals that the Sheriff's Office is lacking a roof in order to light the set from above (author's collection).

Introduction

"What makes a man to wander…?"

"…and turn his back on home? Ride away…"—Theme song from *The Searchers* (1956)

In many ways, John Wayne was like the ultimate drifter, Ethan Edwards, his multifaceted character in The Searchers. *Almost to his dying day, the actor talked about his next movie. To him, making movies meant traveling. To "ride away," like in the theme song to* The Searchers. *He needed the often-harsh environment of the locations to help shape the portrayal of his outdoor men. Even after what was probably his toughest location, the Sahara Desert, which almost killed Sophia Loren and tested everybody's endurance, Wayne summed it up: "I would not have missed this location for anything."*

When asked how he prepared a shot, legendary director John Ford had a simple answer: "Walk on the set, look at the set. Look at the locations."[1] In other words: He let himself be guided by his feeling for the place. Directors have the same mantra as real estate agents: "Location, location, location!"

Most actors prefer working outdoors, being in touch with the elements. Wayne's features needed the space of the land. When he makes his entry in *Stagecoach* or *Hondo*, he is a lone figure coming out of nowhere, dramatically appearing in the scenery. The camera positions the familiar Western figure comfortably at home on the open range, framed between the Mittens in Monument Valley. When Davy Crockett arrives, wild animals jump up. Yet the landscape also isolates him. It sets him apart from the community, as it so often happens in the Ford canon. He has to duck doorways as he enters the houses of civilization. The emphasis on landscape is evident in most of his films. His fans around the world came to associate the John Wayne movies with striking outdoor shots. He would horseback into these compositions, from his very first appearance in *The Big Trail* to his very last ride, into his death valley as *The Shootist*, a man who had been "taught to survive by the wild country." This wild country is more than just a background. It is a participant. In *3 Godfathers*, it takes on Biblical proportions. The desert—in this case, the Mojave—is the garden of the Lord and it cleanses the three badmen.

"Eddie Albert was right. Air France is terrific!"

World Traveler: In this advertisement from March 1961 (shortly before production on *The Longest Day* started in France), John Wayne endorses Air France (author's collection).

In front of Jack Cardiff's famous Technicolor camera: even though the Tripoli location tested everybody's endurance and almost killed Sophia Loren, Wayne's personal conclusion was that he "would not have missed this location for anything" (author's collection).

"We're blazing a trail"

His outdoor men feel the itch to keep moving. "We can't go back," Breck Coleman tells the settlers in a howling snowstorm. "There'll be no quitting along the way," Tom Dunson warns his trail hands, "not by me and not by you." At the end of their struggle, the trailblazers would usually reach a specific location. Ole Olson just wants to go home to Stockholm, Ringo's destination is Lordsburg, and Sean Thornton's yearns for Innisfree. Yet Ireland's Innisfree is just as much a fictional place as Hawaii's Haleokaoloa. In some of Wayne's movies, the land is a memory or a dream. Like in the poem that Mississippi keeps reciting, "Where can it be, this land of El Dorado?" When Sean Thornton remembers what his mother told him about their homestead, we hear her dreamlike voice: "Don't you remember it, Seaneen, and how it was?" And Tom Dunson dreamily muses as he carves his cattle empire, "Wherever they go, they'll be on my land…. My land." However, to make those reel dreams come true, the filmmakers had to find a real place. The Empire Ranch in Arizona, then the largest in Arizona, was Howard Hawks' blueprint for the Red River D Ranch. In John Ford's *Stagecoach*, even though Monument Valley is a real place, it functions as an imaginary geography. The director felt very strongly about his favorite location, as he told *Cosmopolitan* in March 1964: "We bring the land to [the audience]. I feel at peace there. I have been all over the world but I consider this the most complete, beautiful and peaceful place on earth."

To make their magic work on the chosen locations, the filmmakers often executed their own rituals. Ford had an accordionist on set who would play different themes as the protagonists arrived. Whistling was prohibited, as Ford believed it brought bad luck. Henry Hathaway once fired an assistant just for humming because "this is not a goddamn holiday camp."[2] When John Wayne directed for the first time, he had a priest bless his *Alamo* set.

"We'll find her in the end"

Mark Rydell, director of *The Cowboys*, liked to mention that some of the fun of it was to find the locations. During pre-production on *Rooster Cogburn*, producer Hal Wallis had something very essential to say about picking the right sites: "I have my production manager out now looking

Wearing his "lucky hat": On the first day of shooting, John Wayne had a priest bless his *Alamo* set for good luck (author's collection).

for locations. He was in Arkansas last week and is in Georgia today. He's coming back here and then he's going up to Oregon and Washington." Wallis' location scout took photos of the sites that might fit the action. They needed rapids and mountains; therefore, Wallis said, "We'll probably be

shooting in Oregon or Washington. As a general rule, it's far better to use actual locations because they give a sense of reality to a picture." Wallis also knew about the limitations of the actual location: "In some cases, it isn't possible. You travel with an army—any number of trucks, station wagons, cars, 80 to 100 people on a crew. You have to transport them, you have to house them, and it's a very expensive operation."[3]

Maureen O'Hara was very strict in setting the record straight about Lord Killanin's participation in scouting the *Quiet Man* locations, which have since become places of pilgrimage, a deep-rooted attachment to the Irish cultural heritage. Killanin might have suggested, she said, but Ford chose all locations. Communication in location work isn't always easy. When director Burt Kennedy went south to pick the locations for *The Train Robbers*, they had to build a train depot, some tracks, a barn, a water tower, a hotel and a cantina. Back at the studio, the art director drew the layout on a piece of paper to get Wayne's blessing on how they wanted to build the set. He even drew little bumps on the paper to indicate where the mountains in the background were. Wayne took one look at the sheet and declared, "The mountains are too close to the set."[4]

Lack of Air

On the set of *The Cowboys*: He was able to stay patient while the crew prepared the next setup because he knew everybody's job and how long it could take to do it right (author's collection).

Wayne had developed a sense of how the location influenced good storytelling. "Get it out of doors, let some fresh air and sunlight into the story. Give the cameraman a chance to photograph something besides walls and doors and tea tables. Don't let your story expire for lack of air."[5] Some of his outdoor dramas were flawed by obvious studio shots. On the enormous *Tycoon* set on an RKO stage, a *Chicago Tribune* reporter wanted to know why the studio, instead of building this set including a giant stretch of canvas sky, didn't just shoot the scene in Lone Pine. "That," said Wayne, "I cannot answer. It would have been, perhaps, just as cheap, maybe cheaper. But I suppose the producer had his reasons for keeping the picture on the home lot." Wayne then gave the questioner a lecture on shooting on location vs.

"Don't let your story expire for lack of air": Working in the confined spaces of the RKO Studio, playing a love scene with Laraine Day, observed by director Richard Wallace and the director of photography, W. Howard Greene (Museum of Western Film History in Lone Pine).

in the studio: "Using natural backgrounds involves a lot of things. Unless the cameraman and director know how to get the upper value from them, they may prove not only ineffective but also dangerous. It often happens, you know, that backgrounds, if they are too beautiful or majestic, steal the show from the actors."[6] When television had come to stay, Wayne knew that studio sets would no longer do. The audience expected movies to be as big as the land itself.

"The John Wayne thing"

"That town down there, this wonderful old mission," Wayne said as he showed a TV crew around his Alamo set in Texas, "well, we know we've got them pretty close to right. We took the measurements from the old and original drawings and plans. But the men who fought here? How do you measure men…?" He knew the importance of the right location. It took him 14 years to find the place to put his Alamo. But how do you measure men? He started to work on "this John Wayne thing," as he once called his creation, first unconsciously, during the early sagebrush dramas. Even their titles made a direct connection to the land: *The Man from Utah, Somewhere in Sonora, 'Neath Arizona Skies.* "I

knew I was no actor and I went to work on the Wayne thing. I figured I needed a gimmick so I dreamed up the drawl, the squint, and a way of moving meant to suggest that I wasn't looking for trouble but would just as soon throw a bottle at your head as not."[7] The Wayne thing certainly worked for him. Years later, he drew a positive balance: "I play John Wayne in every part regardless of the character, and I've been doing okay, haven't I?"[8]

He learned how to talk low, talk slow, and not talk too much. He learned how to walk like John Wayne. He convincingly played the country boy to the hilt. As early as *Idol of the Crowds* in 1937, he refuses a lucrative offer from the big city: "You see, I was born here. Lived here all my life, and I like it. New York, well, it's too big, too many people." Even when in love, all that outdoor men could talk about was their plot of land. In *Stagecoach*, when Ringo asks Dallas to marry him, he tries to endear her to his ranch with "trees, grass, water…" One year later, in *Dark Command*, he tries to win Mary's heart with the same kind of talk: "Don't know what lovely country really is 'til you've seen Texas … in the springtime." In *The Alamo*, Davy Crockett leads the woman he loves under "one beautiful tree," telling her that it's the "kind of a tree Adam and Eve must have met under."

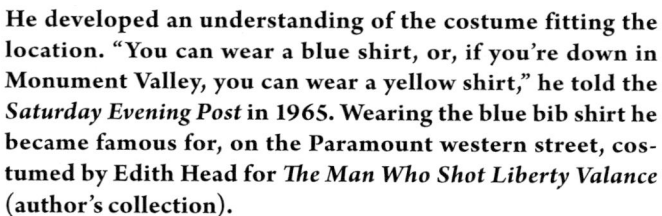

He developed an understanding of the costume fitting the location. "You can wear a blue shirt, or, if you're down in Monument Valley, you can wear a yellow shirt," he told the *Saturday Evening Post* in 1965. Wearing the blue bib shirt he became famous for, on the Paramount western street, costumed by Edith Head for *The Man Who Shot Liberty Valance* (author's collection).

In real life, however, being away on remote locations was one of the main reasons for the failure of his marriages. "We were always in some awful location doing Westerns," his third wife Pilar said in an interview with *Orange Coast*. She demanded, "Why don't you learn to sing and dance like so we can go to Paris like Gene Kelly and Fred Astaire?"[9]

Wayne was a slave to his energy, Pilar once sighed. In the road movie *A Lady Takes a Chance*, he plays a wandering rodeo rider who zigzags through the West. In a campfire scene, the reel John Wayne looks up at the stars (actually the ceiling of the RKO stage) and tells Jean Arthur about this way of living: "It's great, you oughta try it some time." They could just as well have been the words of the real John Wayne.

"A mountain lion in a cage"

In the Western genre, action plays out in front of the unique qualities of the American landscape. "The West—the very words go straight to that place of heart where Americans

Courting a lady in the Old West: The Old Tucson mission wasn't used in *Rio Bravo*, yet the still photographer had the star pose with newcomer Angie Dickinson in front of the church nevertheless (author's collection).

feel the spirit of pride in their Western heritage—the triumph of personal courage over any obstacle, whether nature or man."[10] That's how John Wayne felt about the landscape that was as much a part of making him into an international star as his mentor, John Ford. About their shared experiences, Ford once said, "We went to the most desolate places to film our Westerns. Duke was able to spend time outdoors in close contact with nature. I am sure that he would have been quite unhappy had he been confined to work in the studio sets; it would be the equivalent of putting a mountain lion in a cage. …Duke needs to challenge and be challenged by nature."[11]

The action men in his movies accepted this challenge just as he embraced the discomforts in those remote places. Frank Nugent's *Searchers* script describes Ethan Edwards as "a man as hard as the country he's crossing." In the films he is best remembered for, he is a character who has a deep unity to the land. "Nothing out there is friendly," desert guide Joe January calmly advises. Rooster Cogburn knows, "everything in these woods'll either bite ya, stab ya or stick ya!" Trail boss Wil Anderson uses the school blackboard to show his young cowhands what they're signing up for: "Four hundred miles of the meanest country in the west." His other

Above: Men of action, like *The Cowboys'* Wil Anderson, accepted the challenge of nature (author's collection).

cattle baron, Tom Dunson, makes almost the same speech: "We got a thousand miles to go. There's going to be Indian territory. How bad I don't know."

Crossing the Great American plains is "a fight all the way." Privately, Wayne had his own opinions about the value of this land the forefathers conquered. In his infamous 1971 *Playboy* interview, he made a controversial remark that haunts him still, about the taking of the land from the Native Americans: "Our so-called stealing of this country was just a question of survival. There were great numbers of people who needed new land, and the Indians were selfishly trying to keep it for themselves." Such remarks sounded like they were written for one of his westerners, like his young deputy in *The Big Stampede*, who puts his two cents in about New Mexico being a great cattle country: "It shoulda been colonized long ago."

He started out in the business as a prop man and never forgot how important dressing a set is to the success of a picture: admiring a rare wooden cigar store Indian placed on the *El Dorado* set (author's collection).

"We're building a nation!"

There was "land for the taking." The words of John Chisum, another one of his cattle barons. "These huge ranches," so the narrator in *Big Jake* informs us, "were held together only by having enough men and guns." In these films, the land was never gifted. It had to be taken and defended. As Tom Doniphon puts his idea about frontier justice across to a pilgrim, "Out here, a man settles his own problems."

In his war movies, taking the high ground had strategic reasons. "North by east!" he hammers into the soldiers' heads on the eve of *The Longest Day*. "The Germans have flooded large swamp areas behind the coast. Avoid them if possible. We came here to fight, not to swim!" Adventure types, like the Big Game Hunter from *Hatari!*, are in total command of their surroundings. Sean Mercer knows exactly where to find rhinos at this time of the hunting season, whereas *Legend of the Lost*'s Joe January knows the Sahara like the back of his hand. "It's a lot to know about the desert," he says. When asked if he really likes this hellhole, he replies, "It's mine…. It's all I own."

The cops Wayne portrayed late in his career operate in an urban landscape. The mob rules Seattle and London. McQ and Brannigan only have the advantage when they challenge their adversaries outside the city limits (and outside the law). Wayne told interviewers on the sets of his detective movies that he had to get used to new surroundings. "I feel kinda uncomfortable, fighting in these clothes," he said, rolling his shoulders, as if they needed more space. "I'm used to a big hat and a loose shirt."

"It's our heritage"

By the time he got himself on the cover of *Time* for the first time in 1952, the magazine's editors knew that the screen personality was in sync with the personality of the land; they painted him into a Sedona western landscape. In his 50-year career, John Wayne, the actor, melded with John Wayne, the movie personality, and his screen persona melded with the American landscape, until the public did not know any more where one began and the other ended. However, he kept his reel persona close to his real self. Working in the movie industry allowed him to see the world. When asked in his last TV interview about the new woman in his life, he highlighted

He loved the great outdoors and indulged in many sports, including skiing, as seen in this private moment with one of his children. Although he never mastered the alpine sport, he never quit trying. At the age of 62, he took a skiing lesson in Sun Valley, Idaho, later sending his instructors a thank-you note, "Thanks for the long slide" (author's collection).

Pat Stacy's advantages as a traveling companion: "She likes to travel and likes the things I like to do."[12]

The theme songs of the movies sang the praises of the land and the men who fought to win it. On a recording for *Sons of Katie Elder*, Wayne's distinctive voice personifies the land: "Texas is a woman. She whispers in a boy's ears: Come on out with me and have some fun." Superman had Metropolis for a fantasy landscape. Wayne had Monument Valley. When video companies released his old B-Westerns, they ripped off their customers by using a Monument Valley photo as it had become synonymous with him. No other American actor was ever identified that closely with a landscape. Wayne once said, "No man who ever entered the West was the same again, and neither was the land. And neither are we. It's our heritage. It's the only land we'll ever have. And it's good enough for me."[13]

"We're losing the closeness"

While the outdoor characters he played were blazing trails to Paradise Valley, to him, Hollywood was the Promised Land. But as America was changing, Hollywood too was changing, and so was location work. Spencer Tracy's narration of *How the West Was Won* begins with the words, "This land has a name today, and is marked on maps." Never has the

The international audience identified him with the quintessential American landscape of Monument Valley: the French lobby card of *The Searchers* includes Natalie Wood's portrait (author's collection).

changing of the country been more evident in a western than in the epilogue of that epic. The iconic Monument Valley has just been pacified as the film dissolves to a series of shots of modern (the early 1960s) Los Angeles and San Francisco. It was meant to show progress then. It makes the viewer of today gasp instead. It wasn't just the American landscape that was changing. The landscape of the movie industry that Wayne loved so dearly was remodeled at the same time. Just as the real cowboys had lost the freedom of the open range to the settlers, the filmmakers were pushed back as their locations were homesteaded. A freeway now runs through what has been the busiest Western location in Los Angeles, Iverson's Ranch. The Hollywood studios finally sold out, turning their mythical back lots into parking lots.

Anna Lee, Wayne's leading lady in *Flying Tigers*, recalled: "We made the whole picture out there where Westlake Village is now. It was all country with small little oak trees there; they said it looked as much like China as one of our locales could look. But now, to look at it, there's an enormous city there. There's no sign that we were ever there."[14]

As he contemplated retirement, Howard Hawks discussed the problems of doing a period western on location. "When I first started shooting pictures around Tucson, over 20 years ago, the country was so rugged we had to transport some of our equipment to our locations by mule. Now, we're being ruined by civilization." The master director had many melancholy reflections of his old moviemaking days. "We've got to be very careful to shoot around the paved roads. Even then, we're lucky if we don't end up with some retired millionaire's desert swimming pool in the background."[15]

When Chisum proudly surveys his property, his top hand (Ben Johnson) remarks, "Too many changes," and Chisum replies, "Things usually change for the better." John Wayne, the man, wasn't gloomy about America. His opinion of his home country was well-known. For the cover of his record, *America, Why I Love Her*, he let it be known that he was "born in a country whose immense beauty and grandeur are matched only by the greatness of her people."[16]

He was aware that times would eventually change. Tides in filmmaking were shifting. In his twilight years, he indulged in reminiscences about the good old times on locations. "We lived in a tent city back then and at night we laid

"Those are the people you lean on all the way. They don't miss and they don't fail you," John Wayne said in the news release of his directorial debut. He surrounded himself with co-workers he knew for years. The gruff-looking ex-marine Jack Pennick he borrowed from John Ford's stock company for his own films, as in this case, *The Fighting Kentuckian* (author's collection).

cards or got the Mormons we worked with to sing some of their songs. Sometimes the Sons of the Pioneers were there, and they sang too. It was kind of a captured community and we made the most of it. And most of it was delightful." Talking to *Life* in 1972, he got sentimental about losing those locations, the experiences of living in tents and eating in a commissary. "Now, if there's a road to a location, there's a motel. And at night, when we are through shooting, everybody goes their separate ways. We don't have the camaraderie we used to have. We're losing the closeness."[17]

He was Americana personified. Maureen O'Hara found the right words when she addressed Congress to strike a Gold Medal of Honor for her dearest friend, and that it should just say the words "John Wayne, American": "To the people of the world, John Wayne is not just an actor.... John Wayne is the United States of America. He is what they believe it to be. He is what they hope it will be. And he is what they hope it will always be." The Congressional Gold Medal shows him in Monument Valley. Where else? Like his Ethan Edwards, he is there forever, wandering between the winds.

He came to miss the camaraderie and closeness of the location work in the old days. In the tent cities, the evenings were filled with laughter and music. As he produced his own movies, as seen here on his *Fighting Kentuckian* set with unidentified crewmembers, he used Ford's method of bringing musicians to the set (author's collection).

1

The Big Trail

"We can't turn back"

"We're blazing a trail that started in England. We're building a nation!"
—Breck Coleman (John Wayne) urging the pioneers to get moving

Ironically, no other John Wayne film came even close in using as many locations as the big outdoor drama that was supposed to make him a star. The Big Trail *was shot in no less than seven states. Its shooting schedule (from April 20 to August 20, 1930) easily tops his other epics, like the 81 days he allowed himself to shoot* The Alamo *and the 76 days he was on* Red River.

In 1926, the future John Wayne got his first taste of living on a movie location on the Tom Mix western *The Great K&A Train Robbery*. Young "Duke" Morrison was invited to travel with the production to **Glenwood Springs**, Colorado. The kid from Iowa got to see the Shoshone River for the first time. The crew members were transported in two Pullman train cars and two special baggage cars. The youthful football player and some of his USC teammates were hired to exercise with Mix, to keep him in shape during the location work. Although Wayne's recollections varied in the details as he looked back 50 years later, he remembered never having worked with Mix as he had intended to do. Morrison was re-directed towards moving props. Therefore, on this Colorado location, he also got his first taste of propping. And of movie salaries. Thirty-five dollars a week was good money for a student. But nothing could have prepared him for the four months on location for the film that made him John Wayne: *The Big Trail*.

August 25, 1978. John Wayne had less than a year to live. When Great Western Savings, a large California savings and loan, offered him $350,000 a year to sing their praises, he agreed to appear in several television commercials. That day, they were out in Lone Pine. Many times, he had ridden those trails between the granite outcrops that are scattered over the lowlands in the Alabama Hills. "Beautiful country," he said as he held his horse and gazed over the red rocks. "Y'know, I rode out here about 50 years ago on a little Don Horse and started a film career. Picture called *The Big Trail*."

Half a century before that little scene took place, on April 10, 1930, at exactly 10:30 a.m., a voice shouted: "Walsh 26, scene one, take one!" It was director Raoul Walsh's 26th

"I rode out there fifty years ago": He mentioned his very first appearance as the newly minted western star John Wayne while making his last one in the saddle, in a commercial shot in Lone Pine (author's collection).

picture for Fox. The first take of this massive undertaking got underway. The Arizona sun was already high and blazing. Hundreds of wagons, 1700 head of stock and 1200 persons went into action. It was 100 years after the first wagon train set out from the real Independence, Missouri. On Walsh's set, a young man just a few weeks shy of his 23rd birthday led the wagons westward. He still had to get used to his new name: John Wayne.

Location Scouting, the Hard Way

By 1930, a hundred years after the opening of the Oregon Trail, the original locations had changed a lot. Desert had become farms, orchards and cities. The question of suitable locations was of vital importance, since the new Grandeur cameras (shooting in the 70mm widescreen format developed by Fox) would pick up every detail. Walsh intended to find locations that would replace the actual ones. Not a foot of film was to be shot in Hollywood. He wanted authenticity all the way and buildings were to be real. Where a log cabin was specified in the plot, a real log cabin was built. Walsh traveled 14,000 miles seeking his locations. He even traveled by dog sled through the Blackfeet country over snows 20 feet deep.

He covered 16 states before he was satisfied with his choices. Finally he settled for the desert of Arizona, the Sequoia National Park in California and the big tree section around Klamath Falls in Oregon. In Idaho, he chose the country adjacent to Victor and near Eaton Pass and in Wyoming the Jackson Hole district. Another important scene was laid out not far from Salt Lake City, Utah. In Montana, he scheduled the buffalo hunt. Now the director of this extravaganza, a $1,250,000 gamble, had everything in place. Everything except a leading man.

Enter Duke Morrison

"If there was one thing I did not want, it was an established star for the role of Breck Coleman, the orphan of the plains."[1] Walsh had great confidence in the face he had selected and that the public did not yet know. "I wanted a personality—not an actor." It is fascinating to read this in the Fox souvenir program, issued as the movie was released. Even at this early date in Wayne's career, when

After scouting the locations, the director settled for the Imperial County Sand Dunes west of Yuma for the desert scenes (photo by Roland Schaefli).

memories weren't yet clouded by legend-making, Walsh told the story of how he discovered a property man helping with a set on the Fox lot. "Something one of the others had said had set the boy laughing, and the expression on his face was so warm and wholesome that I stopped and watched."

His first photograph shooting as the newly christened John Wayne took place on the Fox studio lot when the news was released that he would be starring with Marguerite Churchill (author's collection).

Wayne remembered his first encounter with Raoul Walsh this way: "I was goin' to a Ford set, and Walsh asked Eddie Grainger [then an assistant director at Fox] who I was, and Eddie yelled to me. I came over, we were introduced, and then Walsh came over to the set; I guess he talked to Ford then. That night, as I was leaving, Eddie came around: 'Jesus, don't cut your hair—Walsh wants to take a test of you for this picture.'"

Walsh told his story of Wayne's discovery many times, and it never involved John Ford. In his telling, he simply found the young man by accident. Ford sometimes took credit for it. Many years later, in a conversation with Don Siegel, Wayne remarked, "Finally, [Ford] introduced me to Raoul Walsh."[2]

In his 1974 memoir *Each Man in His Time*, Walsh once again described the chance meeting that made Hollywood history: "The tall young fellow carrying an overstuffed chair into the property warehouse had wide shoulders to go with his height. He was unloading a truck and did not see me. I watched him juggle a solid Louis Quinze sofa as though it was made of feathers and pick up another chair with his free hand…" When the prop boy came out for another load, Walsh spoke to him. "What's your name?" Wayne gave him a once-over carefully. "I know you. You directed *What Price Glory*. The name's Morrison."[3]

A guest star on *The Dean Martin Show* in 1965, Wayne recounted again (this time without mentioning Ford) that Walsh had told him not to cut his hair. "Did you know he was a famous director?" his host asked. "No, I thought he was a barber!" Wayne replied.

The Making of John Wayne

Walsh then put young Michael Morrison in front of a camera for a screen test. Wardrobe had fitted him into a buckskin outfit. According to Walsh, they did three tests: the first one without sound, then with some lines spoken. In the third test, Walsh had his prospect read several scenes from the script. He fell into the common trap of beginners, overdramatizing his lines. "Look," Walsh said, "play him with a cool hand like I think you'd do on a football field. Speak softly but with authority, and look whomever you're talking to right in the eye." The young man caught on almost at once. "Now I had my male lead."[4]

Marion Morrison, however, was not even asked how he liked the invention of the new name for him. It took him a long time and he never really became accustomed to the John. "Nobody ever really calls me John. As a matter of fact, when they got to use it, I don't want them to mention my name. No, I've always been either Duke, Marion or John Wayne. It's a name that goes well together and it's like one

On the town set at the Colorado River: Looking a little thinner after a bout with Montezuma's revenge, which almost cost him his job (author's collection).

word—John Wayne. But if they say John, Christ, I don't look around today."[5]

Before they headed off to the first location in Yuma, Wayne saw Walsh about another husky young man. Wayne asked very humbly if the director could find a part for his friend, sounding apologetic, as though he might be asking too much. Walsh hired Ward Bond as a wagon train driver. Bond would drive a lot more wagons in the years to come. "In helping a pal, Wayne had done picture fans a favor," Walsh mused.[6]

"I've been on their trail ever since"

In 1830, Independence was the most romantic spot in the United States, the embarkation point for the way west. The Missouri River could not be used for the epic scene that would start the trek because of the modern aspect of the banks. But in 1930, the Colorado River that flowed past Yuma was as wild as in 1830. Descriptions and sketches of the period varied widely, so Walsh had a sort of composite city of Independence constructed. Art director Harold Miles built it from his imagination, several miles from Yuma, at a river flat of the Colorado, covered by a jungle of willows. Cast and crew traveled from Hollywood to Yuma by special train with eight Pullman cars full of actors and crew, fed by two dining cars, preceded by 21 cars of baggage, livestock, wardrobe and props. They found a pioneer town awaiting them. It was the biggest set ever built on location, as Fox proudly claimed— more than 40 buildings, each of them looking aged and weathered. In addition, every house was "propped." The hotel was used by wardrobe, another building was equipped as a frontier hospital. Five thousand period costumes were issued. Twenty-four people in the location wardrobe department were on the staff list. A mess tent was equipped to feed 500 people an hour. This was Wayne's first tent city on a location, something he would come to miss in later years. On location, a motion picture company, like an army, travels on its stomach. In Yuma, the commissary department met the Herculean task of feeding 800 people for 16 days, three times daily. It cost $2125 a day to feed the troupe.

"I kill my own rats"

Wayne's first day of shooting finally arrived. When the background came alive with extras and livestock, Wayne,

"Well, Zeke, when you get there say the great white mountain Hello for me." With Tully Marshall as Zeke (author's collection).

playing frontier scout Coleman, was cued to say his good-byes to his friend Zeke. Forty years later, Wayne talked about his first dialogue scene on yet another Western set, this one in Old Tucson. For his TV special *Shoot Out at Rio Lobo*, George Plimpton asked him if he had gotten any acting lessons prior to *The Big Trail*. Astonishingly, Wayne still remembered the line his character was supposed to say with sentiment: "Well, Zeke, when you get there, say the great white mountain *hello* for me." Wayne then did an impression of how his dialogue teacher wanted him to say it, very broadly and over the top. In the film, young John Wayne delivers this dialogue like a throwaway line, completely natural. Walsh observed that: "He took direction easily … he was a natural."[7]

Ward Bond recalled in a *Motion Picture Magazine* article that his pal was awkward and ill at ease when acting in front of the camera: "What a horrible struggle it was for him. Duke had no theatrical background, no stage training, no little theater experience, no real feeling for pictures. I used to watch the big guy in those early scenes, see his suffering face, the way he'd literally freeze in front of the camera, and I had to turn away. I couldn't bear to look at him and feel his agony."[8]

"Gone on another trail"

Wayne had more agony coming. "I was three weeks flat on my back with turistas—or Montezuma's revenge, or the Aztec two-step, whatever you want to call it," he told the editors of *Playboy* in 1971. "You know, you get a little grease and soap on the inside of a fork and you've got it. Anyway, that was the worst case I ever had in my life." Dysentery kept him in bed for three weeks. Walsh shot around him until he could wait no longer. Wayne had lost 18 pounds from the *turistas*. In his first scene after that, Wayne was supposed to ride alongside the wagons as character actor Tully Marshall came by on a mule and offered him a slug form his jug. "That blankety-blank Tully Marshall," Wayne recalled. "It was full of the worst rot-gut I ever tasted, and I had to swallow it or ruin the scene." Ordinarily, he wouldn't have minded so much, but his throat was so raw "that the liquor almost killed me."[9] He told biographer Maurice Zolotow, "I had been puking and crapping blood for a week, and now I just poured that raw stuff right down my throat."[10]

For the duration in Yuma, the cast stayed at the **Hotel del Ming**, 300 Gila Street, then just a few years old. It is now listed on the National Register of Historic Places. Walsh moved on to the **Imperial County Sand Dunes**, located west of Yuma, for the desert scenes. Interstate 8 travels through the southern portion of the dunes. Most filming took place in the Buttercup Valley area of the sand dunes, north of the interstate.

"That's what I aim to do"

Wayne was back on these hot sand dunes sooner than he expected. Two years after *The Big Trail*, when he was relegated to making B-movies, he was filming *The Big Stampede* at a ranch west of Yuma. That same year, it was Yuma again for the Mascot serial *The Three Musketeers*. Wayne remembered how the temperature hit 120 degrees during the day. "Now when you shoot on location in the desert, you usually film early in the morning and late in the afternoon, when the sun isn't too murderous. [The producer Nat] Levine would get goin' at sunup and we didn't knock off until it was dark and we were about ready to drop dead from exhaustion."[11] Actress Ruth Hall developed sun blisters which

Back in the Yuma desert for the serial *Three Musketeers*: Wayne (far right) with Jack Mulhall, Raymond Hatton, and Francis X. Bushman, Jr. (author's collection).

became so badly swollen that in some of her latter scenes, she had to be shot from the back. "And you learned," Wayne told Zolotow, "never to give in to the elements."

Levine cut costs wherever possible. He once saved a buck by convincing Wayne to share a bedroom with two older actors. In March 1933, Franklin D. Roosevelt had been inaugurated and ordered a two-week bank holiday. Thus, when the *Musketeers* crew arrived on location, the banks were closed. Ruth Hall recalled, "However, the show went on." Because Levine had refused to spend money to bring good stunt horses up from Hollywood, action performer Yakima Canutt was stuck with a two-and-a-half-dollar horse that had never seen lighting reflectors before. In one scene, the stuntman hauled himself up to the balcony of the Yuma jail. The horse was scared of bedsheets. As Wayne later told the story, Canutt had "to whip the tar out of that horse" to make it go. As he was climbing the top, he hollered at him, "That ain't John Wayne beating that horse!" Yak bellowed back, "Yeah, and this ain't John Wayne doin' this stunt, either!"[12]

The **Yuma Penitentiary** (now the Yuma Territorial Prison State Historic Park at 220 Prison Hill Road) opened

The notorious Yuma Penitentiary had a deterrent effect on the bad men in the Old West but by 1933, quickie filmmakers used its walls and the prison's Sally Port as an Arabian stronghold. In one episode of the 12-chapter serial *The Three Musketeers*, John Wayne is jailed in one of the original cells (photo by Roland Schaefli).

for business in 1876 and closed in 1909. In its 33 years of operation, a total of 3069 prisoners did time here. During the Depression, it was used as a shelter for the homeless. It was at this time that the Mascot serial put it to good use. They gave the prison buildings a facelift so that it remotely resembled an Arab stronghold. Actual prison cells were utilized to jail Wayne and his fellow Musketeers. The Sally Port was used as a fort entrance.

Wayne certainly had no desire to go back to Yuma. He probably agreed with his *3 Godfathers* character Robert Hightower, who shouted in a rage that he did not want to "grow a long white beard in the Yuma Penitentiary!"

"You can call a settlers' meeting to bury 'em!"

Back to *The Big Trail*, where Raoul Walsh, after 26 days in Yuma, got ready to move his company out to get shots of the covered wagons crossing the desert. Before they went on, each of the 185 pioneer wagons was inspected. The wagons each weighed a ton and cost $400 to build. Jack Padgin, in charge of the livestock, "aged" the vehicles by stitching false patches to the canvas and rubbing mud and ashes on it to get a weather-beaten look. More than 700 horse wranglers and stock herders took care of the livestock. Eighteen hundred heads of cattle, 1400 horses, 80 oxen, 110 mules, 200 chickens, 20 pigs and 14 dogs traveled with the 347 pioneers. The lumbering prairie schooners were set in motion. While they went over every foot of the movie trail in reality, it took 123 baggage cars to move the rest of the production. By this time, Walsh had the feeling "we were off to a good start." His protégé looked fine on a horse. "From somewhere he had picked up the natural slouch of a trail rider. Jack Padgin would make a rider out of him."[13] After *The Big Trail*, however, Wayne would get rid of the Indian slouch in the saddle that Walsh had wanted from him. When he directed himself, 30 years later, he gave teenage star Frankie Avalon a little

Breck Coleman leads the wagon train on *The Big Trail*: in his first starring role, John Wayne looked like he was born in the saddle. Ward Bond is right behind him; among the unidentified extras, the pair of badmen to the left and right of the tree stump are Tyrone Power, Sr., and Charles Stevens. The latter was publicized as the "Geronimo's grandson" which was a publicity invention (author's collection).

piece of advice how to sit a saddle: "Feel as though you had a coat hanger in your outfit. And feel like it's just pulling you with the movement of the horse."[14]

"The turning back place for the weak"

Two special trains took the company up to **Sacramento** for the river scenes. The morning after arrival, the bugler woke them at dawn and they boarded an old river steamboat. Walsh had scheduled to shoot dialogue scenes for the movie's beginning as they actually traveled downriver.

Walsh packed up again and went on to **St. George**, Utah, for canyon takes, utilizing the rimrock country of Hurricane Bluffs near **Zion National Park**. Wayne returned to St. George almost a quarter of a century later for *The Conqueror* (see Chapter 8). From Utah, they doubled back to the California Sierra and shot some footage in **Sequoia National Park**, home of giant sequoias, the largest trees in the world. The actual location was south of **Kings Canyon**.

One of the very first publicity photographs taken of the new face, on the Yuma set: Fox executives changed Morrison's name to Wayne, the last name being taken from the American Revolutionary general "Mad Anthony" Wayne (author's collection).

"Their spirit leads"

By the time they packed once more and headed north—in the supposedly westward trek—*The Big Trail* must have been the most traveled motion picture crew on record. They often moved on existing trails where the toppled wagons and broken wheels that Walsh worked into his widescreen compositions were not fakes or purposely contrived. The expensive location shooting was quite unusual for its time and the enormous crew was working under harsh conditions. For a short flashback scene—with Wayne wearing a beaver cap—they went to **Grand Canyon** to make good use of Fox Grandeur. By this time, the female lead, Marguerite Churchill, had decided she liked Duke, who had by then turned 23. Some biographers have speculated about an affair. Walsh gave his protégé credit for giving his full attention to his work. "If Lady Godiva had ridden across the back lot with her hair cut off, it was a safe bet he would not even have glanced at her."[15]

"Praying for peace—but ready for battle"

Only rarely did the cast and crew have the comfort of sleeping in hotels. In Montana, they even slept in their coaches. In Wyoming, their homes were 160 specially built cabins. Each had just a bed and a stove, but there were electric lights and shower baths of a sort. In its attempt to recreate American history, the company actually made American history there, in a small but significant way. "There was a place called **Moran Camp**, on Jackson Lake," Wayne recalled in 1978 in an article for the book *The War, the West and the Wilderness*. "It probably had five or six little shacks when we arrived. We came out with 350 people, and by the time we were through, we had about 500 people working there, with 150 wagons and horses. So we had to have a pretty big setup." The Fox people enlarged the place, built cabins and sets, and they ended up with an establishment that is now called Moran, Wyoming. "It's a township. We started it."[16] You'll find the little settlement on **Moran Town Road**, just off U.S. Highway 26. Howard Hawks used the same terrain 20 years later for the riverboat sequences in *The Big Sky*.

"History cuts the way"

"Have you seen the mighty Tetons?" John Wayne would ask in a poem on his record *America, Why I Love Her*. He himself saw the exceptional mountain range of the Rocky Mountains for the first time when they traveled over Teton's snowy pass at an altitude of just over 6000 feet (now the **Grand Teton National Park**), a month before the road opened. On top of the Teton Pass, six oxen started running with a heavy wagon occupied by three women. Raoul Walsh recalled how Wayne "happened to be in the path of the animals and showed he had nerve. He stood out in front of the team and bullwhacked them into the side of the road. On the other side was a precipice." That was just a sample of the sort of thing that went on every day, according to Walsh's recollections in the Fox souvenir program.

Most movie lovers are familiar with the sight of the Tetons from the Western classic *Shane*, best seen in a burial scene on a hill. John Wayne rode up that same hill 25 years before Alan Ladd, to watch over his wagon train circulated on the **Antelope Flats** below.

"The starting place for the strong"

By far the most grueling scene to shoot was the film's "lowering of the wagons" sequence, shot near **Jackson Hole**. Walsh dreamed it up—it was not in the script—when he spotted the ideal hill as he was coming out of Moran, on the left-hand side of U.S. Highway 26, with the Buffalo Fork River rolling below. (In later years, Walsh mistakenly gave St. George as the place of this specific location. But the Tetons appear in the background of one shot.) "I remembered the coils of stout rope I had loaded into some of the wagons, with no clear idea of where or when I might need them. The ropes were the answer." They constructed primitive pulleys and log booms to lower wagons, horses and other livestock. A few extras could clamber down with the rest of the cast. When Padgin and Walsh showed Wayne and Bond how to anchor the ropes and rig the wagons,

they worked like beavers. Walsh had scribbled some lines for Wayne, but he ad-libbed most of the descent. The last wagon to go down gave the sequence more reality than Walsh had bargained for. A knot must have slipped. The wagon hung lopsided just long enough to heighten the suspense. Then it went crashing to the canyon floor. (According to other sources, probably exaggerated, up to nine wagons met the same fate.)

Although the exact place was not recorded, the scene in which Tyrone Power, Sr., tries to ambush Wayne was probably shot at **Lewis Falls**, at the southern entrance to Yellowstone National Park.

"You're going on with me!"

John Wayne returned to Jackson Hole in 1968 for a few scenes of *Hellfighters* (see Chapter 11). He first set foot into **Cody**, Wyoming, the town named after its founder William F. Cody, when the *Big Trail* company crossed the Yellowstone Park to Jackson. In 1976, Wayne participated in the opening of the Cody Firearms Museum of the **Buffalo Bill Historical Center**, celebrating the Bi-centennial. He was the grand marshal in the Fourth of July parade. The museum at 720 Sheridan Avenue displays several movie guns, James Stewart's Winchester '73 and the six-shooters of the *Bonanza* principals, to name a few. Also on display is a shirt once worn by Wayne.

"Not even the snows of winter…"

The *Big Trail* company was in Jackson Hole for nearly eight weeks. By then they had been working on the picture for nearly four months. "We were tired, eaten up by mosquitoes and black flies," Walsh recalled, "and I guess most of our nerves were pretty much on edge." Still, they moved on to Eastern Idaho to their Fort Hall location. They followed the Snake River, not far from Jackson Hole country (but on the other side of the Tetons). The original Fort Hall was along the Oregon Trail at the Snake. Walsh had ordered that an exact duplicate of the historic fort be built in the wilderness. One of the most spectacular sequences was set in this area: the Indian attack on the wagon train.

The location of the arduous "lowering of the wagons" sequence was improvised on this hill at the Buffalo Fork River just off U.S. Highway 26 (photo by Roland Schaefli).

In this scenic place, Breck Coleman narrowly escaped being shot in the back. The location of Lewis Falls can be seen from the south entrance road coming out of Yellowstone (photo by Roland Schaefli).

"The Indians are my friends"

Seven hundred twenty-five Indians were gathered from a number of reservations. Weeks before the picture started, Walsh made systematic visits to every Indian reservation in the Northwest, conferred with tribal chiefs, reservation officials and chiefs of the Indian Bureau. As a result of this preparation—during which he rode hundreds of miles on horseback—he decided on five tribes: Arapahos, the Blackfeet and the Shoshones at Lander, Wyoming, the Cheyenne, at the Tongue River Agency and the Crows at the Crow Agency, both in Montana. In the attack sequence, nine men—whites and Indians—were knocked out and

the doctor and nurses were busy patching up minor bruises and cuts. Walsh had Hollywood trick riders train the young Indian warriors. A full hospital staff was on duty during the whole shoot: a doctor, two orderlies, and four nurses.

"Not even massacres could stop them"

The shooting was scheduled to come to a close in **Moiese**, in Western Montana, with the buffalo stampede. Walsh shot it about 35 miles north of Dixon, now the **National Bison Range at Moiese**, off Highway 93, located in the Flathead Valley. Moiese was then a small western town, with one hotel and the largest controlled government buffalo herd in the country. It was established in 1908 to protect the remaining herds of the American bison. Washington had given Fox permission to use the herd providing no hardship be inflicted on the animals. "I did not think that some mild hazing by a few hired Indians would hurt the buffalo," said Walsh.[17]

In that scene, Wayne uses a six-gun for the first time, not a movie prop but an authentic nickel-plated, cartridge conversion, Remington Army revolver 1861. The distinctive six-shooter was reportedly also used by cowboy star William S. Hart.

When the stampede was over, Wayne got off his horse, gave Walsh that lopsided grin which was to become one of his trademarks and asked, "How did I do, Mr. Walsh?" He was confident in himself by this time and looked as if he knew the answer. That night, Walsh predicted that John Wayne would have a future in motion pictures. He also thanked him for staying sober when so many of the Broadway actors in the troupe didn't. (Walsh had nicknamed the character actors Johnnie Walker, Gordon Gin and several names of whiskey.) Wayne gave him a straight look. "You hired me to act, not to guzzle booze."[18]

"We're building a nation"

Walsh kept the happy ending for last: Only the final clinch between Wayne and Churchill remained to be filmed. The director wanted it to convey the happy conclusion of many such trails since the world began. He chose the Big Tree Grove of the **Sequoia National Forest** because it seemed to him that nature had there provided a cathedral of the ages. The youngest tree in the grove was then 400 years older than the discovery of America by Columbus. Some final pick-up shots were accomplished on the sand dunes at **Oxnard**. Walsh finally wrapped *The Big Trail* on August 20.

During the four months, the company had traveled through seven states and had covered more than 4300 miles. Walsh hat exposed 1,300,000 feet of film in 70mm Grandeur and standard 35mm format. Out of the footage, he selected 30,000 feet. The ambitious production ran over schedule and broke the budget. The total bill amounted to $1,900,000. Wayne had received $75 per week.

"A low-down coyote left his sign"

The world premiere was a big extravaganza at Grauman's Chinese Theatre in Hollywood (one of only two theaters equipped to show the version in 70mm). On October 24, 1930, Sid Grauman pulled out all the stops. He had assembled so many army searchlights that people all over the Los Angeles Basin could see the glow. The famous forecourt was turned into a frontier encampment. It was the biggest night of Wayne's early life. He got two guest passes to the premiere and invited his parents. They were to sit in the limousine ferrying the young star down Hollywood Boulevard. His parents were divorced by then, and his mother refused to go anywhere with his father. His dad told him to give his mother both passes. Yet Wayne proudly picked up his dad and his new love at their home. It was the only time he ever saw his father in a tuxedo. It took Wayne another 20 years to be invited back to that famous movie theater to leave his bootprints in the cement.

After The Big Trail

Fox sent Wayne on an ill-fated publicity campaign to New York, wearing a fringed buckskin costume, a big hat and a silver-studded belt. He was photographed in his western garb disembarking from the train at **Grand Central Station,** where somebody told him he "looks like Buffalo Bill's ghost" (the newspapers sarcastically pointed to his brand-new Bulova wristwatch). He then held his first press conference at the **Astor Hotel**, 235 West 75th Street. It was a disaster. "That was my first collision with the press," he later wrote.[19] It certainly wouldn't be his last.

As we now know, Fox's gamble didn't pay off. Raoul

The souvenir program (pictured here with Marguerite Churchill) that was sold to moviegoers in the movie theaters. The world premiere was held at Grauman's Chinese Theatre in Hollywood where Raoul Walsh punched his fist in the cement. Above the imprint, he wrote: "His mark." (author's collection).

Traveling by train to New York: John Wayne on his first promotion tour, still wearing his movie costume—plus a new wristwatch (author's collection).

Walsh: "In spite of weather extremes and frequent changes in location, and the bellyaching of the Broadway element [referring to the drinking habits of his stage actors], my new leading man had made a fine frontiersman. His acting was instinctive, so that he became whatever and whoever he was playing." Walsh took a lot of pride in the knowledge that he "discovered a winner. Not only that. I also found a great American."[20]

In its time, *The Big Trail* was a rare vision of nature. The film, as one reviewer noted, was permeated with a powerful, mysterious sense of an always looming, weighty, abstract empty space. The reasons why the epic could not succeed in 1930 are clear now. As Wayne summed it up, "*The Big Trail* laid a very impressive egg."[21]

Not that the newly minted star was not optimistic for success. Forty-five years later, he told his future biographer Michael Munn, "I was sure I'd set the world on fire, and it was hard for a young feller like me to realize the truth." However, in retrospect, Wayne understood that he was "totally unprepared to handle the consequences if *The Big Trail* had been a success and launched me as a star."[22]

Walsh read in the trade papers—30 years after their collaboration—that Wayne was embarking on directing his own epic, *The Alamo*, and sent him a movie still of Breck Coleman in front of the Grand Tetons, and wished him good luck.

Back on the Big Trail

Back to 1978 when Wayne was doing his final acting bits, in the commercials for Great Western Savings. He had some say in the locations. He picked a good one for the August 22 shoot. It brought him back to one of his earliest movie locations: Sequoia National Park, the site of the happy conclusion of *The Big Trail*. When he looked up to the giant trees, he said in awe that it was "like being in a giant cathedral."

2

Hollywood

Home Off the Range

"He was not a cowboy. He was not a sheriff. He was a movie star."[1]
—Michael Wayne explaining that in reality, his Dad was not Davy Crockett

John Wayne's son Michael had to remind people time and time again that John Wayne was a movie star. His audience tends to forget that John T. Chance didn't really ensure law and order in the border town of Rio Bravo, and there was no McLintock town named after him. John Wayne, the screen idol, had made his home in Hollywood. He would frequent its notorious waterholes and leave his mark there.

When he was still a youngster in Glendale, Duke Morrison was already living close to the moviemaking colony; "our glorious industry," as he called it in his Oscar acceptance speech. This industry came to Los Angeles just a few years ahead of him. The first studio in Hollywood, the Nestor Company, was established by a New Jersey company in a roadhouse at 6121 Sunset Boulevard (at the corner of Gower) in October 1911. Three years later, Marion Morrison moved to California. As he became John Wayne, he got around in Hollywood. He defended it as one would his hometown. His star on the **Walk of Fame** is on 1541 Vine Street.

Meeting with Mentors

His movie characters often preferred the desert to a town. As he stated in *Dark Command*, "It's different out there on the prairie." In private, however, Wayne had no objections to the accommodations a modern town had to offer. He told the editors of *Life*, "I've been lucky enough to portray man against the elements at the same time as there was always someone there to bring me the orange juice."[2]

One place in the greater Los Angeles area held a special meaning for Wayne: the home of his boyhood idol Harry Carey at the mouth of **San Francisquito Canyon**, north of Saugus. The silent movie star had acquired the homestead in 1916, established a rancho and even a trading post. The western actor and his novice director, John Ford, occasionally used the rustic ranch as a location for their sagebrush sagas. At one point, Ford had even moved

in with the Careys while learning his craft doing two-reelers for Universal. Santa Clarita Valley was then a busy western location. Harry Carey, Jr., later a fixture in Wayne Westerns, was born in the ranch home in 1921. Because of his red hair, most everybody called him "Dobe," short for adobe, the color of the bricks the rancho was made of. Through his association with Ford, young John Wayne was welcomed into their circle of friends. He spent many hours around the

Famous faces: John Wayne and James Stewart, stars of *How the West Was Won*, are accompanied to the premiere by Irene Dunne (left) and Rosalind Russell. The world premiere was at London's Casino Cinerama on November 2, 1962. The film had an incredible run of 123 weeks (author's collection).

Carey fireplace. The Careys had moved out of the ranch by 1944. The ranch house at 29350 Avenida Rancho Tesoro is now the centerpiece of the **Harry Carey Historic District**; it is being preserved and is open to the public.

When Harry Carey died on September 21, 1947, John Ford was at his bedside. Wayne remained in the next room (the director-star team was completing *Fort Apache* at the time). Ford then went out on the porch, put his head on Olive Carey's breast and cried, "and the whole front of my sweater was sopping wet. For at least 15 or 20 minutes he cried, just solid sobbing, and the more he cried, the stronger I'd get. It was good for me, it was wonderful."[3] Wayne was a pallbearer, along with Ford, Ward Bond and Spencer Tracy. Wayne recited Tennyson's "Crossing the Bar" at Harry Carey's funeral service.

The Harry Carey Ranch in Saugus: a meeting place for real cowpokes and ambitious young filmmakers of the western genre. The property is strongly associated with the development of the motion picture industry in the region (photo by Roland Schaefli).

Cowboy Breakfast

When Harry Carey was at the peak of his career, a street corner on 6098 Sunset Boulevard named **Gower Gulch** was the hangout for many out-of-work cowboys. They came to town because word was out that Hollywoodland needed men who could ride and take a fall. They waited in hopes of being picked for "extra work" in the westerns. Many small, struggling studios were located nearby on **Poverty Row.** These studios made good use of the riding abilities of the cowpokes. When John Wayne started working there, he used to study the mannerisms of these men. They were grateful to pick up a couple of bucks a day for bit parts. And they even brought their own wardrobe.

Cowboy Lunch

When Wayne courted his sweetheart and future first wife Josie, they would take long walks in **Griffith Park**, the large municipal park that borders on Glendale. In 1988, Wayne's old compadre from his Republic days, Gene Autry, established a museum in the park, to explore the history of the American West. The **Autry Museum of the American West** (or "The Autry," as Western aficionados choose to call it) at 4700 Western Heritage Way presents a wide range of exhibitions, including some of Wayne's artifacts. "The Cowboy Lunch" is an ongoing series of events that focuses on Wayne and his co-workers. Wayne had something to do with making Autry into an industry giant. When Wayne told his

Poverty Row producers that he was done with the part of Singin' Sandy because he could neither sing nor strum a guitar (see Chapter 3), they looked around and found … Gene Autry. Wayne and Autry stayed in contact over the years, and Autry often visited Wayne's Arizona ranch. In fact, he stayed at the guest house so often that they started calling it "The Gene Autry Bedroom."

Hollywood Athletic Club

"Sunset Boulevard's Tower of Babylon" is what they sometimes called this Hollywood landmark on 6525 Sunset Boulevard, and with good reason. Wayne used the ninth floor penthouse for drinking parties. Ramon Novarro reportedly used the same rooms for trysts with his many lovers. Rudolph Valentino stayed there whenever he had a disagreement with one of his wives.

Tyrone Power, Sr., had starred with Wayne in *The Big Trail*. Shortly after returning from the exhausting location work, he suffered a massive heart attack at his apartment at the club. He died in the arms of his 17-year-old son Tyrone Power, Jr.

The Hollywood Athletic Club was originally built in 1924 as a health club but it is safe to say that it was more like a hideout of male stars from the '20s through the '50s. The restored structure of one of Tinseltown's most historical buildings still contains the Olympic-sized pool. John Ford often spent his afternoons naked in the steam room (writers found out this was the ideal place to corner the director to pitch him a story). Here, Ford's drinking buddies, young Wayne among them, formed an inner social club, the Young Men's Purity, Total Abstinence, and Snooker Pool Association. (In 1938 it was renamed "The Emerald Bay Yacht Club.") They even held their meetings in the steam room (some of the members were barred from L.A.'s better country clubs). Ward Bond was, of course, a founding member: "I want to tell you that a steam room of an athletic club is a wonderful place to form a yacht club."[4]

Soon the management discreetly set up a bar in an upstairs room for the use of the heavy drinkers. A story often told (and printed in several biographies but with differing locales) actually happened right at the club: Bond bet Wayne $100 that he could stand on a newspaper and Wayne couldn't knock him off. Wayne took the bet. Bond laid a newspaper out on at the floor in an upstairs doorway and then closed the door. "Okay, you dumb son of a bitch, now

One of Hollywood's most iconic buildings: the Athletic Club, home to the "Emerald Bay Yacht Club" (photo by Roland Schaefli).

hit me!" Wayne hit Bond through the door, knocking him off the newspaper.[5]

At the Athletic Club, Wayne also met Bruce Cabot for the first time. The character actor would appear in ten films with him. When Wayne was made a producer and was

The original billiard room: according to a club legend, John Wayne and Ward Bond threw billiard balls at the cars on Sunset Boulevard when they were well gone in their cups (photo by Hollywood Athletic Club).

calling the shots for the first time, he selected Cabot for a lead role in *Angel and the Badman*. Wayne would become good friends with another regular at the club, Johnny Weissmuller, the screen's Tarzan. In years to come, the men would hunt on Catalina Island and even go into the hotel business together in Acapulco.

According to another club legend, one night Wayne and Bond got so drunk that they stood on the roof and threw billiard balls at the cars moving along Sunset. The billiard room was (and is) one of the favorite hangouts in the club. The restoration of the Hollywood Athletic Club is an homage to its original design. The club is available for special events.

"How about the cantina up the street?"

Hollywood's oldest restaurant that is still in existence is **Musso & Frank's Grill** at 6667 Hollywood Boulevard. It has been called "the genesis of Hollywood." Rightly so because since 1919, many a movie deal was made at one of their tables over an excellent steak. Not only has it maintained its classic steakhouse style theme but its classic décor as well. The popularity with the movie industry also continues. However, when Alonzo Castillo (known to his customers as "Panama") retired after 40-plus years, he did not name one of the popular new stars as his favorite customer, but John Wayne.

The **Tam O'Shanter Inn** at 2980 Los Felix Boulevard was favored by nearby Disney Studio employees (and therefore it's sometimes called the Disney Studio Commissary). Walt Disney used the inn for meetings (his favorite table was

In 1967, when this picture was taken at the Cocoanut Grove in Los Angeles, Steve McQueen was the hottest thing at the box office. He idolized John Wayne, calling him "a real pro." The male action stars met on various social occasions over the years and invited each other to their homes (author's collection).

near the fireplace). According to Disney historians, it was also a favorite of Wayne's, whose table was always #15. However, he was a regular even before he became John Wayne. When he was in his sophomore year of Glendale High, he used to bring his first steady girlfriend, Polly Richmond, to the Tam O'Shanter. It is still there.

Chasen's was located at 9039 Beverly Boulevard. For many years, the restaurant was the site of the Academy Awards party. Since it opened for business in 1936, it was frequented by entertainers and famous for its chili. While filming *Cleopatra* in Rome, Elizabeth Taylor had several orders of chili flown to the set. Maureen O'Hara had her own table (she was Dave Chasen's neighbor on Stone Canyon Road in Bel Air) and dined there at least once a week, and she was there on closing night. "We really miss Chasen's. It's a shame it's gone," she said in a 1995 TV interview.[6] Wayne and Howard Hughes had already met at the Athletic Club but they really became acquainted over a meal at Chasen's. The billionaire offered to produce Wayne movies (which would eventually lead to *Jet Pilot*). However, that night Wayne did not want to talk movies. He was maudlin and moaning for Esperanza, who would eventually become his second wife. The aviator let the movie star know he had a little plane always ready in Inglewood, and why the hell didn't they just go to Mexico right now? "What the hell are we waiting for, amigo?" was Wayne's answer, and off they flew to Mexico City where he and Esperanza had a thrilling reunion.[7] When they finally did get married, Hughes personally flew the newlyweds to Hawaii, the first civilian flight since the end of the war.

Chasen's closed in 1995. The original dining room is now a grocery. Nevertheless, the main dining room and the street façade of the original restaurant remain as an eatery. The plaque at the entrance reads, "Through the doors of Beverly Boulevard walked movie stars and moguls, dignitaries and presidents." In fact, Ronald Reagan met a girl named Nancy in one of the booths on a blind date.

The Brown Derby at 3427 Wilshire Boulevard was called the Restaurant of the Stars, and it was said that there was no Hollywood star who had not been in it. That was certainly true in John Wayne's case. He started coming in the '30s, dining with his first wife Josie and her best friend Loretta Young, and he still held a member card in 1955. The restaurant, shaped like a giant Brown Derby hat, closed down in 1985. Fire destroyed it in 1988. The Brown Derby Plaza is named in its memory.

Game show host Ed McMahon remembered a time when he and Wayne were at **Sneaky Pete's**, a classic hot dog joint at 8901 Sunset Boulevard (now the location of the Whisky a Go Go). They were seated at the piano when two long-haired hippie types came up to bait Wayne:

Rubbing shoulders with society bigwigs and the powerful of Tinseltown: in the mid–40s with his boss Herbert J. Yates (left) and director George Waggner, then under contract to Republic (author's collection).

"Hey, John, whaddaya think about long hair?" Wayne spun around in his chair and said, "Jesus Christ had long hair, but he kept it clean."[8]

The man who "can outdrink any man" (as Henry Fonda once called him) liked whiskey but his favorite drink was straight tequila on ice, and always Commemorativo. He used to bring his own bottle to parties and bestow it on the bartender with a generous tip. "Here you go. This is what I drink."[10] Wayne told *Playboy* magazine in 1971: "You hear about tequila and think about a cheap cactus drink, but this is something extraordinary."

As a reminder that Wayne was one of its famous guests, **Mike Lyman's Grill**, 424 West Sixth Street, had Wayne's right handprint cast in clay (which made it special since the more famous cement print at Grauman's doesn't feature a hand print but a fist print). Wayne had signed his cast and it hung over Lyman's bar for many years. Lyman's restaurants were loyally populated by the A-listers from the worlds of show biz and sports. In *The Black Dahlia*, crime novelist James Ellroy described a victim's face as looking like "the steak tartare at Mike Lyman's Grill."

"I drink for comradeship"

On any given night, one might find the **Mocambo Night Club** at 8588 Sunset Boulevard filled with the leading men and women of the *picture* industry. There was another

"I never trust a man that doesn't drink"

One night in the 1950s, Wayne went out with director Budd Boetticher and actor Walter Reed to **Tail o' the Cock**, then at 44 South La Cienga Boulevard. It claimed to be the first place in L.A. to serve Margaritas. After a lot of those, Wayne simply disappeared. The man at the door told his group that Wayne had left, feeling no pain. Wayne had an arrangement with the police: They would take him home whenever he felt he had one too many. In return, he made personal appearances for the LAPD. His drinking buddies were astonished since no one brought enough cash. The manager came over and told them, "There's no bill. Mr. Wayne left a blank check!"[9]

Wining and dining with colleague James Stewart in the early 1960s. Wayne called Stewart "Jimmy Boy" which he liked because Stewart was almost exactly one year younger (author's collection).

address close by, that helped the strip live up to its reputation for glamour with its French-themed late nightclubs: the **Café Trocadero** (or the Troc, as some called it), 8610 Sunset Boulevard. Agents and publicity departments staged dates there because the columnists would write stories of possible love affairs, which helped promote upcoming movies. During Wayne's rather public fling with Marlene Dietrich, he showed up at the Troc, rather unconcerned about the media coverage. The press also documented the pair at the South American–styled Mocambo.

Today, there are no hints on Sunset Plaza that the leading nightspots were located there. Wayne took Pilar to the Mocambo when his divorce from Chata was almost finalized. "We're celebrating the fact that it's a great world!" he told reporters.[11]

Wayne was also the holder of a (personally authorized by Dean Martin) member card of **Dino's Lodge**, 5824 Sunset Boulevard.

In her biography, Maureen O'Hara tells the story that John Ford got Wayne drunk on some occasion and then ordered her to take him home: "You're responsible for him." So Duke was poured into her car. She decided to take him to the **Lakeside Country Club** (now Lakeside Golf Club, 4500 Lakeside Drive, a short distance from the Warner Brothers), then a favorite Hollywood hangout.

The worst kept secret in Hollywood: the public affair of John Wayne and Marlene Dietrich, pictured here between scenes of *Pittsburgh*—the diva would later claim she had hated playing chess with him (author's collection).

During the drive there, Wayne wanted to get out, insisting, "I need another drink." He then started banging on the doors of complete strangers. Imagine the reaction of any resident who opened the door to find John Wayne and Maureen O'Hara standing on their porch in the dark of night. Nonetheless, when he declared with a loud slur, "Good evening. We need a drink," they invited them in. In the end, O'Hara managed to get him to the Country Club, telling the manager, "He's your responsibility now."[12]

The Hollywood Canteen

The famous **Hollywood Canteen** was located at 1451 Cahuenga Boulevard. Bette Davis, John Garfield and Jules Stein founded the USO nightclub exclusively for enlisted men and women (no officers). Admission was just their uniform. Servicemen could dance with (say) Hedy Lamarr and be served doughnuts by (perhaps) Rita Hayworth. It opened on October 3, 1942, and closed on November 22, 1945. During that time, the Canteen entertained three million military personnel. On Thanksgiving in **1943**, 3500 soldiers were served and entertained by Bob Hope. Wayne helped carve the 76 turkeys.

During the 1940s, Hollywood was the nightspot

Business aside, the fun part of going to a movie premiere is being picked up by a driver. In this case, in a Jeep from *Hatari!*, to the Egyptian Theatre on Hollywood Boulevard (author's collection).

destination for visiting servicemen. The **Earl Carroll Theatre**, 6320 Sunset Boulevard, welcomed many men and women in uniform. In 1953, it became the Moulin Rouge, featuring Vegas-style shows. It lasted into the 1960s. It was not inside the club but rather in its parking lot that Wayne and Frank Sinatra almost came to blows, in the infamous aftermath of a "Share" benefit gala (the organization helped mentally disabled children). Wayne had groped his way through "Red River Valley" in his usual cowboy duds. Frank Sinatra sang "The Lady Is a Tramp." Some time before that event, Sinatra had hired Albert Maltz, a blacklisted writer, and then was pressured to let him go; Sinatra blamed Wayne. When they met in the parking lot, Sinatra stiffened. "You don't seem to agree with me," he said, to which Wayne replied, "Let's discuss this some other time." Then Frankie took a swipe at him. Friends intervened. Sinatra got into a nasty fight with a lot attendant instead. There are now Nickelodeon studios in the former Earl Carroll Theatre building.

Wayne told the editors of *Today* magazine that he only had one public brawl in his life, and that was at the Ship Café. He was then still a bit player. "A guy made fun of my Western sideburns. All kinds of men tried to pick fights with me."[13] **The Baron Long's Ship Café** was then standing along the Venice pier. Built in 1905 and fashioned after a Spanish galleon, it featured booze during Prohibition (which is maybe why Wayne went there in the first place). It was razed in 1946.

Checking In and Out

The grand Spanish castle-like structure at 8221 Sunset Boulevard is hard to miss. It's impossible to describe the **Chateau Marmont** without name-dropping. Garbo and Monroe were guests. So were Bogart and Flynn. The establishment has witnessed the misbehavior of generations of stars. Robert Mitchum got himself arrested in one of the rooms for drug use (he always insisted he was framed). John Belushi was found dead in his bungalow.

In May 1943, Wayne moved in. He had finally separated from Josie to shack up with Chata in a penthouse apartment in the Sunset Tower. According to one of the hotel's legends—probably exaggerated but too funny not to mention—Wayne kept a pet cow on the balcony.

The Beverly Wilshire was built in 1928 at 9500 Beverly Wilshire Boulevard. During its rich history, stars like Elvis and Steve McQueen lived there. The hotel exterior was the setting of *Pretty Woman*. Wayne told the story of how he once bedded down Spencer Tracy. Spence got drunk, so Wayne dragged him upstairs and slung him on the bed. As he was taking Tracy's shoes off, Tracy reared up and punched Wayne in the mouth. Wayne shot one back, "in a reflex action on my part." That put Tracy to sleep for good.[14] Wayne came

back to the Beverly Wilshire in later years, once for a private party hosted by Henry Kissinger. Mary St. John, Wayne's secretary and confidante since the Republic days, finally retired in 1975, and Wayne threw her a farewell bash at the Beverly Wilshire. The same year, he met the Japanese emperor there, at the request of the State Department. Wayne found Hirohito's wish to meet him a bit odd since he had knocked out the whole Japanese army on the screen.

The legendary **Beverly Hills Hotel** at 9641 Sunset Boulevard (or the "Pink Palace," as it was called) was another haven for the rich and famous and sometimes served as a film location. Michael Caine always relished telling the tale how he met Wayne in the lobby. After the young British actor made a big splash with *Alfie*, the promoters put him into the hotel with nothing to do. Therefore, he just hung out in the lobby, watching for movie stars. A helicopter landed and Wayne, in full western garb, ambled in. That's when he noticed the young actor. "Are you in that movie *Alfie*?" he inquired. Caine introduced himself. Wayne then predicted, "You gonna be a star, kid." He gave him a piece of advice: "Talk low, talk slow, and don't say too much." Caine got it from Wayne personally to never wear suede shoes: "Because every time he would go to a gent's room, the guy next to him would recognize him, turn around and pee all over his shoes!"[15]

In May 1956, Wayne hosted a lavish wedding reception in the Beverly Hills Hotel ballroom for his daughter Toni. In a November 5, 1966, meeting between Batjac and United Artists, it was agreed that UA would cancel all of Batjac's debt (they carried a $350,000 *Legend of the Lost* debt in their books) in trade for the re-issue and TV rights to *The Alamo*.

In April 1970, the night that would finally bring him the Academy Award, Wayne flew in from the *Rio Lobo* set in Tucson and stayed in Bungalow 3 of the Beverly Hilton. He had convinced himself that Richard Burton would receive a long-overdue Oscar. As it turned out, the Burtons were in an adjoining bungalow. Pilar never forgot how Wayne and Burton embraced and swore undying loyalty, no matter what the outcome. The two men had been friends for years: While Wayne was shooting *Legend of the Lost* in the Sahara, Burton was acting nearby in *Bitter Victory* under the direction of Nicholas Ray (Wayne's *Flying Leathernecks* director). When Burton and Ray heard that Wayne had injured himself falling from a camel, they brought over a saddle to mark the occasion.

Wayne returned to the Pink Palace a final time in 1978. He was staying in one of the bungalows for several days when director Peter Bogdanovich brought over an award he had accepted for him (the "John Ford Medallion for outstanding contributions to Americana on the screen," presented by the Utah Film Festival). Even though Wayne was ill, he made Bogdanovich a job offer on the spot: to direct his next picture, a period piece called *Beau John*. Wayne had bought the rights and had already announced it as his next project to the press. He also wanted to reunite with his *Shootist* co-star Ron Howard, promising the young actor a great part. "It's you and me or nobody!"[16]

"There aren't enough words"

Grauman's Chinese Theater, 6925 Hollywood Boulevard, opened in 1927 and is now the TCL Chinese Theater. Each year, several million people want to take a look at the famous forecourt where the stars left handprints and footprints in the concrete. Twenty years after the premiere of his first film *The Big Trail*, Wayne joined the ranks of immortal movie legends: He was the 125th star to be immortalized outside the theater. On January 25, 1950, he put his cowboy boots in the wet cement and etched his name next to it. With the sentiment, "To Sid—there are not enough words," Wayne paid his respects to the man who had created this Hollywood landmark, Sid Grauman. Atypically, this honoree did not push his hands but his right fist into the cement. When his future wife, the Peruvian Pilar Pallete, first came to Hollywood, the first thing she did as a tourist was check out his footprints. In "Lucy Visits Grauman's" (1955), a hilarious episode of the popular *I Love Lucy* TV series, Lucille Ball decides to steal Wayne's cement slab.

Across the street is Grauman's other famed movie house, the **Egyptian Theater**. Sid Grauman started the tradition of lavish premieres on October 18, 1922, with *Robin Hood*. Wayne premiered *The Alamo* at the Egyptian on October 26, 1960.

Going on Stage

Wayne even performed at Grauman's in the stage play *What Price Glory*. He squeezed this in his already busy 1949 schedule as a favor for John Ford. The director mounted that production for charity, for the Purple Heart Association. Everybody chipped in. The play starred Ward Bond and Pat O'Brien, with cameos by Wayne, Maureen O'Hara (actually their first acting appearance together), Gregory Peck and Oliver Hardy. They rehearsed at the **Masquers Club** at 1765 North Sycamore Avenue, founded in 1925. The troupe held the dress rehearsal there on February 21, 1949. That night, James Stewart explained to the 450 invited guests how the play's proceeds would be used to help veterans. Then they performed the play as a six-city tour of one-night stands from February 22 through March 11, 1949: Long Beach, San Jose, Oakland, San Francisco, Pasadena and finally back in Hollywood. The last show was planned for March 2 at the Philharmonic Hall, which was owned by the Methodist Church. But there were complaints about the profanity in the rowdy play, and the church did not allow it to go on. Ford moved his show across the street to Grauman's Chinese.

Wayne made his entrance at the end of the second act;

The only time the two giants of the screen appeared together was on stage: backstage with Gregory Peck at the *What Price Glory* play (photograph by Roland Schaefli).

Made from the real Sands of Iwo Jima: the cement for John Wayne's footprints at the Chinese Theatre (photograph by Roland Schaefli).

so he had plenty of time to sit around with Oliver Hardy. Wayne was very much in awe of the great comedian. This led to Wayne offering him the part of his sidekick in his upcoming production *The Fighting Kentuckian*. "Duke learned a lot from [the *What Price Glory*] experience," Ward Bond said. "It was his first and only stage appearance and he freely admits he had an acute attack of stage fright—and so did I."[17]

Wayne had come close to being on stage before: at the **Las Palmas Theatre**, 1642 Las Palmas Avenue. When it was a stage of the performing arts in the 1930s, Wayne's longtime friend Paul Fix (he would later pen the script of *Tall in the Saddle*) wanted to put on his own stage play. Wayne helped his buddy out by working as the stage manager. At one point during the play, Wayne was to ring a bell for the phone, and Fix was then supposed to answer it on stage. The play was in progress when Wayne realized he had forgotten to put the phone on the table upstage. So he grabbed a phone, ran backstage and shoved his fist, with the phone in it, through the scenery. He dumped the prop on the table and pulled his hand back out, so Fix could answer it.[18]

In *Shooting Star*, Zolotow wrote about another of Fix's failed attempts to lure Wayne to the theater: In the early 1930s, Fix rented a theater on Figueroa Street in San Francisco to do the play *Red Sky at Evening*. Wayne was supposed to be in it. To remedy his flutters, he took a bottle of Scotch backstage. When he got on and was hit with a breakaway vase, he said, "Where am I?" But that line wasn't what Fix had written.[19]

Cutting a Record

At the **RCA Hollywood Studio**, 6363 Sunset Boulevard, Wayne and John Mitchum recorded their record album *America, Why I Love Her* in 1972. It happened almost by accident: On the set of *Chisum*, co-star Forrest Tucker asked Wayne to listen to a song he had heard Mitchum sing. Wayne was playing a game of chess with Mitchum's nephew Chris. Wayne stopped the game and drawled, "Well, go ahead. I'm listenin'." John Mitchum recited, "Why Are You Marching, Son?" Halfway through, Wayne had tears in his eyes. They made a handshake deal to record it. When they cut the record at RCA, Wayne had a difficult time recording the lyrics with a sore throat. He would take sips of Jack Daniels to ease his pain. "Most of the time he would spit the whiskey out," John Mitchum recalled, "but once in a while he would look at us apologetically and say, 'Oops, that one slipped away!'" Wayne did the vocal recordings; the music was later added. In hindsight, it was obvious to Mitchum that Wayne's former cancer operation was hindering his breathing. When they recorded "Taps"—a single trumpet would play Taps before Wayne's voice would come back in—Wayne looked

at Mitchum with tears welling from his eyes. "Mitch," he whispered softly, "aren't the people gonna get mad at me for talkin'?"[20]

Wayne was no stranger to the microphone. From 1934 to 1955, NBC broadcast *Lux Presents Hollywood*, a popular radio show featuring adaptations of film scripts, often hosted by Cecil B. DeMille. Whenever possible, the original cast members performed in front of a live audience at the **CBS Playhouse Theater**, 1615 Vine Street. On March 7, 1949, Wayne reprised his role from *Red River* (Jeff Chandler played the Montgomery Clift part). On March 12, 1951, Wayne was Nathan Brittles two years after he played the character in *She Wore a Yellow Ribbon* (Mel Ferrer in the John Agar role). Messages from the sponsor, the Lux luxury soap, would interrupt the program. The Beaux-Arts building of the CBS Playhouse Theater, constructed in 1926, was sold to the Montalban Foundation in 1999 and re-opened as the **Ricardo Montalban Theatre**.

Wayne had been on the air before the *Lux Presents Hollywood*. On April 12, 1943, on *The Louella Parsons Show*, he had relived his experiences from *Pittsburgh* with Marlene Dietrich.

On January 9, 1949, ten years after *Stagecoach*, he was the Ringo Kid again on the airwaves for *NBC Theater*. John Ford introduced the first Screen Directors Guild production: "Now the story and the cast are united again" (except that Ward Bond had taken over for Andy Devine). CBS had beat NBC by three years in putting *Stagecoach* on; they'd had Randolph Scott as the Ringo Kid, along with Claire Trevor.

If you tuned in on August 5, 1949, you would had heard Wayne's voice in a *Screen Directors Playhouse* adaptation of *Fort Apache*. Ward Bond filled in for Henry Fonda that night.

Wayne even did a radio serial. *Three Sheets to the Wind* was on NBC Sunday evenings from February 15, 1942, to June 28, 1942. His *Seven Sinners* director Tay Garnett helmed it. For 26 episodes, Wayne played an eccentric detective who sometimes pretended to be drunk to throw his enemies off guard. The character might have been unusual for Wayne but having the detective sail his own ship to solve mysteries certainly hit close to home.

John Wayne Theater

Knott's Berry Farm, 8039 Beach Boulevard in Buena Park, is a renowned theme park in the neighborhood of Disneyland. What started as a berry farm began to grow into a family theme park destination. Wayne knew Walter Knott (he called him Mr. Free Enterprise) for ten years when, in 1969, the star helped to open the Timbermountain Log Ride, assisted by his son Ethan. In 1971, Knott named his 2150-seat theater the John Wayne Theater. At a press reception, Wayne

The Grand Opening of the John Wayne Theatre
GALA WORLD PREMIERE
"Big Jake"

The formal invitation to the Grand Opening of the John Wayne Theatre, at Knott's Berry Farm in Los Angeles (author's collection).

said that he felt "rather embarrassed to be here and still alive but I'm not gonna die just so they can call it the John Wayne Theatre." The star premiered *Big Jake* in it (Governor Ronald Reagan attended along with other dignitaries) and the theater even displayed some Wayne memorabilia in a trophy room. However, Knott's rechristened the full-service theater again: It is now the Charles M. Schulz Theatre.

Catalina Island

The island located 26 miles off the Los Angeles coastline was one of John Wayne's favorite places. **Catalina** had a special meaning to him, ever since that fateful October day in 1929 when John Ford shot his submarine movie *Men Without Women* just off the coast of the island. The U.S. Navy allowed the use of a fleet submarine. The scene in which the submarine was abandoned called for stuntmen to surface in a burst of bubbles. Prop man Wayne provided the air bubbles. As the destroyers were swinging back at the right time for a great shot, each actor was supposed to swim out, duck down in the air bubbles, and be picked up. "We were out between San Diego and Catalina," Wayne remembered decades later. "But I want to tell ya, this was one of those gunmetal-gray days—and the waves were about the size of this house, those swells—and these guys took a dim view of what they were supposed to do."[21]

In a *New York Herald Tribune* interview (August 17, 1952), Ford recalled the incident that brought young Duke's abilities to his attention: "I spotted a big guy who worked in props, and I yelled at him, 'Hey Duke, get in there!'" Duke was up on amidships deck, turned the hose over to somebody else and ran to the edge. Without hesitating, he shucked off his clothes and made a clean dive off the side of the tanker they used for a camera ship: "I hit the god-damned water and swam out there, went down under and came up for all of 'em!" Ford made a decision on the spot. "I took a good look at him and decided he was quite a boy—or quite a man." Wayne remembered, "After they hauled me back aboard ship, I was so cold and near drowned, they took pity on me and let me stay in Ford's stateroom to recuperate. Jack acted sincerely worried about me, and even gave me several shots of his best bourbon to warm me up by."[22]

Young Morrison did triple duty that day, as a prop man, a stuntman and playing the bit part of a radio operator. He always pointed out they cheated him out of the stuntman fee he had coming.

Young Wayne felt that after *Men Without Women*, Ford started to appreciate him. He told Peter Bogdanovich that after the incident, he started looking at pictures with a different view. He was beginning to enjoy this work and thought about how long it would be before he'd get any place if he took the law course he had been planning on. "I was going to school with kids whose fathers and uncles all had law firms and I started thinking I'll end up writing briefs in the back room for these bastards for ten years. I tell ya, the picture business started lookin' pretty good."[23]

Catalina continued to be significant in his life. It was on a trip to the island when Ford finally gave Wayne a screenplay adapted from the story "Stage to Lordsburg." Ford dangled the star-making part of the Ringo Kid in front of Wayne's nose like a carrot while Ford's yacht, the *Araner*, was moored in the harbor at **Avalon**, Catalina's main town. After two days, when they were back at the harbor of San Pedro, Ford told him he had the part.

Wake of the Red Witch was partially shot off the island. So many movies were made at the Isthmus/Two Harbors area of Catalina that it was nicknamed "The Isthmus Movie Colony." Wayne was a regular at **Christian's Hut** (now defunct) at the **Twin Harbors**. The restaurant had been built for the cast and crew of *Mutiny on the Bounty* in 1934 (Clark Gable lived above the bar). Wayne's business manager Bö Roos put some of Wayne's money into a yachting marina on Catalina.

Ray Kellogg, the second unit director who shared screen credit with Wayne for directing *The Green Berets*, was with him one night at the **Catalina Casino**, which is right on the tip of **Avalon Bay**. Kellogg saw a man challenge Wayne to a fight. Wayne suggested they arm wrestle to decide who was stronger. They tipped a wastebasket over to serve as the table. It was rusty, so their elbows went right through the bottom. After that, the man offered to buy Wayne a drink, and Wayne accepted.

When his best friend Ward Bond died of a heart attack on November 5, 1960, Wayne was a pallbearer along with Terry Wilson (Bond's co-star in the TV series *Wagon Train*). In his last testament, Bond had included his wish for a burial at sea: "I loved lobster all my life and I want to return the favor."[24] After the funeral, Wayne told Wilson, "You know, you've got a little chore ahead of you. Ward's cremated and he wants his ashes spread in Catalina." At that time, this was against the law, but Wilson and some of the gang fulfilled Ward's last wish. They went to one of his favorite coves and threw his ashes out while drinking toasts with bourbon, gin and vodka.[25]

That's how Wayne wanted to go himself. He had told Pilar he wanted to be cremated, his ashes scattered in the sea by Catalina. Wayne took the final voyage to his beloved island in April 1979. The weekend after his last public appearance at the Oscar telecast, he raised the anchor of his yacht, the *Wild Goose*, once more to take an Easter trip to **White's Landing**. He had taken hunting expeditions on Catalina when buffalo still roamed the island. On the day of this last visit, when he went shopping in Avalon, they did not yet have a museum. Today, the **Catalina Island Museum**, 217 Metropole Avenue, pays homage to the island's frequent visitor. One of the plaques tells an anecdote from the time after the arduous filming of *3 Godfathers* when Wayne invited Harry Carey, Jr., and his wife Marilyn on a trip to Two Harbors. After some

Ward Bond (right, with unidentified player) was Wayne's closest friend, "from school right on through," as he said in his eulogy. He never stopped thinking about Ward, even fantasizing about casting him in movies when he read scripts in the years following Bond's death in 1960 (author's collection).

drinking, Wayne and Marilyn went missing; Carey found them on the dance floor. Wayne was dangling her upside down, her head swaying near his feet. Carey rushed over and ordered Wayne to turn her upright. The next day, when Carey recounted the incident to Wayne, he exclaimed, "Bullshit, I

John Wayne himself said that John Ford directed not only his career but his life: the director (seated, wearing glasses and cap) giving his favorite actor instructions how to play the next scene of *The Horse Soldiers*, on location in Natchitoches, Louisiana (author's collection).

wouldn't do that!" However, upon returning home, Wayne, ever the gentleman, sent Marilyn a huge bunch of flowers—"to be on the safe side."

"I hate solemn funerals"

When John Ford was diagnosed with inoperable abdominal cancer, he moved to a five-bedroom Spanish-style house on 74–605 Old Prospector Trail in **Palm Desert**, close to the Eisenhower Hospital where he would undergo treatment. On a Wednesday, Ford said he wanted to see Duke. On Thursday Wayne flew down. As he rushed to his coach's side, Ford sarcastically said, "Come for the death watch, Duke?" Wayne was used to the roughness of his idealized father. "Hell, no. You're the anchor," he reportedly answered; "You'll bury us all." Ford died the next day, Friday, August 31, 1973, after receiving the last rites.

Ford's grave is in **Holy Cross**, the Catholic cemetery in Culver City; section M, Lot 304, Space 5, Ladera Heights. Admiral John Ford lies just a few plots from his brother Francis. Michael Blake (who would later write the screenplay of *Dances with Wolves*) was present at the funeral: "[Wayne] was crying, Niagara Falls. His eyes were so red. To watch John Wayne cry was an amazing sight to see."[26] Wayne supported Ford's widow and his daughter Barbara. The tattered flag draped on the coffin was from Ford's headquarters at the Battle of Midway. Wayne fought for control of his emotions throughout the ceremonies. Ford biographer Joseph McBride

With Howard Hawks on the set of *El Dorado* in 1965. Both men are wearing a "Red River D" belt buckle. The director had them made up as gifts for some of the crew, with the respective initials in the corner. In a friendship ritual, Hawks and Wayne swapped theirs, so in a total of nine films, Wayne wore the buckle marked H-W-H (author's collection).

observed how Wayne marched behind the coffin, crying hard as a soloist sang "The Battle Hymn of the Republic."

Howard Hawks had lived close to his celebrated colleague and friendly rival in **Palm Springs**, 501 Stevens Road. In his living room, he displayed a painting of two fighting stallions by Olaf Wieghorst, whom he justifiably called "the most famous American western painter today." Hawks had used it in the title credits of *El Dorado*. Hawks died at home on December 26, 1977. His ashes were scattered in the desert near Calimesa, California. Wayne read the poem "Immortality."[27]

"You can't eat awards…"

"I always go to the Academy Awards each year, in case one of my friends, who is out of town, wins an Oscar and I can pick it up on his behalf," Wayne once said. "I have received awards for Gary Cooper and John Ford. But no one—including me—has ever collected one for John Wayne."[28] The first time he was up for an Oscar was on March 23, 1950, at the ceremony at the **Hollywood Pantages Theater** (then known as the RKO Pantages Theatre). The palatial art deco theater at 6233 Hollywood Boulevard was then just 20 years old. Wayne was nominated for *Sands of Iwo Jima*; Winton C. Hoch won Best Color Cinematography for *She Wore a Yellow Ribbon*. Wayne lost to Broderick Crawford for *All the King's Men*, playing a role that Wayne had turned down. (According to some reports, Wayne threw the script overboard on a cruise to Catalina.) When the ceremony ended, Wayne told reporters, "After 25 years in the business, this does not keep me tossing in my bed at night."[29]

He picked up two Oscars on March 19, 1953, at the Pantages—one for Ford's direction of *The Quiet Man* and "one for our beloved Gary Cooper," in a film Wayne himself didn't love just as much as he loved old Coop, *High Noon*. Wayne was up for the award again, this time for Best Picture, as the producer of *The Alamo* (he got the news that his movie was nominated for seven awards while he was in Africa making *Hatari!*). The 33rd Annual Academy Awards were held at the **Santa Monica Civic Auditorium**, at 1855 Main Street in Santa Monica, the first time outside of L.A. The night of April 17, 1961, *The Alamo* picked up only one: for Best Sound. (Jim Hutton, Wayne's future *Green Berets* co-star, presented it.) Audrey Hepburn announced *The Apartment* the winner of Best Picture. Wayne smiled and applauded.

"…nor, more to the point, drink 'em"

His big night finally arrived on April 7, 1970, when he received the Best Actor Oscar for *True Grit* at the

Dorothy Chandler Pavilion, 135 North Grand Avenue (now the home of the L.A. Opera). After the interviews and the awards shows, as the Waynes waited for their limousine, Pilar suddenly realized that her husband was no longer clutching the Oscar. Seven-year-old Ethan gripped the award firmly. Footage of Ethan running up to his Dad to hand him the trophy, and Wayne holding it up to adoring fans, made it into the trailer for *Chisum* that year.

Wayne's last public appearance was at the Dorothy Chandler Pavilion, almost exactly nine years later, on April 9, 1979. That morning, he had gone to **Hoag Hospital** on Hoag Drive in Newport Beach for his daily radiation treatment. Aissa used the Apollo Motor Home to get him to Hollywood. He usually used it as a dressing room on location (Apollo advertised that it added "horsepower" to John Wayne). He had made reservations at the **Bonaventure Hotel** at 404S South Figueroa Street, a few minutes from the auditorium. When his longtime makeup man Dave Grayson arrived at the hotel to prepare him, Wayne instructed, "Go easy. I'd rather not look as if I'd just been embalmed." Wayne's companion Pat Stacy wrote in her memoirs, "I believe Duke was there to bid a glorious and fond farewell—to the industry, to his friends, to the

world."[30] That night, Jane Fonda, Wayne's longtime political adversary, dropped in to say a few encouraging words to her father's close friend, the man who had bounced her on his lap when she was a shy child.

Film historian Tony Thomas met Wayne on several occasions as a publicist. He was the writer for the Academy Awards show and wrote Wayne's final speech for the occasion: his last in public, his last hurrah. "It was a shock to see him. The huge bulk had gone. He was now thin, gaunt, the face ashen and the eyes those of a dying man." The publicist was tempted to write a lot of copy for him but when Wayne looked over the lines, he commanded, "Cut it down."[31]

The minute Wayne made his entrance to the *High and the Mighty* theme, Pilar "began to weep helplessly." Aissa later told her that Wayne was wearing a thick wetsuit under his tuxedo to make him look heavier.[32] After a thunderous standing ovation, he spoke: "I thank you. Believe me when I tell you how pleased I am to be here. Oscar and I have something in common. Oscar first came on the Hollywood scene in 1928. So did I. We're both a little weatherbeaten but we're both still here. And plan to be around a whole lot longer." He delivered this last line with his typical drawl, putting in that little characteristic John Wayne hitch, but everybody knew that it was a lie happily agreed upon.

At the Golden Globes, February 2, 1970: Joan Crawford receives the Cecil B. DeMille Award from John Wayne, at the Cocoanut Grove in Hollywood (author's collection).

He could have lived any place he wanted to, as he once stated in a commercial, "But I chose California." As the producer of *Seven Men from Now*, starring Randolph Scott, not only did he approve the director Budd Boetticher (right) but also the Californian locations (author's collection).

The John Wayne Cancer Institute

In memory of the actor, the Wayne Foundation formed the **John Wayne Cancer Institute** (formerly known as the John Wayne Cancer Clinic) in 1981 to promote leading-edge cancer research and the education of the next generation of cancer physicians. Located at 2200 Santa Monica Boulevard, **Saint John's Health Center** is easily accessible from all points in Southern California. Michael Wayne served as board chairman for almost two decades. After his premature death in 2003, Patrick Wayne took over. The family's goal remains: help to find the cure to the dreaded disease.

3

Shooting Star
of the Golden State
California Straight Ahead!

"I have kicked horses up and down the hills around Placerita Canyon."
—John Wayne in a letter to the Historical Society of Santa Clarita Valley

Governor Arnold Schwarzenegger praised John Wayne for being a Californian: "John Wayne lives forever in the hearts of Americans, and particularly in the hearts of the people of our state, which was his home from the age of six years until the day he died in 1979."[1] The majority of John Wayne movies were shot In Old California.

On December 12, 1913, when young John Wayne was living in a desert just outside Los Angeles, Cecil B. DeMille boarded a westbound Southern Pacific train. His plan was to scout locations in Arizona. However, he had heard that other filmmakers were already shooting further west, in Los Angeles—even in winter. That's how it came to pass that DeMille didn't step off the train in Flagstaff. Some movie pioneers were using Glendale as a filming site. Yet DeMille chose to

Kicking up horses around Placerita Canyon—sometimes even jumping on them. In 1932's *Ride Him, Cowboy*, with Duke, the Miracle Horse (author's collection).

rent a Hollywood barn, to function as his studio. Soon he was making *The Squaw Man*, the first Hollywood movie.

When Wayne came to the Hollywood scene in 1928, the dream factory had been at it for years. Around three decades after DeMille stayed on the westbound train, the founding father of Hollywoodland directed Wayne in *Reap the Wild Wind*.

"I'm always the straight guy"

Shortly after the misfire of *The Big Trail*, Wayne found himself in B-movies. Until the end of the decade, he would work for the so-called Poverty Row studios. Those modest films would usually confine themselves to locations within easy reach. Those early oaters helped the young actor shape the John Wayne screen persona. In a 1972 interview with *Life*, he revealed how the surroundings and the weather would influence a performance: "Your character changed with the effect of the elements." During those long days on location, Wayne spent a lot of time with the cowboys who had been forced off the range by the Depression and had migrated to Hollywood looking for work. "In the evening, I spent my time with them playing poker. There was always somebody who'd bring along a guitar or a banjo, and we'd all sit around the fire singing with the stars shining bright above us."

He added, "Great times."[2]

When the cowpoke in *Westward Ho* got into a romantic mood, he would serenade his gal around the campfire. With Sheila Mannors in the Lone Pine meadows near what is now Highway 395. In 2001, Mannors revealed that they had an affair. After their third picture together, the spark just burned out, but they remained friends until he died (author's collection).

"A lot of unhappiness back there"

Yet at the time, it must have been a bit of a shock for the struggling young star to find himself back where he began: in Antelope Valley. It didn't look like *Rainbow Valley* to him. The Morrison family had lived there under harsh conditions. As a kid, he often used the **Mint Canyon Road**, then just a dirt road, which ran through Antelope Valley. Now film companies shot chase scenes on that strip. His first Mascot serial, *Shadow of the Eagle*, was made there in just 21 days, between December 1931 and January 1932. Wayne may have hated the harsh surroundings since his childhood days—yet it was there that he formed a lifelong friendship during his three weeks on that 12-chapter serial. One night the crew worked until midnight. Most of the company decided to bed down in the desert for the night rather than return to town. Wayne and Yakima Canutt shared a bottle of bootleg whiskey that night by a fire. As they exchanged the bottle, the ace stuntman said, "Well, Duke, it don't take very long to spend the whole night here." Wayne, with a pull at the whiskey and a chuckle, agreed, "Sure don't."[3] Yak was a real cowhand, Wayne observed. He would work closely with Yak in the years to come.

"My build-up was done through constant exposure"

Wayne was back in Antelope Valley the next year. *Riders of Destiny* was filmed in the desert communities he called home as a kid: Palmdale and Lancaster. Producer Paul Malvern recalled that he found fresh locations for those movies even if they were cheap westerns because "people don't want to see the same thing" all the time. Therefore, he utilized filming locations he knew as a hunter and fisherman. "Hell, we had background! I found places where you couldn't even get a major company into today."[4]

Wayne found *Riders of Destiny*, released October 10, 1933, a humiliating experience. As Singin' Sandy, he became the first singing cowboy on screen. Wayne had to sing and strum a guitar. Some 40 years later, he was still fuming about it. In 1955, on the TV show *Warner Bros. Presents*, he called this period "the short and unhappy career of Singin' Sandy." In 1971, talking with the editors of *Playboy*, he described the embarrassment on personal appearances when the kids insisted that he sing a song. "But I couldn't take along the fella who played the guitar out on one side of the camera and the fella who sang on the other side. So finally, I went to the head of the studio and said, 'Screw this.'"

The Lucky Texan, next on the Monogram assembly line, was also filmed in Antelope Valley. Just when Wayne may have thought he had escaped the quickie Westerns and Antelope Valley for good, they sent him right back: *California Straight Ahead!*, one of six non–Westerns he made for Universal, was made in the vicinity. In 1938, the first of his *Three Mesquiteers* series, *Pals of the Saddle*, brought him back to Antelope Valley yet again. Right after *Stagecoach*, he had to go back once more as the leader of the Mesquiteer trio: *Wyoming Outlaw* was shot in May 1939 in the foothills of his old hometown, Lancaster.

Bronson Canyon

Students of John Wayne will come to recognize that even after he became the world's box office champion, he kept returning to the same old B-movie grind. **Bronson Canyon** is the most evident example of this. On August 12, 1955, Ethan Edwards took Debbie in his arms in the last reel of *The Searchers*. Wayne was a giant to Natalie Wood: "He was able to lift me as though I were a doll."[5] Yet the moment that made film history was not made in a cave in Monument Valley. Nor was it Wayne's first trip to those caves in the Hollywood Hills. The studios had used Bronson

"One look that works is better than twenty lines of dialogue," John Wayne occasionally said about the monosyllabic characters he often played. Working overtime at the Poverty Row Studios, he is back at Antelope Valley in *Pals of the Saddle* in 1938 (author's collection).

Canyon—actually man-made tunnels—countless times. Wayne had been there, done that, more than 20 years before. He first defended these stark rock faces in the Mascot serial *The Hurricane Express*.

He was back in the horseshoe-shaped canyon for *Sagebrush Trail* in 1933 for an action-packed shootout (he actually drives a stagecoach from one end of the tunnel to the other). To get to Bronson Canyon, exit the 101 Freeway North at Hollywood Boulevard, drive Bronson Avenue and go left at **Canyon Drive**.

"Guess you don't remember me"

"We'd start before dawn, using flares to light close-ups. When the sun came up, we'd do some medium-range shots. In full daylight, we'd do the distance shots, following the sun up one side of the hill and down the other side." That's how Wayne recounted (for the January 28, 1972, *Life*) how he rode the Santa Susana Mountains and the trails in Simi Valley.

The city of Santa Clarita keeps its Western heritage alive with the Cowboy Fest. The Western Walk of Stars is

Young John Wayne defends Bronson Canyon at gunpoint in *Hurricane Express*, **at the same cave entrance later used in** *The Searchers* **(author's collection).**

a salute to the screen idols who worked there. Inductees are honored with a bronze star stamped into Main Street of Old Town Newhall. In the heyday of the Western, Newhall was one of the most filmed areas in the Los Angeles area. When Wayne first got to Newhall, he was playing second fiddle to Western stars Buck Jones and Tim McCoy. He was the hero's best friend in *Range Feud* and *Two-Fisted Law*. Both were lensed at the **Walker Ranch**, named after the area's first homesteader, at Placerita Canyon Road. When Wayne moved up into lead roles, *Riders of Destiny* used the Walker ranch as well. The cabin is still there, now at the Placerita Canyon Park.

It was the Walker Ranch that got Wayne back in contact with the people in the Santa Clarita Valley in 1978. The Historical Society wrote him a letter, pointing out that he had made a false statement in one of his Great Western Bank commercials when he stated that gold was "first"

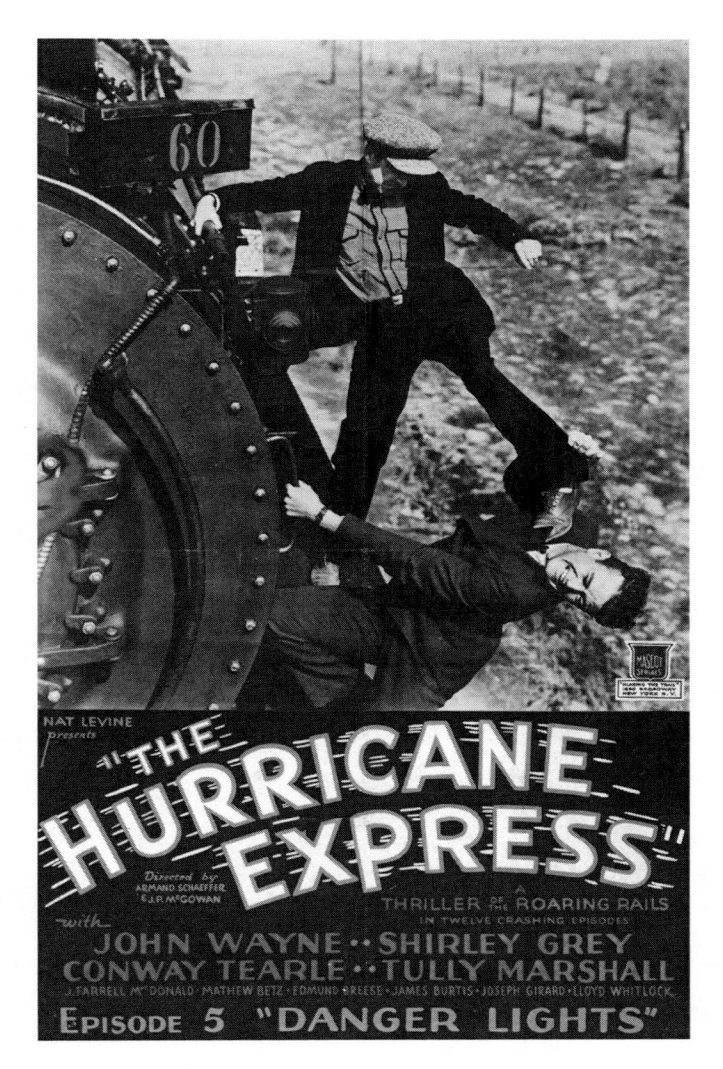

The *Hurricane Express* serial used the Saugus train station. Early one morning, before filming started at the railroad site, Wayne joined a hobo for a stew (author's collection).

discovered at Sutter's Mill. "Knowing that you have shot more Indians than ever lived here in the Santa Clarita Valley, we of the Historical Society are shocked that you did not know that the gold was first discovered right here in Placerita Canyon at the location of many of your Western films—near the Walker cabin." And yes, gold was found there seven years before the discovery in Sutter's Creek. Wayne replied immediately: "You are so right! I have kicked horses up and down the hills around Placerita Canyon and stepped on every foot of it. Matter of fact, they built that Western street that used to be there off my back, so I certainly knew that the first gold was discovered in Placerita Canyon." He thanked the Society for calling the mistake to his attention and went back to Great Western to have the word "first" removed.[6]

One of *Hurricane Express'* primary locations was the **Newhall train depot**. The Saugus train station (as it was also called) remained in use, not just as a station but a movie location, until the late 1960s. Saved from the wrecking ball, it was moved on June 24, 1980, about three miles from its original location. Now located at 24101 Newhall Avenue, it was dedicated as a State Historic Landmark and now serves as the headquarters for the Santa Clarita Valley Historical Society (SCVHS).

Also on display among the buildings in the **Heritage Junction Historic Park** is the Ramona Chapel. It was built in 1926 and moved from Mint Canyon to its current location in 2001. This is where Gary Cooper was inducted into the Sioux Nation. The Historical Society claims it was also used in one of Wayne's B-movies yet it's difficult to pinpoint which one.

"It's meat-and-potatoes roles"

The hilarious *Lucky Texan* action sequence in which Wayne chases Yak Canutt on a motorized railroad track car was shot at **Lang Station** in Soledad Canyon, on Lang Station Road. Canutt, playing the bad guy as usual, had to be in the same shot as Wayne's hero, who was to leap from his horse onto the car. Producer Paul Malvern had neglected to bring out another stuntman. When they were setting up to do the stunt, it dawned on them that if Canutt would have to double Wayne, someone else would have to double Canutt. While they were trying to figure things out, Wayne looked questioningly at Canutt; the stuntman nodded in agreement. "Which one?" he asked with a grin. "Give me your wardrobe," Wayne answered.[7] They changed clothes. In the scene, Canutt doubled Wayne and Wayne doubled Canutt. After the stuntman had made the transfer from horse to handcar, they switched back to their own costumes.

Ramona Chapel now stands at the Heritage Junction Historic Park, next to the old Saugus train depot (photograph by Roland Schaefli).

"All I do is sell sincerity"

Wayne's mission statement during those busy years in the Placerita Canyon: "My main duty was to ride, fight, keep my hat on, and at the end of the shooting still have enough strength left to kiss the girl and ride off on my horse, or kiss my horse and ride off on the girl, whichever they wanted."[8]

He made movies along the Placerita Canyon Road one after the other: *Randy Rides Alone* in late April to early May 1934, *The Star Packer*, *The Lawless Frontier* and *Texas Terror* in November the same year, followed by *The Desert Trail* in February 1935. On March 27, he began shooting *The Dawn Rider* in ten days. It was soon followed by *Paradise Canyon* in early April. It was on this picture that Canutt recalled they had to do a rugged fight and, "believe me, Wayne can put on a better fight than the majority of stuntmen." In one stunt on *Paradise Canyon*, Canutt was doubling Wayne and exposed a bald spot on the top of his head. No one noticed while shooing it, but when the picture ran at a local theater, everyone saw it: "After the show, Wayne, the director, and the producer really chewed me out." From then on, whenever Canutt doubled

for Wayne, the actor would say, "Get the shoe blacking on that bald spot!"[9]

Wayne was on *The Lonely Trail* from April 14 to April 20, 1936. In one scene, somebody shoots a water dipper out of Wayne's hand. A live bullet did that. Wayne recalled, "An old man came onto the set wearing thick glasses and carrying a suitcase." The man opened the case, took out a two-piece rifle and assembled it. "We all wondered what would happen as we started filming the scene. Well, during the filming, this old man proceeded to shoot up the set, sending live ammo flying all around us. Then he took his gun apart, put it back in his case, and left the set as quietly as he came there."[10]

The old-timer was a sharpshooter, hired to lend some realism to a shootout. Director Joe Kane backed up Wayne's story. He refused to direct the scene. The first slug went through the dipper without taking it out of the star's hand. So they filled another one with water and did it again. "Doubly dangerous because water can deflect a bullet," said Kane. "That's how films were made then," Wayne concluded. Actually, the B-movie veteran carried a scar on his leg as a souvenir from those days: He was burned by a blank, which can be quite hazardous when shot at close range.

Wayne didn't turn his back on Santa Clarita after he made it into the big leagues with *Stagecoach*. In *New Frontier*, he saves the day by closing the flood gates of the **Van Norman Reservoir** in Granada Hills. This was his last *Three Mesquiteer* outing but not his last visit to Placerita Canyon. Even though his *Dark Command* character claimed that he "aimed to see them mountains" of Kansas, it was also shot in Placerita Canyon, from November 29, 1939, to February 1, 1940. Wayne told *Life* in 1972: "There were a great many days when it was fun, especially on the action shots, with the open air, the setting, the background. But the scenes were work, they were always work."

"Hold it!"

Wayne had waited to break out of B-movies for a long time. Yet when the "Stage to Lordsburg" finally arrived, he found himself acting in his former B-Western surroundings. Even Lordsburg, the town of Ringo's salvation, was just the backlot of his home studio, Republic.

This book breaks with the tradition of calling *Stagecoach* a "Monument Valley picture." As a matter of fact, it stresses the point that the majority of the locations were found in California. The Ringo Kid had it right when he quipped, "I guess you can't break out of prison and into society the same week."

Stagecoach was in production from November 10 to December 22, 1938. The "road" that took the Ringo Kid

The Ringo Kid takes a break on the rocky outcroppings at Iverson Movie Ranch. His *Stagecoach* hat was displayed at the Cinémathèque Française in Paris for decades (author's collection).

from Tonto to Lordsburg and John Wayne from obscurity to superstardom started at the **RKO Encino Ranch**, then located on the outskirts of the city of Encino, near the Los Angeles River. RKO Radio Pictures had purchased the property in 1931 for the epic *Cimarron* (one of the few Westerns to win the Best Picture Oscar). *Stagecoach* director John Ford used the Western street constructed for *Cimarron* as his starting point, Tonto. As the stagecoach leaves the RKO Ranch, Ford cuts to Arizona the first time, as the coach rolls in the direction of **El Capitan**, the volcanic mountain considered sacred by the Navajo, seven miles from **Kayenta** (see Chapter 5).

"Some things a man just can't run away from"

At that point the film reaches Monument Valley, but when Wayne twirls his rifle to stop the stagecoach, he's at **Iverson Ranch** on Santa Susana Pass, well-known to him. He had been shooting B-Westerns in Chatsworth for a whole decade. The movie ranch in the Simi Hills was in operation as early as 1912. When he makes his now-famous entrance, he is backed up by Wyatt Earp Rock, the distinctive boulder in the Iverson Gorge.

As the stagecoach arrives at the first relay station, it runs between a famous rock formation in Lower Iverson (Tower Rock) to the left and the Sphinx to the right. The place is now

John Wayne makes his classic entrance, stopping the *Stagecoach* at Iverson to hitch a ride. George Bancroft has a gun on him while Andy Devine holds the six-up (author's collection).

the backyard of a private home. If you turn from the Santa Susana Pass into **Red Mesa Road**, you will stand in the middle of the **Garden of the Gods**, as this heavily filmed area became known. But you'll find a row of condos in its place, part of the Cal West Townhomes which went up in the late 1980s.

When the stagecoach reaches the second relay station, it's actually the same set as before, seen from a different camera angle. As it departs on the last leg of the trip, it's heading out in yet the third direction at Iverson. In the movie, the travelers then get to Lee's Ferry, burned to the ground by the Apaches. Ford put the smoking ruins on one

The stagecoach runs between Tower Rock and Sphinx at Iverson, now in the back of a private condominium (photograph by Roland Schaefli).

The neglected landmark of Beale's Cut: John Ford used this location again for *Stagecoach*, as a transition between Monument Valley in Arizona and the dry lake in California (photograph by Roland Schaefli).

of the most frequently used spots at Iverson, with Batman Rock and the Happy Slab in the background. Today, it's a parking lot.

"There's a nice place, a real nice place"

Now the stagecoach must cross a river. It was in fact the **Kern River**, three hours north of Chatsworth, close to Kernville.

Again, this wasn't unknown territory for Wayne: He had been to Kernville for no less than ten B-Westerns between 1933 and 1935 (see Chapter 16). Before *Stagecoach*, Yak Canutt had done countless stunts at the lagoon area, south of the current dam. There is a jumping-off rock used many times when the hero escapes the heavies by jumping his horse into the water below.

Ford gave Canutt the script to study, and Canutt found "one gag which had never been done before": The passengers attach logs to either side of the coach to float it, and the six horses swim and pull the coach across the river. Canutt figured this would be tricky. On location, he weighed the stagecoach and the eight passengers. It was heavy. He then hired a Paramount special effects expert who supervised the building of four hollow logs, two for each side of the coach. They were made so that they could be secured to the boom poles located on the understructure of the coach, but would allow the wheels to turn. The logs had enough air in them to float the vehicle. The stuntman devised an underwater cable that was attached to the front lead tongue. The cable ran through a pulley to an off-stage truck on the opposite riverbank. The rigging took three days, and everything worked the first time.[11]

The largest artifact of the **Kern Valley Museum** at 49 Big Blue Rd is the wagon Canutt used to make that crossing. It is slightly different from the Concord type of stagecoach. For this long shot of the river crossing, he converted the "mud wagon" that today stands in the backyard of the museum into a regular stagecoach.

As an aside, Ward Bond declared in his will that he owned an interest in two parcels of real property located in Kern County, 320 and 80 acres. "I hereby give, devise and bequeath to my friend, Marion M. Morrison, also known as John Wayne, an option to purchase."

"I know all I wanna know"

After the river crossing, Ford makes another clever transition: To get from rocky Monument Valley to the chase sequence on the flat plains, he uses **Beale's Cut** in Newhall. He had filmed at the pass between the San Gabriel and the Santa Susana Mountains before, in his Harry Carey western *Straight Shooting* and in the epic *The Iron Horse*. Tom Mix made it famous in 1923 by "jumping" it. (Actually, he rode his horse Tony across a wooden bridge and special effects spliced it in.) In 1938, the Sierra Highway was the main roadway from Los Angeles to Newhall. The cut in the mountain suffered a partial collapse during the 1994 earthquake and is not easy to find as the road leading up from Sierra Highway is now closed. Even the historical marker is gone. Expect a march up from the former parking area, now used as a dump.

"You may need me and this Winchester"

After Beale's Cut, the Indians chase the coach to **Lucerne Dry Lake**. Ford had shot the landrush of *Three Bad Men* on the dry lake bed east of **Victorville**. When Peter Bogdanovich interviewed him in 1969 for the TV special *Directed by John Ford*, he asked how Ford shot the land rush in his 1926 film. Ford replied in his usually sardonic tone: "With a camera!" The lake is five miles wide and almost four miles in length. Highway 247 runs through it. Ford filmed on both sides of the road. On the right side (looking north), he had the cavalry coming to the rescue (with the San Bernardino Mountains in the background, to the south). The incredible stunts were accomplished on the left side of the road.

Producer Walter Wanger visited the Victorville set and to his horror he saw Wayne climbing to the top of the careening coach. Wayne was quoted about it in *Time* magazine (August 8, 1969): Wanger screamed to get the movie star off there before he killed himself. Wayne assured him that he had been doing things like that for some time now, "just to eat."

Even this iconic *Stagecoach* location wasn't new to Wayne. He had been near Victorville in 1932 to shoot *Somewhere in Sonora* at **Deadman Hill**, in the southern portion of the Granite Mountain, at the eastern edge of Apple Valley. Highway 18 runs along the southern edge of the hills. They used the then unpaved highway, heading west. When in Apple Valley, Wayne stayed at the **Apple Valley Inn**, an area landmark, on the Apple Valley Inn Road. When Roy Rogers and Dale Evans became Apple Valley residents, they leased the inn and restaurant and renamed it Roy Rogers Apple Valley Inn. It closed in 1987 and was restored in 2003.

The Apache assault on the stagecoach was shot in two days (three, according to Canutt's memoirs). Ford had mounted his cameras on automobiles that could go over 40 miles an hour on the bed of the dry lake. Interviewed for the TV special *The American West* almost 40 years later, Wayne said about Canutt's legendary stunt of jumping from the coach to the lead horses, "I was happy to settle for the close-up."

Wayne had a little to do with getting Canutt the job of *Stagecoach* stunt coordinator. When Canutt walked into Ford's office to be interviewed, Ford studied him for a moment, then remarked, "Well, Enos, how are you?" Few people knew Yakima's real name since he always went by his rodeo nickname. "I see Wayne has given you all the inside dope on me," Canutt shot back.[12]

Canutt had a farmer with a tractor disc up 15 or 20 acres of the lake bed to give the stuntmen good soft ground for the falls. Henry Wills, a longtime stuntman on Ford Westerns, recalled that the Victorville location was "freezing. We didn't have any clothes on as Indians!"[13]

After Ford had enough footage of the Indians splitting to either side of the running coach, he waved his stunt coordinator over. "Yak," he said, "we'll do that Indian routine of yours now. So get into your war paint." Canutt had done a similar stunt earlier in some of the quickie Westerns but this would be the first time on a

Cut to the chase: the location of the famous chase sequence in *Stagecoach*, the dry lakebed east of Victorville (photograph by Roland Schaefli).

major motion picture. The stunt of him falling under the coach, letting the six horses pass by—three on either side— and the coach pass over him is now a cherished moment in film history. Steven Spielberg and George Lucas made their reference to Canutt in the first of their Indiana Jones movies (exchanging the stagecoach for a Nazi truck). "All in all, it is a gag that you could easily rub yourself out with if you make the wrong move," he declared.

Canutt picked a section with hard surface so the wheels would not sink into the ground, then told Ford to run the camera car at 37 miles an hour. After he had done the transfer from his pinto to the lead horses, Ford called him over. "A hell of a lot you know about how fast a team can run," he snorted. The coach was going 45 miles per hour. Ford predicted he could never top that transfer with the finish of his gag. Yet Canutt did. When Wayne fired his first shot at him,

he fell between the team, dragging along. Wayne gave the action performer his due even in his last written interview with *Real West* magazine (March 1979): "His falling down between the horses has never been duplicated." Canutt was "looking back between the horse's flying legs and the undercarriage of the coach. It was a little spooky, but the horses were running straight." When Wayne fired again, "I let go of the tongue, keeping my legs together and my arms flat on my body." As the back of the coach went over him, he rolled over and tried to get up. He heard Ford holler "Cut!" The cameramen weren't sure they got it. But Ford shook his head when Canutt offered to do it again (and make more money): "I'll never shoot that again. They better have it."

That evening, Ford, Wayne and Canutt celebrated at the restaurant of the **Green Spot Motel** in Victorville where they were staying. Canutt would rig up a stunt in *Stagecoach*

The *Stagecoach* cast assembled for a group shot at the Samuel Goldwyn studio in Los Angeles: Claire Trevor, John Wayne, Andy Devine, John Carradine, Louise Platt, Thomas Mitchell, Berton Churchill, Donald Meek and George Bancroft (author's collection).

fashion just a year after, for *Dark Command* (on the Melody Ranch location): He let Wayne ride between the horses of a carriage. This was the start of Yakima Canutt's unparalleled career as a second unit director.

"Will you go?"

After Ford's cavalry arrives in the nick of time, the stagecoach finally reaches Lordsburg. Familiar surroundings for Wayne as that Western street was on the Republic backlot. Ford completed his masterpiece with the interiors at the **Samuel Goldwyn Studios**, located at 1041 North Formosa Avenue. Wayne said about the process shots inside a mock-up of the stagecoach, using rear projection, "It would have been useless to try to shoot those with the grinding and rattling of the wheels and the clippity-clop of six horses."[14] The studio lot on the corner of Formosa and Santa Monica Boulevard had changed hands several times and was leased by different independent producers. By the time Ford filmed on the interior stages, it belonged to Mary Pickford and Douglas Fairbanks. When Fairbanks died in 1939, he left his share to Mary. The lot was auctioned in 1955. Warner Brothers sold it again in 1999 when the name was officially changed to its longtime unofficial nickname, The Lot. A legendary Hollywood hangout across the street is still there: the **Formosa Cafe** at 7156 Santa Monica Boulevard. The Chinese-influenced restaurant was threatened by demolition as plans evolved for the Hollywood Gateway shopping center, next to The Lot. Due to preservationist efforts, the landmark was preserved. According to a Formosa legend (printed on the menu card), Wayne passed out in his booth after a night of imbibing at the café. The staff was not able to wake him and simply locked up. In the morning, they caught him in the kitchen making scrambled eggs. The story inspired the Duke's All Nighter cocktail.

When Andy Devine said, "If there's anything I don't like, it's driving a stagecoach through Apache country," he needn't have worried as the road almost never cut into Indian country. Instead, John Ford's renaissance of the Western genre was firmly rooted in the grounds of B-movie country.

"Shoot what you're pointin' at"

The Saugus Café is Los Angeles County's oldest continually operating eatery. It has been open 24 hours for more than a century (except for closure during World War II, due to food shortages). It's now called the Original Saugus Café, at 25861 Railroad Avenue. The stars didn't just eat there, they came to shoot their shows. Wayne appeared right in the back of the café—now the parking lot—in a Raquel Welch TV special called *Raquel!*, aired April 26, 1970. He taught Raquel how to handle a six-gun.

Wayne was familiar with Saugus ever since he appeared just a short distance from the café, in the Saugus Rodeo on the old Gibson Ranch in 1939. That day, the 18-year-old Harry Carey, Jr., laid eyes for the first time on the man who would have a great influence on his career in Westerns. His father Harry Carey was the rodeo's grand marshal and the officials had chosen Wayne, fresh from his success as the Ringo Kid, to ride in the parade. "When Wayne stepped out of a big black Packard twin-six Cadillac, you could tell he was drunk," Carey Jr. recalled.[15]

The Waynes were staying in the guest wing of the Carey ranch that weekend. They got him into the house and on a couch, where he explained that he had been out all night honoring the *Stagecoach* actors at the **Ambassador Hotel's Cocoanut Grove** (he probably meant the Academy Award ceremonies; his co-star Thomas Mitchell won for Best Supporting Actor). In 1968, Robert F. Kennedy was shot

John Wayne and Claire Trevor have reached the final destination in *Stagecoach*: Lordsburg is actually the backlot of John Wayne's home studio, Republic (author's collection).

at the Ambassador. It was demolished in 2005. Olive Carey fetched Wayne a bottle of Old Taylor. That helped him to straighten up. After consuming large quantities of black coffee, he was human again by noon and then even managed to drink a lot of the local beer, called Brown Derby. "So by the time he rode in the parade around the arena he was really soused," Harry Carey, Jr., remarked.[16] The rodeo grounds were on **Saugus Speedway**, 22500 Soledad Canyon Road. The racetrack now hosts weekly swap meets.

"Still the same shameless witch"

Stagecoach stars Claire Trevor and Wayne were quickly reteamed in *Allegheny Uprising*, filmed from July 10 to September 3, 1939, in the Santa Monica Mountains and **Lake Sherwood**. This lake near Thousand Oaks, east of Hidden Valley, is surrounded by Sherwood Forest, named after the forest in the Douglas Fairbanks vehicle *Robin Hood*. Another forest area, south of the lake along the Upper Lake Road, was used for the Errol Flynn version, *The Adventures of Robin Hood* and is now aptly named Maid Marian Forest. It was here that RKO had *Allegheny Uprising*'s impressive frontier fort constructed (and then removed after filming). Wayne was back in Sherwood for the lake scenes in *Dark Command* one year later, and again in 1944: The Albertson Ranch in *Tall in the Saddle* was located at Lake Sherwood.

"Don't try to win this war all by yourself"

The tracks the stagecoach made were still fresh when Wayne returned to Chatsworth, the neighborhood in the northwestern San Fernando Valley. *Flying Tigers* was shot between April 28 and June 26, 1942, at Russell Ranch—that's where **Westlake Village** now sits. Republic carpenters built a headquarters command complex replete with barracks, aircraft hangars and an airstrip. Seven wood-and-canvas replica P-40 planes were manufactured, with the now-famous shark's teeth painted on their bellies. Two flyers of the actual American Volunteer Group, Lawrence Moore and Kenneth Sanger, were technical advisors.

Studio publicity revealed that some aircraft sequences were shot at the Curtiss-Wright Aircraft Co. in Buffalo, New York. According to the film's pressbook, the Curtiss people "painted up a squadron of real P-40s with the well-known tiger shark design to be used in these scenes and the company made their test pilots and stunt flyers available to depict some of the precision flight formations for which the 'Tigers' were famous." The pressbook further notes that these scenes "had to be sent to Washington, D.C. for censorship, so that no vital information could reach the enemy." No

scene showing the interior of a plane could be shown. In fact, Republic had to design an instrument board of its own for cockpit closeups.

Flying Tigers was the crowning achievement in special effects by the Lydecker siblings, Howard and Theodore, under contract to Republic. Model airplanes on wires were used in some 150 aerial segments. "Few people outside of the film industry were even aware of all the miniatures they were viewing," said Ted Lydecker. "And I'm sure they didn't know the Lydecker Twins were working together making that small, detailed world seem so huge."[17] Unlike other studios who shot their miniatures indoors against painted backdrops, the Lydeckers were convinced that their large-scale models would look the most realistic when shot against real cloud formations. The aerial combat footage was shot under the Santa Fe sky. When Flying Tiger Wayne bombs the enemy railroad in the finale, it is a miniature train, placed in the foreground of a New Mexico landscape. Ironically, the

For their issue of June 1, 1950, "John Wayne Adventure Comics" used a picture of Wayne as the leader of the *Flying Tigers*. Cartoonists at Walt Disney created the famous insignia of the Republic of China Air Force (author's collection).

Lydecker brothers lost the Best Effects Oscar this year to another Wayne movie, *Reap the Wild Wind*.

Shortly after the war, in 1946, Wayne was back in Chatsworth again. *Without Reservations* was basically done on the RKO lot but for the few outdoor sequences, they came out to the wide-open spaces that are now the various recreation parks around Chatsworth.

"Risking the lives of these men is my business"

From November 6, 1944, to March 2, 1945, Wayne was working on another war movie that got its release while the fighting was still going on: For *Back to Bataan*, RKO transformed its backlot, the **Encino Ranch**, into the islands of the Philippines. The famed backlot covered 89 acres, bordered by Louise on the west, Balboa Park on the east, Burbank Boulevard on the south and Oxnard on the north. Just months before that shoot, Wayne had fought a range war at the RKO Ranch, in his usual western duds: *Tall in the Saddle* was in production from April 17 to June 19, 1944 (with additional stunt work at Flagstaff and on the outskirts of Tucson).

Local Filipinos, lettuce pickers from the Salinas Valley, pitched in as guerrilla fighters. When the makeup men dirtied the clothes worn by the guerrillas, the technical advisor who had been evacuated from Corregidor blew his top.

The Filipino fighters, he maintained, never allowed their uniforms to get dirty. Dirt photographs with difficulty, particularly in black and white. For a realistic appearance, a great deal more must be applied than seems normal to the naked eye. However, the colonel stomped off the set to phone Washington, "but the brass decided to keep out of what was strictly a parochial affair," according to Edward Dmytryk's memoir. So Dmytryk insisted on even more dirt on the costumes.[18] When newsreels of liberated guerrillas arrived, they showed the fighters wearing threadbare clothes.

In the January 1989 issue of *Los Angeles Magazine*, screenwriter Ben Barzman recalled watching the execution of a stunt he had dreamed up. In the script, Wayne would be blown out of his foxhole by a shell. Dmytryk had a special leather harness custom-tailored for the star. Very thin but tough wires were attached to the harness and then to an enormous crane. The control of the crane was high up in a tower above camera range. An explosive charge was placed right next to Wayne. At the fraction of a second the explosion happened, the crane lifted him high in the air and then dropped him a few inches from the ground, so it would look to the camera as if he had been blown sky-high. "There was a breath-holding moment as the smoke cleared away," Barzman remembered. "Then all sighed in relief as the tall figure pulled himself to his feet and staggered away." Dmytryk shouted, "Let's do it again! We need a protection shot." Wayne signaled back that a second take was okay with him.

When they shot the bit in which Wayne and Anthony Quinn were hiding in a pond, supposedly a rice paddy, sucking air through a reed, it was so cold that they had to break the ice on the ranch pond first. The actors went into the freezing water in their thin jungle fatigues just as soon as the cracked bits of ice were carried away. The soaked actors sipped bourbon between shots, and after a while they were laughing hilariously. The "Bataan Death March" sequence was shot near **Mulholland Drive** in Los Angeles.

Back to Bataan opened on July 18, 1945, at the Fox Wilshire Theater, now the **Saban Theater** at 8840 Wilshire Boulevard, with a charity premiere for the war wounded. Around ten years after

Copyright 1949·RKO Radio Pictures Inc. Country of Origin U.S.A.   Property of National Screen Service Corp. Licensed for display only in connection with the exhibition of this picture at your theatre. Must be returned immediately, thereafter.   49/389

John Wayne rides the range of the RKO Ranch. Also *Tall in the Saddle* are Frank Puglia (middle) and Ella Raines (author's collection).

Fighting the battle for Bataan, actually, the RKO Ranch. During that time, John Wayne was living with his friend Paul Fix (author's collection).

Back to Bataan, when RKO folded, the ranch property was sold to the Encino Park housing development. All the sets were bulldozed in order to erect the Encino Village subdivision on the grounds.

"If I ever hear you hurt her, I'll come back and kill ya"

The *Back to Bataan* guerrilla fighters also fought on the Baldwin estate in Arcadia. When the State of California and the County of L.A. purchased 111 acres of what is known today as the **L.A. Arboretum**, moviemaking history could be made. The same year *Back to Bataan* hit theaters, another classic war movie used the jungle site, Errol Flynn's *Objective, Burma!* Because of the large lagoon and the lush foliage surrounding it, this location was often used for jungle-type pictures. Tarzan had his home there; so did Gregory Peck in *The Yearling*. And the evil owner of the Batjak

Shipping Company in Wayne's *Wake of the Red Witch*. He supposedly lived in the 1880s **Queen Anne Cottage**, located in the middle of the park at Baldwin Lake. The sea adventure was filmed between July 14 and August 21, 1948. Some pick-ups for *Tycoon* were also shot on the Arboretum premises. The entrance is directly across from the Santa Anita Race Track, at 301 North Baldwin Avenue.

"I didn't get famous doing drawing room comedies"

Wayne had played shipmates before. *Adventure's End*, shot in 13 days in July 1937, is considered one of the lost films of John Wayne. Director Arthur Lubin recalled how they got the idea for this B-movie: "The reason they selected it was that there was a boat on the Universal lot and they could use it. They said, well, what sets are up these days that we can use to make pictures on that won't cost money?"[19] Some scenes were shot off the coast of **Laguna Beach**, then an artist colony. For these shots at sea, the four-masted whaling schooner *Mary Drew* was towed to the beach. "That's the way the pictures were made," Lubin recalled.[20]

They also did not cast off to sea for *The Long Voyage Home*. John Ford filmed aboard the freighter the S.S. *Munami*, anchored at **Wilmington Harbor**, San Pedro Pier 195 to be exact (according to *Lights! Camera! Action!* from May 11, 1940). It was the last time the vessel was under the American flag for it had been sold to the French government and was soon to play a role in the real war zones. Ford started the production on April 18, 1940, and finished interiors on May

From this porch, the evil Batjak owner conducted his business in *Wake of the Red Witch*: actually the Queen Anne Cottage inside the L.A. Arboretum (photograph by Roland Schaefli).

Adventure's End **got made for the simple reason that a ship was available on the Universal lot, left over from another film. As this lobby card (with Diana Gibson) proves, the film was re-released but was lost nevertheless (author's collection).**

27, again at Samuel Goldwyn where he had an exact replica of the SS *Glencairn* built. Wayne had to step out of character for the part of the Swedish sailor. "The hard thing about it," he recalled in a 1975 *Film Heritage* interview, "was that John Qualen with the same accent must be funny, and I must not be funny and have an accent. It was a tough spot to be in."

"Out here a man settles his own problems"

The Man Who Shot Liberty Valance was another Ford masterpiece with very little location work. Actually, Ford had

written to Wayne that he could expect a change of pace with this one, for there would be no location work at all. As a matter of fact, the bulk of the picture was shot from September 5 to November 7, 1961, on the Paramount soundstages where the entire town of Shinbone was constructed (see Chapter 9). The Western street is seen just once in bright daylight, when James Stewart returns to a more modern version of Shinbone. Because Ford needed a shot of a railroad arriving at the train station, the filmmakers seem to have rented space on the MGM lot No. 3, as the studio in Culver City had a rail connection.

The only outdoor sequences involved Tom Doniphon's ranch. Several biographers pointed to the Paramount Ranch in Agoura because it would seem logical for a Paramount picture to use their own premises. However, since Ford did not work on an outdoor western street, the **Janss Conejo Ranch** was a more likely choice. The Cartwrights rode this wide spread (originally 10,000 acres) in a great number of episodes as Paramount had leased a portion of land. Even the opening credits of *Bonanza* were shot on a dirt road at the ranch. (After two seasons,

In Thousand Oaks, Tom Doniphon waits for his cue in *The Man Who Shot Liberty Valance's* only outdoor sequence. William H. Clothier (in the middle on the camera platform, with two unidentified crewmembers) first started working with John Ford on *Fort Apache* (author's collection).

Trying hard not to sound like John Qualen in *The Long Voyage Home*, aboard the S.S. *Munami* at San Pedro Pier (author's collection).

Paramount decided they could afford to redo the opening at the now-famous Lake Tahoe location.) In 1969, the Hawaiian Land Corporation acquired the Janss Conejo ranchland and developed it into the vast city of Thousand Oaks. However, 1765 acres were spared, and they're now **Wildwood Park** at 928 West Avenida De Los Arboles. It's sometimes still used for location shooting.

Wayne's occasional use of colorful language became apparent in this interview about his part as Tom Doniphon: "Well, *Liberty Valance* was a tough assignment for me because dammit Ford had Jimmy for the shit-kicking humor; he had the Irishman, [Edmond] O'Brien, playing the sophisticated humor; and he had the heavy, you know the dashing, wild, terrific guy…. Christ, there was no place for me. I just had to wander around in that son of a bitch and try to make a part for myself, and he let me, too. I mean, he just, goddamit, he forgot I was around!"[21]

In 1956, Wayne had met that "dashing, wild, terrible guy"—Lee Marvin—on the Lone Pine set of *Seven Men from Now*, a Budd Boetticher Western produced by Wayne's own company. Screenwriter Burt Kennedy remembered how Lee came out with his coat on. "He went up to Duke who introduced himself and Lee said, 'This coat had your name in it at wardrobe but it's a little tight for me.' That's what Marvin said every time he saw Wayne, and Duke loved it."[22]

Marvin always suspected that Wayne had something to do with his casting as Liberty Valance. The year before, they had shared the screen for ten minutes in *The Comancheros*, Marvin delivering his scene-stealing characterization of the half-scalped Tully Crowe. But when Marvin was on a flight to be interviewed for the part of Liberty Valance by Ford, he feared that the master filmmaker would recast. Filming an episode of *Route 66*, co-star Martin Milner had broken Marvin's nose wide open. So now his face was swollen, his nose stitched up. Nevertheless, Ford took an instant liking to Marvin and rearranged the schedule. One day he gave him a piece of direction that people in the old Ford Stock Company never heard the old man give anybody before: "Lee, take the stage!" When Wayne came over to Marvin's house after the film's release, the actor's son Christopher wouldn't shake Wayne's hand because he felt he had to dislike his father's film enemy. "Duke got off on that. He loved it!"[23]

"There are only two parties: the quick and the dead"

Vasquez Rocks, located in Agua Dulce, was overexposed, especially through television shows. *Star Trek* fans like to call Vasquez Rocks "Kirk Rock." The first to use these magnificent rock formations, however, were the Tataviam Indians. Outlaw Tiburcio Vasquez lent the pointed rocks his name. Wayne fans recognize the striking rock from *The Lawless Range*; Wayne passes it singing a song and playing the guitar on horseback. He returned to the natural area park on Escondido Canyon Road in 1945 for *Dakota*, which paired him with Vera Ralston for the first time. The Olympic ice skater was Herbert Yates' protégé and would eventually become the wife of the Republic boss. Wayne didn't dislike her; she simply did not fit the Wayne Westerns in which Yates cast her. "She didn't have the experience, and she didn't have the right accent," Wayne is quoted as saying.[24]

"I had the longest legs, I guess"

Wayne came to **Taft** in 1943 to film the railroad scenes of *In Old Oklahoma*. The city at the edge of the San Joaquin Valley lies about midway along the old Sunset Railroad line, which serviced the oil companies. Fittingly for the story about the fight for oil rights, Taft was then located in the oil-rich fields of Kern County. It's still one of the largest

Vasquez Rocks made many appearances in popular culture, including two Wayne westerns. It is located just a short distance from his boyhood home in Palmdale (photograph by Roland Schaefli).

oil fields in California but there is nothing left to see from the movie. It was retitled *War of the Wildcats* after the New York Theatre Guilds sued Republic, arguing that the title was unfair competition to their musical *Oklahoma!*

"We're awful hard to see down here"

Universal movies had bigger budgets than the Republic quickies. Although still considered a B-movie, the lumberjack drama *Conflict* could afford to go on location to **Tuolumne County**, near Sacramento, in September 1936. Wayne went even further up north for *Island in the Sky*, in production between February 2 and April 1953 (with interiors at the Goldwyn Studios). The valley, six miles from Truckee in the Sierra Nevada, served as an airplane runway during the summer. It was surrounded by pine trees similar to those in Labrador where the story was set. California Forestry Service rangers felled trees to make airplane runways in the four-foot-deep snow. Actor James Lydon "never had a more difficult location" in his life. The only way the crew could get from the hotel five miles away to the location was a Greyhound bus. Then a Snowcat took the personnel to the location at Donner Lake and dropped them off in the snow about a quarter to eight in the morning. They were picked up about five in the afternoon when the light would fade. Lydon: "We didn't even have chairs, because where are you going to put chairs in 14 feet of snow?" At mealtime, the Snowcat would take them back to the bus, where they ate.[25]

Improvised script conference on the set of *Island in the Sky*: director William A. Wellman and old buddies Andy Devine (middle) and John Wayne seem to not mind the cold (author's collection).

When Wayne's company acquired the rights, they had made tentative plans to shoot on location in Canada. Wayne also considered filming in the San Bernardino Mountains, a place he knew well. Lack of snow that year forced them to move to Northern California.

"The bigger the man, the deeper the imprint"

Wayne's first film in the San Bernardino Mountains, *The Shepherd of the Hills*, was also his first Technicolor film. During production (September 9 to November 14, 1940), near **Big Bear Lake,** at **Moon Ridge, Cedar Lake** and **Bartlett Lake**, forest rangers and members of the Civilian Conservation Corps supervised the filmmakers. Wayne always thought the following incident was funny: After director Henry Hathaway set up a scene in a cabin, a horse outside began to whinny. Hathaway ran out but couldn't find a horse. This was repeated three times until Hathaway went berserk and found Ward Bond, laughing himself sick. Bond was able to whinny just like a horse.

Wayne's other experience in the San Bernardino Mountains was less funny: He crashed his car. He had finished *Seven Sinners* just the week before, but having to start *The Shepherd of the Hills* on January 12, at **Lake Arrowhead**, didn't end his affair with Marlene Dietrich. She stayed at a hotel by the lake to be close to him. Henry Hathaway remembered, "I didn't like having her around because her ardor sometimes made him late, which was unlike Duke." Hathaway told biographer Munn that one morning Wayne came rushing in and hit a corner and turned over his station wagon.[26] He had spent the night with Dietrich in Arrowhead and was walking back to Big Bear when Harry Carey's wife Olive picked him up.

It was also on this location that Olive gave John Wayne "the best advice of my life," as he often called it. At this point in his career, he was tired of playing Western types; he wanted to stretch his acting muscles. Olive told him not to change his ways because "the American public decided to take you into their homes and their hearts."[27]

The area was often used as a Canadian-looking backdrop or as a substitute for Alaska. *The Spoilers'* title card reads, "This is the story of the frozen North." Yet even though this

Universal Western was set in Nome during the Gold Rush, the Big Bear location seemed close enough, as it even had its own gold rush in 1860. The discovery of gold in the hills north of Bear Valley had caused the San Bernardino Gold Rush. *The Spoilers* was in production until February 25, 1942. A second unit shot some outdoor scenes in Sunland, close to Los Angeles.

Wayne made his comeback to San Bernardino 20 years later, for the lumberjack scenes in *North to Alaska*. The mill set which was built on **Cedar Lake** for *Shepherd of the Hills* can be spotted in the background of the lumberjack picnic scene. Those log structures, originally constructed by movie carpenters, stood for decades before they were removed.

The San Bernardino Mountains held another memory for Wayne and his pal Ward Bond. Wayne had borrowed Bond's 20-gauge for their hunting trip. "We were strung out in a line, with Wayne on a ridge above me, in brush

With Capucine at the lumberjack picnic on the Big Bear location of *North to Alaska*, with the old Cedar Lake Mill in the background (author's collection).

"Want culture with your sunshine?" In 1970, the Californian promoted vacationing in the Sunshine State (author's collection).

so high it was almost impossible to see each other," Bond recalled in a *Motion Picture Magazine* article.[28] Bond had turned his back to the ridge and was stringing down into the valley when Wayne flushed a covey of quail and let go with the shotgun. His friend got the charge "in my shoulders, arms and the back of my head, and for a moment I thought my skull was gone." Bond let out a yell and Wayne rushed down. "I was afraid to have him take off my cap; I thought I was already dead and only dreaming of what had happened." Wayne, of course, was all but overcome. "I'm roughly the size of a baby elephant, but he half carried, half dragged me two miles to a hospital, where they picked 40 birdshot out of my back," Bond later told *The Saturday Evening Post* (reprinted in an August 1979 special issue). The hunting party bought a quart of bourbon and poured a huge slug into the wounded man. The local doctor started prying those lead pellets out of Bond: 13 in his head and about 50 in his back, legs and arms. In later years, he would claim that he was "still carrying some, even today." Relieved seeing his friend alive and yelling, Wayne wisecracked, "That shotgun you loaned me is really good. It made a nice pattern." Wayne would have loved to have the rifle. Over his dead body, Bond would tell him every time he asked. After his untimely death in 1960, Bond bequeathed to his friend his 20-gauge. In May 1970, Wayne had some 30 guns stolen from his home. Eventually, most were recovered, but he didn't get Ward's shotgun back. "I wish," he told Ford when the director visited him on location for *The Cowboys*, as usual, "he was around so I could shoot him again."

"Sure, we can go to California"

More than once, Wayne had lent his name to support California. At one time, he endorsed Ducks Unlimited (DU), an American nonprofit organization. As he introduced a documentary about their conservation work, he issued a warning that rings true today: "We could perhaps survive without certain flowers or trees or wildlife—we may in fact someday have to."

In 2007, California Governor Arnold Schwarzenegger inducted Wayne into the California Hall of Fame. The honoree spent most of his life in California and often spoke on behalf of the Golden State. In 1970, as a tie-in for *Chisum*, he even became an advertising figure for the Southern California Visitors Council, inviting tourists to "take the Duke's grand tour of Southern California." In the ad, he stated, "The water's fine. A whole Pacific to surf in, fish in or cruise in." He listed the Huntington Art Gallery, the Los Angeles Music Center, Disneyland, Marineland and the San Diego Zoo as places to see, and he didn't fail to mention his old alma mater USC. He urged potential visitors to "Come on out!"

4

Ireland

"Peace and quiet came to Innisfree"

"This is Ireland, Sean, not America."
—Michaeleen (Barry Fitzgerald) tells Sean (John Wayne)
that he cannot marry Mary Kate without her brother's consent

The Quiet Man did much for Irish tourism. There is a saying that every St. Patrick's Day, every Irishman goes out to find another Irishman to make a speech to. It is also true that every St. Patrick's Day, they take particular delight in watching The Quiet Man. Maybe it's because it still speaks to Irishmen. It talks to John Wayne fans, too. Outside the U.S., Cong is the movie location most sought after by his fans. Not for nothing are they called the "Quiet Maniacs."

He was holding court in his own bar, named Mellotte, paid by his wages as John Wayne's stand-in. Big Joe Mellotte he was called, and he had become something of an ambassador to the many fans who flocked to his pub at the Neale. (His family now calls it **the Pyramid Restaurant**, on Neale Road.) Joe loved telling the story of how he was picked from a group of well-built men on the first day of shooting. "We stood in a line that morning and it was John Wayne himself who appeared, to carry out an inspection of the troops. He walked back and forward a couple of times, pointed at me and said in that drawl of his: 'That's him.'"[1]

"All I want is to get to Innisfree"

However, as Ward Bond says in his narration, let's "begin at the beginnin.'" Wayne and Maureen O'Hara had kept their summer schedule open for several years until John Ford could find the money to make his pet project. The time finally came in 1951. On June 5, Wayne, O'Hara and Victor McLaglen arrived at **Shannon Airport** on Ireland's west coast. Wayne had brought his four children over during their summer vacation. His daughter Toni remembered, "We lived in California all our lives with palm trees. All of a sudden, there's a huge castle there. There's a great big river there. It was absolutely fabulous."[2] By the "huge castle," she meant what is today one of the great hotels of the world,

The "Quiet Maniacs" take private chauffeur tours on the bus at the Quiet Man Museum to make a pilgrimage to the location. Even Wayne's children and his widow have visited this shrine to the movie classic (poster: *Quiet Man Museum*).

Ashford Castle, on Leaf Island near Cong. The 22 double rooms and three singles weren't quite as luxurious in those days, with little heat and no elevators. In her memoir, O'Hara wrote that Ford "deliberately assigned me to a room that was

Republic Pictures sent this campaign manual to exhibitors, emphasizing that "there had to be a fight" in this love story. Until the film received the International Prize at the Venice Film Festival, Herbert Yates didn't realize he had a hit on his hands. *The Quiet Man* was among the top ten grossers of the year (author's collection).

The grounds of the medieval Ashford Castle formed the backdrop for much of the action. As a leading hotel of the world, it is still enjoying *Quiet Man* fame (*Fáilte Ireland*).

very beat up, with holes in the worn-out carpet and wallpaper peeling off the walls. Duke, on the other hand, had a gorgeous suite. I thought, 'Oh, that old bastard. He did this on purpose, just so I'll make a fuss and complain.'" O'Hara never said a word. "I would never have given him the satisfaction."[3]

The crew filled the local **Ryan's Hotel** on Cong's main street and all the guest houses in town. One night, Wayne went out with the Irish heavyweight champion "Marching" Mairtin Thornton. When they returned to Ryan's, it was obvious that they had been drinking and Wayne loudly announced that he wanted to fight Thornton, shouting only one would "survive." All in good fun, of course.[4]

"I was born in that little cottage"

Ford made a trip to **Spiddal**, where he was reunited after an absence of 30 years with his cousin Martin Feeney and visited the cottage where his father had been born. The infamous "Young Men's Purity, Total Abstinence and Yachting Association" held a meeting near Spiddal Pier during the filming. (A photograph shows the group wading through the shallow water without visible cause.)

Many of the costumes were tailored by the O'Máille family. Cast members including Wayne and O'Hara visited their shop, creating a major sensation in Galway City. The **Original House of Style** was then on Dominick Street (it's now located at 16 High Street). When Wayne shopped in Dominick Street, word quickly spread among local schoolboys. He put his hand in his pocket, extracted a generous handful of coins and scattered them in all directions to make good his escape. Mary O'Máille went to Ashford Castle to complete fittings for O'Hara's outfits. The association with *The Quiet Man* has brought the O'Máilles international acclaim and to this day, the Quiet Maniacs travel to the store.

The filmmakers needed electricity and their schedule prompted its arrival. Yet when the Electricity Supply Board started blasting holes for the erection of the electrical poles, the blasts were picked up on the soundtrack. The company agreed to postpone their work. Local tradesmen were employed, some using their skills to make Celtic crosses and headstones out of cardboard. The shops did well because many things were still rationed. The likes of tinned fruit and chocolate were plentiful and the visitors bought up everything to post home.

"I'm getting real fond of you"

The first day of filming was June 7. Frank Nugent's shooting script, dated April 30, 1951, starts with a very unusual explanation about the locations: "MAIN TITLE. Behind the Title and the Credits there will be a series of shots in and around Galway, which the director knows like the back of his hand—the same back of the hand which this writer would get if he risked suggesting the shots." Nevertheless, Ford didn't go for "a series of shots." Just one: He used the Ashford Castle pier at the end of the bay as his background for the credits, even though Ashford is never fully seen during the movie. Probably he just tipped his hat to the hospitality of the owners.

In Peter Bogdanovich's documentary *Directed by John Ford*, released 20 years after *The Quiet Man*, Wayne claimed that Ford was so sensitive to colors that he would even relate them to an actor. "You're like a color to him. And he knows how he's going to use you. He always uses blue where blue should be and red where red should be. That's why it's wonderful to work with him. You never feel displaced."

The opening shot couldn't have been more colorful. A train steams into **Ballyglunin** station. The now-famous railway station is on an unknown road a 40-minute drive from Cong, virtually in the middle of nowhere, just off the road between Athenry and Tuam. Victor McLaglen favored the steaks at Tuam's Imperial Hotel (now the **Corralea Court Hotel** at the Square). Right outside Ballyglunin station stands the bridge that the train goes under in another picturesque shot (the man who sits in Wayne's place on Michaeleen's sidecar is one of his stand-ins). Ballyglunin has not changed much, but the old green metal passenger-bridge across the track isn't there any more. It is now doing duty at **Ballinasloe Station** in County Galway.

The Castletown Station, as Ballyglunin is named in the film,

The restoring project of the Ballyglunin Railway Station even includes the sign "Castletown Station." Maureen O'Hara sent the non-profit organization a letter, stating: "John Ford loved the name Castletown used for the station and I can still remember sitting in the last carriage of that grand old steam train waiting for John Wayne" (*Ballyglunin Railway Station*).

has been in a bad state of disrepair for some time. The local community is raising funds to restore it. Actors like Liam Neeson endorsed the project: "We must save this iconic building, otherwise it will be lost." Gabriel Byrne backed the campaign as well: "The image of Ballyglunin station is known to millions all over the world and is part of film archaeology."[5]

Nugent's script describes the series of shots covering

The Leam Bridge has long since its appearance in the classic film become part of Ireland's cinematic history. It is now usually just called the "Quiet Man Bridge" (photograph by Roland Schaefli).

Michaeleen's (Fitzgerald) sidecar trip to their destination, Innisfree: "The director intends to take dramatic liberties and play the countryside for all it is worth—with one shot in Killarney, another in Clare, a third in Galway, one passing the ruins of Muckross Castle, etc." In the script, Sean (Wayne) watches Innisfree from a hillcrest yet Ford decided to stop the sidecar on the humpbacked **Leam Bridge**. You'll find this lovely stone bridge on the right side off the Galway-Clifden road (from Maam Cross on the N59 to Oughterard). It hasn't changed one bit since 1951, being preserved by Galway County Council and signposted for the Quiet Maniacs. Ford cuts to Sean's point of view, actually a shot of **Clifden**, the capital of Connemara. Then Michaeleen's mood-shattering interruption ends the dream: "That'll be the pub down there to the right."

"There'll be no locks or bolts between us"

Ford then shows Sean's point of view, his first sight of **White O'Morn**, the "wee humble cottage." Actually, the cottage is 13 miles from Cong, in **Maam.**

If *The Quiet Man* is hailed as Irish America's most beloved film, then the remains of the cottage are its shrine. To get there, take a left at Maam Bridge. After the first corner on this road at Teernakill there's the bridge over Failmore River. It flows in front of White O'Morn. The stepping stones are still in the stream. O'Hara said about the place that it was "just what we wanted…. One would think some set designer just dreamed it as it is."[6]

Ironically, Nugent imagines that dreamy place thusly: "The yard is weed-grown and neglected, the thatch roof is ragged and with gaps in it. Yet the place is far from a ruin." Which is exactly its state today. For years, a legal battle over the ownership has postponed the restoration of the iconic building. On the left of the ruin, you can still find the little concrete bridge on which Michaeleen tells Sean he'll "talk a little treason."

Ford often repeated that the weather was awful all during the shoot, which according to O'Hara was not true at all. The single day that it did rain was just when Ford needed it, in the sequence where O'Hara runs from the cottage, crosses the stream, and then falls. "That was real rain. The wind actually blew me down in that scene, but I kept going because Mr. Ford always made it clear to his actors that 'You do not stop acting no matter what happens in a scene until I say cut.'"[7]

A replica of the cottage can be seen at **Maam's Cross**, right at N59.

"Innisfree—this way!"

Innisfree is described in the screenplay "as serene an Irish Village as might be found, with the play of shadows on its cobbled streets and rooftops, a river or brook running by, stone fences and the dappled fields and cottages beyond." **Cong** doubles for two Irish towns, Innisfree as well as Castletown.

Pat Cohan's Bar is the easiest location to find, right at the Market Cross on Main Street. Even Michaeleen's horse knew exactly where the pub was. However, the place wasn't a bar when Hollywood came to town. It was then a shop, and all the interiors of the pub were shot later on a soundstage. Even the part of the proprietor Pat Cohan wasn't cast until Ford had returned to Hollywood. The original owner of the general store was Jack Murphy, who was an extra in the film. Joe Mellotte was

When John Ford had to make several cuts to shorten the film on Yates' demand, this scene ended up on the cutting room floor: after breaking through the door at Pat Cohan's, Victor McLaglen and John Wayne shake hands for the second time. Jack MacGowran (left), Ward Bond, Barry Fitzgerald, and James O'Hara (as the young priest) look on. Many locals from Cong were used in the crowd scenes (author's collection).

asked to crash through the door of Cohan's Bar in place of Victor McLaglen. According to stuntmen Gerry McNee, "It was a nice soft landing because they had cushions on the street. The replacement doors were made of the thinnest plywood."[8]

"How's that bettin' going?"

In the last scene, the villagers cheer "like protestants" when the bishop's car passes, followed by Michaeleen carrying the soon-to-be-wed couple. That was all shot on **the Circular Road**. You'll also find the Quiet Man Museum and another replica of the Thornton cottage there, in the exact spot where Ford filmed Michaeleen taking bets during the fight. From that road leads the Cong street called **"Blazes Lane,"** to the dying man's house (played by Ford's brother Francis), the third one on the left.

Ford used the upper part of Main Street for the Castletown scenes. What is now a delicatessen was in 1951 the thatched whitewashed building called Currans Pub, where McLaglen sells his sheep. A craft shop named "Emily O'Connor" is seen in the background as Sean and Mary Kate quarrel about the money (actually the last scene shot in Ireland).

"Some things a man doesn't get over so easy"

The statue of John Wayne sweeping Maureen O'Hara off her feet stands on the corner of **Abbey Street.** Looking from there towards the **Church of Ireland**, that's Corcoran's Field. The three children who ran up through that field were Wayne's kids. However, Ford used just the outside of the church. For the inside, he went to the Catholic Church **Saint Mary's** with its magnificent Harry Clarke stained-glass window. (The Cong window is not included in the official list of the artist's work.) The director of photography, Winton C. Hoch, had to slow down the camera speed to capture Clarke's work on the slow Technicolor film, and Wayne, coming down the aisle, had to move slower, which makes the distinctive Wayne walk look a little strange. (Michael Wayne is the altar boy.) The church has long since been demolished and a modern building was erected. The window itself has been split in two to fit the smaller dimensions of the new sanctuary.

The Pat Cohan Bar as it is today: reality finally caught up to movie magic when the new owners actually turned the grocery store into a pub, serving traditional Irish Dishes (photograph by Pat Cohan Bar & Restaurant).

For the "patty-fingers scene," they took the holy water font from the Catholic Church and placed it at the door of the Church of Ireland but left it there by mistake. When the Protestants turned up the following Sunday, they objected strongly to their minister who had given permission for filming. Just across the Catholic parish, you'll notice the beautiful ivy-covered home of the Reverend Playfair.

John Wayne rereads the script while character actors Victor McLaglen and Barry Fitzgerald obviously see no need to learn their lines (author's collection).

"The sight of a girl coming through the fields"

What is now the third fairway of the **Ashford Castle Golf Course** was the field where Sean first lays eyes on his red-haired colleen. Later in the movie, as Sean has been abandoned and is walking home, he marches through the **Ashford Deerpark**, the castle towers just visible through the trees, and a flock of birds takes flight. The film is back in that deerpark for the scenes in which Sean drags Mary Kate and kicks her behind.

Ford and Wayne played a joke on O'Hara. When he drags her through the fields, they kicked all of the sheep dung they could find onto the hill where she was to be dragged, face down. "Of course, I saw them doing it, and so I kicked it right back off," O'Hara remembered. "They'd kick it in, and we'd kick it out. Duke had the time of his life dragging me through it." Wayne told Bogdanovich that Ford "didn't have to lay down horse manure. There was pig shit all over. And actually, there was nothing we could do. I had to drag her through it."[9]

The Widow Tillane's House was a big two-story whitewashed house in the park. At some point in the past, they knocked the house down to make way for the new car park. That must have happened before the locals became aware of the global Quiet Maniacs movement.

Under John Ford's watchful eye, John Wayne drags Maureen O'Hara along on the location known as the Meadow Field. On the last page of Ford's script, O'Hara wrote the Gaelic word for "bastard" (author's collection).

"It's your custom, not mine"

The bishop and the Reverend Playfair watch the big fight from **Ashford Castle Bridge** over Lough Corrib. The movie shows the banks of the Cong River several times. In the courting scene, Sean and Mary Kate "walk correctly together" along that pathway. The same spot, with the castle bridge in the back, is used for the fishing scene when Father Lonergan (Ward Bond) unsuccessfully tries to catch "the king of all salmon." (A local man named Jim Morrin pulled on the line outside the shot.) Bond became a fisherman during his stay in Cong, landing some fine salmon. J.J. Murphy, a young local angler (he later authored the brochure *Guide to The Quiet Man*) was sitting at Ashford castle pier when the character actor asked, "Any fish in the hole?" His knowledge of fishing was obviously very limited because "the hole" he was referring to was Lough Corrib, the biggest lake in the republic. Murphy pointed him in the direction of the fishing tackle shop, where Bond got himself a spinning rod and reel to catch some real salmon. One Sunday evening, he brought a five-pound trout off the lake. Bond decided against having it mounted and instead ate it for breakfast.

"Sit down, that's what chairs are for!"

The Danagher house, Victor McLaglen's home in the film, is just around the corner from Ashford Castle; the farmyard is on the castle grounds on Broad Avenue. The road straight ahead takes you to the wall from which Mary Kate observes how Sean gets his huge bed (White O'Morn is, in fact, 15 miles away). Follow Broad Avenue further and you will reach what is locally known as the **Meadow Field**, the location for the beginning of the classic Wayne-McLaglen fight.

"You'll never hear the man count ten"

The Meadow Field was a hayfield in 1951. The five-bar gate that Ward Bond vaults after hearing about the fight stands in the corner of that field, at the far end of the "Danaher" farm. (They filmed a tandem scene in the other corner

The house of "Squire Danaher" as it looked in 1998. It still stands on the grounds of Ashford Castle Estate (photograph by Roland Schaefli).

of the field, at the old **Ashford Schoolhouse**.) When the villagers join in the fight, some roughnecks in the mob felt they had a license to a real fight, as Ford had ordered the extras "to kick up hell." Local extra Jack McGauran got trampled on. Wayne rushed to his assistance, lifted him up and carried him to the trailer where the lady doctor was always in attendance in case of such emergencies.

Sean knocks Danaher into the river on the grounds of **Cong Abbey**, one of the country's most famous monastic sites, founded about 1120.

Thoor Ballylee is known today as Yeats Tower. The Irish poet W.B. Yeats purchased the property around 1916 for £35 and created several works there. After his family moved out in 1929, it fell into disuse. In 1951, John Wayne and Maureen O'Hara ran across the river in front of the castle (Yeats Thoor Ballylee Society).

"If anybody had told me six months ago…"

During the courting, Michaeleen points out "the ancestral home of the ancient Flynns": In reality, that's the **Ross Errilly Friary**. After the couple escapes from the matchmaker, they get to the tourist attraction **Thoor Ballylee**. Where Sean has to follow Mary Kate across the stream was once a favorite haunt of Irish poet W.B. Yeats.

As Sean and Mary Kate travel to Castletown in their trap, they cross a bridge in view of the imposing **Kylemore Abbey**. When Mary Kate leaves Sean after their bickering, she passes an Ivy Lodge at **Clifden**. Then Sean has to walk all the way back. As he rests on a stone wall, there's a small island on Lough Corrib in the background with the ruins of **Castlekirk** on it. The same field at **Carrowgarriff** is used twice: as Sean is getting rid of his bowler hat during the courting and later, as he angrily walks home, kicking stones.

The hundred-foot-high **Joyce's Tower** (also known as Leonard's Tower), near the Ashford farm, provides a dramatic background for the moment in which Wayne double jumps his black horse over a wooden fence. According to Hollywood legend, Ward Bond climbed Joyce's Tower to carve the words "Fuck Herb Yates" on the inside of a wall. He then told Wayne (who had his own troubles with the Republic boss) about the spectacular view there. Yates complained after viewing the dailies that the film looked too "green."

"I don't give a hang about the money"

Wayne might have even spared a buck or two for Yates. When Ford fell sick for three days, he took over the directing of the Innisfree horse race with second-unit cinematographer Archie Stout, whom he called "a terrific outdoor man." The script called for 400 spectators in the sandhills of **Bunnageeha Bay**. Wayne held the horses back on the beach, and the people spread out coming up toward the camera, and finally, he yelled, "Hold still everybody!" And so he had "about 400 people in there where we only had about 50 extras. And everything was working just right." Still, Ford didn't take kindly to Wayne's claim that he had done "the whole goddamn race for Ford."[10]

The **Lettergesh Beach** is the main beach used for the race, a beautiful stretch of coastline about 20 miles north of Clifden. In one shot, the riders cross the Clufin River.

According to Lord Killanin (at the time of the filming, he was the head of Ireland's Olympic Council), he was helpful to Ford in setting up the locations. He recalled filming at the beach, which he remembered being Tully

John Wayne is about to throw that bowler hat on the ground of Carrowgarriff (author's collection).

Strand. Wayne's black horse was actually Lord Killanin's own hunter. "What a f***ing awful horse you've given me," complained Wayne. Killanin realized the actor had never ridden on a hunting saddle before. The production had a suitable saddle flown in from the States.[11]

Sean and Mary Kate come close to the Lettergesh Beach when they pedal their tandem up on a minor road from **Kylemore Abbey** to Tully Cross. They finally drop the stolen bike on the road from Lettergesh to Tully Cross, in the village of **Gowlaun**. (In the shot, Sean points out to Killary Harbour.)

Towards the end of location filming in July, Wayne made a big night of the arrival of electricity in one of the pubs as the paraffin lamp went out for the last time and the Electricity Supply Boards switch took over from the tinderbox. Ford, always the consummate director, gave the signal for the big switch-on. The director also agreed that he and the cast would take part in a fund-raiser for the County Galway Volunteer Memorial Fund in the Seapoint Ballroom

in **Salthill** near Galway Bay on July 3, 1951. Wayne was master of ceremonies. It was truly homeric.

"I have brought the brother home to supper"

Two weeks of interior lensing commenced at Republic on August 3. On the set, the White O'Morn cottage was reconstructed with whitewashed walls and freshly thatched roof. Art director Frank Hotaling had an Irish countryside painted behind it, covering the whole of an expansive wall. Ford gifted Lord Killanin with Sean's big bed. Look carefully and you will notice there are two different beds: the one brought across the stream in Ireland and the one used in the studio mock-up of the Thornton cottage. All interiors were set in the same hangar; next to the cottage set was the interior of the Danaher house, dressed for the wedding. In fact, in one of the studio fight scenes, the White O'Morn set can be glimpsed in an early stage of construction.

The scene in which Sean and Mary Kate are caught in a thunderstorm in a cemetery was originally scheduled to be shot on the cliffs of Moher (Nugent had dared to write it in the script as a specific location, risking "the director's back of the hand"). But Ford had to reschedule it as a set as the lighting proved unsatisfactory.

The famous kiss in White O'Morn (Steven Spielberg paid tribute to the iconic shot in *E.T.*) was also accomplished on the stage. Ford used two large wind machines

The jaunting cart used in *The Quiet Man* had gone missing for decades. The prized relic was located at Maureen O'Hara's former home in Glengarriff (shortly before she moved to Boise, Idaho). One of her final wishes was to donate this ancient cart to the John Wayne Birthplace in Iowa (Carol Bassett/ The John Wayne Birthplace).

to blow their clothes and O'Hara's hair for the effect. "There were two large airplane propellers on a stand that Mr. Ford controlled by sending hand signals to an operator," O'Hara recalled. She recalls that day for another reason: "I was mad as hell at Duke and Mr. Ford for something they had done earlier. My plan was to sock Duke in the jaw and really let him have it." But Wayne was no fool and he saw it coming: "He saw it in my face." So he put his hand up to shield his chin, and her hand hit the top of his fingers and snapped back. "My plan backfired and my hand hurt like hell." Wayne came over and said, "You nearly broke my jaw. Let me see that hand."[12] He lifted it out of hiding; each one of her fingers had blown up like a sausage. O'Hara had suffered a hairline fracture in one of the bones of her wrist, but in the end got no sympathy. She was taken back from the doctors to the set and put to work.

In her biography, O'Hara wanted to get something out of the way once and for all: "I did not have an affair with John Ford while we were making *The Quiet Man*, or at any other time." There had been rumors, repeated in many books. "I'm sorry, guys, but you have it wrong." It is true that he sent her love letters, though.

Wayne's summary of the experience was somewhat different: "That was a goddam hard script. For nine weeks, I was just playing a straight man to those wonderful characters, and that's really hard."[13]

"Is that all you Danahers think about? Money?" Maureen O'Hara and John Wayne on the last day on location, in the jaunting cart on Cong's Main Street, in front of Emily O'Connor's shop. Note the microphone on the top edge (author's collection).

"Impetuous. Homeric!"

The world premiere of *The Quiet Man* was at the **Adelphi Cinema** in Dublin. You can still see the façade on Middle Abbey Street, but it is now closed. The internationally famous **Abbey Theatre** at 26/27 Abbey Street in Dublin where Ford auditioned a number of actors for the great character parts is still playing. Frank Nugent's original shooting script can be viewed by making an appointment with the **Irish Film Institute**, 6 Eustace Street, Dublin.

As the narrator informs the audience: "And so the village of Innisfree is at peace again…." Yet Cong never got over

The statue in front of the Quiet Man Museum. It houses the original fishing rod used by Ward Bond when he tries to catch the "King of All Salmon," as well as the harness of Barry Fitzgerald's horse. Wayne's widow Josephine Wayne wrote in the guestbook: "Duke would have loved this!" (photograph by Quiet Man Museum).

The Quiet Man. Road signs point to "Quiet Man Country." Tourists surge to come see for themselves. At some point, life began to imitate art. The grocery store they used as a set for Pat Cohan's Bar was converted to a real bar. Ashford Castle continues to house luminaries. In 2001, it was the chosen venue for the wedding of Pierce Brosnan, then the screen's James Bond. The 800-year-old castle received massive interest from abroad following the high-profile reception. Still, the story the locals love to tell about the hotel bar, the **Pigeon Hole**, is how John Wayne got a little drunk off the lethal local brew and had to be carried upstairs.

5

Monument Valley

"Let's go home, Debbie"

"Medicine country, huh…?"
—Ethan (John Wayne) as he finds Scar's camp at the Totem Pole

Geologists date the area on the Utah-Arizona state line as 25 million years old. Film historians disagree. For them, time began in 1938. That's when John Ford, the Columbus of Western film, found the new world in Monument Valley. Stuntman Chuck Roberson had this to say about it: "If you listened to the story long enough, you'd come away believing that God had consulted the Old Man before He created the place, with Ford ordering two buttes—about a thousand feet high—on either side of a dry valley bed, topped off with some fantastic cloud formations."[1]

The story of exactly how Ford "found" those stark rock formations on an ancient sea floor is clouded in myth. Ford told Peter Bogdanovich that he came across the area as he was driving through Arizona on his way to Santa Fe, New Mexico (highly unlikely, but Ford loved a good yarn as much as he loved misleading Bogdanovich). Dan Ford, his grandson, printed the legend that Ford first heard about Monument Valley from Harry Carey, "who had stumbled into it while exploring the Navajo country in the 1920s."[2] George O'Brien, who had starred in some of Ford's silent Westerns, claimed it was he who had pointed the valley out to the old man.

The version that gets repeated the most and is commonly accepted is also not the most plausible. Harry Goulding came to Monument Valley in 1923. A sheepherder by trade, he saw prospects for the little-known area and established a small trading post on the north side of Red Door Mesa. Goulding said he heard a Western movie should be made (even though in those days literally hundreds were made) and he decided to pitch Monument Valley as a location to the Hollywood honchos. Somehow he got ahold of Ford and showed him photographs. The story is colorful myth, just like the movies shot on those windswept plains. The question of the "discovery" of Monument Valley as a movie location will probably never be settled. The book *Tall Sheep*, which researches the details of Goulding's history, gives the best explanation: "Perhaps what Harry Goulding did was to offer the practical possibility of setting up a complex movie location in such a desolate place."

"Don't mean nothin', not in the long run"

However, there was one more discovery claim: John Wayne's. His stunt-double Chuck Roberson gave him credit for the

Goulding's Lodge today: the trading post was added to the National Register of Historic Places in 1980 (photograph by Matt Morgan).

locating. Roberson explained that Ford had "sealed Duke's lips with one of his open-your-mouth-and-you're-going-home looks."[3] Wayne repeated his account in front of Bogdanovich's TV cameras—even as Ford was still alive. He also told his biographer Zolotow about "a secret I've kept for many years. I was the guy who found Monument Valley." Wayne researcher Fred Landesman found that "Duke" Morrison was serving as a wrangler, stunt double and bit player back in '29 as he was "proppin'" for a George O'Brien location in Arizona. Wayne probably referred to *The Lone Star Ranger*. This Zane Grey Western was partially filmed in the area of Monument Valley. He took a car, as he wanted to get away by himself. He reached the valley at sunset, parked the car and looked at it. Wayne described this moment of destiny: "[T]hat evening it looked, well, kind of like it was another world."

"Those buttes sure would frame a composition," the young man thought and kept it in mind. Almost a decade later, when Ford was looking for "a new fresh location" for *Stagecoach*, Wayne told him about it. When Ford declared to the crew that he had found the perfect location, he looked Wayne straight in the eye—and Wayne kept his mouth shut.

Even when he had only weeks to live, after his final public appearance at the Academy Awards, Wayne tried to set the record straight. In an April 27, 1979, letter to the editors of *The Saturday Evening Post* who were preparing a complimentary article about his life, he wanted to correct "some slight misinformation." He let them know that it was his job as an assistant for a George O'Brien western to get 400 head of cattle into Blue Canyon, which was 150 miles from any paved road. A preacher who had a little church on the Hopi Reservation agreed to help him gather them. "In gathering those cattle we horse-backed into Monument Valley," Wayne wrote. "For ten years I held that back as a possible future location." Then Ford announced he had found "the most colorful location that can ever be used for a picture." And from that moment on, Jack Ford discovered Monument Valley. "But actually," Wayne finished his letter, "who cares."[4]

"A man's only good for one oath"

It should also be noted that Bert Glennon, *Stagecoach*'s director of photography, was an assistant cameraman on some of the George O'Brien films made in that part of Arizona. In any event, the whole pleading might be useless as a Richard Dix silent, the first feature produced in southeastern Utah, got there 13 years ahead of *Stagecoach*. In September 1923, to be exact, famed western novelist Zane Grey (he actually lived in the area), took Paramount production executive Jesse L. Lasky on a ten-day horseback expedition that included Monument Valley. The trip convinced Lasky to make *The Vanishing American*, based on Grey's book, in this locale. As indicated in the 1925 souvenir program published by Famous Players-Lasky Corporation, Grey wrote to Lasky in a telegram after the first screening: "That first sweeping view of Monument Valley made me homesick."

What's certainly true is that by the end of Wayne's life, the star and the landscape were irrevocably partnered in the public eye. And Monument Valley had become so identified with Ford that other directors felt it would be plagiarism to make a picture in Ford Country. The truth is Ford had made Wayne and those red sandstone massifs into one mythical symbol of the Wild West.

"He can't enter the spirit-land"

Talking about Monument Valley, Ben Johnson once said, "The actors don't have to be too good. The background sells it."[5] Director John Milius, who was greatly influenced by *The Searchers* said about Ford, "He was genuinely having a love affair with this land."[6]

As director of photography, William Clothier shot 15 pictures with Wayne and was for many years under exclusive contract to Batjac. He knew what he had to watch out for when filming in Ford Country. The grumpy director never would allow a water wagon onto the set. "Two things make Western pictures: horse manure and dust," Ford

One of the iconic places in Monument Valley: John Ford Point, named after the Columbus of the Western during the filming of *The Searchers*, ranked number 12 in the installment of the American Film Institute's 100 greatest American movies of all time (photograph by Utah Office of Tourism).

would repeat like a mantra. When some cameraman still got a water wagon, he blew his top: "Hell, that's why I came out here, I want the dust." Dust, especially in backlight, adds to the drama. But Clothier heard actors scream because they got their eyes full of dust, including Wayne: "I can't see in the dust." Clothier told the star, "Well, the script said they want dust and wind, so we've got wind machines and we've got dust. Close your eyes or get a double!"[7] Wayne was very believable when, as Ethan Edwards, he proclaimed, "I don't stand talkin' in the wind."

The first chance Wayne got to produce a picture of his own, he used Monument Valley right away. The principal location for *Angel and the Badman* in 1946 was Sedona. Yet he sent Yakima Canutt and a couple of stunt riders up to Monument Valley to shoot the title sequence. He didn't get involved in it himself and resumed filming in Sedona.

A number of books incorrectly list *Rio Grande* as a Monument Valley film while still excluding *Angel and the Badman*.

"You got yourself surrounded"

In the early years, Harry Goulding and his wife "Mike" would try to accommodate Ford and his primary stars in their own home. In 1953, they tore down their two rock cabins and built a row of motel rooms up on the bench next to the post. Once the one-story lodge rooms were completed, Ford would always want to be in the far west room, with Wayne in the next room. *Time* magazine featured the lodge as "one of the first to cater to the country's new fashion in travel—motels."[8] In 1956, they doubled the number of rooms. Ford continued to use Goulding's as a headquarters and always stayed in the last room along the motel row.

Ford once hired a gorgeous woman to wait on Ward Bond's table and act as though she was enamored of him. She told Ward her husband wouldn't be back until the next day and that he should bring a six-pack and a watermelon that night. So Bond set out for her bungalow. Little did he suspect that Ford, Wayne and four others were waiting with blank-loaded pistols. When Bond opened the door, they started firing away. He dropped the six-pack and raced for his life, still carrying the watermelon.[9]

Nowadays, the original Trading Post is a museum at 1000 Gouldings Trading Post Road. The upstairs has been brought back to a close facsimile of how it appeared during the years when the Gouldings called it their home and houseguest John Ford stayed with them.

The mess room was added on as a makeshift dining facility for the crew that shot second unit footage for MGM's *The Harvey Girls* in 1946 and it was turned into a museum with movie memorabilia. Today's main dining room is standing in the same place as the old dining room building, which was also the post's general store and bar. Wayne inscribed the guestbook after his stay for *Fort Apache* with "Thanks for making our work easier." When they asked him to sign again the next time, he doodled, "Don't know why I'm still signing this—this is home!"

Stagecoach

The legacy of the legendary Ford-Wayne team starts with *Stagecoach*, in production from November 10 to December 22, 1938. When Paramount produced the Zane Grey Westerns, the novelist insisted they be filmed in the locales where his books were set. The crews on these movies always used the **Wetherill's Inn** and trading post in **Kayenta**. When Ford brought the *Stagecoach* company to town, he set up headquarters at the Wetherill's Inn as well. Fourteen people stayed at the inn, 22 bunked in a Civilian Conversation camp's barracks and 26 camped at Goulding's below the trading post.

In those days, it was still a long way from the location. Their days were hot, the nights just as cold. Wayne, not yet an A-lister, didn't exactly learn how the other half lived on *Stagecoach*. Goulding's wife recalled that the movie

This French lobby card of *She Wore a Yellow Ribbon* shows cavalryman Nathan Brittles (John Wayne) jumping his horse over the corral in the Square Rock area (author's collection).

star shared a snake cabin below the Trading Post during the few days of filming in the Valley. Bear in mind that none of the principals can be seen in any of the compositions made in Monument Valley (not even Wayne); Ford only filmed long shots of the coach traveling through endless expanses of desert sand.

In the film, the coach drives on the same dirt road that is now winding through the park. Iron Eyes Cody, who played one of the Indians for Ford, recalled, "We had to lay plank-boards over the dirt paths and sand, which the trucks had to follow carefully, or sink."[10] Therefore, Ford didn't travel too far into the backlands, saving those spots for later films.

"Is this an invite to a necktie party?"

On May 11, 1947, Wayne told Hedda Hopper: "John Ford is a master at getting the most out of backgrounds. Take *Stagecoach*, for instance. You'll rarely see a picture filmed against such an enormous background. Yet the vastness of the landscape but served to point up the isolation of the action rather than engulf it."

It's well-known that Ford was overcritical with Wayne while making *Stagecoach*. Claire Trevor remembered, "It was tough for Duke to take the pressure Ford put on him, but he took it. And he learned eight volumes about acting in that picture."[11] It is a lesser-known fact that in 1970, Wayne actually helped rescue the movie. The first negative of the film was chopped to bits by independent distributors, then completely lost due to nitrate decomposition. Wayne had saved his personal pristine print (see Chapter 22).

Fort Apache

The director-star combination returned to Monument Valley for *Fort Apache*, in production between July 24 and September 13, 1947. Article 14 in the agreement that Argosy Pictures Corporation and Wayne entered into on May 26, 1947 (his fortieth birthday), is enlightening because it establishes the rules of accommodations on location: "If the services of Artist are required to be performed elsewhere than within a radius of twenty-five (25) miles from Producer's studio in Culver City, Producer agrees to furnish Artist's first-class transportation from such studio to any other place or location, where Artist's services shall be required to be performed, and to pay all of Artist's reasonable living expenses at any such place, together with similar return transportation to such studio."

Ford discouraged his actors from bringing their spouses on location. The night before Wayne left for Monument Valley, his Mexican wife Chata got drunk and hurled all the verbal abuse she could think of, "in both English and Spanish."[12]

"That'll *be the day*"

The Cavalry Trilogy gave Wayne the reputation of a Western character set against all Indians. Navajo officials recollected that the actor "always was real nice to the Navajos. They got along with him right well." One Navajo official, Linda Rodriguez, recollected the occasion when Wayne and friends invited everybody to a barbecue. Wayne asked her why she looked rather sad. She replied, "If we gonna win just once in your next Western, I'll look happy."[13] (As a child, Rodriguez was an extra in *Cheyenne Autumn*.) In a 1975 *Film Heritage* interview, Wayne philosophized about his image as an Indian hater: "It's a funny thing, the Indians now, this AIM group [American Indian Movement] have started something and are against me for some reason. But I am the only man in pictures that always gave them their human dignity. I never was in a picture, I never allowed myself at any time to do anything that would take their human dignity away from them, and that to me is a most important thing in a man." Wayne added that he said it the best he could in his production of *Hondo*: "It was the closest thing to my having anything to do

This rare publicity photograph shows Wayne, in costume as *Fort Apache*'s Captain York, observing the work of an unidentified Navajo woman and her children right outside the Trading Post (author's collection).

with the writing of a piece. At the finish, the Indian is dead— it was an impersonal thing. And I'm saying, 'Yeah, he's gone, things changed. It's a good life, sorry to see it go.' It was not saying, 'Oh, that dirty scavenger son of a bitch.'"[14]

In July 1970, Wayne found himself surrounded by real Apaches. They had invited him to a traditional lunch at Alchesay Hall in **Whiteriver**, the capital of the Fort Apache Indian Reservation. He toured the old fort, and fans surrounded him everywhere, calling out *hon dah*, "welcome" in the Apache language.

When biographer Joseph McBride asked Ford in 1970 if it was correct that Wayne felt uneasy about being in *Fort Apache* because he thought Custer (on whom the Henry Fonda character is based) was a disgrace to the cavalry, Ford answered, "Oh, that's a lot of crap. I don't think he's ever heard of Custer."[15]

She Wore a Yellow Ribbon

Ford shot *She Wore a Yellow Ribbon* in just 31 days, October 28 to November 27, 1948. Back then, the crew would travel to Flagstaff by train. After that, it would take another full day to get into Monument Valley by car. In his wonderful account about his life in the John Ford Stock Company, Harry Carey, Jr., remembered his first trip there on roads that were just dirt and very rutted. When he arrived on location, an aged Navajo woman who had been engaged to work in the Indian scenes greeted him enthusiastically.

She proved to be a nurse he had during his early childhood on the Carey Ranch at Saugus when his father maintained an Indian trading post on the grounds. He also discovered that the living conditions were very "out West." The only women in the cast, Joanne Dru and Mildred Natwick, stayed at the Gouldings' home. There were five special cabins for the stars. Wayne and John Ford each had a cabin to themselves. The rest of the cast doubled or tripled up and everybody shared toilets and shower. The shower was an old five-gallon oil tin with holes in the bottom, hanging from a wooden beam. Then you just stood under this shower and "asked some sadist" to turn on the cold water. In the middle of the cabin stood an old-fashioned kerosene heater. The crew was housed in a beautiful Anderson Camp about a mile below the Post. The floor was swept, hard dirt with a Navajo rug on it.

While Ford utilized the Trading Post buildings as the cavalry headquarters, a false fort front was built miles away, at the base of the Mitten Buttes. The film would cut back and forth from Goulding's to this palisade. In reality, this would have been the worst place to put the fort entrance. Right outside was just a hundred yards of level ground, then it dropped off at a 45-degree angle all the way to the floor of the Valley (this is where the View Hotel now stands). In the scene when Carey, Jr., drives a buggy out the gate, Wayne had taken it upon himself to throw a rock at the horses at the same time as Carey let them go. "I had runaways on my hands…. I thought of bailing out, but it was all cactus and rocks. Stunt ace Cliff Lyons stopped the team at the last moment."[16]

They surely kept the editor busy on this film. When the horse soldiers in Monument Valley point to buffalo, the film cuts to the actual beasts over in **Houserock Valley**, Arizona.

"I finally arrived," Wayne said after Ford had given him a birthday cake with just one candle to mark his first year of maturity as an actor. "And I think it's the best thing I've ever done."[17] Others thought so, too. On May 13, 1950, Wayne was honored at the Silver Spurs Award Ceremony. Ford recalled that trip: "Last summer I went to Reno with him to attend John Wayne Day, during which he received the yearly award that the city gives him for his role in a western. Duke was far more interested in the people he met than in the trophy he received. 'Nice, eh?' he said as he showed me the award. 'But it is not as important as the ideas behind it.'"[18]

John Ford (with pipe, left of unidentified crewmember) turned Goulding's into a cavalry fort for *She Wore a Yellow Ribbon*. Ben Johnson is standing left of Wayne. Note the new guest cabin in the back (author's collection).

The Searchers

"He is Ethan Edwards. A man as hard as the country he is crossing." In his *Searchers* script, writer Frank Nugent followed this introduction of the Wayne character with "a study of hoofprints, deeply etched in the ground, picking their way through scrubby desert growth, late afternoon." Ford had informed him that he would use the Navajo reservation once more. The script shows that he had specific locations in mind. *The Searchers* went into production on June 15, 1955. This time, they stayed 50 days at Monument Valley, followed by nine days of indoor shooting on RKO-Pathé's Stage 15. Ford wrapped his masterpiece on August 16, 1955.

"You'll love it," Wayne promised his third wife, Pilar, when he told her they'd be spending the entire summer hundreds of miles from civilization in the middle of the Navajo Reservation. "I don't think anyone, including the Navajos who live there year-round, really enjoys summering in 115 scorching degrees," Pilar thought. To her, the red rock buildings at Goulding's looked as if they'd stood in that spot since the days of the Indian wars. At sunset, they'd wait outside the Trading Post until Ford approached. "Then our host rang an old dinner bell, and we followed Ford inside as if he was a Biblical patriarch."[19]

Everything really eventful seemed to happen on the porch at the lodge. It was here that Ford decided Ken Curtis should play the role of Charlie McCorry with a Colorado dryland accent. Curtis was telling a hilarious story, using this accent. When Ford heard the hillbilly accent, he told him to use it. But Curtis didn't want to make an ass of himself. For posterity, Harry Carey, Jr., recorded Wayne's reaction to Ken's refusal: He burst into Ken's room that night and, subtle as always, said, "Bullshit! Listen, you're a nice-looking fella, but ya' ain't as good-lookin' as this Jeff kid [Jeffrey Hunter], an' on toppa' that, yer playing the second lead and there's nothin' more thankless than a second fuckin' lead! Play it like the Old Man says, fer Christ's sake, an' you'll be noticed in the goddamned picture!"[20] Curtis followed this advice and it eventually led to his winning the role of Festus on TV's *Gunsmoke*.

"Long as you live, don't ever ask me more"

Even in 1955, there were just a few cabins at Goulding's. A tent city, again located below the Trading Post (complete with street signs "Hollywood and Vine"), housed 300 cast and crew personnel, approximately where Ford had erected the town of Tombstone for *My Darling Clementine* ten years earlier. Actress Pippa Scott: "The tent city glowed at night with campfires. Frankly, quite a bit of drinking, gambling, carousing. Great fun."[21]

Wayne bunked with Ward Bond in a little cabin at Goulding's. One night he invited the usual group of stuntmen up to his room. "So this is how the other half lives," snarled Chuck Roberson, who was living in an old army tent with a wooden floor. Wayne opened the refrigerator, revealing a half-dozen six-packs of German beer. He tossed each of the men a bottle, stating, "Only the best for my friends." They knew they were drinking Ward Bond's beer. When they saw him coming back, they loaded all the empties back in their cartons. Wayne fixed an innocent smile on his face. As the stuntmen passed Bond walking through the door, each of them called up the loudest belch. "You drank my beer, you sons of bitches," they heard as they ran like hell for their tents.[22]

Natalie Wood celebrated her seventeenth birthday on location. She and Patrick Wayne were the only teenagers on the remote location and naturally drifted together, enjoying a mutual crush. Patrick recalled, "We didn't have to fake being on the frontier, we were living in it, so you were really looking anywhere for any kind of amusement. There were no movies, there was no radio, there was no television, there was nothing!" John Wayne gave the youngster a bit of fatherly advice as he realized that Pat, barely 16, had a great deal of

Dolores Del Rio visits the Burbank set of *The Searchers*. John Ford (in glasses) is about to direct the scene where Ethan (Wayne) and Martin (Jeffrey Hunter, right) try to find Debbie at the snowbound cavalry fort (note the fake snow on Wayne's boot), assisted by a gruff sergeant (Jack Pennick). The set is roofless to allow for lighting (author's collection).

fondness for Wood, even puppy love: "Just be careful where you're going."

The cast semi-roughed it. One day, Bond got bitten by a scorpion. As Wood watched them drain the poison from the wound, she felt faint at the sight of it. "Ford sat holding court at this long table at the Goulding Trading Post mess hall and we were all there to do his bidding," remembered Lana Wood, Natalie's sister. Although Natalie thought it was "a big deal" to do a picture with John Wayne, the true reason she accepted the movie was that Ford had agreed to her mother's idea to cast eight-year-old Lana as young Debbie. Ford had only one stipulation, according to Lana: "I was brought into the office to meet John Wayne, and John Ford said, 'Can you pick her up?' So he lifted me off the ground, held me up and said 'Okay,' and that was it."23

Harry Carey, Jr., recalled that Wayne was different on this movie, portraying the Indian hater. "When I looked up at him in rehearsal, it was into the meanest, coldest eyes I have ever seen. I don't know how he molded that character." He was even Ethan at dinnertime. He didn't kid around on the set as he had done on other shows; "Ethan was always in his eyes."24

Carey was in the scene in which Wayne ordered "Don't ever ask me more," on a sand dune south of the **Mitchell Butte**. "It really was something. That emotion he found. This rage." Ford was very pleased with the scene and usually printed the first take. But Ward Bond went over to the generator and unplugged the camera so he could plug in his electric shaver. So the camera stopped in the middle of the shot and the actors had to re-do it. Ford never knew what happened. "If he had, he would have gone crazy!" Carey recalled.25

Wayne was suffering from a hangover in the iconic final shot, as Ethan walks away and the door closes. (He once called it "an unhappy happy ending."26) Carey urged there should be a sign put on the room in Goulding's, "In this room, John Wayne got drunk before he shot one of the most famous scenes in motion picture history."

"Why don't you finish the job?"

Once a day, a Cessna would take off from the little red-dirt airstrip down below Goulding's and fly the film to Flagstaff, from where it was sent on to the Warner Brothers lab. Wayne had his own plane at his disposal. When a two-year-old Navajo girl contracted double pneumonia, he offered the plane to transport her to the hospital, which probably saved her life. The Navajos

gave him a special name for his deed: "The Man with the Big Eagle." And Ford was made a full-fledged member of the tribe. They picked a day when Ford wanted to rest the company. The company got three beef in there and a truckload of watermelons. They put on horse races (Ford advised Chuck Roberson to lose the race so the competing Navajo wouldn't lose face). Wayne and Bond were picked to accompany Ford when the tribe presented him with a deerskin in a ceremony. It had all its feet and the hoofs, for not even a hair was supposed to leave that skin. Ford was inducted into the tribe as "Natani Nez." Ford treasured the lettered deer hide. The *Searchers* sets were donated to the Navajo Tribal Council, who chose to dismantle them for the lumber.

"Never apologize, it's a sign of weakness"

They were back in Monument Valley for the last hurrah, the television special *The American West of John Ford,* broadcasted on CBS on December 5, 1971. Ford stayed over an extra day in his usual cabin. "To me, this will always be John Ford Country," Wayne said in his introduction to the show, standing on **Ford Point** as it was called since the days of *The Searchers*, just as he had as Ethan Edwards (but wearing the costume of his recent Western). In view of the knowledge that it was he who suggested Monument Valley to Ford, it's even more touching to hear him say, "Pappy found it and brought me with him…"

Then his mentor directed him for the last time: Wayne was simply shot off his horse Dollor, being doubled by Chuck Roberson in the long shot. Ford shouted into the scene to "tub your butt," after Wayne finds he had landed on

"Tub your butt": John Ford's very last direction of John Wayne, filming a CBS special in their favorite location (author's collection).

a rock. His expression is a reminder of a similar situation in *The Quiet Man* (Sean sits on a manure fork). In the final shot of the TV segment, the two men stand on the outlook on the three famous mittens. They agree that this was the location where the Indians were waiting to attack the stagecoach. Ford came to say goodbye. He looked over the Valley and remarked, "The memories come back."

Two short days of shooting in Monument Valley ended with a last big feast, a barbecue thrown by the Navajos in honor of Ford and Wayne. Wayne said, "I came back to reminisce, and I got the feeling that maybe Pappy came back to say good-bye."[27]

Wayne's last visit would come seven years later, unfortunately an unhappy one. He had suggested Monument Valley as the backdrop for a new aspirin substitute that the Bristol Myers Company wanted to launch, Datril 500. Calling it "strong medicine" ironically echoed Ethan Edwards as he finds Scar's camp: "Medicine country, huh?"

Wayne was incensed by what he considered the crew's total disregard for proper lighting and camerawork. When

This advertisement gave him a headache: John Wayne's last stand in Monument Valley was shot at North Window, the spot where he found the butchered cow in *The Searchers* (author's collection).

the commercial was aired, even his gardener asked, "Why did they have to use that phony-looking background?" Actually, the testimonial was shot in a particularly beautiful spot called the **North Window**, with its commanding view of the north end of the valley. During the few days at that location, he was back in the past, as Pat Stacy noted in her memoir. He missed his old buddies. "All gone," he said sadly, "never to return."[28]

Maybe John Milius—a famous director in his own right, and greatly influenced by Ford (he named one of his children Ethan)—put it best when he said, almost angrily, that Wayne and Ford should have been buried in Monument Valley, side by side.

"Me, I go on searchin'…"

Another moviemaker once called Monument Valley Ford's "moral battleground." At the beginning of *Fort Apache*, Col. Thursday (Henry Fonda), unfamiliar with the terrain, asks the name of a distant outcrop and if they could go there. He's told its name is Blue Mesa and that "it's not as close as it seems." In this natural architecture of Monument Valley, Western director John Ford found the perfect setting for the following scenes on the Arizona side of Monument Valley:

As Tim Holt is leading the cavalry down into the valley in *Stagecoach*, that's **El Capitan** on the horizon, near Kayenta, formed by cooled lava and basalt. It is visible from U.S. Route 163 and is also known as Agathla Peak.

West Mitten Butte to the left, the **East Mitten** in the middle and **Merrick Butte** to the right make up the formation probably the most famous. In *Stagecoach*, Ford uses this natural composition twice, once as the voyage begins and then when the Indians finally appear on the crest, which is now the location of the Tourist office.

In *She Wore a Yellow Ribbon*, Brittles' patrol is attacked by Red Shirt on the back of West Mitten—in the same place Ethan discovers that the Edwards farm is on fire. The rough "road" across the desert floor behind the rock group was dubbed **Hollywood Boulevard** by the Navajo because so many riding sequences were shot there; the ground was ideal to drive a camera car along with the stars on horseback.

The now-famous opening door in *The Searchers* was shot south of the Mitten Buttes looking north (the best long-distance shot in the area): Ethan is framed by **Gray Whiskers** and **Mitchell Butte**. Nugent's revised final screenplay dated January 12, 1955, did not detail the shot. Even though in the original novel Ethan's quest takes him from Texas as far as Wyoming, Ford shot it in a six-mile radius of that point.

Normally locations are chosen once the writing is finished and the production can logistically determine where they will film certain scenes. In this case, Ford knew where he wanted the scenes to be shot. The set of the Edwards farmhouse was placed in front of **Sentinel Mesa**, and Ford detailed in his notes where the ill-fated homestead should be: "It sits alone in a vast expanse. I suggest it be located in Monument Valley."

For Scene 89 (Ethan finds Lucy's body in the canyon), the note reads, "the gap in the rocks near Medicine Country." The script also determines the location for Scar's camp to be at Yei Bi Chei, the formation with the Needles Monument tower, now called the **Totem Pole**. (The last time this photogenic pinnacle was allowed to be climbed was in Clint Eastwood's *The Eiger Sanction* in 1975.) **Sand Spring** is the place they call the sand dunes and a dry wash close to Totem Pole; that's where Wayne tries to shoot Natalie Wood and orders Jeffrey Hunter to "stand aside!" Also on Sand Spring, the bloodthirsty Ethan starts chasing Debbie in the final scene (before the scene cuts to Bronson Canyon in the Hollywood hills).

The **arch-shaped cave** in which Wayne and Jeffrey Hunter take shelter from the Comanche has been a nameless dumping ground for the Navajo for years.

At **North Window,** which is formed by Elephant Butte, Cly Butte and Camel Butt, Ethan finds the butchered cow. The **Three Sisters** are prominently seen in the background of Ethan's "Don't call me uncle" dialogue.

The dramatic location on which Ethan watches Scar's camp at night is called **John Ford Point.** The scene was shot day for night, so assistants with mirrors were placed in the camp below. In the final film, the reflections looked like campfires. The cliff got its name when Navajos inquired about being hired as extras, and production personnel then pointed to Ford. Ever since his first picture in the Valley, Ford insisted the Navajos working as extras be paid the same rate as their Hollywood counterparts (usually $10 to $15 a day). About 5000 Navajos worked as extras or in various other capacities on *The Searchers*, which earned the tribe $35,000 (in 1955 dollars).

"As long as the regiment lives…"

Locations on the Utah side include Goulding's Trading Post, used as a location in *Fort Apache* (as a stagecoach relay station) and *Yellow Ribbon* (as the fort's headquarters). For *Yellow Ribbon*, Ford added a blacksmith shop on the backside.

Just behind Goulding's stands the little building where every Wayne fan has to have his picture taken: Originally used by Mike Goulding as a potato cellar for storing fruits and vegetables, it became "Captain Nathan Brittles' Cabin," maintained just as they left it. (It's also a fine example of how

"You're an actor now": John Wayne in his most mature performance to date, as the retired Nathan Brittles in *She Wore a Yellow Ribbon*, standing in front of his cabin (author's collection).

an interior built on a Hollywood stage usually offers more space than the original room.) The large stone on top of it is a prop from *Cheyenne Autumn*—a fake rock.

From Goulding's, you'll reach the junction to **Oljato Road**. That's about where Brittles led the troops under thunder and lighting in *Yellow Ribbon*. The famous storm scene won the movie the Academy Award for photography. In the same area, on **Rock Door Mesa**, Ford had built the town of Tombstone for *My Darling Clementine*. That set was turned over to the tribal council to be rented to other studios or disposed of in a manner the Indians saw fit. For five years, it rested quietly in the sun. Then, in 1951, the make-believe western town was sold for salvage and dismantled, the wood used for building new houses or just firewood. Some of it now lies in the original Trading Post.

As you turn onto **Red Door Canyon Road**, there's a small pocket canyon to your left. This is where Wayne rode into Cochise's camp in *Fort Apache*. It's now the site of one of Goulding's lodges. As you come up Red Door Canyon, you will recognize the place where Henry Fonda's troop got massacred in the same movie. The same spot was also the location of the Indian Camp in *Yellow Ribbon* (Nathan Brittles' powwow with Chief Pony That Walks).

The road brings you up to the **Square Rock** area. Henry Fonda insults Cochise on the plain south of Square Rock.

Captain Nathan Brittles cabin from *She Wore a Yellow Ribbon*, still standing at Goulding's Lodge. The fake rock on the roof is a *Cheyenne Autumn* prop (photograph by Roland Schaefli).

Although a spectacular location, John Ford used it only once: in *Fort Apache*, John Wayne takes a drink at Goosenecks State Park (photograph by Roland Schaefli).

Wayne rides to the rescue of John Agar's troop in *Fort Apache* on the same flat stretch of sand where Ben Johnson stops the leaderless coach at the beginning of *Yellow Ribbon*. As Ward Bond "gets himself surrounded" in *The Searchers*, they're again on the Square Rock location.

"How far's the river from here, Mose?"

Mexican Hat is a tiny village on the banks of the San Juan River, a 30-minute drive from Monument Valley on U.S. 163. Ford used it for river-crossing scenes in *Fort Apache, Yellow Ribbon* and *The Searchers*. The sombrero-shaped rock is visible in the scene where Ethan keeps killing retreating Indians. In the first take of the river crossing, Chuck Roberson dropped his rifle. "The thing must have been at least a hundred years old and worth a fortune. I knew for a fact that it was heavy as hell, and as we searched the depths, everyone was impressed that instead of sinking straight to the bottom, it had been swept downstream." Maybe it's still there, they never retrieved it. When Ward Bond fell off his horse in the next take, Ford changed the location for the next day to a dirt reservoir only about three feet deep.

U.S. 163 takes you to another spectacular location as you turn left on Rte. 316 to **Goosenecks State Park**. The astonishing view from that overlook includes the meandering canyon carved by the San Juan River 1000 feet below. Ford used it only once, in *Fort Apache*. Wayne and Pedro Armendariz share a drink of rotgut on their way to Cochise's camp, then Wayne throws the empty bottle into the abyss—not something you should repeat.

6

Military Bases

"Just wanted to say hello to the boys"

"Have you been to Southeast Asia?"
—Col. Mike Kirby (John Wayne) to reporter
Beckham (David Janssen) in *The Green Berets*

One track on his surprise hit album America, Why I Love Her *was the sentimental piece "Taps." It paid respects to the U.S. Armed Forces. In the book that was a follow-up to the record, Wayne wrote, "In my picture-making, I've done a lot of shows where the cavalry would bed down for the night in a desert outpost. Even in a movie, the sound of that lone bugle would send a shiver through me."[1]*

Next to his westerns, Wayne is best remembered for his military roles. His war movies were supposed to be morale-boosters. Many times, the U.S. military didn't just supply the filmmakers with personnel and material but with the locations as well. The film dedicated to the forming of the United States Naval Construction Battalion, better known as the Seabees, brought John Wayne to **Camp Pendleton** in California for the first but not the last time. Pendleton had then just been established to train Marines for war.

"I want them armed"

In *Guts & Glory*, his book about the creation of the American military image on film, Lawrence H. Suid wrote that the Wayne movie *The Fighting Seabees* came about because a truck driver on the Republic lot told Wayne about this new organization. Since the actor did not yet "have enough pull to do what I wanted to do," he sent the man to see a producer, who co-opted the idea. Ultimately, the president of the studio, Herbert Yates, informed

This picture was taken on June 20, 1966, with corpsmen from Bravo Company, 1st Tank Battalion, 1st Marine Division, on Hill 55 in the Chu Lai/Da Nang area of Vietnam (author's collection).

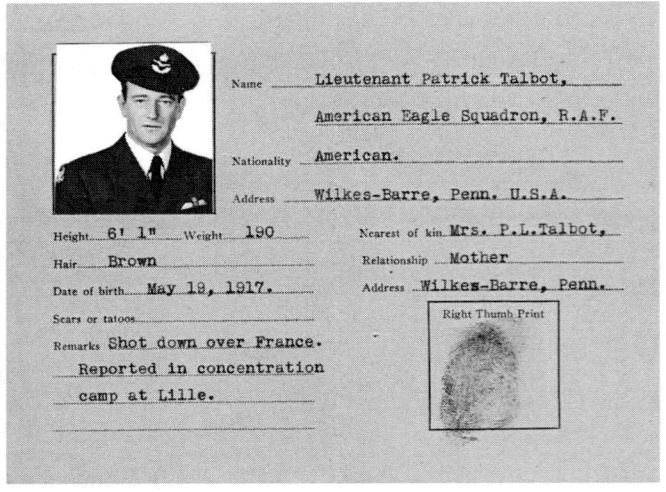

This prop identity card made for *Reunion in France* is never seen that close in the movie but gives detailed information about Wayne's role as a member of the American Eagle Squadron, "shot down over France" in his first war movie (author's collection).

Wayne, "Duke, I've got the greatest idea that's come up so far. We're going to do a story on the fighting Seabees and put you in it."[2]

Republic produced *The Fighting Seabees* from September 20 to December 5, 1943. The main location was the reliable Iverson Ranch in Chatsworth where 250 Seabees worked with the filmmakers to lend some authenticity to the battle scenes. The studio also secured locations on military bases. For the parade ground scenes, they went to **Camp Endicott** in Davisville, Rhode Island. They featured footage of real Seabees marching in review before the Secretary of the Navy. This vast Navy facility was then just one year old. It's now mostly demolished.

"Fix your bayonets and follow me"

Training scenes with Navy equipment show **Camp Rousseau** at Port Hueneme, California, homeport of the Seabees. What they called Splinter City back then was the Bees' last stop before shipping out. Camp Rousseau had been in operation for just four months when the film company arrived. The real-life unit made Wayne an honorary member and presented him with his own uniform. They also took the opportunity to crown leading lady Susan Hayward as their first Seabee Queen. The filmmakers moved from Los Angeles to San Diego to take advantage of more military support at **Camp Pendleton**. The sprawling, 125,000-acre

After the morale-booster *The Fighting Seabees*, **John Wayne kept in contact with the men at Camp Pendleton. On March 23, 1950, he attended the annual dress blues parade at the Marine Barracks, with Calvin T. Durgin (left), Graves B. Erskine (middle), and other USCM officials) (photo courtesy of the Camp Pendleton History and Museum Division).**

Marine Corps base hosted several patriotic epics during World War II.

Actor-friend Paul Fix recalled that Wayne often drank with off-duty Marines. At times Wayne had a little too much, and a Marine would occasionally pick a fight with him. Director Edward Ludwig remembered that there was a saloon near the location frequented by servicemen. Every time Wayne would go there, some guy would pick a fight with him, wondering why he wasn't in uniform and instead only play-acting that he was in the military service. "Wayne would lose more fights than he won and I had to forbid him going there if I expected to get him through the picture in one piece."[3]

"Then let 'em have it"

After *Seabees*, Wayne reported for duty at the U.S.O. When his movie was released in January 1944, he was on a tour of the South Pacific and Australia, entertaining troops. He toured the southwest Pacific bases and battle lines from **Brisbane**, Australia, to New Britain and New Guinea. He also carried out a secret commission for the commander of the Office of Strategic Services, William "Wild Bill" Donovan. The Brisbane newspapers reported that the Hollywood star arrived a few days prior to Christmas. Wayne traveled with accordion player–singer Vikki Montan. Wayne told reporters, "I never knew there was so much water in the world till we crossed that great Pacific." He also let it be known that his stage performance was not overplanned. "I'm here to entertain the troops. I have no special act but hope to get by on appearances."

One newspaper published a story on Wayne spending four hours at a military hospital near Brisbane on Christmas Day. "White Christmas" was the most popular tune the patients wanted to hear from Montan. A reporter asked Wayne why he visited the hospital prior to his scheduled tour in northern battle zones. "It was Christmas. I was here and I just wanted to say hello to some of the boys in the hospital. That's all there is to it."[4]

A few days later, December 27, 1943, he made an appearance at Albion Park Raceway at Breakfast Creek, Brisbane. He was dressed in military uniform.

"I'm strictly a one-man band"

During the war, Wayne's mentor John Ford served as head of the photographic unit for the OSS and made documentaries for the Navy Department. He was commissioned as a commander in the Navy Reserve. During the Normandy invasion, Ford spent five days and nights aboard John Bulkeley's PT boat. The book *They Were Expendable*, relating the story of Bulkeley's PT boat unit, had already been published. Fatefully, Robert Montgomery, who was to portray Bulkeley in the movie version of *They Were Expendable*, was also in the Normandy landings, and waved to the two men from a destroyer.

MGM had requested that Ford would be made available by the Navy for the film version "because Commander Ford is ably qualified by reason of his motion picture experience and his naval experience." Secretary of the Navy James Forrestal then wrote to the director of the OSS, and the movie version came about.[5] Ford claimed he was forced to do the picture against his will. "I knew Johnny Bulkeley well [the name was changed to Brickley in the film]. He dropped me on the coast of France several times during the war when I was working with the French underground. I guess it's all right for me to say this, now," he told *Films in Review* in 1964.[6]

"We'll try to put 'em where they belong"

Ford shot the film in 84 days in South Florida, starting February 11, 1945, and finishing just after the war with Japan had ended. By several accounts, Ford gave Wayne a hard time during the making because he had not served. Robert Montgomery told Ford biographer and filmmaker Lindsay Anderson about one of their first scenes. Montgomery and Wayne had to salute the admiral who inspects the outfit. They did the shot once, then Ford called out for another take. "We didn't know why. After the second take—the same thing again." Wayne murmured to Montgomery, "What's wrong with it?" It seemed to have gone perfectly well. Halfway through the third take, Ford called "Cut!" Then—and according to Montgomery's recollection there must have

With Jack Holt in *They Were Expandable*, on the top-secret location off Miami Beach, code-name "Coconut Island" (author's collection).

In *They Were Expandable* with Robert Montgomery, who portrayed war hero Robert Bulkeley. During the war years, Montgomery had joined the U.S. Navy, rising to the rank of lieutenant commander (author's collection).

been at least a thousand people crowding around, watching the shooting—he yelled out to Wayne, for everyone to hear: "Duke—can't you manage a salute that at least looks as though you've been in the service?" Montgomery was outraged. He walked over to Ford and put his hands on the arms of his chair and leaned over and said: "Don't you ever speak like that to anyone again." Wayne walked off the set and went back to the hotel.[7]

There is a mystery surrounding the location of *They Were Expendable*. All official MGM documents reported **Key Biscayne**, south of Miami Beach, as the filming site. A batch of production photographs was recently discovered and published in the book *Behind the Scenes of* They Were Expendable. The pictures give reason to believe that Ford shot on a small, inhabited island off the coast. The bluejackets involved in the making of the film called it the "Coconut Island," for lack of an official name. Since the fighting was still raging at the time and they were filming in uncharted waters, there may have been security reasons for the officials to provide a "wrong address."

The Navy loaned MGM several squadrons of PT boats. Ford and his stars would pile into the boats, which were docked in Miami, just a few blocks from the Submarine Chaser Training Station, and race each other to the island. It took 20 minutes to reach it. To simulate the Philippines, the art department had constructed sets out of bamboo, straw and wood (just the façades).

In a letter to his small children at home, Wayne said that the **Blackstone Hotel**, Miami Beach, was where they should direct their letters. (It's now Blackstone Apartments, 800 Washington Avenue.) Some of the crew members were staying at the Roney Plaza in Miami Beach. Wayne also let his children know that he was working on "a little island off the coast," a place covered with palm trees, rattlesnakes, tarantulas and sand flies. "The flies worry us the most."[8]

Shooting on the island lasted 30 days. Capt. James Havens, a former Marine sergeant, mined the harbor and set explosive depth charges to go off, simulating near-misses on the PT boats. The Japanese battleships were detailed replicas. One day, a large brushfire provided Ford with enormous billows of gray smoke. Never one to miss what nature would provide, he promptly sent a second unit to get it on film, as it would be perfect for the burning of Manila.

The scenes early in the film dealing with the Manila base of Motor Torpedo Boat Squadron 3 were filmed on the bayfront of Miami Beach. Those sets were built just three blocks away from Biscayne Boulevard, not far from Collins Avenue. Either the camera was always shooting out to the sea, or the skyline was matted out of the film.

Taken on an occasion at the Field Photo Farm: John Ford makes Wayne and Harry Carey, Jr., (right) sing when they are obviously over the limit on booze, with Hugh Farr and Lloyd Perryman of the Sons of the Pioneers in the back (author's collection).

MGM announces the wrap of *They Were Expandable* in the trade papers, using a publicity shot of Donna Reed, Robert Montgomery, and John Wayne. Note that John Ford is credited as Captain U.S.N.R. (author's collection).

"Listen, sister, I don't dance!"

Ford resumed shooting on the MGM lot on May 14. Three days later, while directing from a camera scaffold, he slipped off and landed on the concrete 20 feet below, prompting Wayne to shout: "Jesus Christ, you clumsy bastard!"[9] Ford spent two weeks in traction in Cedars of Lebanon Hospital.

There was one more accident before they wrapped it up, and Wayne remembered it as probably the only time he got close to a fight with his mentor. They were shooting a process scene where Wayne's boat is strafed by an airplane. The special effects person shooting ball bearings at the boat had forgotten to replace the windshield with a non-breakable plexiglass one. According to Wayne, "Real glass went flying into my face. In a rage, I grabbed a hammer and went after the guy." But Ford stepped in front of him and said, "No you don't. They're my crew." Wayne shouted, "Your crew, goddammit, they're my eyes!"[10]

Ford donated his salary for a "living memorial" to his men and their Field Photographic Unit. He bought a 20-acre estate in the San Fernando Valley and built the Field Photo Farm (see Chapter 19) at an estimated cost of $225,000. Wayne chipped in $10,000.

"Let's get back in the war"

Sands of Iwo Jima has become something of an unofficial recruiting film for the United States Marine Corps, and Wayne's portrayal of the tough-as-nails Sergeant Stryker has long since entered their do-or-die mentality. In retrospect, it's surprising that not only was the story developed without Wayne in mind but the star was reluctant to do it. According to director Allan Dwan, Republic tried to sign Wayne only when they realized they needed some box office insurance because the studio could not do a large-scale war movie on its usual shoestring budget. As the shooting date came near, Dwan still had no main actor and even kidded Gen. Graves B. Erskine, then in command at Camp Pendleton, that he should consider playing the part himself.

Producer Edmund Grainger went after Kirk Douglas first and was already negotiating with his agent when Wayne expressed interest in the part. But he just wasn't that enthralled with the screenplay. According to Michael Wayne, "He wasn't sold on it until the USMC came to him and explained their need for a strong picture that would show the public the importance of the Corps."[11] At this time, four years after the war, the Senate was cutting military budgets and there was talk about cutting out the Marine Corps' elite unit completely. That, as Michael recalled, was one of the main reasons for his father to do the film. But not before Wayne had brought in his personal writer, James Edward Grant, to rewrite some of his dialogue. When Wayne finally okayed the script, he called it a "beautiful personal story. A man takes eight boys and has to make men out of them."[12]

Marine Corps assistance was essential. "Without Marine cooperation," Grainger estimated, "the picture would have cost at least $2,500,000." Therefore, it had to be both logistically feasible and operationally acceptable to shoot at Camp Pendleton, home of the First Marine Division and 16,000 Leathernecks. The USMC went all-out in assisting the moviemakers. Still, Marine Headquarters was aware that

Sands of Iwo Jima **was a team effort between Hollywood and the USMC: Forrest Tucker, John Wayne, director Allan Dwan, producer Edmund Grainger, and Gen. Graves B. Erskine at Camp Pendleton (photo courtesy of the Graves B. Erskine Collection at the Marine Corps Archives).**

the exigencies of making a motion picture required the occasional bending of military procedures.

"You gotta learn right and you gotta learn fast"

Filming of *Sands of Iwo Jima* began in the summer of 1949. A veteran filmmaker, Dwan was familiar with San Diego County—he had made more than 150 short features there in 1910 and 1911, mostly in the back country near La Mesa. Now, with a million dollar budget, he had the resources to make a technically challenging feature. The Corps supplied Sherman tanks, planes, Jeeps, trucks and any other military gear seen in the movie. Twelve hundred off-duty Marines were recruited as extras, in full battle equipment. On the daily call sheets, some of them were even assigned to play "Dead Marines." Semper fi!

The camp's vast and varied topography was perfect for the filmmakers. The outdoor set spanned two and a half miles. Art director James Sullivan consulted historical photographs of the battle sites to create believable facsimiles. The two major battlegrounds in the film, Tarawa and Iwo Jima, looked different. To recreate the Tarawa beachhead, Sullivan brought in 500 plastic palm trees from Hollywood. Scores of plaster pillboxes and bunkers were erected, thousands of feet of barbed wire stretched. To recreate the barren terrain of the volcanic island Iwo Jima, flame throwers burned off foliage from hillsides. The ground was covered with oil and lampblack to simulate volcanic ash. The film's two amphibious landings were re-enacted on the beaches at **Camp Del Mar**, Pendleton's

A Marine at Camp Pendleton took this snapshot of John Wayne with two of his USMC corpsmen, working as uncredited extras in *Sands of Iwo Jima*, in June 1949 (photo courtesy of the Camp Pendleton History and Museum Division).

Marine amphibious base. Thirty amtracs and several landing ships were at Dwan's disposal. Two squadrons of Corsair fighter planes from the Marine Air Station at El Toro flew overhead when the equivalent of a battalion invaded a mile and a half of beach. During this period, the Marine air units at El Toro were molded together with the 1st Marine Division troops at Pendleton. This combination embarked for Korea soon thereafter.

"If you don't, you'll be dead"

Dwan shot the battle for Mount Suribachi in two parts. The first piece of the sequence was set in a vast stone quarry, prepared to resemble the slopes of the dormant vent of a volcano. For the second part, which included the moment of the famous flag-raising, Dwan chose the site of an artillery observation post, modified to resemble the Suribachi.

USMC Captain Leonard Fribourg's job was to check the script for authenticity. He even suggested "Saddle up!," which became a trademark line for Wayne—Fribourg had heard another Marine instructor use it. It suited the Stryker character fine. He scrutinized dialogue like, "That shelling didn't help at all" (in the scene when Marines approach the beach and comment on the accuracy of naval gunfire). "The Navy might take exception to this," Fribourg opined. He also criticized the scene essential to the plot: Stryker orders that a wounded Marine *not* be rescued, as doing so would give away the platoon's position. "Marines would not leave wounded Marine," Fribourg wrote in his revision. The Marines also took offense at the scene where Stryker teaches a recruit a lesson. Fribourg even recommended that headquarters in

On the San Diego set of *Sands of Iwo Jima*, Sergeant Stryker consults technical advisor "Len" Fribourg about the authenticity of Marine Corps drill instructors (photo courtesy of the Camp Pendleton History and Museum Division).

Washington prevent the scene from being shot: "Marines don't hit Marines with a rifle butt."[13] Washington overruled the technical advisor and the scene was retained because it was important to develop the Stryker character—but they added the scene in which Stryker and that recruit make up for it. Still, Dwan never rolled the cameras without asking his military advisor, "Does that look okay?"[14]

"I'm gonna get the job done"

Fribourg said that Wayne would have made a good commander in real life "because he got enough guts to tell the truth and put it the way people would understand."[15] However, making Marines out of a platoon of movie actors presented a problem even to Sergeant Stryker. "Wayne used to like to stay up at the bar quite late," the director recalled, "and he could put away a lot." His leading man never found it difficult to be ready for action the next morning no matter how late he had stayed at the bar. Co-star John Agar remembered one party lasted into the wee hours of the morning, and Wayne had an appointment with the Marine Corps at eight o'clock. "And by tosh, he was there. He was there."[16]

Since the younger actors tried to keep up with Wayne, according to Dwan, "they'd be a pathetic sight in the morning." To turn his hungover actors into Marines, Dwan asked for help from General Erskine. The camp commandant gave him "the toughest drill sergeant there," who worked Dwan's actors in full packs and rifles for hours each day. The men hardened up, went to bed at ten and "avoided Wayne like a plague."

Dwan told Peter Bogdanovich of one time when some of the younger cast members were a little sulky in their response to the director's orders. Wayne came up and peered over Dwan's shoulder. "God damn it! Will you bastards do what he tells you!" And they did.[17]

The actors stayed at the **Carlsbad Hotel**, 5720 Paseo Del Norte in Carlsbad, 20 minutes from Pendleton.

"You have your orders, don't move!"

Under the expert supervision of special effect wizard Howard Lydecker, 19 men of his Republic staff laid a mile and a half of wire connected to 2000 sticks of dynamite and 50 black powder bombs. The explosives were carefully marked, then covered with truckloads of sand, peat soil and cork. They were encased in directional containers which sent the explosive force out at certain angles to avoid the extras who were dodging these orchestrated movie explosions. Gas machine guns spurted flames instead of bullets, and air valves gave off puffs of smoke from the ground. When Dwan called action, six cameras rolled simultaneously.

The authenticity amazed even battle-hardened veterans. Gen. Howland "Howlin' Mad" Smith—who had been in command of the U.S. forces at Iwo Jima and portrayed himself in the film—told reporters: "I felt as though I were back in the South Pacific. It's so real, it's almost frightening." David M. Shoup, Medal of Honor winner at Tarawa, also played himself. Regarding the Tarawa recreation, he said, "It was a fearsome thing to look at because having experienced the battle, goddamn, I didn't want to go through it again."[18]

The movie even weaved in archival newsreel battle footage, selected with Fribourg's help. Erskine was impressed enough to ask Grainger to leave the sets standing after the filming, to use for training purposes.

"Forevermore, he don't walk away"

It was Fribourg's suggestion to use the real lieutenant who took the patrol up Suribachi as he "is alive today and still a member of the USMC." Capt. George Schrier was ready to re-enact his actions. Republic also recruited the three surviving members of the six-man team that raised Old Glory in Joe Rosenthal's iconic photograph, probably the picture that was reproduced more than any single picture about World War II. So when Wayne tells a group of soldiers to "find something we can use for a standard and we'll put this up," he hands the original flag to Ira Hayes, John Bradley and Rene Gagnon, who then went into action as the flag-raisers. "Howlin' Mad" Smith was in attendance as a technical advisor in this pivotal scene. The Corps even let them use the actual flag. It was returned to the **National Museum of the Marine Corps** in Virginia, where it is displayed to this day, at 18900 Jefferson Davis Highway, Triangle. The credits included an unusual historical note: "The first American flag was raised on Mount Suribachi by the late Sgt. Ernest I. Thomas, Jr., U.S.M.C., on the morning of February 23, 1945." Four years after Rosenthal took his famous photo of what was actually the *second* flag-raising on Suribachi, it was already surrounded by controversy. In advertisements, Republic used the photo with the tagline "The Marine's Finest Hour!" In 1954, the Iwo Jima memorial, a huge bronze monument west of Arlington Cemetery, was unveiled, based on the Rosenthal photo. Sculptor Felix W. De Weldon had advised the actors in the flag-raising scene of how to assume the proper position.

"Any questions? That's all"

Filming at Pendleton took three weeks. Dwan finished up on the Republic stages the following month. *Sands*

John Wayne, producer Edmund Grainger and Gen. Graves B. Erskine briefly discuss the next scene while the camera is set up for the next scene of *Sands of Iwo Jima* (photo courtesy of the Graves B. Erskine Collection at the Marine Corps Archives).

dwarfed the expense of any previous Republic film. But when Yates saw the result, for once he didn't complain, even though the final bill was four times higher than the usual budget.

The Pendleton Scout, the official newspaper of the base, proudly informed its readers about the December 28 premiere of "their" film at the Fox Carthay Circle Theatre in

The three survivors of six men who raised the historic flag on Mt. Suribachi are back in Marine uniforms: Ira Hayes, John Bradley, and Rene Gagnon. They made the Hollywood version for *Sands of Iwo Jima*, on July 27, 1949 (note the sound trucks in the background) (photo courtesy of the Camp Pendleton History and Museum Division).

Los Angeles. "Some 503 Marines from the 5th Regiment, 1st Marine Division, paraded down Wilshire Boulevard in dress blues. The red-carpeted walk to the theatre was lined with Marine Staff." In addition to *Sands'* stars, Maureen O'Hara, Rhonda Fleming, Janet Leigh and Robert Mitchum were there. Commanding General Graves B. Erskine attended along with several other high-ranking officers.

Sands of Iwo Jima was an instant critical and commercial success. It grossed over $5 million in the U.S. and garnered Academy Award nominations (something unusual for Republic), including Wayne's first for Best Actor. When Wayne had his footprints placed at Grauman's Chinese Theatre on January 25, 1950, two hundred-pound sacks of original "Sands of Iwo Jima" were shipped in to make the cement. Allan Dwan was correct in observing, "After this movie, Wayne was King." The USMC shared in its success. Many years later, Marine recruiters claimed that volunteers increased whenever the movie appeared on television. Pendleton was given the affectionate nickname "Hollywood South" and would go on as an occasional movie location. Even though Sgt. Stryker had to die in the climax of *Sands of Iwo Jima*, John Wayne would live to fight another day at Camp Pendleton.

"Drop your dive brakes"

In the credits, *Jet Pilot* starred John Wayne, Janet Leigh and the United States Air Force. Quite a statement! Yet if one takes into account how much of their time the pilots devoted to the making of this Cold War comedy, they certainly earned it.

Captain Chuck Yeager was a technical advisor on the film and piloted a supersonic plane, the X-1, for the first time. Wayne acted out the flying scenes in front of a rear-projection screen in a plane mock-up. The Navy sent a pilot to the RKO lot to instruct Wayne on how to "fly" a jet fighter. Director Josef von Sternberg, discoverer (and former lover) of Marlene Dietrich, demanded seemingly endless rehearsals. Wayne told his leading lady Janet Leigh that if he'd allow his temper to explode, "I'd kill the S.O.B."[19]

Jet Pilot started principal photography right after *Sands of Iwo Jima* wrapped. It ran from October 31, 1949, to February 13, 1950. However, RKO boss Howard Hughes felt additional aviation scenes were needed, and resumed filming one year after Wayne had wrapped the film. The first version was eight hours long, and Hughes could never decide how to cut it. More than 16 months of actual aerial footage was filmed. Camera operators flew more than 40,000 miles and spent over 250 hours in the air. Hughes went crazy dispatching second and third camera crews on zigzags across thousands of miles looking for the right clouds.

As late as March 1953, William Clothier—the fifth cameraman hired—filmed additional sequences. (He went on to shoot the *High and the Mighty* and *Island in the Sky* aerial sequences.) Clothier had served in the Air Force during the war, heading a film unit and photographing aerial combat in the European Theater. When Hughes screened the footage he shot at Travis Air Force Base, he demanded "clouds that look that good or better."[20] Clothier then filmed for 15 more months, often at speeds of over 500 m.p.h. He always made sure there were clouds.

The company used **Air Forces bases** in California: March Field, Hamilton Army Air Field and Edwards Air Force Base; in

Premiering *Sands of Iwo Jima*: John Wayne standing next to Herbert Yates; General Graves B. Erskine is next to actress Adele Mara (middle), with other USMC officials and their wives. Producer Edmund Grainger stands to the right (photo courtesy of the Graves B. Erskine Collection at the Marine Corps Archives).

leader (minus Stryker's nuances) and a James Edward Grant script, and again backed by the USMC hardware-wise. In June 1950, following meetings with Grainger, Marine Corps officials in Washington granted the production permission to use its facilities. But the Navy later reneged on its agreement to allow the use of the carrier *Bataan* for filming at sea: It was suddenly needed more urgently in Korea. Nevertheless, they did provide several planes. The Marine pilots came from Marine Training Squadron VMT-2 and Marine Fighter Squadron VMF-232, stationed at El Toro Air Station. They flew the Hellcats and Corsairs down the coast to perform the aerial sequences (even though the F6F-3 Hellcats had not been available in 1942 when the story is set). The USMC even provided the filmmakers with a few airplanes to use as the Japanese enemies.

Some of these fighter pilots were shipped to Korea after they were done with the movie. "Those pilots were a fearless bunch," recalled John Mitchum (Robert's brother), who

This publicity still announcing *Jet Pilot* was released in 1950, a full seven years before the movie actually appeared on the movie screens. Among many more military airfields, location filming took place at Edwards Air Force Base and Hamilton Air Force Base in California (author's collection).

Colorado: Lowry Field; in North Dakota: Fargo Air National Guard Base; in South Dakota: Ellsworth Air Force Base in Rapid City; in Texas: Kelly Field and Lackland Air Force Base in San Antonio; in Florida: Eglin Field; in Nevada: Reno Stead Airport and Nellis Air Force Base in Las Vegas, as well as Pensacola-Eglin Air Force Base in Florida. Seventeen months of shooting was the longest shooting schedule in RKO history. In the end, *Jet Pilot* didn't get a release until 1957. By then, Wayne had already made *The Wings of Eagles* in Pensacola. "It was just too stupid for words," Wayne commented.[21]

"Schedule that mission"

On October 28, 1950, Wayne signed a new contract with RKO. He returned to Camp Pendleton for *Flying Leathernecks*, made from November 20, 1950, to January 27, 1951. Producer Edmund Grainger used the *Iwo Jima* formula: Wayne as a seemingly emotionless

"Marine Air-Devils in hot pursuit": *Flying Leathernecks* **relied heavily on Hellcats and Corsairs at Camp Pendleton, north of San Diego. Some of the Marine pilots were shipped out to fight in Korea after the movie was done (author's collection).**

played one of the pilots in Wayne's Wildcat squadron. One fighter pilot unit had already seen action in Korea, and "these guys from Georgia were the wildest bunch of fliers I have ever seen. They would be drinking until five in the morning, then suck straight oxygen out of tubes, and go straight in the air."[22]

The set designers built a replica of Henderson Field "that was so realistic that the pilots who had actually flown into the base on Guadalcanal shook their heads in amazement," Mitchum wrote in his memoir.[23]

"You haven't got the guts"

When Wayne arrived in Buffalo for a premiere of *The Searchers*, the Marines gave him a personal escort. On December 12, 1959, during a lull in production on *The Alamo*, Wayne filmed three one-minute commercials for the Corps. In one appearance on Rowan & Martin's *Laugh-In* show, he

John Wayne doing his own stunt: this barracks on a hill in Camp Pendleton, representing Henderson Field on Guadalcanal, is about to explode. Robert Ryan is on the left, Carleton Young is ahead of Wayne, with unidentified extras (author's collection).

On the Brackettville set in Texas, Wayne is taking time off his busy schedule on *The Alamo* to film commercials for the Marine Corps (with unidentified corpsmen) (author's collection).

comically recited his version of a poem: "The sky is blue/the grass is green/get off your butt and join the Marine!"

Between August 1968 and April 1970, Wayne and John Ford teamed up once more for *Chesty: A Tribute to a Legend*, a made-for-TV tribute to Lt. General Lewis "Chesty" Puller of the USMC, a "sweet, tough, gentle, hard-boiled Marine," according to host-narrator Wayne. (Howard Hawks didn't mind that Ford used his *Rio Lobo* stage and "borrowed" his lead actor, wearing western garb, in his scenes.) Years earlier, after the battle of Guadalcanal, Ford paid Chesty a visit with his Field Photographic Unit and took Wayne along. Ford introduced Wayne to the Marine commander who right away ordered him to "put on boots and a big hat and circulate about my wounded," because there never was a Marine who didn't love a Western. When Wayne walked among "those clovered-up kids," some broke into grins just to see someone they were familiar with. Chesty then said, "Duke, you're better than all the goddamn pills in the world." In the documentary, Wayne said with feeling, "I think that was my proudest moment." Sad to say, the film never found a buyer; the documentary's first public showing was after Ford's death, on April 4, 1976.

On August 13, 1973, Wayne received the U.S. Marine Corps Leagues Iron Mike Award, given for Americanism. He told his *Playboy* interviewers, "I know the Marines and all the American Armed Forces were quite proud of my portrayal of

Stryker." At an American Legion convention in Florida, General MacArthur told him, "You represent the American Serviceman better than the American Serviceman himself."[24]

His custom-made Pontiac had a distinctive bubble top. Wayne had Barris of Hollywood, the self-proclaimed "King of the Customizers," raise the roof seven inches so that he could wear his Stetson while driving. The bumper sticker on the Pontiac was much simpler: "The Marines Are Looking for a Few Good Men."

"I'm gonna move that toe!"

The narration of *The Wings of Eagles* begins with, "I guess now in Pensacola they still talk about the admiral's tea party…," and John Ford made it a point to shoot it where it happened, at the actual **U.S. Naval Air Station** in Florida. The film they made between September 10 and October 4, 1956, depicts the life of Frank F. "Spig" Wead, the daredevil Navy aviator who turned to screenwriting. Wead had crafted the script of *They Were Expendable*.

A highly personal film: In *Wings of Eagles*, Ward Bond (left) is playing a movie director called John Dodge, a thin disguise for director John Ford (standing); and John Wayne plays the real-life Navy hero "Spig" Wead, who was a friend of the trio (author's collection).

Group shot with the Navy personnel on the deck of the USS *Philippine Sea*: John Ford (white pants) and Wayne, cinematographer Paul Vogel by the camera, next to Danny Borzage who used to play the accordion on Ford's sets to get the actors in the right mood. Also in the crowd are cast members Ken Curtis, Jack Pennick and Louis Jean Heydt (author's collection).

They had been working in the heat and humidity of Pensacola all week long. Still, the Old Man wouldn't have the men drink a cold beer. Wayne, Chuck Roberson and the usual gang checked the production schedule and found out they could sleep off hangovers, as they were not on the next day's call sheet. They decided to hit the town. By the time the steaks arrived, they were feeling no pain. Wayne kept the drinks coming "as if the bourbon had been mineral water," Roberson wrote in the often hilarious retelling of his life. They got back to the motel as the sun was lighting up the Gulf of Mexico. A short while later, they heard knocking on their doors: the Skipper wanted them to go to work! Ford had changed the schedule after he heard that the men had broken his rule.

"Oh man," was all John Wayne said, sitting in the back seat with his head in his hands, being transported to the set. Ford didn't even use them in front of the camera, he just had them standing there. "There can't be any place in the world more humid than Florida in July, and putting that together with the worst hangover of a lifetime, you're about as close to hell as a man can be," Roberson recalled. Wayne sweated all day long, smelling "like an old onion."[25] Stuntman Terry Wilson added that after a while, Wayne said, "If I'm working, I might as well run the train." As they were setting up the scene in which an airplane flies over a train, he got up with the engineer, asking him to "show me how to do this."[26]

"Thanks for the ride"

The heartbreaking finale was filmed on the aircraft carrier USS ***Philippine Sea***, off the coast of South California. Ford asked his star to ride a bosun's chair for the shot that ends the picture, as Wayne is transferred from carrier to destroyer. Wayne knew Ford was challenging him and bravely consented. Pilar recalled, "Duke looked at the fragile rigging and suddenly the other ship seemed a hell of a long way off. But Ford was acting so matter-of-fact that Duke didn't dare express a single doubt. He gave everyone a big grin and a thumbs-up sign and the terrifying crossing was underway."[27]

Wayne spent four hours suspended 40 feet over the water for

this shot. Two ships were 80 yards apart while Wayne was on the breeches buoy. Afterward, the crew of the Navy destroyer gave Wayne the following citation: "You have bravely allowed yourself to be carried over the raging waters of the Pacific. To the immortal shouts 'Don't give up the ship!,' 'Damn the torpedos, full speed ahead!' and 'Fire when ready, Gridley!' you have added the fighting phrase 'Get me down out of this son of a bitch!'"[28]

Ford held the press preview aboard the carrier ***Lexington***. "The bluejackets were with it every minute, and during the dramatic moments there was complete silence in the great big hangar deck, which, as you know, is bigger than St. Peter's," Ford proudly informed Wayne.[29]

"You tangle with me, I'll have your hide"

The Civil War western *The Horse Soldiers* was on location in Mississippi and Louisiana from October 28 to December 5, 1958, followed by 19 days of interiors at Columbia and MGM. The production headquarters was in Alexandria, Louisiana. John Ford used the **Jefferson Military College** in Mississippi (the alma mater of Confederate president Jefferson Davis) as a location for the scene when 150 cadets between the ages of nine and 16 charge Wayne's cavalry. Ford's reliable Jack-of-all-trades, retired marine Jack

"Get me down out of this son-of-a-bitch!" Wayne spent hours in this position, transferred from carrier to destroyer, with the Pacific Ocean underneath. The USS *Philippine Sea* was decommissioned on 28 December 1958 and sold for scrap in 1970 (author's collection).

Pennick, spent a week drilling the boys in preparation for their big scene. Ford regular Anna Lee played the mother who tried to get her boy out of the cadets' ranks. To get the emotion he wanted, Ford had asked her to be on the set at a specific time and when she arrived, he berated her in front of the whole crew for being late. The tears she shed in that scene were real.

The facility closed just five years after *The Horse Soldiers*. The historic campus at 16 Old North Street in Natchez is operated as a museum.

"War isn't exactly a civilized business"

The climactic *Horse Soldiers* fight for the bridge was shot in December in **Natchitoches**, Louisiana. **Oakland Plantations** in Natchitoches (near the Cane River Creole National Heritage Area) portrayed Constance Towers' estate in the movie.

William Holden didn't stay with the rest of the company at a place then called Bill's Motel in Clarence but set himself up in **Shreveport**, out of Ford's reach so that Ford couldn't stop Holden from having a drink. Holden then cooked up a scheme to spring Wayne. He claimed that Wayne's teeth looked discolored in the dailies, and consequently Wayne was sent to Shreveport to have his teeth cleaned. Holden, of course, insisted that he'd drive him to the dentist since it was on his way. They really had a night on the town. Constance Towers remembered that the next morning, they looked "'like they hadn't been to bed at all,' and Pappy Ford had all the stuntmen lined up to smell their breath."[30] Wayne returned to Shreveport to premiere the film.

When Wayne got to know the woman that would be the last one in his life, Pat Stacy, he learned that she was from Shreveport. Laughing, he asked her why she didn't call him while he was there making the Ford western. Wayne returned to Shreveport once more, on December 14, 1978. He was

John Ford (holding sign) even directed Christmas cards: in December 1958, he had several youthful cadets stand at attention in front of Jefferson Military College for this picture, accompanied by stars Anna Lee (sitting left), William Holden (standing next to Wayne), and Constance Towers (author's collection).

presented with the Omar M. Bradley Spirit of the Independence Award at the **Independence Bowl**, 3301 Pershing Boulevard. Wayne went to the stadium in an escorted motorcade. Leonard Phillips was instrumental in this. The men knew each other since 1942, when Phillips served as a film industry liaison officer for the U.S. Army Air Corps. During his stay in Shreveport, Wayne stayed at the Phillips' home, and the Phillipses spent time on his yacht.

"I've got a ship to run"

The controversies *The Longest Day* created because of the amount of assistance Darryl F. Zanuck received from the Army (see Chapter 12) shook up the relationship between Hollywood and the military branches. The Pentagon rewrote the regulations for assistance. Filmmakers would have to meet certain criteria. By the time *In Harm's Way* (1965) went into pre-production, new regulations had been issued. If they wanted to use Pearl Harbor as a location, they needed military cooperation. Director Otto Preminger went through normal channels and paid for the support he received, as new guidelines required. Preminger emphasized that he reimbursed the Navy: "I remember very well that there was never the taxpayers' money involved."[31] The Navy gave extensive cooperation including filming at **Pearl**

After receiving the **Omar M. Bradley Spirit of Independence Award** at the **Independence Bowl in Shreveport, Louisiana** (seen here with several unidentified officials of the award), Wayne flew back in a private plane. While he and other guests were waiting at the hangar, a woman was calling her husband to explain why she was running late. Wayne got to the phone and let him know the reason for her being late was talking to him (photograph by Diane Gainey).

Harbor. Between June 24 and September 1964, scenes for *In Harm's Way* were shot aboard several Navy ships: the USS *St. Paul*, USS *Braine*, USS *Capitaine*, USS *O'Bannon*, USS *Philip*, USS *Renshaw* and the USS *Walker*. One day, Kirk Douglas held a Jewish worship service for the Jewish sailors on the *St. Paul*.

"We'll try to make it in"

On December 26, 1965, Wayne wrote directly to President Lyndon B. Johnson. He wanted to "'tell the story of our fighting men in Vietnam' in a manner that will inspire a patriotic attitude." The most effective way he could think of explaining to the public why the involvement in Vietnam was necessary "is through the motion picture medium."[32] To make a successful film, Wayne told his commander-in-chief, he would need the cooperation of the Pentagon. Johnson supported Wayne's efforts.

Wayne flew to South Vietnam in June 1966 to get a first-hand look. This tour is often misinterpreted as having given Wayne the idea for making a film about the servicemen in Vietnam when in fact it was the other way around. At this time, Wayne already had the film rights to Robin Moore's novel *The Green Berets* and was deep in pre-production. He wasn't just visiting troops this time, he was getting ready to make the first movie about the Vietnam War. In Saigon, he stayed at the **Rex Hotel**, (now Hồ Chí Minh, at 141 Nguyễn Huệ). Later on, he got proof that Maoist spies were watching him.

"Out here, due process is a bullet"

He visited the 101st Airborne Division based at Dak To in South Vietnam. While signing autographs in Chu Lai, sniper fire landed less than 50 feet away. "He continued signing autographs," Army periodicals reported, "and posing for pictures as though nothing was happening, but the Marines who heard the incoming rounds reacted differently. They unlimbered weapons and raced toward the outer perimeter of 7th Marines Area."[33] He told the episode to his biographer Munn from his own view: "I didn't notice and just kept signing autographs but the Marines automatically scrambled for cover. So I took cover also, 'cause I'm not stupid enough to stand out there and be a sitting duck."[34]

At Pleiku in the Central Highlands, the Montagnard tribesmen presented him with a bracelet he wore on his wrist for the remainder of his life. When he came down with a severe eye inflammation, he had to be treated in the Third Field Hospital. The only empty bed was in a neuropsychiatric ward. Wayne went over to the patient in the next bed and said, "I'm John Wayne. You're going to pull out of this." The wounded soldier started laughing and whispered to the nurse, "That guy is really crazy. He thinks he's John Wayne."[35]

"You always knew it could happen"

While Wayne was touring the front lines, screenwriter James Lee Barrett, a former Marine, was already adapting the book. Robin Moore would have been a logical choice to write it based on his novel. Yet Moore had offended too many Army officials by insisting that the Green Berets' raid into Cambodia he presented in the book was based on fact. Batjac president Michael Wayne had to ensure Pentagon officials that Barrett would use only a few incidents from the original book. (As a matter of fact, the two major portions which have nothing to do with each other, the capture of the general and the VC attack on Fort Dodge, are two separate chapters in the Moore book.)

In April, Wayne and Barrett discussed the script development at the Defense Department in Washington. At the suggestion of the Pentagon, they traveled on to the John F. Kennedy Special Warfare Center at **Fort Bragg**, North Carolina, to get the feel of the place where the Special Forces were trained. Barrett had his first draft ready by August 1966. As expected, the Defense Department PR office vetoed the covert mission into North Vietnam to seize the VC general. They insisted that this was not a mission that the Green Berets would undertake (their job was reconnaissance, surveillance and training). The Department granted the request of the producers to have Barrett make a trip to Vietnam, to familiarize himself with the jargon, equipment and procedures.

"So you decided to volunteer"

Michael Wayne and Barrett went to another Washington meeting on September 29, 1966, to talk about the "faults" the Department

found. They agreed to delete the kidnapping in Cambodia. It was fixed easily enough: Barrett just left out the specific geographics. The beautiful Vietnamese spy would simply lead the high-ranking enemy officer to a place where the Americans could get ahold of him—without illegally crossing any borders. Barrett finished his next draft by the end of 1966. In February 1967, the Army pointed out mistakes in technical matters (like the wrong type of aircraft). They also suggested dialogue changes. Barrett recitified matters so that the South Vietnamese soldiers defended the camp. However, the producers managed to keep two major plot points in: the brutal treatment of a prisoner (off-screen) by a Vietnamese officer (George Takei) and a war correspondent's (David Janssen) decision to pick up a gun and become a combatant.

The Pentagon formally approved the script on March 30, 1967—more than a year after Barrett was commissioned to write it—and Batjac was asked to submit their list of requirements. They would eventually be granted the use of several UH1-Huey attack helicopters and a C-7 Caribou light transport. The Air Force supplied two C-130 Hercules transports and two A-1 Skyraider attack aircraft as well as film footage of an AC-47 "Puff the Magic Dragon" gunship. In addition, an HC-130 Hercules employing the Skyhook Fulton recovery system could be used (for the scene in which the enemy general is lifted into the air). The Army also

In the thick of the action (with unknown extras) at the "Dodge City" set at Fort Benning, Georgia: After another script revision, the South Vietnamese soldiers defended the camp, aided by *The Green Berets* (author's collection).

provided uniforms, including the OG-107 green and "Tiger Stripe" Tropical Combat Uniform (jungle fatigues), with correct Vietnam War subdued insignia.

"He won't quit"

Wayne had always wanted to film in Vietnam. The American public saw that war daily on TV, so he knew they would not accept a location other than the real thing. The Pentagon talked him out of it because "if you start shooting blanks over there, they might start shooting back."[36]

Army facilities on Okinawa were considered. During his stay on the Japanese island in April, Wayne took time out to visit the U.S. Army Hospital at **Camp Kue**. One of the hospitalized Green Berets remembered how Wayne reached out his huge hand and asked how he was doing. All the stunned young man could utter was, "I'm fine, Mr. Duke."[37]

Okinawa offered tropical terrain and an Army helicopter facility. But when Wayne inspected it with his co-director Ray Kellogg, they found the aircraft would not be available on a regular basis. Fort Bragg was also ruled out as a location because base officials could not provide a reliable schedule for use of aircraft. It was the Army's idea to consider shooting the film at Fort Benning. Wayne himself doubted that he could make Georgia look enough like the Vietnam jungle (which many critics would point out as one of the weaknesses of the film). Kellogg went on a scouting trip and found that Fort Benning regularly had 20 to 30 Huey helicopters in the training program, and that the brass would make them available. This was the main reason for Wayne to settle for Benning. In May 1967, John and Michael Wayne took a look for themselves. Fort Benning's commander also guaranteed the use of locations for special effects and facilities for housing the crew.

Wayne lived with the rest of the cast in the **Camellia Motel** in Columbus, 53–55 Fort Benning Road. Cast member Rudy Robbins roomed with Chuck Roberson. "The folks in Georgia were great," Robbins said, "the camaraderie was terrific."[38]

During their stay, the eagerly awaited finale of the television series *The Fugitive* aired on August 29. Of all U.S. households, 49.9 percent of all U.S. watched. So did David Janssen, who had played Dr. Kimble, in his Columbus motel room.

The decision to use Fort Benning as the primary location was made because the Army had twenty to thirty UH-1 Huey attack helicopters in their training program. David Janssen sits in the Huey with unknown extras (author's collection).

"We all get steak or nobody does": the director, producer, and star of *The Green Berets*, having his lunch on the set (author's collection).

"What you saw in there was nothing"

Fort Benning is on the outskirts of Columbus in Muscogee County with its entrance on Victory Drive. Wayne shot there from August 9 to November 15, 1967. (Benning is the largest military base in Georgia where elite infantry was trained before departing for Vietnam.) He was allowed to use the briefing rooms at **Infantry Hall** for interiors and **Todd Field** for barrack scenes. The scene in which his troops first arrive in Da Nang was shot at **Lawson Air Field**.

Colonel Lamar Asbury "Bill" Welch, the actual commander of Benning's Army Airborne School, made a cameo, shooting trap with Col. Mike Kirby (Wayne). The soldiers exercising on the drill field when Wayne calls out to them were actual Airborne recruits in training. A platoon of Hawaiians was flown down from Fort Devens in Massachusetts to appear as Vietnamese and Viet Cong. All extras in Benning were paid a total of $305,000 for 70 shooting days. John F. Schultz played roles as an extra as well as a U.S. soldier and a North Vietnamese Regular. He once recalled, "At lunch, the producers were going to feed us peons hamburgers and hot dogs while the main characters ate steak. John Wayne said 'We all get steak or nobody does.'"[39]

From the scene on the skeet shooting range, they moved to Benning's golf course where army personnel enjoyed their free time. Wayne's frequent castmate Ed Faulkner recalled that an officer spotted the star wearing a colonel's uniform and tried hard to remember where he knew that colonel from. The officer finally walked over to Wayne and extended his hand; he read the name on Wayne's uniform and said, "Colonel Kirby, I'll be damned if we haven't served together somewhere."[40]

On August 9, Wayne captured a parachute landing onto **Eubanks Field,** which he would edit into the parachute jump sequence. Batjac was permitted to build the Dodge City sets and the Vietnamese village in a backwoods area. Combat footage was shot at a C Camp near **Kelley Hills**.

"We won't go back without the general"

The capture of the enemy general was filmed at the **Eakle's home**, a mansion in the Hilton district of Columbus. This typical Southern mansion off Hilton Avenue was built in 1838. Its classic neo–French architecture served as a perfect facsimile of a South Vietnamese plantation house. From its balcony, some of the last shots of the Civil War were fired. It saw action again on October 11, 1967, when Wayne shot the night scene. The house burned down in the 1990s but the non-native plants—another reason why they choose this location—still grow on the grounds.

Major Jerold R. Dodds, a real-life Green Beret, was delegated by the Pentagon to serve as technical advisor. He told Wayne biographer Mike Tomkies, "If I'm in half the shape he's in when I'm his age, I'll be happy. His leadership qualities are real."[41]

Co-director Ray Kellogg took four Panavision cameras to **Fort Rucker**, Alabama, to get footage of 96 helicopters flying in formation at the graduation ceremonies of the Helicopter School of the U.S. Army Aviation Command.

"This is Bulldog"

The shooting script dated May 15 had a much different beginning. It starts with Wayne's character being attacked by gang members in Central Park in New York where he's visiting his estranged wife Vera Miles. (Their single scene together didn't make the final print.) Also, the explanatory press information scene is placed as a pre-title sequence, before the credits start to roll. Barrett's script suggested a

The Green Berets **capture the VC General (William Olds) at a mansion in the Hilton district of Columbus: Wayne is abseiling from the balcony with actress Irene Tsu (author's collection).**

montage of training scenes much like the one in *Sands of Iwo Jima*: men who crawl ropes, train karate and hand-to-hand combat with fixed bayonets, all to be shot on the Benning training grounds. A scene of Wayne inspecting the shooting range was filmed but not used.

"I think Puff broke their back"

The film's large set-piece battle was loosely based on the Battle of Nam Dong, fought in July 1964. Two Viet Cong battalions and the People's Army of Vietnam had attacked a mixed defense group as portrayed in the film. This set was constructed on an isolated hill within Fort Benning. Several tons of dynamite practically flattened it during the battle sequence. Fifteen hundred black powder bombs were exploded and 6000 rounds of blank ammunition fired. Robin Moore made a cameo appearance as a Special Forces member: "It was startling to walk through the movie sets, which were authentic replicas of similar South Vietnam sites, then watch the realistic recreations of battle actions." He remembered the scene of the night attack: "The special effects men had set charges out all over the ground, and you couldn't see where those charges were, since it was night. And yet we had

to be running around like in confusion. I was deadly afraid I was gonna run up on one of those charges."[42]

The realistic "village" set was left intact and was used by the Army for training troops destined for Southeast Asia. Batjac spent $171,000 to construct these sets and $18,623 for the use of government-furnished equipment.

The film's pressbook offered newspapers the use of an article titled "Action Still Exploding on Sets Given Army by Green Berets": "Army personnel, undergoing counter-guerrilla training, is now employing materials and equipment the film company left behind: six Vietcong villages, built from bamboo; barbed-wire and thatch; thousands of rubber pungi sticks, simulating the lethal bamboo ones used as man-trap weapons. Also, control shacks were built from lumber left after the filmmakers dismantled their Montagnard villages. Thousands of rice bags, stuffed with sawdust, are being used in training. Trainees now execute raids on prisoner camps used as movie sets."

Before the company left the compound, Fort Benning staff members presented Wayne with an engraved letter opener in the form of a bayonet.

"God willing and the river don't rise"

Nature played a trick on John Wayne. In the middle of November, with work nearly completed, an early frost hit, most unusual for that time of year in Georgia. It turned the lush green of their "jungle" to yellow and brown. Nothing could be done but to build a substitute jungle in Burbank. At Warner Brothers, they shot the scene in which the captured VC general is lifted into the air. U.S. Army Captain William Olds, familiar with the technique, got jerked 50 feet up into to the air to simulate the air rescue. The stunt involved the use of a giant crane, an electric winch, and a system of slip ropes. When the slip ropes let Olds down, Wayne clapped his hands and kept a straight face: "Now let's have some film in that camera this time!"[43]

Wayne shot the closing scene on the Californian beach at **Point Mugu** where, as many film

John Wayne hangs on by himself for the shot in which the command tower collapses; it was edited together with a shot using dummies in the actor's places. With him in the scene are Ed Faulkner (right) and George Takei (middle) who missed season 2 of *Star Trek* while appearing in Wayne's film (author's collection).

critics loved to point out since Vietnam has no west coast, the sun sets in the east. More striking is that Wayne added the final line to Barrett's script there, telling the orphan kid: "You're what this is all about."

"You let me worry about that, Green Beret"

On the Fourth of July 1968, Wayne headed the Salute to America Parade in **Atlanta**. He was grand marshal and his co-stars honorary grand marshals. They then premiered their film in the magnificent **Fox Theatre**, an Atlanta landmark, 660 Peachtree Street NE.

The day before, at a Lockheed installation in **Marietta**, just outside Atlanta, Wayne had toured the Air Force's new C5A cargo plane and had unveiled one last testimonial to the men he held in such high esteem. Its inscription reads, "In tribute to the men of the Green Beret, United States Army Special Forces, whose valiant exploits will ever inspire mankind: John Wayne, July 4, 1968." The five-and-a-half-foot white granite stone was shipped to Fort Bragg where it stands today, in front of the **Special Forces Memorial Chapel**.

Critics went out gunning for Wayne's Vietnam statement. He felt their "overkilling" it actually helped the box office. "The left wingers are shredding my flesh, but like Liberace, we're bawling all the way to the bank."[44]

As the producer, Wayne maintained a personal interest how his movie was received overseas where theaters showing *The Green Berets* were sometimes controversially boycotted. For instance, he sent a thank-you note to the head of Warner Bros. in Switzerland because they found ways to successfully release it despite the people who picketed the movie theaters.

"It's pretty good shooting"

A full year after the premiere, a Democratic Congressman accused the filmmakers and the Army of making a pure propaganda film; he publicized a General Accounting Office report showing that Wayne was billed only $18,623 for service (including the fuel) provided during the 108 days of shooting at Benning. Wayne explained that the money was the exact amount for government equipment they could not get elsewhere. He also claimed to have paid almost half a million dollars to the Army in salaries, housing and food

for off-duty personnel used in the scenes and construction of sets left standing for training purposes. They were able to use army equipment as long as it was not tied up in training. The soldiers were available if they could get a two- or three-day pass, and they got paid regular extra pay. Wayne told the Associated Press: "We received good treatment at Benning—within the letter of the law."[45]

In July 1969, Wayne set the record straight in writing: "We were allowed the use of four helicopters for a combined 85 hours, averaging about 20 hours apiece. And the use of them even for that limited time was at the convenience of the fliers who were fulfilling their normal need of time in the air in those copters." Furthermore, Batjac was allowed the use of one of their cannons for only an hour (even though the base had acres of howitzers). Wayne's company even brought in its own Jeeps. Lastly, "we paid for our own ammunition and explosives."[46]

In 2011, the John Wayne estate raised a total $5.3 million from the sale of more than 700 of Wayne's costumes and personal items. (A portion went to the John Wayne Cancer Foundation.) Among them was the green beret he wore in the picture. "This is crazy," Ethan Wayne whispered astonished, as the bids for the beret started to climb way over the estimate. It sold for almost $180,000.[47]

On May 24, 1973, Wayne was invited to the White House. President Richard Nixon held a reception for former Vietnam prisoners of war. Wayne told the group, "I want to say thanks for showing the whole world what the kind of men in a free country could put up with when the going gets rough. You're the best we have. And I'll ride off into the sunset with you any time."[48]

"Besides that … it sings!"

Many veterans have said their reason for serving was in some part related to watching John Wayne in war movies. To this day, his name is attached to various pieces of gear, such as the P-38 "John Wayne" can-opener, so named because "it can do anything." C-Ration crackers are called "John Wayne crackers." The Swiss army's name for a C-Ration can of beans is "a John Wayne." A rough mountain pass used by Army tanks at Fort Irwin in San Bernardino County goes under the name of John Wayne Pass. The national veterans service AMVETS named their Post 57 in Fort Worth after him. And the RAH-66 Comanche helicopter is nicknamed "Duke."

7

Hatari!
Big Bwana's Bootprints in Africa

"Calling Arusha Control, calling Arusha Control…"
—Sean Mercer (John Wayne) informs the hospital
that one of his men was horned by a rhino

One thing about movie locations: They change over the years. Roads are built, buildings erased, trees cut down. It's different with the Savanna, though. In Africa, you're right back in Hatari country. There, this Swahili word still means "danger" and the Location Hunter can find the tracks of Big Game Hunter John Wayne.

With a hunter as a guide, associate producer Paul Helmick went on a seven-week survey trip to East Africa. His task: find shooting locations for *The African Story*, as *Hatari!* was called in the beginning. He settled for Momella in today's Tanzania (former Tanganyika) as the basic location. Then he successfully negotiated with the government in the capital,

Dar es Salaam, for the cooperation of the game department. He hired Willy de Beer, a highly experienced animal catcher who had invented the process of catching wild game from a car (he got a technical advisor credit on *Hatari!*). Willy was able to cut through a lot of red tape.

In the meantime, director Howard Hawks had hammered out a script with frequent collaborator Leigh Brackett. He even had to clear the word "Hatari" with African authorities—the officials were convinced the title could have dangerous political implications. Hawks was burning up his confirmed budget of $4,275,000 before he even had a finished screenplay. Helmick had been filming animals from his car with a 16mm camera to prove they would need to build a completely new camera, "otherwise you make your audience dizzy or even seasick."[1] Russ Brown, head of Paramount's technical department, had to develop a special camera car that would absorb the bounces. Hawks even tried an outfit from a destroyer gun stand, $25,000 worth. It didn't work at all. "We ended up by getting a big fat inner tube, putting a kind of gimbal on the camera and setting it in the inner tube and it took everything just beautifully. Probably cost about ten bucks."[2]

"Let's go, start out easy"

Finally, *Hatari!* was set to go to Africa. The advance team, again helmed by Helmick, had been filming since

Films shot on location in deep Africa were still a rare exception in 1960. John Wayne in the Masai steppe at Ngasumet Wells, with unknown Tanzanian extras (author's collection).

September 1960 when the main actors arrived for principal photography starting November 28. As Gerard Blain landed on the dusty airfield, which is still called **Arusha Airport**, he was in for his first adventure: Nobody had been sent to pick him up. He got himself into a cab and drove 250 kilometers to the set. The cabby got 200,000 francs. Blain had been working at French racetracks, nearly becoming a professional jockey, and he caused a sensation when he rode a zebra.[3]

"Can't use fuzzy heads in the morning"

Wayne bonded with his younger co-stars in his typical bombastic way. It was on the lofty **Lake Manyara Hotel**, overlooking hordes of flamingos, that Wayne told Hardy Kruger over dinner, "Kid, afterwards we're gonna have a drink at the bar." Kruger had been an international sensation as *The One That Got Away*. Only he couldn't get away this evening. Friends warned him that he was in for some serious drinking once he bellied up to the bar with John Wayne. So Kruger prepared himself by drinking sweet corn oil. Wayne kept the brandy coming. But when Wayne wanted to hit the sack, it was Hardy's turn to challenge him. Having the advantage of the oil in his stomach, he managed to drink Wayne under the table. The next day, Wayne was nonplussed by his "defeat." As usual, he was first on the set and he handed Kruger a cup of coffee, saying, "You're gonna need that."[4]

The Momella Game Ltd. Farm, as it was called in the movie, was complete down to the last detail. De Beer was also instrumental in giving the animal cages authenticity. But they didn't have to build the main house. It was rented from

Entrance to the Momella Game Farm as it looks now. After the movie, Hardy Kruger ran it as a lodge for thirteen years until he had to leave the country when the socialist regime took over (photograph by Roland Schaefli).

its famous tenants, the Trappe family. The first woman to settle in this part of East Africa was pioneer Margarete Trappe. Her son Rolf cemented the deal to use the property.

The actors were housed in town, at the **Arusha Hotel** and the **Safari Hotel**. Furnished private homes were rented for Hawks, Wayne and others who commuted to the main location, about an hour away, mostly over unpaved roads. Elsa Martinelli told the author: "We were there four months and it wasn't quite as comfortable as it looks today." Still, the Indian merchants in town were catching on fast that many dollars would be spent and stocked their shelves with items that the cast and crew asked for.

"That's a challenge we'll try to meet"

Hawks had wanted to make *The African Story* with Gary Cooper and Clark Gable. When Cooper died, Hawks tried to team Gable with John Wayne. As Paramount was taken over by a cost-cutting lawyer, Jacob M. Karp, they would afford just one star: Wayne. In the end, Hawks never got to make his ultimate buddy movie. "As much as moviegoers seemed to like what we finally made," remembered Helmick, "what a hell of a great movie it might have been had we only made the yarn that Hawks spun." Hawks never got over it: "The story did not live up to the great stuff that was around it." He had to make his vision of two big white hunters who hunt the same girl into a subplot, casting Hardy Kruger and Gerard Blain in the Gable-Wayne roles. Wayne played an undisputed individualist leader, without a strong presence to play against. "There was no fight," Hawks lamented, "there was no argument."[5]

As Dallas couldn't shake the baby elephants, she tried to escape into the Safari Hotel in Arusha. This is as it looks today, baby elephants still not admitted (photograph by Roland Schaefli).

"Don't start in by spoiling her!"

Every morning a fleet of 42 Jeep vehicles stood ready, each car a production department on wheels: wardrobe, props, grips. Helmick had struck a deal with Kaiser-Jeep to furnish all the vehicles. They were delivered to the harbor of Mombasa. Kaiser-Jeep got three commercials in return, all of which were made during the filming.[6] Unfortunately, the cars weren't half as rugged as advertised, so the mechanic worked a good deal of overtime. Hawks also had a Piper Cub airplane at his disposal. The pilot would spot animals and radio their position. Once the pilot told them about a rhino that looked "mean." Suddenly, a big crash was audible over the radio and the pilot laughed, "I told you it was bad."[7] Exposed film was flown 200 miles north to Nairobi, then by commercial plane to England for processing by Technicolor. In Arusha, two editors had to keep pace with production. Rushes were screened in a small movie theater. When cinematographer Russell Harlan watched the dailies, he knew that all his headaches were "more than worthwhile." The country was perfect for Technicolor with its ability to pick up those subtle pastel tones. Harlan had 22 cameras ranging from VistaVision plate cameras to 16mm

This lobby card uses a behind-the-scenes snapshot of an encounter with unknown Warusha tribesmen. Wayne is at the wheel of one of forty-two jeeps, with Elsa Martinelli (middle), Hardy Kruger, and (standing) Red Buttons, Michèle Girardon and Gerard Blain (author's collection).

remote-controlled gun cameras at his disposal. "At night our service tents looked like Mark Armistead's."[8]

"Your little pets, the rhino"

From the very beginning, it was clear that Helmick would develop a team capable of photographing the catching (Willy de Beer drove the catching truck). He used the actor's doubles for those scenes. After Hawks had approved the footage, the director would then move in and take over the camp with his first unit. Helmick called this scheduling "haphazard, but generally it worked." According to Wayne, "There was only one thing wrong—[Hawks let Helmick] do the second unit work. Shit, we did everything the second unit did. They didn't come up with any new values in action or anything. I did all the crap that you see in the picture."[9] Stuntman Ted White remembered it differently: "He wasn't even there yet when we filmed some of that. Duke got there when we were half through with the picture."[10] What actually happened was that Wayne checked out the footage. "I looked at the stuff—they'd been over there for three months when I got there—and I said, 'Christ, Howard, there isn't anything there that we can't do.'" So

"There isn't anything there that we can't do": John Wayne opted to do his own animal catching. This French lobby uses a behind-the-scenes photograph in which one of the professional hunters (with cap and glasses) gets in the shot. Valentin de Vargas stands to the left (author's collection).

Hawks went out with his actors and rode around and before long he put his own infant son on the car. Wayne: "Why, then all the second unit stuff went out of the window, we didn't need it. What I did was exciting, but it wasn't dangerous."

Wayne felt the catching sequences were dull. "You know, you just can't catch animals the same frigging way all the time."[11] When the director didn't like Helmick's giraffe catch, he re-shot the sequence using some of the real actors and some doubles. Like so often in Hollywood history, the truth lies in between. In some scenes (like the buffalo catch), doubles are so obvious, one can even see their faces.

But make no mistake about Wayne's actual contribution. There's the legendary rhino anecdote. According to Hawks, "Wayne had the time of his life chasing those rhinos. He didn't want a stuntman. One time the rhino got in closer than he wanted, and for a moment, Duke was in trouble. It made for a great scene."[12] What Hawks describes in typically laconic fashion, Aissa Wayne saw a little differently through the eyes of a girl: "My father … hung off the side of the Land Rover during a zebra-hunting scene. From the blind side of the Jeep rushed an uninvited bull rhinoceros. The startled driver veered, the Jeep bucked, almost flipping, and my father was nearly catapulted into what might have been a fatal landing."[13] Wayne himself recalled, "The rhino was a little rough. The fucking kids let the rope burn out of their hands and didn't scream 'Look out!' or anything. I just looked up and see this son of a bitch is loose and they're just standing there…. Shit." Wayne got himself into the truck just as the rhino stuck his horn right through the metal. "And then he stood there a minute and he started to move his head and goddamn he tore that cab all to hell."[14] And that's the truth. Only, it's not in the movie.

"Whatever it is, I'm doing it right"

When *Ciné Monde* did a story about Gerard Blain, a year prior to the film's release, the French journalists elaborated about Hawks' "improvisational style" and compared him to their favorite, Godard. Of course, there was no way *not* to improvise. According to the conversations between Peter Bogdanovich and Hawks, they never even worked from a script: "You can't write on your desk how a rhino is going to act."[15] Elsa Martinelli remembered: "Hawks was a

As dangerous as it looks: John Wayne ropes the rhino himself. This U.S. lobby card uses a behind-the-scenes photograph that makes no secret of the fact that uncredited animal catchers support the actors. The doubles of Hardy Kruger and Valentin de Vargas are seen behind the beast as well (author's collection).

strange man, a fantastic man to work with. But he was quite a hard man. He knew what he wanted. So, you had to be prepared: prepared to realize what he expected from you. Usually, there was no script. So Hawks used to get on the set at five in the morning and write the lines and tape them and as

John Wayne checks out one of the cameras Howard Hawks (left) had made up especially for the filming on rugged terrain. Note that the director is wearing the Red River D buckle with the initials "JW," originally Wayne's buckle, and Russell Harlan (left of Wayne) is wearing his own buckle, too (author's collection).

soon as you arrived, he gave them to you. And you had to be quite fast to memorize them."[16]

The cast would just talk each morning about what Hawks wanted them to do that day. Almost every night they would gather for a conference where the professionals would explain what the actors should watch out for. Wayne: "If the ostrich really gets mad, he'll crush you to death by dumping his full 400-pound weight on top of you!" Hawks: "You couldn't control the animals. We chased nine rhinos, filmed them all, and we caught four."[17] The agreement with the game department was they would not hold an animal longer than three to four minutes. Wayne would use a lot of profanity, which Hawks had to figure out how to censor. Hawks would yell "Gobble!" which meant they would loop the dialogue later. Most of the lines in these scenes were ad-libbed. All dialogue involving character development occurs in the scenes at the lodge. "The boys got very good at it," Hawks found, "they'd turn around to one another and just said anything."[18] In the written dialogue, he'd put a few unnecessary words on the front and a few on the end of a sentence, so people could overlap their talking.

"This is a mean one!"

Hawks had nothing so dangerous in the can to justify the title Hatari! Even the Cape buffalo, considered the most dangerous of all African beasts, wasn't that much of a dramatic capture. Eventually, production got permission to shoot in the sacred **Ngorongoro Crater**, the bottom of which had only recently become accessible by vehicle. Elsa Martinelli: "Back then, we were the first to actually go down there."[19] However, Helmick's unit was only permitted to go

The *Hatari* company broke new ground when they filmed at the sacred Ngorongoro Crater, a protected World Heritage Site. A great variety of animals are present and the rare specimen of rhinos can still be sighted (photograph by Roland Schaefli).

after some cloven-hoofed animals that weren't high on the priority list. They were secretly hoping to get a rhino attack on film. The game warden had already explained it would never charge a car, always stopping several meters short. Yet when the second unit gave it a try, the rhino hit the truck full speed. A case of Scotch was presented to the warden the same evening to encourage him into give permission to film the rhino—but without trying to catch it. The very next morning, when the animal hit the Jeep, stuntman Ted White grabbed his leg. The crew thought for sure the beast had gored him. The stunt guys were highly insulted: "Don't you know good acting when you see it?" The enthused Helmick cabled Hawks: "Stop worrying about calling the picture 'Danger in Swahili' because a rhino damn near did in Ted White this afternoon. And we've got it all on beautiful Eastman Kodak color film."[20] The director brought in his unit and created— on the famous yellow legal pad he always used for re-writing dialogue right on the spot—his pre-title sequence. The principal cast got into the thick of the rhino action as well. Hardy Kruger tried to keep the beast at bay but in fact the cameramen told him over the radio where to move for a better shot. It was then that the rhino drove his horn against the Jeep, lifting it up onto two wheels. Kruger thought the vehicle might fall apart.[21]

"What is it, that you liked?"

Wayne claimed that the time he spent in Tanganyika was the most fun he'd had on any picture. In a 1976 TV interview with Phil Donahue, he called *Hatari!* one of his all-time favorites "because I had a three-month safari free."

"You wake up in the morning," he said, "and you hear the savage sounds of these animals and your hair curls."[22] His daughter Aissa describes the experience differently: "Lying in my bed beneath a suspended mesh net I was safe from bloodthirsty bugs but could not tune out the strange sounds of screaming, yowling, jabbering, honking African beasts." She was chased by an ostrich, and a monkey jumped on her back.[23] Her 53-year-old dad felt young again: "You grab that gun and you take a different attitude than you did when you were at home."

Red Buttons recalled that the crew spent a lot of time together, "When you're in Africa with someone for four months, you better get on with them. Duke was easy to get on with, and we had a lot of fun." The comedian relished telling the story of the night they were playing cards and a leopard walked out of the bush. "Duke, there's a leopard walking toward us." Wayne answered, "Buttons, see what he wants."[24] Hawks had gotten himself a pet mongoose named Squeaky which he turned loose on dinner guests. On February 4, 1961, Wayne sent a telegram to John F. Kennedy: "Congratulations Mr. President. It was thrilling reading your inaugural speech here in Tanganyika. It made us even prouder that we are Americans."[25] And this was from a man who opposed Kennedy in the general election.

"Feels good to be finished"

One morning, the Americans were gone. After five and a half months, the phones stopped ringing in Arusha and an African extra, Kisetu, realized that his newfound friends had left without saying goodbye. He is clearly visible in the catching scenes, standing on the back of the truck, giving Wayne a helping hand. And then they had gone. Kisetu remained in the area, got prominent in his own right and eventually became Hardy Kruger's gardener. When Kruger also left, Kisetu still remained. Years after Wayne's death, some family members visited and graciously gave Kisetu some of Wayne's old duds. He never sold them. He wore them out.[26]

Wayne brought home a pair of African antelope skulls and horns to decorate his home. They continued shooting at Paramount where production designer Hal Pereira, who had created *Bonanza*'s Ponderosa ranch on the same lot, had built the replica of the lodge. The set was, in fact, so close

to the original that Kruger immediately got homesick for Africa. They even used stones from Ngare Nanyuki to recreate the fireplace. But Kisetu and the other guys who played the hands on the catch truck weren't around when they shot the process scenes in Hollywood. Other black extras were standing on the truck for the rear projection—there's zero continuity between the location and the studio scenes.

Paramount brought 28 animals back to Hollywood: four baby elephants, two lions, three cheetahs, two leopards, one hyena and assorted monkeys. The modern Noah's Ark took four days to make the trip to Burbank. Buttons was sad to hear his mongoose was not allowed into this country. At the studio, the baby elephants were no longer cute. They delighted in chasing people on bicycles. Aissa remembers her father's birthday surprise: Wayne had made her ride the little elephants back in Africa and believed Aissa's counterfeit smile when in fact she was afraid of the little beasts. Now he had one of the babies over for her birthday party. Aissa: "As if still on Howard Hawks' cue, it stuck its trunk in the pool and sprayed water all over the deck and my dad."[27] The last day of shooting on Stage 14 was May 26, 1961—Wayne turned 54 that day.

This rare French lobby card shows a moment used only in the documentary *Big Game Hunters Without Guns*. Wayne and Elsa Martinelli are rowed over a river by unknown native workers. Since Valentin de Vargas' double is plainly visible in the left of the photograph, it was never intended to use the scene in the picture (author's collection).

Kisetu in 2011: after his bit in *Hatari!* he worked for Hardy Kruger on the Momella grounds (photograph by Roland Schaefli).

"Tell us when you want her"

The publicity department went to work. Wayne was quoted as saying that after the experience of sitting on the mudguard, "riding a horse is like sleeping on foam rubber."[28] Peggy Page, one of the foremost names in the fashion world, set a national campaign: They created "that Peggy Page look," inspired by jungle colors. The women's magazines wrote about how Elsa Martinelli took her spaghetti on safari and how a modern woman can make life more comfortable in a tent. The marketing people went so far as to suggest to theater operators to "borrow any unusual animals from a pet shop or local zoo and display them in cages in your foyer."[29] After the work on the Paramount lot was completed, the baby elephants were put in the San Diego Zoo. "They were growing quite big," said Martinelli.

"I already have one patient"

As the PR people were turned loose, they also invented the story that no one got hurt, no animal got killed. They even produced a featurette titled *Big Game Hunters Without Guns*. Unfortunately, this, too, was a myth. One of the white hunters was killed in a car wreck. Ted White recalled, "He was in a Jeep, coming around a corner at a very hazardous speed. The car dropped off a crevice and that was that."[30] Jan Oelofse, Willy de Beer's head catcher, was injured during the shooting with the baby leopard and badly clawed on his face and arm. "The leopard didn't mean to do it—he was only playing."[31] Far more tragic was the encounter of Elsa Martinelli's double with a supposedly tame lion that ended up killing the young woman.

The marketing department stressed the fact that the catching went "without the firing of a single shot." The chief game warden, Major Bruce Kinloch, affirmed, "Too often the killing of wild game is over-stressed [in movies]."[32] Tanganyika's Game Department had given unprecedented permission to film. To show his gratitude, Hawks donated 14 Jeeps and trucks to the department.

"You mean you're going to shoot him?"

The film's souvenir brochure assured moviegoers, "All game caught, where suitable, were assured a life of ease and safety in American zoos." Twenty-five animals were put into nine public zoos and one private aviary. (In 1998, the San Diego Zoo had to put down the elephant named Hatari.) Despite the press campaign, one mystery kept popping up: the infamous killing of an elephant. It was kept out of the papers. Wayne was obviously filmed shooting a large specimen, but this was sliced from the release print because producers feared fans would object. Actually, Wayne himself said in an interview for a hunting magazine that he shot the elephant with the .458 Winchester Magnum rifle he carries in the picture.[33] And in 1971 he told one of his first biographers, Mike Tomkies, that he got the charging elephant with one shot between the eyes. "They got it all on film because the camera was right behind me," Wayne said. It would have made a great sequence, he speculated, but they couldn't use a foot of it. "John Wayne shoot a poor elephant? I guess they felt it would destroy my heroic image or something." In the picture gallery of his den in Newport was a photo of Pilar and Aissa standing in front of the elephant, their noses wrinkled. In later years, Hawks wasn't quite so reluctant to talk about the actual shooting of an elephant. He said they had been looking for an especially mean specimen that had been terrorizing the local population. The natives were hoping the filmmakers could get it.

"If you're gonna shoot an elephant, as he got closer to you, you'd shoot lower because he was higher. We had skull practice all the time." Hawks told Wayne he would determine the exact timing for this shot. The gun was loaded with live ammunition and precautions were taken to ensure the star's safety. The animal was racing towards him and Wayne mumbled between closed lips, "You damn son of a bitch, say when!" Hawks finally yelled, "Now!" Wayne scored a precise hit, felling the elephant.[34] In 2011, some of Hawks' possessions were auctioned off, among them a collection of photos showing him and other crew members on hunting trips. As early as 1961, *International Photographer* illustrated a story with two photos of Wayne dropping the animal "with just one bullet." Aissa remembered that a dangerous elephant had charged the men on the set, including her dad, and "he and the men had killed it." Whether this was the truth or whether her memory had been influenced by myths surrounding the incident will probably never be known. In any event, it's apparent why the elephant affair never made it into the film or the publicity materials, as it would have nullified the promise that *Hatari!* was a film "for people of all ages."

"Nobody can ever say your inventions don't work"

The world premiere was held at the Egyptian, June 19, 1962, a full year after shooting wrapped. *Hatari!* had to recoup its final bill of $6,546,000 against strong competition from such epics as *Mutiny on the Bounty* and *Lawrence of Arabia*. By the end of the year, it had raked in more than $14 million. Wayne received ten percent of the gross receipts against a guaranteed minimum of $750,000 (he got additional checks for the re-issues). The annual poll of the theater owners saw him as number four at the box office that year. Hawks may have never made the movie he set out to do. But for a movie that didn't turn out the way he wanted it, big game hunters sure made big bucks.

The One That Didn't Get Away

For Hardy Kruger, the Hatari adventure went on long after the film's run. In the evenings, as the Americans in their tents were playing poker, the young German lay awake, listening to the strange African sounds. He hadn't been a star long. *The One That Got Away* provided his international breakthrough, making him the first German actor to play the lead role in an English movie after the war. He instantly fell in love with Momella. "I've seen the garden of Eden," he wrote in his memoir *Eine Farm in Afrika*. Here, time was measured by "the day we caught the rhino with the broken horn…"[35] When he tried to rent a Jeep to explore the grounds, he learned that Paramount had utilized just about every vehicle around. That's how he met Jim Mallory, who let him have his Range Rover. From then on, Hardy wasn't dependent any more on Paramount drivers. Free to explore on his own, he had more dangerous encounters than written in the script. One day, he and a local Englishman gave Hawks the coordinates on a herd of buffalo they had sighted. Hawks radioed him to stay put. Suddenly, his companion whispered, "Don't move!" Kruger now realized that a female lion was so close that he could see the dried blood of the last kill on her mouth.

The location for the scene that introduced the world to the memorable Henry Mancini tune "Baby Elephant Walk": The waterhole is accessible by foot from Momella and is dry most of the year (photograph by Roland Schaefli).

Ever so slowly, he moved back to the Jeep and escaped. The lion never moved. But the herd of buffalo was gone.[36] The pressbook relates this incident—but suddenly, John Wayne appears in the tale as well. The publicists happily wrote him into this scene.

Wayne wasn't unsympathetic with Tanganyikan nationalists' attempt to throw off British imperialism. But when nationalist leader Julius Nyerere took control in December 1961, Wayne was prophetic that his "half-baked socialist schemes" would ruin the country: "The whole damn place won't be worth a shit in ten years."[37] Kruger thought otherwise. As a matter of fact, it was Nyerere himself who advised him to open a bush hotel. Kruger made a deal with the landowner, Rolf Trappe, and went into partnership with Mallory. In November 1961, they opened the hotel, which was built on the very compound seen in *Hatari!* Kruger lived at Momella for 13 years, and a lot of his Hollywood earnings were put into the enterprise and later an ill-fated meat processing plant. After Kruger finally left Africa, the **Momella Lodge** was in a state of disrepair for a long time, but it still exists today, on Momella Road. Another hotel opened next to the Momella Lodge, under the management of a German couple. That venue, the **Hatari Lodge**, utilizes the former homes of Mallory and Kruger for accommodations.

The locals accurately call it "John Wayne Rock": This is where Sean watched Dallas wash the elephants. However, for reasons of lighting and camera angle John Wayne was not looking in the direction of the waterhole (photograph by Roland Schaefli).

"Where are we going today?"

In terms of setting, Hawks liked the audience to know exactly where it is, and so the place namess ("Where are we going today?" "Manyara, I guess") are correct. Hawks always felt he needed his plot to be confined to a basic location and later called it a mistake to break this up by having the group move out of the main lodge to a tent camp, although geographically right.[38] Just off the main road leading to the Hatari Lodges, the shooting contest was filmed in a beautiful strip of trees. The waterhole Elsa Martinelli where washes the elephants can still be found, although dried up most of the year. It is accessible by foot from Momella Lodge. What the natives accurately call John Wayne Rock, where he is leaning in the film, is an easy find in the same area. Probably for reasons of lighting, Wayne actually looks away from the waterhole when he observes the elephant washing cycle.

The crocodile attack was filmed on the last day of exterior shooting at the **Ruvu River**.

The landmark of **Arusha** is the clock tower, seen in several shots. The shop into which Tembo pursues Martinelli, the **Clock Tower Supermarket**, is still in business, at the roundabout in the middle of town. So is the **Lutheran Church** on Goliondoi Road, visible in the background when the men hand over Dallas' clothes on the street. The Safari Hotel in Arusha still exists on Boma Road but underwent major reconstruction (more recently it's called the New Safari Hotel). The **New Arusha Hotel** at the Clocktower roundabout wasn't used in the movie but it housed cast and crew. Nowadays it cashes in on the film's ongoing popularity with a Hatari Bar that showcases some original posters.

Initially, the cast lived at the **Lake Manyara Hotel** (now

The clock tower of Arusha: at this roundabout, the elephants chase Dallas into the grocery, still located there (photograph by Roland Schaefli).

called the Lake Manyara Serena Safari Lodge, on the B144 in Karatu) and in two-man tents near the lake, on Mto Wa Mbu River. On the **Lake Manyara Plain**, a flat dry salt lake bed (20 miles wide and some 50 miles long), Hawks shot scenes with giraffes and zebras. The white plains on which the rhino is caught in the climax are called the **Seven Sisters** (accurately named in the dialogue), close to the Kenyan border. The crew lived in a camp at **Longido** for these sequences. The shot in which Wayne hides in high grass and beckons the car is a rare eucalyptus forest just off the A104 between Longido and Arusha. The wells where the hunters get water for their motor can still be found deep in Masai territory, in **Naberara**. The natural wonder of the crater in the **Ngorongoro Conservation Area**, 110 miles west of Arusha, is accessible today via the same road used by the filmmakers. It's a Jeep-wide path cut in the side of the crater walls over a period of seven years by convict laborers.

8

Utah

"The Gobi Desert seethed with unrest"

"For the real outdoor dramas, you have to go where God
put the West … and there is no better example of this than around Moab."
—John Wayne on the Utah location of *The Comancheros*[1]

"A conqueror who's coming changed the face of the earth": This introduction launches The Conqueror, *generally regarded as the most ludicrous of John Wayne's major films. Superimposed over a shot of Snow Canyon State Park in Utah, the rolling titles read: "In the twelfth century, the Gobi Desert seethed with unrest." The place is St. George. The location scouts could not foresee that it would be the center of lengthy litigation over the impact of radioactive fallout.*

Because of its proximity to I-15 and an airport, **St. George** is a popular gateway city to Zion National Park. Republic was the first studio to arrive, with *The Painted Stallion* in 1937. Three years later, Howard Hawks made the place look like Cary Grant's air freight enterprise in South America: Zion Canyon doubled for the Andes Mountains in *Only Angels Have Wings*. But St. George wasn't considered a major movie location until Dick Powell, *The Conqueror's* director, set out in 1953 to find the setting for the Mongolian epic. The director and a group of eight RKO location scouts had

already searched eight western states when a member of the St. George Chamber of Commerce advised them to look at their canyons. (He had been a flyer in World War II and knew how the Gobi looked from above.). The city lies in the northeasternmost part of the Mojave Desert. The RKO group did not mention that they were representing billionaire Howard Hughes, neither did they reveal anything about a Genghis Khan movie. And they kept their mouths shut about who was going to play the title role.

Several months later, on March 10, 1954, 4800 residents found themselves hosting an exotic invasion, headed by John Wayne as Genghis Khan. Cast and crew filled the motels and enlisted locals as laborers and extras.

Almost all the 22 motels in town were booked for the more than 500 crew members. RKO got permission to use the high school for dressing rooms and the storage of 1200 costumes. However, a local paper had to ask parents to limit the time in which their teenagers could ask for autographs.

"Yer beautiful in yer wrath"

For Wayne to reside during his five weeks in St. George, RKO rented the private residence of Wendell and Betty Motter. Susan Hayward lived in the Howard Schmutz house. Their houses were on the opposite sides of the same street, and Hayward frequently came over to flirt with her leading man. Pilar Wayne went with her husband to St. George and her presence aroused Hayward's jealousy. "One night a group congregated at Duke's house

This painting of John Wayne and Susan Hayward was used as the background for *The Conqueror* movie posters. The unknown artist painted the Utah desert in deep black, the skies in flaming red (author's collection/photo: Julien's Auctions/Summer Evans).

for one of those impromptu gatherings that are so much a part of life on location," Pilar remembered. Hayward came up to her, a wild gleam in her gorgeous eyes. "Take off your shoes," she challenged Pilar, "and fight me for him!"[2]

Even the local Boy Scouts pitched in: They gave up their tables and chairs to accommodate the feeding of up to a thousand people on location at one time. All nine buses from the school district were employed to transport the crew to the "Gobi Desert." Restaurateur Dick Hammer served lunches from a chuck wagon he called his "stainless steel kitchen on wheels." He fed 320 hot lunches every 20 minutes out of his locally famous eatery, Dick's Cafe, located at 100 East 100 North (it even served as a set for the Jane Fonda movie *The Electric Horseman*). According to the historical society, Wayne became friendly with Hammer, who later decorated his place with Wayne memorabilia. It was demolished in 1999. The Cache Valley Bank building now stands there.

They screened the rushes in the local movie theater. The baseball games in town offered another diversion. The local team of the St. George All-Stars challenged the cast and crew to a game. Wayne (with his boys Michael and Patrick), Pedro Armendariz and Susan Hayward participated and the Mormons gathered. The stands were full, and big washtubs were full of beer.

RKO hired 300 Indians from the Shivwits reservation as the Mongol villagers. In fact, the Anasazi Indians had inhabited the region 2000 years ago. Paiute then used the canyon to the mid–1800s. Mormon pioneers "discovered" Snow Canyon in the 1850s.

Rolling in the red dust of St. George with Susan Hayward for *The Conqueror*. A number of researchers linked their causes of death to radiation in the Utah desert (author's collection).

Everybody associated with *The Conqueror* remembered it being hot. The thermometer often read 124. To put their feet in the hot sand, the oxen wore lean-tos made of canvas. The weather proved to be difficult. They had built a waterhole on the ridge above Snow Canyon. When a heavy summer rain turned the red sand into a muddy goo, a crew member said, "Yesterday we build an artificial waterhole and today they are a dime a dozen."[3]

"Chase them like rats across the tundra"

A total of ten shooting sites was chosen among Utah's scenic red bluffs and white dunes. Advance road crews had begun building a road into the principal location of **Snow Canyon** in late March. They also shot at the Bench near **Harrisburg**, 12 miles north of town, which had then been a ghost town for 60 years. The plains there became the setting for the climactic battle between Mongols and Tartars, filmed over a six-day period. Powell also took his Technicolor cameras to **Warner Valley**, 15 miles from St. George. Different types of dinosaur tracks are evident in its rock strata.

Just five years after the filming, 7400 acres were converted into a state park. Utah State Route 18 travels through Dammeron Valley. To get to the park, located in the Red Cliffs Desert Reserve, turn onto Snow Valley Drive. As is always the case when looking for movie locations, just find the trails that enabled the moviemakers to bring in their heavy equipment. The filming sites run along the paved roads. Wayne paid St. George a nice compliment: "This is the way we like to think of

Genghis Khan and his Tartar woman: On location in Utah, Susan Hayward developed a crush on her leading man. Far from a box office failure, *The Conqueror* ranked number 10 on the list of 1956s top grossing films. Nobody could beat *The Ten Commandments* that year (author's collection).

America—people cheerfully helping people simply because that's a good way to live."[4]

"My blood says take her"

But he wasn't as cheerful about his contract with RKO. During the filming, on April 29, 1954, he sent a letter to Howard Hughes about some "very simple beefs": At the other studios and at his own company, "I seldom get involved for more than eight to ten weeks overall." Wayne complained that while he gets paid top terms at the competitors, he winds up giving six months of his time at RKO. "And it's hectic, uncomfortable and unpleasant times—for a fraction of the compensation paid me by the other studios and for only a portion of my present market value."[5] Wayne proposed that Hughes resolve this problem by paying him what the others do.

When *The Conqueror* wrapped on August 17, 1954, St. George wasn't finished as a movie location. The following year, Ray Milland used the same sites for his picture *A Man Alone*. Wayne and Milland had become fast friends on *Reap the Wild Wind* but had a falling out after Milland introduced Wayne to his second wife Chata.

"I am Temujin, the Conqueror"

Wayne went to England for a Command Performance attended by the queen's sister, the Duchess of Gloucester. *The Conqueror* opened on February 2, 1956, at the famous **Odeon Leicester Square.** This prominent cinema building in London's West End is the place for lavish world premieres (like the James Bond outings). On August 8, 1978, Wayne granted *Real West* magazine what would become his last written interview, and even though more than 20 years

Ted de Corsia, the Brooklyn actor, tortures the Mongol chief. John Wayne complained to RKO-boss Howard Hughes that making *The Conqueror* was "hectic, uncomfortable and unpleasant." (author's collection).

had passed since that night in London, he recalled, "After it was over, you know, I went over expecting to get congratulations." But the queen's sister just quipped, "What a terrible thing to do to those horses!" Wayne drawled, "Well, Your

Ancient lava flows and sand dunes in Snow Canyon State Park, the primary location of the epic *The Conqueror* (photograph by Matt Morgan).

Tarzan pays a visit to Genghis Khan: Gordon Scott had a mutual acquaintance with *The Conqueror*: After appearing with Wayne in *The Searchers*, Vera Miles played the love interest in Scott's first Tarzan movie, an RKO-film. They married in 1956.

Highness, I'm telling you, and my word is good, there were no horses hurt."[6]

Wayne went on to Berlin to attend the German premiere on January 28, 1956, at the **Film Bühne Wien**, at Kurfürstendamm 26, then a movie house with a lengthy history, now remodeled as an Apple store. He received an award as Hollywood's Macho Man, met Berlin's well-known mayor, Willy Brandt, and posed for news photographers in front of the **Brandenburger Tor**, the gate between East and West, soon to become the focus of the Cold War. Oddly enough, the Soviet Union had expressed a desire to show the picture in Moscow. Wayne had made plans with Gary Cooper to stay in the Russian capital. But after the Soviet Embassy in Washington had a private screening, they decided to ban the film. After all, it was about the war between the Mongols and Tartars, now Soviet citizens all.

Wayne himself probably knew that it was one of his biggest mistakes to volunteer for the role. "A fucking disaster," he called it.[7] True, his Genghis Khan went down in movie history as a massive instance of miscasting. Over the years, it was ridiculed as a turkey, making it easy to forget that the film was far from a box office disaster. It earned a whopping $12 million and outgrossed, for instance, the year's Hitchcock thriller *The Man Who Knew Too Much*, starring James Stewart and Doris Day.

"For good or ill—she is my destiny"

The Conqueror was the last film Howard Hughes ever produced. After he sold RKO, one of the "Big Five" studios of Hollywood's golden age ceased to exist. Desilu Productions

then purchased the physical lots for $6.1 million. That's how it becomes possible to spot Wayne's Genghis Khan costume on a Klingon in a *Star Trek* episode. Hughes sold the rights to 700 films in the RKO vault for $25 million. A few years later, he bought two of them back for the unbelievable sum of $12 million: *Jet Pilot* and *The Conqueror*. The eccentric plutocrat screened his favorites over and over. He never explained, but he refused to let them appear on TV. *The Conqueror* wasn't seen for decades.

As the years passed, more and more participants fell sick, and the movie acquired a dark reputation. Dick Powell died of lymph cancer in 1963. The same year, Wayne's friend Pedro Armendariz shot himself after being diagnosed with terminal cancer. When Wayne heard of the death of his three-time co-star, he told his son Michael, "I don't blame Pete. I'd do the same thing that he did."[8] One of the first members of the company to make a connection between the film and the fallout was actress Agnes Moorehead. Long before she developed uterine cancer that killed her in 1974, she recounted rumors of "some radioactive germs" on the Utah location, observing: "Everybody in that picture has gotten cancer and died." As she was dying, she told best friend Debbie Reynolds: "I should never have taken that part."[9] Susan Hayward died of brain cancer in 1975. Soon, the Genghis Khan movie would be dubbed an "RKO Radioactive Picture." Shortly after Wayne's death, a number of researchers finally linked his fatal cancer to radiation in the Utah desert.

"Operation Upshot-Knothole" involved the detonation of 11 atomic bombs in 1953. The continental Proving Ground at Yucca Flat, Nevada, was only 137 miles from St. George. More A-bombs were detonated there than anywhere else in the world. St. George inhabitants were told they had nothing to fear. Residents said they could even see the mushroom clouds (the roll of thunder took 18 minutes to reach them). The bomb codenamed "Harry," a 32-kiloton shot, detonated on May 19, 1953 (inhabitants renamed it "Dirty Harry"). Almost all of them were larger than the bomb dropped on Hiroshima.

"Come and take me, mongrels!"

The Wayne movie was made less than a year later. Although no bombs were tested during the filming, radioactivity from previous blasts probably lingered in Snow Canyon. The tests certainly weren't kept secret. Nobody worried about radiation. There was no concern. Wayne took his sons on an excursion into the desert, using a Geiger counter to measure radioactivity. To make matters worse, the company took truckloads of the red sands back to the RKO to match interior shots, possibly exposing the actors to fallout once more.

2nd unit director Cliff Lyons put impressive action on the screen: John Wayne takes the arrow in the first part of the horse fall which then cuts to the stuntman doing the fall (author's collection).

St. George is plagued by an extraordinarily high rate of cancer. In 1990, the U.S. Congress passed the Radiation Exposure Compensation Act. It established a fund for the so-called downwinders with serious illnesses apparently linked to nuclear weapons testing. Conspiracists insist that the filming so close to the testing site allegedly killed dozens of the people who made *The Conqueror*. At one point, a TV crew even tested Susan Hayward's costume, on display in a Hollywood museum, with a Geiger counter (establishing no radioactivity at all). *People* magazine reported in 1980 that of 220 cast and crew members, 91 had contracted cancer, with 46 of them dying. Michael Wayne responded to the idea of suing: "Suing the government is not going to bring my father back."[10]

Wayne's widow Pilar had another theory. His chain-smoking (up to four packs of cigarettes a day) was a likelier cause of death: "He lit he cigarette with the butt of the last one."[11]

Many of the rest of *The Conqueror*'s cast and crew were also heavy smokers. Pilar attributed the deaths of some of these people to "their constant, incessant smoking. Duke never smoked fewer than three packs a day."[12] In the 1950s, half the men in the U.S. were smokers. Wayne even endorsed his favorite cigarette brand in ads.

However, after his bout with the "Big C," he became a spokesperson for the American Cancer Society. "They found a spot on the X-rays," he told his audience in an appeal to get a check-up. "It was lung cancer. If I waited a few more weeks, I wouldn't be here now." Wayne had been a smoker for many years and he missed the habit. Even after he had lost one lung, he infrequently smoked cigars. Did his smoking habit cause cancer? He answered that question on the set of *The Cowboys* with a plain "I don't know."[13] But "the smoking certainly didn't help," he usually answered when asked that question.

At about the same time, he narrated a documentation for the American Cancer Society. "It has only been recently, that most of us have become aware of the risks. It's unfortunate that we as a society have to learn the hard way."

Stuntman Jack Williams was a Tartar who gets lanced by Wayne and also doubled Wayne in the horse fall. "Doing all those stunts in that goddamned radioactive sand," he lamented years later. "We're up there six weeks and then they took a lot of that stuff back with them to reproduce sets at the studio. Gosh darn, there were a lot of people who died of cancer who worked on that thing." However, both he and Chuck Roberson were in *The Conqueror* and when they were alive almost 30 years later, Chuck said, "Hell. They'll never get me now!"[14]

"We can build that house by the river"

Wayne had been a conqueror in Utah a good ten years before *The Conqueror*. *In Old Oklahoma* (aka *War of the Wildcats*) was in production on Utah locations between June 28 and September 4, 1943. The movie was headquartered in **Kanab.** Unusually, there was no catering, so the cast and crew had the privilege of eating at the cafés about town. This was probably the first time Wayne stayed at the now-famous **Parry Lodge**, 89 East Center Street. The colonial-style hotel with its columned structure got started in 1931. The Parrys housed and fed movie crews for decades, Wayne's leading ladies Maureen O'Hara and Claire Trevor among them. According to the Lodge's history, the kidney-shaped swimming pool and patio were added at the request of Wayne, who wanted a "place to cool off" the next time he stayed at Parry's. When he offered to pay half the cost of constructing the pool, Whit Parry agreed. (Pool and patio were used as a location in 1956 in *The Girl in Black Stockings* starring Lex Barker.) In the summer of 1965, the principals of *The Greatest Story Ever Told* were housed in the lodge. Wayne was not among them as all his scenes as the Roman centurion were done at the studio. A John Wayne Room and more than 250 autographed photos in the lobby are a reminder of the Parrys' glory days when Kanab established a reputation as "Little Hollywood."

"Well, we're sure gonna try!"

In Old Oklahoma deals with oil drilling and Republic was able to construct a set where oil fields still existed, near the small town of **Virgin**, in the scenic area of Washington County. Yakima Canutt had become the top Republic

The historic Parry Lodge, the Hollywood hub in Kanab: John Wayne was responsible for the building of the pool in the back (photograph by Roland Schaefli).

stunt man in the meantime. Many times, he would receive a script that would have blank pages and scene numbers in the main action spots with a caption saying, "See Yakima Canutt for action sequences." He was also in charge of the climactic sequence of *In Old Oklahoma* in which horse-drawn oil tanks get blown sky-high. He bought the wagons from the real farmers in the area and fit oil tanks on the running gears.

At the Union Pacific train depot, in the west of **Cedar City,** Wayne's cowboy character is introduced, as he gets on the special train uninvited.

A trail winds down from Kanab into the **Kanab Canyon**, off Highway 89. The dirt road leads five miles to the Paria town site, at the Paria River (meaning "muddy water" in the Paiute language). **Paria Canyon** (sometimes called Pahreah) is one of the most famous—and certainly most beautiful—of western locations. The original Mormon settlement was abandoned and then put to use by Hollywood cowpokes. The black-and-white Wayne movie was just a little bit ahead of director William Wellman, who would make Paria's vibrant colors famous with his Technicolor Western *Buffalo Bill*, shot just months after the Wayne vehicle. The Rat Pack western *Sergeants 3* enlarged the ghost town, causing visitors to confuse the movie set with the real Paria. That will not happen any more. A flash flood damaged the set in 1998. The structures were then replaced and distinguished from Paria itself. But then, in 2006, the rebuilt set was destroyed by fire.

"If you desert, you'll be found"

It's every marketing manager's dream, having John Wayne coin a phrase to advertise your place: "Where God

put the West." Meaning no disrespect to Monument Valley but even John Ford needed a fresh location after he had filmed several pictures there in a row. The director traveled north on U.S. 191 into southeastern Utah. Once in Moab, so the story goes, the editor of the Moab *Times-Independent* introduced him to local cattle rancher George White (later the founder of the Moab Film Commission). White understood what Ford was looking for. He drove him up State Route 128 to **Professor Valley**. After Ford had a look at the region of the Fisher Towers on the Colorado River, he declared he would shoot his next feature, *Wagon Master*, there. Moab had an advantage over Monument Valley: Ford had a lot of fording river scenes to do and the Colorado River runs right through the redrock country.

"Any liquor in this village?"

Ford was true to his word: Shortly after *Wagon Master*, he returned to Moab, in the spring of 1950, to scout locations

A series of towers made of sandstone and caked with a stucco of red mud: Fisher Towers was looming in the background of *Rio Grande* and *The Comancheros,* now world-renowned as a subject for photography and for classic climbing routes (photograph by Matt Morgan).

The principal players of *In Old Oklahoma* take a walk in Kanab: John Wayne, Martha Scott, and Albert Dekker (author's collection).

for what would be the first pairing of John Wayne and Maureen O'Hara: *Rio Grande*. He reused some locations and added **Castle Valley** to his list. The advance team covered the roads with oil to make them drivable for the 32 cars, trucks and buses. The majority of the crew arrived on June 14, 1950, at Moab's airport. Back in those days, Moab was just a one-horse Mormon town in the middle of nowhere. One hotel and three motels weren't enough to house the Ford company. A tent city was erected just off Main Street: 29 army tents with wooden-planked floors, housing five men per unit. Chuck Roberson remembered they stashed their supply of alcohol under a loose plank. On this picture, Ford christened Roberson "Bad Chuck" because he was a ladies' man and at one point even managed to smuggle a girl into his tent where other stuntmen slept. The name stuck.

An old wooden school cafeteria had been rented to serve as a mess hall. A catering truck was always packed with donuts and coffee. On a Ford set, everybody was on location at seven o'clock sharp. Everybody, that is, except Ford himself. The master filmmaker would sometimes arrive 20 minutes late. The entire company would snap to attention as he stepped from the car, and accordionist Danny Borzage would play

Army tents were pitched on the George White ranch, the primary location of *Rio Grande*. J. Carrol Naish (standing next to Wayne) is playing Gen. Phil Sheridan. Jack Pennick is holding the horse while stuntman Chuck Roberson, far right, at Peter Oritz' side, is doing his little acting bit (author's collection).

Ford's favorite tune, "Bringing in the Sheaves." Ford liked his Horse Soldiers dirty, so the uniforms were not to be washed for the entire duration. Stuntman Terry Wilson told Wayne historian Tim Lilley that the day you got to the location, they'd issue your uniform and you wore it every day until the day you left; "So you had the sweat and the stink and the whole thing going all the time."[15] Ford would line everybody up in the morning and fix kerchiefs, but it was really a breath check to see if anybody had a drink.

Michael Wayne remembered the picturesque pioneer town on Highway 191 as a much better place to visit than Monument Valley: "You had motels with air conditioning ... and you had a great restaurant, the Red Door."[16] And Patrick Wayne swore the best steaks in the world were prepared in a little old Moab restaurant. He was probably referring to **Milt's Stop & Eat**, 356 Millcreek Drive, the oldest eatery there; Milt's been around since 1954.

"Put out of your mind any romantic ideas"

Ford took the liberty to remodel George White's ranch on the banks of the Colorado as the cavalry outpost. They

Publicity still with Peter Oritz, playing Wayne's aid in *Rio Grande*: Oritz was a most decorated Marine officer and the youngest sergeant in the French Foreign Legion. He knew John Ford from his service in the OSS and the director occasionally gave him supporting parts (author's collection).

built a palisaded entrance and tents and tie rails out in the alfalfa field. The riding track (for the "Roman riding" scene) was a circle all around the outer edge of that field. A wooden bridge spanned Castle Creek below where the soldiers held the Indians captive. White recalled the day they shot the Indian attack on the cavalry tents: "Hoping to catch a special angle of the warriors as they hit the camp, cameraman Archie Stout was stationed behind one of the tents." One of the riders, carried away with the excitement of it all, ran over Stout with his horse, knocking him out. White: "He was taken to the ranchhouse. The damage was minor."[17]

Karl Tangren, later a prominent figure in the Moab Film Commission, was a 19-year-old extra in the scene where wounded soldiers were brought back to the cavalry post. The men were dragged on stretchers behind horses on a travois. Tangren recounted, "We were going to choke to death on that hot and dry day dragged behind a horse."[18]

"Soldiers' fight, eh? Carry on"

The Rio Grande fort was reused in later Westerns and then dismantled. The George White Ranch is now the location of **Red Cliffs Lodge**, Milepost 14, Highway 128. The lodge also maintains the **Moab Museum of Film and Western Heritage**.

The renegade Apaches in *Rio Grande* used a pueblo city for a hideout. Ford built this set in **Castle Valley**, located 14 miles east of Moab off State Route 128. The pueblo was located between Castle Rock and Fisher Towers. Turn right before crossing the highway bridge at milepost 19, then follow the dirt road.

Ford often put Castletown Tower in the background. He filmed Wayne's cavalry fording the Rio Grande (a shallow area of the Colorado) at the gravel site at **Ida Gulch** (one mile east of the junction of Castle Valley Road and State Route 128, milepost 16).

Follow the Colorado on route 128; it'll get you to **Professor Valley**. A series of sandstone towers (**Fisher Towers**) are easy to spot in the movie. The jagged peaks of the towers are now a world-renowned photography subject. At **Hittle Bottom**, a low-lying area along the Colorado, a peculiar rock formation is evident; Wayne christened it **Locomotive Rock**. That's where in a wide shot, with Fisher Towers in the far background, Wayne's cavalry crosses the river into Mexico at night. Wayne then leads his determined troopers through a canyon; that's the **Onion Creek Narrows**.

White told the story of how he and Wayne went up **Onion Creek** to check out a location. He shouted the name of the notorious Hollywood columnist Louella Parsons into the canyon. She had recently reported something not to

Wayne's liking. Listening to the multiple echoes for too long, they returned late for lunch. Ford had already removed the sunshade from Wayne's table, prompting Wayne to explain to White, "The Old Man is getting even with us."[19]

"A man's word to anything, even his own destruction, is his honor"

The crew put on a special show at Moab's **Grand County High School**, 608 Fourth East Street. Chill Wills acted as master of ceremonies, Maureen O'Hara sang three solos, and Wayne and Victor McLaglen performed a skit as prizefight promoters with stuntmen taking pratfalls. "When we went to places like Moab, Utah," Wayne fondly remembered in a 1972 *Life* interview, "we'd put on entertainments for the kids. Actors who loved histronics would do recitations. Victor McLaglen and I worked up an act in which we managed boxers, who were stuntmen. We'd meet in the center of the ring and start punching, showing the things they weren't supposed to do. The thing became a free-for-all. I broke it up, throwing a bucket of water on the fighters and another bucket, full of confetti, at the kids."

The three-week shoot that began on June 15 ended on

The cavalry colonel has reached his target, the hideout of the renegade Apaches. This elaborate set was built in Castle Valley for *Rio Grande* (author's collection).

July 7. The next day, the company was bused to Grand Junction and flown back to Hollywood. Ford wrapped *Rio Grande* at Republic studios on July 21, 1950.

"We found the hideout"

It took Wayne more than two lustrums to return to Moab. On June 18, 1961, he was back for the rousing *The Comancheros*. Like *Rio Grande*, it turned Utah into Texas. Wayne and other cast members stayed at the **Apache Hotel**, at 166 Fourth East Street, usually in room 34 when he was alone, room 20 when his family accompanied him.

On June 1, 1961, Twentieth Century–Fox had begun construction of 23 buildings in **Professor Valley**. The largest was the stucco-and-tile headquarters of the Comanchero boss, on a flat in the shadow of Fisher Towers, on milepost 21.

It was on the *Comancheros* set that Wayne was asked why they shot on location instead of a comfortable studio set. "TV you can make on the backlot," he replied, "but for the big screen, for the real outdoor dramas, you have to go where God put the West."[20]

"Look at that scenery," acknowledged *Comancheros* co-star Stuart Whitman. "The art director didn't have much to do."[21]

Admittedly, the Comanchero hideout was the result of the imagination of art director Al Ybarra, put to work again after the construction of Wayne's Alamo in Brackettville. He had to watch his impressive Spanish villa burn to the ground in the big finale. (Three years later, Fox built another set on the same spot, for *Rio Conchos*, and they would again rub out the mansion.) Clever editing made it seem like the Comanchero encampment was located in a much deeper valley. The filmmakers enhanced the Texas Ranger's ride down in the wagon by adding shots on steeper hills.

"Words are what men live by"

William Clothier, director of photography, laid dolly tracks along the canyon walls of **King's Bottom**, for the dialogue scene in which Wayne's Texas Ranger reminds

Before *The Comancheros*, the jaw-dropping overlook from Dead Horse Point, towering 2,000 feet above the Colorado, had already been used in the Henry Fonda western *Warlock*. In more recent years, the area was seen in *Thelma & Louise* (photograph by Shay Read).

Whitman's gambler, "Mon-sewer, words are what men live by." King's Bottom is now a campground, three miles from downtown Moab. The farm that is attacked by the Comancheros was on a plateau right on the shores of the Colorado.

"Big country," Wayne's Texas Ranger muses as Clothier's CinemaScope camera pans from an outlook on the **La Sal loop**, a beautiful scenic drive that offers incredible views.

The Comancheros: John Wayne and Stuart Whitman ride the wagon at breakneck speeds on La Sal Mountain Loop Road (author's collection).

"Once more would be too often"

Different sources confirm that Wayne took over from Michael Curtiz when the director was not able to continue. According to Paul Helmick, "It was well known that Mike was in great pain with cancer during the location shooting and lasted only because John Wayne took the helm on the days Mike couldn't make it."[22] Principal photography ended on August 9, 1961.

The Comancheros was Wayne's last movie in what is often referred to as "the Heart of the Canyonlands." In 1978, the Utah Film Festival wanted to present its first John Ford Medallion for outstanding contributions to Americana on the screen to Wayne. Director Peter Bogdanovich accepted it for Wayne, who was too ill to attend.

9

The Studio Backlots

A Tree Is a Tree

"I guess my mind wasn't in Bavaria."
—John Wayne about his first job on the Fox lot

Nowadays filmmakers use the whole world for a location. But until the invention of television, the studios built their make-believe world in their own backyard. Even though John Wayne felt that his movies needed space, fresh air and sunlight, he worked on the backlots of all the major studios during Hollywood's Golden Age—and on some of the little ones, too.

Wayne preferred the lifestyle on location to working in the studio. "Nothing is so discouraging to an actor than to have to work for long hours upon hours in brightly lighted interior sets," he explained in a guest column even while he was churning out the B-westerns. "On western locations, which are generally three or four hundred miles from Los Angeles up in them mountains, we arise at five in the morning, then spend practically the entire day in the saddle—running, riding, chasing and jumping."[1]

The bosses at Poverty Row calculated differently than the moguls of the leading studios. While Monogram and Mascot relied on the real outdoors for their cheap programmers, the majors built the foreign locations on the backlot. In the days before TV invaded the American living rooms, a common saying among studio executives was, "A rock is a rock, a tree is a tree. Shoot it in Griffith Park." Wayne never forgot the experience of having to improvise to get a picture done. When the director of *Rooster Cogburn* called him on ad-libbing too much, he announced, "I haven't said lines just as they were written in a script since I worked for Mascot Productions."[2]

Twentieth Century–Fox

Marion Morrison apprenticed on the Fox lot when the studio was still the William Fox West Coast Studio. The Fox facility was then situated at 1401 North Western Avenue, the grounds William Fox had purchased in 1916. Early movies had been shot in roofless glass buildings in order to take advantage of natural light—the number of sunny days had brought the film pioneers to Hollywood

to begin with. Yet even in California, sunshine is inconsistent. That makes it hard matching morning shots with shots taken in the afternoon. So when Wayne started to work for Fox, the early buildings had already been replaced by windowless stages, with electric lights replacing the natural light. They would have to be rebuilt soon to be soundproofed, with the coming of the talkie movie era. When Wayne summed up his apprenticeship, he didn't feel the least bit sorry about

John Ford once compared John Wayne to a mountain lion who was unhappy when confined to working in the studio. However, the movie star was aware of the necessity of working on the stage. Waiting patiently for his cue on the *Fighting Kentuckian* set at Republic Studio, with Dutch actor Philip Dorn (author's collection).

116

having to come up through the ranks the hard way. "In those days, you could operate in every department of pictures. You didn't need a union card. I was a carpenter. I was a juicer. I rigged lights. I helped build sets. Carried props. Hauled furniture." In other words, he got to know the nuts and bolts of making pictures. "That is why I know what a scene is going to look like on film."[3]

"Bring him back"

Fox employed young Duke for periods stretching over several years, from 1926 to 1931. He served in many a crowd scene as an extra and earned his first screen credit in 1929 for *Words and Music* (billed as Duke Morrison). More importantly, it was here that the fateful meeting between the USC student and an already well-established director occurred, his future mentor John Ford. After the filmmaker had taken a liking to this 6'4" kid, he made it a habit of using him as a prop man or assistant of sorts. Ford remembered

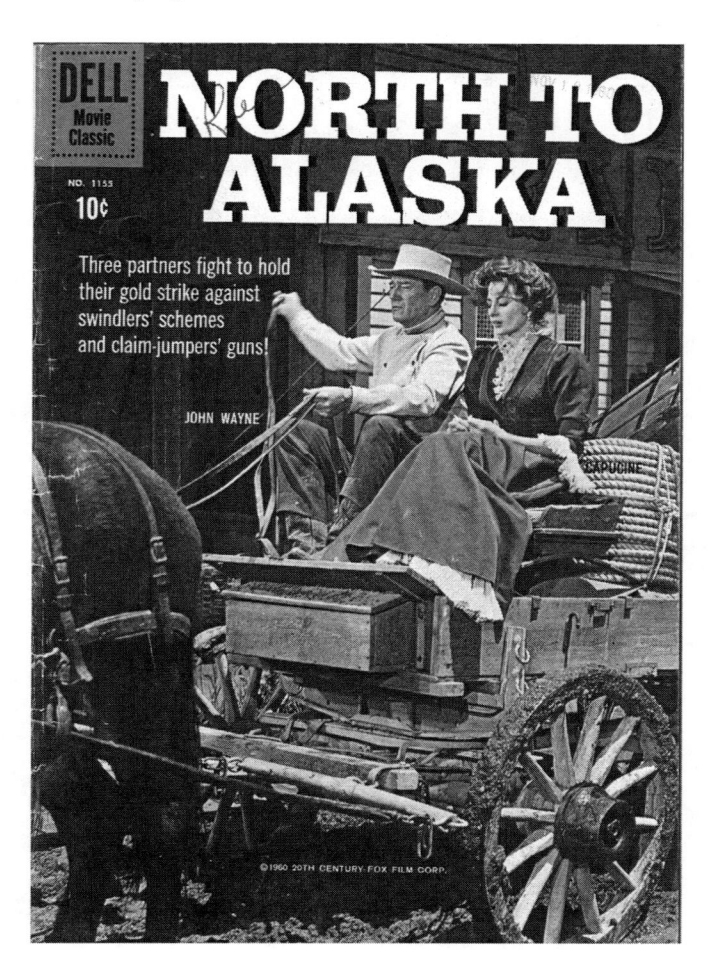

This Dell comic book adaption of *North to Alaska* displays John Wayne and Capucine working on "Tombstone Street" on the old Fox lot, shortly before Century City went up in its place (author's collection).

that Wayne was "the second or third assistant prop man" in his *Four Sons* (1928). In one dramatic scene in which the mother had just received notice that one of her sons had died, she had to break down and cry. Autumn leaves were falling. Take after take, young Wayne would sweep the leaves up for the next take. When Ford just got the shot perfectly, Wayne walked into the shot with his broom, reacted with horror when he saw the camera going, and started running for the gate. Wayne felt the embarrassment even decades later: "Shit, there I was. I just threw down my goddam broom and started to walk off."[4] Ford recounted it as well: "We were laughing so damn hard—I said, 'Go get him, bring him back.' Fortunately, they finally caught up with him and he came back so sheepfaced."[5]

In an episode of TV's *Warner Bros. Presents* in 1955, Wayne even reenacted his funny *faux pas* for host Gig Young. "I guess my mind wasn't in Bavaria. Because all of a sudden I caught myself onstage sweeping when I shoulda been offstage tossing. And I looked over my shoulder and I saw that I got my picture taken."

From then on, Ford put him into his films as a bit player. Like in *The Black Watch*, Ford's first all-taking feature, filmed on the Fox lot from January to February 1929: Wayne worked as a prop man as well as an extra in a dinner scene— he's almost cut off at the edge of the frame. Ford eventually put him in the middle of a shot in *Rough Romance* (1930), as an uncredited lumberjack, and even gave him some lines.

Duke Morrison, Production Assistant

That same year, when he was again doing double duty as a prop man and a bit player in *Born Reckless*, he ran into Raoul Walsh. It will forever remain a mystery under which circumstances the *Big Trail* director made his discovery. Did he just happen to spot Wayne when he walked on the Ford set? Or did puppet master Ford point Wayne out to his director friend? Walsh said that he was pretty much persuaded at first sight: "His height gave him authority and his voice was developing the familiar twang that would come to be expected by millions."[6] Wayne himself told the story, probably for the first time, in a *Motion Picture Magazine* interview in February 1931. In this account, the encounter happened on the *Born Reckless* set—a John Ford set. Hence, it might just be that Ford had a hand in suggesting the promising propman to Walsh. The one-eyed director recalled the first sighting very well: "He had a good height. ... It was a hot day. He wasn't wearing a shirt. He had a certain western hang to his shoulders.... A certain way of holding yourself and walking is typical of a real westerner and he had it."[7] His studio ID card identified him as Duke Morrison, Production Assistant. The studio heads decided to change that. According to a popular story, production chieftain Winfield Sheehan came up with "Wayne" and Walsh added the "John."

"You're working, ain't you?"

After *The Big Trail* misfired, Fox wasn't so sure about the future prospects of their contract player. They put him in *Girls Demand Excitement*, shot on the lot from November 24, 1930, to January 1931. An anecdote that has been repeated in various biographies has the struggling young actor trudging to the Fox parking lot one evening where he ran into Will Rogers, America's folk hero. The movie veteran inquired about his young colleague's low spirits. Wayne complained about the thankless part the Fox front office had him playing. "Waal, I'll tell you something, young feller," Rogers drawled. "You're workin', ain't you?" When the young actor replied in the affirmative, the homespun humorist advised, "Just keep on workin'."

It took Wayne almost 30 years to return to the Fox lot. It had become Twentieth Century–Fox in a merger with 20th Century Pictures in 1935. The corporation had started selling off large hunks of its lot when Wayne came back to shoot the western town scenes of *The Comancheros* (1961) on the often-used Tombstone Street. It was being razed even as Wayne was filming. At the time, 20th-Century Fox proudly proclaimed, "It will be the site of a huge new housing development known as Century City." For Wayne, even for the short remaining time on the old Fox lot, this last return was something of a nostalgic experience. "A couple of my old buddies were still on the payroll," he noted. It was like old times. Only they now were grandfathers—"and so am I!"[8]

In the TV special *The American West of John Ford*, Henry

On the Warner set of *The Man from Monterey*: an unknown production assistant points to John Wayne's next line in the script (author's collection).

Back to his old stomping ground, the former Fox lot, now the Century Plaza Hotel: John Wayne receives the Hebrew University Scopus Award from the hands of Frank Sinatra (author's collection).

Fonda and John Ford reminisced about that backlot, standing on a hill where the Western street used to be, looking down on the paved streets of Century City. "It's been homesteaded," Fonda quipped, only half-jokingly.

Scout's Honor

In 1977, Wayne returned to the place where he started out as Duke Morrison of the prop department (he had kept his union card all these years). Only it wasn't his Fox backlot any more. The once sprawling 225-acre film factory was by then fully developed into Century City. At the **Century Plaza Hotel**, on the Avenue of the Stars, he received the Hebrew University Scopus Award from Frank Sinatra. In the same place in September 1978, the Boy Scouts of America gave him their annual award and announced the formation of the **John Wayne Outpost Camp** near Lake Arrowhead. Wayne had been a Boy Scout himself; he recited the Scout Law at this dinner and thanked the Scouts for putting his name on the outpost camp: "I would rather see it there than on all the theater marquees the world over."[9] President Gerald Ford then presented him with the plaque that lauded him "as an example of the spirit of America and the ideals of scouting."

It was probably unintentional but when Wayne's estate was sold off in October 2011, the auction was held at that same hotel at 2025 Avenue of the Stars. Ethan Wayne, head of Wayne Enterprises, announced that this would be a chance for fans to get a piece of the Duke, "and we're not going to do it again."[10] The Wayne clan wasn't anticipating that the fans would dig quite so deeply into their pockets to collect Wayne artifacts. The bids in the Heritage auction climbed way over the estimates. The total of the two-day sale eventually exceeded $5.4 million. A portion of the proceeds funded the John Wayne Cancer Foundation.

Metro-Goldwyn-Mayer

MGM was the most prodigious of the dream factories. It has been estimated that historically a fifth of all movies made in the United States were partially shot somewhere at MGM studios. When Wayne walked onto this lot, it was still relatively new. MGM was founded in 1924 when Metro, Goldwyn and Louis B. Mayer Pictures merged in Culver City. The historical marker for the Ince/Triangle Studios that formed the original lot is located at 10202 West Washington Boulevard, on the landmark MGM colonnade. The lion in the logo had just been introduced when Wayne was working there for the first time, in the summer of 1926, as a costumed extra, wearing a kilt, in *Annie Laurie*, starring one of the greatest stars of the silent age, Lillian Gish. Around the same time, he also was a spear-carrying guard in the gallows scene of *Bardelys the Magnificent* (it was considered lost because MGM chose to destroy the negative in 1936; a nearly complete print was found in France in 2006 and it has been restored).

"I'm Superman"

Wayne walked through the MGM colonnade again in 1942, to star in the Joan Crawford melodrama *Reunion in France*. MGM recreated the streets of occupied Paris on the lot.

The war was still on when Wayne was invited back on the MGM lot for a story conference on *They Were Expendable*. John Ford held it in the **Thalberg Building**, the MGM administration headquarters. The iconic building was adjacent to the famed East Gate, which could be accessed by Grant Avenue. This was the primary entrance until Sony purchased the studio in 1989 and the gate became too small for modern truck traffic. In the above-mentioned conference, Wayne met the man he was to portray later, after Frank W. Wead's death. "Spig" Wead wrote the screenplay of *They Were Expandable* and was in his naval uniform at that meeting. So was Robert Montgomery, who was cast for the leading part. Wayne was wearing gray flannel slacks, a brown sports shirt, and a brown hounds-tooth jacket. That's when he started to feel like an outsider. According to biographer Zolotow, Wayne went to the private bathroom in Ford's office suite. He felt disgraced by his civilian clothes. Ford gave him the cold-water treatment. "Listen, you dumb bastard, get the

On screen, it will look like John Wayne is all alone in the deserted streets of "Newton Station." However, John Ford's camera car is following him closely on the MGM backlot for *The Horse Soldiers*.

hell out of this office. We got a picture to make and we go to Miami for our locations in three weeks."[11] The movie's sea battles were shot in MGM's tank, a controllable "ocean" upon which miniature of full-size aquatic sequences were shot. A five-story-high cyclorama with any painted backdrop encircled the back. The tank held more than three million gallons. Years later, *Ben-Hur's* sea battle was filmed in that tank.

In 1957, Wayne played naval aviator "Spig" in the biopic *The Wings of Eagles*. The hilarious scene in which he belly-flops the airplane in the admiral's pool was shot on the MGM lot in the **Esther Williams Pool**. Elvis Presley used the pool the same year as Wayne, in *Jailhouse Rock*. Ford filmed the rest of the admiral's garden party on the grounds of the *Gone with the Wind* Atlanta setting.

"That's a mighty pretty name, B. Sweet"

MGM called the largest Western movie location in the world its own, a large spread around Culver City, with a standing set of a western town on it. In 1948, Ford used it for the *3 Godfathers* scenes of the friendly town of Welcome, Arizona. (Just before Wayne's ride down that Western street, it had been Gregory Peck's turn in *Duel in the Sun*.) Ten years later, Ford used the same western town for parts of *The Horse Soldiers*.

Star and director teamed up again for the Civil War sequence of *How the West Was Won*. The massive MGM epic was in production from May 26 until November 1961. Wayne worked for five days making his cameo appearance as General Sherman on the backlot, on one of the 77 individual sets that were designed. The stages had to be built higher, wider and more complete than usual because the Cinerama camera magnified each detail. Henry Hathaway, who shot most of his sections outdoors, was particularly critical of Ford's "Civil War stuff," which to him looked "a little stagy. He shot the whole sequence on a soundstage and it … needed air."[12]

Wayne was back on the MGM lot one more time, for another cameo: the Roman centurion in *The Greatest Story Ever Told*, in production from October 1962 to July 1963. George Stevens directed the crucifixion sequence on a soundstage. Wayne's single line, "Truly this man was the son of God," was taped later in a recording studio. The studio complex is now Sony Pictures Studios.

Columbia Pictures

Movie mogul Harry Cohn funded Columbia Pictures Studios in 1918, in the Poverty Row area of Hollywood, bounded by Sunset Boulevard on the north, Gower on the west and Beachwood Drive on the east. After Fox dropped Wayne's contract, Cohn picked the young actor up. His six-month contract was a step down as Columbia was a minor studio.

Cohn put Wayne in three B-Westerns in which he was eclipsed by their stars, Tim McCoy and Buck Jones. The actor formed an admiration for Jones. Jones became a victim of the tragic Coconut Nightclub fire ten years later. Legend has it that Jones returned to the blazing building to rescue others. Actual evidence indicates that he was trapped and succumbed, as most did, trying to escape. Wayne was a believer in the "hero" version. "How sad," he once ruminated, "that

our industry doesn't realize that Buck Jones is one of the real heroes of the business."[13]

Wayne soon fell out of favor with Cohn, who ordered him to appear as a corpse in *The Deceiver* (1931), a humiliation Wayne would never forget. More than 30 years later, he recalled, "The son of a bitch [Cohn] called me in one day and told me to lay off the bottle and broads. I asked him what the hell he meant and he said he had documented evidence that I'd been boozing it up on the set and making eyes off-camera at one of the leading ladies."[14] Cohn dropped him, and Wayne would refuse to make a picture for Columbia for the rest of his life. When you prowl around the former location of the studio, look up **Beachwood Street**. That's where the Columbia gate was, and that's where the gateman refused Wayne admittance—on Harry Cohn's orders.

Mascot and Monogram

Young John Wayne didn't have to go far after the Columbia mogul was finished crushing him. He ambled over to Gower Gulch and signed on with Mascot to do serials, considered the lowest work in the movie industry. Mascot didn't even have its own studios. Company operator Nat Levine rented all of the equipment and facilities. He had leased the lot of comedy pioneer Mack Sennett, 20 acres called "the Valley lot." Today, this part of North Hollywood is called **Studio City**. At the time of Wayne's arrival, Mascot's offices were at Santa Monica Boulevard, now the site of Hollywood Forever Cemetery.

In 1933, Wayne went with Trem Carr's Monogram Pictures, then headquartered at 6048 Sunset Boulevard, to make a series of cheapie westerns under the Lone Star brand. The brick stone buildings can still be seen on **Hoover Street**.

Jerusalem on the MGM stage: Sidney Poitier, as the man who helps Jesus carry the cross, is talking to the toupee-less supervisor of the crucifixion, for *The Greatest Story Ever Told* (author's collection).

No marker identifies this brick building on Hoover Street as the former Monogram Studio. Sometimes, they would just get out of the studio door and start cranking (photograph by Roland Schaefli).

Sometimes the moviemakers would just go out onto the street and start shooting a scene. In 2011, Scientology bought the old lot.

"Learn to fight"

On the Trem Carr quickies, Wayne first worked with legendary stuntman Yakima Canutt. "Dear Yak," Wayne wrote as an afterword to Canutt's autobiography, "if you capture a mite of the printable experiences that we went through during the Wayne period of your life, the feeling of our industry in the '30s and '40s will come to life for the generations since." The team worked out a routine of film fisticuffs. In the early days, the fight consisted of wild swinging in which the actors would hit each other's shoulders. The stunt ace and the aspiring actor knew there had to be a better way. "My advice to any actor who wants to work in outdoor pictures,"

he would advise in later years, "is to learn to fight. Above all, it has to be convincing."[15] They worked together so often that the director usually left them choreograph their own fight scenes. Wayne and Canutt were both so competitive, both so eager to top whatever previous bit they had worked out, that this might have been dangerous if they had not become such close friends. "When I was a kid," Wayne recalled on a movie set 45 years later, "they didn't hire you for your acting abilities for those quickies. But for how agile you were!"[16]

The duo devised a technique of near-miss swings with long follow-throughs which looked realistic when the camera photographed them at a precise angle. Even as late in his career as *McQ*, Wayne could give fellow actor Al Lettieri a little advice: "He taught me how to really throw some movie-type punches. I've done that thing before but with John Wayne, it's a kind of a science."[17] Canutt and Wayne had developed this "pass system" into the fine art of screen

Duke it out: John Wayne helped to invent the technique for movie fighting, currently in use in this brawl from *Tall in the Saddle* (author's collection).

fighting on the Poverty Row flicks. According to Canutt, "I'd rather do a fight with Duke Wayne than with any stunt man. That's how good he is." Late in life, Wayne still offered tips to screen fighters: "In order to do this kind of work, you have to be completely relaxed, because otherwise, you tighten up."[18]

Republic Pictures

In the fall of 1935, former tobacco executive Herbert J. Yates absorbed Wayne's employers Mascot and Monogram as well as other production entities and formed Republic Pictures. This new studio complex, on Ventura and Radford in the **San Fernando Valley**, would become Wayne's home studio for approximately the next 17 years, the longest he was ever associated with one company. Yates put him to work in a string of B-Westerns. Even after the success of *Stagecoach*, it took Yates a while to catch on that he had a potential A-list star under contract. In time, he would give the Wayne films higher budgets. For *Dark Command*, Republic's follow-up on *Stagecoach*, six of Republic's seven soundstages were utilized for interiors.

"With the compliments of the house"

Republic had another big asset: the Lydecker siblings. Howard and Theodore Lydecker were the special effects wizards of their time. On many of Wayne's films, they were in charge of effects like matte paintings and miniatures. Their effects in *Flying Tigers* earned them an Academy Award

He knew each corner on the Republic lot, his home studio for seventeen years. Walking between the huge studio hangars with Vera Hruba Ralston, in costume for *The Fighting Kentuckian*. The ice-skater from Czechoslovakia became Mrs. Herbert Yates the same year (author's collection).

nomination. In *Three Faces West*, they created the Depression Dust Bowl conditions. In *Lady from Louisiana*, they let the Mississippi rise and flood their miniatures. *Flame of Barbary Coast* (Republic's "Tenth Anniversary Film"), primarily shot on the studio lot from July 6 to August 19, 1944, was a particular delight. The Lydeckers created the San Francisco earthquake, splitting sidewalks apart and cracking roofs in their detailed miniature.

"You get a panicky feeling"

Yates went all-out with the seafaring adventure *Wake of the Red Witch*. He had a full-scale replica of a three-mast sailing vessel built on one of his largest soundstages, an exact duplication of the 200-foot schooner used in the sequences filmed on location in Catalina. Yates also allowed for the construction of a water tank. It was a truncated cone, measuring 55 feet in diameter at the top, 33 feet at the bottom, and 16 feet deep. The Lydeckers supervised the underwater setups. Howard designed an elaborate filtration system to purify water, which could be rapidly warmed with flash heating. The camera could get a crystal-clear look through the glass window near the

John Wayne appreciated working with pros. Pictured here with director of photography Lee Garmes, who won the Oscar for the Marlene Dietrich vehicle *Shanghai-Express*, and director George Waggner, who had the horror classic *The Wolf Man* to his credit (author's collection).

bottom of the tank where Wayne had to battle a nightmarish octopus. "You know it's a fake octopus but when you get down there and those long arms wrap around you, you get a panicky feeling," Wayne told a reporter as he prepared to descend into the tank.[19] Six puppeteers controlled the movement of the creature. The tank's walls were blue, with seaweed and rock formations painted on the walls. Helping Wayne get to the bottom were the heavily weighted shoes he wore. He breathed through a facemask with an oxygen tube, descending on an iron ladder. An assistant would empty a bucket of live freshwater bass and carp into the tank. When the cameras were rolling, Wayne would take off his facemask and the shot would last as long as he could stay underwater. Many years later, Wayne told the captain of his *Wild Goose*, "I picked up a fungus infection in my ears doing the diving scenes in *Wake of the Red Witch*. Whenever I go swimming, it bothers me."[20]

You might get wet: In *Wake of the Red Witch*, John Wayne drifts in the new Republic Studio tank, tied to a raft as the condemned Captain Ralls (author's collection).

In 1954, the eccentric director Edward Wood, Jr., stole the sea monster from the Republic prop department to use it in his own horror quickie *Bride of the Monster* with Bela Lugosi. The incident is portrayed in the Tim Burton film *Ed Wood* with Johnny Depp.

"Republic—I like the sound of the word"

Even though most likely a product of the publicity writers, an article in the 1950 issue of *The Film Show Annual*, supposedly written by Wayne himself, is an interesting read about the making of *Rio Grande*. "Hi, there! Welcome to Hollywood!" Wayne starts out. "All set? Fine, we'll drive over to Republic. We shot most of the footage on location in Utah but there are a few odds and ends we have to wind up here

before the film is completed and in the can." Wayne proceeds to tell the reader about the "'big sign across all those sound-stages stretching for two blocks!' Let's go inside the sound-stage and see what's going on." He then describes the interior scene in which Claude Jarman, Jr., and his fellow players hide on the church set.

The day Wayne left his Republic home over a final dispute about cutting costs on his *Alamo* project, he called the movers and asked his secretary Mary St. John to pack and come along. When Yates lost his temper and told her to stop packing, she refused. "Who are your working for, him or me?" he screamed. "Wayne," she answered.[21]

The Hollywood Reporter announced on November 13, 1952, that Wayne had come to an impasse with the head of Republic and that their falling-out meant the end of a picture-making partnership. "Yates will have to make me a damned good offer to get me to make another picture with him," Wayne said. He added that his difficulties with Yates arose over the proposed filming of his pet project *The Alamo*. Wayne didn't feel that he owed Republic anything. "I've made a lot of money for the studio."[22]

By the end of the decade, the "biggest of the little studios" was out of the moviemaking business. In May 1962, the CBS Television Network took over the lot. Many TV series were then produced on what once was the Republic lot. CBS attempted to recruit Wayne for their new TV series

Returning to the old Republic lot for interiors of *Big Jake*: By then, Herbert Yates was long gone and the studio was absorbed by CBS Studio Center. Wayne and production manager Lee Lukather (right) went way back at Republic, from *Sands of Iwo Jima* (author's collection).

Gunsmoke. Wayne had James Arness under contract: "I told the producers I had the guy for them and all they had to do was pay him a salary and give him a piece if they wanted to. I fought with the producers, drank with 'em, argued with 'em and finally, they agreed to talk to him."[23] Wayne then insisted on doing an introduction for the first episode, in full Ethan Edwards' gear, as *The Searchers* was in production on the Warner stages at that time.

"If you don't mind drinkin' with a Bluebelly"

It must have given Wayne a feeling of *déjà vu* when he returned to his Republic stamping grounds for the interiors of *Rio Lobo.* Of course, by 1970, Yates was long gone. The interior shots took 22 days on Soundstage 18. Maurice Zolotow observed how Howard Hawks got a saloon scene in the can in five takes: When Wayne heard the buzzer, he became Colonel McNally, in 1866. "His blue eyes harden. His jaw stiffens. His muscles tense. He speaks his lines perfectly. He sits where he has to sit. He does not forget lines. He enters completely into the dramatic moment. This saloon becomes a real saloon outside a Union prison camp."[24] Someone asked him if he remembered where his old dressing room had been. Wayne answered that he didn't have one. "I had a hook."[25]

During his *Rio Lobo* work on the old Republic lot, Wayne stayed at the nearby **Sportsman's Lodge**, 12825 Ventura Boulevard. That place he knew from way back: He had taught his kids to fish in their large trout ponds.

It took Wayne almost 20 years to make another appearance on CBS-TV television, in the *Maude* episode "Maude Meets the Duke" (September 9, 1974). This was, finally, his last visit to the former Republic facilities. **CBS Studio Center** at 4024 Radford Avenue is still used primarily for television. Several memorial markers in the ground outside their walls remind visitors of its former glory (Security doesn't like you to take pictures). Where the old Western street was, there's now a parking lot. The Dakota Street which was added for Wayne's *Dakota* has vanished.

When Harry Carey, Jr., first went to work for Republic in *Rio Grande* on Stage 11, he found it looked like a huge Spanish hacienda. But in later years, there was nothing left that reminded him of those days; it was replaced by an ugly building, and what little was left of the hacienda smelled bad inside. It always depressed the hell out of him to have to go over to the former Republic studios.

RKO Radio Pictures

In 1945, Wayne signed a multi-picture contract with RKO, one of the "Big Five" studios of the Golden Age of Hollywood. It was located along **Gower Street**, adjacent to Paramount. *Without Reservations* was Wayne's only movie dealing with the making of motion pictures. The opening shot shows a movie studio—that's the actual RKO building at 780 Gower Street. For this footage, the RKO signs were replaced with signs that said "Arrowhead Pictures." (This historic structure now bears the Paramount logo.)

This comedy was soon followed by RKO's *Tycoon.* Hollywood columnist Hedda Hopper (she had played a small part in his *Reap the Wild Wind*) visited the set in May 1947 and found Wayne in a corner of the soundstage, oblivious to a couple hundred extras who were milling about the set while waiting for the next scene to be set up. He was absorbed in a matter at hand, Hopper reported: a hand of playing cards. "At that particular moment the only thing producer Wayne was trying to produce was a royal flush."[26]

"Come on, Wildcats, make us proud today!"

Three years after Wayne had joined forces with RKO, industrialist and part-time moviemaker Howard Hughes acquired a large share of stock and gained control. Hughes and Wayne had been casual acquaintances for years. *Jet Pilot* was the first picture Wayne made under Hughes's leadership; then another aviation picture was lined up, *Flying Leathernecks* (1951). With this war movie, Wayne started his "mug tradition." In the plot, each fighter pilot has his own coffee mug with his name written on it so every time one of the squadron doesn't return from a mission, they take his mug off the wall. RKO had approached artist Bob Williams to produce these props. That's where Wayne got the idea to commission mugs for the cast and crew members, a tradition that would eventually span 25 years. The hand-painted personalized mugs were made of heavy Wallace China. From *Hondo* on, Williams stamped the address "515 N. Main Rm 20 in **Santa Ana**" on the bottoms. The Mug Shop at 3024 East Coast Highway in **Corona Del Mar** produced the mugs from *Sons of Katie Elder* on to *The Cowboys.* When they too stopped making them, Ketchum Originals at 1105 Long Beach Boulevard in **Long Beach** produced the mementos from then on.

Wayne's association with RKO came to an end on a summer day in 1956. He was on the set of *I Married a Woman* just one day to do a cameo, fulfilling his contract. RKO folded soon thereafter. Within the Hollywood studio's ever-changing borders, some of the old RKO stages were situated on Paramount grounds after the Desilu merger. RKO Stage 10, where the rice paddies of *Back to Bataan* had been created for the underwater close-ups, became Paramount's Stage 32. A year after Wayne held his breath in the artificial pond, it became a river with falling snow, observed by a suicidal James Stewart in *It's a Wonderful Life*.

Warner Brothers

After Wayne escaped the Mascot serials, the door opened to Warner Brothers, on what is now Warner Boulevard in North Hollywood. The struggling actor had managed to get a six-picture deal. The so-called 4-Star-Westerns started with *Ride Him, Cowboy* in 1932. To be precise, Wayne had been working for Warners even before they signed him to that contract. Long before Wayne could ask for—and get—the sum of a quarter of a million dollars for his cameo in Darryl F. Zanuck's *The Longest Day*, Zanuck made the Biblical epic *Noah's Ark* in 1928 for Warners. "They called the schools and wanted kids over six feet to come out for $15 a day and swim while they broke the temple down on top of us," Wayne recalled in a conversation with Peter Bogdanovich. Young Andy Devine came up beside Morrison and said, "Hey, give me a hand, will you?" And he put a hand on Wayne's shoulder and a hand on another guy's shoulder, "and he's that big around, he's the first one they picked...." Both were hired as stunt swimmers, among 7500 other extras. The flood's destruction of the Temple of Moloch was filmed on a huge set constructed within the concrete lake which was Warners' studio tank. Three extras died on that set, and many were injured. *Noah's Ark* was directed by Michael Curtiz. "So that's how far back I went with Andy Devine," said Wayne.[27] And that's how far back he went with Warner Brothers.

"Give me a break in a fair fight!"

Warners was a well-greased factory in its heyday. The brothers had staked out their empire in Burbank in 1929 when they gained control of First National Pictures. They built their Western sets early. What is now **Forest Lawn Cemetery** on Forest Lawn Drive was once the Providencia Ranch, where several outdoor movies, as well as Wayne's early Warner Westerns, were filmed. By 1948, the property was transformed into the cemetery, which borders on the Warner premises. The six western flicks Wayne made back to back in the 1932–33 period were well-produced. They all used the same studio stage but since the sets were dressed differently each time, nobody ever noticed.

Even though Warners starred their young man in his own westerns, they used him in bit parts just as well. *Central Airport*, in production from November 21, 1932, to February 10, 1933, is noteworthy as the first time Wayne dies on screen. As the co-pilot of a plane that crashes into the ocean—back at the Warner wet tank—he tries to save

Operation Pacific **was studio-bound even when the setting was the Pacific war theater. Gary Cooper drops in on John Wayne not so much because he likes submarine mock-ups. The studio still photographer welcomes the opportunity to get two stars for the price of one (author's collection).**

a passenger and loses his life, in a matter of a few seconds on film. After this appearance without even a word of dialogue, Wayne would work for the film's director again. Ironically, William Wellman, the hard-nosed former World War I flyer, would helm Wayne's "flying" pictures *Island in the Sky* and *The High and the Mighty*, also released through Warner Brothers.

After being absent from the studio for 18 years, Wayne returned as the country's number one box office attraction to Warner Burbank. His first, *Operation Pacific*, is a perfect example of a studio-bound film. Even though the story is set in Honolulu, not a foot of film was shot there, apart from some establishing shots and stock footage. The Navy had allowed the use of the submarine *Thunder* for outdoor shots but when Wayne commands, he is standing on a full-size mock-up in the studio tank. In the scene where the servicemen watch a Warner war movie in the submarine set, somebody utters without a hint of irony, "The things those Hollywood guys can do with a submarine." During the days on the set, between September and November in 1950, Gary Cooper was an almost constant visitor because he was madly in love with Wayne's co-star, Patricia Neal.

"I just got tired of picking myself up"

Trouble Along the Way, shot from August 28 to December 1952, is another textbook example of a Warner studio film that manages without location work. The story plays on the East Coast yet just one single shot was made in New York (with a double of child actress Sherry Jackson,

John Wayne working the "New York Street," home to the Warner gangster pictures. With Charles Coburn in *Trouble Along the Way* (author's collection).

walking away from the camera). This establishing shot places Wayne's home in the vicinity of Manhattan Bridge. However, all scenes that play out in this neighborhood were photographed on Warners' New York Street, where the hoods from the studio's "Murderers' Row," the Bogarts and the Cagneys, used to play hide-and-seek with the coppers. A shot of **Yankee Stadium** is rear-projected.

In one of the crowd scenes, there is an uncredited extra named James Dean. This goes to show that when you were a contract player for Warners, they would certainly put you to work.

On location for *Trouble Along the Way* at Loyola Marymount University from which his sons were graduated. John Wayne was personally acquainted with Charles Coburn as the character actor had served as vice-president of the Motion Picture Alliance for the Preservation of American Ideals (author's collection).

"I'd say that was raw courage"

Director Michael Curtiz used the inside of the **Cathedral Chapel**, 923 South La Brea Avenue in La Brea, for the chapel scenes and edited the footage together with the entrance of the Hall of Music at **Pomona College**, 333 North College Way, Claremont. That's where Wayne calls out to Donna Reed in the farewell scene, "Nice legs—for a copper!" More college scenes were shot at **Loyola Marymount University**, 1901 Venice Boulevard. Wayne's sons Michael and Patrick were both graduates of Loyola High. Patrick never forgot how in 1956, when he was playing football for Loyola and they had a game against Glendale High, his father showed up and sat on the side of his alma mater, Glendale.

Sherry Jackson remembered Wayne being very protective of her. After her screen test, Curtiz let her know that they would cut her pigtails off. "Tears welled up into my eyes. And Duke was standing next to me and when Curtiz walked away he came over and says, 'Don't worry, I won't let them cut your braids.'"[28]

Wayne had the screenplay rewritten by James Edward Grant, but producer Melville Shavelson had his own ideas about the storyline. So he gave Wayne one version of the script; on the days that he was not present, Shavelson prepared another version, to film with subsidiary characters, that changed the plotline to his liking. Only one thing went wrong: Wayne showed up on the set on a day he wasn't supposed to. Shavelson remembered, "When double-crossed, he can make an underground nuclear explosion seem like a baby's sigh."[29] They finished the picture Wayne's way. (Years later, Wayne proved he did not hold a grudge long when he gave Shavelson a deal with *Cast a Giant Shadow*.)

On the last day of *Trouble Along the Way*, Wayne ran into Pilar, his future wife. She was dubbing the movie she made in Peru where they first met. He hadn't seen her since their chance encounter in Tingo Maria (see Chapter 10) and asked her out.

"You look like the vermin-ridden S.O.B. you are"

Over the years, Wayne worked on the Warner stages time and again. His Warner release of 1959, *Rio Bravo*, cut back and forth between the streets of Old Tucson and the interiors on Stage 4 (now Stages 5 and 10). Stage 1 was of particular meaning. In 1938, Nottingham Castle was built on this soundstage for *The Adventures of Robin Hood*; in 1942 it was the home of the fogbound *Casablanca* airport. And in 1972, that same 30,856-square-foot stage saw the fight to the death between Wayne and Bruce Dern—the haunting night scene from *The Cowboys*. (Today, Stage 1 is divided into Stages 12 and 18.) Wayne warned his co-star Dern that he would never be forgiven for shooting him in the back. The cocky New Hollywood actor quipped, "Yes, but they'll love me in Berkeley."[30] Wayne was to be proven right in the end. Not only did that scene have an effect on Dern's career but he was once held by the police because they felt he was wanted for *something*.

The heavy's role was originally offered to David Carradine, who was at that time doing Warner's *Kung Fu* series. He turned it down: "I didn't want to be the guy who killed John Wayne." One of Carradine's brothers, Robert, played one of Wayne's young Cowboys in the film. David rejoiced: "They taught him how to ride and shoot, and the Duke taught him how to act."[31] David got his chance to appear with Wayne in early 1978 when ABC celebrated its twenty-fifth year on the air with a show called *The Silver Anniversary Celebration*. The network rounded up all the cowboys who had worked for them over the years.

As a director, Wayne used the Warner backlot in 1968 for *The Green Berets*. He dressed the French Street (the Paris scenes of the *Casablanca* flashback were set there) as well as the New Orleans Street (Sgt. Provo points the "hero signs" out to Colonel Kirby) as Saigon streets. Some of the Vietnam jungle scenes were shot in the jungle section of the Warner backlot.

"What'd stop me? Fear of dying?"

Wayne was back in the Burbank studios for his final movie, *The Shootist*. Most of the Carson City set was built on Midwest Street (Warners had rented it out to Paramount). That street has lent a familiar small-town feeling to a great many movies. The homes of the juvenile delinquents of *Rebel Without a Cause* stood there. The courthouse structure on that same street found cinematic significance as it was converted into the Metropole Saloon, the place of Wayne's final showdown. The same area was dressed with snow for 1984's *Gremlins*. *Shootist* interiors were lensed on Stage 25, which had been home to the beloved Warner classic *Giant* (Wayne had already used that stage for a few short *Green Berets* interior scenes). Stage 25 was dubbed the *Big Bang Theory* Stage in 2019, to celebrate a total of 279 sitcom episodes that were taped there in front of a live audience.

Wayne returned to Burbank for the TV segment *An All-Star Tribute to John Wayne*, which aired November 26, 1976, and featured several of his past co-stars—Glen Campbell, Lee Marvin, James Stewart, Angie Dickinson, Ron Howard, Maureen O'Hara, Claire Trevor. Host Frank Sinatra presented Wayne with a bronze statue, to which Wayne said, "Tonight you made an old man and an actor very happy. You are happy, aren't you, Frank?"[32]

Wayne did his last work on the Warner Brothers lot on December 7, 1978, when he took part in a fundraiser, *All-Star Tribute to Jimmy Stewart*.

The Warner Bros. Studio Tour (3400 Warner Boulevard) offers a behind-the-scenes-look in a combination of a tram and walking tour that takes visitors through exterior street sets and into soundstages. Years back, the tour included a museum that displayed the miniature plane from *The High and the Mighty* and one of Wayne's large loop Winchester rifles from *Rio Bravo*.

Paramount Pictures

Paramount, once RKO's next-door neighbor, is now the sole member of the classic "Big Five" still located in the L.A. neighborhood of Hollywood. Its Bronson gate, one of movieland's iconic symbols, is located near the intersection of Melrose and Bronson. For decades, actors whispered, "I'm ready for my close-up, Mr. DeMille," for good luck, when they touched the iron gate. Hollywood's "Arc de

"They'll love me in Berkeley": Bruce Dern (shooting) could never live it down to have killed John Wayne in *The Cowboys* on Warner Stage 1 (author's collection).

Triomphe" can't be seen any more, since it is no longer the studio's main entrance, not open to traffic and now inaccessible to the public. (The Windsor Gate, constructed on Melrose Avenue in 1988, was designed to mimic its more famous sister.)

Coffee break on Paramount Stage 9: John Ford is making *The Man Who Shot Liberty Valance*. Note the letters on the wall: The Jerry Lewis movie *The Errand Boy* was made on that stage a short while before (author's collection).

Wayne walked through that gate between May 26 and August 19, 1941. Even though the film is set in the Florida Keys, *Reap the Wild Wind* was produced entirely on the Paramount lot. The famous film pioneer Cecil B. DeMille had virtually built Paramount, just as William Holden said in *Sunset Boulevard* (in which DeMille played himself). In 1936, Wayne had lobbied for the part of Buffalo Bill in DeMille's epic *The Plainsman*, starring Gary Cooper. When asked about regrets in his career, Wayne used to say it was never having made a movie with his friend Gary Cooper. Wayne told the story of how he went to see DeMille in his office (formerly Gloria Swanson's dressing room; in the 1990s, it was occupied by Eddie Murphy and producers Don Simpson and Jerry Bruckheimer). Wayne: "[I sat outside] the bastard's office and I could look in there and see him just thinking. He was talking to a casting director. So after about

an hour—the son of a bitch kept me waiting that long—he came out and said, 'Well, I'm going to lunch.' My agent said, 'You asked John Wayne to come over for an interview.' DeMille said, 'Oh yeah, so I did. Come along.' That's what you say to a dog." As he was walking along with DeMille's entourage, the director said, "Oh, you were in *The Big Trail*. But that was some time ago, wasn't it?" Wayne responded that he had been doing quickie pictures since, "and I think I've learned to read bad lines as well as anybody, and how to throw them away." DeMille looked him up and down and said, "A lotta water's under the bridge, and I'll get back to you."[33]

That was the last Wayne heard of *The Plainsman*. After *Stagecoach*, DeMille called Republic and again asked for him to come over, to play a Canadian Mountie in *North West Mounted Police*, another Cooper western. Wayne did not go. He had them send the word back, "A lotta water's under the bridge!"

The next opportunity to work for DeMille came up two years later when he was up for the part of the *Reap the Wild Wind* sea captain. Finally the head of Republic said, "Duke,

"I'll bring you a rainbow fish for breakfast": the romantic couple John Wayne and Paulette Goddard make the cover of the UK fan magazine *Picturegoer* in wartime. His first Paramount film *Reap the Wild Wind* had the biggest budget since *The Big Trail* (author's collection).

I want you to go over there and talk with this fellow." So he did and DeMille explained, "Mr. Wayne, I don't want to work with you if you don't like me, but I've admired your work." Wayne still hesitated to play the second lead: "The only reason you called me here is to make Ray Milland look like a man." DeMille leveled with him: "That's right." The respectful attitude softened Wayne's resolve to snub the director. During the picture, they had lunch together every day and Wayne came to admire the man for his principles. When they shot the fight scene on the boat set, DeMille openly asked Wayne for assistance. "John, I want you to show them how to play this scene."[34] Wayne gladly demonstrated his way of throwing a movie punch.

"I'd make a topsail out of Cutler's hide!"

Ray Milland recalled they spent hours in Paramount's large water tank fighting the giant squid. The mechanical rubber creature was operated by electric motors so it could lash out with its 30-foot tentacles. While his stars were underwater, DeMille directed them through telephone wires attached to the diving helmets. It cost $70,000 to create the monster. The studio donated it to the war effort in 1942 since the Japanese had conquered Malaya and Indochina, the source of most of the world's rubber.

The 175 × 195 foot tank (referred to as "B" tank on the Paramount lot) cost $50,000 to build and was first used in this film. It held 91,423 gallons. There was no filtration system, so the water tended to stagnate quickly. DeMille was back there for the parting of the Red Sea sequence for another epic, *The Ten Commandments* (1956). For Humphrey Bogart's *We're No Angels*, they built a dock and a street at the water's edge.

Built in 1922, Stage 1 is one of Paramount's oldest. It held the cave set of the Kirk Douglas classic *Ace in the Hole* and the chapel for *Donovan's Reef*'s Christmas scene and the cantina set of *El Dorado*, where James Caan makes his entrance.

"Take this one, Pockets!"

Stage 2 was Paramount's process stage. When an actor is seen in (for example) a moving car, he would be positioned in front of a transparency screen. Footage of any chosen landscape would then be projected on a screen behind him. Wayne shot the *Hatari!* process shots here, standing on the mock-up of the

herding car, as well as the speedboat process shots from *Donovan's Reef*. *El Dorado* used Stage 4 for Maudie's place and the barn. On Stage 5, the largest on the lot in terms of square feet, the interior of Wayne's home in *Donovan's Reef* was built.

Wayne's Paramount releases *Hatari*, *Donovan's Reef* (the bedroom sets) and *The Man Who Shot Liberty Valance* utilized Stage 9. Hard to imagine, but true: The same stage that was an African big game farm in *Hatari!* was also the setting of many galaxies where no man had gone before: It is sometimes called the *Star Trek* stage.

"You were pretty good in there"

Paramount Stages 12, 13 and 14 were combined in one building. For *Hatari!*, they were made up as the inside of Sean's bedroom, the Arusha hotel (the elephants catch up with Dallas) and the Safari bar (the gang gets blind drunk) as easily as Birnbaum's store in *McLintock!* In *El Dorado*, Stage 12 was the home of the saloon set, where Robert Mitchum's rifle bullet drove a bunch of bartop splinters into the hand of the crooked bartender, played by Mitchum's brother John. Hawks told John the squib would go off on the count of three but he had it set to off on *one*. The look on John's face was not acting. The insides of *El Dorado*'s church and bell tower (the famous shot of Chuck Roberson falling directly onto the camera) were on Stage 14. All interiors of the sheriff's office were done on the same stage.

Paramount's longtime production designer Hal Pereira used the stones from Ngare Nanyuki to recreate the fireplace of the Momella Game Farm for *Hatari!* on Paramount Stage 9—what Trekkies like to call the "Star Trek Stage." In a replay of Howard Hawks' *Only Angels Have Wings*, Elsa Martinelli plays the piano, accompanied by Red Buttons, while Hardy Kruger (left), Wayne, Valentin de Vargas and Michèle Girardon listen (author's collection).

Stage 15, built in 1938, was used for *True Grit*, probably for the night scene in which Rooster tells about his past.

"Run this scum out of town!"

Stage 18 had been known for years as the DeMille Stage because from 1941 on, C.B. had shot spectacles like *Reap the Wild Wind* in its vast expanses. When Gloria Swanson asks about DeMille's whereabouts in *Sunset Boulevard*, she is naturally directed to Stage 18. The largest indoor set ever built at Paramount was also built on Stage 18, Hitchcock's legendary *Rear Window* courtyard set, and the Cartwrights rode up to their Ponderosa ranch inside this soundstage for a number of years. Ford had part of the town of Shinbone in *Liberty Valance* placed inside Stage 18 as well as out in the open. While the night scenes were all shot on the stage, the day

Kim Darby (wearing skirt) wasn't supposed to be in the photo, but Wayne just asked her to come over, put out his arms, lifted her up and put her in the center. She shakes Barbara Streisand's hand who reported with Yves Montand (top row, right) to the studio for *On a Clear Day You Can See Forever*. The Star turnout on the Paramount lot includes Lee Marvin and Clint Eastwood (to the left and the right) who were making *Paint Your Wagon*. Rock Hudson (top row, left) came over from the *Darling Lili* set (author's collection).

scenes (James Stewart's arrival in modern Shinbone) were filmed on the lower part of Paramount's Western Street (the Virginia City Street in *Bonanza*). Wayne had shot assorted town scenes for *McLintock!* on the upper part of the street. Western Street was torn down in 1979 to make way for a parking lot. A long-standing rumor holds that Paramount had been afraid to remove it while Wayne was still alive.

Universal Studios

In 1915, Universal opened what was then the world's largest motion picture facility on a 230-acre converted farm just over the Cahuenga Pass from Hollywood. It's now called **Universal City Plaza**. Wayne took a break from Republic to make six action pictures for Universal in the 1936–37 period. Even though Wayne's series of non–Westerns, beginning with *The Sea Spoilers*, had bigger budgets, the six films didn't help Wayne break out of his B-movie rut. "We were trying to sell cotton hose in a silk stocking market," he commented later.[35] After the Universal series failed to catapult him higher, he got back to Republic to make more Westerns. Just as he came to the conclusion in *Idol of the Crowds*: "I guess I'm just a country boy after all."

"Pickings are plenty tough"

Two years after that batch of B-movies, Wayne had the success of *Stagecoach* under his belt when he returned to Universal. The studio used to have a complete Western set and Wayne had his longest screen fight there, in *The Spoilers*. Randolph Scott remembered the saloon brawl that made movie history: "We actually fought it out, for real on the set." Scott admitted that he did not particularly like Wayne in the beginning. Adding such feelings to Wayne's determination to make his action scenes authentic was like adding fuel to the flames. "The cameras, unfortunately, kept rolling and got every punch, show of blood and fall. Duke and I sustained injuries from the brawl, scars I still carry on me today. However, we eventually became good friends and today we're on the best of terms." Wayne suffered a broken nose and Scott a chipped hipbone.[36]

Wayne made *Pittsburgh* at Universal later in 1942. It then took him 25 years to do another picture for the company: *The War Wagon*. A few years back, visitors of the Universal Studio Tour got treated to a rare sight by the side of a tram tour road: one of the largest props ever built for a Wayne film, the War Wagon itself. Sad to say, because of exposure to the elements, the black paint on the plywood had faded away, and the top-gun turret was long gone. It was left to rot with other movie cars not used any more.

On the lower part of the Paramount Western Street, hometown of the Cartwrights, the *Donovan's Reef* saloon was built: Elizabeth Allen, Jack Warden, Jacqueline Malouf, Cesar Romero, Dorothy Lamour, and Jeffrey Byron witness John Wayne punching out a very cooperative Lee Marvin (author's collection).

"Imagine finding you here"

Up until about 1940, there had been rumors that Wayne was quite a ladies man, about brief affairs with Osa Massen, his accent coach in *The Long Voyage Home*, and with Sigrid Gurie, his *Three Faces West* co-star. "How could any woman not be charmed by John Wayne? It's impossible," Gurie once adoringly answered when a newspaper inquired about the depth of their feelings.[37] When asked about this period in

The tagline read, "When the War Wagon rolls, the screen explodes," but then the largest prop ever filmed for a John Wayne western just fell apart on the Universal lot (photo by Roland Schaefli).

his life, he once jokingly admitted that until he met Pilar, he thought it was obligatory to sleep with the leading lady. If the rumors were true, those were just flings. Yet the stormiest affair in his life would go on for three years and three films. Director Tay Garnett not only gave a detailed description of this fateful first meeting—he had actually set it up. Garnett wanted to cast Wayne opposite Dietrich in *Seven Sinners* but he needed her approval. Therefore, he had a lunch date at the Universal commissary with Marlene to let her see the guy he had in mind for the lead. "Dietrich, with that wonderful floating walk, passed Wayne as if he were invisible, then paused, made a half-turn and cased him from cowlick to cowboots. As she moved on, she said in her characteristic basso whisper, 'Daddy, buy me *that.*'"[38]

Their relationship got off like a fireworks display. According to a July 20, 1940, article in *Lights! Camera! Action!*, the producer toasted the beginning of the shooting with champagne. La Dietrich drained her glass and smashed it on the floor. Wayne followed suit. Very dramatic to everybody but the property man. One of the very few outdoor scenes was shot in Saugus, an area Wayne was familiar with: the **Saugus Airfield**, later known as Newhall Airport. On the Universal set, Wayne met Anna Lee for the first time. She would be his love interest in the upcoming *Flying Tigers* and become a fixture in the John Ford films. She had just come out of England when Wayne asked her, "Are you a Republican?" She had no idea what a Republican was and thought he said "publican," somebody who keeps a public house. So she answered, "No, I'm very fond of beer but I couldn't say I'm a publican."[39] Dietrich asked the producers to dye Anna Lee's hair jet-black—she didn't want any competition from other blondes.

The last day of shooting *Seven Sinners* was September 14. Yet that wasn't the last day of their love affair. Paul Fix summed it up: "Duke was caught up in this incredible love affair with Marlene who really beguiled him with her vast experience as a lover."[40]

"You'd look good to me, baby, in a burlap bag"

Dietrich held a special place in Wayne's heart for years after. When asked in 1976 in a TV interview by Phil Donahue what his most dangerous stunt was, Wayne smirked: "Talking back to Marlene Dietrich."[41] Even in his very last TV interview by Barbara Walters, shortly before he had to check into the hospital, Dietrich was the only name that came to his mind when asked about women he

The Universal picture was called *Seven Sinners* but actually, they were just two: According to the director, Marlene Dietrich looked at John Wayne as though he were a prime rib at Chasen's (author's collection).

came to like on his films. He mentioned that she slapped him good. The slapping Wayne kept referring to through the years happened on *The Spoilers*, their next Universal picture. The magazine *Lights! Camera! Action!* covered it in its January 31, 1942, issue: While rehearsing, Marlene pulled her punch, but in the take she really brought one up from the floor. Wayne's cheek was red from the blow as he left the room. Unfortunately, he jerked the door open so hard that it jammed on the thick rug. They had to re-do the scene. This one went well enough but director Ray Enright again ordered another take. "What was the matter with that one?" inquired the twice-slapped Wayne, and he was informed that he forgot to put his hat on when exiting. After the third shot, Marlene complained that the kiss he forced on her in the scene smeared her makeup. Normally, an actress' lips are powdered before the caress. But Wayne was a powerful kisser. Wayne most certainly wasn't blind to the fact that Dietrich had thrown her former lover, Richard Barthelmess, an acting job in *The Spoilers* while they were carrying on their own affair. Most biographers agree that it was over before they started the third Universal picture, *Pittsburgh*, released at the end of 1942.

"If you have to shoot, aim low"

Sexual encounters reportedly still happened years after the affair had ended. When asked about his single most exciting sexual episode in his life, he told his close friend Cecilia Presley, granddaughter of Cecil B. DeMille, "Rome. The Excelsior Hotel. Dietrich. I took her on the staircase."[42]

Pilar recounted how one day in 1954, Howard

Hughes offered to fly up to Vegas and catch Dietrich's new nightclub act. The minute she appeared on the stage of the Sahara, she threw Duke a suggestive kiss. "From then on, she played to him alone," Pilar noticed. When the house lights went on at the end of her act, Dietrich swayed to the edge of the stage and invited Wayne's party to her dressing room. He insisted on introducing Dietrich to his future wife. Dietrich looked at her former lover coldly, turned her back on them and began a lively conversation with Hughes. Pilar recalled, "Duke and I walked out unnoticed a few minutes later."[43]

Twenty years after the affair, the cast of *Donovan's Reef* was having lunch at a long table. Wayne took a look at Michelle Mazurki, who was working odd jobs on the set and told her father, character actor Mike Mazurki, "She looks like Marlene Dietrich." The girl was flattered since she knew that Wayne and La Dietrich had that thing many years before. She wrote the diva in New York and told her about Wayne's remark. Dietrich autographed her picture, "To Michelle, my lookalike."[44]

Somewhere along the road, Wayne must have aroused Dietrich's anger as she kept telling stories that put him in a bad light. As late as 1977, the old diva wasn't finished with him, lambasting him for doing the Datril 500 advertisements. "A he-man of the great outdoors on horseback with his hat and all the other trappings of a real cowboy on, praising the effect of a headache tablet. Too funny for words."[45]

Marlene's daughter Maria once asked Wayne over dinner in London how he had provoked the goddess. He just laughed it off. "Never liked being part of a stable."[46]

The set of *The Fighting Kentuckian* is dressed according to the period of 1812. Producer John Wayne seems content with the uncredited assistant director Lee Lukather, along with director George Waggner and director of photography Lee Garmes (from right) (author's collection).

10

Durango

South of the Border

"Let's go to Mexico."
—Lane (John Wayne) to his mercenaries
as they cross the border in *The Train Robbers*

Long before movie star John Wayne made pictures in Mexico, he had discovered the land south of the border as a private person. He had also fallen in love with Latin women. All three of his wives were of Spanish descent, his first being the daughter of a Panamanian diplomat, his third the daughter of a Peruvian senator. So his dialogue exchange with his leading lady in 1947's Tycoon had a ring of truth about it: "What's wrong with South America?" she asks, and Wayne, an engineer who loves working abroad, answers, "What's wrong with it? Nothing's wrong with it! Some of the nicest people I know come from South America!"

John Ford usually kept his yacht the *Araner* moored at the harbor in San Pedro. On summer days, he would sail to Catalina. In wintertime, he would bring her to Mexico with Wayne, Bond and Fonda, for some sport fishing but mostly for carousing. In 1938, Wayne hooked a marlin that

John Wayne was an admirer of the Mexican Carlos Arruza, one of the most prominent bullfighters of the 20th century. He was already retired when Wayne cast him as Santa Anna's messenger in his *Alamo* film (author's collection).

he remembered as "the biggest damn thing I've ever seen." Sweating mightily, he played it for over two hours, only to have it throw its hook just before coming to the gaff. Wayne was so disappointed that, according to Ford's grandson Dan in the biography *Pappy*, he sat panting and cursing for half an hour until a sudden rain squall came and cooled him off.

With the Gang in Mazatlan

At the mouth of the Gulf of California, **Mazatlan** was their favorite "liberty port": The gang would prowl through the bars barefoot, unshaven and dressed in khaki work clothes splattered with fish blood, sometimes accompanied by a mariachi band playing the director's favorite sentimental Mexican tunes. Fonda remembered a vacation they took right after *Fort Apache*. "We'd start at the Hotel Central, and then we'd pick up a three-piece mariachi band and got from bar to bar, saloon to saloon, whorehouse to whorehouse. You went to the whorehouses just to sit and drink and listen to the mariachis play. You didn't fuck. You didn't think you should. Those whores looked grungy." The hotel **Belmar** at Paseo Olas Altas 166 was one of the places where Wayne lodged. Today it's Mazatlan's oldest still-functioning hotel. Wayne said, "There was an ambiance about it."[1]

The master's ships' log for New Year's Eve 1934 reads: "1:18 p.m. Went ashore—got the owner, Fonda, Wayne, and Bond out of jail. Put up a bond for their behavior. 9:30 p.m. Got the owner, Fonda, Wayne, and Bond out of jail again. Invited by Mexican officials to leave town." The entry the following day: "Owner went to Mass—brought priest to *Araner*—purpose to sign pledge [to quit drinking]—celebrated signing of pledge with champagne, later augmented with brandy."[2]

A live snake played a big part in the adventures of the movie stars. No animal wrangler was involved. Dan Ford retold this story. Their favorite bar was in the Belmar Hotel ("or one of the local whorehouses," Ford added[3]), located on the beach. The owner had a pet boa constrictor. One night, Bond passed out early, as was his custom. Rude awakening: When he came to, he saw the snake on his lap, courtesy of Wayne. Bond popped up like a coiled spring and threw the snake back at Wayne. In his own memoir, Fonda wrote how Wayne played the same trick on him. (Fonda placed the incident in the Hotel Central. Maybe more than one Mazatlan hotel had pet snakes back then.)

Fonda and Wayne got drunk at the hotel bar. Fonda could not keep up with Wayne and passed out. Wayne tipped somebody to get the snake. "Now I opened my eyes and saw this damn snake glaring at me, and for some reason,

I'll never know why—probably I was anesthetized by the Mexican beer—I wasn't frightened." Fonda just called out, holding up the snake: "'Duke! Hey Duke! Look what I got!' Scared him to death."[4] Fonda repeated the story to Peter Bogdanovich: "I'm not afraid of snakes and Duke didn't know this." Then Fonda wanted to give the snake back to Wayne, who ran through the lobby clear outside. "You know those long legs of his. Four steps and he was out of the hotel."[5]

In Active Duty

Ford's yacht was the center of their activities. He had the roof of the *Araner*'s teakwood deckhouse raised so Wayne would stop bumping his head. Bond got married on the *Araner*.

Wayne was aboard on the most unusual cruise of the *Araner*. In the fall of 1939, they urgently set sail for Mexico. Europe was at war already. Ford was on a mission for a chief intelligence officer. The *Araner* made the usual stops in Magdalena Bay, Cabo San Lucas and Mazatlan. From there, the yacht motored up into the Gulf. They pulled into the harbor of Guaymas, at the northern end of the Gulf. Ford was supposed to make a detailed report on Japanese activity there. On December 16, they sighted a fleet of Japanese fishing trawlers. Ford was certain these vessels weren't fishing boats, but spy ships engaged in some sort of espionage activity. Ford and his pals also took a close look at the crews on liberty. "It is my belief that the crews and officers of this shrimp fleet belong to the Imperial Navy or Reserve," Ford wrote in his report to Naval intelligence.[6]

Meeting Chata in Mexico

In 1976, Wayne jokingly described his vacations in the South as his reasons for marrying only Spanish type women. "The only times when I didn't work, I headed south. So I've seen more of them and been in closer contact to them," he said with a wink on *The Phil Donahue Show.*

In August 1941, Wayne's business manager Bö Roos (Marlene Dietrich put them together) took a group of clients to Mexico City to examine an

In 1938, John Ford's Christmas card pictured the *Araner*. He sent his Christmas wishes out from onboard (author's collection).

independent film company he was thinking of buying: the **Churubusco Studios**. (Wayne shot many of his later Westerns there.) The group stayed at the exclusive **Del Prado Hotel**. During that trip, Wayne met the woman who became his second wife, Esperanza Baur, or Chata, as he nicknamed her. Ray Milland, his *Reap the Wild Wind* co-star, introduced Wayne to Chata at the **Reforma Hotel,** Avenue Paseo de la Reforma 64. The Reforma eventually became the favorite point for many personalities, including Orson Welles. It was the first hotel to open its own nightclub. Wayne and Chata danced there for the first time.

Back in Hollywood, at John Ford's house on Odin Street (across the street from the Hollywood Bowl), Wayne went down on his knees to declare his love to Chata. They were married in 1946 and were divorced by October 1953. At the divorce trial, she claimed that her husband had dragged her the full length of the corridor in the Del Prado. The hotel used to be located next to the Alameda Centro Park, near the historic district of Mexico City. It was destroyed in the 1985 earthquake. At the time of her death on March 10, 1961, Chata was back in Mexico City: She was found dead of a heart attack in a hotel room.

Despite the trouble with Montezuma's revenge, John Wayne shares a laugh with his contract player James Arness on the *Hondo* **set in Mexico (author's collection).**

Meeting Pilar in Peru

Wayne met his third wife in **Lima**, Peru, in 1951. He was on a working vacation, scouting locations for *The Alamo* and staying at the **Crillon Hotel**, Avenue Nicolás de Piérola 589. In the evenings, he could be spotted at the famous bar at the **Gran Hotel Bolívar**, at Jirón de la Unión 958. Hemingway loved the hotel's Pisco Sour, a typically South American cocktail. Wayne was invited to watch a Peruvian film crew shoot *Green Hell* in the South American jungle near **Tingo Maria**. The 22-year-old Pilar Palette was starring in it. When he arrived with his entourage, she was dancing barefoot by firelight, wearing a low-cut gypsy costume. It was like a meet-cute scene in a screenplay.

As she was introduced to the tall, imposing man, "all I could do was stare. He was the handsomest man I'd ever seen. I couldn't believe anyone's eyes could be so turquoise, so piercing." In her memoir *My Life with the Duke*, Pilar remembered that her head didn't even reach his shoulder. "That was quite a dance," he commented.[7] That evening, RKO gave a dinner party in his honor at the **Plaza Hotel**, Avenue Alameda Perú 588. At movie conventions later in life, Pilar would tell a story that still made her cringe: As she tried to make small talk with Wayne, she told him, "You were wonderful in *For Whom the Bell Tolls.*"

Bullfights and Tequila

In 1951, Wayne produced *Bullfighter and the Lady*, giving director Budd Boetticher his big break. They shot it in Mexico City's federal district and in a small settlement then called **Xayai**. Importantly, the John Wayne production got permission to shoot in the **Plaza de Toros México**, the world's largest bullring, then just four years old. Boetticher made good use of the statues (dedicated to bullfighting) lining the square at Augusto Rodin 130. Wayne was on the set just the first day of shooting, making suggestions. Boetticher told him to make up his mind about who was directing this picture. Wayne said to the crew, "One of us has to go home." He only returned on the day the shoot wrapped. Boetticher recalled that at the wrap party, Wayne got so drunk on his favorite tequila that he fell off a veranda into a bush.[8]

"A man oughta do what he thinks is best"

Now under his own Batjac flag, Wayne produced *Hondo* in **Camargo**, in the State of Chihuahua, between May and August 1953. He said about Camargo that it was "a one-horse border town."[9] With the divorce trial coming up, Chata was trying to collect evidence for infidelity. She even sent some detectives to Camargo to investigate his new love, Pilar.

Leo Gordon played the baddie and had instructions to take a taxi to the location once his plane arrived in Mexico. When he learned that the town was 110 miles from the airport, he figured they really didn't mean he should take a cab. So he rode the local bus with chickens and pigs. Everybody got quite a laugh out of that. The taxi fare would have been something like ten bucks.[10]

"Everybody gets dead"

The food in Camargo was bad, the water undrinkable. After a 14-hour working day in the hot sun, the crew of 130 would race to the run-down **Baca Motel** and hit the bar. They'd order anything just so the glass was full of ice. Most of the company got sick. Wayne had arranged for the crew to have distilled water to ward off dysentery. But James Arness, then under contract to Batjac, recalled that everyone came down with Montezuma's revenge after a few days. "I vividly remember being ill, but we had to keep working anyway. We'd be out in the blazing desert during a take on horseback, and the minute they'd say 'Cut!' we'd all jump off our horses, drop our pants, and hit it!"[11] Grudgingly, Wayne admitted, "I'm payin' five bucks a bottle for distilled water, and it's not doin' a damn bit of good." Chuck Roberson discovered the reason: The stuntman watched the deliverymen with their water-delivery truck pulling into a gas station where they filled empty bottles with a hose.[12]

Chuck Roberson rides his stunt horse Cocaine through the window in *The Train Robbers*. **He was Wayne's main stunt double but he also stunted for Clark Gable, Robert Mitchum and Gregory Peck (author's collection).**

"It didn't happen in the low way you heard it"

By the time of *Hondo*, "Bad Chuck" was Wayne's permanent double. One complicated stunt involved him in the same shot with Wayne. Roberson was to ride hell-for-leather down a gully where Wayne was waiting. Wayne was to come up shooting right after his stuntman made his horse fall *behind* Wayne; it would look as though it was one continuous motion. Roberson's falling horse Cocaine (who carried Roberson through glass windows in *Chisum* and *The Train Robbers*) knew the word *action* and took off like a torpedo.

Roberson cued Cocaine the instant he reached Wayne in the ravine. He described in his memoir how "the horse dropped on the spot, so close to Duke that I could see his spurs as he jumped out of the ditch, shooting up into the face of the camera." But the fall had been too close for Roberson to even raise his left stirrup to Cocaine's shoulder and out of the way of his crushing weight: "I felt my ankle bone crack as he came down on top of it." John Ford, a visitor to Wayne's set, noticed Roberson's limping. "Hurt your foot, Bad Chuck?" Roberson told him that it was "nothing a little ice won't take care of." Wayne slapped him on the back: "That horse of yours is really somethin'. One minute I think he's gonna run over the top of me, and the next minute, he's breathin' down my boots!" When a fellow stuntman offered to cut the boot off Roberson's swollen foot, he protested: "These are John Wayne's boots. I'll be damned if you're going

Shooting up the Camargo scenery with his trusty large loop Winchester as *Hondo*. Batjac had originally envisioned Glenn Ford in the title role (author's collection).

to cut them off of me." He never told anybody. For the next few weeks, he taped his boot-top around his ankle.[13]

"You smell all over like a woman"

In Wayne's later years, Andrew V. McLaglen would become his championed director, but he was still a production manager at the time of *Hondo*. He recalled one priceless moment from the shooting, at **Lake Tamargo**, below Chihuahua. "One day, it was raining like total hell. I was in having a Coca-Cola at the bar and Duke came in and said, 'Geez, I wonder where the company is.'" McLaglen had an idea what do to about it: "You know, the governor told us that we could always use his little yacht." He suggested they take it out on the lake and look for them. "That's a hell of an idea," Wayne said. So they went out on this "little, lousy boat" with two flashlights. Finally, on the shore in the distance, they saw campfires going. The whole crew was in a flooded area and couldn't get out. Wayne and McLaglen piled the whole

Five bucks for a bottle of distilled water and **"it's not doin' a damn bit of good"**: with Broadway actress Geraldine Page, Tom Irish and Ward Bond on the Mexican location of *Hondo* (author's collection).

company into the governor's boat. "And I swear, this boat was just one inch from being underwater." Wayne and McLaglen laughed about that experience for years afterward.[14]

Geraldine Page, fresh from Broadway, had the room adjoining Ward Bond's, and every night during the location, she could hear him, Wayne and the stuntmen drinking and playing cards until the wee hours. "All night long I had such a refresher course in all the foulest language … an endless stream of it … like rhythm, like music … on and on and on, it's fantastic."[15]

"That dog don't take to pettin', son"

In one of the back rooms of the Baca Motel took place what Wayne called "the longest damn poker game in history." It had been raining for several days. James Edward Grant had already rewritten a scene so that director John Farrow could continue shooting. But after a few days, most of the company holed up in that motel had nothing else to do than play poker. They started on Friday afternoon. Wayne had wandered in and out to watch yet did not join in until the second day. By then, "Bad" Chuck had broken everybody else, including Rudd Weatherwax. The animal trainer had wagered and lost the dog who portrayed Hondo's dog Sam in the picture. Wayne was the only one left with cash. He then ordered a bottle of his special bourbon. For the rest of the game, he made sure that Roberson's glass was never empty. After 24 hours without sleep, it didn't take the stuntman long to feel the booze clouding up his game. Wayne beat Roberson's full house with a straight flush. He had even bet the dog in the pot. Wayne let Rudd know that he now owed

Some costume pieces became icons in their own right: the battered hat, deerskin shirt and large loop Winchester from *Hondo* were some of the items gifted to USC (courtesy of the USC School of Cinematic Arts).

"that damn dog!" The story about that poker game has been told many times, often spreading the false report that Wayne had become the owner of the original Lassie. According to the Weatherfax family, the collies in *Hondo* (and also in the later Western *Big Jake*) were Lassie siblings—but not played by Lassie himself. Wayne gave the dog back, of course. Burt Kennedy even circulated the story that the dog was kidnapped in Camargo and they were forced to pay a lot of money to get him back from the Mexican dognappers.

Years after *Hondo*, only some ruins of the Baca Motel that used to stand in Camargo's Calle Abasolo were left standing as a reminder of the place where "the longest damn poker game in history" took place.

Fun in Acapulco

The **Las Hadas Hotel** on the Avenida Vista Hermosa in Manzanillo was another favorite stopping place in Mexico. Once Wayne and Pilar sat in an expansive restaurant at Chapultepec Park in Mexico City when the mariachi band

This French magazine published a John Wayne movie in the form of a photocomic, marketing it with Wayne in action as cavalry scout *Hondo* (author's collection).

recognized him and played the theme from *The High and the Mighty*. Wayne had been in and out of Mexican hotels so often that he decided he wanted to own one. Together with Johnny Weissmuller, another member of the Emerald Yachting Club, he became a part-owner of the **Hotel Los Flamingos** in Acapulco (see Chapter 19), another venture his business manager Bö Roos had set up for his clients.

Business in Panama

Wayne had business and personal ties in Panama for decades. His Panamanian connections went back to his first marriage. At one time, he considered shooting his *Alamo* picture in Panama. In 1959, he went into business with the sons of Harmodio Arias, the former Panamanian president. They invested in a shrimp boat business in Panama; Wayne put a half million into the venture. The Waynes were such close friends with the Ariases that they asked Tony Arias to be Aissa's godfather. Roberto Arias was later revealed to be the leader of a small band of rebels who tried an unsuccessful invasion coup. Panamanian officials cleared the Hollywood star: "Mr. Wayne was in no way connected with the attempts to overthrow the Government. His deals with Arias were strictly business."[16]

In 1978, Wayne went public about the ownership of the Panama Canal and helped lobbying Republican Senators to ratify the Treaties (favored by President Jimmy Carter and opposed by Ronald Reagan). When the leader of Panama, General Omar Torrijos, invited a Senate delegation to **Contadora Island**, where the treaties had been negotiated, Torrijos announced there would be a special guest, someone well-known to the American delegation. Sure enough, that guest was Wayne. He went out of his way to say how much he disagreed with Reagan's views about the issue.

Waiting for his cue to jump into action in *The Train Robbers*, on the sand dunes of Torreón (author's collection).

In the *Washington Post* on June 17, 1979, days after Wayne's passing, Torrijos said how the opinion leader had made up his mind about the Canal. Wayne had met with Torrijos at **Rio Hato**, a former U.S. military base. Wayne talked with U.S. soldiers who were on maneuvers with forces of the Panamese National Guard. These soldiers "who in the last analysis are the ones who risk their lives for our country's political mistakes, have told me that the only way to keep the canal open is to reach a just accord between Panama and the United States. I believe them, not the politicians who would sell their own mothers to be reelected."

On October 10, 1977, Wayne wrote a letter to the U.S. Senate in support of the treaty: "I support it based on my belief that America looks always to the future and that our people have demonstrated qualities of justice and reason for 200 years. That attitude has made our country a great nation." In his closing remarks, he said that the new treaty modernizes an outmoded relation "with a friendly and hospitable country." Wayne pointed out that the treaty also solved an international question "with our other Latin American neighbors."[17] On May 11, 1979, just days before his death, the government of Panama accorded Wayne their highest civilian honor, the Order of Vasco Núñez de Balboa in recognition of his support.

"Something I gotta do myself"

In 1965, Wayne made the city of **Durango** in the Valley of Guadiana in northern Mexico his base of operations for a number of Westerns to come. Then the first one they intended to make, *The Sons of Katie Elder*, got delayed. A week before they were to leave for Mexico, Wayne invited producer Hal B. Wallis to his office on the Paramount lot. He had already called in director Henry Hathaway, and Wayne's son Michael was also present. Wayne indicated that Wallis should sit down and said, "Well, Hal, I'm going to hit you with it. I've got the big C." Wallis remembered being too shocked to speak. All he could say was something practical like, "Are you going to have cobalt treatments?" Wayne's replay was decisive: "No. None of that stuff. I'm going to have the lung removed. I'm checking in for surgery tomorrow morning." He said it matter-of-factly. It was typical of him, Wallis wrote in his memoir *Starmaker*, "to be more concerned with the schedule than with his own health." Wayne added, "The doctors tell me it may be six weeks." Wallis postponed the picture, ready to wait as long as it took. Some time later, Wayne was ready—against the advice of his doctors and his wife. He shook Wallis' hand in his giant fist and said, "Let's go to work."[18] On January 4, 1965, he got up from his hospital bed and left for Durango.

"You fight us every step of the way"

The Sons of Katie Elder was in production from January 5 to March 5, 1965. Fourteen weeks after two major operations, Wayne was back in the saddle in a "ridin', fightin', jumpin' picture," as he called it when he announced to the press that he had beaten cancer. However, a portable inhalator (for a "lift" with some pure oxygen) was always at hand. From then on, he kept supplies of bottled oxygen on his locations.

In addition to its elevation, Durango was not an easy location. Aissa Wayne remembered it as a town of dirt streets with no names, one horseshoe-shaped motel "and one hole in the wall that everyone called a diner."[19] Batjac production manager George Colman had to deal with a granary near Durango which was infested with rats. He couldn't get the poison that was fatal to these huge Mexican rats, so he ordered every member of the company coming down to fill one suitcase with American rat poison.

Burt Kennedy would direct Wayne in two Durango Westerns. He remembered one night at the **Campo Mexico Courts Hotel** at Avenida 20 de Noviembre: "Duke's asleep in the next room. Here's a guy with a million-dollar boat docked at Mazatlan, a million-dollar plane in the air flying back to L.A., a million-dollar home in Newport Beach, number-one box office in the world, and he's asleep in a lonely, flea-bitten motel room in Durango, Mexico. Beats the hell outta me."[20]

It seems only Wayne defended the cactus-studded grazing land of Pancho Villa country for what it was: "Durango isn't phony," he once said. "It's one place that is still pretty much untouched. The country there gives you the feeling that it must have been the same many years ago when the kind of action you see in Westerns today was a reality."[21]

Sometimes it got so cold on the *Katie Elder* set that Hathaway postponed exteriors and finally shot them inside the **Estudio Churubusco**, the studios in Mexico City (still in operation, on the Ciudad de México). Wayne, the 20-inch scar still throbbing around his chest wall where doctors had removed one lung, never complained, but he growled like "a big, old bear with a thorn in his paw," Roberson remembered. The stuntman offered to double him in the icy waters of the Rio Chico, but Hathaway insisted Wayne do it himself, following his strategy of not pampering Wayne so he would not start to feel like an invalid. Wayne pulled through that tough day himself (although he later confessed to Pilar that the water was far colder than he had anticipated).

They used the river near the triple waterfall **Cascada El Saltito**, reached on Route 45 to the east of Durango, a location they used in almost all the subsequent Mexico Westerns. The area's monumental trees, the large-sized Montezuma cypress, added their beauty to these scenes. However, on that particular day, Wayne did not have a chance to admire nature. He blacked out when he was dragged into the icy mountain stream, but he quickly came to. The set was thronged with media. Now the paparazzi would get what they had been waiting for. They described the star as ashen, shivering violently, struggling for breath as he staggered out of the water. The photographers reached his side before anyone could interfere. Someone ran up with Wayne's oxygen, clamped the mask on his face, and the crisis passed. When a reporter snapped a picture of him taking a whiff of oxygen, Wayne scared the hell out of him; the reporter tore out the film and threw it on the ground. But photographs of the incident did survive and were published.

Hathaway was a tough taskmaster by all accounts. Supporting player Dennis Hopper called him "the meanest man on the set and the nicest man to have dinner with."[22] Karl Malden simply called him "Screaming Henry."[23] Wayne called him "the most irascible, most talented, most fascinated bastard" to his face,[24] at Hathaway's 80th birthday party at the Bel-Air Country Club. After Hathaway had chased him into the cold water, he confessed to the director: "I thought I was gonna die in that water, but I didn't. Now I know I can do anything."[25]

Hal Wallis remembered a similar incident on the *Rooster Cogburn* location, ten years later. They were shooting the river scenes at Grants Pass, Oregon, in perfect weather. Wayne was able to pull through with few indications of the fact that he was relying on one lung. Then during the wrap party, a night when bitter cold and high altitude finally got to him, he started wheezing and gasped, "I can't breathe." Wallis recalled, "We rushed oxygen to him and he rallied, but I realized for the first time the strain under which he had been working." In his biography, Kirk Douglas recalled when he and Wayne flew down to Mexico to do *The War Wagon*: Wayne suddenly experienced difficulty breathing and they had to put an oxygen mask on him.

"This is no time for lying"

According to the Durango state tourism department, **Chupaderos**, a dust-blown village on Mexico's central plateau, has lured nearly 50 American film crews south of the border. The *Katie Elder* production started that tradition when the chalky streets portrayed the town of Sweetwater. Pretty soon, as many as three movies a year were being shot in the western town. Of course, U.S. producers were also interested in the non-union workforce eager to work as extras. Townsman Domingo Flores recalled, "John Wayne would walk around our streets, greeting people, speaking very bad Spanish."[26]

Dean Martin kept everybody well supplied with food. He had ordered his steaks flown down from the Sands in Las Vegas; but then the manager of Mexico City's **Hotel Bamer**, at Avenida Juárez 52, refused to let him set up a brick barbecue in his room. Hence, his mother, a real Italian momma, shipped homemade food to Durango by air two or three times a week. Martin had her send Pilar the recipe for her pasta fasul (Pilar reprinted it in her own cookbook). Martin became very friendly with the Waynes. One morning, he came on the set without his spurs, causing the youngest Wayne, Ethan, to announce seriously, "You forgot your propellers!"[27]

Production hit a long spell of heavy rain. "For days we went to the set and got nada," George Kennedy remembered. Insurance still required they made the 50-minute drive over mostly unpaved roads and wait until three p.m. for it to clear. It didn't. When Kennedy sat in a small portable dressing room, he heard a repeated whup sound. "There was Dean Martin in a poncho, swinging a seven-iron at manure. 'I'm not getting the distance I got last year with my horseshit.'"[28]

Actually, Martin was glad Wayne talked him into coming to Durango. On his first Sunday there, Martin got his first-ever hole-in-one on the Durango Country Clubs nine-hole golf

Disregarding all advice even from the stuntmen, John Wayne dove into the icy El Saltito mountain stream, together with his movie brothers Michael Anderson, Jr., Earl Holliman, and Dean Martin. This lobby card uses a shot not used in the film and was made for double use in France and Germany (author's collection).

Homemade food from his Italian momma: Pot gazers Dean Martin and John Wayne (author's collection).

course. It happened on the 140-yard seventh hole with the actor using an eight-iron.

Hathaway was especially pleased with the performance of novice actor Michael Anderson, who played the youngest of Wayne's brothers. The director ordered him his own chair, with "Big Mike" tooled on the back, and gave him a big hug. "You see that?" Anderson asked Wayne. Wayne gave him the smile, the nod, the final accolade: "I saw it, kid."[29]

On April 21, 1965, *Variety* revealed that United Artists intended to reuse Paramount's Durango sets for a production titled *29 to Duel*, but plans were canceled when area villagers looted the property.

"Fighting for a wagon full of gold"

Wayne was back in Durango and Mexico City the next year, shooting *The War Wagon* from September 15 to December 1966. In just six weeks, the art director Alfred Sweeney had enlarged the Chupaderos location by another 20 buildings. Some of the houses featured detailed interiors so they could photograph people coming in and out. The *Los Angeles Times* reported on October 9 that the construction of the new western town in Durango was finished. The following day, *Variety* revealed that the $100,000 set would be preserved as a movie museum designed to attract tourists and other American and Mexican movie companies. (That didn't happen.)

They again stayed at the Campo Mexico Courts Motel. When the Durango locals recreated Grauman's on the motel porch, Wayne put his fist in the wet cement. His cabin was next to director Burt Kennedy's. On Cinco de Mayo, the Mexican Independence day, Gene Evans showed Kennedy an antique, double-barrel, 12-gauge shotgun he had bought. At that moment, the Mexicans shot off firecrackers. Kennedy recollected that Wayne woke up and came crashing out of his cabin. "The first thing he saw was me standing there holding the shotgun." Wayne chewed Kennedy out for "shooting that goddamn shotgun" when he was trying to sleep! For years after that, when he'd see Kennedy, Wayne would say, "You're the guy who shoots shotguns while I'm trying to sleep!"[30]

"Mine was bigger"

Wayne and his *War Wagon* co-star Kirk Douglas had been up against each other in the Oscar race of 1949, his Sergeant Stryker vs. Kirk's boxer in *Champion*. When Douglas arrived on the *War Wagon* set in his gunfighter outfit, he wore a black glove with a ring over one finger, because his character was kind of a show-off. The *American Film Magazine* reported Wayne's reaction: "You gonna play in that effete style?" To which Douglas replied, "John, I'll try not to let the homosexuality come through."

In his memoir *Hollywood Trail Boss*, Burt Kennedy had one thing to add to the infamous ring affair: Wayne had threatened he'd walk off the picture "if you don't get that

"All men are fighting for a wagon full of gold": *The War Wagon* **gets into Chupaderos, the town that had been Sweetwater in the** *Katie Elder* **film the year before (author's collection).**

faggot ring off that sonofabitch." So when the director found himself in the crossfire of the stars, he asked Douglas, "Don't you think the ring is a little much, Kirk?" Douglas gave him that familiar grin and answered, "No, I think it's just fine." Then, holding the ring up to Wayne: "What do you think?" Wayne, according to Kennedy, didn't even bat an eye. "It's great, just great." Kennedy complained that this was not the first time Wayne put him out on a limb and cut it off.[31]

Kennedy sometimes seemed to forget that it was Wayne who gave him his first writing gig, buying and producing his script *Seven Men from Now*. Wayne made no secret what he thought about Kennedy's talent as a screenwriter: "Burt Kennedy writes Broadway in Arizona."

"You caused me a lot of embarrassment"

Kennedy had noticed the **Sierra de Órganos National Park** in the 1955 Clark Gable Western *The Tall Men*: its director Raoul Walsh had shot an elaborate cattle stampede in that valley. The Los Organos park is located

After Hal Needham changed horses, the revenge-seeking Taw Jackson safely arrives in Chupaderos, the dust-blown village on Mexico's central plateau, to hold up *The War Wagon* (author's collection).

in the northwest corner of Sombrerete. So Kennedy drove Wayne all the way in a car—about 85 miles from Durango—to look at it. When you come upon Los Organos, you come around a corner to a panoramic view of all those towering rock formations, looking like organs. Wayne gasped, "Oh, my God! We've gotta shoot here!"[32] That's how it came to be they built an airport, got themselves a C-47 and flew the crew up from Durango.

When a scene was halted midway because the sound engineer heard a dog barking in the distance, Wayne let him know: "Dogs bark all over the world, and they barked the same in 1870 as they do today."[33]

While Wayne didn't let a dog stop the production, a horse almost did. Wayne saw stuntman Hal Needham exercising with his horse Hondo and suggested that he'd ride that one in the next scene where he simply had to come into town. Needham handed him the reins and Wayne mounted. So far so good. But as Wayne was riding around getting a feel for Hondo, Pilar appeared on the set. Needham remembered the shock of the next moment for a long time: "Duke made a move with his right hand to wave at his wife." The trouble was that Needham's cue for the trained stunt horse to fall was to grab the right rein and pull it back. When Hondo saw Wayne's hand move, he started down. A split second later, Wayne and Hondo were on the ground. He wasn't hurt, but he changed his mind about riding Hondo, whispering to Needham, "That horse is a danger to mankind."[34]

Burt Kennedy is directing Kirk Douglas in *The War Wagon*— or is it the other way around? John Wayne just noticed the ring over Kirk's glove (author's collection).

Supporting actor Keenan Wynn whispered a secret to the writers of the pressbook about the hat he wore in the picture. When MGM first tested Wynn in 1942, the studio wardrobe department assigned him the hat. Wynn never returned the topper. It was Leslie Howard's cavalry hat from *Gone with the Wind*, and Wynn decided it was a collector's item.

"Windage and elevation"

Wayne was back in action in Mexico for *The Undefeated*, shot between February 4 and mid–May 1969. To people who asked director Andrew V. McLaglen why he loved going to "this horrible hole" (Durango) with Wayne, he answered, "There are some beautiful houses where we always live when we got there. In the evenings we eat something of a specialty ... a little suckling goat roasted over a spit that they butterfly, and with it, you drink a little tequila to keep you relaxed."[35] Almost out of tradition, they went to the Campo Mexico Courts again. Supporting actor Robert Donner (Milt in *El Dorado*) told Wayne historian Tim Lilley how actress Marion Moses found a mouse in her room and ran to the hotel manager, crying, "I found a mouse in my room." The manager just looked up and said, "I'll get you a cat."[36]

Hal Needham was made stunt coordinator and put in charge of the biggest herd of horses ever filmed—the 2500 head that Wayne's character would stampede to run the French troops over. The wranglers kept asking Needham how he was going to pull this one off.

The cocky young stunt director had diamond-shaped wooden fences built as safety zones. The diamonds would divert the stampeding herd around the stuntmen. Each diamond safety zone would be a hundred feet long. The fence would need to be lower than the height of the backs of the horses so the fence would disappear from camera view. This would make the men appear as though they were doing battle in the middle of the stampede. They looked as if they were falling under the running horses where they were really falling safely in the "diamonds." Pretty clever, but he still managed to lose 60 horses. "Those damn horses took off like goats," said William Clothier. "We had horses all over Mexico."[37]

"Conversation kinda dried up"

After Durango and Los Organos, the production moved on to Louisiana. At the **1600 Acre Plantation**, Rock Hudson was supposed to set fire to the plantation set in Baton Rouge. The prop man had forgotten to put out the sprinklers, so the system went off.

According to Pilar, Wayne and Hudson got along fine. "What Rock Hudson does," Wayne told his wife when they discussed Hudson's sexual preferences, "in the privacy of his room is his own business. He's a professional on the set and a real gentleman—and he plays a hell of a hand of bridge."[38]

"Trouble? Well, let's see..."

In April 1969, McLaglen was shooting the pre-credits sequence in Baton Rouge (Wayne's cavalry attacking the last Confederate position) when the star's saddle cinch slipped and his stirrup came loose. "I twisted around in the saddle," Wayne recounted, "and the damn stirrup was completely loose. I fell right under that dog-damned horse; I'm lucky I didn't kill myself."[39]

Daily Variety noted on April 21 that although the star was rushed to the hospital, he reportedly returned to the set the same day and continued acting. The fall had dislocated his right shoulder. During his stay in Mexico, he had already broken two ribs. When old man Ford heard about this, he sent his protégé a telegram: "Dear Duke, what's new?"[40] This injury is sometimes mixed up

Andrew V. McLaglen (wearing sweater) directs John Wayne and Rock Hudson on the Los Organos set in *The Undefeated*, while unidentified crewmembers take care of the horses (author's collection).

The Undefeated set a record: 2,500 head was the biggest herd of horses ever filmed. With Rock Hudson and Tony Aguilar (back to camera) (author's collection).

with the Baton Rouge stirrup accident. However, the rib fracture had happened a few days prior to the start of filming. Wayne fell in a restaurant in Guaymas, Mexico, as reported in *Daily Variety* on February 5, 1969. The actor went home to recuperate, and he was due to return to the set on February 17. Wayne ultimately admitted that he had been drinking before the fall. Yet it certainly seemed the movie was jinxed.

Back in 1965, Wayne had complained to a *Life* reporter on location in Durango that the only really painful part after the cancer operation was getting onto a horse: "Using my left arm and leg put pressure on the area and it hurt like hell. I mounted like a cheechako [tenderfoot]."[41]

Two years after the *Undefeated* accident, he told *Playboy*, "What the hell, in my racket I've fallen off a lot of horses. I don't have good use of one arm anymore and it makes me look like an idiot when I'm getting on a horse."

Principal photography was completed by early May 1969. The final cost was cited as $7 million. The price of shooting in Durango had not been as low as initially expected, as was noted in *Variety* on May 14. Local vendors reportedly overcharged for food, housing and other services. Angered by the price gouging, Wayne allegedly threatened never to shoot in the city again. By August 26, the governor

of Durango had personally promised the overcharging would not be repeated.

"I don't have to be neighborly"

"There was land for the taking. And the keeping. No place on God's earth more beautiful," rancher Chisum proudly tells his niece. Wayne and McLaglen did decide to return to Durango for *Chisum*, in production between October 6 and mid–December 1969. In September, Batjac's executive producer Michael Wayne had laid the cornerstone of a new $1.6 million filming complex, financed by the state of Durango, where production was set to take place. Thirty-five miles from Durango, a complete ranch complex was erected on the grounds of the **Rancho Marley.** They even planted the single tree where Chisum surveys his cattle empire. (The same spread, sometimes just called the Durango Ranch, also became "the great McCandles ranch" in *Big Jake*.)

This time, Batjac had to build its own western town near Durango because they would pretty much destroy it in the final shoot-out. McLaglen had a cattle stampede rolling through Main Street, the beasts ripping the sidewalks. He said, "We didn't have to rig a lot for that—they just did it!"[42] If anybody had wanted to use the set after that, they would have found almost none of the buildings undamaged.

"You're going to shoot us, ain't you, Chisum?"

Geoffrey Deuel was introduced to movie audiences in the part of Billy the Kid. The newcomer took the acting business very seriously. But when he discussed his motivation for a scene for five minutes with the director, Wayne finally had to chime in, "Motivation? Mo–ti–va–tion, huh? Well, you're getting paid, goddammit, that's your motivation! Say the line!"[43]

Christopher Mitchum got his first acting break as one of Billy's companions. "I don't think I ever went to sleep without hearing gunfire at night," he remembered about Durango. Pancho Villa's son, Jose Trinidad Villa Casas, was a pistolero who stayed with the young cast members all the time to make sure they were safe. Almost everybody in town carried a gun.[44]

In the fight to the death between Chisum and his adversary, Chuck Roberson doubled for Wayne and Jim Burk took over for Forrest Tucker. McLaglen (who was once described as "one of the greatest sadists in the history of the motion picture industry") didn't make it easy for the doubles to fall off the balcony. "He made a big point of me having to land on my back on a pair of steer's horns," recalled Burk. "I had to come off the balcony backwards, counting on Chuck to help me because he could see the horns." Just as they were ready to go, McLaglen mentioned to Burk, "You don't mind, do you?" and pointed to a real set of horns which he had put on the catcher. Burk told him he got the wrong man. "The horns are rubber, or I don't go!"[45]

"Splatter gun's useless"

In 1970, Howard Hawks ordered production manager Paul Helmick to find him a Civil War–era steam train and period railway station, a location with railroad tracks that ran through a forest of trees. And, of course, Hawks wanted complete control for this action sequence that would start off *Rio Lobo*. Some assignment! Helmick headed for Mexico, the land where the expression "no problem" originated. He found the railroad locations a short distance from **Cuernavaca**. Regular trains used the line twice a day so they would have to clear the tracks for them. *Rio Lobo* went into production on March 16.

Yakima Canutt was put in charge of that logistically challenging sequence. A quarter of a century had passed since Yak had last worked with Wayne. In the meantime, he had become a celebrated second unit director, responsible for the chariot race in *Ben-Hur* and exciting action sequences in the epics *El Cid* and *Spartacus*. He brought with him his sons Joe and Tap, both expert stuntmen in their own right. They did the falls of the Union soldiers from the train. Yak

found a nice sandy embankment where they could get some good jumps of the Yanks when they had to jump off the car because of a swarm of hornets (drones with no stingers). He had special effects trim an old, dead tree snag so that his son could break it up when he hit it falling down. But when Canutt rolled the cameras and Tap hit the tree, it didn't break. "He glanced off and did a fast roll," Canutt recorded in his memoir. "He was jarred up a bit."[46]

When the train hit the ropes, which were tied to the trees, it was something to watch—trees falling in all directions and being dragged. Still, Canutt asked Hawks for a second try because the brakeman brought the cars to a stop too early. The next day, Canutt had the crew dig all around a big tree, exposing the roots, and cut the center root nearly through. Then all the dirt was shoveled back. He put the camera near this tree so he could pan with the oncoming cars and get on film how the huge tree was actually pulled out. Hawks admitted that Yak was right on that retake.

"I've been called a lot of things"

On March 26, while shooting was underway in Cuernavaca, an accident took place. Hawks had directed a railroad scene from the back of a speeding train. When an engineer had to stop abruptly to avoid an automobile crossing the tracks, the 73-year-old director was thrown against the camera platform, suffering a deep gash in his leg that required stitches. He was treated at nearby Social Security Hospital.

During his stay in Cuernavaca, Wayne learned about an American priest who ran the "Our Little Brothers and Sisters orphanage. Wayne "adopted" all 1040 of the orphans, becoming one of their principal benefactors. (Footage of a visit was presented in the Raquel Welch TV special *Raquel!*) Wayne then arranged a *True Grit* premiere in Cuernavaca as a benefit for the orphanage. On this occasion, the youngsters gave him a trophy they themselves had won as soccer champions.

"I thought you was dead"

Wayne was back in Durango the same year. *Big Jake*, in production from October through December 1970, brought him to the top of

The western town built near Durango for *Chisum* was destroyed in the final shoot-out. That's stuntman Jim Burk in the long shot, impaled by rubber horns, while Wayne is helped up by his foreman Ben Johnson (author's collection).

the list of box office attractions for the fourth time in his career. Harry Carey, Jr., played a desperado older than his actual years. For this unusual casting, they darkened his beard and added a lot of dirt. He was chewing tobacco and the juice was running down the side of his mouth. So Carey hoped Wayne would say something like, "You look really tough." Instead, his comment was, "You look like the Cowardly Lion!"[47] Carey and the other bandits of Richard Boone's gang go down in a furious firefight, filmed in the famous arched courtyard of **Don Luis Flores** in Durango, one of the remnants of the old Mexico. Pancho Villa and his men had slaughtered 750 persons in it.

"Something to do!"

Burt Kennedy had picked Torreón, three hours outside Durango, for the desert locations of *The Train Robbers*, filmed between March 23 and mid–June 1972. It was art director Alfred Sweeney's idea to put an abandoned train on the sand dunes. "That was all built and put in there," Kennedy recalled, "that's a wonderful location, too. It was terrible to work in, but great on the screen."[48] The fictional settlement of Liberty was built north of Durango.

Big Jake **arrives with his sons, Patrick Wayne and Chris Mitchum, at the arched courtyard of Don Luis Flores in Durango, followed by stalwart Bruce Cabot (author's collection).**

The town that was subsequently destroyed to film the story's climax cost $100,000 to construct. Once more, the film used the triple El Saltito waterfall east of Durango, in the municipality of Sombrerete.

One Sunday evening in May, Wayne's publicist Jim Henaghan was on hand as Wayne, Rod Taylor, Christopher George and Bobby Vinton went out to a Greek restaurant in **Torreón**, after a week of outdoor shooting. Wayne had some martinis, then hot shrimps, a big steak and a bottle of wine, and then settled down to some serious brandy drinking. One by one, the others dropped out, leaving only Rod Taylor. The Australian of stout physique finally had to give in even though he was 20 years younger. In the early morning, they all staggered happily back to the Torreón **Hotel Rio Nazas**, Avenida Morelos 732.

For *The Train Robbers*, **the art director put an abandoned train on the sand dunes at Torreón (author's collection).**

"Any of you want to surrender?"

Up until November 1972, if you drove north out of Durango, you would pass a sign about 20 miles along the way reading **La Joya.** This road would lead you to an assortment of burros, cattle and horses in the high desert hills covered by cactus, scrub oak, mesquite and sagebrush. Then Batjac moved in and built a Western street for *Cahill, U.S. Marshal.* From sketches drawn by art director Walter M. Simonds (responsible for the *Green Berets* Vietnam sets), 250 artisans worked for 26 weeks building the period western town that would portray Fort Davis, Texas. Batjac spent over $500,000 to convert the little Mexican town of La Joya into a western town and make the houses look a century old. "Not a big town," director Andrew McLaglen said, "kind of sparse but actually that what was called for."[49]

Cahill was in production from November 13, 1972, to January 1973. McLaglen took pride in the short pre-production time and his way of shooting fast. (Wayne later remarked that the film needed a little better care in making.) McLaglen was able to cut costs by setting up soundstages in Durango. For the magnificent pre-title sequence—Cahill (Wayne) confronting a bunch of bad guys at night—McLaglen had a large warehouse in Durango dressed up like a snow-covered landscape.

"Yes sir, you got style!"

Cahill, U.S. Marshal featured Marie Windsor in her third Wayne picture (after *The Fighting Kentuckian* and *Trouble Along the Way*), but her first in Durango: "You just couldn't find a good restaurant in Durango, it was awful." The actress didn't feel comfortable with the Mexican eating habits. "One of the things that would turn your stomach is that they always had a lamb tied up at a stake that you could see out

Back at the Sierra de Órganos National Park for more action: John Wayne leads his gang of mercenaries deep into Mexico in *The Train Robbers* (author's collection).

Efficient movie making: For the cool pre-title sequence of *Cahill, U.S. Marshal,* they didn't go back to the studio nor did they actually have to shoot in the snow: a large warehouse in Durango was dressed to look like a snow-covered landscape (author's collection).

of the dining room window which they were keeping to kill for the next people who wanted to eat. So, if the lamb was gone, you knew you were going to get lamb that day."[50]

George Kennedy played the meaty part of the main heavy but had to wait several weeks after he was sent the script until he was called into the office to read for the part. By that point, he "was boiling mad because I was sure they had signed someone else." There was a lot of anger in his reading and he got the part. The Batjac people told him afterward that they had never seen such a convincing display of anger and hate.

The *Cahill* world premiere was held in Seattle, during the making of *McQ*, on June 14, 1973. Protesters appeared at the opening, calling the film unfair to Native Americans (even though the only Native American portrayed in it was Neville Brand's likable tracker).

Cahill was Wayne's final Mexico movie. But his love for Mexico never faded. When he was laid to rest in his unmarked grave, he faced south. He had long before mentioned that he would like his memorial stone to have a Spanish inscription, *Feo Fuerte y Formal*: He was ugly, he was strong, he had dignity.

Marie Windsor didn't care much for what they served in La Joya. In *Cahill, U.S. Marshal*, Gary Grimes and Clay O'Brien (left) play Wayne's sons; the latter had been the pint-sized kid in *The Cowboys* and went on to become a multiple Rodeo world champion (author's collection).

11

Exotic Places

East of the Divide

"The bleeding heart of China. You can pin one on me, Baby."
—Captain Tom Wilder (John Wayne) to his invisible companion
in *Blood Alley*

"Having traveled extensively throughout the world," Wayne wrote in the companion book to America, Why I Love Her,
*"those travels only increased my love for the United States."1 However, audiences around the world loved the American
actor. In 1955, fans in more than 50 nations had selected him for a Henrietta award as the most popular international
star. It seemed reasonable enough when John Huston announced that he wanted to send this symbol of the west to the east:
"Who better to symbolize the big awkward United States of 100 years ago?"2*

Blood Alley was a Cold War statement, with Wayne's ferryboat captain transporting the people of the Chinese village of Chiku Shan out of Red China to the British port of Hong Kong. The Batjac production never left American soil. They found their China in Northern California.

"If you want to take a last look at home…"

On the north coast of San Francisco Bay, you will find San Rafael. **China Camp**, on the shore of San Pablo Bay, is now a state park, surrounding the historic Chinese American

Well-acquainted with international colleagues: the renowned Swiss character actor Michel Simon greets Wayne in Paris (author's collection).

shrimp-fishing village and a salt marsh. The village at 100 China Camp Village Road looks pretty much the way director William "Wild Bill" Wellman left it after he spun the adventure yarn from January to March 15, 1955. Chinese immigrants had developed the village. The first people there harvested the abundant shellfish. The remaining buildings are the last evidence of an important era in California history. "Those of you who live up near San Francisco Bay will recognize the scenery," Wayne revealed when he plugged his movie on the telecast *Warner Bros. Presents*. "Only now our art department has been at work. We built that Chinese wall atop the hill, we moved out the commercial fishing boats and moved in sampans. I think we disguised this bit of California so that even the Chinese would say: Darn clever, those Americans."

The art department also fabricated the shell of a large castle on the hillside above the village (all scenes inside the castle were photographed on the Warner Brothers stages). Building the outdoor sets amounted to an expenditure of $220,000. During filming at China Camp, Wayne strained his back and was hospitalized at **Marin General Hospital**, 3950 Civic Center Drive, San Rafael.

"300 miles down Blood Alley?"

Rat Rock, a distinctive reef at China Camp, has a prominent function in the plot: It serves as a point where the villagers lay a trap for the Communist patrol boat (actually a rescue boat on loan to the film company by the Air Force). Stockton's California Delta played the choppy waters of the Formosa Strait. Wayne was familiar with the area since he had been on location in San Joaquin Valley for *Dakota* ten years before.

For the ship graveyard, they used a real wreck on the mudflats of Richmond, the marina of **Point San Pablo** at Stenmark Drive. The crew was largely based in San Pablo Harbor. The stars stayed at the **Hotel Stockton** at 133 East Weber Avenue in Stockton. Opened in 1910, the grand building had been popular with entertainers. Locals remember that Wayne signed autographs until there weren't any more to sign. The actors would sometimes frequent the popular Stockton bar Chet's (now **Growers Hall** at 122 North Wilson Way).

Wayne put his discovery Anita Ekberg, Miss Sweden of 1950, in the movie. *Blood Alley* won her the Golden Globe for Most Promising Newcomer. Lauren Bacall found her leading man "to my surprise warm, likable and helpful."[3] On the final night of shooting the interior scenes in Hollywood, Wayne brought Bacall home after a few drinks and he had gotten somewhat drunk. Her husband Humphrey Bogart was waiting and Wayne was noticeably awkward around him. Bacall called the moment "ridiculous."[4]

The principal location of *Blood Alley*: China Camp, north of San Francisco, with its historic Chinese American shrimp-fishing village (photo courtesy of Friends of China Camp).

"We're coming into Hong Kong"

Wayne's skipper steers a 100-foot long, three-stories-tall ferryboat down the 300-mile route to "Hongkong" (actually, not a very convincing miniature, shot on the Warner stage). The vessel used for outdoor filming was real enough. The *Putah* was originally created as a snag boat. The Berkeley Steel Construction Company built it in 1952 for the U.S. Army Corps of Engineers. Its purpose was to remove obstructions so that other boats could safely pass through. Batjac purchased it from war surplus and gave it a makeover. A superstructure was added, disguising the diesel engine and making it appear to be a wood burner. It cost $200,000 to convert the *Putah* into the movie's *Chiku Shan*.

"Nobody's leaving this ship"

After its starring role, the boat was sold to a Sacramento businessman who renamed it the *Mansion Belle*, cruising it up and down the Delta River. In August 1957, the boat apparently rammed into a cottage and lost ten blades from the stern wheel. The dinner cruises continued for several more years. In 1991, the boat was sold once more and renamed the *Spirit of Sacramento*. It was then docked at the Old Sacramento Waterfront. The sightseeing ventures stopped on February 3, 1996, when the boat was damaged by fire. Even though it was almost completely reduced to ruins, the boat found a new owner with intentions of restoring and even christening it *The Duke*. It was then sometimes

The Chinese vessel runs aground at the China Camp reef: Rat Rock stopped the Communists in 1955 and could still smash a ship (photo courtesy of Friends of China Camp).

John Wayne goes over the *Blood Alley* script with an unidentified production assistant on the landing stage at China Camp (author's collection).

advertised as Duke Riverboat Steakhouse. It was eventually abandoned, tied up along the Sacramento bank.

But the *Chiku Shan* still wasn't ready for the ship graveyard. Ten years after the fire, the *Blood Alley* ferryboat woke again. The vandalized, partially sunken boat was raised and cleaned. In 2012, a court ordered the large vessel removed from the water and placed on land because people in the river area feared that it might break free and destroy anything in its path. As of this writing, it's still sitting on what appears to be its final resting place: on the west side of **Garden Highway,** north of the Sacramento airport, left to rust on private property. It's visible from the road. The fate of the *Chiku Shan* is finally sealed.

"A whole village scratched off the Red map"

In his autobiography, director William Wellman collected all his memories about this movie in just one paragraph: "I started out like a racehorse, with *Island*

in the Sky and *The High and the Mighty*, and then fell on my skinny butt with *Blood Alley*."[5] His failure to discuss the film might have something to do with the infamous Robert Mitchum incident, which is now the stuff of Hollywood legend. Mitchum was signed as the star and pre-production had already begun. In some stories, Mitchum threw Wellman into San Francisco Bay; in others, the victim was the production manager. Andrew McLaglen was there that day, in his capacity as an assistant director: "Mitchum really hadn't done anything wrong." The star got into an argument because he wanted to join in a conversation between the production managers and they turned their backs on him. Mitchum made sure they understood that he didn't appreciate that: "Don't ever do that to me again. Don't walk away when I'm trying to find out what's going on." He then kiddingly insulted Bill Wellman: "I couldn't hit an arthritic old man like you."[6] The producer called Jack Warner, Warner heard him out and said, "Okay, fire him."

Wayne was then in New York. With Batjac producing, Wayne had a stake in this film but was overruled. He told McLaglen, "Andy McSandy, for God's sake, don't let him fire Mitchum." But it was too late. McLaglen and others always suspected that Wellman wanted Wayne for the part from the beginning, even though Mitchum was more suited for it. Mitchum's brother John also wanted to set the record straight in his own book. Robert had told him: "It never happened!"[7]

Pilar would hold a lasting grudge against Mitchum for causing the premature termination of her honeymoon. When Wayne felt the time had finally come to invite the Mitchums to his Encino home, Pilar dutifully came out to greet them. But Bad Boy Mitchum insulted her again. He

A whole Chinese village escaped on John Wayne's ferry boat but now the fate of the Putah is finally sealed (photo courtesy of Rick Rockwell/CalExplornia).

peered down her gown and muttered, "Boy, do you need a new bra." All her stored-up anti–Mitchum fury returned in a lash. "Leave here! This instant!"[8]

But Mitchum and Wayne remained good pals. Production manager Paul Helmick remembered a welcome party for Barbra Streisand: "And who shows up stumbling around in the garden but Mitchum and Wayne. Just the two of them, crashing this party." Helmick told them, "What the hell are you doing here? This is a formal thing; they don't want a bunch of cowboys here!" But the pair demanded, "We want to meet Barbra!"[9]

"I'm the consul general to Japan"

To this day, fans shake their heads in dismay at *The Barbarian and the Geisha*. Wayne's decision to play Townsend Harris, the first American diplomat to Japan, had something to do with his fondness for location work. Twentieth Century–Fox "played on one of my weak points—I would have a chance to go to Japan, a place I had never seen," he told Peter Bogdanovich years later.

On November 4, 1957, Ford wrote to Wayne wishing him and John Huston a lot of luck and recommending that Duke get in contact with his (Ford's) friend Akira Kurosawa,

the Japanese director of *Seven Samurai*: "He is a great admirer of ours and would like to have the pleasure of visiting you while you are in Tokyo. He is a terribly, terribly nice guy." If that meeting ever took place remains unknown.

"Wonderful record, let's drink to it"

It is well-documented that Wayne and Huston had different working styles. The stories of their clash are legendary. But they started out on the right foot. At a press conference, the enthusiastic Huston announced that he wanted to "send Duke's gigantic form into the exotic world that was the Japanese empire in the 1800s. Imagine!"[10] Wayne allegedly went to see the locations with Huston. "I got up early with him, went hunting with him, went on location with him. I did every single thing to try to establish some rapport, but it was like sticking your head in a pail of cold water."[11]

Waiting for John Huston to light the *Barbarian and the Geisha* set to his liking: Townsend Harris is one of only a handful of real-life persons John Wayne portrayed (author's collection).

His action pictures usually drew in international audiences yet this souvenir program, sold in cinemas in German-speaking countries during the short run of *The Barbarian and the Geisha*, uses an unusually static pose of John Wayne, with Eiko Ando (author's collection).

The Barbarian and the Geisha was in production in Japan from December 1957 to February 1958. **Kyoto** had been the capital city of Japan for a thousand years. Its Buddhist and Shinto shrines provided the colorful background backdrop, situated at **Lake Biwa**. Some exteriors were filmed at the **Temple of Flowers** and the **Nijojo Castle**, one of several historic monuments designated by UNESCO as a World Heritage Site. In fact, it was this picturesque scenery that Huston wanted Wayne to "absorb": Wayne wrote home to Pilar, "I ask him what's on tomorrow's shooting schedule, and he'll tell me to spend more time absorbing the beauty of the scenery and less time worrying about my part."[12]

"It's the only way to stop cholera"

When they shot the scenes of the burning Shimoda in the fishing village of **Kawana** on the Izu Peninsula, they had a crisis on their hands. In the sequence, the American diplomat would take the bodies of the cholera victims, pile them on boats and run them out to sea to be burned. They had constructed a barge some 40 feet long, which was supposed to be full of bodies. The special effects men set fire to it and launched it on log rollers from a beach near the village of **Ito**. Somehow, the mooring cable attached to the barge as a means of controlling it was severed as it rolled into the sea. An inshore wind caught the flaming barge and drove it toward Japanese fishing boats. Huston: "We stood by

helplessly, watching this huge, floating torch—burning furiously by now—drift right into the middle of those boats." A number of them immediately caught fire. Ito itself was little more than a collection of paper houses stacked closely around the cove. One spark would have sent the village up in flames. Fortunately, a Japanese man found the end of the cut cable and hauled it to the nearest spot on shore. The filmmakers were able to march the barge away from town. The villagers had rushed out to help the fishermen fight the fires.

Then the riots started. Anglers and townspeople attacked the Japanese connected with the movie company. Many were clubbed unconscious, "and why no one was killed I'll never know," said Huston.[13]

"That's in the past, it's best forgotten"

By then, Wayne and Huston were hardly speaking. In the parade scene, with quite a number of extras, Huston got a bunch of Japanese kids to light firecrackers and throw them at the feet of Wayne's horse. Wayne: "[I realized] that the sonofabitch was trying to get me thrown off this horse in front of all these people."[14] Chuck Roberson was on hand for the limited number of action scenes. He remembered that Huston "drove Duke up a pagoda, the way he hemmed and hawed over directing a scene."[15]

Wayne once acted out such a confrontation, showing Bogdanovich how he had resolved an argument with Huston. Wayne actually grabbed Bogdanovich by his shirt front in reenacting the incident, and cocked his arm back as though to throw a punch. Wayne's face was suddenly close to Bogdanovich's, his teeth clenched fiercely. Bogdanovich laughingly exclaimed, "Jesus!" Then Wayne shook his head once and let go of the young *Paper Moon* director. "Sorry," he said, "that guy really sets me off."[16]

"Show his excellence in"

Interiors were shot at the **Eiga Studios** in Kyoto. While filming on the Japanese stages, Wayne's weight made the floors creak, making the recording of sound difficult. A second floor had to be constructed for support. The studio's movie village, the **Toei Kyoto Studio Park** at Ukyo Ward, is open to the public.

Huston claimed that he handed over a well-balanced work to Fox. "John

No one of the familiar crew hands or his usual cronies around: John Wayne looks lost amidst the unknown Japanese players in the Eiga Studios in Kyoto. Seated in the back is Hiroshi Yamato as the Shogun (author's collection).

Wayne apparently took over after I left. He [carried] a lot of weight at Fox, so the studio went along with his demands for changes."[17] Wayne had the final word in the matter: "Considering [Huston] never told me at any point what he did want, I consider his comments a little unfair."[18] He gave it his best shot when he tried to sell the movie personally in the original trailer: "Just as this white Barbarian from the West, as they called him, was the first man to raise the American flag on Japanese soil, so will his story for the first time bring you the mystery and color and exotic splendors of the Orient that no other medium could open up to you."

Even though Wayne called his Japanese movie one of the worst experiences in his career, he took souvenirs: He bought out the original woodcut blocks form a Buddhist temple. The prints of the wallpaper in his home were then made from these woodblocks.

Casper residents were able to see huge pillars of fire when the special effects department burned gas on the *Hellfighters* set (author's collection).

"Did you get your well capped?"

In *Hellfighters*, Wayne played a firefighter with exotic workplaces around the world. But Wayne never left the U.S. to film it. When his character "Red" Adair is called to put out an oil fire in Bolivia, Wayne went to **Casper**, Wyoming. The action movie was loosely based on the life of Adair, who found fame and made millions with his ability to put out oil field fires. On *Hellfighters*, Adair and his specialists "Boots" Hansen and "Coots" Matthews were consultants for the methods of handling the various fire sequences. Incidentally, filming in Casper wasn't long after Adair had actually put out a real fire in Gilette, just a bit north of the Wyoming filming location. It took his team nine days to snuff it out. Universal didn't miss the opportunity to get some footage out of it. They landed a DC3, a camera crew of 14 people who hauled 6600 pounds of filming equipment, and started pre-production for *Hellfighters* right away.

Officially, principal photography began on March 14, 1968. By mid–May, production had moved to Casper. Residents could see huge pillars of fire in the scenic bluffs west of their town. Follow Wyoming Highway 220 15 miles out of town to get to **Bessemer Bend**. The distinctive red terrain to the right was the site of the oil field where Wayne's crew fends off Bolivian guerrillas.

For the sequence in which Wayne's freight plane lands on a South American airfield, production made use of **Wardwell Field**, a former Casper airport that contained six miles of paved runways. It was ideal because grass was already growing on the abandoned landing strips. Nowadays, the hangars are used for boat storage. The runways are still evident. One sequence *not* involving Wayne was shot at a former *Big Trail* location, **Jackson Hole**: The scene in which

It's Bolivia to the movie audiences of *Hellfighters* but to the people of Casper, Wyoming, it's the red bluffs of their own Bessemer Bend (photograph by Roland Schaefli).

Jim Hutton picks up Katharine Ross was shot on the **Jackson Hole Airport**, 1250 East Airport Road.

"Somebody wake me up!"

Coming out of retirement for *Hellfighters*, special effects engineer Fred Knoth devised five 125-foot fire jets for the explosive scenes. Special nozzles were designed for the fires. An outer ring nozzle shot out the flames and an inner one shot out a mixture of water and India ink to simulate oil. When it was time to work close to the blazing fires, Wayne told the director, "I'll only go if Red tells me it's safe!" As Wayne came out of the flames unharmed, he quipped, "I'll never steam a clam again!"[19]

"The hottest movie I ever made," Wayne's voice drawled in the trailer, and stuntman Hal Needham could confirm that statement: "It was unbelievably hot." In one stunt, he drove the Jeep that accidently runs into a lake, and even though Neeham had to drive just a hundred yards, the heat burned "the goddamn hair off my arm."

Accidentally, the Wyoming fire sequence had to be achieved in the absence of the original firefighter team: Adair was called away to a real fire—in Bolivia, ironically enough. More Casper exteriors were reportedly shot on the grounds of **Snodgrass Ranch**. Stuntman Gary Combs watched an interesting incident on the set in Casper. Usually, visitors would be kept away from the main actors but a little boy of about ten managed to wander up to Wayne, who was playing chess. When the actor noticed the boy carrying something like an autograph book, he said, "Can I do something

John Wayne (still wearing the cap he picked up on the Fort Benning location) plays a game of chess with young fans on the *Hellfighters* set (author's collection).

for you?" By then the boy had watched some of the chess play and mentioned that he liked chess himself. Wayne sat him down and played a game of chess with him before signing his book.[20]

"The old headache gag?"

Before moving the production to Wyoming, director Andrew V. McLaglen had already shot the first oil fire in Texas. **Goose Creek Oil Field** in Baytown provided views of a multitude of derricks next to onshore and offshore wells at **Tabbs Bay**. The headquarters of Wayne's outfit in the film, the Buckman Company, was located just off Interstate 45 in **Houston**. The windows looked out over the skyline of Houston.

The gripping pre-title sequence was also shot in Houston. It marked Needham's first time as official stunt coordinator. One of his stuntmen hits a light bulb with his steel helmet, causing a spark. The well explodes, and all five men are engulfed in flames. "Red" Adair was on the movie set with his fellow workers. He asked Needham to warn them if he planned any more of those kinds of scenes so they could leave because that's exactly how their worst nightmare looked.

True enough, in one big fire scene, Chuck Roberson, doubling Wayne, slipped and fell, landing on his back. He couldn't get up and Needham was the only one who realized that he was in trouble. The young stunt ace ran into the flames, aiding Roberson. When he came out of the flames, Needham's clothes were smoking, his hair was singed and half the skin on the back of his hands was curled up and blistered. Special effects men hit him with foam. Wayne wanted to know what happened to all the stuntmen who were supposed to be working safety. Turned out that the production manager had two of them sent home to save money. "Duke was in shock. He bellowed the production manager's name. The guy came running out of his trailer and proceeded to get a tongue-lashing, along with orders to catch the stuntmen as they got off the plane and get them on the next flight back to Houston."[21] Stuntman Ronnie Rondell (who traded punches with Wayne in *The Wings of Eagles*) was one of those stunt guys: "We came back to California and did our laundry. I went to the beach. When I came back, there was a phone message: Be on a plane tomorrow morning. The tickets will be there." At their return, the stuntmen found out that Wayne would not come to the set until he got all the stuntmen back.[22]

Even though Wayne himself was not in that pre-title sequence, he stayed during the nights they shot it, chewing tobacco filched from the stuntmen. When someone asked him why he chose to do this picture, he deadpanned, "Oh, about a million dollars."[23]

"Can't say I blame you"

McLaglen shot the remainder of the interior scenes on Universal's **Stage 32** (the Special Effects Stage, demolished in 2010 to make room for the *Transformers* ride). By the time the film wrapped, Wayne and Adair had formed a lasting friendship. But it was six years before Wayne saw him really put out a fire. That was in 1974, in the foothills near Burbank. Wayne was limping after an injury filming *Rooster Cogburn* (he had hurt himself in the raft scene). A sudden change in wind pushed the flames in their direction. Wayne yelled at Adair, "You got me up here and you're gonna have to get me out!"[24]

12

Normandy

D-Day for the Duke

"We came here to take Sainte-Mère-Église. We're gonna take it and hold it."
—Lt. Col. Benjamin Vandervoort (John Wayne) to his paratroopers
on the eve of the invasion

"Remember every bit of it, 'cause we're on the eve of a day that people are going to talk about long after we are dead and gone." Rod Steiger's line from The Longest Day *rings true today. Not just for the real heroes of D-Day but for the monumental war movie as well. It will help future generations to remember. It feels real because it wasn't made on the backlot but on the original French locations.*

Now more than 75 years after the Allied invasion, the Normandy coast is peaceful, with lovely seaside towns and picturesque beaches. Still, the memories of war are engrained in the landscape. In almost every village, monuments have been erected, like the statue for Easy Company, inaugurated decades after the Normandy action because of its newly won *Band of Brothers* fame. On the annual commemorative days, veterans and re-enactors come out in force. Once a year, on June 6, like some sort of military Brigadoon, D-Day comes alive again; in many a bistro that was "liberated" on that day in 1944, the Longest Day march is played. The only connection most visitors have to Operation Overlord is through this enormous Hollywood undertaking. On the Normandy beaches, movie history seamlessly blends into war history.

"I don't think I have to remind you"

The Longest Day began with a long night in Paris. Well-known executive Elmo Williams, an amiable and unflappable man in his early 40s, was actually on his way to Munich to take an assignment offered by Walt Disney. Before taking off, he chose to say goodbye to Darryl F. Zanuck. DFZ, as they called him, had set up offices in Paris after his departure from 20th Century–Fox. It was Zanuck's darkest period. The 59-year-old had exiled himself when the days of the moguls were numbered. Zanuck was once one of the most powerful men in town; now he couldn't get a film project off the ground. Sure, he still had a seven-picture Fox contract. But so far, all his European ventures had been duds.

Williams had heard that Zanuck was drinking heavily.

So when he rang the bell of the apartment at **44 Rue du Bac**, he was prepared for the worst. But not for a nurse to open the door and doctors padding around. Zanuck was propped up in bed, having one of his beloved cigars despite the fact the "frog" doctors had told him to lay off of them. His girlfriend had left him, his whole staff had abandoned him. Worse: Zanuck feared he had lost his famous touch.

He wasn't sure about the screenplays he had in development. His hand trembled as he lighted the giant cigar. There

Before shooting started, Zanuck had a new girlfriend: Irina Demick. He gave the Dior and Givenchy model her big break by casting her in the only main female part of the film, as Janine Boitard of the French Resistance, pictured here in a publicity still with one of Johnny Jendrich's uncredited Germans in Port-en-Bessin (author's collection).

was just one more property: A fat book was lying by his bedside table. French producer Raoul Lévy had tried to turn this into a movie but nobody wanted to bankroll such a costly epic. Zanuck staked him with $75,000 and now held an option on the book. "Maybe there's a film in it," he mused.[1] It was Cornelius Ryan's bestselling account of the invasion, *The Longest Day*.

Williams read it that night and came back enthused. He warned the old man it would be a hazardous project. But the old man was already transforming back to his former self, the mighty movie producer, itching to get out of sickbed. Exactly because it seemed an impossible undertaking, Zanuck wanted to do it.

Williams cancelled his Disney assignment and started to work on the project right away. After he had sketched an outline, Zanuck offered a lucrative contract to Cornelius Ryan for the film rights and a screenplay based on his book. On December 2, 1960, Ryan signed on for $175,000.

Zanuck knew two things: First, to make this the success he so badly needed, the giant Allied invasion would have to be shot where it actually happened: Normandy. Second, he wanted the tin hat hero who, in the eyes of the moviegoing public, had single-handedly won the Second World War; he wanted the name of John Wayne on the marquee.

"God willing, we'll do what we came here to do"

Zanuck's nickname "The General" was certainly appropriate. "I believe I have a tougher job than Ike had on D-Day," he claimed. "At least Eisenhower had the equipment. I have to find it, rebuild it, and transport it to Normandy."[2] For instance, they found two Messerschmitts in Spain, now on duty in General Franco's air force, and were able to locate three Spitfires in the Belgian Air Force, being used for target practice. They were fitted with new engines and repainted in new colors. A 20mm Wehrmacht cannon was discovered in England.

The values contributed through military and naval assistance were priceless. The four governments concerned—the U.S., France, Britain and West Germany—even extended assistance through 48 technical advisors. Landing craft, battleships and G.I.s storming the beaches—all of that Zanuck arranged by asking favors of men he knew when he was a colonel in World War II. Charles de Gaulle authorized the use of 1,000 commandos brought back from the Algerian War. The NATO command promised 700 Special Forces troops. Somebody once counted the numbers: Zanuck had 23,000 soldiers as extras under his command, more than any single general during D-Day did.

But there was an aftermath to the use of U.S. troops:

At the crucial moment when U.S. soldiers were doing their acting bits, the Berlin Wall was surprisingly erected. The news reached Zanuck on August 13. Army units throughout Europe were put on full alert. Zanuck was then just recreating the assault at Pointe du Hoc. A direct line was kept open to the Ranger headquarters in Wiesbaden in case they needed to move to Berlin at once. The Senate ordered an investigation. Assistant defense secretary Arthur Sylvester had to answer questions about the extent to which Zanuck was given support. He argued that the film "will give the public a better understanding of a most crucial combat operation." He also expressed the hopes of the PR people that it "should prove beneficial for recruiting and in creating general interest in the Armed Forces."[3]

"We're 11 minutes from the green light"

In **Fort de Vincennes** in Paris, the production set up a boot camp to train the extras with special warfare duties like marching and throwing grenades. Zanuck had made up his mind to cast well-known stars even in minor roles. Actors pocketed $40,000 for their cameos, a much smaller fee than most of them were used to. He persuaded them that the real reward would be the connection with his great movie. Zanuck also made good use of Fox's roster of contract players as he assembled his star armada.

He was still negotiating star deals when the actual shooting had to commence. The U.S. 6th fleet was doing landing exercises in the Mediterranean, and the filmmakers couldn't miss this opportunity. The fleet commander was sympathetic to the cause and was persuaded to let his 22 ships simulate an invasion and allow it to be photographed. And the Marines were dressed like 1944 G.I.s. Williams got the art department to work overtime to have simulated objects and props in place. As a naturist resort was not far from the beach, they posted signs warning them not to approach the water during filming.

Beginning June 21, 1961, the CinemaScope cameras captured the 1600 American soldiers in maneuver, wading ashore on the **Plage de Saleccia**—while they avoided getting the aircraft carrier in the shot, as they weren't part of D-Day. The beach, off the **Désert des Agriates**, has perfect soft sand. (Zanuck was scammed out of $15,000, paying a "representative" of the beach owners who demanded payment for the use. It turned out there were no private beaches in Corsica. Zanuck got his money back after a long lawsuit.) The crew hosed down the beaches to make them appear darker, like a Norman shore. To cool the cameras on the broiling Corsican battlefield, they flew in ice, as opposed to filming on the Normandy beaches where they soon learned that they sometimes had near-zero visibility.

"You can't give the enemy a break"

Zanuck set up headquarters in the **Malherbe Hotel** in Caen where he screened the rushes for his five different directors in an improvised projection room. During the war, the hotel on the Rue du 11 Novembre had been occupied by the German Feldkommandantur. In later years, it was reduced to an apartment building and is now permanently closed.

From his HQ, "The General" (Zanuck) commanded the operation where the sequences were simultaneously shot over a period of ten months in 31 locations. But his most formidable battle was a battle of egos to bring John Wayne on board. Wayne had rejected Zanuck's offer cold. He gave the diplomatic excuse that he and his wife were "thinking of taking a vacation."[4] In fact, Wayne was still smarting from a remark Zanuck once made in an interview about actors who want to be directors: "Actors are now producing, directing and writing, they have taken over Hollywood completely, together with their agents. What the hell—I'm not going to work for actors."[5] He then provided a quote which Wayne later called "the most expensive interview a movie producer ever gave": Zanuck attacked Wayne for producing and directing *The Alamo*: "Look at poor old Duke. He's never going to see a nickel for his film and he put all his money into finishing it."

Now it was payback time for Wayne. The producer kept calling, raising the salary every time, and Wayne kept declining. When the offer reached a quarter of a million, "poor old Duke" finally agreed. "What the hell," he said, grinning with satisfaction. "It might be highway robbery, but it serves the bastard right."[6] When Wayne arrived in France, their

"**One click has to be answered by two clicks**": Still photograph with Fox contract player Steve Forrest of a moment not in the film (**author's collection**).

friendship was renewed. "He was so pleasant that I kinda wished I hadn't charged him that much money."

Zanuck had first offered Wayne the part of army officer Norman Cota, famous for rallying demoralized troops on Omaha Beach (Robert Mitchum eventually played him). Negotiations with William Holden to play Benjamin Vandervoort, the airborne commander who reaches his objectives despite having broken his ankle on landing, fell through. Then Charlton Heston decided that he liked the part. By his own account, he threw his weight around, the weight of "a 600-pound gorilla," in an effort to get the part. But when Wayne made up his mind, Zanuck snapped him up at once. "The Duke was the thousand-pound gorilla," Heston wrote in his diary, "if ever there was one."[7]

Zanuck spent just $2 million on one of the largest casts in history—a comparatively small amount for a cast of "42 international stars," as the movie marquees would boast.

"You're as ready as we could make you"

The Longest Day was a logistical monster. During the months on location, the company served 63,000 full meals. The total cost of putting on the feedbag came to $968,000. Six hundred thousand blanks were shot, hand manufactured in five different countries (a Belgian gunsmith produced handmade blank shells for a German anti-aircraft gun, at $10 per shot), 15 tons of demolition charges used, 25,000 tires burned, 3000 meters of barbed wire laid out. The depiction of the first 24 hours of the invasion was hailed as the most realistic war film of all time, and that claim was certainly cemented by using the real locations. Zanuck wanted to shoot in original places whenever permissible and technically possible. Yet the 15 years since the invasion had already taken its toll: The bunkers had completely overgrown. It cost him $800,000 to transform the beaches back into the 1944 Atlantic Wall. Monuments to the war-dead were covered up, burned-down buildings reconstructed and years of underbrush cut away. Frequently, old shell holes were re-exploded. Great care had to be taken since the Germans had buried four million mines along the coast and in 1961, it was still dangerous to stray off the marked paths. On one beach section, Zanuck's movie engineers unearthed a British tank. After its restoration, it joined Zanuck's tank corps.

The supreme compliment to Zanuck came during the creation of the Omaha Beach sequence. Sgt. Charles Pace, an original participant, was standing on the beach littered with bodies and burning equipment. He shook his head in wonderment. "This is like living the most terrifying moment of my life over again."[8]

The church tower of Sainte-Mère-Église: come June, a rubber paratrooper reminds visitors of that fatal night in 1944 (photograph by Roland Schaefli).

"'Til hell freezes over"

Sainte-Mère-Église on the Cotentin peninsula is the objective of Wayne's paratroopers. Each June, the townsfolk make sure there is a rubber paratrooper hanging from their famous church tower in memory of that fatal night. The unique Airborne Museum in the town's center features life-sized scenes of the nightly drama. The church's interior and its pulpit from which Jean-Louis Barroult delivers a flaming sermon remain unchanged. For the dramatic landing of airborne troops right smack on the town square, Zanuck had recreated the house which burned down that night—just to burn it down again. For three weeks, the inhabitants got little sleep as guns rattled in the square and helicopters roared overhead. For each jump, the electricity had to be cut in case anyone came down on a wire. Sudden winds would carry the paratroopers off—just as in 1944.

According to director Gerd Oswald, who was assigned to this sequence, "The Normandy winds were simply terrible." Twenty-five French stuntmen, a number of English paratroopers and a contingent of soldiers from a nearby French air force base jumped from two

The recreation of the paratrooper drop on the town square of Sainte-Mère-Église proved complicated: Sudden Normandy winds carried the stuntmen off (author's collection).

helicopters but could never land in their proper places (one of the jumpers broke both his legs). "They were always being blown away. Week after week, we had to resign ourselves to getting little pieces of film at a time."[9] Oswald finally solved his problem by putting construction cranes next to the

The cliff-top overlooking the pock-marked Pointe du Hoc: Zanuck recreated the dramatic assault on the original location where the blasted bunkers still stand unchanged (photograph by Roland Schaefli).

church. He would then just drop the paratroopers from the guidelines strung across the square.

The 150 men who portrayed German troops in this and other scenes went to special training at Fort de Vincennes. Johnny Jendrich, former German paratrooper and uncredited technical advisor, put them through drills. How much sensitivity to the Germans still remained was demonstrated when Jendrich thought it amusing to parade his little army into Sainte-Mère-Église. The disgruntled inhabitants had to be calmed down by shouting through a megaphone: "These are only extras!"

"Your assignment tonight is strategic"

Zanuck received permission from the French army to use flame throwers on the pockmarked **Pointe du Hoc** to "clear the area." That wasn't always easy: Even though in 1961 the number of monuments erected was small compared to today, in the shot of the landing crafts approaching Pointe du Hoc (actually a rear projection), the monument erected for the fallen is seen, camouflaged yet clearly visible. They also cleared out 600 live land mines in the area. One hundred fifty Rangers of the Eight Division, transported from their base in Wiesbaden, Germany, were assigned to help the moviemakers recreate the daring taking of the 80-foot cliff. "The one we're after," George Segal tells the matinee idols Tommy Sands and Fabian when he gets a thick-walled bunker in his sights. This main objective of the Pointe du Hoc sequence is still located on the former battlefield. It appeared again in Zanuck's 1969 documentary *D-Day*

The battery of Longue-sur-Mer was put to use in several sequences. It retains its original guns and remains in a good state of conservation (photograph by Roland Schaefli).

Revisited, with which he hoped to promote the re-release, and he is actually landing on top of that bunker in a helicopter in true showman-style.

Nearby is another half-sunken bunker. It was the backdrop of a very daring scene at the time: Tommy Sands shoots Germans who want to surrender. Ryan described the situation in his book; however, veterans of Pointe du Hoc objected to the scene. The shooting of unarmed soldiers by Americans, accidental or not, had not been accepted up to that point. It would take *Saving Private Ryan* to get audiences used to that.

The fierce firefight lasts ten minutes of screen time. It was shot in 12 days and cost half a million dollars. Today, the huge shell craters remain. The memorial for the Rangers Battalion stands on a casemate. The bodies of soldiers still lie under the ruins.

"I got the best battalion in this division"

One series of concrete bunkers was used in particular: the battery of **Longue-sur-mer**, the only one in Normandy that still retained all its original guns. A historical monument, it remains in good condition. The largest bunker of the garrison at 39 Rue de la Mer, overlooking the sea, was used as the German command post, in addition to several night scenes. The production actually filled in bullet holes and painted on a new camouflage.

"Hit the dirt and open fire"

The beaches are still known today by their D-Day code names. **Utah Beach** was easy to access and back then existed just by a strip of sand dunes. The place where

During the filming of the assault on Pointe du Hoc, American soldiers were suddenly needed in Berlin as another war was about to break out (author's collection).

German actor Gert Fröbe would go on to play *Goldfinger*. The scene in which he is slowly becoming aware of the massive fleet is the only footage actually shot in the sector of Omaha Beach (author's collection).

Henry Fonda delivers Gen. Theodore Roosevelt's famous line, "We're starting the war from right here," was shot approximately where his memorial now stands. The son of U.S. President Theodore Roosevelt is buried on the **Normandy American Cemetery & Memorial**, on a bluff overlooking Omaha Beach in Colleville. It is home to the graves of 9387 American soldiers. Steven Spielberg shot the opening and ending of *Saving Private Ryan* there. Not far from Colleville, in a place called **Honorine des Pertes**, on the

Rue de la Mer, they filmed the episode of the German (Gert Fröbe) who gets the surprise of his life as he spots the Allied armada while on horseback.

"Do I make myself clear?"

One of the most ambitious sequences was the French commando assault, beautifully orchestrated in one

Top: Not far from the American Cemetery at Colleville, Honorine des Pertes is the movie location of the house where the Frenchman watches Gert Fröbe fleeing from the whole Allied Armada (photograph by Roland Schaefli).
Middle: Rather unusual for a lobby card to reveal how movie magic is made: the helicopter taking the famous continuous shot of the fighting is clearly seen, hovering over the Port-en-Bessin canal (author's collection).
Bottom: The fishermen village of Port-en-Bessin stood in for the real Ouistreham. The picturesque stretch of houses along the canal remains unchanged since the filming (photograph by Roland Schaefli).

continuous four-minute helicopter shot. As the real Ouistreham didn't resemble the town at wartime any more, the nearby town of **Port-en-Bessin** (in which some bombed-out buildings were still in existence) stood in. The small fishing town was evacuated for two weeks as the capture of the casino was recreated. When oyster bed owners complained that some of Zanuck's forces were destroying their crop of crustaceans, Charles de Gaulle threatened to imprison them. The picturesque stretch of houses along the canal is the same as it looked in the sequence. So is the old **Vauban Tower** at Rue du Castel. Special effects men filled in old shell holes just to blow them out again. The tower overlooking the harbor has been restored to its original appearance.

The most important construction job involved the casino at the estuary. The three-story building was reconstructed, then blown up. It stood in the place where a memorial was later erected. The French forces battle the Germans from a bullet-riddled house—now the location of the local tourist office. Zanuck was interviewed on French TV in front of this detailed set and asked how much his film would cost. "I really have no idea," he answered in French. "Mais c'est cher [but it's expensive]."

Traces left by *The Longest Day*: The paint is peeling where the art director wrote "Bazar de Quistreham"; revealing the original lettering "Port-en-Bessin" (photograph by Roland Schaefli).

There is one amusing reminder of the filming in Port-en-Bessin: A building seen in the long tracking shot is painted with the words "Bazar de Ouistreham." The sign originally said "Bazar de Port-en-Bessin"; it was painted over to say "Ouistreham" for filming, then restored to "Port-en-Bessin." Years later, the paint of the lettering has faded to the point where "Ouistreham" has reappeared.

"Sometimes I wonder which side God's on"

At the canal bridge, Richard Todd must have felt *déjà vu* in September 1961, playing Major John Howard. The actor had parachuted into Normandy and participated in the holding of this strategic object in **Bénouville**, renamed **Pegasus Bridge**. Howard coached Todd on how to play him. (Many real-life veterans came out to meet their film counterparts and received "technical advisor" credits for their assistance.) In the movie, Todd wears the beret he wore on D-Day and

Filming the bloody attack of the French troops, led by France's star actor **Christian Marquand** (center) and unidentified players, with Vauban tower in the background. Note that the camera is protected by pads (author's collection).

donated his original gear to the **Café Gondrée**, 12 Avenue du Commandant Kieffer, where it is still displayed. This national monument was the first house in France that got liberated. When Zanuck wanted a shot of German soldiers jumping out of windows, Madame Gondrée insisted she had never allowed Germans to sleep in her house, and Zanuck had to back down. In 1992, the bridge was transported to a museum nearby, on Avenue du Major Howard, and can be admired there, thanks to Howard and the veterans who protested when authorities wanted to replace "their bridge" with a rather different one and also send the old one to Caen.

Zanuck built a number of gliders for the sequence. They sent the ships crashing down at the exact same spot. A monument for the fallen paraglider troops stands there today.

"All right, let's go"

Time was running out. At the end of summer, the weather had closed in. Zanuck vetoed suggestions to postpone all remaining scenes until the next year. He had moved the vast company to the **Ile de Ré** on the west coast; the completely flat island facing the Bay of Biscay offered beaches that were good for shooting over wide distances. By November, Zanuck virtually took over the Ile de Ré. With the exception of Utah Beach, its beaches were used for the recreation of all the landings.

At a May 24, 1961, board meeting, Fox executives, frantically trying to prevent more losses as the colossal *Cleopatra* drained the studio's lifeblood, had determined that *The Longest Day*'s final cost could not exceed $8 million. (By that time, *Cleopatra* had eaten up $15 million and was nowhere near completion.) The money ran out when the filming on the Ile the Ré was in progress. Zanuck used his own resources from then on.

The bunker-strewn **Conche des Baleines**, to the north of the island, was wisely chosen to portray Omaha Beach. The German fortifications had never seen action, because they were abandoned when the Wehrmacht retreated. The half-submerged remains are now a popular meeting place of the island's teenagers. Zanuck's engineers even unearthed several 50mm German anti-aircraft guns. A passage was dug out for the scene in which the G.I.s finally breach the seawall and storm inland.

The assault on Omaha was complicated, to say the least. Waves hit the beach and filled the air with stinging sea spray. Special effects men had placed explosive charges, simulating land mines, invisible to the camera. They were marked for the stuntmen with either red or green flags (the green ones marked the lighter charges, the red ones meant: stay away). On the day they filmed Robert Mitchum storming the beach, the star and the extras waded into the icy water to board their landing craft, which then motored back to the starting position of the sequence. All landing craft had to be in their assigned places. Like the men in the original landing, some extras got seasick and threw up everywhere. One soldier, Mitchum claimed, discharged a blank cartridge into his (Mitchum's) backside. When Andrew Marton, director of the American battle scenes, finally gave the signal, the Conche des Baleines became a scene of pure chaos. To each camera, Marton had the name of the main actors attached. Mitchum leaped out of the vessel and an explosive (planted near the water) went off. The tide had shifted and so it sent off a giant plume of water, soaking everything. Much to Zanuck's annoyance, Mitchum's remark that the real American soldiers were afraid to get their feet wet in the scene made the headlines.

"We came here to fight, not to swim"

To the east of the island, **Rivedoux-Plage**, the sickle-shaped **Sablanceaux shore** was converted into the

The Longest Day was nominated for the Oscar for Best Art Direction. Along the Conche des Baleines, a realistic-looking papier-mâché wall was constructed and breached in the explosive finale. The place was renamed "Pas Zanuck" (author's collection).

landing beaches Sword, Gold and Juno. For this memorable sequence, Zanuck borrowed 30 landing craft from the U.S. Army (they made the filming part of a tank landing exercise). Ken Annakin had to calculate exactly how long it would take to get the craft ashore and the British commandos on the beach to coordinate it with the German air raid. Six cameras were set up. The Americans weren't too keen about being directed by a Limey director. The U.S. sergeant in charge of the boats made no secret of how he felt about his British cousins. He let down the ramps too early and gave Peter Lawford a good soaking. By the time they got the Rat Pack star out of the water, he was completely waterlogged. Zanuck showered Annakin with profanity. The shot took six hours to set up again. Another sergeant was used for the retake. Sean Connery was in the same sequence. The young Fox contract player had just come in from Jamaica where he was making a low-budget spy picture. Nobody at Fox had high hopes for him. "If I'd drowned him," said Annakin, "there would have been no James Bond."[10]

French soldiers from the nearby Rochefort Air Base acted as soldiers of the landing forces. (With the money Zanuck paid for the use of the young recruits, the Air Forces Saintes built a movie theater in their barracks, still operating today.) As the extras approached the camera, Annakin cried out: "Now come on, you're doing this for king and country." Zanuck roared, "Not for king and country, for 20th Century–Fox!" During the weeks of filming, the stars were housed in La Rochelle. Zanuck would screen their rushes at the movie house in the **Café de la Paix**, 54 Rue Chaudrier.

The historic **Château de Chantilly**, about 30 miles

"**Get them down, down!**" John Wayne's powerful close-up in the moment he sees the dead paratroopers with Steve Forrest, accomplished on the Boulogne stage (author's collection).

north of Paris, is well known among movie lovers as a James Bond location. In *A View to a Kill*, the famous horse stable was the estate of super gangster Christopher Walken. In *The Longest Day*, it became the headquarters of German field marshal Rommel. When a swastika was flown over the castle, it nearly started a riot.

"Get those bodies down!"

Zanuck set a trend for future international productions when he used the French **Boulogne studios** in Paris. The 52 sets included the full deck of a destroyer. A landing craft was constructed ingeniously to simulate movement in the heavy sea. A wide expanse of typical Normandy countryside, divided by a running stream, covered two full stages, the largest movie set ever created in France. Sad to say, the once-mighty Studios de Boulogne is cut down to being a TV facility at 2 rue de Silly, with all its former glory lost.

Zanuck claimed he did not use models. But models *were* used, back in the studio—pretty neat ones, too. The Eiffel Tower as seen from a German headquarter is a detailed model, and so is the church of Ste-Mère-Eglise, when seen through a window. Wayne never went to that town. His fine bit of action—the reaction shot when he "sees" his dead men—was photographed as he stared at a blank studio wall in Boulogne. The shot of dead

Before the famous Château de Chantilly became the headquarters of a James Bond villain, it was Feldmarschall Rommel's headquarters in *The Longest Day* (photograph by Roland Schaefli).

bodies hanging from telephone poles in the town square, filmed in Ste-Mère-Eglise, was intercut with Wayne's footage. The same is true for Red Buttons' hanging from the church tower: A section of the tower was recreated in safe studio surroundings (the comedian suffered from fear of heights, anyhow). As Zanuck had Wayne for just four shooting days, it is safe to say they stayed in the Paris countryside for his one outdoor shot (the typical Norman hedgerows are tellingly absent). They shot his outdoor scene on a cold day. While everybody was freezing, Wayne was calmly playing chess undisturbed. Stuart Whitman noticed that every once in a while, Wayne would take a little cognac with his coffee. Ironically enough, while Wayne never did enter the strategically vital village, his uniforms from that movie did: A French dealer of military artifacts bought them for $14,340 at the 2011 Wayne family auction and displayed them in his shop—in Sainte-Mère-Eglise.

Work was swift at the studio. The American stars were flown in on a clockwork schedule and put through their paces as quickly as possible. Most of them weren't even needed on location. Roddy McDowall's scene in the Utah landing was shot with a double, shown from the back. Clever cutting to the interior shot gives the impression that he is fighting in the thick of the beach. Richard Burton had a brief vacation from the *Cleopatra* set to shoot his two scenes.

James Gavin, then ambassador to the U.S. in France, visited the filming in Paris and pointed out that his counterpart, Robert Ryan, should wear a West Point ring. Wayne helped out by lending Ryan his own similar-looking ring. According to legend, Marlene Dietrich, when on tour entertaining the U.S. troops in wartime, had a stormy affair with Gavin. Did the two men ever discuss the romantic interest they shared?

Each national contingent spoke its own language during the filming. The dubbing into English was also done at Boulogne.

"The most crucial day of our times"

Sixty-six hours of raw footage were edited into the three-hour epic. When all the bills were added, they amounted to ten million dollars. Zanuck premiered his movie in the **Palais de Chaillot**, on the Place du Trocadéro. A large section of Paris was lighted. Charles de Gaulle and all commanders from NATO headquarters were guests of honor. From the third level of an illuminated

Eiffel Tower, Edith Piaf sang the theme song, which had been written by Paul Anka. The fireworks burst over the City of Lights. One critic remarked, as he finally reached his seat having walked the red carpet along fanfares: "I feel as if I've just gained entry to Valhalla."[11] For the New York premiere, Zanuck turned Broadway into a military parade. General Omar Bradley attended with other high-ranking brass.

Cornelius Ryan had written the script at the **Prince de Galles Hotel**, 33 Avenue George V., in Paris. After he turned in his first draft, Zanuck secretly enlisted the help of other writers to get the script he envisioned. Ryan went before the Screen Writers Guild to argue about credits—and received sole credit in the end. On Oscar night, *The Longest Day* took home awards for Photography and Special Effects. The film wasn't just the most expensive black-and-white film up until then—it held the position of the highest-grossing black-and-white film until *Schindler's List* in 1993. At Zanuck's funeral, the Longest Day march was played over his grave (at the Westwood Village Memorial Park Cemetery in Los Angeles). It's that same piece of music one can hear in Normandy in June when the bands are playing it on the beaches.

Even though John Wayne didn't use all the costume pieces, 20th Century–Fox issued a full set. They were sold for $14,340 at the John Wayne family auction in 2011 and then displayed in a military shop in Sainte-Mère-Église (Heritage Auctions, HA.com).

13

Arizona

Meanwhile, Back at the Ranch

"It's right friendly of 'em. Welcome is more neighborly."
—Robert Hightower (John Wayne) as the Three Godfathers reach
the town sign of Welcome, Arizona

"I love Arizona." John Wayne made this simple but heartfelt statement to a Historical Society *interviewer on the set of* Rio Lobo, *his last film on an Arizona location. He didn't just love shooting films in the Grand Canyon state. He loved staying there. Moreover, he came often.*

Wherever Wayne went in Arizona to make a picture, other film companies would soon trail him. Attracted by the natural wonders put on the screens, tourists would eventually follow suit. To this day, hotels all around the state proudly remark, "The Duke slept here."

"I may own property in Arizona…"

"I'm about as big a rancher as there is in Arizona," Wayne boasted in his *Playboy* interview. He was a cattleman for 15 years. He and his partner Louis Johnson of Stanfield, Arizona, broke records with their bull sales. But the outlook on his Arizona ventures wasn't so bright in 1958. He had borrowed $4 million to buy 4000 acres of prime cotton land, financed through a cotton broker. But then the Clari Land Company south of Phoenix got in trouble. One good thing about that doomed venture: Louis Johnson became his neighbor.

Wayne hoped he could get Johnson to manage his cotton. On December 19, 1958, Johnson took him up on his invitation to his Encino home. They shook on the deal. Johnson made him a profit in the very first year. When Wayne visited his fields, he stayed at the **Mountain Shadows Hotel** in Scottsdale. (Rebuilt in 2017, it is now the Mountain Shadows Resort at 5445 East Lincoln Drive.) Over dinner, the two partners decided to put together their 6000 and 4000 acres. That's how it came to be that in 1964, the cotton men Wayne and Johnson became cattlemen. Wayne went along with Johnson's plan to raise purebred Herefords. Like Tom Dunson looking at the wide expanse of grassland to

form his Red River D cattle empire, the team looked at the valleys near **Springerville** in Eastern Arizona. The partners first purchased the **26 Bar Ranch** as their headquarters. They then systematically bought up 14 adjoining properties, with 30,000 acres of Forest Service leases in the mountains. They bought only top-of-the-line cows from the country's three leading registered Hereford breeders. Finally, they called a herd of 800 outstanding animals with proven bloodlines their own. In 1967, when they began their annual production sale, they wrote a new chapter

Inspecting his Hereford cattle with Louis Johnson (left), a business friend he trusted, and an unidentified hand of the 26 Bar Ranch. John Wayne appointed Johnson executor of his will with respect to his Arizona estate (author's collection).

in Hereford history. The sale became number one in the nation for 18 consecutive years.

In August 1968, Wayne rode at the head of the parade from Eagar to Springerville in the big John Wayne Day celebration. Many people would run up to him and ask for his autograph. He yelled back that they should all meet him afterward at the Holiday Inn where he was staying to spend some time with him—and that's exactly what he did.

He always made it a point to attend the annual auction. When he kicked off the 1978 auction, he drawled into the mike: "My favorite food is beef. My favorite beef is Hereford. My favorite people are Hereford breeders."[1]

"I'll have the Red River D on more cattle than you've ever seen"

Bob Hope visited the ranch in 1976 to type an interview by the fireplace for his *Christmas Special*. He asked his host, "How can you stand it here, Duke? There's nothing for miles and miles." Wayne continued to tell the comedian that there was an Indian reservation just down the road, and as Hope inquired if they were friendly, Wayne answered with a line that might get him into trouble with a contemporary perspective: "They better be or they won't work in my next picture."

Wayne even used their spread as a location for a TV announcement in 1977, asking for the appreciation of American farmers on Agriculture Day. As they were about to film his monologue, some steers in the background decided to move through the frame and ruined the take. He had to wait until they settled down. Cattleman Wayne became irritated with his own cattle, growling: "This is a Red River stampede!" Well, he and Johnson didn't name the largest privately owned cattle feedlot in the U.S. after his classic western, the Red River Land Co., for nothing.

He allowed a German TV crew to interview him at the 26 Bar Ranch. They chose a roof, which offered a look down at the corrals. Wayne lost his temper with the female journalist who tried to corner him about the parts women played in his pictures. Wayne tried to change the subject and pointed out the scenery and "the beautiful old mill" in the distance as he felt they were part of his life, too. He asked the camera operator to pan over there. He didn't follow Wayne's direction of the interview, and Wayne walked off in the middle of it.[2]

While he stayed at the ranch, he was always approachable. In 1976, when he appeared on Phil Donahue's talk show to promote *The Shootist*, an audience member wanted to know the exact location of the ranch house as she would soon be moving to Springerville.

Wayne immediately offered, "Stop in and have a cup of coffee next time!"

After his death, Johnson sold the 26 Bar Ranch and its affiliated properties for $45 million. In his will, Wayne appointed Johnson one of his trustees and executor of his will "with respect to my Arizona estate." He wrote in his testament, "I anticipate that at the time of my death I may own property in Arizona...."

The rock sign for the 26 Bar reads "26 Herefords." It's still there, on a hillside along State Route 260 west of Springerville. The 26 Bar Road leads there. For a stretch of 28 miles, Arizona State Highway 347 is now known as **John Wayne Parkway**.

"I am the Hollywood yahoo S.O.B.!"

Wayne sometimes engaged a private pilot to fly from Los Angeles to Stanfield. William T. Brooks, aka "Chili Bill," recalled the first time he picked his famous passenger up at the Orange County Airport to take him to the Hearst Castle in San Simeon. It didn't take Wayne long to ask Brooks if he would mind him sitting upfront. "Like to see where I'm going." The pilot then told him that as a teenager, he had been an extra in *Angel and the Badman*, as he lived around the Sedona area back then. Brooks later became a fixture at the 26 Bar Ranch as a cook of his own chili recipe. Wayne once asked him to fly five gallons to the *Brannigan* set in London. Brooks' favorite anecdote dated from the time when Wayne and Johnson had purchased the 26 Bar Ranch. Wayne asked to scout the high country he now owned himself. When a

For the first time, the credit in the movie titles read "A John Wayne Production": John Wayne calls the shots in *Angel and the Badman*, instructing unidentified key personnel (author's collection).

thunderstorm came up, he found the line shack up on the mountain. Some ranch hands had already taken refuge inside. They talked about the ranch being sold and that some "Hollywood yahoo S.O.B" had bought it. Wayne, not wearing his hairpiece and not having shaved for some days, went his way unrecognized. The next morning, all the people who worked the ranch lined up to meet the new owners. Wayne stood up and said, "I guess I am the Hollywood yahoo S.O.B.!" From that day on, the line shack became known as "John Wayne's S.O.B. line shack."[3]

"Vengeance dance. They'll dance until dawn"

In his second home, Wayne often stayed in his unpretentious bedroom down a hallway at Johnson's—a plain bed, an old oak rocker, windows looking out on pecan trees. He'd watch the sunset color Table Top Mountain. During the sale weekend in November, when accompanied by his family, he would rent rooms at the **Francisco Grande**, an hour's drive from Scottsdale. The San Francisco Giants built this golf resort outside Casa Grande at 12684 West Gila Bend Highway for their spring training. One night before a cattle auction, it was hard for Wayne to hide in the throng at the cocktail party in the Francisco Grande ballroom. Residents remember that the star wasn't shying away from multiple offers to dance with the female guests in the large ballroom. "The old widows here in town used to love to go out there and dance with John Wayne," John Hindman, a docent at the Casa Grande Valley Historical Society, told the editors of *Arizona Highways*. At the Grande, the John Wayne memory never fades. You order from "Duke's Menu" or enjoy the casual atmosphere at "Duke's," the resort lounge named for the famous guest. His usual room, #804, is now the John Wayne Suite. The newly renovated bar is named in his honor as well.

But Wayne was also known in Arizona as an unrepentant speeder. He shrugged off a number of tickets. Sometimes he would drive his partners to **Nogales** just to have a slice of hot apple pie à la mode at **Zula's Cafe**, his hangout at 982 North Grand Avenue.

"I thought you weren't allowed to work on Sunday"

Gary Cooper was once asked why so many film colony marriages fail. He put much of the blame on location work and the fact that the actors get separated from their families for long periods. The idea that Wayne and Gail Russell carried on an affair on the *Angel and the Badman* location in Sedona has occupied his biographers and loyal fans for

years. Even when Wayne was elevated to producer status for this first time, he still stayed in a little cabin at the **Sedona Lodge**, ate in the mess hall, and mingled with the townsfolk. The Lodge was built just in time to house the crew and became the production hub supporting a boomlet of subsequent Sedona films. It has since been torn down. Bob Bradshaw, a carpenter who built Wayne's western town below **Coffee Pot Rock** for the film, remembered that one time at the lodge, "[Wayne] got drunk and kicked in all the doors of the bunkhouse."[4] However, some of these nights in 1946 he spent elsewhere. In subsequent publications about the making of this western, the consensus is that leading lady Gail Russell developed a crush on Wayne. Yet the oral history of the **Cottonwood Hotel** describes that crush as mutual.

When John Wayne put *Angel* in production in April 1946, he regularly viewed the rushes at the Rialto Theater in the little town of **Cottonwood**, some distance from Sedona. (The Rialto is today's location of the **Tavern Grill,** 914 North Main Street). His co-star would accompany him to the movie house. On several occasions, Wayne and Russell wouldn't return to Sedona but check into the **Cottonwood Hotel**, just a few doors from the theater at 930 North Main Street. The hotel had been part of the movie set of Burt Lancaster's *Desert Fury* the previous year, so locals were already used to show business people. Actually, Mae West had roomed here some 20 years before. According to residents, the romance was a secret but not-so-secret love affair. The story was told by old-timer Josephine Becchetti. Her father owned the Rialto, and his friend Bob Bradshaw had rented his **Sedona Ranch** to the movie people as the main location for the Wayne Western. The ranch between Cottonwood and Sedona was used for no less than 144 films. Jean Hall Redmond was then working in the Robinson's Clothier/Western Wear on the ground

The "Angel" and the "Badman": Are Gail Russell and John Wayne just playacting? (author's collection).

floor of the Cottonwood Hotel. Jean claimed that Wayne had been buying Western wear at the store. She said she also vividly recalled Wayne and Russell standing in the doorway of the hotel entrance, holding hands and smooching. Then they would go upstairs to their hotel room. At that time, one of the ten rooms could be rented for just $1.50 per night. Early in the morning, they'd get up and sneak back into their Sedona lodging location, before other crew members would wake up. Bradshaw confirmed the story.

"We water our horses at the same trough"

Suite #2 has been called the John Wayne Suite—the hotel's largest room today. However, the hotel units were a lot different back then. Wayne had requested one of the rooms with the bathroom and clawfoot tub (which is now the Mae West Suite). He couldn't always get one, so his second option was to be adjacent to the common balcony. The three small rooms put together is what the Cottonwood now calls the John Wayne Suite.

Did John Wayne really romance Gail Russell at the historic place? Whether it was a steamy affair or not, the movie couple kept seeing each other privately even after their time in Sedona. The shoot lasted from April 22 to June 6, 1946. Wayne threw a wrap party after they finished shooting interiors at Republic.

Wayne's wife Chata had begun to suspect that the "Badman" was spending just a little too much time with the "Angel." In November 1953, at the divorce trial in the Superior Court of the County of Los Angeles, Chata testified that Wayne had committed adultery with Russell. When Gail took the witness stand, she said, "Wayne and the director had surprised me by telling me they were presenting me with approximately $500 because they believed my salary had not been in keeping with the caliber of my work as feminine lead…. John took me home after the party. He had celebrated too much and apologized to my mother for his condition. He called a taxi. My brother helped him into the taxi and he left about 1:00 a.m. The next morning he sent my mother a box of flowers with a note of apology for any inconvenience he might have caused her."

When he didn't come home at all that particular night, Chata suspected he was at a hotel in Studio City with Russell. Chata later claimed that she called the home of Russell's mother and was told that because of the late schedule, Russell was staying at a motel. When Wayne finally did come home after spending a few hours drinking, he discovered he was locked out of his Encino home. Wayne broke a glass panel of the front door with his fist, let himself in and, still drunk, reclined on the sofa. A few minutes later, a drunk Chata came running into the living room packing a loaded gun. Her

"Absolutely not": John Wayne had to testify in court that he did not commit adultery with co-star Gail Russell (author's collection).

mother grabbed it and prevented her daughter from killing Wayne. (Some reports say Chata actually fired a round.)

The party Wayne hosted was at **Eaton's Rancho Restaurant**, modeled after early California hacienda-style. Just a block away from Republic at 12012 Ventura Boulevard, it was popular with their stars. (On the menu, it had a "Three Mesquiteer," a three-decker hamburger for 35 cents.) A McDonald's went up on the property in 1976.

"Does a lot of foofaraw have to go with it?"

Wayne's story differed a little from Chata's. When the wrap party ended early, he and some others headed for another bar. He drove Gail's car, but en route, they lost sight of their friends, and ended up at a restaurant on the Santa Monica beach. When he finally arrived home, he had to break into his own house because he didn't have his key. This led to Chata aiming the gun at him. In the divorce battle, Wayne claimed she tried to kill him with a .45 automatic. He testified that he and his wife had struggled over the .45 she owned. When Wayne took the stand, he denied ever having sex with Gail.

His attorney Frank Belcher asked, "Were there any improprieties between you and Miss Russell?"

Wayne: "Absolutely not."

"Were you at a motel any time that night?"

"Absolutely not."

"He swung a wide loop in his younger days"

Wayne's long-time secretary Mary St. John never asked her boss about the rumors of affairs. But she did notice

Chata "got so jealous that any time Gail even came toward his office, Duke would head out the back door."[5] Mary didn't believe they had an affair, nor did Michael Wayne. But Jeannette Mazurki Lindner, the wife of character actor Mike Mazurki, said, "They did have a love affair. After the picture, it was over."[6] According to Harry Carey, Jr., "My mother said he and Gail definitely had tremendous chemistry between them. Yet I don't think it ever got into a big affair." Olive Carey, who was on the set, said, "He had a definite attraction to Gail."[7]

Wayne very much resented the fact that the trial caused Gail trouble. "Why did Chata have to drag that poor kid's name into this? I never had anything to do with Miss Russell except to make a couple of pictures with her!"[8]

Three years after the trial, Gail made a comeback in Wayne's Batjac production *Seven Men from Now*. Director Budd Boetticher had this to add, "I think Duke had a crush on her. I think she was the only leading lady that he really cared about in anything but a professional way."[9]

Russell died of alcoholism at the age of 36 in 1961. Years later, Wayne still got agitated at the very mention of her name. "Gail was just such a beautiful young girl and some of those fucking sons of bitches at the studios had taken advantage of her. You know about the old casting couch. She'd been there a number of times."[10] Wayne stressed the fact that this didn't happen with him and that he gave her the part on her merits.

"I'll catch up with ya"

Tombstone, the town associated with the Wyatt Earp legend, had earned the moniker as "the town too tough to die." Wayne has never been in a movie about the infamous Gunfight at the OK Corral (although his character's backstory in *Angel and the Badman* has him as Earp's deputy). In real life, Wayne stayed in Tombstone more than once, at the **Sagebrush Inn** at 227 North 4th Street, a short walking distance from the spot where Virgil Earp was ambushed on March 18, 1882. One wonders if Wayne met Wyatt Earp in the silent movie days when the old lawman came to Hollywood in the capacity of a technical advisor. John Ford claimed Earp told him the story of the gunfight the way "it really happened," and young Duke Morrison might have been Ford's prop boy at the time.

In 1947, when Wayne stayed for the first time in the Sagebrush Inn's room #4 (now a John Wayne shrine), the motel was new. Wayne was filming *Red River* scenes at the nearby San Pedro River. That was long before Tombstone became a tourist magnet. Back then, the Sagebrush

John Wayne in the courtyard of the Hacienda Corona in Nogales, admiring a well-preserved mural of Salvador Corona. The Mexican-American bullfighter and artist created folk-art style, pastoral paintings on everyday objects (photo courtesy of Hacienda Corona).

motel was the best one could expect in the old mining town. Wayne returned in 1963 as he was filming scenes for *McLintock!* in the **Dragoon Mountains,** which can be seen from the porch.

According to the motel history, Maureen O'Hara occupied a room at the opposite side of the inn. After years of deterioration, the place was purchased in 1998 by the present owners, who invested in "making sure their guests wouldn't miss out on a single aspect of the past preserved in this historic inn." According to legend, the BBQ out front

Starting with the location work for *Red River,* John Wayne stayed at the Sagebrush Inn whenever he got to Tombstone, "the town to tough to die" (photograph by Roland Schaefli).

The Hacienda Del Sol as it looked in the 1960s when Wayne stayed at the Spanish Colonial style guest ranch. The historic hotel was the secret hideaway for Spencer Tracy and Katharine Hepburn (photo courtesy of Hacienda Del Sol Guest Ranch Resort).

was specially built for Wayne. In Tombstone, when the legend becomes fact, they certainly print the legend in bold letters. In any event, it is true that Wayne loved to visit with the locals. They snapped his picture relaxing at the bar of the **Big Nose Kate's Saloon**, a notorious waterhole of the Earp brothers on Tombstone's main street.

"Well, I'll take that chance"

Noted as being Arizona's longest continuously operated hotel, the **Copper Queen** at 11 Howell Avenue in Bisbee was constructed between 1898 to 1902. Famous guests included Lee Marvin, Marlon Brando, Julia Roberts and Harry Houdini. Wayne fans will want to look up just one signature in the hotel's register, and then spend the night in his bed. If you're able to find any sleep. Because there are reportedly three ghosts in some of the 48 Victorian-styled rooms. An older gentleman leaving a trail of cigar smoke, a prostitute who took her life there and can be heard whispering, and a little boy who drowned in the San Pedro River. Guests swore they saw objects being moved in their rooms. Wayne never told any such story after having slept there peacefully.

"Two dollars will buy a lot of sleep around here"

When shooting at the Old Tucson set was finished for the day, Wayne would drive back to Tucson to a hotel which is recognized as a historic resort: the **Hacienda Del Sol**. Today, it is included in the National Registry of Historic Places in Arizona and is a member of the Historic Hotels in America. The place attracted notable stars like Clark Gable and was the secret hideaway for Spencer Tracy and Katharine Hepburn who carried on their discreet affair for 26 years. It is therefore quite fitting that the hotel at 5501 North Hacienda del Sol Road advertises "lots of privacy." Originally a boarding school for girls, the 43-acre property was converted in 1948 into a Spanish Colonial–style guest ranch. It changed hands a few times and fell into disrepair. In 1995, a group of investors took over management and rebuilt and expanded the hotel.

"The big house will be down by the river"

During the making of *Red River* in Elgin, Ralph Wingfield, the owner of the Guevavi Ranch in Nogales, supplied

300 head of cattle to add to Dunson's herd. Wayne began staying at Wingfield's ranch in the early '50s. The actor liked to sit under the mesquite tree outside his room, on the little brick patio overlooking the duck pond. The Wayne family would often return on Wingfield's invitation to what is now the **Hacienda Corona de Guevavi**, 348 South River Road, Nogales. "He liked it out here," said Wingfield. "It was quiet."[11]

The month before Wayne died, the Arizona rancher went along on Wayne's last trip to Catalina. When they returned to Newport Harbor, Wayne gave Wingfield his Stetson hat, casually saying, "It looks better on you."[12]

"It was quiet": Looking out of the window from his favorite place in Nogales. The Wingfield ranch is now the Hacienda Corona where this photograph is proudly displayed to guests. The star saw the ranch as a hideout from the demands of celebrity (photo courtesy of Hacienda Corona).

14

Hawaii

"Does the word aloha *make you warm?"*

"Don't you wanna spend eight weeks on Hawaii this summer?"[1]
—John Ford talks Lee Marvin into accepting *Donovan's Reef*
without reading the script

John Wayne felt a longing for Hawaii. His first voyage to Honolulu ended quickly and abruptly. He didn't let the failed attempt stop him. Ultimately he filmed five films on the islands and even honeymooned with two of his wives there. It's an easy guess how he would have answered the question he posed himself in his album America, Why I Love Her: *"Does the word* aloha *make you warm?"*

According to an article in the November 1940 *Silver Screen* magazine (Wayne confirmed it in several interviews), as a young man he embarked on a foolish adventure after being dropped from the Trojan football team. He headed for San Francisco and stowed away on the SS *Malolo*, a steamship bound for Honolulu. Duke Morrison slept in an unoccupied stateroom, but turned himself in on the fourth day at sea when he got too hungry. They handcuffed him and threw him in the brig. As soon as the *Malolo* reached Honolulu, he was transferred to a Matson liner going east. Back in San Francisco, he was handed over to the harbor police. So he didn't get to see Hawaii the first time around.

When Wayne returned a full-fledged movie star and number one box-office champ, the Honolulu police didn't just welcome him with open arms—the police chief even played a real-life part in his movie, *Big Jim McLain*.

"Scares most people, I guess"

Jim McLain, an investigator for the House Un-American Activities Committee, goes after the Commies in the most unlikely of places: the Hawaiian island of **Oahu**. The part was a natural for Wayne because it expressed his own political ideology. During the Red Scare, he served as a president of the Motion Picture Alliance for the Preservation of American Ideals.

Big Jim McLain was in production from April 30 to June 16, 1952. "And it was shot on the spot in Hawaii," the trailer proudly informed audiences. Which was still quite unusual for its time. Just a year before, *Flying Leathernecks*

had used just stock footage to show soldiers on leave, surfing on **Waikiki Beach**. Now Wayne was riding an outrigger boat in that same spot, with **Diamond Head** in the background. The Outrigger Canoe Club had turned over its grounds to his production company. On the marquees, the star was advertised as "the toughest storm that ever hit the beach at Waikiki!"

Honolulu's native-born police chief Dan Liu portrayed

Quality time with dad: Michael and John Wayne on the Kona coast in 1954, during production of *The Sea Chase*. The film was based on the factual story of the German steamer *Erlangen*, who made a successful escape when war broke out (author's collection).

174

No scenes for *Big Jim McLain* were shot on the outside of the Honolulu Police Department but Wayne posed for publicity photographs at the entrance to the historic precinct (author's collection).

This *Big Jim McLain* lobby card depicts a scene with Nancy Olson not in the film, simply to promote the Hawaiian location of Hanauma Bay (author's collection).

himself in the picture. He also made Wayne a duly appointed officer of the **Honolulu Police Department**. Wayne was allowed to shoot scenes in the real offices. The precinct is at 842 Kukui Street.

Wayne knew that J. Edgar Hoover had his film investigated. "He sent agents to Hawaii to check us out. He thought we were playing FBI agents and he wanted to know how the FBI would come across."[2]

Wayne's investigator does quite a bit of lolling around the popular Hawaiian spots. He takes his romantic interest Nancy Olson to view **Hanauma Bay**, a natural pool formed in a volcanic crater on the southern end of Oahu. After that, Hanauma Bay quickly became a hot tourist spot and suffered from overuse. In the 1990s, the county of Honolulu started preserving the area and limited the number of visitors. Location filming is no longer permitted.

"She still carries a full crew"

Wayne had made a private pilgrimage to the wrecks of the *Arizona* and *Utah* battleships before. He got special permission to shoot a scene in which the investigators witness the wreck of the **USS *Arizona*** at the Pearl Harbor base. This footage stands out as a contemporary document, because it captured the memorial just one decade after the attack on Pearl Harbor. Built in 1962, the memorial is visted by more that two million people annually. In his den at home, John Wayne had a piece of polished wood from the *Arizona's* deck.

One sequence shows the investigator at Honolulu's

Shingon Mission, located at 915 Sheridan Street. It is one of the most elaborate displays of Japanese Buddhist temple architecture in Hawaii. The moviemakers tried hard to make *Big Jim McLain* a film noir, even filming the island paradise in black and white. McLain even tracks a clue to the **Molokai leper colony**, known as Kalaupapa. The territorial government gave permission for the shooting at Kalaupapa Settlement for Hansen's Disease victims on Molokai island.

The manhunt leads to the **Medical Arts Building** at 1010 South King Street. Finally, Wayne brings his suspects to justice at the **Aliʻiolani Hale** at 417 King Street, currently the home of the Hawaii State Supreme Court.

When in Honolulu, Wayne liked to visit his friend Duke Kahanamoku. The Hawaiian legend had popularized

The same lovely spot today, also used in *Blue Hawaii*, the movie that linked the islands forever with Elvis Presley. However, location filming is no longer permitted at Hanauma Bay (photograph by Roland Schaefli).

the ancient Hawaiian sport of surfing. The five-time Olympic medalist had played a cameo in *Wake of the Red Witch* and the two men shared a love of the ocean. When they got together, they would test out the first pairs of aqua lungs, as the breathing apparatus for divers had just been introduced.

"You're comfy without French fries"

In one continuous dolly shot, Wayne escorts Veda Ann Borg the full length of the elegant lobby at the **Royal Hawaiian Hotel**. The famous hotel at 2259 Kalakaua Avenue occupies ten acres of prime Waikiki beachfront and has been in operation since 1927. The structure was fashioned in a Spanish-Moorish pink-color style. The hotel's oceanfront **Mai Tai Bar** is said to have been one of Wayne's favorite waterholes. But his memories of the luxury resort were not all happy ones. After marrying Chata on January 17, 1946, the couple honeymooned at Waikiki Beach, occupying the Royal Hawaiian's Presidential Suite. It rained every day of their three weeks there. They were back the same year, in December, to celebrate the completion of his first film as a producer, *Angel and the Badman*, accompanied by James Edward Grant and his wife. This time, they stayed at the **Ala Moana Hotel** at 410 Atkinson Drive. As Chata would testify in court a few years later, it was at the Ala Moana that Wayne grabbed her by the foot and dragged her from her bed to the floor.

When *Big Jim McLain* came about (his first venture as an independent producer), he had planned the cruise to Honolulu as a second honeymoon in an attempt to patch things up. However, when they landed in Honolulu, the marriage was in deep trouble. During *Big Jim*, the Waynes stayed at the **Edgewater Beach Hotel**, which had opened the year before at Kalia Road in Waikiki. (It also served as the production's headquarters.) For interior shots, Wayne moved his company back to Burbank and wrapped on June 9, 1952. He returned to Hawaii on August 28 that year, to premiere his anti-Communist film close to Waikiki.

"We're takin' this bird all the way to Frisco"

The disaster movie *The High and the Mighty*, one of Wayne's most successful ventures as a producer, was in production from November 25, 1953, to January 11, 1954. Even though the plot centers around the flight of a CD-4 airliner from Honolulu to San Francisco, only minor work was done on location in Hawaii: just a few establishing shots on Waikiki. For one of the brief flashback scenes, Wayne again utilized the Royal Hawaiian

Hotel. Take-offs of the aircraft were captured at **Oakland International Airport**, 1 Airport Drive. In the credits, the producers offer thanks for assistance to Oakland Airport. However, according to former employees of Transocean Air Lines, which provided two TA DC-4s, the takeoff scene was shot at the Flying Tigers hangar at Westchester (now on the grounds of Los Angeles International Airport). The planes were flown by Transocean Air Lines pilots. One of them simulated the emergency night landing on Runway 28R at **San Francisco Airport**. Fire trucks sprayed water on the runway to make it appear that it was a rainy night. Several years later, Steve McQueen chased a gangster down the same runways in *Bullitt*.

Producer Wayne put in two nights of shooting at the **Glendale Grand Central Air Terminal**, 1310 Air Way, not far from his Glendale home turf. According to Transocean's logbooks, their chief engineer designed the fire-damaged engine there. The scene as scripted called for tilting the engine at a 30-degree angle. A large amount of oil was accidentally spilled onto the side of the cowling. This made the make-believe damage look authentic, and director William Wellman congratulated the mechanics for their artistry. The actors played the majority of their scenes in the mock-up airplane on the Goldwyn stages.

"I'll take my chances"

Although the Caribbean and Mexican coastline were scouted as possible location sites, *The Sea Chase* put Wayne back on the Hawaiian Islands the same year he premiered

Even though the doomed CD-4 airliner starts his voyage in Honolulu, all interiors of the plane were shot on a stage in the Goldwyn studio. With Jan Sterling, David Brian, Claire Trevor (from left) and his discovery, John Smith (right) (author's collection).

The High and the Mighty at the Egyptian Theatre. Location shooting near **Kona** on Big Island started September 24, 1954, and lasted until October 30 (with interiors shot in the Warner Burbank studios).

Key members of the cast were booked in the 20 rooms of the **Kona Inn**, a hotel and spa on Alii Drive then, a restaurant today. The rambling two-story Hawaiian structure was instrumental in developing the Kona Coast as one of the great fishing areas. The place had attracted marlin anglers from all over the globe. Since many American tourists frequented the inn, Wayne found himself constantly hounded for autographs. After one week, he asked for a private residence for him and the new love in his life, Pilar. From then on, they traveled 14 miles in a water-taxi from the filming location down the coast to the home of William H. Hill, one of Hawaii's first Senators. The stunning oceanfront estate is nestled in the sun-drenched shores of **Keauhou Bay**. The historic three-acre tropical retreat called Hale Kai (Ocean House) was auctioned off in 2013.

They had Lana Turner booked into a single room at the Kona Inn. She was furious when she found that her room adjoined John Farrow's, for the director was noted for dramatic flirtations with his leading ladies. When the glamorous star arrived, she learned that Wayne, Farrow and the two writers were still working on the script. "That didn't bode too well," recalled Turner. The story was indeed weak, and Wayne did not wear the unlikely role of a German freighter captain comfortably. The freighter he commands, the *Ergenstrasse*, was actually a steel-hulled tramp steamer anchored in the Kona harbor, 45 minutes away by speedboat. "We had

to wake up at the break of dawn," Turner complained, "to take advantage of the light." When the sun shone, the crew couldn't touch the hot steel. Turner: "They set up fans to cool the metal, but they didn't help much."[3]

"We'll burn this ship in her own fires!"

The main filming site was **Kealakekua Bay**, 12 miles south of Kailua-Kona. The historical sites include the spot where Captain James Cook was killed: Scenes were shot near the brass plate that marks the site.

James Arness, then under contract to Batjac, brought his experience as a logger to the picture. He was furiously chopping away at those logs. "Seems no one else in the cast really knew how to handle an axe."[4] Jim was looking forward to the time they would move to Oahu because he loved to surf. To him, the famous waves at Waikiki looked rather disappointing. Therefore, when somebody suggested going 40 miles west to Makaha, Arness rented a car and took Gil Perkins, a stuntman who also played one of the shipmates. Arness told him, "If I ever make any money in this business, I'm going to have a home here in Makaha."[5] The next year, Wayne introduced his protégé to the CBS executives who were looking for the lead in *Gunsmoke*. Three years later, Arness had that home in Makaha.

"Don't confuse sincerity of purpose with success"

One time, when they were lunching at the Kona Inn, Pilar Palette—not yet married to Wayne—came in and started screaming at Turner about staying clear of Duke. She

Another visit from Tarzan: Lex Barker, then married to Lana Turner, drops in on John Farrow (in director's chair) and John Wayne. Four years after *The Sea Chase*, controversy surrounded the movie goddess when her 14-year-old daughter stabbed Turner's lover to death during a domestic struggle (author's collection).

Jack L. Warner (right) looks rather proud to welcome this famous guest to the *Sea Chase* set: Field Marshall Bernard Montgomery (in uniform). John Farrow, Mia's father, stands to Monty's left (author's collection).

just vented her feelings and Gil Perkins thought to himself, "Boy. What a broad!"[6]

The event that occurred two days after wrapping the location was probably more important to Wayne. His lawyer called after the final divorce papers came through, and Wayne turned to Pilar with a big grin and said, "How would you like to get married today?" The wedding took place on November 1, 1954, in the garden of Senator Hill's home. In a small, quiet ceremony, John Farrow acted as best man and Wayne's secretary Mary St. John was the maid of honor. The entire town closed its shops. When some 150 natives came to the house to stand outside, Wayne invited them in. In the end, he ended up inviting about everyone on the island to the wedding. Guests lined up with the cast to kiss the bride. "I was well-bussed," remembered Pilar.[7] "Wayne was quoted as saying something to the effect: 'You can bet this will be a hot marriage. The ceremony was performed on a lava bed.'"[8] They spent their wedding night at Honolulu's Royal Hawaiian Hotel. The next day, the newlyweds left for California. At the airport, the photographers snapped a picture that was reprinted numerous times over the years: Wayne gallantly lifting Pilar in his arms and carrying her over deep puddles. "To me, Honolulu is the garden spot of the world," Pilar reminisced, "the lushness of the scenery, the beautiful clear warm waters, it is truly paradise."[9]

"Look, we're noble allies"

Some call the almost perfectly round island of **Kauai** a magic place for its outrageous beauty. Filmmakers call it

The fictitious village of Haleakaloha was created on the palm-tree-lined Hanamaulu Bay. The unspoiled beach looks exactly the same as when the *Donovan's Reef* company arrived (photograph by Roland Schaefli).

magical because its 550 square miles can be Africa, Australia, England, Tahiti, Vietnam, even Arizona—all within a 40-minute driving radius. For *Donovan's Reef* director John Ford, Kauai turned into the fictional island of Haleakaloha, a Hawaiian word that can be translated as "Home of Laughter and Love," and that is exactly the atmosphere Ford wanted to create. When Lee Marvin was hesitant to take second billing once again, Ford worked on him, explaining that the entire Marvin family could partake of the tropical paradise. The director asked Marvin, "Don't you want you and your family to all get brown as berries?"[10]

The light-hearted Technicolor comedy about a couple of expatriate Navy veterans who occasionally trash the island saloon Donovan's Reef became the last screen collaboration of Wayne and Ford. They made *Donovan's Reef* between July 23 and September 1962 under the working title *The Climate of Love*.

"We got blown off our can"

True to form, Ford did his own location scouting on the *Araner*. He sailed across the Kauai Channel, from Honolulu to Nawiliwili. He once told Peter Bogdanovich he wouldn't like to live on an island like that; "I like to go to Honolulu for a couple of weeks on leave, but after that, the island closes in on me."[11]

When he surveyed the palm tree-lined **Hanamaulu Bay**, the next major bay north of Kalapaki, he decided this would be the place for the fictitious native village of Haleakaloha. The production put 31 grass shacks on the balmy beach. As the characters moved up and down from the customs port and the South Seas bar of the title, clever

Elizabeth Allen is about to give John Wayne a swimming lesson on Hanamaulu Bay. Director John Ford scouted this pristine beach for *Donovan's Reef* himself (author's collection).

editing brought the location together with the Paramount studio lot where the upper part of Haleakaloha was created. The natural paradise lies hidden off HI-51. Hehi Road gets you to the beach park.

On the right side of the bay lies the old **Ahukini Pier**. The cement pier with its signal tower was perfect as the setting of the communications hut in which Wayne and Marvin send the arriving doctor a message about their scheme. The remnants of Ahukini Landing, once the main port of Kauai, had already been closed down for ten years when Ford utilized it. (It had been the location for the Esther Williams film *Pagan Love Song*.) The wooden walkway is situated at the mouth of the Hanamaulu Stream, at 3651 Ahukini Road.

For the scene of Elizabeth Allen's tumultuous arrival, William Clothier turned his camera to the white-sand beach at **Kalapaki**, just north of Nawiliwili, now a resort strand fronting several hotels. When Allen drops into the water, she falls into the center of **Nawiliwili Harbor**.

"Not the brandy, you dope!"

The cast was housed just a few minutes away, at the **Kauai Inn**, at the small boat harbor at 2430 Hulemalu Road, Lihue. One day, the actors were rehearsing in the banquet room. Ford was not pleased with Wayne's delivery of the line, "Ann, bring me some coffee." He asked him to repeat it several times. Wayne did, but louder each time. Ida Lovell, working in the adjacent bar and overhearing, fixed a pot of coffee and brought it to Wayne.

The Kauai Inn was the first hotel on the island. It underwent a renovation in 1991 only to be hit by Hurricane Iniki. After years of repairing, the new owners brought the historic hotel back to life.

The locals still tell the story of Wayne swimming ashore from the *Araner* to Nawiliwili Harbor and, dripping wet, entering Club Jetty, at the time Kauai's leading nightspot. The feisty proprietor, Emma "Mama" Ouye, wanted to stop him from making this a habit, so she told him that she would chant at night to attract a shark which she personally fed. Wayne never swam into the club again. Another legend concerns Lee Marvin, who liked to go out on drunken binges. One time, he was so drunk that he reportedly stripped naked and danced at a bar in Nawiliwili Harbor—probably the same club.

Marvin's wife Betty recalled the production: "Duke would talk slow. The more he drank, the slower he talked. He was a big kissy bear." Her husband, on the other hand, was fast, like a leopard. "So, you have these two animals, you can imagine."[12] One night, after a pub crawl with Wayne, Marvin plum forgot what he was doing in Hawaii.

In a minute, John Wayne will drop Elizabeth Allen into Nawiliwili Harbor in *Donovan's Reef*. The first movie appearance of the *Araner*, John Ford's yacht, is also its last (author's collection).

He went to the airport shoeless and caught a plane to L.A. They brought him back the next day.

"You're quite a gal"

Ford shot the colorful Coronation Ball sequence featuring 200 local extras costumed as Polynesian dancers at the **Allerton Estate** at 4425 Lawai Road, Koloa. In the film, the Allerton Estate home stood in as the home of the French island governor, portrayed by Cesar Romero. The white beach house was the former residence of Hawaiian Queen Emma and is now a part of the National Tropical Botanical Garden. The scenes on this location were edited together

During the making of *Donovan's Reef*, cast and crew were housed at the Kauai Inn in Lihue. They still tell hilarious stories about their famous guests (photograph by Roland Schaefli).

with Wayne's first entrance in a canoe, which was actually filmed at **Smith's Boat Landing** at the Wailua River in

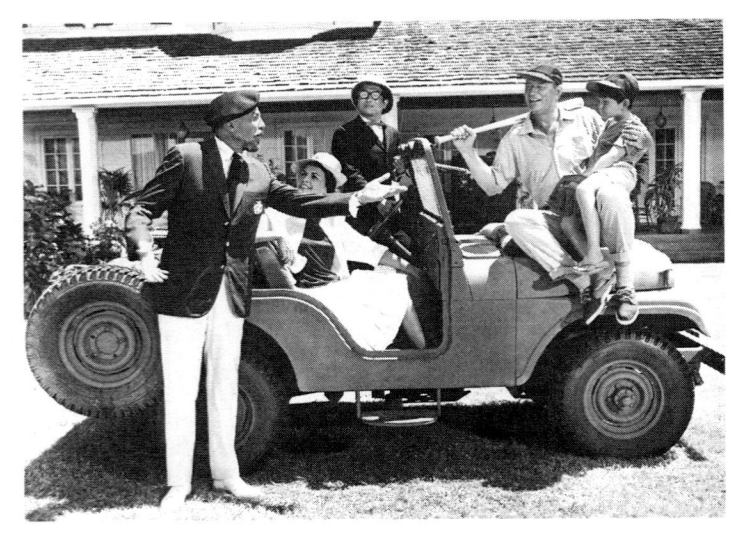

This publicity photograph was snapped in front of the former residence of the Queen, the Allerton Estate in Koloa: with Cesar Romero, Elizabeth Allen, and Jon Fong. Child actor Jeffrey Byron (on Wayne's knee) made his debut in *Donovan's Reef* and went on to a long career on TV shows, including *Dallas*, *The Bold and the Beautiful*, and *Baywatch* (author's collection).

An unlikely place to look for a Christmas tree: John Wayne at Waimea Canyon in a posed shot for *Donovan's Reef* (author's collection).

Kapaa. The Wailua is the only navigable river in all of Hawaii. Right in front of where the Grotto tour now starts, at 3–5971 Kuhio Highway, Ford also shot the speedboat scenes. The fake rock Elizabeth Allen jumps on water skis was set in the middle of the river.

Close to the river location was Dr. Dedham's house, on Wailua Beach just north of the Coco Palms Hotel (famous for Elvis' wedding scene in *Blue Hawaii*). It has since been moved up into the hills and now stands on the grounds of the Horner mansion at Waipouli Beach.

"Those gold stars don't stand for good behavior"

Production trucks moved up on windy Kokee Road to **Waimea Canyon** where Ford directed a pictorial highlight of the film, Wayne felling a tree for Christmas on the sandy hills of the Waimea lookout. Mark Twain once called it the Grand Canyon of Kauai. Still, Ford cheated a bit when he showed **Waipoo Falls**, the waterfall streaming down the mountainside, closer than it actually is.

"…threw 'em a few spitballs"

When in Honolulu, the *Araner* would often anchor at Ala Wai Harbor. *Donovan's Reef* was a farewell to Ford's boat as well. He had bought the 110-foot yacht in 1934. At the time he made his last film with Wayne, the director could no longer support this way of life. So with this reunion of old friends, he commemorated his yacht on film. Elizabeth Allen sails into the film on the *Araner*, and Wayne even calls the boat by its proper name. "It was summer fun," Lee Marvin said, "his last return to paradise."[13] Ford took his family on this last voyage, along with Wayne and his children, Marvin and his children, and Anna Lee's children. After that, the beloved boat was sold for a song and became a tourist cruise boat called the *Windjammer*. Wayne had been a guest on the *Araner* so often that sightseeing boats that used to go by would say, "That's John Wayne's boat." And John Ford would stand up and say, "Yeah, this is John Wayne."[14]

"Permission to speak"

Betty Marvin remembered Wayne being very honest about himself: "Look, I'm not an actor," he would say, "I just stand and move." Betty did not remember the two stars ever discussing filmmaking: "They were instinctual."[15] Later in that decade, Wayne turned down the movie that fully cemented Marvin's star status: *The Dirty Dozen*.

Back at the Paramount lot, Ford matched the grass huts

with the nineteenth-century western town set. The lower part of Western Street—for years it had served as the Virginia City Street on *Bonanza*—was turned into the South Pacific Island village. The Native American actor and singer Branscombe Richmond, who became famous with the TV series *Renegade*, was one of the children cast as bit players. To this day, he calls "watching John Wayne work" one of the highlights of his long career.[16]

Wayne sometimes said that the only guy he ever hit unintentionally in a screen fight was "Iron" Mike Mazurki. It happened on this set, in the big fight scene on the saloon set. Wayne had told him, "Mike, I'm gonna throw-boom! But before I throw it, I'm gonna reach up and yank your white hat down, and then throw it!" But when Wayne "boomed" it, instead of leaning back, Mazurki came forward. "And damn it, I just hit him as hard as I could and took all the makeup off his face and put it in his white hat, and it didn't hurt him a damn bit! He just stood there and blinked!"[17] After the fight, the slot machine pays out 2700 silver dollars. These were borrowed from the Bank of America. Five armed guards observed the shooting of that scene on the Paramount lot.

"All battles are fought by scarred men"

In Harm's Way, the war movie that dealt with the aftermath of Pearl Harbor, was Wayne's last Hawaii film (and also his last black-and-white film). It was in production from June 24 until September 1964. During the filming, he lived at the newly opened **Ilikai Hotel** on Waikiki Beach. For over 50 years, it has been a Waikiki landmark, a symbol of the

The "Grand Canyon of Kauai": the natural wonder of Waimea Canyon was one of the visual highlights of the Technicolor film (photograph by Roland Schaefli).

moment when centuries of Hawaiian culture merged with a vision of a modern, urban Waikiki. When seen from the air, the hotel at 1777 Ala Moana looks shaped like a peace symbol. It was made famous in the opening credits of the TV series *Hawaii Five-O*.

Director Otto Preminger shot a scene with Wayne and leading lady Patricia Neal in downtown Honolulu, a section then known as Hell's Half Acre. During the dinner scene, Wayne proved that deep down he was still a prop man when he suggested that Neal's nurse shouldn't have her cigarettes in a case but carry a pack, and have the matches tucked into the pack, as he'd seen some nurses do.

Preminger didn't shoot the interior takes on a Hollywood soundstage but in the cramped confines of actual bungalows, the homes of military personnel on Oahu. He had rented several for the various scenes showing the servicemen in their private quarters. The exteriors of the base housing were shot on **Ford Island**, Pearl Harbor.

Wayne filmed his scenes aboard the Navy ship on the USS *Kearsarge* anti-submarine naval vessel. He believed that the climactic battle was poorly done because, after showing these mighty ships, Preminger relied on miniatures for the final sea battle. Paramount's special effects department usually shot trick scenes like that on their B-tank. They towed those "boats in bathtubs" on cables across the water in front of a painted backdrop. The technique was still used by Paramount in 1983 when they shot the epic miniseries *The Winds of War*. Wayne: "He really had a fine picture going for him until he got all enamored with miniatures. Christsakes, you didn't believe one thing because you saw these phony miniatures going back and forth."[18]

"Full report"

Wayne's persistent cough, developed on the set of *Circus World*, continued into the filming of *In Harm's Way*, sometimes ruining takes. Pilar had been praying that Hawaii's temperate climate would restore his health. Instead, his cough grew worse. Aissa Wayne remembered, "Even in the crystalline air of Hawaii, it became so torturous that some days he had to stop shooting his scenes."[19] After he finished the Preminger picture, Wayne was diagnosed with lung cancer.

After the somewhat unexpected success of the record *America, Why I Love Her* (it sold 100,000 copies in the first two weeks), a companion book was published under the same title in 1977. In it, Wayne again expressed his love for the United States, helped along by writer John Mitchum. Together, they recommend that you "watch a Hawaiian island sunrise from the old Lahaina Inn or Maui."[20] Wayne certainly didn't need someone to put words in his mouth when it came to praising the beauty of Hawaii. His memories never faded. Just months from his death, he told a writer about the time he "caught a giant mahi-mahi in the waters of Hawaii. I weighed the fish, then ate it." Later, when the boat docked, he discovered he had eaten the world's record for that species. "I should have had that son of a bitch mounted!"[21]

Pilar summed up how the Waynes felt about the island paradise: "The Hawaiian people are so dear. Duke will always live in their hearts."[22]

15

Venture Abroad

"Got a great idea: European tour"

"The Sahara desert! Straight ahead, then turn to the left."
—Desert guide Joe January (John Wayne) discusses the route
in *Legend of the Lost*

Matt Masters (John Wayne) thought he had a great idea: a European tour. But European ventures didn't turn out to be great, neither for the Circus World entrepreneur nor for movie producer Wayne. He made deals with Italian and Spanish companies. All resulting films were duds. Joe January had suspected as much when he told his pack mule, "Out in the middle o' nowhere, lookin' for nothin' in the wrong season! Jeanette, you have a pal on this trip. A fellow jackass. It's me!"

As an independent producer, Wayne made the deals. He hired the talent. And he took the blame for the failure of a film. That was the case with 1957's *Legend of the Lost*. Like the adventurer he portrayed in it, he went into the desert to look for treasure. But the prospects of *Legend of the Lost* proved to be a movie fata morgana, and box office was weak.

"I like my chippies in a room"

For his first Batjac production based outside the U.S., Wayne boarded the French liner *Liberte* on May 10, 1956, in New York. The ship had been the replacement for the legendary SS *Normandie* that was lost during World War II. Now the *Liberte* was the flagship for CGT French Line. For Wayne, the filming of the grim *Timbuktu* (the working title of *Legend of the Lost*) was a good excuse for a holiday, European style.

The trip started out well enough. Batjac had gotten Henry Hathaway as director and a story by renowned scriptwriter Ben Hecht. (In an early draft, he had written Joe January as a crapulent Foreign Legionnaire.) He would play opposite the Italian star Rossano Brazzi, who was made famous by appearing as a Latin lover in Hollywood movies based in Italy: *Three Coins in the Fountain* and David Lean's *Summertime*. But most of all, Batjac was able to secure the services of the exciting young Italian star Sophia Loren, a last-minute replacement for Gina Lollobrigida. Famed British cinematographer and multiple Oscar winner Jack Cardiff would lens the intimate three-character drama in glorious Technicolor.

John Wayne, Claudia Cardinale, and the Columbus Monument: the scene of Matt Masters' arrival in the harbor of Barcelona was shot with a rear-projection but didn't make the final cut (author's collection).

As head of Batjac, Wayne sealed the deal with co-producer Dear Films, an Italian company based in Rome. Up until the Batjac venture, they had spawned a number of French films. One condition was that Cinecitta in Rome had to be used for the studio scenes.

"Best desert remedy on the market"

Wayne passed through Rome to do screen tests. His arrival in the Eternal City made headlines and he held a press reception at the **Hotel Excelsior**, at the famous Via Vittorio Veneto 125. Enrico Mazzega, a syndicated writer who covered all the Hollywood stars coming to work in Cinecitta, had a vivid memory of that night. Other stars would usually just give the press some printable statement of how much they loved Italy and how much they loved working here. "Wayne, however, appeared to be cautious about the whole affair." The star gave his interviewers the flinty-eyed look they knew so well from his American movies as if he wanted to say, "What d'ya really want from me?" The waiters at the Excelsior kept the Italian wine coming, and after an evening of heavy drinking, Mazzega realized that Wayne was no longer able to get up. With the help of a friend, the publicist got the tall American in a cab, then dragged him up to his hotel suite. The next morning, Mazzega came to check on how Wayne was doing. The star looked him up and down, then inquired, "Who are you?"[1] Harry Carey, Jr., once confirmed that Wayne did have blackouts when he didn't remember what he did when he was out drinking.

"A great town for thinkin'. No distractions"

Wayne was at the **Grand Hotel**, Via Vittorio Emanuele Orlando 3. Richard Burton and Liz Taylor were loyal guests, usually staying at the Royal Suite with their sizable entourage, occupying nearby rooms, and their frequent visits had brought glamour back to the Grand Hotel. In later years, stars Meg Ryan, George Clooney, Brad Pitt, Richard Gere and Hugh Grant stayed there. Sophia Loren celebrated Christmas 1956 in Wayne's hotel suite. The whole crew went to **Piazza Navona** to buy gifts from the market stands. Wayne also went to a gala at the **Teatro Sistina**, Via Sistina 129, and he had spaghetti at the **Alfredo Restaurant**, Via della Scrofa 104. The Alfredo alla Scrofa had been operating since 1914 and is still known as the birthplace of fettucine alfredo. On January 2, they were off for Libya.

"Out in the middle o' nowhere…"

The first thing Wayne noticed upon meeting with the key people on location: Nobody had hired professional

Finding a treasure trove: While in Rome, Wayne had a photograph shooting for an advertisement scheduled which would be timed to coincide with the release of *Legend of the Lost*. He had endorsed Rheingold Lager Beer for several years during the 1950s. His promotional slogan was "My beer is Rheingold—because it's extra dry!" (author's collection).

wranglers. An Italian trainer was supposed to prepare the mules. They were brought all the way from Sicily. Wayne and Hathaway checked on them, and when the director walked behind them, one mule almost kicked his head off. So Wayne declared, "I'm going to call a couple of guys and have them come over." On New Year's Eve morning he had his secretary Mary St. John get ahold of stuntmen Terry Wilson and Chuck Hayward. They left the same day and got into Rome the next day. At first, they figured this would be a quick job: They had to work out all the things the donkeys would have to do, smell the water and so on. They stayed on the payroll for three months.[2]

Ghadames in Northwestern Lybia was the headquarters of the Batjac/Dear Films Produzione. It is one of the oldest pre–Saharan cities. The rustic town was an oasis situated at the center of an ancient camel route leading to Tripoli and the sea. One shabby hotel was the only habitable accommodation. Its half-dozen small grotty rooms had once served for a retreat of Italian General Italo Balbo. Now they housed

Wayne's key crew members. The production manager had an extra-large bed installed in Wayne's room.

"Shows you how serious the situation is"

"It was a surreal and fantastic place, brimming with magic, but with hazards, too," Loren told the readers of her memoir. "Cockroaches, scorpions, snakes, sandstorms, the heat, the thirst … and the Tuaregs." Those "blue men" both attracted and frightened the young Italian star: "It's a good thing John Wayne was there to protect us!"[3]

There was soon more for her to fear. The desert was a shimmering, ferocious furnace during the day but it turned numbingly cold as soon as the sun went down. One of those freezing nights almost cost Loren her life. Her small room was heated by a gas stove (a film crew technician had installed it for her). She sealed the windows because the room was on the ground floor and she feared the scorpions. During the night, the young actress tried desperately to wake up from a terrible nightmare. She was asphyxiating from the gas stove's fumes. She managed to crawl to the door before she fainted. Rossano Brazzi found her unconscious and called for help, and she was saved in the nick of time. While Hathaway's biggest concern was how he would have replaced the leading lady, Wayne was more concerned for Sophia than for the film.

"You live your way, I live mine"

The Batjac crew organized the preliminary work. Even though Europe is famous for its camping equipment, Wayne's employees preferred to ship a boatload of surplus Army junk from Hollywood to the port of Genoa in Italy, thence to Tripoli. Outside Ghadames, they built a tent city. Entertainment journalist David Hanna (he would publish *The Life and Times of John Wayne* in 1979) observed how the crew lived in two-man tents. To him, the tent city "resembled the Hoovervilles of the Depression."[4] The tents were shabby, stained, full of holes. The septic toilets were too small and too few. Once they were installed, the showers functioned erratically, leaving half a dozen soap-covered men to make out as best they could until water pressure resumed, "sometimes, the following day," Hanna added.

Ghadames in the Sahara Desert: probably his toughest location ever—and that means something (author's collection).

Practicing the fight scene in the fake sand dunes of Cinecitta studio. *Legend of the Lost* almost became the last epitaph of the young film career of Sophia Loren. She had replaced Gina Lollobrigida on short notice (author's collection).

Even Terry Wilson, who had toughed it out on many rough locations, had to admit, "The conditions were rustic, to say the least."[5] And Jack Cardiff, who had filmed *The African Queen* under equally harsh conditions in Africa, said, "The work was pure hell."[6]

One day, Hanna found Loren crying, miles away from the campsite. No toilet facility had been provided in her dressing room trailer, nor for the only other two women on the set, her hairdresser and the script girl. An accommodation was made the next day. Loren later called it the harshest conditions of any location she had ever been on. Wayne seemed to be the only one who liked his tent city! It probably reminded him of his early Poverty Row films.

"That's an easy faith to lose"

Loren never ceased to be amazed at the fact that the king of Westerns seen up close was "exactly as I expected him to be." To the young star, Wayne really was a cowboy, a big, solid, authoritative one, "and very sure of himself." But he was always with his wife, a petite Mexican woman, "without whom he felt lost."[7]

Pilar, just having given birth to their first child, had initially refused to join him. Then she received a frightening cablegram: "Please hurry here. I need you."[8] There were no phones on the Saharan location, so she left for North Africa at once, fearing the worst. It took her four days to get to Ghadames. When the tiny plane taxied to stop on the primitive dirt strip, she rushed out straight into Wayne's waiting arms. He had just wanted her here so she could see the sunset with him. Pilar remembered their mud-plastered, thatch-roofed room: "Every evening, a houseboy would water the room's dirt floor to keep the dust down. Duke and I would slip and slide on fresh mud like a pair of Keystone Cops."[9]

In terms of experiences of other cultures, Batjac was a beginner. The Americans had shipped the kind of food that suited the particular tastes of American crews—hundreds of cans of pork and beans, cases of pickled onions, corned beef, canned tomatoes, pancake mix, cans of maple syrup, corn flakes, canned corn. And canned American coffee. The members of the Arab crew refused to eat the canned stuff, fearing it might contain pork. The Italians loathed corn and demanded pasta. There was a threat of a strike unless more suitable food was provided and camp conditions improved. Wayne and his men couldn't quite understand the resentment. A new cooking staff was soon installed. Rossano Brazzi, fresh from his success in *South Pacific*, kept asking himself why he had to work in such conditions. "I didn't know such places could exist in this century."[10]

"A million years of dead sand"

Every morning, the Batjac caravan set out on a two-hour journey to the shooting location. Pilar estimated that it must have been 20 below zero when they got started in the dark. Jack Cardiff described the numbingly cold nights: "We slept in every garment we possessed, a couple of pullovers, as many socks as we could manage, overcoats—everything."[11] When they got up, they were already dressed. They even wore special Norwegian ski boots.

The trucks' engines were always frozen and had to be started by putting flaming torches under them. The road was a dusty track on which at least one truck always sunk axle-deep in the sand and had to be dug out. By nine in the morning, the temperature had risen from arctic cold to blazing heat. The extreme changes of temperature caused desert pebbles to "crack open like fretful fireworks," Cardiff observed.[12] Loren had to take a bath in a stream that, in the movie story, was supposed to be hot. It was ice cold. Her lips turned blue.

Hollywood Reporter's editors came out to see some of the filming. Wayne told them how his company moved out of the village each morning at five in four- and six-wheel vehicles equipped with special desert tires. "We move around until Henry Hathaway finds a background he wants and we start to work; finishing with that, we dash off to another location." He added, "I would not have missed this location for anything, but when I leave it, I'm certain that I would never want to make it again."

"Even camels can't make it sometimes"

The everpresent gusts of desert wind wafted sand into eyes and throats; it got into everything, "including our lunch," Cardiff mentioned. "Screaming Henry" was at his worst: Hathaway screamed maniacally at everybody who left footprints in the sand until, as Cardiff recalled, "we were all afraid to move." A crew worker remembered how Hathaway used to peer through a viewfinder, apparently dissatisfied with the footprints some character's safari boots had left. He wanted these dunes to have that pristine, untouched-by-human-foot look. So he turned to an assistant who grabbed a megaphone and bellowed to the shimmering horizon: "Get some men and dust them doons!"[13]

Even Wayne, their stoic producer, was not above moodiness. When the publicity manager asked Sophia to pose with the Tuaregs, the veiled Arabians were superstitious about being photographed. Hanna recalled that Wayne was furious when the publicity man couldn't hold the tribe long enough to get a picture with him too.

In those diabolical conditions, the suffering comrades

of Batjac worked with mechanical stoicism. On one opportunity, they even rallied to the aid of the mayor of Ghadames. His wife needed to be flown to a hospital, but a plane could not land because the runway had no lights. The crew used the lights from the set and lit up the runway so the woman could be rushed to the hospital.

Wayne was the undisputed leader, but according to Loren's recollections, he never took advantage of his power. One day, however, the legend ran the risk of cracking. That was when Wayne fell off his mount. "Hard to imagine, isn't it?," Loren asked in her 2014 biography. Wayne broke his ankle in the fall. "The crew expected him to swallow his pain with a shot of whiskey," Loren remembered. "Instead he started howling like a madman." *The Hollywood Reported* stated on March 28 that Wayne's injuries caused a three-week delay (he is clearly limping in the scene when he gets the donkeys ready for departure). Years later, when Wayne had to undergo cancer surgery, Michael Wayne used that accident

Joe January and Zita have reached the lost city: actually the ancient Roman port of Leptis Magna, Lybia's Roman heritage. To Sophia Loren, John Wayne was really a cowboy and "exactly as I expected him to be" (author's collection).

for an excuse to the press that his father had pulled a tendon in his ankle making that movie and had to have it corrected. Sophia kept the stirrups Wayne used in the movie as a souvenir. To this day, they hang on the wall of her office.

"You're a couple of fakes"

One evening, Loren and Wayne were walking on the sand dunes when Wayne boyishly handed her a desert rose. After that, she never thought of him in his popular image of the rough'n'tough he-man. Rumors about Sophia having had an affair behind the scenes of *Legend of the Lost* never quieted down. Sophia herself wrote in her memoir that Brazzi, the embodiment of the Latin lover, was so focused on his good looks that he never even realized she was just joking when she told him how adorable he was. "Maybe he took me seriously."[14] Of course, Loren was one of the most beautiful women on Earth, blue lips or not, and a photographer's delight. When Jack Cardiff looked into Sophia's "wonderfully lucent eyes," he was lost. In 1997, he revealed the secret about their falling in love in this preposterously unromantic atmosphere. They kept their fervent love secret throughout the film. Cardiff: "We had secret codewords and phrases which passed between us on the set." They did such a good job of hiding their feeling that Brazzi was boasting to people on the unit that Sophia was making a play for him and was knocking on his wall at night. Sophia swore that she would get her revenge for this wild untruth.

Wayne actually believed the rumor. Several of his biographers picked up on it, saying that Wayne didn't approve what went on between his leading lady and the other Italian actor on the set, Brazzi, because the head of Batjac knew that Sophia was engaged to the renowned Italian producer Carlo Ponti.

Still, to Wayne, Sophia was just a little girl. He liked watching her play around. On the grim location, she was hugely popular with her sense of fun, and whenever someone tried to put a damper on her exuberance, he'd say: "C'mon, leave her alone, she's young…. Let her laugh." When she was close to him, she felt safe.[15]

"It's goodbye, waterhole"

Hathaway and Wayne dreamed up a helicopter shot that would fill the Technirama screen, with the lost trio like specks in the desert. Wayne asked a retired general, Clarence A. Shoop, then a vice-president of the Hughes Aircraft Company, for help in arranging military logistical support in Libya. Shoop asked for assistance from officials at Wheelus Air Force Base on the coast of Tripoli, then the largest U.S. military facility outside the U.S. (Today it's

Mitiga International Airport.) Air Force Colonel William J. Cain, Jr., agreed to offer as much assistance as possible, largely because of Wayne's "past assistance to the Air Force."[16] A chopper was provided and the occasion resulted in a jolly evening.

Unfortunately, they never got the shot they wanted. Cardiff had angled his camera on the train of pack mules with the actors. The star trio was swaying and plodding across the desert, all alone in the Sahara. When the camera was too close, Cardiff ordered the French pilot, "Au-dessus." He forgot "au-dessus" is the French word for "high" but "au-dessous" means lower. The helicopter sank noisily down. The animals panicked (unseating some riders) and galloped in all directions over the Sahara.

When they finally got all the desert scenes in the can, they moved to the sea. Hathaway shot all the "Timbuctoo" scenes that set up the story in the town of **Zliten**, east of Tripoli. Zliten has been targeted in the Libyan Civil War by terrorists.

"2,000 years of busy bats"

The company moved on to the ancient Roman port of **Leptis Magna**, the film's visual highlight. Leptis Magna was called one of the jewels of the Kingdom of Lybia. The roman ruins aren't in the middle of the desert as the movie makes us believe but on the coast. When Cardiff's camera showed the front view of the Roman theater, he did not show the building in its whole height, because then viewers would see the sea in the background. The ruin is a two-hour ride from Tripoli, which the world perceives to be the second-worst city to live in. Leptis Magna might be a high-risk destination but curious travelers are still magnetically drawn to the stunning UNESCO site.

After five weeks of exteriors, the company left Ghadames. Not too many crew members remember it for its moniker, the "pearl of the desert." Loren called the experience one of the most physically challenging of her career. Pilar concluded: "[Wayne] was right about one thing, the sunsets were glorious. That is the only positive thing I can say about Ghadames."[17]

"A half a degree error can mean 40 miles!"

By March, Hathaway had moved the company into Rome's **Cinecitta Studios**, Via Tuscolana 1055. The fascists had founded the studios in 1937. The Allies had bombed Cinecitta during the war. After Rome fell to the Allies, they used the former studios as a displaced persons' camp. An estimated 3,000 refugees lived on Cinecitta grounds for a period of two years. When Wayne's company utilized the sets, the studio had already been dubbed "Hollywood on the Tiber." Beginning with the Bible spectacle *Quo Vadis* in 1950, MGM set the trend to make epics set in ancient Rome with the help of their descendants. In 2014, "Cinecitta World" opened. The movie-themed amusement park is located 16 miles southwest of the studios on the site of a former movie studio built by Dino De Laurentiis (one of the producers of Wayne's final film, *The Shootist*).

In those fake sand dunes, Loren finally got her revenge on Rossano Brazzi. In the sandstorm scene, she had to struggle with him in a tent. During the take, Brazzi suddenly yelled in pain and ran off the set holding his bruised manhood.

Legend of the Lost wrapped in April. Budgeted at $1,750,000, it earned domestic rentals of $2,200,000 and was considered a failure. Even the eerie score, composed by Italy's Angelo Francesco Lavagnino, didn't sound much like the score of a John Wayne picture. The Italian co-producers lost the tapes; the full soundtrack was

"The third legion of Rome made this city to last forever": A two-hour ride from Tripoli lies the archaeological site of Leptis Magna, one of the most surprising of all John Wayne locations (photograph by Tidwa Tourism Services).

never recovered. John Wayne kept his Joe January vest and used it in private. When it was sold at auction in 2011, it was still splattered with fish blood.

"Man, I smell as sweet as lilies in the valley"

During his stay in Italy, Wayne took a vacation. Secretly and silently, he went to **Ishia**, the volcanic island in the Gulf of Naples. The Burt Lancaster flick *The Crimson Pirate* had put Ischia on the movie location map a few years back. By the time Wayne visited, it was already known among celebrities for its natural hot springs. He bathed in hot water at the **Regina Isabella**, on the Piazza Santa Restituta, in the village of Lacco Ameno. The hotel was then new, built by Italian film producer Angelo Rizzoli. It can be assumed that Wayne stayed there because Rizzoli was a partner in the Dear Films venture. Never one to disappoint a photographer, the bronzed star posed in shorts on the stairs of the spa. Within a few years, the Regina Isabella became the center of attraction for the international jet set.

"The same raw material Homer used"

Wayne still longed to see European sites. He traveled to Greece and visited the **Acropolis,** the ancient citadel above Athens. Ironically, the film Sophia Loren had made before *Legend, Boy on a Dolphin*, was filmed on the rocky outcrop. (That was the first time city officials had given permission to film at the Parthenon.) Wayne was back in the Greek capital when he was promoting *McQ*. Mayor Dimitrios Ritos gave him a gold Key to the City for launching an anti-pollution campaign. When in Athens, he used to stay at the **Astir Palace**, a resort on a private 30-hectare peninsula in the southern suburb of Vouliagmeni. At the time, it was called the Athens Riviera. Richard Nixon was a guest as well. It opened in 1958 and is now the Four Seasons Astir Palace.

Wayne gave credit to the Europeans for their understanding of western folklore: A Western deals in life and sudden death and primitive struggle, and with the basic emotions love, hate and anger. "In other words," he lectured, "they're made of the same raw material Homer used." He told the editors of *The Saturday Evening Post* that Europeans had a better understanding of that than the Americans did. "They recognize their relationship to the old Greek stories that are classics now, and they love 'em."[18]

"If there's anything I'm gonna miss in Europe"

The experience with the Italian producers didn't teach Wayne not to make deals with European movie moguls. Samuel Bronston was described as a sort of Cecil B. DeMille character, driven to make big films. No amount of money was too great to spend on sets and costumes. By 1964, he had

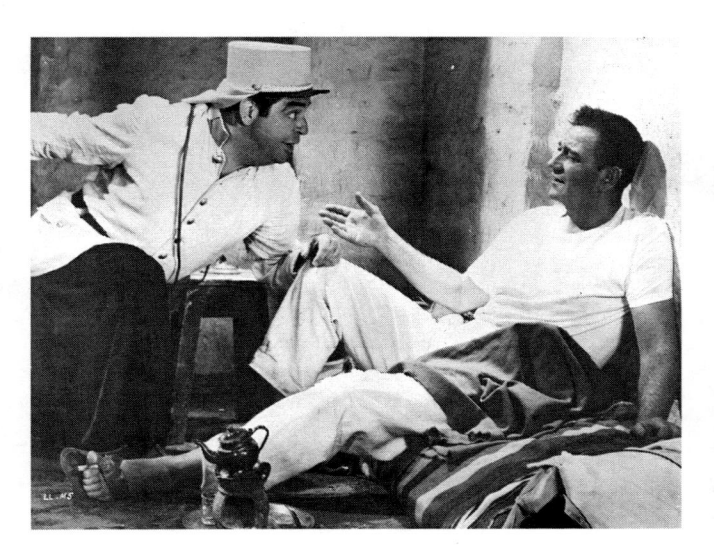

At the tail end of production in the Cinecittà interiors: John Wayne is jailed by Kurt Kasznar. Originally born in Austria, the character actor was one of the first U.S. Army photographers to film the ruins of Hiroshima (author's collection).

Anchoring the *Wild Goose* in the Port Hercules, the harbor of Monaco: Like circus entrepreneur Matt Masters, John Wayne went to Spain by boat (author's collection).

enough pull to get Wayne to star in his next extravaganza, *Circus World*, to be filmed in Spain.

Like his character in the movie, circus director Matt Masters, Wayne traveled to Europe by boat. The names of the destinations "got a nice sound," as the magnificent showman had stated. While the first trips in the *Wild Goose* had been relatively easy excursions, up and down the Baja coast, Wayne was anxious to put his ship to the ultimate challenge: a transatlantic crossing. His daughter Aissa remembered him "leaning over the maps spread on the desk in his trophy room," breathlessly explaining the route.[19] The Bronston engagement was the perfect opportunity. According to Pilar, Wayne planned to cross the Atlantic "with the same care and attention to detail that he put into the pre-production of *The Alamo*."[20]

"Send it to Matt Masters, somewhere in Europe"

So they headed down to Acapulco, paying his Los Flamingos Hotel a visit (see Chapter 10). In Acapulco, the *Wild Goose* was usually docked at the **Club de Yates**, on the Avenida Gran Via Tropical. Then they moved on to Panama.

Strange place for rifle practice: John Wayne is standing on the bottom of the artificial lake in Madrid's Parque del Retiro while it was drained (author's collection).

From the Canal, they sailed across the Gulf of Mexico to San Blas Island and on to Bermuda. The next leg of the trip across the Atlantic took six days of steady steaming. After the *Goose* had reached Lisbon on the Portuguese coast, they steered her through the Straits of Gibraltar. The *Wild Goose* reached Spanish soil in Palma de Mallorca. Wayne made headlines even when he didn't have a film to promote. "I love France," he told *Paris Match*. When a storm broke out, the *Wild Goose* was in jeopardy because she was too big to maneuver between the other yachts. A hauler pulled her into the big sea. The headline read that Wayne "went like a lamb."[21]

They went on to Monaco. When the yacht moored in Monte Carlo, Princess Grace came aboard. Next was Porto Fino on the Italian Riviera. From there, the crew brought the *Wild Goose* back and anchored her in a small Mexican fishing village called La Paz, near the Baja California tip, while Wayne flew to Madrid to begin working on *Circus World*.

"You got guts. I hope you win"

The script wasn't in the shape Wayne had been promised it would be. Frank Capra was set to direct and had been developing the screenplay for months. For a long time, the legendary director had in mind to do a picture with Wayne, whom he regarded next in line to his former stars Cooper and James Stewart, who had played American Everymen in Capra's *Mr. Deeds Goes to Town* and *Mr. Smith Goes to Washington*, respectively. At first glance, the story about a patchwork family in a circus appeared to be ideal sentimental material for his style. "I was sure in that big chunk of solid man there was the depth and humanity of a Mr. Deeds, a Mr. Smith, or a John Doe," Capra noted in his memoir. Wayne kept one of the Capra scripts on file; he scribbled all over it, outlining his complaints about the lead character: "Here is what is really wrong with this script: Capra has Duke mixed up with Gene Autry…." On another page near the end, he sums it up: "This is typically Jimmy Stewart."[22] He had analyzed the basic problem: Capra wasn't out to do a typical Wayne picture. In a Capra film, the lead character was the underdog, the small-town man who must be helped by the community to succeed in the end. On one back page, Wayne noted, "Capra just don't know a John Wayne picture."

"You can't say I didn't try"

Wayne had director and script approval and Capra had to realize that once you agreed to work with Wayne, you agreed to work with his entourage. His usual writer James Edward Grant was part of it. Grant caused friction and Capra

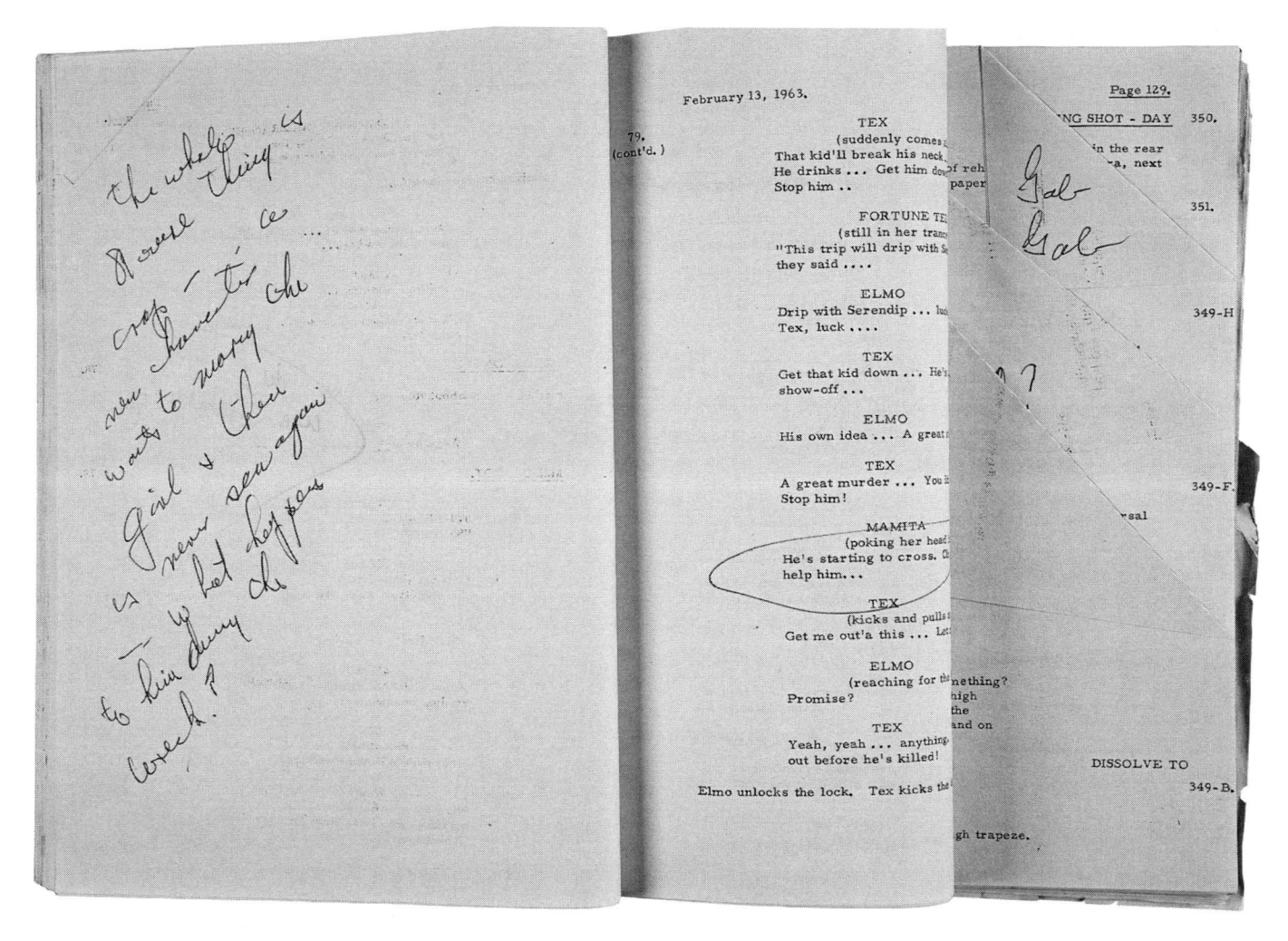

"Capra just don't know a John Wayne picture": the star kept the *Circus World* script that he refused to make in his files (Heritage Auctions, HA.com).

changed his mind about working with Wayne. Rather than lock horns with Wayne and force a great performance out of him, the director decided to opt out: "By that time, I hated the story, I hated circuses, I hated animals. I hated Wayne. I hated everything."[23] The Bronston people met with Wayne in Portugal to talk about an urgently needed director, and the actor made it clear: "I'm not going to just go with any old director you pick."[24] Wayne figured there was only one director who could salvage the wreck: "Screaming Henry."

Bronston had made it a habit to put his stars at the **Castellana Hilton** on the Paseo de la Castellana (now the Hotel InterContinental Madrid). When Henry Hathaway arrived in Madrid, he demanded to see Capra. After months of work on the script, Capra told his colleague that he was fleeing Madrid the way one flees from Siberia. Sad to say, the great director never got another major motion picture off the ground. After Capra quit, David Niven (who was to play the Lloyd Nolan part) dropped out, too, complaining that the film turned into a John Wayne movie. Rod Taylor was already in Spain when he realized that his role had shrunk to a supporting part. Even though Wayne and Taylor had wanted to make a film together for some time, the Australian actor left amicably and Wayne saw to it that John Smith got the part. (Wayne had already given Smith his big break with *The High and the Mighty*.)

When Wayne read Capra's autobiography *The Name Above the Title*, he said that he deeply resented the "rotten things this son-of-a-bitch said about Jimmy Grant and me."[25] Ironically, Hathaway didn't think much of Grant's script either, and he brought in script fixer Ben Hecht for yet another rewrite.

"She's been hurt once, that's enough"

The shooting script wouldn't be ready before September, so the Waynes had plenty of time to take in the sights of the capital of Spain. **Madrid** was not new to them: His daughter Melinda was attending the University of Madrid.

They stayed at a villa rented from Ava Gardner. The place was "barely livable," as Pilar recounted.[26]

"You got a circus to get movin'"

Russian-born Samuel Bronston was a salesman for MGM in France before moving to the U.S. at the outbreak of the Second World War. He became a production executive at Wayne's former studio, Columbia, but he had bigger dreams. In the early 1960s, he tried to turn Madrid into his own mini–Hollywood. Admiral Chester Nimitz was a supporter of Bronston's project of a film biography of Navy hero John Paul Jones. It was Nimitz who introduced Bronston to the regent of Spain, Generalissimo Franco, a strategic ally of America. Franco understood the possibility of making Madrid the European film capital and offered support. From then on, the self-proclaimed mogul tried to eclipse everything the Americans were doing at Cinecitta: colossal epics with star casts, big crowds and huge sets. Bronston even let the Pope bless his script for *King of Kings* in which he cast Wayne's *Searchers* co-star Jeffrey Hunter as Jesus. Bronston

This illustration of the Japanese souvenir program suggests that *Circus World* would feature the Arc de Triomphe. Even though the film plot involved many European landmarks, production never left Spain (author's collection).

Production built a platform on the artificial lake in Retiro Park, with the impressive Alfons XII. Monument in the background as a stand-in for Vienna's Gloriette, for the finale of *Circus World* (photograph by Roland Schaefli).

played for an even higher amount with his next epic about Spain's national hero, *El Cid*, getting Charlton Heston to star and Yakima Canutt to direct the second unit. Franco commanded his foot soldiers to play Roman legionaries or Chinese boxers, whatever Bronston's latest extravaganza called for.

For *55 Days at Peking*, the film czar built a huge studio in **Las Matas**, a district northwest of Madrid (it was a Spanish Civil War battlefield and is now a football stadium). With that epic, Bronston's winning streak came to a sudden end. The production history was a succession of problems. He then wanted to surpass himself with the monumental *The Fall of the Roman Empire* and had the Roman forum rebuilt in Las Matas, true to his mantra "Make it real!" It turned out to be a gigantic flop. Bronston lost $18 million. That was when he tried to get *Circus World* off the ground.

"Let's go into the opening act!"

September 23, 1963, was the first day of shooting *Circus World*. Bronston was betting a $9,000,000 budget on Wayne's draw as a box office champ. The film went over budget and took until February 1964 to finish.

The 125 horses, which were trained for *The Fall of the Roman Empire*, were now pulling circus wagons and stagecoaches. In the film, the circus show moves from one European capital to the next. Might be that was what attracted globetrotter Wayne in the first place. But in Madrid, his European sightseeing tour came to an end: Matt Masters' "European tour" would never leave Spain. For the first time, Bronston was cost-conscious.

Some of the publicity material places Wayne in the foreground of the Paris landmark, the Arc de Triomphe. But when showman Matt rides a stagecoach down the Champs-Elysées, Wayne is actually still on the Parkway in the **Retiro Park**, Madrid's recreational area. The six-up running wild is stopped at the roundabout of the **Fuente de la Alcahofa** in the Parque del Retiro. John Ford wouldn't let Wayne's usual stuntman Chuck Roberson leave his *Cheyenne Autumn* set to go to Madrid. That's why Bob Terhune (son of Max Terhune, Wayne's partner in the *Mesquiteer* Westerns) doubled Wayne in the transfer from horse to coach.

The artificial lake in the middle of the park was drained so the big circus set for the movie's acrobatic climax could be built. That gave Hathaway the chance to get the magnificent Alfons XII monument at **Plaza Maestro Villa** into the shot. Even though the sequence (with the doubles of Rita Hayworth and Claudia Cardinale twirling about on the ropes) was exquisitely staged and beautifully

When the Matt Masters' circus travels to the legendary Berlin Wintergarten, it is in fact Velázquez Palace in Madrid's Retiro Park (photograph by Roland Schaefli).

lit, Hathaway never thought it made for an exciting ending. After the lake was drained, Hathaway used the grounds for the sequence in which Matt signs on with another Wild West show. Wayne was supposed to jump off a ten-foot platform onto his horse and he actually practiced the stunt. Then the second unit took over and had Bob Terhune do the stunt. Terhune sprained his ankle and a wrist and broke his hip.

Hathaway remembered that Claudia Cardinale "was young and full of life, and Wayne treated her like she was one of his daughters."[27] Cardinale is still very fond of the experience: "I was having John Wayne for my father and Rita Hayworth for my mother—it can't get better than that!"[28]

Wild West show in the world-famous bullfighting ring of Chinchón: John Wayne rides to the rescue in *Circus World* (author's collection).

"Make up your mind
or you're forever dead"

Bronston had ensured that filming in the world-famous bullfighting arena in **Chinchón** was possible. In the **Plaza Mayor**, ringmaster Wayne rides a cavalry charge against the Indians. The Plaza with its typical Castile balcony rails and galleries is considered one of the most beautiful in the country. The Plaza de Toros had been cinematically used for the first time in 1956 in *Around the World in 80 Days*. The old town center is now classified as a cultural asset. Movie fans must not miss the opportunity to see the **Cuevas del Vino** at Calle Benito Hortelano 13. In the extensive wine cellars, visiting movie stars are always asked to sign the massive wine jugs. One of them was Yul Brynner as he was filming a sequence for the *Magnificent Seven* sequel in the same arena. In one of the rustic dining rooms, Wayne and Rita Hayworth played the scene of their bitter reunion.

"Bring out those cargo nets!"

The sequence in which Matt's steamer sinks in the **Barcelona** harbor cut even deeper into Bronston's finances: First they made the scrap-ready *Cabo Huertas* seaworthy again. The effect of the side-sinking ship was achieved by pumping 300 tons of water in one-half of the empty oil tanks. The capsizing sequence took place in the old part of the harbor, on the **Moll de Bosch**. The beautiful old customs building appears in the background. Bronston was able to conceal the fact that the departure of the steamer in New York was also shot at the same Barcelona seafront; they just decorated the customs building differently.

A logistical nightmare: In this impressive sequence of *Circus World*, the SS *Cabo Huertas* is sunk in the harbor of Barcelona (author's collection).

Because two units were working at the same time, Bob Terhune was called over from Madrid to Barcelona, to double Wayne in the shot when Matt climbs a rope as the 250-foot-long ship is turning on its side. Due to his accident in the horse stunt, Terhune wasn't able to perform it. The action sequence benefits from this, as it is clearly Wayne doing his own stunt.

Six hundred extras in contemporary costumes were swimming in the harbor basin. The ladies were held up by cork corsets. The men were kept afloat by cork belts hidden under their costumes. Hathaway was surprised that they got away with it without injuries or deaths: "I've been making pictures for 40 years, and this was the greatest job of its kind I have ever been involved in."[29] Bronston got the help of the Spanish Coast Guard, and a fleet of local fishermen was hired to rescue any waterlogged extras. Even the *Wild Goose* stood by, out of camera range.

Barcelona also served as another one of the establishing shots, giving the impression that Matt Masters travels all over Europa. In the movie, he visits the Hamburg Hansa circus at the turn of the century. In actual fact, it's the **Gran Teatre del Liceu**, the world-famous opera house on La Rambla 51–59, dating from 1847. Even though the Liceu had to be rebuilt after a fire (it reopened

The Plaza de Toros in Chinchón, considered one of the most beautiful arenas of Spain, was used in several movies, including the *Magnificent Seven* sequel with Yul Brynner (photograph by Roland Schaefli).

John Wayne doing his own stunt: Climbing a rope on the vertical deck of the sinking ship in *Circus World* (author's collection).

in 1999), Wayne fans will immediately recognize the superb interior: From one of the plush theater boxes, Wayne and Cardinale watched the lion tamer. After that number, Wayne wanders backstage. This landmark in European music history can be visited on a backstage tour.

"Nothing to be ashamed of—then or now"

The inside of the Berlin Wintergarten scene—Matt watches the clown perform on a high rope—was shot at the Circo Price in Madrid. It was almost equally famous as the Teatre del Liceu, but the Circo was not as fortunate: it fell victim to a fire soon after the filming. (The original circus is not to be confused with the new Circo Price that stands on a different location.)

Hathaway then moved the circus to **Toledo**. On the banks of the picturesque Tajo River, in the **Safont Park,** they filmed the scenes in the winter quarters, against the backdrop of the **Alcázar.** This rock fortress of the late Renaissance has a symbolic significance for the Spanish Civil War as a victory for Franco's army.

"Screaming Henry" Hathaway directs Wayne and Claudia Cardinale at the Gran Teatre del Liceu. Barcelona's opera house stood in for the Hamburg Hansa circus. The opera with an international reputation was restored to its former glory (author's collection).

"It's out of control!"

There was still the spectacular fire sequence to be filmed. They moved a short distance to the town of **Aranjuez,** also on the Tajo River. The circus tent goes up in flames right on the **Plaza de Parejas**, in front of the **Palacio Real,** supposedly Vienna in the film but actually the summer residence of the Spanish kings (and now a UNESCO World Heritage Site). The shooting of the big top catching fire took five days, during which time artificial and real fires were constantly being set, quenched and re-set. "Hell, Pilar, it's my job. It's what I get paid for," Wayne said, waving his wife's concerns aside. When he came home at night, he was exhausted, barely able to eat a decent meal before falling into bed. But he coughed so hard that he could not really rest. The inhalation of smoke aggravated his already besieged lungs.

While filming the scene in which Matt is knocking down circus seats with a hammer, the raging fire was blown out of control by an unexpected breeze. Wayne was oblivious to the danger. Though he wore fireproof underclothes, the heat became unbearable. Looking up, he saw that the tent was on fire for 50 feet behind him. When he finally fled, he realized that the Technirama cameras had been abandoned. "No one yelled or even threw a rock to warn me or anything. Their first reaction when the burning canvas started to fall was to take off fast!"[30]

"Cut it and get outta there!"

This wasn't a publicity stunt. The incident made headlines even back home in American newspapers. *Record*

The fire suddenly turned real: John Smith, Claudia Cardinale, and John Wayne in the burning tent (signed by Cardinale) (author's collection).

American printed Wayne's statement, "Nobody said Cut!" in its edition the very next day, December 27, 1963. When the pyrotechnics lost control, stuntman Bob Terhune said it burned the whole tent. Bronston was crying to Hathaway, who still wanted to do the rest of the fire scenes, "We haven't got any more tent!" To which Hathaway responded, "You should have thought of that before you started the picture. Burn it!"[31]

Aissa heard her father viciously coughing that night. A Madrid physician prescribed a codeine syrup so that he would not cough during the filming. The interior scenes were waiting. Bronston made complicated deals. He settled with Paramount to distribute his movie in the U.S. and other territories, but he made another deal with the British Rank

Organization (which released the film as *The Magnificent Showman* in Great Britain). That's the reason why Wayne, like in *Legend of the Lost*, couldn't work in the familiar surroundings of a Hollywood studio. Interiors and process shots were done at **Pinewood**, west of London, a studio now forever linked with the James Bond franchise. In fact, the first 007 movie had just been finished when Rank rented the stages for *Circus World*. The cold London weather didn't agree with Wayne, and his hacking cough continued. That's when Pilar started begging him to see a doctor. When the picture wrapped, Wayne flew to La Paz via small plane to join the crew of the *Wild Goose* for the trip home.

"You had your fun, come on down"

Bronston rushed *Circus World* into release in June 1964, just three months after the disastrous box office results of *The Fall of the Roman Empire*. Yet his gamble didn't pay off. His dream of becoming Spain's Cecil B. DeMille was over for good. For the next 20 years, Samuel Bronston was paying off millions of dollars in debt.

His proud Samuel Bronston Studio on the Avenida

In this Chinchón scene, John Wayne was leaning against this wall built in 1925… (photograph by Roland Schaefli).

…therefore, to prevent an anachronism, the set dressers of *Circus World* filled in the number 9, making it look like 1825 (author's collection).

de Burgos in Madrid was closed in 1984. (It was resurrected some years later as a television studio, the "Estudios Buñuel.") Although Bronston Films folded, Spain wasn't finished as a film location. Three years after the *Wild Goose* left its shores, a young American actor arrived to make a spaghetti western based in Madrid: Clint Eastwood.

"That's all the help they'll get from us"

Even before he underwent cancer surgery, Wayne let himself be talked into yet another ill-fated venture that would bring him back to Europe. A year had passed since *Circus World* when he agreed to meet with producer Melville Shavelson. Shavelson appeared to the sentimental side of John Wayne when he tried to sell him on the story of the Jewish fight for Independence, calling Jerusalem a "Jewish Alamo." Wayne glared at him: "You out of your mind? The picture lost so much money I can't buy a pack of chewing gum in Texas without a co-signer!"[32] But Shavelson got a handshake deal the same day and *Cast a Giant Shadow* became a Batjac co-production with the companies of Shavelson and Kirk Douglas; the latter played the leading part in this superficial biography. The war movie went into production on May 17, 1965, and the complicated filming schedule took well into

With Kirk Douglas on the Dachau set in Rome's Cinecitta Studios. John Wayne's character in *Cast a Giant Shadow* was based on the real-life General George Patton (author's collection).

August. Shavelson had to wait until Wayne was well enough to do his cameo after his cancer operation. His scenes were filmed at the tail end of production.

"If I were running the Pentagon…"

On March 14, 1965, the international crew arrived in Tel Aviv and took over the **Dan Hotel** at HaYarkon Street (Kirk Douglas holed up in the David Suite). The first day of shooting, the battle scenes indicated that the production would soon turn into a producer's nightmare. After eight hours of shooting, the rented Israeli soldiers and tanks were suddenly called away because of a "skirmish" between Israel and neighboring Jordan. That was just the beginning of a series of hilarious problems that plagued the production. Five years later, Shavelson filled a whole book with these experiences: *How to Make a Jewish Movie* is one of the best takes ever on the production of a large-scale film and anything that can possibly go wrong. Kirk Douglas let Shavelson know that, instead of writing a funny book, he should have made a better picture.

Among the locations were Jerusalem, the Negev Desert, the village of Nazareth, Galilee, the Palmachim Beach south of Tel-Aviv, and a fortress at Iraque Sudan.

"I don't care who you have to steal them from"

By July, Shavelson had returned from Jerusalem to start filming at Cinecitta Studios. Wayne reported to Rome for his scenes and hit every nightspot in the Eternal City. Angie Dickinson's scenes were also shot on the Rome stages. They even built the Dachau concentration camp in Cinecitta. Wayne's biggest moment in his cameo came when the "Camera moves to an extreme Close Shot of Randolph," as Shavelson's script indicated. "All we see are his eyes and the three stars on his helmet." Shavelson didn't know how effective his close-up of Wayne's blue eyes was until he saw the rushes.

Shavelson used locations close to Rome for the remaining exteriors. The **Alban Hills** above Frascati substituted for the Hills of Jerusalem in a battle scene between the Arab Legion and elements of the Israeli Army. Wayne had to do just one exterior there, in **Santa Maria di Galeria**, north of Rome. The little town was chosen to represent a Normandy village on D-Day. He hurt his back in the scene where he ducks a sniper's bullet behind a Jeep. He was driven to the nearby **Villa Clara Hospital** where X-rays showed he had a slipped disc. *Cast a Giant Shadow* didn't earn back its negative cost. That flop ended Wayne's European tour. At least until he went back to London to do *Brannigan* with the Brits.

16

Road Trip

Wayne's Way to Work

"A wonderful thing about Alaska is that matrimony hasn't hit up here yet.
Let's keep it a free country!"
—Sam McCord (John Wayne) to his partner George (Stewart Granger)

When Sam McCord strikes gold in Alaska, he's off to Seattle to fetch his partner's fiancée back to Nome. Wayne went North to Alaska *without even leaving California. As this road map shows, he could reach his workplaces in a matter of a few hours, all along the U.S. 395, and all in a day's work.*

North to Alaska was in production from May to August 1960. The first exterior in the script called for a sandy shore in Nome, busy with gold diggers. As soon as Johnny Horton gets through singing about crossing the Yukon River in the title song, the credits informs us that we are in "Nome, in the year 1900." Yet that beach is **Point Mugu** in Ventura County. The Naval Base installations are visible on the northern tip of the coastline.

Point Mugu State Park is near the city of Oxnard. When Wayne arrived at the first location, he had to learn that the script wasn't finished yet (Hollywood writers went on strike in early 1960). Wayne complained to Fox executives. When the script still wasn't finished in June, he told *The New York Times*, "They're supposed to have been preparing this thing for a year. Henry is a fine director, but he shouldn't have to be making up scenes."[1] Not for the first time, Hathaway had to improvise all the way. When Fox president Spyros Skouras instructed Hathaway to trim the budget, initially projected at $3.5 million, Hathaway cut $36,000 mainly by eliminating backgrounds and some of the local shots. He got around to filming the whole Alaska movie in some of his reliable Californian locations. When Wayne had to find a substitute for a Vietnam beach for the poignant ending of *The Green Berets*, he chose to come back to what had served well as the Nome waterfront: Point Mugu.

"A fella gets sore, that's all"

After the beach sequences, Hathaway moved the company north on State Highway 14 that connects L.A. to the Northern Mojave Desert. Several Wayne locations lie along this route. Take his old hometown Lancaster as a starting

Taking direction from Henry Hathaway (behind the camera, wearing cap) at Point Mugu. The beach near the Naval station was standing in for Nome harbor in *North to Alaska*. Capucine (in costume) got the chance to play opposite John Wayne because she was the girlfriend of agent Charlie Feldman whose talent agency also represented Hathaway (author's collection).

point. Within the hour, Red Rock Canyon is reached. CA 14 cuts directly across **Red Rock Canyon State Park.**

Countless westerns were shot between these rock formations and sandstone peaks. The terrain that John Wayne location hunters seek is on the left side. From the car park, a hiking trail leads to **Hagen Canyon.** In 1934, Wayne shot *The Lawless Frontier* there, followed five years later by *Pals of the Saddle.* Red Rock Canyon became so overexposed in films and TV shows that the satire *Westworld* made a statement by having a gunslinger robot (Yul Brynner) chase a hapless tourist around the colorful canyons. The area became a state park in 1968 and now comprises 27,000 acres. Red Rock Canyon was considered as a location for the sequel of *Rooster Cogburn* (working title: *Someday*), which was no to be.

The stream that Yakima Canutt almost drowned in: the Kern River, location of a large number of low-budget westerns (photograph by Roland Schaefli).

"I aim to see them mountains"

During the silent movie era, Highway 14 was simply a road blacktopped with oil sand. They started paving it in 1931 and finally completed it in the year that Gregory Peck and Gary Cooper shot Westerns back to back in Red Rock Canyon, *The Big Country* and *Man of the West* respectively.

After you go north for another 15 minutes, take a left on CA 178. It will bring you to **Kernville,** a busy western town during the silent movie era; they even had a Western street. The Isabella Dam across the Kern River was built in 1948, and Old Kernville was covered by Isabella Lake in 1953. Several of the original buildings were moved to the present location of Kernville. There are John Wayne locations in them

thar hills. For instance, *The New Frontier* was shot in the area in August 1935. His biggest movie in Kernville was *In Old California*, in production between March 13 and April 20, 1942. "It was a beautiful little western town close to the Kern River," he remembered years later in the March 1976 *Saturday Evening Post*, "so it had pleasant vegetation and trees in its square. It is now at the bottom of a man-made lake to keep it from interfering with progress."

The **Kern River** was a favorite for stunt scenes involving jumping horses into the water. Yakima Canutt performed a spectacular stunt in *Dark Command*, driving a wagon with a team of horses over the cliff and into the river. They used a high cliff overlooking a lagoon for gags like these; now it's a favorite spot for cliff divers. In his autobiography, the master stuntman recalled one time on a Wayne western that he almost lost his life in that river. Canutt was to slide down a rope. He had checked out the landing spot carefully and noticed a rock in the water. As he jumped off the cliff, he realized he would hit that rock. Pure instinct helped Canutt to survive the situation. Wayne, who had seen it coming, was in the water in no time. He got ahold of Yak and helped him out.

"I thought you were all steamed up about goin' to Alaska?"

Track back to SR 14 to follow it further north until it turns into U.S. Route 395. Soon you will have **Olancha** to your right. The sand dunes to the east of town saw a lot of action over the decades. In the Batjac Western *Seven Men from Now*, Randolph Scott drops a couple of attacking Indians there. Producer Wayne later regretted having given this great part to Scott instead of playing it himself.

Countless westerns were shot at the colorful Red Rock Canyon, including two of Wayne's—a third one was planned (author's collection).

More recently, the Marvel hero Iron Man landed in those sand dunes.

"We must band together"

The mostly dry lake in the Owens Valley is up next, to the right of U.S. 395. It was sometimes used for desert scenes. When the Mormons in *Brigham Young* (1940) looked out over the Owens Valley, they saw the dry **Owens Lake** bed and said, "Looks like Salt Lake City to me." The Owens Lake was the natural collection point for all the streams flowing into the Owens Valley. Before the Los Angeles Aqueduct was completed in 1913 and diverted the water, the lake covered 100 square miles.

"Fill up the canteens, Kid"

Almost in Lone Pine now. But before you get to that movie lovers' paradise, swing to the right at the visitor center. Running along the northern edge of Owens Lake, CA 136 leads to the semi-ghost town of **Keeler**. That's where John Ford shot the railroad scenes for *3 Godfathers*. The Carson & Colorado Railroad narrow gauge line was discontinued to Keeler in 1960. The depot remains intact although it's not in use and falling into disrepair.

From Keeler, the route runs further into Death Valley. Much of the *3 Godfathers* filming was done between May 3 and June 9, 1948, in the Furnace Creek area, such as **Zabriskie Point**, noted for its erosional landscape. On the ridge on the **Amargosa Range**, Wayne finds that Ward Bond has hit the waterbag. The canyon through which Wayne stumbles is the same one where Gregory Peck rides in *The Gunfighter* two years later.

In Wayne's book, this was "one of the most difficult locations I ever worked on. We were out in the desert sun in soaring temperatures for much of the time." Ford had his company going from eight in the morning until 11, then broke for a four-hour lunch during the hottest part of the day when it was impossible to work. Then back to work again until around six in the evening. According to Wayne, "I drank gallons of water to try to keep from getting

Studio cars are parked on the flat area just outside Lone Pine, probably for *Westward Ho*, the first production under the new Republic banner (Museum of Western Film History in Lone Pine).

dehydrated, but my lips still cracked and I got terribly sunburned. That wasn't all makeup on my face."[2]

Two huge wooden airplane propellers created the windstorm effect. It took days to shoot what Wayne called "that fucking scene" and the sand lodged itself in the actor's pants, shirts, boots, ears and eyes.[3]

"One of the most difficult locations I ever worked on": John Wayne is trying to save the orphan as the last of the *Three Godfathers* (author's collection).

"Drove 'em plain loco"

This certainly wasn't the place to bring a newborn infant. It was a well-kept secret that whenever the Godfathers nurse the baby, they're holding a doll. The real baby is shown only in close-up, delicately lighted on an MGM stage. Fun fact: The baby boy was a girl. Playing "Robert William Pedro" was Amelia Yelda's only screen credit.

Ford shot the three bank robbers crossing the dry lake in a place called the **Devil's Golf Course**, not far from Badwater, which is the lowest point below sea level in the Western Hemisphere. The director kept giving Harry Carey, Jr., directions until the novice actor was completely confused, then let him lay out alone in the sun to prepare him for his death scene. After work, they rode back to the Furnace Creek Ranch in one station wagon. Ford seated in the front next to the driver, and the other three actors cramped in the back. At the two-room cabin motel, the stars slept two in a room, Wayne and Pedro Armendariz doubled up. As they sat on the porch of the green cabin that evening, sipping Wayne's Poland Spring Water (he kept everyone supplied with it, having it sent up from Maine), the older actor told the kid that Ford had given him the same treatment ten years earlier on *Stagecoach*. "Ha-ha—He's just giving ya' the business. He's breaking you in, Ol' Dobe."[4] The Death Valley motel is now **Furnace Creek Ranch**, an oasis on Highway 190. Back in Ford's days, there was, of course, no air conditioning.

"I've always been a lucky sort of a cuss"

The picturesque town of **Lone Pine** has given birth to many movie legends. It came to the movies—or rather the

This still was not released to the press as it clearly shows that the baby is a doll: enduring the heat of the Death Valley location with Pedro Armendariz and Harry Carey, Jr. (author's collection).

other way around—in 1920, for *The Roundup*. The old **Lone Pine Hotel** (now the residence of the Chamber of Commerce, 120 South Main Street) accommodated the earliest movie stars. Some companies would shoot their town scenes right out on Main Street.

In 1935, Republic contract player John Wayne stayed for the first time at the Dow's, as it was called then. Originally, the hotel at 310 South Main Street had 55 rooms. In one of them, Glenn Ford and Rita Hayworth were having an affair in 1948, making *The Loves of Carmen*. In 1957, the hotel's name was changed to the **Dow Villa** and the first motel units were added. During his last visits to Lone Pine, Wayne preferred to stay in Room 20.

Inside the **Native Trading Post** at 124 North Main Street, visiting movie actors signed the wall: Gary Cooper, Steve McQueen and Errol Flynn, to name a few. Back in the old days, Lone Pine counted two saloons. Three, including Richard Boone's room, as Harry Carey, Jr., recalled.

Lone Pine could provide what the small studios could not: production value. The trip north was worth

If only the walls could talk: John Wayne stayed in the historic Dow's for the first time in 1935, for the last in 1978. The hotel is and remains the center of Lone Pine (photograph by Roland Schaefli).

the trouble because they would get the snow-capped Sierra Nevada Mountains—free of charge. They found all the western scenery just two miles west of Lone Pine, in the **Alabama Hills**. Turn onto Whitney Portal Road at the only stoplight in town. Follow the road all the way to the Whitney Portal area. When mountain man Henry Fonda built his cabin up there in *How the West Was Won*, it was still called Hunter's Flats. It is now a quiet camping area, 4000 feet high above Lone Pine.

Wayne first came to this rock-studded splendor in 1933 for *Somewhere in Sonora*, a remake of a Ken Maynard Western, recycling action sequences from the 1927 film. Producer Leon Schlesinger okayed a brief location jaunt to Lone Pine so that the newly shot scenes of Wayne (in costumes identical to Maynard's) would match the stock footage.

The Narrow Gauge Road to the east of town leads to a completely flat area. On that barren playa, Yakima Canutt's

gang ambushes Wayne's family as they travel over the lake bed in the first minutes of *Westward Ho*.

"What do you want me to do— get snake-bit?"

More than any other Californian location close to the studio, Lone Pine added a majestic touch to those B-movies, the picturesque 14,496-foot-high Mount Whitney looming in the background. The young star returned early the next year for *Blue Steel*, filmed in the Big Pines section. *The Man from Utah* was in production between the end of March and April 3, 1934. "Each one was lousier than the last," Wayne reflected later on the modestly made movies.[5]

In 1935, Wayne was especially busy in the Alabama Hills as the newly founded Republic Studios provided a bigger budget. *Westward Ho* was first in the assembly line, shot from May 19 to June 3. If you turn left on **Horseshoe Meadow**, there is a distinctive formation of rocks on the left. This is where Wayne and his Singing Riders captured the outlaw gang in *Westward Ho*. Wayne also strung a rope across the trail to trip some riders following him in an area the local Paiute Indians call the Garden of the Gods. Canutt had rigged that stunt using the Running W

The rock-studded splendor of the Alabama Hills: This bulky rock marked the start of the Indian chase in *How the West Was Won* (photograph by Roland Schaefli).

Hidden on a flat area north of town and seldom found by location hunters: the dramatic playa where Yakima Canutt ambushes the Wayne family in *Westward Ho* (photograph by Roland Schaefli).

Two actors sharing the same role in *King of the Pecos*: This rare photograph on the location in Lone Pine shows child actor Bradley Metcalfe who plays John Wayne's character as a kid (author's collection).

method; a dangerous procedure which has since been outlawed by the Humane Society. However, the stunt coordinator declared late in life, "I have done some 300 Running Ws and never crippled a horse."[6]

Lawless Range was simultaneously filmed in those brown, orange and gray rocks, from May 19 to June 3, 1935. In August 1935, *The New Frontier* was there for some shots, too. They squeezed in *The Oregon Trail* between December 14 and 23. This is the one Wayne film that must be considered lost forever. Whether Republic just threw the original materials out, or it was displaced or the nitrate material had deteriorated, all hopes that a print might surface over time have now evaporated.

On this picturesque spot just off Horseshoe Meadows Road, John Wayne and his vigilantes took time off for a singalong in *Westward Ho*. Four years after, George Stevens built the evil temple for the classic *Gunga Din* on the other side of these outcroppings.

Collectors and historians have looked all over the world for it but *The Oregon Trail* remains a lost John Wayne film. The star is about to fire the cannon on top of the boulder (Museum of Western Film History in Lone Pine).

"Gonna get you that chance you've been waiting for"

As you come up from Lone Pine, turn right to the Alabama Hills at the intersection, which is marked by a white rock with a plaque. This will put you onto **Movie Road**. It got that name because it has the flattest terrain for shots of riders galloping, and because it was so smooth, they could let the star do his own riding in traveling shots. Locals still call this whole area **Movie Flats**. Literally hundreds of films were made along that scenic loop. A narrow road twists through the rocks on the east side of Movie Road, called the **Lone Ranger Canyon**. It's the place where Wayne shot it out with his parents' murderer at the end of *King of the Pecos* (made between February 5 and February 11, 1936). Towards the end of Movie Road, there's a steep arroyo, sometimes called **Stuntman Canyon** because it was their favorite place for sending a wagon over the edge. This resulted in *How the West Was Won*'s awesome Cinerama shot in which the camera is actually placed inside a covered wagon, rolling down that hill. The bad guy in *King of the Pecos* deservedly went over the same edge.

Ann Rutherford, just a couple of years shy of her role in *Gone with the Wind*, was the romantic interest in some of these Wayne entries. She remembered she was "not so fond of the working conditions!" She described Lone Pine as a windy, dusty place "where there were no union representatives from the Screen Actors Guild to protect you. They would take you out into nowhere. The stillness, the quiet, there'd be no noise, with nothing but rocks— no plumbing, no accommodations, no restaurant; you just work out there in the elements seven days a week from sunup to sundown and get dirty!"[7]

"Makin' a new start in life"

Wayne certainly knew what his leading lady was talking about. The year 1937 saw him back in the red dust for *I Cover the War*, made on a short shooting schedule in April. The Alabama Hills doubled for rugged Middle Eastern terrain. Imported palm trees helped sustain the illusion that Wayne was acting in the middle of the Arabian Desert.

"You keep your trap shut when they get here"

After *Stagecoach* put a higher value on Wayne, he still came back to Lone Pine on occasion. In Republic's *Three Faces West*, made between March 27 and April 16, 1940, he leads another wagon train—modern trucks this time—from a North Dakota Dust Bowl to new farming land in Oregon. To get there, they of course cross Lone Pine.

The Alabama Hills' volcanic and granite rocks and their contrast with the high alpine peaks made the location a substitute for the Khyber Pass and many other exotic places. In 1947, RKO decided to sell it to the public as the Andes. *Tycoon* was Wayne's biggest Lone Pine picture, in production between January 6 and April 26. RKO initially intended to shoot it at its new studio in Churubusco, Mexico. Shortly before the start of production, plans were changed. Anthony Quinn remembered that he and Wayne thought, "Hey, RKO is giving this special treatment, because the Mexican location would add some authenticity." Doubts about the lighting facilities in the Churubusco studio and perhaps a few concerns about the political stability prompted the decision. So they moved to Lone Pine instead. "That was typical RKO," Quinn said later.[8]

"I've got a railroad to build"

Yet location filming reportedly broke expenditure records for RKO, with $65,000 spent for a mock road strip and train tunnel. As you come up from Lone Pine towards the Alabama Hills, that's the first John Wayne location you'll see to your right, a granite formation called **Face Rock** (in the neighborhood of Gregory Peck's *Yellow Sky* gold mine). Ruiz Hill, the *Tycoon* mine entrance, was a fake façade built between the two massive outcroppings in the **Ruiz Hills** area so that Wayne, as the construction engineer, could blow a tunnel through it.

On that location, Wayne did something he never did before: he ordered the set closed to visitors. It so happened that leading lady Laraine Day was just married to baseball player Leo "The Lip" Durocher. The athlete misinterpreted the screen kisses as the real thing. Wayne recalled that Durocher watched him like a base runner who was preparing to steal home. So "The Lip" stood around the set each day, seething with jealousy, until Wayne couldn't take it any longer.

When Laraine Day collapsed on location and required medical attention, the *Tycoon* shoot had to be reorganized (which might be the reason for later pick-up shots at the Arboretum in Arcadia).

"Make yourself at home"

When Henry Hathaway and his *North to Alaska* star Wayne arrived in Lone Pine in 1960, they certainly weren't strangers to the layout of possible locations. The director chose the area on the left of the Whitney

On the *Tycoon* location in Ruiz Hills: Russ Spainhower was Hollywood's contact man and trusted location scout in Lone Pine. A written tribute said: "His opinion and judgment were highly respected by the movie directors and his friendship treasured" (Museum of Western Film History in Lone Pine).

Paul Fix and John Wayne wait for the technical crew to set up the next explosion in *Tycoon*. Plaster of the fake tunnel can still be found in the area. Unfortunately, the movie was a box-office dud (Museum of Western Film History in Lone Pine).

Portal Road for the hilarious moment when Wayne crashes a wagon into some claim jumpers, resulting in a mud fight in the creek. That happened where **Lone Pine Campground** is today, at Lone Pine Creek.

Wayne and his co-star Stewart Granger had known each other before co-starring in *North to Alaska*. The British actor and his wife Jean Simmons owned the 5280-acre

In *North to Alaska*, gold miner Sam McCord was confronting claim jumpers with a runaway wagon at the gravelly slopes of Lone Pine Creek. The snow-capped Sierra Nevada Mountains helped to give the audience a Yukon feeling (photograph by Roland Schaefli).

John Wayne had to get wet for the scene in which he crushes a wagon into a gold wash: Henry Hathaway (with cigar) keeps him company on the set, which is today Lone Pine Campground (Museum of Western Film History in Lone Pine).

Estancia Yerba Buena Ranch outside Nogales. Wayne and other stars like Elizabeth Taylor had been their guests. During the time of *North to Alaska*, Granger was secretly divorcing Simmons and, according to Granger, "my nerves were beginning to go." In his memoir, Granger confessed that he had a lot of money problems on his mind then. It was his first film for a year and he nearly failed. He called his first scene with Wayne "a nightmare": He could not remember his lines. The more he fluffed, the more Hathaway glared and chewed on his ever-present cigar. Wayne, Granger remembered, was "slightly bewildered by the behavior of an actor who had starred in 50 films yet didn't seem capable of saying one line of dialogue." The truth was that Granger was terrified. He muttered that he had a touch of flu and excused himself to his dressing room where he took a belt of brandy and two tranquilizers. After that, he "sailed through the scene."[9] After wrapping the slapstick comedy, Granger put the Nogales ranch up for sale. It is now **Kino Springs Golf Course**, 187 Kino Springs Drive.

It was on Movie Road that Wayne rode into the sunset for the last time. On August 25, 1978, he did the Great Western Savings commercials. According to its director Peter Vanlaw, Wayne came a day early to pick the locations himself. He rented a vehicle at the local car dealership to go off-road. But he got the truck stuck in the sand and had to hitchhike back to town. This visit to Lone Pine also marked his last stay at the Dow's. He spontaneously invited a hotel employee and her kids to the set. According to their observations,. Wayne was polite, rather quiet and obviously did not feel too well. Wayne used some of his familiar costume pieces in the commercial (like the *Cowboys* hat, which raked in nearly $120,000 in the 2011 Wayne estate auction).

"Beautiful country," Wayne remarked as he rode a horse (borrowed from Ben Johnson) into his farewell shot. Then he galloped away on Movie Road, towards the towering Sierras, telling his audience not to forget what he said about setting aside some money. After Wayne's death, Great Western went through a number of celebrity spokespersons, including Ben Johnson.

The annual Lone Pine Movie Festival brings back some of the stalwarts to reminiscence. The festival, held every Columbus Day weekend, is highly recommended. The **Museum of Western Film History** at 701 South Main Street features great movie artifacts and some Wayne mementos, too.

"That's White Peak all right"

Continue north on U.S. 395. Shortly before getting into Mammoth Lakes, turn left on Convict Lake Road. **Convict**

Lake is the scenic background of the first moments in *How the West Was Won* (James Stewart paddles off in an Indian canoe). **Mammoth Lakes** lies west of State Route 395. The Mammoth Lakes Basin numbers six lakes. In *Flame of Barbary Coast*, when Wayne takes a break after driving the cattle, he looks out at **TJ Lake**. Wayne had been at Mammoth more than ten years earlier: In *The Trail Beyond* (made in July 1934), the Eastern Sierras doubled for the Canadian Rockies. In one of the chase scenes (this little action-packed western has more than one), the dramatic peak of **Crystal Crag**, close to Lake Mary, appears in the background. Right after that, Wayne has to rescue a Mountie at **Rainbow Falls** in a canoe. This waterfall on **Red's Meadow** looks like it was put there for action scenes.

"I'm here to fetch you back to Alaska"

The area around Mammoth Lakes is geologically active. Some rhyolite domes are less than 1000 years old. In the hot springs of what is now **Hot Creek Geological Site**, Henry Hathaway found a location in Inyo National Forest that he used numerous times.

Hot Creek is an ancient volcanic region with boiling water, geysers and fumaroles. There are warning signs

Paul Lauten who visited the set on Movie Road took these snapshots of John Wayne's last ride into the sunset (Paul Lauten, Museum of Western Film History in Lone Pine).

Publicity still of John Wayne at Mammoth, in character as the lovesick cowpuncher, looking at TJ Lake in *Flame of Barbary Coast* (author's collection).

about their harmful effects, and visitors are advised not to get into the hot water. They didn't think of security in the scene where Wayne dunks the hungover Fabian into the steaming water, even though he acknowledges Hot Creek with his line of dialogue, "Why don't you find the coldest spot in that hot creek and go sit down in it?" About the improvising of scenes

The location of three John Wayne films: the amazing canyon of the Hot Creek Geological Site, seen from where Rooster found his spot to ambush the Ned Pepper Gang (photograph by Roland Schaefli).

in the absence of a finished script, Wayne said, "All I know is, I'd go broke if I tried this in an independent production."[10]

Coming up from U.S. 395, turn right onto Hot Creek Hatchery Road and follow it to the car park. As you look down in the narrow valley, you'll enjoy Rooster Cogburn's view on Lucky Ned Pepper's hideout in *True Grit*. Sam McCord found gold in that same spot in *North to Alaska*. That vista is also included in *The Comancheros'* title sequence although the film didn't include any Hot Creek scenes.

The dugout in *True Grit* was built against a rock formation on the upper part of the creek. This is also the spot where the actual *North to Alaska* gold mine is seen for the only time in the movie. Follow the bank a bit further down to the bend: Stewart Granger built a wooden bridge to his Honeymoon Cabin there.

Wayne had been in the valley of the hot waters years before, 1945 to be exact, for *Flame of Barbary Coast*: It cuts together nicely with the studio shot of him jumping off a train and rolling down the hill (doing his own stunt) at Hot Creek. The place is a bit upstream from the Hathaway locations. As Wayne and his cowpokes drive the cattle herd, they're actually moving the doggies along Hot Creek Hatchery Road, with the Mammoth Mountains prominent in the background. It's now one of the largest ski resorts in the western U.S.

"Nome is no place for a girl like you"

Back to U.S. 395 and on to **Mono Lake**. Clint Eastwood erected the town of *High Plains Drifter* on its shore and

Patrick Wayne takes time off to visit his dad on the "Honeymoon Cabin" set in *North to Alaska* (author's collection).

This German lobby card shows the exact position of the gold miner's hut at the banks of Hot Creek in *North to Alaska*. John Wayne tells pop idol Fabian to sit in the hot creek to cool off while French model Capucine gives them a skeptical look (author's collection).

painted it red. According to Eastwood, Wayne expressed his dislike for his film: "John Wayne once wrote me a letter telling me he didn't like *High Plains Drifter*. He said it wasn't about the people who really pioneered the West." Eastwood realized that there are two different generations and that Wayne "wouldn't understand what I was doing." He meant his film to be a fable. "It wasn't meant to shoot the hours of pioneering drudgery."[11]

"I got myself a real gold mine!"

North of Mono Lake, off U.S. 395, on CA 270 (also known as Bodie Road), lies the last stop on this road trip: **Bodie State Historic Park.** (Don't use the rough road leading out there in wintertime.) On November 29, 1970, approximately 77,000,000 people saw the John Wayne television special *Swing Out, Sweet Land* (later retitled *John Wayne's Tribute to America*). It was then the most expensive single show ever produced for television; sponsor Budweiser put roughly $2,000,000 into it. The whole show was pre-recorded on Universal stages. Just one sketch was shot on location: Wayne rides old Dollor into the mining ghost town of **Bodie**—and discovers in one of the broken-down saloons that Budweiser is still foaming. "The Old West, the wild west, is long gone," he tells himself as he wanders the empty town in the whistling wind. "What does matter is that nothing ever dies if folks don't want it to." Indeed, half a century after he shot his scenes in Bodie, the buildings where he listens to the voices of the "ghosts" still remain, making the empty town one of the most fulfilling trips for John Wayne location hunters.

So there it is, a road trip that covers about 300 miles and ten major John Wayne working places. All in a day's work for the Duke.

Looking for a cool glass of beer in the ghost town of Bodie: the only outdoor footage shot for his highly successful Budweiser television special *Swing Out, Sweet Land* (author's collection).

John Wayne rolled down this hill from the top to the bottom in *Flame of Barbary Coast*, just a few steps from the spot where, twenty years later, Steve McQueen would have his final shoot-out in *Nevada Smith* (photograph by Roland Schaefli).

Only a small part of the once-thriving mining camp of Bodie survives, preserved in a state of "arrested decay." The good news is half a century after Wayne's Budweiser segment, all the buildings used are still standing; the hotel, the saloon, and even the slanting shack they used as a jail (photograph by Roland Schaefli).

17

Two Roosters

Patching It Up

"They'll be happy to know that some part of Arkansas looks like that."
—Director Henry Hathaway explains to author Charles Portis
why he won't film *True Grit* in Arkansas

When John Wayne received his Academy Award for the portrayal of one-eyed Rooster Cogburn, he was moved to tears. "Wow!" he said, "If I'd known that, I'd have put the patch on 35 years earlier." This despite the fact that he disagreed vehemently about wearing the eye patch: "Hell, the fans pay to see me—not some son of a bitch who looks like a pirate in an Errol Flynn movie"[1]

John Wayne had a very definite idea about how his audience wanted to see him. When *Legend of the Lost* cinematographer Jack Cardiff came on the set the first day, he was astonished to see Wayne wearing a large Stetson hat, cowboy boots and a pistol belt. He whispered to Henry Hathaway, "Why is he wearing the cowboy outfit?" Hathaway stared at Cardiff as though he was mad. "He always wears the cowboy outfit."[2] But when it came to eye patches, Hathaway had some convincing to do.

"No way"

"I'm not an actor to begin with," Wayne argued with Hathaway, who was to direct him for the sixth time in *True Grit*. "I'm a reactor, and no way will I wear the patch." Hathaway then had old clothes out in the costume department for his star to try on, and when he let him look in the cheval mirror, he had that little patch hanging on a hinge. "You're a pretty smart son of a bitch," Wayne admitted. But he still said no. On the second fitting, the patch was hanging there again. Hathaway had the patch made with black gauze in it, so he could see through it perfectly. Wayne finally tried it on, stepped back, looked at himself, turned around and said, "Shall I try on a coat?"[3]

"Where the hell is my suit?"

The *True Grit* costume fitting took place at **Western Costume Company** (WCC). Founded in 1912, it outdates any studio or production company. For decades, the massive

and labyrinthine building stood in front of Paramount, facing Melrose Avenue.

Wayne had his own ideas for costumes. In interviews, he often repeated that he changed the custom of the hero wearing a white hat. "When I went into Westerns, I didn't like to wear the rodeo clothes that Tom Mix and other Western stars of the era were wearing. ...I'm the first one to ever use those brown Levis that they have now. I got Western Costume to make some for me to kind of take the place of booger reds."

At the American clothing company Levi Strauss, they still remember that Wayne wore 1938 Levi's 501s in

Cowboy boots made by Lucchese's in San Antonio, displayed at the Century Plaza Hotel in Los Angeles. John Wayne used the same boots in *True Grit* and the sequel, *Rooster Cogburn* (photograph by Roland Schaefli).

Stagecoach. Historically accurate or not, his outfit would typify a generation's image of the cowboy. Wayne usually bought his own boots at **Lucchese's**, 255 East Basse Road in San Antonio. Once he instructed gun leather craftsman John Bianchi how to make his gun belt. He even included a drawing that showed how "the gun should ride just below belt." Wayne had always used reinforced leather on the front of his holster. "Carry the holster over the gun belt but with enough of a drop so that the gun hangs at the bottom of the belt."[4]

In the lovable account about his years in John Ford's stock company, Harry Carey, Jr., described the wardrobe fittings for *3 Godfathers*. Ford had a selection of Western Costume pieces over and handpicked the hats and boots. During this routine, Wayne reminded the newcomer: "Fer God's sake, kid, keep yer mouth shut and yer ears open!" The veteran also told Carey not to make any suggestions. "An' be careful, 'cause he'll try to suck you into it." When Carey did just that, offering an opinion about the hat Ford wanted to put on him, Wayne turned and faced the wall. Deadly silence. And then Ford chewed Carey out: "Oh, so you're going to direct the goddamn picture."[5]

Howard Hughes took such an interest in *The Conqueror*'s Genghis Khan helmets that he was present at WCC when Wayne was fitted for his Mongolian wardrobe. The billionaire sat in an antique Morris chair and observed the goings-on with unsmiling detachment. Contrary to popular belief that Wayne hated the way he had to look for the part, he thought that Yvonne Wood's costumes were great and said she'd get an Oscar nomination for them. She didn't.

"I want the cuffs"

When Wayne came in for a fitting at WCC, he asked the costumers, "Remember, I want the cuffs" (he liked his western pants with a cuff). When the first shooting day arrived and his pants did not have the cuffs, he told them, "Add 'em."[6]

Hathaway knew that Wayne was "more particular about the pants he wears than anything in the world because he's got such big hips. He's just boney. And unless he gets the thinnest kind of material, it drives him crazy."[7] On their first collaboration, *The Shepherd of the Hills*, Hathaway told him: "You've got to wear homespun. You can't wear cotton gabardine, for Chrissake, or poplin or something." Years later, when Wayne came to Hathaway's office on the Paramount lot to discuss the upcoming *Sons of Katie Elder*, he noticed a picture on the wall from their earlier movie. He looked at it for a long time and he said, "Do you remember those damn pants?"[8]

Howard Hawks did not like bright red colors in his Westerns. So when Wayne wanted to wear a red bib shirt in *Rio Bravo*, Hawks said, "Let me have this overnight and I let you wear it tomorrow." Hawks had wardrobe take all the color out "until it was faded pink!"[9]

For *The Man Who Shot Liberty Valance*, Wayne had Stetson custom-make a high-crowned, broad-brimmed felt hat with a one-hand crease. When he got his Tom Doniphon costume at Western Costume, he asked for a bandanna. Costumer Ron Talsky asked about the color and Wayne told him, "Coffee," since it was by then decided to shoot it in black-and-white. (The first costume sketches were made for a color movie, which requires a different kind of costume.) Three days later, Talsky met Wayne and the actor said he had everything but the bandanna. The costume designer reached in his pocket, handed him a black bandanna and explained, "I drink my coffee black." Then he pulled out the right (coffee-colored) bandanna. Wayne roared with laughter.[10]

Ranse Stoddard and Tom Doniphon in costume: James Stewart and John Wayne were dressed by legendary costume designer Edith Head, winner of a staggering eight Academy Awards. *The Man Who Shot Liberty Valance* added another nomination (author's collection).

"I don't need to buy that, I confiscate it"

Wayne had given Talsky his first break, fitting a large number of costumes on the set of *The Alamo*. (John Jensen, Cecil B. DeMille's former costumer, did the costume sketches.) Wayne also rented a sizable batch from WCC. He had gotten estimates for leather uniforms made in Mexico for $15 apiece against a $150 weekly rental from Western Costume. And since WCC owned the uniforms already used in previous Alamo movies like Republic's *The Last Command*, he reused them. Ironically, since Wayne left Republic after a dispute over his *Alamo* budget, the uniforms his soldados wore also bore the Republic costume stamp.

After *The Alamo* wrapped, the custom-made clothes were returned to WCC and put back in stock. Before the value of such costume pieces was realized, they would be reused, often altered for other productions. Even for his main *Alamo* actors, the cost-conscious Wayne rented many costumes instead of having them made. For instance, the pants worn by Frankie Avalon were originally made for *Saskatchewan* star Alan Ladd, who wore the same size.

The warehouse kept older costumes ready for stars to re-use. In Wayne's case, they put his movie duds on a special rack, and whenever he planned his next film, they'd pull the rack out. New clothes he would collect three weeks before the first shooting day because he liked to get used to them. That's how Wayne was able to use the same costume pieces over and over, even when under contract to different studios. If the viewer pays attention to the costumes, he'll recognize the same heavyweight khaki-grayish cotton jacket (called a stockade jacket) on him in *McLintock!*, *Circus World* and *The Sons of Katie Elder*. He finally retired the garment after *The War Wagon*. As an homage to "Spig" Wead, Wayne used the USN jacket that he wore throughout *They Were Expandable* in the poignant farewell of *The Wings of Eagles*. Yet when somebody in the audience of the Phil Donahue talk show told him she had noticed he kept wearing the same vest, he shook his head. "I change vests," he stated—except in the early years when he had to wear the same clothes, as the pictures were made that cheaply.

When he helmed *The Alamo*, he rented a large batch of Mexican uniforms from Western Costume to dress Santa Anna's soldados: on location in Texas, surrounded by unidentified Batjac employees (author's collection).

The original costume sketch for a navy-blue pea coat that would serve two sea captains who both went down with their ships: Captain Jack Stuart and Captain Ralls. The Western Costume label gave his chest measure as 46" (author's collection).

After Wayne passed away in June 1979, an inventory was made of the contents of his Newport home, including many costume pieces he kept handy at the house. The Wayne Estate also bought some of the WCC costumes when they became available in the 1990s. When the estate auctioned off hundreds of costumes, Ethan Wayne pointed out a pea coat as the one piece he would like to own himself: it was tailored the part of Captain Jack Stuart in the 1942 Paramount film *Reap the Wild Wind* and was put into use a second time six years later, for Captain Ralls in Republic's *Wake of the Red Witch*.

The largest costume house in the U.S. had been co-owned by several studios over the years. In 1988, Paramount bought it all. But they were only interested in the five-storey building, in order to tear it down (angering some preservation societies) to extend their lot out to Melrose Avenue. The Western Costume company itself was sold again and moved to North Hollywood. The Mecca of motion picture wardrobe garment is now at 11041 Vanowen Street.

"I always go backwards when I'm backin' up"

Back to 1968 and the *True Grit* eye patch. Customer Luster Bayless provided the actor with a new one each day to protect him from eye irritation. That film started Wayne's association with Bayless, who became his costumer in all his later pictures. As Rooster, Wayne wears the same black felt hat that WCC made for *The Alamo* (and which Wayne reused in *The Comancheros*). According to Bayless, he just changed the block around. The office of his American Costume Co. was at **12980 Raymer** in North Hollywood.

True Grit's first day of shooting was September 5, 1968. Wayne: "We shot in the autumn so it was extraordinarily beautiful as the leaves changed color and then dropped."[11] Dean Smith, who stunted in the film, remembered how they "watched the changing of the aspen trees; they went from green to yellow to red."[12]

Those rich colors in the San Juan Mountains were the reason that Hathaway chose Colorado. The hard-nosed director had put his mind to making the movie look like a fairy tale. But when producer Hal Wallis had asked Charles Portis, the author of the novel *True Grit*, for his thoughts, he strongly objected to Colorado. After all, the setting of *True Grit* was Arkansas. "Look," Hathaway told him, "in Arkansas, nobody's been ten miles from their house in their whole fucking lives. And when they see the picture, they'll be happy to know that some part of Arkansas looks like that."[13] Hathaway thanked Portis for his comments and didn't change his mind one bit.

"There's not hut grub or warm beds"

Hathaway was familiar with the town of **Ridgway** ("Gateway to the San Juans"), located on scenic U.S. Route 550: He'd previously used it as a backdrop for his *How the West Was Won* segment. The **Hartwell Park** in the middle of town is where Gregory Peck offers his services to Debbie Reynolds. Now Hathaway put the town park to good use again: He ordered the construction of the Fort Smith

Western Costume designers originally made this black felt hat for Davy Crockett. Wayne's later customer Luster Bayless changed it into Rooster Cogburn's headgear. The photograph also shows one of many eye patches Bayless provided because Wayne wanted a new one for every day (photograph by Roland Schaefli).

Ridgway's "Fort Smith Saloon" where Mattie's father gets shot. Montrose local Bob DeJulio painted the sets. His lettering is still apparent half a century after he applied them. Locals tell the story about a couple of kids asking John Wayne if he'd pose for a photograph. An assistant tried to chase them out but Wayne got up, took the camera and handed it to the assistant. Standing between the youngsters, he put his arm around them and said, "Now you take the picture" (photograph by Roland Schaefli).

gallows and the shell of Judge Parker's courthouse from which the "Hanging Judge" supervises the execution on **Lena Street**. When Rooster Cogburn makes his entrance, delivering his prisoners in a paddy wagon, he walks downstairs to take a side entrance. In 1985, the **True Grit Café** was built on this empty lot. It honors the movie and its star. The place is special because it actually encloses an original John Wayne location: The external wall on which the art department painted "Chambers Grocery" is now the internal south wall of the restaurant. It specializes in Cowboy Cuisine, of course. Rooster's paddy wagon,

Kim Darby (with bag) watches John Wayne making his entrance in Ridgway: the paddy wagon from *True Grit* is still parked in the area and… (author's collection).

… the wall that was painted "Chambers Grocery" is now the internal wall of the True Grit Café. It encloses the original John Wayne location (photograph by Roland Schaefli).

recently renovated, is usually parked in its place of honor downtown.

Mattie's father got shot down on Lena Street, in front of the Fort Smith Saloon. What used to be a movie saloon is now the site of an Adventure Sports store. On the corner of North Lena and Clinton, the Old Ridgway Fire Station bell tower was added for the movie (it was originally a high school building). Across the street, on Clinton, is an old stone house—that's where Hank Worden acted as an embalmer (also seen in the background of the abovementioned Gregory Peck scene). To the left of Clinton Street is the lot where Cheng Lee's shop was located.

"Well, that didn't pan out"

Ridgway is a former railroad stop. Paramount borrowed the antique caboose from the Rio Grande Railroad. (For the scene of Mattie's arrival, the train was pulled into the shot.) In 1971, a newspaper reported that some citizens complained to Paramount that the caboose had not been restored. Reportedly Paramount paid the community $700 to cover paved sidewalks with dirt and got permission to close the park and build the gallows. The company restored everything with the exception of a number of roofs over privately owned porches; those houses' owners liked them better the way they looked in *True Grit*.

Hathaway was able to use the real courthouse in **Ouray**, ten miles from Ridgway on Highway 550. The time-honored county courthouse stands on 4th Street.

Hathaway merged the inside scenes (the courtroom and Rooster's first encounter with Mattie on the staircase) with the outdoor shot as Rooster exits the shell built for the movie in Ridgway. During his stay in Ouray, Wayne had steak at the **Outlaw Restaurant** at 610 Main Street. The restaurant calls itself "the home of John Wayne's hat."

The art department built the snake pit in the Ouray area, where Million Dollar Highway cuts to the right onto **Camp Bird Road**. The remains of the pit are on private property.

"She reminds me of me!"

The **Blue Mesa Reservoir** east of Montrose on Highway 50 was the location of the ferry sequence. The water was much lower then; the locations are now underwater. Stuntwoman Polly Burson doubled Kim Darby in all riding

Rooster retrieves Mattie (Kim Darby) from the snake pit. The *True Grit* art department built fiberglass boulders to add to the hole in the ground (author's collection).

scenes. She made the scene in which Mattie swims the river on her horse look easy. In fact, Polly went through six or seven horses until she found one that would swim straight like that. All horses swim differently. One of them needed a little help, as Polly recalled: "They threw a line to me. I got a rope around his neck and they drag him ashore."[14]

During the shooting in Montrose, Wayne stayed (supposedly in two rooms) at the **Lazy IG Motel** in Montrose (now the Country Lodge at 124 East Main Street). The motel is filled with film history. Locals remember he had his supper at the **Red Barn Restaurant**, down the road a piece, and breakfast at **Mary's**, still at 13 Leith Road.

The first image in the film shows the Wilson Peaks, three closely related 14,000-foot mountains in the San Miguel Range. The credits roll over a shot of an old homestead, the Ross Ranch in the movie. This shot was taken from **Wilson Mesa**, spread along the Big Bear Creek, on Last Dollar Road, off Highway 62, which leads from Ridgway to Telluride. It is on private land. Nowadays, Mattie's neighbor is Tom Selleck. Quite a land baron himself, he bought up most of the parcels surrounding the remains of the "Ross homestead."

"Come see a fat old man some time!"

The final scene at the Ross cemetery—and Wayne's famous line "Come see a fat old man some time!"— were shot on top of the hill overlooking the farmhouses. Hathaway had most of the scene in the can but when they came back the second day, it had snowed during the night. The director decided to re-shoot the whole scene. Rooster's jumping the four-rail fence was achieved in two shots: Wayne's medium shot riding towards the camera and jumping a lower fence cuts to a long shot of stuntman Jim Burk riding away from the camera. "To ride a jumping horse is not an easy thing to do for an actor," observed Gary Combs, a member of the stunt crew. They had set the camera low for Wayne's jumping Chuck Hayward's old sorrel horse Twinkletoes about two feet high. "It made a nice cut to the shot from behind, with Jim Burk."[15] Burk is also recognizable as one of Crockett's Tennesseans, as the drover who has to go up against Merlin Olsen in *The Undefeated* and as one of the cutthroats in *Big Jake*, the dastardly villain introduced as "Trooper … name unknown." The all-around stuntman made his last contribution in Wayne's final scene: He took the dive over the bar in *The Shootist* and was then gunned down by the bartender; the shotgun blast in the back sent him crashing to the floor.

McAlester's Store is close to Last Dollar Road. Follow Highway 62 a bit further up and take a cutoff to the right. Follow the dirt road to an area called **Horsefly Mesa**. All that remained a few years back were some planks on the ground but the hitching post still stood.

Mattie asks Rooster to be buried in her family cemetery. Note that there is no snow on the ground; this was the first take of *True Grit*'s farewell scene. It was reshot when snow fell the next day on Hastings Mesa (author's collection).

"**Well, come and see a fat old man sometime**": The place where Rooster jumped the fence. Three buildings remain on the Hastings Mesa homestead, now unofficially called True Grit Cabin (photograph by Roland Schaefli).

The dialogue maintains the novel's references to place names in Arkansas and Oklahoma. Hathaway even incorporated his favored Californian location in the film, **Hot Creek**, near Mammoth Lakes on the east side of the Sierra Nevada (see Chapter 16). The footage of Rooster raiding the dugout as well as carrying Mattie after the snake bite cuts seamlessly

to the Colorado locations, even though the peaks of the Californian mountains Morrison and Laurel can be spotted in the background.

"Fill your hand, you son of a bitch!"

The Montrose locations were nearly 6000 feet above sea level so Wayne kept his portable oxygen tanks close. "I looked for weeks, literally, for that natural arena surrounded by aspen trees for the final shoot-out," Hathaway said about finding **Owl Creek Pass**.[16] With Chimney Rock rising above **Deb's Meadow**, near the summit, this was the perfect place for Rooster's showdown with Lucky Ned Pepper. Hathaway had used the same spot before in *How the West Was Won*: Gregory Peck tries to tow a covered wagon stuck in the mud. Follow U.S. 550 north out of Ridgway, then turn right on County Road 10, which leads up up to Owl Creek Pass. "I shot it from high on purpose, so it looks like a bullring, with knights jousting," Hathaway remembered about the location. "Mixed metaphors, I know, but it worked."[17]

Obvious to the eye of the movie buff, Wayne's close-ups as he charges the outlaws weren't done on a running horse but on a camera car. (So were Robert Duvall's.) It's not possible to frame a medium shot like that one from a galloping horse; not on this bumpy terrain anyway. Secondly, you don't put a star of Wayne's stature in any kind of danger, and riding without reins certainly is dangerous. Therefore, that's Jim Burk riding for Wayne in the long shots. Neil Summers doubled one of the Pepper gang. He remembered Wayne sitting in the saddle on the barrel screwed onto the side of a camera car and a still photographer taking a picture. Wayne ordered that film ripped out. "That will be on every magazine cover in the world!"[18]

Rooster shows "True Grit" at last, charging the outlaws: John Wayne in his Oscar-winning performance, at Owl Creek Pass (author's collection).

"**First time you ever give me reason to cuss you!**" The particular boulder on Deb's Meadow marks the spot where Rooster gets his horse Bo shot out from under him (photograph by Roland Schaefli).

A small stream runs through Deb's Meadow, the place where Rooster made camp. (Robert Preston proposed to Debbie Reynolds there in *How the West Was Won*.) The large boulder where Rooster's horse Bo dies under him is still there. So is Sleeping Rock, as the locals call it now. Follow the road up to the summit of Owl Creek Pass (10,114 feet) until you reach the little loop. The cave-like rock where Mattie sleeps is located just next to the road. That is Cimarron Range in the background of the scene where Rooster hits the bottle.

True Grit wrapped in mid–December. Producer Hal Wallis took the closing words "Come and see a fat old man" literally. About six years later, they resurrected Rooster Cogburn.

"If you ever need a one-eyed peace officer…"

For the *True Grit* sequel, Wallis chose Oregon over Colorado. *Rooster Cogburn* was in production in Deschutes County from September 5 to October 30, 1974. Wayne's second-to-last picture also marked the last time he worked at Universal City. The interiors of the courtroom and Rooster's home, which had been on the Paramount stages in the original movie, were recreated at Universal for the sequel. Chen Lee was portrayed by a different actor.

But first, it was back to the costume department. Some of Hollywood's finest costume designers had dressed Wayne in the past. Walter Plunkett, famous for his *Gone with the Wind* creations, was responsible for Wayne's costumes in *Lady for a Night*, *In Old Oklahoma* and *How the West Was Won*. Yet not even Plunkett was held in the same high esteem as Edith Head. *Rooster Cogburn* was the last time the legendary dressmaker worked on a Wayne movie. For providing the *Man Who Shot Liberty Valance* costumes, she had garnered a very unusual Oscar nomination for a Western. For *Rooster Cogburn*, her last Western, "we had to solve the problem of how a very proper Bible-toting lady in a period skirt was going to ride a horse bareback." She solved it together with Katharine Hepburn. The actress liked to bring a bag of fabrics to costume meetings, and Head brought a fake horse into the fitting room. "We experimented with a number of skirts until we found the one that worked best," Head recalled. They still had to split a side seam of the skirt so that it would function properly. "Some of the newcomers in the wardrobe department asked why she didn't just ride sidesaddle, but that simply showed that they didn't understand the script."[19]

When Wallis saw the wardrobe tests, he told Head she had made a mistake: Hepburn wore a dashing-looking hat with great style and a smart shoulder bag. Hepburn, the complete pro, didn't argue for a minute. "She and Edith went over

As *Rooster Cogburn*, John Wayne takes a second shot at playing the *True Grit* character while Katharine Hepburn replays her role of the spinster from *The African Queen* (author's collection).

to Western Costume and selected a wardrobe of old clothes, just right for a priest's daughter."[20]

"Payday! Come and get it, boys!"

Hepburn satisfied her 18-year desire to "star in a Western with Wayne."[21] Their discreet sizing-up of each other was short-lived; soon he was calling her Sister and she was calling him Duke. As one veteran crew member observed, "Goddamn, there ain't nothing like a couple of old pros when they get going."[22] Wayne took one look at her doing her own riding and said, "She's on there by the grace of God Himself." And Hepburn said afterward: "Of course, he was a terrible reactionary. But funny. And fair. He had tiny Irish feet. About that long, you know, size eight and a half. Enormous man. Tiny feet. Big hands. You leaned against him and it was exactly like leaning against an oak tree."[23]

"Ain't that the way it works, Hawk?"

The two old pros began the film in **Bend**, Oregon. West of town, in the Deschutes County, they shot all their mountain scenes. **The Ryan Ranch Meadow** in the Deschutes National Forest was one of the scenic backdrops for Wayne and Hepburn's scenes of bickering. The wetland just south of Dillon Falls is on public land. At **Sparks Lake**, also in the National Forest near the crest of the central Cascade Range, a prominent scree is the place where Rooster revealed that his real name was Reuben.

Smith Rock State Park in Terrebonne was the setting for a saloon scene featuring the bad guys. The building at the park entrance was built as a set for the movie, Kate's Saloon. Smith Rock is a world-renowned rock-climbing destination, known as the birthplace of American sport climbing. When the outlaw gang is trying to follow Rooster's raft, they jump from cliff to cliff on the steep face at Crooked River. The Old Stern Cabin, built in the early 1900s as a mining shack near Sunriver, was moved to Smith Rock State Park to make an appearance. The cabin was later moved again to its current location at the Riverhouse Resort in Bend.

"It's a dangerous business"

During the Bend location, cast and crew stayed in the town of **Sunriver** with a marvelous view of the Three Sisters Mountains, which is a short distance from the filming location Bend. Joining Wayne on location was Pat Stacy, who had rented a house at Sunriver. His companion described the place as "the most perfect house we ever lived in while on location: big rooms, the walls all lined in cedar, a kitchen-dining area overlooking the patio and pool."[24]

This scene in *Rooster Cogburn* ended up on the cutting room floor but was still used on this German lobby card: after Rooster blows up the nitro, Richard Jordan (later a heavy in a James Bond movie) manages to get to the raft and makes a last unsuccessful attempt at killing the marshal (author's collection).

One day, Wayne was giving golf lessons to his daughter Marisa on the Sunriver golf course. He stood behind her when her follow-through was so healthy she hit him under the eye with the end of the club. He received eight butterfly stitches from the local doctor. When Wayne called Wallis about the purple bruises, he said, "It's just your luck, you son of a bitch. The eye she hit is the one with the patch on it!"[25]

Hepburn stayed at the Sunriver Resort at 17600 Center Drive until she found a house better suited for her. *Life* photographer John Loengard was there to take pictures: "It is 5 a.m., a morning so cold that first snow must be near. Cars move the cast and crew up into the pine forests of the Cascade range; then, an overland trek to a location so rugged that the usual portable toilets have not been brought in. Bushes serve."[26] They watched the rushes in the **Tower Theater** in Bend, still existing at 835 Northwest Wall Street.

In Seattle, Wayne would eat at his friend **Peter Canlis'** place at 2576 Aurora Avenue N. When Wayne gave Hal Wallis a birthday party in his hideaway house in Sunriver, he had the famous restaurateur fly food in from Seattle.

Portable oxygen tanks were on the set at all times to help Wayne when he struggled to catch his breath with just one lung. (When Walt Disney had to undergo a similar lung cancer operation, Wayne sent him a telegram: "Welcome to the Club—the only problem is height."[27]) At a Halloween party in Sunriver, Wayne started wheezing and gasped, "I can't breathe."[28] They rushed oxygen to him. Wallis realized for the first time the strain under which Wayne had been working ever since *Katie Elder*.

"Damned if she didn't get the last word in again"

The whitewater rapids were shot on the Deschutes River, the calmer river scenes on the **Rogue River** in the Josephine and Curry counties, west of **Grants Pass**, Oregon. "Fortunately," said Wallis, "the insurance people were not around when Miss Hepburn went white-water–kayaking down the dangerous Rogue River."[29] At Grants Pass, Pat Stacy joined Wayne at a small motel not far from the shooting site. Wayne played a trick on the crew, to introduce them to Stacy: He told them she had a fake leg and everyone took him seriously. "Now you can see what a really good actor I am!"[30]

The forest location where Rooster takes the nitro away from the outlaws was 5500 feet high in an area where fine red volcanic dust kicked up all the time. Visitors noticed that this caused an irritation to Wayne's voice and his breathing and he had to use the oxygen. But Wayne was not going to be prevented from shooting at Grants Pass once more. When Great Western Savings gave him editorial control over their commercials, he chose to shoot the very first one at the Grants Pass ranch of his friend Chick Iverson. It was filmed on October 25, 1977. The camera pans over his children Ethan and Marisa cuddled in sleeping bags, then sweeps up to the tall man standing at a fireplace. "Good morning," he says. "Great time o' day, first light."

"Ain't nothing like a couple of old pros when they get going": The first pairing of screen legends Wayne and Hepburn, seen here in Deschutes County with Native American actor Richard Romancito (right), was assessed positively by movie critics but plans for the sequel *Someday* did not materialize (author's collection).

18

Beaches and Bridges
Duke's Detectives

The role of an urban cop fit John Wayne's screen persona like a glove. He had been looking for a contemporary thriller and he made no secret of the main reason for making a police movie: "Because somebody else made a detective story that grossed $30 million. That's why."[1] Late in his career, two cop movies brought another ingredient to his film oeuvre: the urban locations of large metropoles.

Batjac went on the lookout for a project in the same vein as Clint Eastwood's *Dirty Harry*. Harry Julian Fink, who penned *Cahill, U.S. Marshal*, had been one of the *Dirty Harry* writers. In the same year as *Dirty Harry*'s successful release (which cemented Eastwood's superstar status), Wayne had

Change of pace and location: as Seattle cop *McQ*, armed with an unregistered MAC-10 submachine gun. With this police thriller, the compact gun first registered in America's collective imagination. After that, it became a standard prop gun (author's collection).

produced another one of Fink's scripts, *Big Jake*. Wayne called Fink one of his favorite writers. Yet when *Dirty Harry* was offered to Wayne, "like an idiot I turned it down," he self-critically said afterward. So as soon as he was approached with this new Fink script about a lawman named Cahill, "I said yes right off." Even though it's easy to see how this story about an old marshal who neglects his children was first conceived as a modern-day story, Fink's screenplay of *Wednesday Morning* was adapted to Wayne's natural setting and retitled *Cahill, U.S. Marshal*. It would take another year and a Seattle cop to have the Western hero trade his trusty Winchester for an unregistered MAC-10 submachine gun.

"The hell I can't!"

One of the reasons why Wayne passed on the part of Harry Calahan was the language the homicide detective used: "Hell, everyone knows I talk that way in person, but never on the screen." Up until his famous line as Rooster Cogburn, Wayne had never said "son of a bitch" onscreen. Yet even Ronald Reagan had once observed Wayne "could use some pretty salty language."[2] Harry Carey, Jr., once found that Wayne "just didn't know how to give an order without sounding like he was a buck sergeant."[3] Maureen O'Hara said, "Duke would often use language that would make a sailor blush but usually just in the company of the guys. When there was a woman present, he was a different man. He always tried to curb his language out of respect for the ladies."[4]

When preparing *The Shootist* with Don Siegel, Wayne asked the *Dirty Harry* director why Eastwood made such violent pictures with such profane language. "There's very little gratuitous violence, sex or bad language in an Eastwood film," Siegel said in defense. Wayne exploded, "Bullshit! His films are full of fucking, goddamn obscenities. It's a bad image to paint himself into." According to Siegel's memoir, Wayne then added, "A fucking shame."[5]

"It kept him off the streets"

"Hell, it's just me t'try somethin' different, now and then," Wayne told interviewers about his decision to ride a different trail for a change. "It ain't anything unusual for me, 'cause I've done it lots of times in the past."[6] During his six weeks on the *McQ*'s **Seattle** location, he lived aboard the *Wild Goose*, very much in character: Seattle detective Lon McQ also lives on a boat. On the weekends, Wayne sailed the *Wild Goose* around the island of **Puget Sound**, along the northwestern coast, an inlet of the Pacific Ocean. Wayne knew the waters around Seattle, as he had taken the *Wild Goose* up coastal British Columbia to Glacier Bay several times over the years. As the captain of his boat, Wayne liked to explore the Sunshine Coast and Discovery Passage areas of lower British Columbia. His first mate and subsequent skipper, Bert Minshall, knew that the **Princess Louisa Inlet**, about 70 miles north of Vancouver, was one of Wayne's favorite cruising spots. Wayne watched the **Chatterbox Falls**, a popular destination for boaters around the world, from the *Wild Goose*'s bow. About a hundred miles north of Vancouver is an angler's nirvana called **Big Bay**, Stuart Island. Wayne would embark on various salmon marathons

Something new for the hero of *McQ*: at the Ocean Shores location, the woman (Diana Muldaur) turns out to be working for the other side (author's collection).

there. He once caught a 40-pound salmon. When the *Wild Goose* was docked at Victoria, in her usual slip in front of the **Empress Hotel** at 721 Government Street, Wayne would haunt the shops of the lovely Canadian cities located on Vancouver Island for presents. Sometimes, the *Wild Goose* sailed as far north as **Juneau**, Alaska. In one year, they lassoed a small iceberg, towed it to the yacht and hoisted a large chunk of it onto the deck.

So when Wayne sailed to Seattle, he certainly wasn't a stranger to the seaport city. During the shooting of *McQ* (from June 4 to August 1973), the *Wild Goose* was berthed at Max Wyman's private dock at the **Seattle Yacht Club**. It was a place with significance for his relationship with secretary Pat Stacy. She remembered fondly in her *Love Story* book, published four years after Wayne's death, that it was here that she and Wayne "became lovers for the first time in June 1973."

"Why d'you blast through those stop signs?"

The production team bounced all over town. The action flick shows off the grittier side of 1970s Seattle. McQ's best friend is gunned down in Post Alley at University Street, and McQ sets out to find the killer. The boat harbor where McQ lives is **Northlake Marina** at 1059 North Northlake Way. The Fremont Boat Company which is seen in the background is still situated there, and older employees remember McQ's deadly encounter with a hitman well. The Aurora Bridge appears prominently in the sequence.

The moviemakers were allowed to shoot in the

Swift justice: McQ shot the hitman on the run at Northlake Marina. The Aurora Bridge provides a dramatic background for the assassination attempt (author's collection).

actual police headquarters, whose entrance was on Cherry Street. The entire building has since been demolished. Another building long gone is the warehouse used by the gangster Santiago, located off East Marginal Way. A cultural icon of the city, **Smith Tower**, Seattle's first skyscraper, was home to the office of McQ's friend Pinky, the private investigator.

As the investigator follows a van around town, the movie provides a sightseeing tour. McQ follows the drug shipment south of 6th Avenue and turns left on the Yesler Way overpass. While waiting for the next setup at Yesler, Wayne played an eight-game chess marathon at a nearby bar with his personal photographer, David Sutton. Some people said Sutton was on the payroll of many Wayne movies for the simple reason that Wayne liked playing chess with him. The chase continues up **Beacon Hill**, McQ passing through the intersection of 12th Avenue and Golf Drive. The van reaches its destination: the **PacMed** building. McQ uses the back entrance on 12th Avenue. In the rear of the building, the detective trades shots with Santiago's mobsters. In hot pursuit of the van, he races down South Dearborn Street. He then takes a shortcut, driving under the freeway bridge. You don't want to try that yourself.

"The new national sport called grabbing"

One of the highlights of any John Wayne location tour is the **J&M Café** at 201 1st Avenue South: This is where McQ walks up to the bar to learn that his friend just died and, in a rage, beats up Santiago in the rest room. The restaurant remains virtually unchanged. The rest room took up the space that is now a storage room.

McQ meets the local drug dealer inside the **Coliseum,** which is now Key Arena at 305 Harrison Street; he corners a man on the steps of 119 1st Avenue South; and he exits Harborview Medical Center on 8th Avenue.

When McQ allows himself to take a break, he sees his ex-wife at **Medina**, on the other side of Lake Washington. The production used the Thurston Mansion on Groat Point Drive. The home has since been torn down. This was Julie Adams' only scene as McQ's ex-wife. She remembers that her main acting problem was "to erase the image, the icon of John Wayne and put in his place this cop that I used to be married to. But he was absolutely delightful."[7]

McQ plays a trick on his police friends as he has an unmanned car roll down Spring Street, crashing into the **National Building** at Post Avenue (and of course, exploding,

McQ takes a couple of shots at the robbers on the back entrance of the PacMed building. Note that Wayne is wearing the bracelet the Montagnard tribesmen presented him on his visit to the front in Vietnam (author's collection).

Northlake Marina looks almost the same as it did when renegade cop McQ had his boat lie at anchor and so is the wooden staircase from where Wayne took aim with his Colt Python (photograph by Roland Schaefli).

The investigator follows the drugs to the PacMed building on Beacon Hill. The back entrance is unaltered since 1973 (photograph by Roland Schaefli).

as is the custom in cop thrillers). McQ is watching his diversion from the stone archway at 107 Spring Street.

"I'm up to my butt in gas!"

Ten years before *McQ*, director John Sturges had been attached to the *Sons of Katie Elder* project. He was then already an old hand in directing action flicks, having *The Magnificent Seven* and *The Great Escape* under his belt. In 1973, the long-rumored pairing with Wayne finally became a reality. McQ's investigation culminates in a car chase filmed at the beach. "God knows, we needed something in that picture," Sturges said. The director claimed he got the idea for this location when he went to **Olympic Peninsula** and noticed a guy driving up the beach. He thought it was "a terrific place to stage a chase." That's the reason why he issued the hero a supercharged Pontiac and had the second unit set up shop at the further edge of the Olympic Peninsula, at **Ocean Shores**.

"I feel kinda silly about that, too"

One morning in 1959, young stuntman Hal Needham watched on **La Tuna Canyon Road**, which was also known as Stuntman Canyon because so many of them lived there, how all the stuntmen were heading out to Brackettville. Wayne cleaned Hollywood out that day, taking 28 stunt guys out on his Alamo location for four months. That morning, Needham waved at each one passing by. He had not been chosen. His time was yet to come. Needham first took a couple of blows in the *Donovan's Reef* barroom brawl and he was in the covered wagon rolling down the hill in *How the West Was Won*. After that, Wayne saw to it that the young daredevil got a nice speaking part as one of his ranchhands in *McLintock!* On *The War Wagon*, Needham got his chance to push himself into the foreground when the stunt coordinator had difficulties setting up Wayne's fisticuffs on the street, taking out some of Bruce Cabot's bad guys in a flash. Wayne got impatient and walked away, telling them, "When you figure it out, let me know. I'll be over here playing chess." So Needham figured it out. "Okay," Wayne said, "let's see how Mr. Needham would do it."

After they shot the scene Needham's way, Wayne gave him an attaboy wink. "Needham, if I'm ever in a fight, I want you on my side."[8] When they did the big saloon brawl in the same picture, Wayne finally let "Mr. Needham" take over completely. "Damn it, Needham, why don't you use one of your young Supermen to do this?" Wayne gave him permission to move in his newly trained stuntmen because "we've been around too long to do this kind of stuff." In his biography, Needham plays down the part that Wayne played in helping him come up through the ranks (at one time, Wayne called the eager man a "young pipsqueak"). Needham even boasted how he had to demonstrate to Wayne (in 1969!)

Action director John Sturges discusses the next set up of *McQ* with his star in the streets of Seattle. The two pros had long wanted to make a picture together (author's collection).

JOHN WAYNE
McQ – schlägt zu

After the big shoot-out on the northern end of Ocean Shores, John Wayne lets the waves wash away the suitcase full of drugs in *McQ* (author's collection).

how to throw a correct punch. Because Needham repeated that story so often, his long-time pal Burt Reynolds repeated it in *his* biography as well.

"Come and get the stuff!"

When stunt coordinator Ronnie Rondell was trying to find a solution for the signature stunt in *McQ*, flipping a car on a flat beach, he turned to Needham. There was nothing on the sandy Ocean Shores to hide the customary ramp. So Needham dreamed up what would become the first-ever cannon-roll car stunt in the movies. Rondell decided it was too risky and complicated to try for the first time on the set. Needham was left with a try-out in Los Angeles. His regulars rigged an old wreck of a car, cut a hole in the back floorboard, then put a small cannon in the hole with the muzzle pointed down. They brought five four-ounce black-powder bombs to a dry lake outside L.A. The first one lifted the car just about six inches. Needham clearly remembered their next move: "There were five of us with maybe a total of ten years education among us, but we came to a decision: put all four remaining bombs in." Needham strapped himself in the beat-up car. As it went into a broad slide at 55 MPH, he hit the bomb button. The explosion blew the vehicle 30 feet into the air. When Needham opened his eyes in mid-flight, he was upside down and going backward: "I knew this wasn't going as planned." The next thing he heard was the boys: "Holy shit, he's still alive!" He had a cracked vertebra, six broken ribs, and a punctured lung. He counted the missing teeth himself: three. "John Wayne would have to finish the movie without me."

"I need the cover of your license"

The inventor of the stunt still insisted the same men get on the plane to Seattle and tell Rondell how to do it right. Rondell had chosen the special section of the pristine beach at **Grenville Bay**, just off State Route 109, north of **Moclips**. "It was hard-packed, like Daytona, when that tide went out, and you could fly down that stretch."[9] In the stunt that became a science in stuntwork, they used eight ounces of black powder. When the stuntman steered the Chevy Impala at 55 MPH to the right, he triggered the cannon and catapulted the car into the air, flipping it 12 times. The wreck covered 40 yards in four and a half seconds. Gary McLarty (who flew over the bar with the help of a trampoline in *The War Wagon*) was at the wheel. A member of the Hollywood Stuntmen's Hall of Fame, he was tragically killed in a car wreck in 2014.

The advertising banners proclaimed: "Wayne on Wheels!" and for a while, they called it the "McQ cannon." In time, it was given the name of its inventor: "the Needham cannon." Look for it when James Bond crashes the Aston Martin in *Casino Royale*.

"He bumped into a chair"

When Rondell was asked how the stuntmen felt about working with Wayne, he acknowledged, "You know, he's our Dad!"[10] In the '60s, young stuntmen came into the business, usually hanging onto the shirttails of an established stuntman. Chuck Roberson had shown Needham the ropes. According to Roberson, young Hal went "from being a kid who didn't know which end of the horse to put a bridle on, to one of the most sought-after stuntmen around."[11] The scene on the beach marked the changing of the guard: In *McQ*, Roberson played a heavy in the wrecked car (McQ guns him

JOHN WAYNE
McQ – schlägt zu

A car stunt for the history books: the Chevy Impala is blown up by the Needham cannon and will do twelve flips (author's collection).

The beach at Grenville Bay just off Moclips was chosen for *McQ* because it was hard enough to have cars drive on it (photograph by Roland Schaefli).

down in the surf), his last appearance in a John Wayne film (apart from his horse fall in *The American West of John Ford*). Roberson had been on the road with Wayne ever since *The Fighting Kentuckian*. Roberson stunted for Mitchum and Gable but Wayne always referred to him as "his" stuntman. In fact, Wayne didn't shy away when somebody would take their picture even as they were both wearing the same costume—something other stars would have vetoed.

Roberson's grandson was on the set one day. When he saw Wayne dressed up the same way as his "Gwampa," he stomped up to the star and said, "And what do you do?" Wayne laughed loudly, bent down and put his nose right next to the kid's nose. "You mean you don't know? I stand in for your Grandpa on the close-ups!"[12]

"Lousy damn junk"

During the shooting at Ocean Shores, Wayne and the crew lived at the **Polynesian Resort** at 615 Ocean Shores Boulevard. He knew the "Poly" well; the kitchen staff remembers he found their cooking to his taste. He returned every once in a while, in the years after, when the *Wild Goose* cruised the waters off the Washington coast.

At the northern tip of Ocean Shores (note the rocks sticking out of the water at low tide), *McQ*-director John Sturges walks Wayne to the camera (author's collection).

"There's a bar": since McQ's final line was not in the shooting script, they just used this beach house in Moclips to have the hero "get a drink." (photograph by Roland Schaefli).

One scene remained to be shot in the nearby beachfront town of **Moclips**. The scene looks easy enough but Wayne and Sturges had long discussions about it. Earlier drafts had McQ continue his investigation in City Hall because the one corrupt police officer probably wasn't acting alone. McQ summarized: "In narco stuff, the threads run deep. I think Tom was too small to have laid it all out by himself. I think he took his orders from somebody sitting dirty some place. That's where I want to go." At the time of shooting, the Nixon hearings were in full swing. Wayne didn't want to have anything to do with an exchange that smacked of liberal paranoia. He was loyal to the police: "These men and women are ready 24 hours a day to put their lives on the line to protect you the way the Army and Marines are. They deserve much better than they get, in most cases."[13] Screenwriter Lawrence Roman rewrote the scene several times, "but I could never satisfy him. He saw it political, anti–American." So when Sturges rolled the camera on the final scene, Wayne ignored the "Threads run deep" speech and just pointed to the wooden shack that still stands at 2nd Street and Pacific Avenue. "There's a bar over there. Let's get a drink."[14]

"You can't get a decent burger anywhere"

As early as 1964, a trade paper had announced that Wayne would begin filming a detective story in the Near East. That never happened. However, one year after *McQ*, they dusted off that project. It became a British production under the working title *Joe Battle*. Wayne plays a fish out of water, again in the same vein as Clint Eastwood, this time like Eastwood's cop in *Coogan's Bluff*: a professional lawman who finds himself in unfamiliar surroundings. To work for a

British company was all new to Wayne. "This is my first time with a full English crew. Great guys! Good sense of humor," he told a Dutch TV crew that interviewed him between scenes. Wayne was clearly enjoying himself: "Hard work but a few laughs to have along the way."

What would eventually become *Brannigan* started principal photography on June 17, 1974. Filming in 60 London locales went on until August 1974. Wayne told the makers of the featurette *The Duke in London* that he was having "a very enjoyable time. I'm kinda new to it but I'm beginning to enjoy it."[15]

"You're a real bush-leaguer"

The film about a Chicago cop who exclaims "Knock, knock!" after breaking down doors starts out in Chicago but just very few settings were shot there. The British company shot the Chicago-based scenes in London. The scene which was supposed to be a Chicago neighborhood—an American squad car summons Brannigan—was actually shot with U.S. cars in the area of the London docks. Brannigan then flies to London from **Chicago's O'Hare's** terminal 1, which has been razed and replaced since.

Most of the crew stayed at the **Penta Hotel** on Oxford Road. For the nine-week schedule, its star was booked at the **Athenaeum Hotel** at 116 Piccadilly, but Wayne soon let the production manager know he did not like the arrangements. That had something to do with his wish for having Pat Stacy live close to him. So they rented a charming house for him at 20 **Cheyne Walk** at Albert Bridge Gardens in Chelsea. (The featurette *The Duke in London* shows him going to work in the morning. As he leaves the Cheyne house, a driver picks

"It's a men's club—rules strictly enforced": the Garrick Club, seen from where Brannigan gets out of the car, one of the sixty London locations (photograph by Roland Schaefli).

him up.) The 200-year-old house cost $2,500 a month to rent.

Ironically, the movie has the mobster boss (John Vernon) stay in one of London's most famous celebrity hotels, the **Dorchester** on Park Lane, east of Hyde Park. To this day, the five-star hotel is associated with famous film stars. Press junket interviews are often conducted in its suites. Elizabeth Taylor and Richard Burton spent their honeymoon in the Oliver Messel Suite. Peter Sellers considered the Dorchester his one true residence. David Lean cast one of his films in the marble reception hall.

Meanwhile, Brannigan is collected at Terminal 3 of **Heathrow Airport** and driven through the **Heathrow road tunnel**. The gangster boss is abducted from the extravagant **Royal Automobile Club** at 89 Pall Mall. Brannigan is introduced to the rules of a British gentleman at the **Garrick Club** on Garrick Street. It's been said that the club only allowed cameras because Richard Attenborough, Wayne's co-star, was a long-time member. The Garrick Club is one of the oldest members' clubs in the world. Writers such as Charles Dickens and H.G. Wells had been members. The film uses the art collection of the club to its advantage: When Wayne and Attenborough discuss police work, portraits of members Laurence Olivier and John Gielgud are on the wall behind them.

The establishing shot of the famous revolving **New Scotland Yard** sign was photographed at its correct location at the Victoria Embankment. But when the movie then jumps to an indoor shot, supposedly Attenborough's Scotland Yard office, they are at the **St. Thomas Hospital** on Westminster Bridge Road, with a view of the former County Hall. (That same year, it was Anthony Hopkins' office in the suspense thriller *Juggernaut*.)

As Brannigan departs, the end credits are shown over a shot of the Tower Hotel sundial with London's Tower Bridge in the background (photograph by Roland Schaefli).

Brannigan has to move house quite a lot: in Little Venice, he lives on Maida Avenue, as a neighbor of *A Fish Called Wanda* (photograph by Roland Schaefli).

In *Brannigan*, Judy Geeson takes John Wayne out to dinner at the Terraza in Soho, which was frequented at the time (author's collection).

"I really walked into that one"

Until the hitman booby-traps the place, Brannigan lives at 61–80 **York Mansions** on Prince of Wales Drive. His room was the one with the oriel. The explosion of the bomb in the toilet results in a hole in the wall and reveals a view of the **Albert Memorial** in Kensington Gardens, actually quite a distance from Battersea Park. Brannigan quips that the gangster "paid 25 grand to get me that view." The moviemakers never made a secret of their desire to

Waiting for the bar brawl in *Brannigan* to start, with director Douglas Hickox and producer Michael Wayne. The covered Leadenhall Market dates from the 14th century (author's collection).

show off as many London sights as possible, so during several car rides, the viewer gets to see Buckingham Palace as well as Trafalgar Square. After Brannigan moves out of York Mansions, his new accommodation is at 6 Maida Avenue, in **Little Venice** (next door to the place where Jamie Lee Curtis lives in *A Fish Called Wanda*). Brannigan is wined and dined in a restaurant at 50 Dean Street in **Soho.** It was then the famed eatery Mario and Franco's Terraza. Mario and Franco defined the new eating style of swinging London. The restaurant has changed owners, cooks and names several times since; it is now Le Relais de Venise l'Entrecôte.

Wayne took Pat Stacy out to the most romantic restaurant in town: the White Elephant on the banks of the Thames. It attracted quite a few celebrities in its heyday but it is closed now.

"Mind if I butt in, partner?"

In a satire of Wayne's usual saloon brawl, Brannigan tears one of London's finest pubs to pieces: the **Lamb Tavern** at **Leadenhall Market,** located on Gracechurch Street. This beautiful covered market dates from the 14th century. Younger movie audiences might recognize it as a *Harry Potter* location: the "Leaky Cauldron" is in real life an optician at Leadenhall. Probably more important to Wayne fans is the fact that Clint Eastwood used the awesome structure in his film *Hereafter.* Brannigan observes the goings-on in the pub from a butcher's shop, which is now a Pizza Express. During the filming, the shopkeepers treated Wayne to a local brew. He remarked with mock surprise, "It's cold! Room temperature." He told bystanders that he "enjoyed the new surroundings and the little differences in customs." The quintessential American star found his London experience

"very refreshing." The inside of the Lamb Tavern was built at the studio. "English stuntmen are very cooperative when it comes to breaking furniture," Wayne said after they had torn the set down.

"Can you swim?"

Location hunters had problems deciding which dock they used for the scene in which Brannigan shoves a motorcycle courier into the waters. According to Tony Robinson who played the courier, they shot his backward fall at **King George V Dock**. Back then, it was not an appealing site. It has since been rebuilt to meet the requirements of a modern dock.

Wayne held up traffic in one of the busiest parts of the capital, **Piccadilly Circus.** This was one of the last times local authorities would allow filmmakers to shut down the famous location. For the drop of the ransom money, a red mailbox was put in the middle of a pedestrian island. Which wasn't even close to reality, but "we've got to show the American audience London landmarks they recognize, or they won't believe it's London," Wayne explained to biographer Munn. "And there was nowhere else to put the damn thing."[16]

When Katharine Hepburn heard that Wayne was shooting in Piccadilly Circus (pre-production of *Rooster Cogburn* was already underway), she drove over, walked straight up to him, put out her hand and announced: "I'm Katharine Hepburn and I'm so happy we're going to be in a picture together!" Wayne couldn't have been more surprised.[17]

The Lamb Tavern in Leadenhall Market has been a part of the tapestry of the City of London since 1780. In 1974, however, it was the place of the barroom brawl in *Brannigan,* easily one of the most charming John Wayne locations (photograph by Roland Schaefli).

JOHN WAYNE dans **BRANNIGAN**
JOHN WAYNE dans BRANNIGAN
avec
RICHARD ATTENBOROUGH
JUDY GEESON · MEL FERRER · JOHN VERNON
RALPH MEEKER · DANIEL PILON   United Artists
distribué par LES ARTISTES ASSOCIÉS

"A false bottom": John Wayne and Richard Attenborough (under the mailbox) draw a large crowd on the *Brannigan* location at Piccadilly Circus (author's collection).

"The view from the bridge was terrific"

Like *McQ, Brannigan* has to include the obligatory sequence of police thrillers: the car chase. After the company managed to showcase virtually every iconic building in London, the biggest coup was setting up the film's signature stunt at **Tower Bridge.** The chase that leads up to that action highlight starts at **Warriner Gardens,** close to Battersea Park again. Brannigan chases a suspect down the road, then confiscates a Capri on Beechmore Road, shouting, "Follow that car!," only to realize he got himself into a right-hand-drive car. To get some footage of Wayne actually behind the wheel, they had him driving the car on a lot at Battersea, with a camera contraption attached to the hood. "It's easier than driving a six-up, with six horses on a stagecoach," he laughingly told a TV crew that covered that part of the shooting.

Brannigan faces the hitman in his 1966 Jaguar at the decommissioned **Beckton Gasworks** on the banks of the Thames. Today, virtually no trace of the large industrial park exists. The brownfield land was redeveloped as an exclusive residential area. The Beckton Retail Park now occupies parts of the former site. The gasworks was an ideal location for action sequences. After Brannigan disposed of his nemesis, James Bond dropped Blofeld into one of the industrial chimneys in *For Your Eyes Only.* Director Stanley Kubrick was the last to use the deserted gasworks in 1987: It portrayed a besieged Vietnamese city in *Full Metal Jacket.* Kubrick had the buildings selectively demolished.

Brannigan moves a third and last time, to the then-new **Tower Hotel** on St. Katherine's Way where he says his final goodbye. The large hotel on the north bank was built in a

Shoot-out at Beckton: the decommissioned gasworks were used in a variety of thrillers after *Brannigan* but are gone now (author's collection).

modern style which is considered rather unattractive today (it has been voted one of the ugliest buildings in London). Still, it gave the camera the opportunity to pan from Brannigan's departing taxi to the sundial and Tower Bridge. The same site was used soon thereafter for a scene with Roger Moore in *The Wild Geese.*

"Unless you wanna sing soprano"

After Wayne worked at Pinewood Studios for *Circus World*, *Brannigan* provided his second opportunity to work in a famous London studio: **Shepperton**, an hour outside of London. On its 15 stages, they built interiors like the abovementioned Lamb Tavern. During the 1970s, the number of films produced at Shepperton was falling rapidly. The year before *Brannigan*, the studio grounds had already been reduced from 60 to 20 acres. In 2001, Shepperton Studios was sold to the Pinewood Group.

British actor Tony Robinson watched the filming of the scene when Brannigan bursts in the door, telling the astonished gangsters, "Knock, knock!" The set was a rickety office with a blown-up photo of Beckton behind it. But when the camera assistant clapped the board, announcing, "Thirty-seven, take one," and director Douglas Hickox shouted "Action!," nothing happened. Then there was a rattling noise and a muffled but familiar voice said, "I can't open the fucking door." Robinson remembered how "assistant directors and carpenters raced out of nowhere like Israeli commandos on a deadly mission. In 30 seconds the edges of the big door had been re-planed, re-sanded and re-oiled."[18] In take two, the door exploded open, sugar-glass shuttered, and in burst Wayne, practically as big as the door.

The Tower Bridge sequence was part real stunt and part studio work. A scale model of the bridge was built and a model car was propelled over the half-raised bridge; the footage was shot with a high-speed camera. The model shot was edited into the footage so expertly that hardly anybody ever noticed it.

"One less detective to worry about!"

After playing two detectives back to back, Wayne summarized his thoughts about his change in routine: "Every once in a while I feel like I'm gettin' in a rut and, well, that's when I start to look at other scripts. Then, once I do a couple adventure or detective pictures, I'm ready to get back in the saddle again and grind out more Westerns. But I just gotta have a little versatility, now and then, to keep my head on straight."[19]

"They pulled a Murphy!" Unaccustomed environment for Chicago cop *Brannigan*: London's King George V Dock (author's collection).

19

Without Reservations

"What do I have?"

"Actors aren't supposed to be businessmen."
—John Wayne on his private investments

So John Wayne told Hedda Hopper in a February 1949 interview, adding "I guess I'm luckier than most that I do have something to show for it."[1] He told the gossip columnist that he had a finger in a couple of business things. This chapter is about what kind of pie he had his fingers in, places he stayed in as a private person, and places he never actually went to but is still remembered in.

When a rather bold interviewer on the set of *The Cowboys* questioned Wayne about his possessions, the actor was clearly uncomfortable. "Let's see, what do I have…" he said, and, just to oblige, he rattled off a number of possessions, like oil wells and hotels. He put his company Batjac first.

Taking care of business: John Wayne at his Batjac office building (author's collection).

Building Batjac

Before Wayne formed Batjac Productions, he had bought an office building for his Wayne-Fellows company at 1022 Palm Avenue, right off Sunset Boulevard. On June 1, 1954, Wayne-Fellows became Batjac. He hired people he felt comfortable working with. "I know that we have in our Batjac organization a group of men unequaled in this business in ability, experience, all the special skills that are required, and in devoted loyalty to the company." The boss went on to praise his company workers, calling them "the best in the business."[2]

John Ford had rented an office in Wayne's Batjac building. The owner was sometimes absent-minded. Early-arriving employees could find him sitting on the steps of the building, reading the morning paper, waiting for someone to let him in because he'd lost his key. Michael Pate was interviewed in Wayne's Batjac office for the part of Chief Vittorio in *Hondo*. He described it as "more like an outdoorsman's den." Wayne's Girl Friday, Mary St. John, would sit in the outside office.[3] Wayne sold the Batjac building in February 1965 and relocated his company to Paramount, on the second floor of the Cecil B. DeMille building. During his years with Paramount and well into the 1970s, Wayne's letter stationery gave this Batjac address as **5451 Marathon Street**. When he set his mind on directing again in 1967, his Directors Guild of America member card was made out to this address as well. The May 1970 *Photoplay* reported how Wayne spent a morning at the office: He winged in by helicopter from Newport, arriving at his office by 9:30. The morning agenda opened with taping radio promotion spots for the Marine Corps,

JOHN WAYNE

BATJAC PRODUCTIONS
1022 PALM AVENUE
HOLLYWOOD, CALIFORNIA

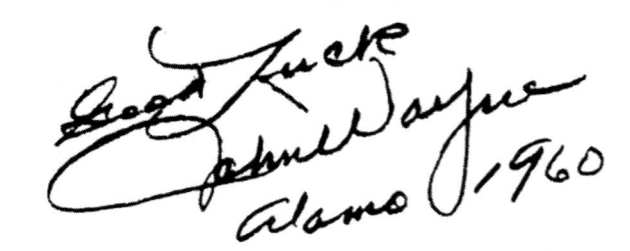

When approached by too many fans at once, Wayne handed out this business card. It had his Batjac address on one side… (author's collection).

followed by a magazine interview, then by looking over some TV films on Vietnam.

After *Brannigan*, he moved the Batjac office again, this time to **9570 Wilshire Boulevard**. From Suite 400, Wayne conducted his business until his last year of life.

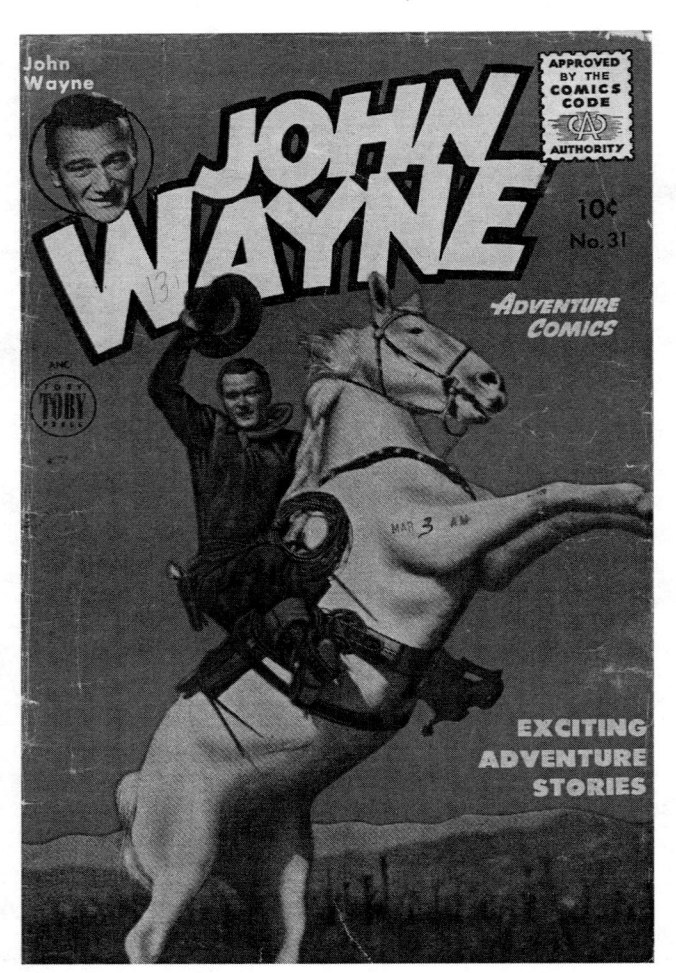

John Wayne had an interest in the comic books published by Toby Press. "John Wayne Adventure Comics" featured photograph covers with scenes from former movies, in this case from *Ride Him, Cowboy*. The short-lived series ran 31 issues from 1949 to 1955 (author's collection).

… and his pre-printed autograph on the other. This one he had made up especially for the Alamo premiere (author's collection).

Owning the Flatiron

When celebrity columnist Hedda Hopper asked Wayne the business question, he named a few oil wells, part of a country club and "the Flatiron building in Culver City."[4] By that, he meant the **Culver City Hotel** at 9400 Culver Boulevard, then a few blocks from MGM studios. It was indeed the case that the movie star had a special liking for owning hotels. This one partially belonged to him, his business manager Bö Roos and Red Skelton. The Flatiron was changing hands ever since it opened in 1924. Charlie Chaplin was one of the first owners. It was used as a movie location as early as in the Laurel & Hardy pictures. Wayne always made it available for fundraisers even though he wanted to get rid of it. He eventually donated it to the YMCA. The six-story Renaissance Revival building is now a national landmark.

"Let's go down to Acapulco"

After the divorce from Chata came through, Wayne told Pilar, "Let's go down to Acapulco for a while. It's time we had some fun."[5] Wayne knew exactly where they would go. During the 1950s, he owned a piece of the **Los Flamingos Hotel**, along with several entertainment personalities, among them his friend Johnny Weissmuller. Director Edward Dmytryk observed that "both men drank well, if not wisely." The director also said that, more than once, people tried to goad the Duke and Johnny Weissmuller (another Flamingos Hotel co-owner) into battle, but it never happened. "Neither of them ever got so boxed that he lost respect for the other's prowess."[6]

The Flamingos Hotel can be spotted in Orson Welles' *The Lady from Shanghai*. The gorgeous building is located on the Avenida Lopez Mateos, atop of the highest cliffs of Acapulco, 450 feet high. The famous cliff divers perform daily at the edge of La Quebrada. One day Wayne sat on the patio watching the divers jump off the famous 200-foot precipice. His publicist Jim Henaghan bet Wayne that he (Henaghan) could do that. Henaghan then paid a diver to put on his red trunks. From a distance, you could see only that the man was

Wayne owned a piece of the uniquely shaped Culver Hotel, also known as the "Flatiron." It has a distinguished role in cinematic history, having hosted the casts of movies such as *Gone with the Wind* and *The Wizard of Oz* (photograph by Roland Schaefli).

John Wayne and Gary Cooper on the way to the Acapulco beach from the Flamingos Hotel. The two stars were great friends and had made plans to do a movie in Mexico. *Vera Cruz* was ultimately made without Wayne, his part rewritten to suit Burt Lancaster (author's collection).

wearing red trunks. When the publicist returned, claiming, "I did it!," Wayne bought drinks all around. He never found out.[7]

An incident that occurred at the Flamingos became fodder for the press: Wayne's second wife Chata claimed that he dashed a glass of water in her face. According to witnesses, she threw a bucket of ice back. Today, the Los Flamingos still advertises "John Wayne's Room" and, in the restaurant, Johnny Weissmuller's table.

Wayne would take a yearly cruise to Acapulco, first in his *Nor'wester*, then in the *Wild Goose*. Once, when the latter was moored in the Acapulco harbor, astronaut Buzz Aldrin

During the photograph shoot for an advertisement of photographic equipment: Even though his audience saw him as an outdoor he-man, John Wayne often endorsed household products (author's collection).

swam out, climbed aboard and introduced himself as a John Wayne fan.

Casting Off Taborcillo Island

Wayne traveled to Panama extensively. In the early 1960s, he reportedly purchased the island of **Taborcillo**, 25 miles off the coast of the Central America country. The 50-acre island is a bird sanctuary with miles of sandy beaches. After Wayne's death, his estate sold it. It changed owners many times before being opened as a tourist resort, sometimes called John Wayne Island, complete with a Western-themed park.

Without Reservations

During the shooting of *Brannigan*, Wayne took the liberty to take Pat Stacy to Paris over the weekend, as she felt very romantic about it. Pat had hoped they could stay at the **George V Hotel** where Wayne had already been a guest. The hotel told her they were booked up, but Wayne went right to the famous hotel (located near the Arc de Triomphe, at 31 Avenue George V) and asked to speak to the manager. Five minutes later, they were being "escorted royally to Suite 152."[8] He then wined and dined her at **La Tour d'Argent**, the 400-year-old restaurant at 17 Quai de la Tournelle. It has hosted the world's rich and famous for centuries. The couple

Top and bottom: In this vintage ad from 1957, the Waynes advertise Remington shavers. Pilar is credited as "Mrs. John Wayne." The two-page spread appeared in *Life Magazine* and plugged *Legend of the Lost*. Before that, John Wayne had endorsed Gillette on TV (author's collection).

John Wayne was among the motion picture stars who appeared in *The Saturday Evening Post* advertisements endorsing Whitman's Chocolates. Compensation came in the form of boxes of chocolates and a mention of the star's upcoming feature (author's collection).

also got a private tour of the famous wine cellars. After that, they made it up to the third landing of the **Eiffel Tower.**

Wayne used another short break in the London shoot for what would be his last visit to his ancestral homeland, Ireland. During another trip with Stacy, they toured the **Napa Valley** wineries and stayed at the **Silverado Resort,** 1600 Atlas Peak Road. The southern mansion was built in the 1860s.

Wayne's last trip to Japan led him to the **Imperial Hotel** in Tokyo, overlooking Hibiya Park. Back then, it was grand and old-school luxurious. A new era is currently in the making: An entirely new structure is being built for the two-tower building.

For some time, Wayne had a suite year-round at the **Hampshire House** on Central Park South in New York. Always on the lookout for business ventures, he invested in a string of Arizona motels. During the 1950s, he became friendly with Duro Gurovich. The son of an Arizona copper miner, Gurovich operated the **Gurovich's Copper Hills Motel,** built in Globe in 1952. His silent partner liked to overnight at the motel. When it was damaged by fire in 2003, it was called the Copper Hills Inns and Suites, located on U.S. 60 & 70, halfway between Globe and Miami, in the heart of the Pinal Mountains. An America's Best Value Hotel stands in its place today.

Marion, Illinois

On July 11, 1975, Wayne was in **Marion,** Illinois, scouting a possible location for a coal degasification plant. This would remove methane gas from coal and leave oil as a by-product. He also backed a California company called Deco (Duke Engineering Company) which reclaimed old tires and yielded petrochemical oil for fuel. Patent rights, for whatever they were worth, would remain with Wayne. It was another unsuccessful venture, probably the last one he was involved with. Just one of his many business ventures was extremely fruitful: the **26 Bar Hereford Ranch** (see Chapter 13). After Wayne passed away, the ranch was sold to Tom Chauncey, who carried on the tradition of raising prime beef. Following Wayne's death, the ranch was sold to the Hopi Tribe, who converted the headquarters into a Bed and Breakfast. Hereford cattle still graze on the prime Arizona ranch land. The town of Eagar celebrates the annual John Wayne Days to preserve the memories.

Travel by train

The **Durango-Silverton Narrow Gauge Railroad** can be seen in the 1957 James Stewart Western *Night Passage*. The heritage railroad operates 45 miles of track between Durango and Silverton, Colorado. That is their steam locomotive in the title sequence of *Katie Elder*. However, Wayne himself is not in the shot. Nevertheless, the museum at the Durango depot proudly devotes some rolling stock to him.

As the locomotive reaches the station, the film cuts to the Mexico location. Interestingly, the revised final script dated December 24, 1964, does not describe the train steaming up through the canyons. Instead, it begins with the depot "on a bleak and lonely expanse of prairie," where "grim-faced men await the arrival of the train." Therefore, after the credits, the movie doesn't just change locations from Durango, Colorado, to Durango, Mexico, but also locomotives: The Durango-Silverton Narrow Gauge Railroad becomes the locomotive No. 650 of the National Railway of Mexico. It was put to use in all of Wayne's Durango westerns. For 70 years, this old steam locomotive traveled between Durango, Mexico, and the silver-gold mining town of Tepehranes in the Sierra Madres. Plans had been made to scrap the 650 after *Katie Elder*. Somebody must have changed his mind because it is that same old locomotive doing duty in *Big Jake*, *The Train Robbers* and *Cahill, U.S. Marshal.*

During filming of *The Sons of Katie Elder*, Wayne climbs up to the Mexican crew to take a closer look at the old locomotive No. 6540 of the National Railway of Mexico (author's collection).

Speaking of *Katie Elder*: There is another Ouray connection to John Wayne in addition to the *True Grit* courthouse. The judge of Ouray wrote down the story of the five Marlow brothers in 1892, and it became the basis for *Katie Elder*. The Marlows were arrested for stealing cattle and an angry mob attempted to lynch them. The screenwriter who originally developed the story for the screen paid the descendants for the film rights. The brothers later lived on the ranch at **Billie Creek**, not far from Ridgway, the principal location of *True Grit*, and two of the brothers even served there as deputies. A few structures of the Marlow ranch still stand.

Before John Ford started principal photography on *The Searchers*, the second unit shot the buffalo scenes in Edmonton, Canada, on a frozen lake at **Elk Island Park**. Chuck Hayward doubled Jeffrey Hunter in that sequence. One buffalo was actually killed on camera as part of a culling of the herd to avoid overpopulation. Hayward remembered, "We shot buffalo, just one is all. Then they butchered him and gave him to the Indians."[9] Terry Wilson wore Wayne's costume: "It was a little scary because every so often you could hear that ice ping as it kind of cracked beneath you."[10] The two stuntmen

also served as photo doubles in the sequence where the two Searchers reach the military outpost to inquire about Debbie. In that sequence, they used a ranch 11 miles north of **Gunnison**, Colorado, 60 miles east of Montrose on Highway 50. (Ford also used the location in *Cheyenne Autumn*.) On the river along that road, Winton Hoch got the beautiful river crossing of the cavalry herding Indian prisoners in the can.

Missing Out the Rain Forest

The production schedule of *The Searchers* kept Wayne from playing the lead in *Seven Men from Now*. It is possible that it also prevented the production of an adventure film for which locations had already been picked in the Amazon Rain Forest. The film, director Sam Fuller's pet project *Tigrero!*, was never made. Wayne was set to play a jaguar hunter, Ava Gardner would have been his love interest, and Darryl F. Zanuck had scheduled it for 1954. The maverick director and Wayne would have made an interesting pair. Forty years after the project was abandoned, filmmaker Jim Jarmusch

"It's a good thing it was a Stetson," John Wayne drawled in *Circus World*. **Stetson Hat took out this ad in the *Saturday Evening Post*. Earlier, in 1943, Wayne had endorsed Adam Hats (author's collection).**

Glenn Faris, executive vice president, is showing John Wayne and other unidentified visitors the construction progress of the Cowboy Museum in Oklahoma in 1963 (© Dickinson Research Center, National Cowboy & Western Heritage Museum, Oklahoma City, Oklahoma).

followed Fuller on a trip into Brazil's Mato Grosso, to the village of **Santa Isabel Do Morro** on Bananal Island, where filming remained a dream of the inhabitants. The result was the unusual documentary *Tigrero: A Film That Was Never Made*.

Cowboy Hall of Fame

Wayne had established a close relationship with the **National Cowboy & Western Heritage Museum** in Oklahoma. When construction began in 1960, he took a red-hot branding iron and burned a "W" into a wooden concrete form. The *Oklahoman* quoted him on September 16: "It's great to have a part in something like this." Five years later, the museum at 1700 NE 63rd Street was ready to go. The day of the opening, June 25, 1965, grand marshal Wayne led a parade through downtown Oklahoma City. In 1973, Norman Rockwell was commissioned by the Western Heritage Center to paint Wayne's picture, to commemorate his induction in the Hall of Great Western Performers. Wayne was flattered

"If it ain't loaded and cocked it don't shoot": the gun expert with one of the valuable weapons from his private collection. It ranged from an 1860s Mexican rifle to the Russian-made AK-47, captured from the enemy and given to him from the troops in Vietnam. The shotgun Ward Bond left him also went to Oklahoma (author's collection).

by the honor and visited the painter's studio in **Stockbridge**, Massachusetts, on November 29, 1973, to sit for the 38×31" oil on canvas. It was auctioned in 2018 for $1.3 million.

Wayne served on the board of directors until he passed away. Upon his death, he left part of his collection to the museum. When Olive Carey died, she willed Harry Carey's memorabilia to Wayne—so it is now also in the cowboy museum.

"You may need me and this Winchester"

In the entryway of the Oklahoma museum is a letter dated May 15, 1979: With a shaky signature, John Wayne willed his possessions to the Cowboy Hall of Fame: 63 guns, knives and other assorted weapons. Also exhibited in the John Wayne Collection are his trademark large loop Model 1892 carbines, serially numbered 987XXX (1927) and 991XXX (1928).

When Wayne was set to play the Ringo Kid, he was summoned to John Ford's office for the costume fitting. There was a holster and a gun and Ford asked him if he could use it. "So my father put the belt on, twirled the gun and did all kinds of tricks of the gunslinger trade," his oldest son Michael told the editors of *Cowboys & Indians* in January 2002. Ford smiled and said, "Well, that's pretty good, but you're not going to have a pistol in this picture. I'm giving you a rifle, and what you are is a plowboy. Not a fast gun like you were in all those B Westerns." So Wayne had to start thinking about the scene in which he would carry a saddle in one hand and this rifle in the other, shooting and cocking it. He got together with Yakima Canutt. As a kid, Canutt had seen a Buffalo Bill's Wild West show. One rider had carried a rifle with a large ring loop, which allowed him to spin the gun in the air. That's how the two of them came up with a large loop Winchester. Ford instructed the prop department to manufacture a ring loop and install it on a standard-issue 1892 Winchester carbine. They sawed an inch off the end, so it would pass beneath Wayne's arm. When Wayne presented his famous rifles to the Hall of Fame, he quipped, "Take care of it. It's killed a lot of phonies."[11]

On the mantelpiece in his den, Wayne had proudly displayed his entire collection of kachina dolls. "I've been collecting them since 1928. They were made by the Pueblo Indians."[12] The frequency with which he was involved in making films in Hopi country led to his knowledge of the kachinas. All 64 of his dolls are now exhibited in the Cowboy Hall of Fame. "As for my collection of memorabilia," he pointed out to an interviewer shortly before he willed it to the Cowboy museum, "they weren't given to me; most of this stuff I had to buy."[13]

The way Wayne willed his prized collection to the

museum echoed the scene in *McLintock!* when the cattle baron tells his daughter that she isn't going to inherit his empire. "I'm going to leave most of it to, well, the nation, really, for a park were no lumbermen'll cut down all the trees for houses with leaky roofs." In April 1988, Michael Wayne answered questions about his father's collection on the Discovery Channel TV show *Take Charge!* Michael somewhat bashfully recalled the day he and his father were looking at a great Charles Russell bronze, "Changing Outfits," and his father said, "You know, Michael, you like this Western art, don't you?" His son nodded. But the family patriarch had to inform him, "Well, I want you to know you're not getting any of it." His seven children might have expected to receive pieces from the collection, as he had collected works of Russell, Jackson, Remington and Wieghorst. Michael understood that his father was unwilling to allow the collection to be broken up like that. "I'm leaving it to the National Cowboy Hall in Oklahoma City, where it is going as a collection and then the whole world'll get to see it. That's a lot better'n sittin' in your living room." His gift was valued at $1.4 million at the time. The collection, comprised of more than 200 items, is housed in a special gallery.

John Ford's Portland

John Ford's hometown Portland honored its famous son with the statue at **Gorham's Corner**, across the former site of Feeney's (Ford's family's) Saloon. His family had lived over the establishment on Center Street in Portland for 14 years. He had lived on Danforth Street, not far from the statue. The ten-foot-high bronze depicts a middle-aged

The ten-foot-high bronze statue honors a Portland-raised filmmaker: For a long time, no trace of John Ford could be found in the Old Port. The statue was created in 1993 in the heart of the former Irish immigrant district (photograph by Roland Schaefli).

"Pappy" sitting in his director's chair, looking across Center Street where his father's saloon stood. The names of his favorite movies are engraved in the socket.

Field Photo Farm

Ford used his salary from *They Were Expandable* to found the **Field Photo Farm** in the San Fernando Valley, as a shrine to the fallen and a meeting place for the veterans of the OSS. The clubhouse was located at 18201 Calvert Street in Reseda. Studio art designers and set builders helped to construct a non-denominational chapel from an old gatehouse. The stained glass windows came from the chapel in Ford's Oscar-winning *How Green Was My Valley*.

After Ward Bond died, his body was placed in a flag-draped casket in the chapel. When Harry Carey died, Ford also put on a funeral. Wayne read the same poem he had recited over the dead soldier in *They Were Expendable*.

The original chapel of the Field Photo Farm, rechristened John Ford Chapel, that *They Were Expendable* salaries helped to pay: now at Spielberg Drive, on the grounds of the retirement community at the Motion Picture Country House and Hospital (photograph by Roland Schaefli).

Carey's horse Sunny was hitched outside the chapel. (When Ford paid homage to his early Western star in the credits of *3 Godfathers*, he had Cliff Lyons riding Sunny, imitating a Harry Carey gesture.) In that chapel, Ford and his wife Mary celebrated their fiftieth anniversary by being married again.

Wayne would often visit the Field Photo Farm on Memorial Day. After the clubhouse was destroyed by fire in 1969, the land and remaining buildings were donated to the Motion Picture and Television Relief Fund. The chapel itself was moved to the grounds of the retirement community at the Motion Picture Country House and Hospital in **Woodland Hills**. It was dedicated anew as the John Ford Chapel on October 19, 1969, and it's still there, at 23399 Mulholland Drive. The Motion Picture Country House and Hospital was created by Hollywood's early luminaries such as Charlie Chaplin, Mary Pickford, Douglas Fairbanks and D.W. Griffith, who realized the need to help those in the entertainment industry who fell upon hard times. For his 99th birthday, Kirk Douglas donated $15 million to enable the creation of an 80-resident Alzheimer facility.

On the *Wings of Eagles* set in Pensacola: John Wayne called Maureen O'Hara "the greatest guy he ever knew." She said about him, "There aren't enough words in the English language to describe a person like John Wayne." She is buried in Arlington National Cemetery next to her husband, U.S. Navy pilot General Charles Blair (author's collection).

Virgin Islands

Maureen O'Hara was living in **St. Croix**, the largest of the U.S. Virgin Islands, when she received a postcard from Wayne saying, "In the twilight of your years, when the hell are you going to invite me down to Saint Croix?"[14] Wayne's last visit to O'Hara on that Caribbean island was in 1978. That same year, her husband Charlie Blair had died in a plane crash. Blair and Wayne would often go flying around the islands. One time, they were making a flight to San Juan in a large airplane—the type that would require a co-pilot. When the pair arrived in San Juan, the officials were alerted. Blair just pointed to Wayne, asking, "Didn't you see *The High and the Mighty*?" According to O'Hara, the officials apologized profusely. Of course, even though Wayne had portrayed a pilot, he was not able to fly and got a huge laugh out of the incident.[15]

The house at Herman Hill 52 is known locally as Maureen O'Hara's Villa. Built in 1968, it was largely destroyed in 1989 by Hurricane Hugo. O'Hara had it rebuilt. She sold the property in 2001. The current owners installed a John Wayne Suite and renamed it the Sky Hawk Villa because of the view, and in tribute to the O'Hara-Blair family, whose emblem included a hawk and a cloverleaf.

John Wayne Airport

When Wayne returned from Boston where he had undergone open-heart surgery, he arrived at Orange County Airport. When asked by reporters in an ad hoc press conference if he now planned to slow down, he replied, "Hell, I feel great, what the hell do I wanna slow down for?" He also used the opportunity to announce *Beau John*, a script he was working on, which had a great part for a man his age. "Can't play those young lieutenants," he laughed. That "next movie" was never made.

Orange County Airport became **John Wayne Airport** when a resolution was passed on June 20, 1979, only days after his passing. The lifelike nine-foot bronze statue of Wayne was dedicated on November 4, 1982, and is located in the terminal front, 18601 Airport Way. Robert Summers was able to use Wayne's actual Western garb in the modeling.

Other public locations were named in his honor, including the **John Wayne Marina** for which he bequeathed the land on Sequim Bay Road, near Sequim, Washington. The **John Wayne Elementary School** in Brooklyn, New York, was dedicated in 1982. Inside the public school at 370 Marcy Avenue is the 38-foot mosaic mural "John Wayne and the American Frontier." A 100-plus-mile trail in Washington's **Iron Horse State Park** was referred to as the "John Wayne Pioneer Trail." (In 2018 it was renamed the Palouse to Cascades State Park Trail.) In **Maricopa**, Arizona, John Wayne Parkway (part of Arizona State Route 347) runs through the center of town.

Comes a Horseman

On October 28, 1977, just three days after Wayne finished the first commercial for Great Western Bank at Grants Pass, Oregon, he was at **Sutter's Mill** in Coloma, California, to do the next one. **Marshall Gold Discovery State Historic Park** marks the location of the discovery of gold at Sutter's Mill in 1848. "That's my kind of a gold mine," Wayne says about his sponsor. It does not diminish his credibility that the mill on Coloma Road is not the original one but a recreation.

Great Western Bank was headquartered in Chatsworth, a place with which Wayne was familiar since his earliest days in movies. A few years after Wayne's passing, the company decided to honor its advertising spokesperson: Harry Jackson was commissioned to create a monumental sculpture. The American artist was no stranger to the subject. He had already sculpted "The Marshal" (depicting Wayne as Rooster

Cogburn) for the cover of the August 8, 1969, issue of *Time*. "I had real respect for him," the artist said, "because he was like so many of the people I grew up with as a cowboy in Wyoming. There wasn't anything phony about them."[16] In the massive 21-foot bronze sculpture "The Horseman," Wayne rides tall in the saddle. It took Jackson three years to create the 5.4-ton sculpture, near Florence, Italy. The work of art was first shown in Camaiore, Italy. It was then brought to California by ship. Prior to its debut in Los Angeles, the Beverly Hills Architectural Commission requested the removal of multicolored paint and a motor in its base that would have slowly rotated the horseman. James Stewart unveiled it on July 22, 1984, at Wilshire and La Cienega Boulevards, then known as the Great Western Savings Plaza. "The Horseman" faces 8484 Wilshire Boulevard. A special tribute from President Ronald Reagan was read, in which the President cited the monument as "a reminder to us all of the Duke's dedication to this pioneer tradition."

The almost twice life-size sculpture is mounted on a 27-ton foundation of Italian marble that shows the hardships of a cowboy's life. Michael Wayne who was there with all of the Wayne children and the 23 grandchildren called it "a wonderful tribute to my father."

"The Horseman" riding on Wilshire Boulevard: Harry Jackson's massive 21-foot bronze sculpture is a reminder to, in Ronald Reagan's words, "the Duke's dedication to this pioneer tradition" (photograph by Roland Schaefli).

Wayne himself gave praise to the likeness: the painted Harry Jackson figurine "The Marshal," displayed at the John Wayne Birthplace Museum (Carol Bassett/The John Wayne Birthplace).

20

The Western Towns

From Rio Bravo to Carson City

"How far is it from here to El Dorado…?"
—Mississippi (James Caan) as he joins Cole Thornton (John Wayne)
on the road to a town besieged by outlaws.

It's just a transition scene in Rio Lobo, *a little moment to get from one place to the other. But when Cord McNally (John Wayne) crosses the main street of Old Tucson, from the sheriff's office to the saloon, he looks around and remarks, "Town's growing up." John Wayne had something to do with that. If you gonna do a Western, you gotta have a western town. And he cleaned up more than one.*

When the studios tried to achieve greater scope, they sent their casts and crews on location. Travel expenses soon created a dispute. The studios agreed to pay union workers extra if they worked out of town. The definition of "out of town," however, was grounds for more discussions. Finally, it was settled: "out of town" meant a distance of more than 30 miles from the studio zone. To save these costs, many studios invested in large tracts of undeveloped rural land. The ones that specialized in horse operas bought or leased ranches close to Hollywood. The Simi Hills, the Santa Monica Mountains and the Santa Clarita area were conveniently within the 30-mile perimeter. That started filming on the road that ran through **Placerita Canyon** in Newhall, a landscape suitable for Westerns. A man named Clarence "Fat" Jones started it all in 1928. He leased several thousand acres of land from Standard Oil (now Chevron) and constructed Western street sets.

"Cut them off at the pass!"

Soon, other western sets sprung up along the **Placerita Canyon Road**. Among them were the so-called Monogram Ranch and the Trem Carr Pictures Ranch, where Wayne shot the bread-and-butter Westerns *Sagebrush Trail, Blue Steel, Lawless Frontier* and *Man from Utah*, to name a few. Quickie producers were more inventive than the majors. They rented, borrowed or stole. Seldom did they own the location areas. They leased them. In the case of the historic Walker Ranch, they utilized a real cabin that had been established there in the 1920s. It is part of Wayne's *The Desert Trail* and *Paradise Canyon*. The **Walker Cabin** is now on the grounds of the **Placerita Canyon Nature Center**.

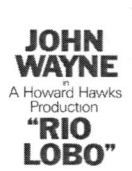

JOHN WAYNE
in
A Howard Hawks Production
"RIO LOBO"

A Cinema Center Films Presentation
Co-starring Jorge Rivero · Jennifer O'Neil · Jack Elam · Victor French · Susana Dosamantes
Screenplay by Burton Wohl and Leigh Brackett · Story by Burton Wohl · Music by Jerry Goldsmith
Directed by Howard Hawks · Technicolor® A National General Picture Release

"Town's growing up": in *Rio Lobo*, **John Wayne rides into Old Tucson for the fourth and last time (author's collection).**

239

Melody Ranch

In 1933, "Fat" Jones moved his horse rental business to North Hollywood where he became indispensable for Western moviemakers. His former site on the left-hand side of the canyon road was later absorbed into the Disney Company's **Golden Oak Ranch**.

Trem Carr, resourceful producer of the Wayne quickie Westerns, had plans for "Fat"'s western towns. Carr even moved around houses. His set designer had created a Western movie town using buildings he imported from Nevada. When Carr's lease ran out in 1936, they trucked their set a couple of miles down the road—and created the Monogram Ranch.

Enter Gene Autry. When the Singing Cowboy purchased the property in 1952, he renamed it **Melody Ranch**. By 1958, more than 80 buildings comprised the ranch. Autry even added a railroad depot. James Arness marched down that dusty Main Street every week to start *Gunsmoke*. Before starting a multi-million dollar beauty business, Max Factor was a makeup artist in a tent at Melody Ranch.

Wayne came to work on his old Monogram stamping grounds just once more, for a June 1958 NBC-TV special, *The Wide, Wide World of the Western*. Wayne, in his *Rio Bravo* costume, appeared with Gary Cooper. That show also marked the only time Gene Autry and Wayne worked together—even though they started at Republic at around the same time. For a while, they even shared the same press agent, Beverly Barnett.

Autry may have saved Wayne's life on that NBC special. The night before the telecast, Wayne lost track of the time while doing some serious partying with old cronies. John Ford, who guest-starred, chewed him out when he arrived late on the set. Then he punished Wayne by demanding endless run-throughs, not giving as much as a drop of water to the hungover star. After this ordeal, Ford gave Autry instructions to give Wayne a slug of bourbon just before the live show. Autry emptied a half bottle of Coke and filled it up with bourbon. Shortly before the show hit the air live, he handed Wayne the bottle. Wayne asked, "You want to get me sick?" and waved the offer aside. "I'm telling you, this is just what you need," Autry sternly replied. Wayne's eyes got "as round as saucers" when he tilted the bottle to his lips. "Autry, you may have saved a man's life!"[1]

On August 28, 1962, a wildfire destroyed most of the Melody Ranch sets and equipment (the TV show *Combat* made use of the remains). The museum Autry had planned would have to wait several decades before becoming "The Autry" at Griffith Park.

In 1990, Renaud and Andre Veluzat bought the highly prized acreage for a reported $975,000. To rebuild the western town, they went to the original source. They used John Wayne—literally—to reconstruct Melody Ranch. With photographs of the young B-Western star ambling along the Western street, Wayne was the blueprint for the resurrection. Since then, the HBO series *Deadwood* was produced at the new Melody Movie ranch on Oak Orchard Road, as well as the *Westworld* series and Quentin Tarantino's *Django Unchained* (2012).

Fox Ranch

The site is variously known as Fox Ranch, Century Ranch and **Malibu Creek Park** (its current name). Filming on this spread in the Santa Monica Mountains began in 1935 with MGM's *Tarzan Escapes*. Wayne worked on the Fox Ranch for the first time from October 28 to November 7, 1938, in the Mesquiteer oater *Red River Range*. Soon after that, John Ford had the entire Welsh village of his Oscar-winning *How Green Was My Valley* built on the Fox land in the Malibu hills.

Wayne's biggest movie in the Agoura Hills surrounding the Fox Ranch came in 1949, and he chose the site as the producer of *The Fighting Kentuckian*. Republic put the Lydecker brothers to work. They turned the Fox grounds and the northwest San Fernando Valley into a passable image of Alabama townships, mansions and countryside. (They even dressed the trees accordingly.) This film marked the first

John Wayne entertains unidentified young fans on his *Fighting Kentuckian* set on the Fox Ranch. Beginning with a number of Tarzan movies, the park was a remote backlot for decades (author's collection).

time that Chuck Roberson doubled Wayne. In one scene, Wayne's character was to straddle his bareback horse in one leap. There was only one problem: He couldn't make the jump. "I sure as hell can't stand flat-footed next to the horse and just hop up like I was jumping a puddle." *All* the stuntmen said it could not be done. "But we had a young stuntman on the set playing a frontier bit part. He heard us talking and said, 'Hell, I can do it!'" Then, he did. Roberson remembered that becoming Wayne's double included having "to practice that pigeon-toed walk of his for days" before he finally got it right. "From that day on," Wayne wrote in the foreword of Roberson's account of *The Fall Guy*, "he's been doubling and stunting fro me—the kind of man I could count on to get the job done. But more than that, he has been my friend."[2]

In 1974, the State of California purchased the Fox Ranch and opened it as public parkland on Las Virgenes Road. Bob Hope donated the majority of the lands. Cary Grant's house in *Mr. Blandings Builds His Dream House* is a fully functional house that still stands today in the park, serving as administrative offices for California State Parks.

Nearby Malibu Beach was a popular spot for filmmakers for years—like for Wayne's entrance in *Flame of Barbary Coast*, throwing pebbles into the waves. When he looks up to the mansion, the film cuts to Villa Leon, at 17948 Porto Marina Way, in **Pacific Palisades**, overlooking the ocean. The Castle Rock Beach may have provided the very first California location to appear in a dramatic film in 1907—Wayne's birth year.

Sedona's Western Town

In 1946, Wayne signed a new five-year contract with Republic. He continued to get ten percent of the gross against a guarantee of $150,000 per film. And he would be allowed to produce. For his first venture as a producer, he selected *Angel and the Badman* and for the first time had a hand in the constructing of a western town for use in his movie.

Call of the Canyon was the first film shot in Sedona in the silent era, based on a Zane Grey novel and using Oak Creek Canyon for a location. Then Wayne and *Angel and the Badman* put the small agricultural cattle town on the moviemaking map. With the help of Bob Bradshaw, a local film location scout and cattle supplier, the Western street was erected beneath **Coffee Pot Rock** in West Sedona. (The rock formation is visible from Highway 89A South.) Location shooting lasted from April 22 to July 6, 1946.

The first frontier town producer John Wayne ever built: the rustic settlement constructed for *Angel and the Badman* lasted a decade (courtesy of Sedona Heritage Museum, Sedona AZ).

After that, Republic took advantage of Wayne's set for later films, including the classic *Johnny Guitar*. *Big Trail* director Raoul Walsh filmed *Gun Fury* in his former protégé's town. It continued to be used for movies until it was torn down in 1959 to make way for a residential community. The neighborhood named the streets after some of the Sedona movies.

The last surviving part of the Sedona West movie town set is the telegraph office, seen early in the movie when Wayne's badman needs to send off an urgent message. The building was actually 100 years old when they trucked it from the Winona, Arizona, railroad depot to the set in Sedona. The historic building was moved again and left to deteriorate outside Sedona. The **Sedona Heritage Museum** restored and relocated it, this time to the museum site at 735 Jordan Road.

The last reminder of the *Angel and the Badman* set: the historic Telegraph Office (where Wayne dictates the telegram), now preserved at the Sedona Heritage Museum (courtesy of Sedona Heritage Museum, Sedona AZ).

Gail Russell's Quaker farmyard was situated on a ranch located at the junction of Hartwell Canyon and Loy Canyon, 12 miles outside Sedona in the **Verde Valley**. Bob Bradshaw purchased the 140-acre ranch in 1960 for $200 an acre. He became Hollywood's point man in the area after the Wayne movie. Many books and websites describe encounters with the supernatural on this spread. After decades of rumors, the Bradshaw family vacated the property. In 2003, the U.S. Forest Service acquired the parcels.

The picture-perfect **Red Rock Crossing** in the Oak Creek Canyon is a fixture in most Sedona movies. Even though it was never used as a John Wayne location, it is included in the visual impressions in the title sequence of his Utah western *The Comancheros*.

Ghost Town of Hornitos

In 1932, Wayne's early Warner Western *Haunted Gold* was in production for two weeks in **Hornitos**, a small town off the beaten path, just outside Yosemite, California. It had existed since before California's statehood and was already a famous ghost town when Warners used it as a set. The structures still stand; it's now a historical landmark.

Carson City: "I intend to die right here"

Hornitos was one of the very first western towns in a Wayne movie; Carson City in Nevada was destined to be his last. As the dying gunfighter J.B. Books, he marches into

Highway robber Gregg Palmer confronts J.B. Books: the sequence of John Wayne's last ride into a western town, filmed at the outskirts of Carson City, had to be reduced for health reasons. The chestnut quarter horse Dollor was written into the *Shootist* script (author's collection).

Sedona's Coffee Pot Rock in the background was almost as attractive to look at as Gail Russell in the foreground. The gunslinger gets convinced to become a pacifist in *Angel and the Badman* (author's collection).

his last saloon in *The Shootist*, in production from January 13 to early April 1976. The first outdoor location scheduled in Nevada was the title sequence, Books' ride down the mountain. Director Don Siegel reminded the location manager that the spot for the opening sequence was limited to 3000 feet altitude. Wayne's doctor refused to take any responsibility if they went higher. The script described the first scene like this: "The small distant figure of Books, dwarfed by the snowcapped mountains behind him, rides alone toward Camera." At first, Jim Burk was called to double Wayne. But since Wayne was fighting a number of ailments all at once, the opening sequences were reduced to just one long shot. The production had to settle for the **Jacks Valley Ranch**, at the base of the snow-capped Sierras, six miles southwest of Carson City. To get the shot at 3500 feet, Siegel had a sign reading "Altitude exactly 3000 feet" tacked on a tree.

When Wayne was driven from the hotel on the **Jack Valley Road** to that first set, the driver stopped short of the location because he could not get the car over the uneven terrain. Wayne ordered him to do so: "Between you and me, damnit, I've got a bad pump and this car is for my convenience."[3] A nurse was assigned to him 24 hours a day to give oxygen assistance whenever needed.

"Why don't you just say it flat-out?"

Production manager Bob Russ had to make sure that the opening shot of the snow-capped mountains would seamlessly cut to the scenes on the Warner backlot. To make sure of that, he had to find a Carson City house with the mountains in the background. He picked a great period house for Lauren Bacall's guest house, the **Krebs-Peterson house** at 1900 South Carson Street. Russ just rang the doorbell and asked if the residents would let John Wayne make a movie at their house. Visitors learn about the historic houses in that district on a "Talking Houses" self-guided tour. The filmmakers used only the exterior of the building. Not only did they create the whole interior on the Burbank lot but part of the outside porch as well, so the movie cuts seamlessly from the real location to the studio set.

Siegel filmed the dialogue scene between Wayne and Ron Howard in the barn in back of the Krebs-Peterson house. The young actor, who would become one of Hollywood's most successful producer-directors, picked something up from working with Wayne. Even at this point in his career, Wayne would shape a John Wayne performance: the way he delivered his lines, the pauses, those little characteristic John Wayne hitches. Howard used to wonder where those moments came from. He saw the elder man rebalancing and refining the way he was going to deliver a line. "He'd do it once and he'd say, 'Let me try it again,' and he'd do it again and he'd actually put that hitch into it—and suddenly the line just had more power and more impact."[4] The sequence in which the gunfighter teaches the young man how to handle a gun was reportedly filmed in the small town of **Genoa**, ten miles away.

"I won't be wronged, I won't be insulted"

For the pensive scene of Wayne's buggy ride with Bacall, the location scouts found a beautiful spot on Willow Beach

Lauren Bacall's boarding house from *The Shootist* is the period house in Carson City, the Krebs-Peterson house (photograph by Roland Schaefli).

"I wish to hell you'd ride with me": Books invited Mrs. Rogers to a buggy ride along the sandy beaches of Washoe Lake (photograph by Roland Schaefli).

in **Washoe Lake State Park**, just a few miles from Carson City, ideally situated next to East Lake Boulevard.

On the *Shootist* location, Wayne occupied a suite at the **Ormsby House**, 600 South Carson Street. When he had dinner with Pat Stacy the first evening of his stay, he was in his robe and pajamas and had already shed his hairpiece for the night. The busboy who removed the dishes asked them excitedly if they knew that John Wayne was supposed to be in town. "I'd like to meet him himself," Wayne responded without missing a beat.[5]

Wayne again had his restaurateur friend from Seattle fly in a load of iced fresh clams, which he served to Siegel, with a chaser of golden tequila.

"I found most men aren't willing"

With the script requirements of a western town at the turn of the century, the real Carson City wouldn't do. But Siegel had reservations about building the Carson City street on the Warner backlot because he "knew it as well as the palm of his hand," having spent 14 years at Warners and still having "the scars on my back to prove it." Bob Russ convinced Siegel by pointing out that building the Carson City street in Burbank instead of dressing the street of a real town would cost less in the long run. They wouldn't have to pay for the usual costs of locations, transportation, living expenses for cast, crew and animals. "We also will have to build certain structures, no matter where we go. Secondly, if you stick to your guns, this ugly, unkempt, nothing street can be transformed into a street much better than anything we could possibly find."[6]

Since the starting date for principal photography wasn't too far off, they had to settle for the old Western street. Several blocks of the turn-of-the century city were recreated on

Hugh O'Brian already bought the farm, now Charles G. Martin takes aim on Warner Stage 25—known today as "The Big Bang Theory Stage." Wayne had always wanted to use this pair of Colt revolvers, given to him by the Great Western Arms Company years before. To give them a bit of a used appearance for *The Shootist*, he dipped the ivory stocks in tea (author's collection).

the lot. A couple of matte shots took care of the problem that Burbank didn't have Nevada's snow-capped mountains. As a matter of fact, Wayne's shooting script reads, "in the distance are the same snowcapped mountains"; he added the handwritten notation MATTE SHOT." And so the Western street which "played" a Virginia City street until *Bonanza* was canceled made the incredible transformation into Carson City's main street—and on a budget just under $300,000.

"The remarkable thing," said Siegel, "was that no audience could possibly tell when we were in Carson City or at the studio." They worked first on the make-believe street, then on the stages. The interior of Bacall's boarding house was created on Stage 14, as well as the interior of Doc Hostettler's (James Stewart) residence. As Stewart pointed out, set decorator Art Parker knew what he was doing: "He knows the period and the story."[7]

For the scene, which reunited silver screen giants Duke Wayne and Jimmy Stewart, the latter as Doc Hostettler waited for his cue outside the door. Siegel gave him the cue—and nothing happened. Again, louder. No movement outside the door. Wayne leaned down to the director's ear and whispered, "He's slightly deaf."[8]

After the final showdown in *The Shootist*, Gillom covers Books with his jacket. Ron Howard remembered that this might be John Wayne's last screen moment but "nobody talked about it" (author's collection).

"Gimme the best in the house"

Art director Robert Boyle designed and built the sets, and received a well-earned Academy Award nomination. With the Metropolitan Saloon, Boyle set the stage for Wayne's last showdown at a cost of $150,000. The set on Stage 25 exactly matched what was shot before in Carson City.

During the work in Burbank, Wayne stayed with Stacy at the **Oakwood Garden apartments**, just a few minutes' drive from the studio at 3700 Barham Boulevard. When *The Shootist* made its Philadelphia premiere, Wayne's entourage settled into suites on the twenty-first floor of the city's midtown **Regal Hotel**.

A lot has been said and written about the difficult relationship between Wayne and his last director, Don Siegel. (Siegel told Clint Eastwood that Wayne "had turned blue" when Siegel asked him to shoot a man in the back.) Siegel devotes a large part of his memoir to his *Shootist* experiences, starting out with the very first script conference, held at Wayne's Newport home. Siegel had been a great editor before he became a great director. He recalled exactly how much footage he used from earlier Wayne pictures, to edit the introduction of J.B. Books: "61 feet from *Red River*, 9 feet from *Hondo*, 13 feet from *Rio Bravo* and two

13-foot sequences from *El Dorado*." At the time of the filming, Wayne did not know how the pre-title montage would look. The script just said, "Through a series of clips from his film career we watch the evolution of John Wayne, the Western star, into the character of J.B. Books … [A]s the clips run in chronological sequence, down the decades, the two men will merge, become one: JOHN BERNARD BOOKS." Clips from some movies could not be included, as the producers asked $5000 and up for the use of only a few seconds of film.

Old Tucson

Carson City was destined to become Wayne's last western town. Nevertheless, no other movie town can match the significance of **Old Tucson.** At a cost of $250,000, the city made of adobe in Pima County's Tucson Mountain Park was put together in 1939 by Wayne's former employer, Columbia chief Harry Cohn. With *Arizona* (starring a very young William Holden), Columbia started a western movie tradition. Wayne would shoot four Westerns at Old Tucson Movie Studio. By 1958, the brick houses had taken on the appearance of a deserted ghost town, like in *Backlash* and *The Guns of Fort Petticoat*. In that year, Howard Hawks

decided to add more structures to what is now the upper part of Old Tucson. Jules Furthman and Leigh Brackett's final screenplay of *Rio Bravo*, dated February 26, 1958, outlined the setting as "a Texas border town with mixed Mexican and American population." The description of the main street read, "On one side is the jail, a strongly built adobe structure with barred windows. Across the street from it is the Saloon…." Hawks had the new main street constructed in four blocks, therefore forever enlarging the pre-existing pueblo structures.

"I said I'd arrest you"

Hawks built the jail as suggested in the script, right at the end of the main street, thus blocking it, making it look like a dead end, which adds dramatically to the claustrophobic feeling of the town that's "bottled up." The shell of the jailhouse was removed after the filming. Director John Carpenter (who likes to borrow from Hawks and calls Hawks his greatest influence) pointed out that all the trappings of the jail and the town were mapped out. "Here's headquarters, here's the enemy street, everything geographically is very simple and direct. It's a very small acreage that these people have to operate in."[9]

"That's what I got"

Ricky Nelson turned 18 during filming. Wayne and Dean Martin presented him with a 300-pound sack of steer manure. The contents were emptied to the ground in a heap. Then they dumped Colorado (Nelson) into his gift.

John T. Chance and "Feathers" take a coffee break: with Angie Dickinson on the Old Tucson set of *Rio Bravo* (author's collection).

A bent over Ricky Nelson receives a strange birthday gift from Dean Martin and John Wayne. Unidentified extras populate the border town of *Rio Bravo* (Old Tucson Studio).

Location filming takes its own sweet time. With unidentified crewmembers during the sequence when "Feathers" throws the flowerpot in *Rio Bravo*. Note that Angie Dickinson is practicing her skills as a card shark (author's collection).

"My Rifle, My Pony and Me"

Rio Bravo was in production in Old Tucson from May 4 to May 28, 1958, followed by interiors at Burbank. As they neared the end of the shooting schedule, one thing remained to be shot in the jail interior: the now-famous song sequence. The only practical way to do a song when the camera cuts to the different players is pre-recording the music and having the actors sing onto the playback. In this case, it took two days to shoot. But it happened that the musicians union had gone on strike, and they didn't have a playback yet because the composer, Dimitri Tiomkin, hadn't done it and could not be persuaded to provide one while on strike. All they got were the lead sheets containing words and music. So Hawks' right-hand man, Paul Helmick, called Ricky Nelson at home and told him of the dilemma. The next morning, when the young pop singer came to work in the jail set, without exchanging one word with Helmick, he handed him a tape. "The playback operator played it, and nobody ever asked where the tape came from."[10] Burt Kennedy was present when they shot that scene. He told Wayne, "You know that's the theme from *Red River*?" Tiomkin wrote the score for both films and "My Rifle, My Pony and Me" was indeed a variation. But Wayne was "tone-deaf and said, 'Like hell it is.'"[11]

"Don't say it's a fine morning or I'll shoot ya!"

Right after Hawks left Pima County, entrepreneur Robert Shelton leased the aging facility. He re-opened Old Tucson as a theme park. But the town needed a boost.

Stuntman Neil Summers recalled that since it wasn't a state park then and not under anybody's jurisdiction, the kids used to party out there. The decrepit buildings would only be renovated when a movie company came in. In 1962, Shelton got his boost when Wayne came to town. Shelton saw him standing behind the Mexican Plaza, the location of the old mission. When he turned around to Shelton, "he looked like the Eiffel Tower standing there." Wayne told him that he had another Western planned and wanted to put a second floor on one of the buildings, maybe build one at another place, and the town would be called McLintock. "I wanna paint your town," he told Shelton and asked, "And what are you gonna do for me?" Shelton answered, "Well, I've got an old pocketknife and a used Cadillac and I'd be happy to give you both if you'd just consider a trade." That's how they started working together. When Wayne shook his hand, Shelton "almost went into cardiac arrest."[12]

The film under discussion, *McLintock!*, was in production from October 24, 1962, to January 1963. Batjac spent $74,000 to build 13 new structures and change *Rio Bravo*'s main street. Wayne's investment promoted Old Tucson and helped attract other productions. "He was a very important part of what we did here," said Shelton.[13] That was when Old Tucson really started to pick up as a big location. Yet a

Enough time for publicity stills between scenes on the *Rio Bravo* set: Angie Dickinson is not wearing her movie costume (author's collection).

John Wayne and Maureen O'Hara prepare for the sequence in which *McLintock* chases his estranged wife around town, an ending similar to the one in *The Quiet Man* (Old Tucson Studio).

location is not just made up of false façades. It's got to have atmosphere. For actor Edward Faulkner, *McLintock!* was his first time on a Wayne set. He remembered, "I've never been on a set like that before. His sets, the ambiance, the whole atmosphere was just marvelous."[14]

"You caused a lot of trouble this morning!"

The famous mudfight was filmed over a period of three days at a cost of $50,000 at an abandoned copper mine in the hills. According to several sources, this location was 33 miles south of Tucson, off the **Pima Mine Road**. When the stuntmen demanded hazardous duty pay before tackling the slide into the mudhole (the material was bentonite that has the consistency of chocolate syrup), producer Wayne drew himself up to his full height. "Well, then, I guess that means I'll have to do it, you white-livered chicken-shits." He told Maureen O'Hara that sliding into the mud was "about as dangerous as diving into a swimming pool," and added, "Maureen and I will prove it, won't we, Maureen?!"[15] As we can see in the finished film, the two of them slid down the hill with gusto.

But the stunt *was* potentially dangerous for O'Hara. She had undergone surgery to remove ovarian cysts only weeks before they started shooting the knockabout comedy. When Wayne found out afterward, he hollered, "Good God. Why didn't you tell me? We could have killed you!"[16]

Many of Wayne's regular stuntmen remembered the mudslide scene fondly. Tom "Bull" Hennesy is easy to spot: He was even called "Bull" in *The Alamo* where he loses the "feather fight" against Crockett. He is on the receiving end of Wayne's punch again as the bartender in *The War Wagon*; Wayne breaks a chair over his head in *The Comancheros*; and in *Big Jake*, Wayne breaks a billiard cue over his head. So when it was time to slide down into the mud in *McLintock!*, O'Hara was supposed to stick Bull's butt with her hairpin. So much was going on in that fight scene, that Hennesy didn't feel the stick. He remembered vividly what happened next: "So Duke yells, 'Cut! Cut!' And he wasn't directing the thing, it was Andy McLaglen, but when Duke's on a picture, why, he's directing it." Wayne questioned O'Hara: "Goddammit, Maureen what happened?" She said, "Well, he didn't jump, he didn't jump." Wayne asked Hennesy, "What the hell is the matter, Tom?" To which Hennesy replied, "Well, I didn't feel it, Duke." So Wayne told O'Hara, "We're gonna do it again and this time I want you to shove that goddamned thing up his ass!" O'Hara hesitated a minute and then said, "No, no. I'm not going to do that, Duke. Not to no Hennesy, I don't!"[17]

Wayne slightly damaged his own pride when he jumped off a second-story balcony (the Alamo Hotel from *Rio Bravo*) onto a hay wagon and landed on the edge of the wagon. "Serves him right!" gloated O'Hara. "Shoulda kept his backside tucked in."[18]

"Drago, I am sleeping in the den!"

According to Neil Summers, the cast members were usually housed in motels along the **Miracle Mile** in Tucson.

The San Rafael Ranch outside Nogales was McLintock's home address. Its French Colonial Revival style is unusual for a rural ranch in Arizona (The Old Pueblo/ Wikimedia Commons).

Before Tucson offered high-rise hotels and gated communities, the stars filming in Old Tucson found a quiet retreat named **Lodge on the Desert** at 306 North Alvernon Way. It boasts that Wayne was one of the high-profile guests who sought out this secluded oasis, followed by many other film industry pros. Evidence of the Lodge's past has been preserved in its original décor.

The title character's brick ranch house was the lavish mansion of cattle baron Colonel William Greene, situated in **San Rafael**, 36 miles east of Nogales. They were allowed to use the outside of the ranch with its white verandas on three sides. The ranch house on 2036 Duquesne Road in Patagonia is now the **San Rafael Ranch**, preserved in the San Rafael State Natural Area that runs along the Mexican border. After *McLintock!*, it was home to other cattle barons: Karl Malden in *Wild Rovers* and Steve McQueen's employer in *Tom Horn*.

In the podcast series *Word on Western*, Stefanie Powers (who played Wayne's daughter in *McLintock!*) revealed that John Ford took over direction for a few days when director Andrew McLaglen got the flu. The whole company awaited "Pappy"'s arrival on a plateau. The cab created a big dust cloud as it came up the rise to the location. Ford got out, "in a terrible stained safari jacket with this horrible hat and the patch," after Wayne had opened the door for him. Ford pushed him aside, walked over to Bill Clothier's camera and said, "Let's get to work."[19]

"I'm your father and I sure love you"

Not far from the San Rafael Ranch, east of Nogales, McLintock goes pheasant hunting on the **Ralph Wingfield Ranch**. Wayne knew Wingfield ever since *Red River* (see Chapter 13). It was here that Stefanie Powers attended a "John Wayne acting lesson." Wayne had taken a liking to her because of her tomboy qualities. Just as she was getting into position to ride into the scene, she saw "himself coming over." The young actress thought, "Oh my God, this is the moment he's going to impart some wonderful wisdom to me about acting." And he came up to her and took a long look at her and he said, "Just remember, kid, it's all in the eyes."[20]

During that scene, Powers fell with the horse and was knocked out. All she realized when she came to was, "John Wayne was over me," with tears welling up in his eyes. And she asked, "Did you get the fall?"[21]

For the scene in which McLintock surveys his cattle, they went to a place called **Curtis** where they built the corrals, right beside the Butterfield Stage route to Tombstone near St. David, about 16 miles north of Tombstone. Hal Needham played the bit part of his ranch hand. The corral is abandoned today and lost to history.

Variety reported on December 7, 1962, that the McLintock company had returned to Hollywood and would begin three weeks of shooting at Paramount. After it wrapped on January 11, Wayne gave Old Tucson a three-year break—and Howard Hawks changed the name of the town once again.

"Next time you shoot somebody…"

Wayne took the daily trip on Kinney Road from Tucson through Gates Pass to get to Old Tucson a third time, for Hawks' *El Dorado*, from October 8 to November 22, 1965. Screenwriter Leigh Brackett wouldn't even go to the trouble of describing the town. There was no layout in the script at all. She would describe this exterior just as "STREET." As a matter of fact, Hawks was even able to reuse *Rio Bravo* footage. He had filmed Ricky Nelson throwing himself in front of the horses of galloping gunslingers. He had to lose the sequence because he felt the good guys had shot a fair amount of bad guys at that point, "too much of a good thing." He cut it out but kept the idea. When he repeated the sequence with James Caan, they were able to splice some *Rio Bravo* stuntwork in because "it was the same street."[22]

Hawks lamented that filmmaking was becoming

JOHN WAYNE **EL DORADO** ROBERT MITCHUM

"You fall off your horse?" Cole Thornton, suddenly paralyzed, rolls into Sonoita Creek in *El Dorado* (author's collection).

increasingly costly. "The shooting schedule of *El Dorado* was at least twice as long as on *Rio Bravo*, which was made in the same location, practically the same cast." He blamed the unions for the fact that it cost them three times as much to make *El Dorado*: "When they had a little two-sided shack put up, it cost $14,000 to build. In the 1920s they'd have put it up for $250."[23]

The 84 buildings then making up Old Tucson underwent only slight alteration at the hands of Hawks' construction crew. They erected the sheriff's office in the same place as the *Rio Bravo* jailhouse, again giving the main street a dead-end look.

Scouting the different outdoor locations allowed Hawks to view the changes occurring over the two decades since *Red River*. Back then, equipment had to be transported by pack mule because the terrain was so hazardous. In 1967, he had to make sure none of his images contained paved roads.

The **Avra Valley** in Pima County was chosen for the long dolly shots of Cole Thornton (Wayne) and Mississippi (James Caan) philosophizing over an Edgar Allan Poe poem. More outdoor scenes followed near the **Sonoita Creek** on the Oak Bar Ranch, located between Nogales and Patagonia, at the present Patagonia Lake State Park. (Cole Thornton, suddenly paralyzed, rolls into the creek.) Other locales included the **Amado Ranch** outside Amado, south of Tucson, where Cole brings in the body of the young man he accidentally shot. Johnny Crawford (the kid from the TV series *The Rifleman*) wore Chuck Roberson's chaps in that scene because they ran out at Western Costume, on account of so many TV Westerns made at that time.

Johnny Crawford bites the dust while Howard Hawks (with viewfinder) and John Wayne still try to make up their minds which angle is best for this dramatic scene that sets up the plot of *El Dorado* (author's collection).

Oldtimers claim that during the shooting in the area, Wayne graced the bar of the **Cow Palace** at 28802 South Nogales Highway.

"Call it professional courtesy"

Peter Bogdanovich observed Wayne on the *El Dorado* set: "I saw Duke playing around with his six-shooter off-camera, or with that repeating rifle he often carried in pictures—as Wyatt Earp himself had told Ford he had done in life—with all the enthusiasm of a kid with a new toy." According to Bogdanovich, Wayne was always ready, always prepared. Wayne did not go to his trailer between shots—as co-stars Robert Mitchum and James Caan did, as most stars do. "Wayne clearly enjoyed watching the process take place, loved the crew, the atmosphere. For Duke Wayne, this was home."[24]

"You're too good to give a chance to"

Hawks had noticed that Frederic Remington's nocturnal paintings always had a great slash of light across

Same jail, same place and almost the same plot: When James Caan and John Wayne arrive in *El Dorado*, Arthur Hunnicutt greets them on the porch of the Sheriff's office (author's collection).

the street coming out of the saloon door. So he asked Harold Rosson to come out of retirement to light Old Tucson at night. (*El Dorado* would be the veteran cinematographer's last work.) Rosson used yellow light and reminded Hawks, "Don't walk your people through it—they'll look like they had yellow jaundice."[25] The perfectionist took hours to light the street. "Am I glad he's not working for my company," Wayne laughed.[26]

Work began in the evenings and lasted until dawn some nights. They worked the graveyard shift for nearly two months. "Some nights until they ran out of dark," Mitchum quipped.[27] During the night, some actors would slip off under a wagon and try to catch a nap. When they needed Mitchum, they could usually find him by the glow of his Gauloise.

One night, when the crew had just finished midnight supper, Rosson was preparing a long shot requiring several lighting units. Without warning, the lighted area was suddenly full of flying bugs. The locusts or grasshoppers were attracted to the large arcs known as brutes. Hawks finally gave up and asked associate producer Paul Helmick to hire some local crop dusters. But the next night, the critters disappeared just fast as they had come.[28]

"Like he said, real easy"

During the 36 days on location, headquarters were set up in Tucson. The 200 crew members trekked ten miles to the location each day. Hawks and Wayne stayed downtown at the **Ramada Inn** (spring training headquarters for the Cleveland Indians), while Mitchum leased the home of former Senator William Nolan. The hotel bar was usually kept

open by special dispensation. When a poker game in Ed Asner's room got out of hand, Asner told the players to keep it down because Hawks was sleeping in the next room. All of a sudden, they heard gunshots from the outside. There was Hawks in his long johns firing away with a six-shooter, shouting, "Goddamn it! If I see anybody not in their bed in five minutes, they're on the goddamn plane out of here!"[29]

Robert Donner (who played the sleazy desperado Milt) said that Hawks "thought nothing of closing down the show and taking everybody down across the border into Mexico to eat at some restaurant he liked." One night, the gang was excited because they thought this must be some incredible restaurant, the way Hawks talked it up. "And we get to this gas station outside Nogales—a café run by the people who run the gas station. But, dammit, the food was just as great as he said it was!"[30]

While *McLintock!* was in production, the outstanding contemporary Western artist Olaf Wieghorst was introduced to Andrew McLaglen in the Mountain Oyster Club at the **Santa Rita Hotel** in Tucson. (Its address, El Dorado Plaza, proved to be prophetic.) The director invited the artist to the set the next day. John Wayne, already familiar with Wieghorst's paintings, asked him to play the small part of the cavalry sergeant. Wayne considered his paintings as background for some of the scenes. But since *McLintock!* was a comedy, Wayne believed it would be best to wait and use them in a serious western. The time came when Hawks decided to

"**Learn how to use a gun**": in the cactus-studded Avra Valley, Cole Thornton is throwing Mississippi (James Caan) a handgun for his first shooting lesson in *El Dorado* (author's collection). Wayne is riding Howard Hawks' appaloosa stallion "Cochise" even though he felt it was too short for him. (author's collection).

Old Tucson, Arizona, is turned into Blackthorne, Texas. John Wayne (middle) stands ready while the *Rio Lobo* crew gets busy (Old Tucson Studio).

open *El Dorado* with a montage of 12 Wieghorst paintings, some of which he created for the film. And the artist played the bit part of the Swedish gunsmith. The star and director called Wieghorst "Swede."

Wayne had collected some fine pieces of Western art. In 1968, he wrote in the foreword of the book *The Cowboy in Art*, "The most authentic and dependable evidence of what the cowboys really were has come from the artists who pictured them in their true environment…. These paintings have come to be a part of the American tradition."[31]

The process of using paintings in a title sequence was repeated in *Chisum* where the paintings of famed western artist Russ Vickers told the backstory of John Chisum.

"You were pretty good in there, like old times"

During the Old Tucson shoot, Wayne had John Wayne Drive named after him through official delegation. With TV westerns still in full swing, Robert Shelton was able to add a complete soundstage to Old Tucson soon after *El Dorado* left town. Up until then, interiors were usually shot on Hollywood stages. The scene of Mitchum taking a bath should have taken place outside the jail. Hawks feared the scene would only be funny if shot outdoors. But when they ran out of time at the location, they rewrote it as an indoor scene. Hawks spent a full nine weeks on the Paramount stages. Interiors were completed by mid–February 1966.

"Don't you know any other songs?"

Hawks had not intended to shoot the next one, *Rio Lobo*, in Old Tucson. For this new Western, Durango made perfect sense, as they had already decided on Cuernavaca for the train robbery scene (see Chapter 10). But producer-director Michael Winner was filming the Burt Lancaster Western *Lawman* around the same time. In an *LA Times* interview (June 28, 1970), Winner claimed that he had fought Hawks over the use of Western sets in Durango. That's why Hawks went back to Old Tucson after all, filming his very last movie between March 16 and mid–June 1970. For the sequence where Wayne gets himself captured and leads the "rebs" into the Union camp, they returned to the two-mile stretch at the Patagonia Creek. The old Fremont Cottonwood trees—a premier birdwatching destination— matched the script requirements without a doubt.

For the final showdown, they put the cantina in about the same place where they exploded the warehouse in *Rio Bravo*. Hawks even had a fake creek dug. Propellers gave the impression of a flow.

"This fight isn't over yet": Assisted by Jack Elam, John Wayne uses the Cantina for cover. This iconic Old Tucson structure was lost to the 1995 fire (author's collection).

After all the *Rio This* and *Rio That*, Wayne and Hawks sometimes got confused. When the two of them tried to tell an Old Tucson anecdote to a TV interviewer, they argued if it happened on the set of *Rio Lobo* or *El Dorado*—and came to the conclusion that it didn't matter at all.

"You got your town back"

On April 24, 1995, at about 6:30 p.m. Tucson time, flames ravaged the old movie set, destroying such landmarks as the Rio Lobo Cantina and the Rio Bravo Hotel. The mission in Mexican Plaza—in *El Dorado*, the bandits hid in the church-tower—was a great loss. Forty percent of the park was gone. All the costumes and memorabilia went up in

A locomotive legend, the Reno, built in 1872. It starred in Cecil B. DeMille's *Union Pacific*. After MGM had bought it, the Reno saw service in Wayne's films *How the West Was Won* and *The Horse Soldiers*. She didn't let the devastating Old Tucson fire stop her (photograph by Roland Schaefli).

smoke. A major loss to the movie industry and Western fans alike.

Old Tucson eventually recovered and rebuilt. Even the old Reno locomotive that had melted in the fire has since been restored. Yet only a few of the buildings from Wayne pictures survived: the shack from which John T. Chance and his troupe fight the opposition (actually the same shack in which the *Rio Lobo* baddies fight Cord McNally); the little wooden bridge where Dude stands watch; the stable where they tie him up. Still there is "Swede"'s shop in which Thornton buys a shotgun for Mississippi. If it wasn't for these precious few buildings, Old Tucson would have to be included in the next chapter, a sad one: about the lost locations.

21

The Lost Locations

Winds of the Wasteland

"There's a fortress all in ruins…"
—"Ballad of the Alamo" (Marty Robbins)

Old Tucson went up in flames but was eventually resurrected. Other Wayne locations weren't so lucky. You can still find the traces. But the following filming sites are lost forever to the movie fan. Maybe Wil Anderson's words might offer some solace: "It's not how you're buried … it's how they remember you."

While some of the former movie ranches in the greater Los Angeles area survived as regional parks, most were sold and subdivided. This was the case with the outdoor ranch Warner Brothers owned in Calabasas, the so-called **Warner Ranch**. Wayne made the last of his Warners B-Westerns there in 1933, *The Man from Monterey*, in a place formally known as **La Providencia**. Soon after, Warners used the spread to develop the western towns for high-profile Errol Flynn Westerns like *Dodge City* and *San Antonio*. In 1963, near the end of the life of the ranch as a movie setting, the Los Angeles County Fire Department practiced firefighting by torching the remaining sets. Houses and a lake now sit on the former filming site on the Calabasas Road.

Gone to Hell Town

In the case of the **Paramount Ranch**, the Fire Department tried to save it. The famous western town on Cornell Road in Malibu burned down in one of the 2018 wildfires. Wayne worked on the premises just once, in his first Paramount Western *Born to the West* (re-released as *Hell Town*), in production from August 20 to September 4, 1937. The Rancho Paramount, as it was known then, had become the property of Paramount Pictures in 1927. *Nevada*, starring a young Gary Cooper, was one of the very first productions shot there. The property went through the hands of several individuals. When RKO sold its Encino Ranch in 1954, the owner of the Paramount lot purchased some of the RKO buildings and actually moved them to the Agoura hills. In 1980, the National Park Service purchased the land and surrounding acreage (436 acres); the scenic western town was

The chapel John Wayne built: Since Alamo Village is left to nature, it is lost for the fans (photograph by Roland Schaefli).

The Paramount Ranch, before the Woolsey Fire tore through the western town in the Santa Monica Mountains (photograph by Roland Schaefli).

then rebuilt and opened to the public. At the time the blaze leveled the Paramount Ranch, the buildings were in use for the hit HBO series *Westworld*. After so many years, the setting of *Born to the West* has vanished. Maybe Wayne's character in that early movie had a misgiving: when asked where he figured Wyoming was at, he answered, "Right over yonder beyond that hill ... unless somebody's moved it!"

"Wherever they go, they'll be on my land"

"We brought nothing into this world and it's certain we can carry nothing out." Wayne spoke those words whenever his cattle baron Tom Dunson was planting a man in the ground. They ring true for the *Red River* location as well: Gone is the railroad town that was the scene of one of the best-remembered screen fights in movie history, Wayne vs. Montgomery Clift.

Even though Howard Hawks relied heavily on Wayne's knowledge of the genre, the director always knew that picking the right locations was almost as important as casting the right people. Hawks even liked to name the characters after the locales. He christened them Colorado, Mississippi, Dallas or just plain Swede and Frenchie. Hawks had sent out scouts in search of filming sites resembling Texas badlands, rivers and Kansas plains. They traveled 15,000 miles by plane, over Texas, Oklahoma and New Mexico, and Sonora and Chihuahua in Mexico, before he settled for **Elgin**, near the border, population seven. That little speck 40 miles east of Nogales became the anchor town for the company. Hawks had the same need as the Montgomery Clift character: At the end of the trail, he needed a railroad to be there. Elgin had a railroad depot. The construction of an 88-mile railroad line had begun in 1882, the New Mexico and Arizona Railroad.

The tiny village rested on the edge of an expansive plain 5,000 feet high. Hawks had the town of Abilene built by adding more buildings at a cost of $150,000. Four hundred people lived in 75 portable tent-cabins wired for electricity and running water. The carpenters even built a crap table in one of the tents and a crude bar in another. Wayne camped out some nights in the tent city.

"Take 'Em to Missouri, Matt"

At first, Wayne was reluctant to play a man older than his actual years (Gary Cooper had been Hawks' first choice). Hawks said, "Duke, you're going to be one pretty soon, why don't you get some practice?" At his office at Republic, Wayne met the young actor who was selected to play his adopted son, Montgomery Clift, fresh from Broadway. Wayne was not impressed. "He's a little queer, don't you think?" he asked Mary St. John after Clift left.[1]

The sensitive stage actor (Hawks called him an "actor's lab guy"[2]) was cast against type. The first days of filming, Clift, practicing his quick draw, burned his thigh with a blank cartridge. Initially, he and Wayne did not get along. Clift stayed pretty much by himself, just occasionally joining the nightly poker games organized by Hawks and Wayne. "They laughed and drank and told dirty jokes and slapped each other on the back," Clift reported later. "They tried to draw me into their circle but I couldn't go along with them. The machismo thing repelled me...." Wayne on the other hand made no secret about his feelings when he told a *Life* reporter, "Clift is an arrogant little bastard."[3]

When they did their first scene together, Clift tried to act very broad, so Hawks took him aside and told him flat-out, he would not get anywhere with trying to trump Wayne. Clift took the advice and underplayed his scenes. After that scene was in the can, Wayne told Hawks, "The kid is all right."

Clift often talked about his big scene coming up: taking

the herd away from Dunson. Hawks told him, "I wouldn't be too sure of this being your scene." When they did the scene, Wayne didn't even look at him until he turned and said, "I'm gonna kill you. I don't know when but I'm gonna kill you." Then the turned and again did not look at Clift, leaving him standing there. "He didn't know what to do," Hawks remembered. The director said into the scene, "Better you get out of there," so Clift turned away from Wayne and just walked off. When Clift complained, "My good scene certainly went to the devil, didn't it?" Hawks replied, "Any time you think you're gonna make Wayne look bad, you've got another thing coming."[4]

In Elgin, Hawks immortalized one of the best-remembered scenes in any Wayne movie: Tom Dunson calmly walking towards his stepson, parting the herd by riding through it. Hawks called getting the shot "pure luck." Wayne had told him that the horse would eventually stop at a certain point riding into a herd of cattle and Hawks asked him to get off and walk on.[5] "You don't have to tell Wayne anything about walking through cattle, Wayne knew. He took his horse right to the cattle, and then he walked through 'em. They just accidentally got in his way, and he just shoved 'em and kept on walking."[6]

The classic fight scene at the Elgin railroad depot took four days to shoot. Hawks claimed later, "My arm's still sore from trying to show Montgomery Clift how to throw a punch."[7] In 1955, the Rodgers & Hammerstein musical *Oklahoma!* used the same set-up at the depot. The line from Fairbank-Campstone-Eglin-Sonoita-Patagonia was discontinued in 1962. If you go looking for this filming site today, you will only find traces. Follow Upper Elgin Road until you cross where the tracks were originally laid. A well and a pump house, visible in the climactic fistfight, exist today on private property.

"You earned it"

When Hawks was looking for a location, he always kept in mind: If you shoot from Tucson to the north, you get a cloudless sky; if you shoot due south, you'll see mountains and always clouds. Near the Elgin area, south of Highway 82 and just east of the Mustang Mountains, he settled for **Rain Valley** for the other outdoor scenes, and rented part of the valley. The first sequence, as Dunson leaves the wagon train, used the eastern side of the Mustang Mountains as a background, just south of Arizona State Highway 82. He got most of the location work done within a 20-mile radius. In later interviews, Hawks would often talk about one particular shot: In the burial scene, a cloud just passed over when he needed it, casting a shadow on the flat-topped hill. For once, he liked to claim, he had that "Ford luck" with the weather.

The area where they moved the cattle herd back and forth boasted a 15-mile range. The **Whetstone Mountains** and **Apache Pass** providing the background. It took eight

On the *Red River* location in Rain Valley with Coleen Gray: Fox lent the contract actress to Hawks only when Darryl F. Zanuck personally gave his permission (author's collection).

"There'd be quite a fight, don't you think so?" Howard Hawks shot a lot of footage of the fight between John Wayne and Montgomery Clift. This angle including Joanne Dru wasn't seen in the finished *Red River* (author's collection).

cattle trucks five days to transport all the steers to the location. It cost an additional $20,000 to supply them with hay.

Red River was budgeted at $2,000,000, a significant sum for an independent production in 1946. The actual cost ran $800,000 higher than that, due to having to transport the cattle all around Arizona. "They'd forgotten to put that in the budget," said Hawks.[8] The cattle were rented at $10 a head— whether they worked or not. He had actually figured to buy the cows and sell them at a profit. Because it was difficult to get that many longhorns, he put the longhorn steers up front and filled the gaps with Mexican cattle. Dimitri Tiomkin, who composed the rousing score, wrote in his autobiography, "[H]undreds of cows died from hoof-and-mouth disease contracted from some Mexican cattle, and the ranchers from whom the herds had been rented had to be reimbursed."[9]

Hawks wanted to hire real cowboys on the spot but Wayne opted for trained stuntmen (they finally got a mixed bunch). The Teamsters, representing the Arizona cowhands, threatened injunctions against the release. They claimed they were owed $20,000 for their services when Hawks' Monterey Production ran out of money. Hawks himself felt they "had earned it," as he liked to put it. "When you have to shift 3,000 head of cattle every time you shoot a new scene, that's hard work."[10]

"Pretty unhealthy job"

They didn't name it Rain Valley for nothing. The crew often ate from a wet dish. However, Wayne told Hawks to go on filming in the rain and said he did not mind acting in the rain. Hawks was making his first Western and he listened

to Wayne's advice. The star told him that on a Western, you worked with the weather and you did not complain about it. The screenplay was rewritten accordingly. Nevertheless, Wayne caught a cold and Joanne Dru got influenza. Hawks was bitten by a centipede and had to be hospitalized.

"Who'll stop me?"

It proved difficult to find an Arizona river that ran enough water for the pivotal scene of the river crossing. Some sources give Sonoita Creek, east of Patagonia, as the location, but people in Tombstone swear that Wayne was their guest for the first time during *Red River*. So the **San Pedro River** near Tombstone is more probable, also taking into consideration that Montgomery Clift was aware of the location being near Tombstone, home of Wyatt Earp: "The tourists are fast ruining this town, before long nothing will stand to show what a hell of a place it once was," he wrote home.[11] Even though they had to move the whole herd over to that location, Hawks was glad to use the property of Stewart Symington, who served as the first Secretary of the Air Force (from 1947 to 1950). There was not enough water in the river for the sequence as Hawks envisioned it, so he had a dam built. Just as the cameras were set up, the dam broke.

"I'll have that brand on the greatest ranch in Texas"

When Hawks set his mind to do the story of the first Texas-to-Missouri cattle drive, he intended to tell the story of the King Ranch, the largest ranch in Texas. He soon found out that would be difficult, and the owners would not allow hazardous stunt work. "So I found *Red River* which was initially the story of the King Ranch."[12] Hawks found the Arizona equivalent of the King Ranch in the Elgin neighborhood: the historic **Empire Ranch**. It had been a working cattle ranch for 140 years.

When Tom Dunson sees his dream of a large ranch realized ("It'll be a good place to live in"), Hawks dissolves to a montage of scenes shot at the Empire Ranch. It is open daily to visitors, from sunrise to sunset. *Red River* started it as a movie location. The grasslands that surround it, with the distinctive dome-topped **Biscuit Mountain** in the background, were later used in classics like *Gunfight at the O.K. Corral*.

"Looks like we'll have to take you along"

Despite all the teasing, Hawks knew he had made another discovery. He even let Montgomery Clift wear

The site of "Abilene" in Elgin: the road that leads to this private home is actually where the railroad tracks were that Dunson crosses to confront Matt. One of the structures seen in the classic fistfight is still standing (photograph by Roland Schaefli).

The Empire Ranch was one of the largest in Arizona. It was placed on the National Register of Historic Places in 1976. *Red River* **started it as a western movie location (photograph by Roland Schaefli).**

his hat—which the director himself had once received from Gary Cooper. To make it look weather-beaten, Coop had taken it out every night and watered it. "Spiders built nests in it," Hawks said. "It looked great."[13] After the first screening, young Clift became aware he was going to be a movie star. The idea of losing his privacy terrified him. So he decided to get drunk anonymously one last time. (Because *Red River* took forever to be released, Clift's next movie, *The Search*, was released as his "first" film.)

Red River had been in production since August 26, 1946. Four stages were constructed in the Goldwyn Studios. A huge set, 110 × 120 feet, simulated a desert exterior, used for the night scenes of the wrangler's camp. Twenty tons of sand and 14 feet of mesquite were imported from Arizona, along with a selection of rocks. The ranch house interior duplicated the historic Empire Ranch house. Coleen Gray, who had shot her only scene as the girl Dunson leaves behind on location, was brought back for well-lighted close-ups. She had to stand on an apple box to kiss Wayne. Production wrapped on December 16, 1946.

"I told you all where you stand in this"

Hawks said in his later days that Wayne had a tendency to overplay a sentimental scene (probably because he had taken Ford's advice to "always play sentimental scenes

to the hilt"). Hawks finally told Wayne, "What do you want to do, this isn't *Uncle Tom's Cabaña*." Wayne replied, "All right, all right, I just tried to put somethin' into that scene." Hawks told him: "There is nothing to put in. Just say your line and get out of the frame." Wayne: "All right, shut up. If you won't say any more, I won't say any more. I just tried to make the scene better."[14] On their next collaborations, Wayne would just ask Hawks, "Hey, is this one of those scenes?" By then he had accepted Hawks' theory that you make just five good scenes in a picture and don't annoy the audience the rest of the time. So they tried to get the dramatic scenes over just as quickly as possible to "not annoy the audience." Hawks was content with his pupil: "Now he preaches that as though it's gospel, and he does a great job of not annoying the audience."[15]

"It's no fort; it's an old mission"

While *Red River* was a movie about "The Early Tales of Texas" but made in Arizona, *The Alamo* just had to be made in the Lone Star State. "14 Years in the Making," the movie marquees boasted. Finding the right location and building the set took up most of those years. "Look, I had to find locations that would look like the areas in those days, build a town, build the Alamo Mission, make a fort out of it," Wayne explained. "It just takes one hell of a lot of time."[16]

On the Goldwyn Studios' sound stage for *Red River*: **In the scene after the stampede, Montgomery Clift, John Wayne, Hank Worden, and Noah Beery, Jr., act in front of a large canvas. Note the director of photography, Russell Harlan, on the dolly tracks to the right (author's collection).**

"This movie is America": John Wayne directing the arrival of Santa Anna's forces in his movie town San Antonio de Bexar for *The Alamo* (author's collection).

On the "Cantina" set, with his son Patrick (left). Cinematographer William H. Clothier (right) prepares the next shot of *The Alamo*. Note that Davy Crockett changed his moccasins to more comfortable shoes (author's collection).

Wayne's Davy Crockett declares in the 1960 film, "When I came down to Texas, I was lookin' for somethin'." It was a sad January day in 2018 when people came down to Texas, lookin' for somethin' to buy from **Alamo Village**. The former tourist attraction had been closed for the past seven years. It opened to the public this one last time: for the liquidation sale. Props and mementos were sold off unceremoniously. Then, finally, "the mission that became a fortress … the fortress that became a shrine" was left to nature. Already, Wayne's most famous movie location looked a lot like Marty Robbins described it in the ballad of the movie: "There's a fortress all in ruins that the weeds have overgrown." Interestingly, the Waynamo, as some fans like to call it, is at this time as old as the original mission in San Antonio was when Santa Anna attacked.

"I like the sound of the word"

Wayne had started to look for locations years before. In 1948, when he and Ford were location-scouting in Texas for 3 *Godfathers*, they stopped in San Antonio. At the Alamo, Wayne was photographed holding Davy Crockett's long rifle, Old Betsy, and told reporters that he had put it in his mind to do a movie about the siege. He had already visited the shrine of Texas liberty with his writer James Edward Grant and had hired a research group to prepare his movie. After that, he explored sites in Panama where he had found an ideal location on the outskirts of Panama City, resembling

John Wayne loved an open set: A constant stream of visitors arrived at *The Alamo* and the location was crawling with reporters (author's collection).

San Antonio of the 1830s. There was even a two-mile airstrip nearby. Late in 1951, he passed up Panama for a perfect site in Sonora, Mexico, and began issuing contracts for set construction. In 1955, local people were already making authentic adobe bricks to build the set.

"Seems like the better part of valor"

Enter James T. "Happy" Shahan of Brackettville. In 1995, Governor George W. Bush dubbed him the "Father of the Texas movie industry." Fifty years before that honor, Happy drummed up additional business for the area by baiting Hollywood producers with the town's advantages. Republic boss Herbert Yates had filmed his cheaper Alamo movie *The Last Command* in the Brackettville area, based on an early draft commissioned by Wayne. His B-movie version of what Wayne had envisioned used walls constructed of papier-mâché.

In 1955, Happy heard that Wayne intended to shoot his version in Mexico or Panama. He got Mary St. John on the phone and let them know that the Daughters of the Republic wouldn't stand for that. When word reached the caretakers of the Alamo that Wayne had no plans to film their fight for independence on Texas soil, they threatened to see to it that he would receive no financing from any Texan and that his movie would not play in any major Texas theater. (For years it was unclear if Happy didn't actually spearhead this campaign.) Wayne had this to say about his standpoint: "They didn't shoot *Gone with the Wind* in the South."[17] But he had to back out of the Durango deal. Nate Edwards, Batjac's production manager, found the right spot on Shahan's ranch on a 1957 location trip. Wayne approved the location the very next day. After that, it took more than a year to build the set.

"You don't get lard less'n you boil a hog"

The story of the making of *The Alamo* has been told many times and has filled several books. Therefore we will provide a digest version, drawing from Russell Birdwell's 184-pages-strong press kit (collectors still call it "the Bible"): The ground was leveled by bulldozers. Several dozens small and large adobe buildings were built with 1.25 million adobe bricks that were made along with the beautiful reproduction of the mission on the 200,000 square feet of land leased from the Shahans. Batjac employed 400 plasterers, bricklayers, carpenters, electricians and other construction union craftsmen. More than ten miles of electric and phone cables were installed underground. Fourteen miles of heavy-duty gravel-and-tar roads were made. Well-diggers dug six deep wells, which produced 25,000 gallons of artesian water per

The director obviously disagrees with the suggestion of his cinematographer. *The Alamo* won William H. Clothier an Academy Award nomination for Best Cinematography. His career began with *Wings* in 1927; he retired in 1972 after *The Train Robbers* (author's collection).

day. The water was filtered and piped to every part of the location. The electricians put in $75,000 worth of small portable air conditioners on each interior set and in the dressing rooms. Adding to the cost: a million square feet of lumber, 40 miles of reinforced construction steel, 125,000 square feet of concrete flooring, 30,000 square feet of Spanish tile roofing. Wayne wanted his crew to have decent toilets, not the usual portable johns. Therefore, they had to lay the sewage pipes. Between setups in Louisiana on the set of *The Horse Soldiers*, Wayne took their long distance phone calls. Did he really need a landing strip to send the dailies to a film lab in Dallas every day? "Yeah," he said, "you're fuckin' right we need an airfield."[18]

"The tall tales folks tell about me"

To build completely finished buildings wasn't Wayne's original intent. "The production manager made a bad mistake," Wayne said. "When we first went down there, we planned to use ordinary false-front sets for the town and the shell of the Alamo. Then we figured the cost of trailers to house actors and crew and got around to the idea of putting up buildings instead." They put dressing rooms in some buildings, used others for warehouses, "and before we got through, we'd built a town."[19]

Working closely with William H. Clothier (pointing) and other Batjac employees to realize his vision. "We have spent 14 years preparing this product. Took us three years to build our set. We got it prepared in time so that we could grow real shrubbery around it. We've done everything that we can to make it measure up as far as the correct size of the city of San Antonio at the time in *The Alamo*," John Wayne said in a radio interview in Oklahoma (author's collection).

The town of San Antonio wasn't an accurate reproduction but built for the camera angles. Designer Al Ybarra looked up the copies of the Alamo's design in the Franciscan archives in Spain but still took some historic license—for instance, putting the chapel in a different spot so that the Crockett palisade could face the town. During construction, first assistant director Robert E. Relyea tried to persuade Ybarra to make the walls as high as possible so they wouldn't have to place thousands of background extras outside every time they shot Bowie and Travis having a discussion. But Wayne told Ybarra, "Don't listen to that son of a bitch. Build the walls of the actual height—I want the extras in the background for scope."[20] Ted White, who had doubled Wayne in *Rio Bravo* the year before, was part of the large group of stuntmen. White remembered when Wayne had them standing on the wall and all the Mexican extras were lined up, and they blew the deguello, "there was no way in hell that you didn't get goose pimples all over your body."[21]

"It's a failing of mine, decidin' for others"

Even though the motives remain unclear, it is accepted as a fact that not only did John Ford direct some of the scenes but some of them were used in the original cut. It is less well-known that Howard Hawks tried to help out in pre-production. Hawks went on record in 1975: "I wrote a whole bunch of scenes for him." Wayne read what Hawks had written and said, "They're great scenes, but I couldn't do it. I couldn't do it." Hawks had the girl in *The Alamo* raped by 20 or 30 people so Crockett would want revenge. "It would have been a hell of a good story," Hawks mused. "That's a good scene," Wayne admitted, "but I don't know how to do those things." So that scene flew out and, as Hawks regretfully added, "he did a corny girl."[22]

Wayne directed his magnum opus in 83 days, from September 22 to December 15, 1959. He summed it up for *Playboy* readers: "I thought it would be a tremendous epic picture that would say: America."

"Tell each other our troubles"

Even though we must consider the Alamo set lost, there are still a lot of locations left to visit, especially the filming sites in and around **Fort Clark**, Brackettville's historic cavalry outpost. It had been used as a film location before, most notably in the Charlton Heston Western *Arrowhead*, where many scenes included the stone commissary, built in 1892. Wayne had leased the premises, and Batjac set up production headquarters in the base officer's club. Pilar called it "a logistical nightmare." To house 342 people, workers were hired to refurbish the barracks, officers' quarters and the mess halls. Relyea remembered it as "a bit like a prison. The structure and its grounds practically made up our entire world for a year." The crew—which numbered over 480 at the height of filming—became so tired of seeing each other across the table three times a day, seven days a week, that nearly every night became "fight night" in the mess hall, according to Relyea's memoir *Not So Quiet on the Set*.[23]

Wayne and his family stayed for almost four months at the spacious **Wainwright House**, the residence of the former commanding officer. General Jonathan Wainwright had surrendered Corregidor and become a prisoner of war. There is a connection to the plot of *Back to Bataan*: The film credits include clips of actual prisoners of war freed from Japanese prison camps. A few years ago, the Wainwright House was up for sale with an asking price of $220,000.

According to Michael Wayne, Batjac built their own interior sets on the fort's grounds "so we wouldn't have to pay the horrendous rates to rent space."[24] **Fort Clark Airport Hangar**, built in 1921 in the southwest corner, was then the second oldest military hangar in the U.S. Two interior sets were created inside: Flaca's hotel room and the room in which Huston puts Travis in command. The makeshift stage in the metal hangar was not air conditioned and the heat got to everybody.

Behind the stables of Clark Springs Horse Club, a small road bridge leads over **Las Moras Creek**. This is where the Tennesseans knock the Mexican sentries over the railing. The bridge has been replaced but the original footings still exist. Following the Las Moras upstream gets you to the brick wall where the Tennesseans watch the Mexican dancers as they wade in the water. Across from the golf course, about 400 yards upstream of Las Moras Creek, is where they put Sam Houston's tent camp. Those scenes were edited together with footage of Frankie Avalon crossing at a small waterfall on the Sabinal River to deliver his message to Huston.

"There's right and there's wrong"

Davy Crockett's speech about right and wrong was filmed on the banks of the **Sabinal River**, eight miles below the town of **Utopia**. Wayne asked for permission from the McCullough family to film on their lands, as it had a wide stream and gorgeous cypress trees. ("That's one beautiful tree!" Crockett enthusiastically points out.) "Flaca's tree" was washed away in a 1986 flood.

The script draft dated July 21, 1959, identified Shahan Ranch as the location of Crockett's arrival. But according to Alamo researcher John Farkis, the scene in which the Tennesseans approach San Antone and startle deer and birds was filmed on **Leona Ranch**, about 14 miles north of Brackettville off of Highway 674. Wayne chose the area as it was well known for the abundance of wild game. Leona was sold in 2016.

"Wearing out horses coming t'wards us"

The creek that the Mexican artillery caissons cross is the **West Nueces River**. Highway 90 runs across it, from Brackettville in the direction of Uvalde, then on the lands of the L.L. Davis ranch. A fortunate accident made one of the most breathtaking shots in the movie. The Todd-AO camera was on remote, positioned on a grip-flat, so the bug-eye lens was just above water level, in the middle of the stream. The riders leading four horses pulling a cannon were supposed to pass on either side. The expensive camera was flipped from the grip-flat. Before anyone could stop him, a well-meaning grip rushed into the water to save the submerged camera, not realizing it was still connected to a generator. "The hair on the grip's head shot straight up when he clutched at it," Relyea remembered. "Well, that takes care of the first shot," Wayne told his first assistant "with that hard-ass grin of his."[25]

Actor Gil Perkins, who played "Scotty," recalled working in that cold water. "We cremated ourselves for six weeks, then, when it came time to do the water work, it turned freezing cold."[26] Perkins also lined up the sword fight between Laurence Harvey and the advancing Mexican soldados. "Before he's taken out," Wayne instructed him, "I want him to kill 10 or 12 Mexicans. But none of that Errol Flynn stuff!"[27]

"Be drunk or sober, however they choose"

Relyea finally just dropped unconsciously in front of Wayne, blood streaming out of his mouth, when an ulcer burst and ate through a main artery. Because of the nature of their job, stuntmen always know their blood type. When the call came from the hospital, 13 stuntmen with Relyea's blood type—most of them drunk, some half-naked—jumped into a pick-up truck and made the 45-minute drive to Del Rio in 25 minutes. If they had arrived 20 minutes later, Relyea would have died. As the doctors pointed out after he was stabilized, "I was now filled with several pints of tequila, Jack Daniels and God knows what else."[28]

The stunt guys were usually involved in card games, and stuntman "Bear" Hudkins was elected "Commissioner on the Hearts Game" which meant collecting the money. When he learned that Ted White had finished his scenes and was on his way home, he told Wayne that Ted owed $4.95. Wayne called Highway Patrol to pick White up. A

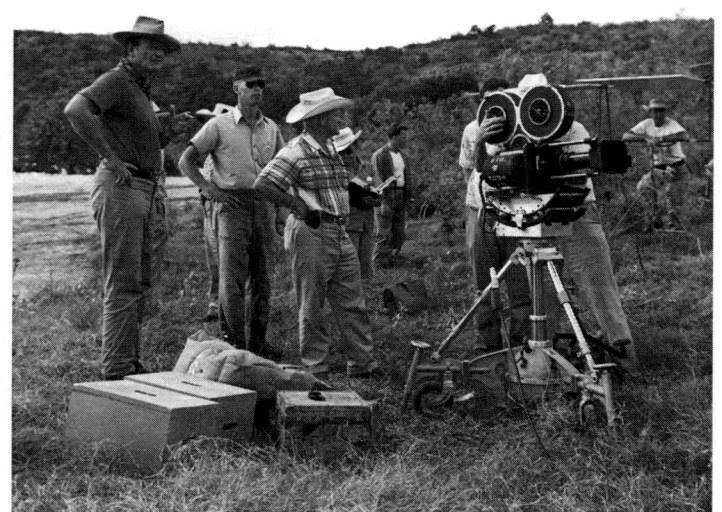

The day the accident happened that made one of the most spectacular shots in the whole picture: filming the Mexican artillery cross the West Nueces River. Robert Relyea (with sunglasses) and William H. Clothier watch the Todd-AO-camera being loaded (author's collection).

little while later, Wayne called the set: "Hey, Bear, we got the money!"[29]

Le Leanne Ethridge was murdered by her boyfriend in a bunkhouse in **Spofford**, Texas, a rail junction town of about 250 residents, 20 miles from Brackettville. Her boyfriend stabbed her to death while she was gathering her belongings to move to Fort Clark, as Wayne had expanded her bit part.

Post-production work was done at the Goldwyn Studio on Formosa Avenue in Los Angeles. The film premiered on October 24, 1960, at the **Woodlawn Theatre**, 1920 Fredericksburg Road, San Antonio. The lavish London premiere on October 27 (Wayne presented Princess Margaret with a silver saddle) was held at the **Astoria Theatre** at 157 Charing Cross Road. The iconic establishment was closed in 2009 and has since been demolished. Wayne stayed at the **Savoy Hotel** while in London. "This is the one big American story, that I didn't think anyone could do better than I," he told *Today* magazine on October 29, 1960. "*The Alamo* will tell what my future is."

"That don't change the truth none"

The *Alamo* script draft dated July 21, 1959, described setups 460 thru 560 as "The Final Assault" with the note: "There is a production department bulletin which lists 100 set-ups for this sequence ... [T]here are short death sequences for all of our principals and supporting players." The blasting of the chapel on December 11 (described in the script as "the explosion dwarfs any of the previously seen explosions") was the last huge special effect shot. After the massive bang, Michael Wayne turned to Happy and said, "Well, Shahan, there goes your Alamo."[30] Not quite. Wayne certainly "blew the smithereens out of it," Shahan said, and he "had to borrow a lot of money to build it back."[31] The Texas rancher often claimed that the idea to make it into a tourist attraction came to him when youngsters kept cutting his wire to take a look at Wayne's set. Yet Shahan probably always had it in mind to use it after the filming. Open daily back then, Alamo Village was located off U.S. Highway 90, to the north of Brackettville. Ironically, that's just what you'll have to do again today if you want to set foot on the John Wayne holy ground: cut the wire.

"Not thinkin', just rememberin'"

Wayne stated that they "make more money from it as a tourist attraction than we will from the picture."[32] Shahan had asked him to join him in the venture but Wayne would not have any part of it. Instead, he sent the cannon and other props to Old Tucson (where most of it was eventually wiped out in the fire). Wayne later regretted his decision. "I'm sorry

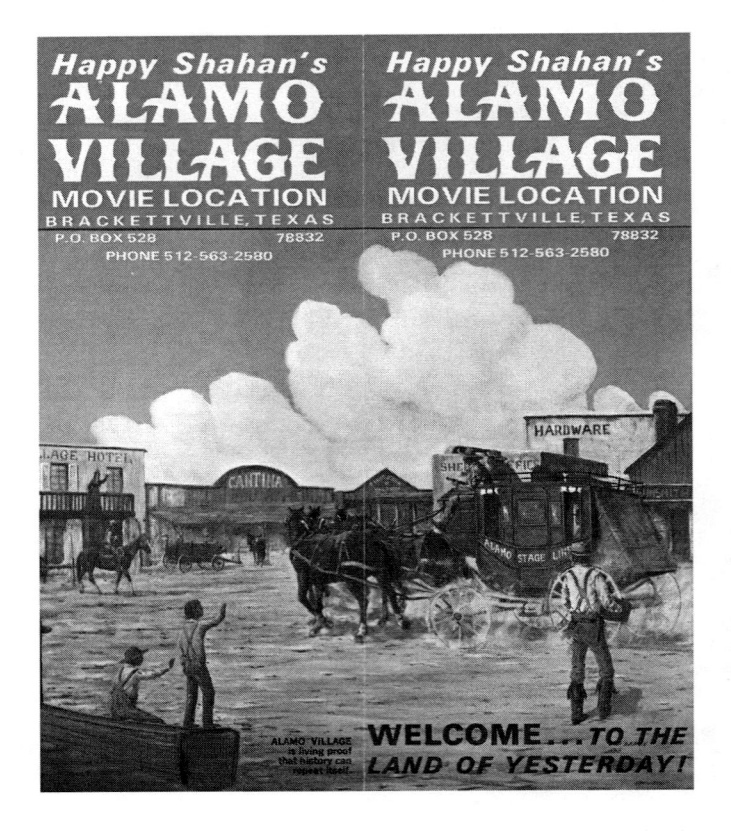

"**Happy**" **Shahan had reason to be happy: after he had rebuilt the set destroyed in the movie battle, he opened Alamo Village as a tourist attraction. Visitors received this brochure that including the timetable of the daily stunt shows (author's collection).**

to say I didn't keep the rights to the location," he lamented.[33] While it lasted, visitors from far and wide traveled to Brackettville. Yet Happy Shahan always used to say that Alamo Village was for sale: "Just make me an offer."[34] Several deals fell through. After his passing, the family struggled to keep it alive. In John Wayne's birthday in 1998, an Alamo Reunion became the last hurrah for the movie location. Joan O'Brien sang songs from the Alamo with Rudy Robbins; stuntman Dean Smith told the story of how he even got married in the San Fernando church Wayne had built. The young Mexican kid that Crockett helped to get his tip was all grown up, and the Champion couple (the flamenco dancer who danced on the table and her husband who played the guitar) returned to the cantina. Several more of the bit players proudly wore the button "I survived the Alamo!" Bill Daniel, who had played Colonel Neill, asked for a moment of silence. For a minute or so, the wind just blew through the old Alamo set. Pilar also attended and stayed at the Wainwright house again.

On August 28, 2010, the Shahan family issued this statement: "After a valiant attempt to keep Alamo Village available to visitors on a limited basis, the family has made the painful decision to close it permanently." The set is still there. But nobody takes care of the buildings. They will not stand forever. On liquidation day, the fortress was already roped off. A tremendous loss to all fans.

For years, Wayne's coonskin cap was featured in a glass case inside the Alamo's gift shop in San Antonio. (Wayne didn't care for it much, as it made his forehead raw.) He had donated it to the Daughters of the Texas Revolution. Then it was kept in storage. The cap was recently re-discovered and is now back on display.

"Get the hell off my spread"

Wayne said about the shooting sites chosen for *The Cowboys*, "This has been the most refreshing location I've been on in more than 40 years of moviemaking. Usually, you end up with the same old bunch of actors, the same old pack of tall tales and lies. But his one is different."[35]

News items indicate that part of the shooting took

Traces of Buckskin Joe: to many western actors, these planks meant the world. The site, now dubbed the Royal-Gorge Ranch & Resort, will be home to 339 mansion sites, according to developers (photograph by Roland Schaefli).

At the 1998 reunion, Joan O'Brien sings her songs from *The Alamo*, accompanied by Rudy Robbins' guitar. Robbins became a fan favorite for his repeated saying of just two words: "It do" (photograph by Roland Schaefli).

place eight miles west of **Canon City**, Colorado, in the movie town known to moviemakers and tourists as **Buckskin Joe** (Wayne rides in to ask Slim Pickens for advice on his cattle drive). MGM built it as a movie set in 1957. Buckskin Joe was different from the western towns built by movie carpenters. Its most important characteristic was that it was formed with around 30 authentic, 100-year-old log buildings from the 19th-century Colorado frontier, assembled there into an old Western-style town. *Cat Ballou*, which won Lee Marvin his Academy Award, was one of the classic Westerns made there. The owners developed the location into a theme park which became one of the largest tourist attractions in the state.

That all ended in 2010 when the owners announced the sale of Buckskin Joe. A Florida billionaire purchased it as a whole. He is known for other record-making purchases on Americana sales (like the only known photograph of Billy the Kid). He moved the movie town to his ranch near Gunnison. A short while later, all that was left of Buckskin Joe were the original entrance boundary stones and a couple of unwanted wooden planks, left in the grass.

"We're burnin' daylight"

When Wayne read the *Cowboys* screenplay, dated March 8, 1971, he came across an expression that he probably hadn't often read in his Western scripts: HELICOPTER SHOT. The chopper was required for the establishing shot of "a vast and peaceful Montana valley, a century ago, swept in the winds of spring." The ranch complex was described as "consisting of several buildings, made of unhewed logs with mud sealing. The main house boasts real glass windows." Director Mark Rydell was inspired by everything that had

"**Bring in the iron, Charlie**": Wil Anderson trains *The Cowboys* on the ranch built for the movie. **The boys holding the cow down are Mike Pyeatt (Homer) and Sean Kelly (Stuttering Bob), Clay O'Brien (Hardy) and Stephen R. Hudis (Charlie) standing to the left and right of Wayne. Robert Carradine (Slim, second from the right) is the son of John Carradine who first acted with Wayne in** *Stagecoach* **(author's collection).**

to do with finding the required filming sites: "Amazing location we were on. We had a wonderful production designer, Philip Jefferies; he built the ranch on this incredible spot where you could see for 50 miles in every direction, without seeing a telephone pole or anything. With the most remarkable research, he made these buildings [Wayne's ranch in the movie] look authentic."[36]

Rydell left for Santa Fe, New Mexico, on March 24, 1971, and filming began on April 1 in the rugged **Sangre de Cristo** mountain range. Three weeks of shooting took place on the **San Cristobal Ranch**, 28 miles from Santa Fe, and on the B-B Ranch. Other scenes were shot at New Mexico's **Pagosa Springs**, 62 miles east of Durango on U.S. 160, on a private ranch in the San Juan Valley of Archuleta County.

"Trail driving is no Sunday school picnic"

One incident happened the day Rydell shot the start of the cattle drive. To get 1500 head of cattle moving takes a while; the drag riders started moving them from behind. Rydell, on his camera crane, had not yet rolled his five cameras because he did not want to waste film. Wayne, on horseback, figured it was time to start the scene because the beasts were on the move, so he rode up to the chuckwagon and delivered his line, "Ready, Mr. Nightlinger?" Rydell blew up and ordered him back to his

mark, realizing at the same time that he would get fired for that. The same evening, Wayne asked him out for dinner. ("To go to a restaurant in Sante Fe with John Wayne is like walking in with Lincoln!" Rydell remembered.) Wayne told him, "You remind me of Ford," and he called him "sir" for the rest of the shooting.[37]

"I like to travel with a man I'm used to"

J.W. Eaves Ranch in New Mexico was a Western bonanza in the 1970 with around 50 shows to its credit. Fourteen miles outside Santa Fe, it was a standing set, built by Gene Kelly for *The Cheyenne Social Club*. For the end of *The Cowboys*, it became the town of Belle Fourche where the young hands bring in Wayne's cattle. A short distance from the movie town was a deep canyon with a running stream; that's where one of the boys is trampled to death. (The box canyon was used again in *Silverado*.) Another *Cowboys* set, eight miles outside **Galisteo**, was the small village of La Fonda. After the Wayne picture, Galisteo served as a location for a number of neo–Westerns, including *Young Guns*.

Rydell shot the first part of *The Cowboys* on the New Mexico locations, using Santa Fe as production headquarters. "Those skies were so incredible to shoot in Santa Fe, with the clouds hovering over those mountains," he mused.[38] They built the schoolhouse near Santa Fe and also the bunkhouse for Roscoe Lee Browne's long monologue, even if it was an interior. In the middle of the film, Rydell changed locations from Santa Fe to Colorado, not in a very subtle way: In the movie, the dry New Mexico plains

The scene that almost got director Mark Rydell in trouble: John Wayne rides up to Roscoe Lee Browne without waiting for his cue (author's collection).

are immediately followed by the rather green Colorado surroundings. In Colorado, they used the Arkansas River for the river-crossing scene. After 12 weeks, the production company finally reached Canon City, for shooting at Buckskin Joe.

"On my worst day, I get to beat the hell out of you"

Location work wrapped on July 21. They went back to Warners' Burbank studios for just a few interiors. Before Rydell directed the Wayne–Bruce Dern fistfight that leads up to Wayne's death scene, they had already shot that poignant moment on the outdoor location of Pagosa Springs. Therefore, Wayne's regular makeup man Dave Grayson had to do the heavy makeup before they even got to the fight. Rydell said it would have been unrealistic for Wayne's character to remain unmarked. In a meeting, Grayson told the director, "It'll take four makeup men" to hold Wayne down to put on "the stuff." Finally, Grayson faced Wayne: "Look, Duke, they want me to mutilate you for this scene, and nobody wants to tell you." Wayne was in his trailer and said, "Bullshit! You know I don't believe in that stuff." After some convincing, he let Grayson "put the stuff on."[39] Grayson had Polaroids of the makeup job he had done at Pagosa Springs so that he could match it for the sequence shot on the stage.

"Tell the truth, Tucson, is this better than ranching?"

Ray "Crash" Corrigan, Wayne's co-star in the *Three Mesquiteer* series and a Republic star in his own right, had purchased a large land property in 1937. While he was starring as "Tucson" in the series, he went on a hunting trip. "Always did like to hunt. While on this hunting trip, I stumbled on this picturesque and peaceful spot in the Simi Valley."[40] Corrigan was in the business long enough to know that the movie companies were always hunting for new faces and new locations. He bought the 2000 acres, called it the **Corrigan Movie Ranch** and offered its wide variety of terrain, including lakes, mines and the western street of Silvertown, for lease to moviemakers. (In some buildings, it was even possible to film interiors.) He lured his home studio Republic up to his place in Simi Valley. Even though Wayne played the leader of the trio, the Three Mesquiteers rode on Corrigan's land. Wayne's Mesquiteer entries in Corriganville include *Pals of the Saddle*, *Santa Fe Stampede* and *Wyoming Outlaw*.

Thirty-five hundred films and television series used the ranch at one time or another. When he told the story of how the Ray Corrigan Ranch became the tourist attraction Corriganville, "Crash" used to say, "It seemed a shame not to share this Last Living Frontier with others." When "Crash" started his amusement park, he named the concrete-lined lagoon Robin Hood Lake. Even the U.S. Post Office realized they were really a town and soon after Corriganville, California, could be found in every post office directory throughout the world.

"Welcome to Fort Apache, General Thursday"

Corriganville was mostly known as a B-movie location. Nevertheless, from July 24 to September 13, 1947, an A-Western was in the making on Corrigan's grounds, destined to become a classic: *Fort Apache*.

When John Ford made the Shirley Temple vehicle *Wee Willie Winkie* in 1937 just a few minutes away, at Iverson Ranch, he had built a complete British fort there. Now he brought Temple back to Simi Valley. They fabricated the cavalry post on flat terrain on **Table Mountain**, surrounded by rocks, so Ford could cut to scenes in Monument Valley without destroying the illusion. As a matter of fact, Temple probably didn't go to Monument Valley. All her long shots in Arizona were done with a double, all her close-ups at the Selznick Studios in Culver City. In her biography, she shared few memories about the making of *Fort Apache*—and she does not mention Monument Valley at all. Ford called for more love scenes between Temple and her real-life husband, John Agar, "not that I intended to keep all this nonsense in the final print," he later admitted. "Just wanted to keep up the morale of the youngsters."[41]

When Wayne returned to his B-movie stamping grounds, he came back a full-fledged star, demanding $100,000 and one percent of the net profits. Just prior to the start of production, his contract was altered to $50,000 and a hefty five percent.

"As long as the regiment lives"

In the last shot taken at Fort Apache, as Wayne takes his company out (Ford uses a big rock at Corriganville to make the transition to Monument Valley), it took three hours lining it up. Anna Lee told Wayne historian Tim Lilley, "It was a boiling hot day, I was wearing tight corsets for the costume. And for the first and, I hope, the last time in my life, I fainted." The next thing the actress remembered, she was being carried down to her dressing room in Wayne's arms: "I'll always remember that." Ford asked if she were pregnant because she was expecting on *How Green Was My Valley* and he didn't know about it then. After that, every picture she did with Ford, he would line up the crew and ask, "Anna, are you pregnant?"[42]

When Peter Fonda was a kid, he visited his first film location, where his dad Henry was working. He remembered the occasion all his life because John Wayne personally drove him to the Corriganville set in his cream-colored convertible with red leather upholstery.

The fort was later expanded and seen in other Westerns such as *Escape from Fort Bravo* with William Holden and in TV's *The Adventures of Rin Tin Tin*. When it was finally dismantled in 1967, the Simi Valley Police Department built a firing range (the cement footings one can find in the ground are remnants of the shooting range, not the movie sets). There is only a marker gone yellow that informs hikers about the making of the John Wayne classic.

According to some sources, John Ford came back to Corriganville for a brief time, for the few outdoor night scenes of *How the West Was Won* (presumably, the volley of cannon shots was filmed at Robin Hood Lake).

Corriganville became Hopetown in 1966 when Bob Hope purchased it for real estate development. On September 25, 1970, a firestorm swept the ranch, destroying almost all of Silvertown. A 1979 fire left just the cement pads of the foundation that still exist today. Only about 200 of the original 2000 acres survive as the **Corriganville Regional Park** at 7001 Smith Road, now part of the Simi Valley Park system and open to the public. The entrance of the amusement park was on Sandalwood Drive. Corrigan's siblings opened a restaurant, **Corrigan's Steakhouse**, at 556 Thousand Oaks Boulevard. It closed in 2018 after the death of Tom Corrigan. For the time being, would-be-patrons are greeted with a message that reads "closed for maint."

"There ain't nobody got me buffaloed!"

From Corriganville, one just needs to cross the Santa Susana Pass to Iverson Road to discover another movie location bonanza, which is now history. "Near a town called Canoga Park are huge elephant-sized outcroppings of rock. This was called **Iverson's Ranch**. Many people tried hard to save it, but it's just a memory now," Harry Carey, Jr., recalled sentimentally.[43] "If you rent an old John Wayne tape, you'll see Iverson's for sure."

It all got started in 1912 when the California Aqueduct brought water to the San Fernando Valley. A man named Karl Iverson left his Chatsworth ranch to lease land on the Valley floor to plant crops. But with no water there, he was running out of options. Then a well-dressed man strode up the trail: a location scout from Hollywood, the small filmmaker community to the south. The craggy landscape was just what they were looking for, the stranger said. Over the years, Iverson's transformed itself to Western locales as well as exotic landscapes or Bible epics such as the silent *Ben-Hur*. *Noah's Ark* could be credited as Duke Morrison's "first Iverson movie": Noah's boat was superimposed on the distinctive rocks known today as the **Garden of the Gods**. Wayne actually set foot into this rocky terrain for the first time in

The Ringo Kid, ready for success: John Wayne on the stage depot set of *Stagecoach*, built on Iverson's Movie Ranch, also known as "the most shot up location in movie history" (author's collection).

On the former grounds of Corriganville: the site of the *Fort Apache* set is marked by a fainted signpost (photograph by Roland Schaefli).

1932, for *Texas Cyclone*. For 35 years, Iverson Movie Ranch was the setting for a host of Tarzan movies, starting in 1919 with the original Tarzan, Elmo Lincoln, and continuing through 1953 with Tarzan successor Lex Barker. Gary Cooper was no stranger to Iverson's: After appearing in five features made there (including *The Plainsman*, for which Wayne had asked Cecil B. DeMille for the part of William F. Cody), Cooper invested his own funds: in 1945, he had a Western set built at Iverson for his production *Along Came Jones*.

Roy Rogers told Joe (son of Karl) Iverson, "I filmed parts of my first movie at your ranch, and parts of my last movie at your ranch—plus parts of most of the movies in between." **Ambush Rock**, named for its ideal place for stuntmen to jump down on stagecoaches, can be spotted in scores of flicks. Thousands of motion pictures, serials and TV shows were made on the rocky plateau in the Santa Susana Mountains, overlooking the town of Chatsworth. Harry Carey, Jr., remembered that at times, "you'd be in the middle of a dialogue scene and gunshots would ruin the take. They'd be coming from another company just over the hill."[44]

"You must be the joker in the deck"

Silent movie star Louise Brooks was reaching the end of her career when she accepted a part in the Three Mesquiteers series, when Wayne's star was rising. One August 1938 morning at sunrise, she was driven in a company car to the ranch where Republic was shooting *Overland Stage Raiders* 1938. She stood "alone in a cloud of dust kicked up by a passing string of horses—that damned dust so cherished by

There wasn't a stagecoach hold-up in years: The Santa Susana Pass Road connects the historical movie locations Iverson, the Garden of the Gods and the Spahn Ranch (photograph by Roland Schaefli).

For *The Fighting Seabees*, the Republic art department turned Upper-Iverson into a Pacific Island (author's collection).

Western cameramen." When her car honked to get a group of cowboys off the road, two men came over to introduce themselves. One was the star of the series, John Wayne. "Looking up at him I thought, this is no actor but the hero of all mythology miraculously brought to life."[45]

When John Ford came to Iverson's to shoot the stage depot scenes of *Stagecoach* (see Chapter 5), he certainly knew where he wanted to put the camera to take advantage of those rock formations. He had been shooting movies up there since the old Harry Carey days. Young Ford even broke an arm there once, when his brother Francis staged an automobile chase through **Cahuenga Pass**.

Before *Stagecoach*, Wayne had filmed *Haunted Gold*, *Texas Cyclone*, *Central Airport* and *The Dawn Rider* at the ranch. So the young star knew all the trails like the back of his hand. Even after *Stagecoach* promised to be his big breakthrough, Republic sent him right back to Iverson Movie Ranch for *Santa Fe Stampede*, from October 11 to October 19, 1938, and *Three Texas Steers*, in March 1939.

"Let them have it!"

In December 1943, Republic rented a large section of Upper Iverson (as the upper part of the ranch was known by producers) to turn it into a South Pacific island on which Wayne battles the Japanese army. As was the case with *Fort Apache* and Corriganville, Wayne came back to Iverson Ranch an A-list star. At $1.5 million, *The Fighting Seabees* had the highest budget in Republic's history to date. Republic made it during the war as a tribute to the U.S. Navy's Construction Battalions (C.B.s).

The area under siege included Cactus Hill and the

South Rim of the Upper Iverson; the landmark **Eagle Beak Rock** is prominently seen. But first, the art directors needed to create the necessary jungle atmosphere. More than ten tall poles were trucked in from San Francisco and planted in spots throughout Iverson. Studio workers asked various L.A. homeowners if they would allow them to trim their palm trees—"for free." They brought the palm fronds back to the set, carefully attaching them to the poles and therefore transforming the ranch into an island. However, after the last blank was fired on *Fighting Seabees*, they found they were unable to remove the well-attached palm fronds. Thus, they removed all "palm trees" intact and transported them to Republic's warehouses for future use.

The *Seabees* art department even built a huge landing strip. In reality, the Upper Iverson Ranch was not wide enough for planes to land or take off. Planes could only just touch down on the short runway to simulate a "landing"; they then had to take off right away. A real plane would merely touch down, then another plane would taxi down the runway and roll to a stop. Joe Iverson recalled, "Many a morning I was jolted from my sleep by the drone of a low-flying fighter-bomber."[46] The sight of military planes circling low over the Santa Susana Mountains also startled Chatsworth residents. According to *Quiet on the Set*, the knowledgeable retelling of those filming days, horseback riders who strayed onto the property had a good chance of running smack into a battalion of "Japanese soldiers."

Several riders faced danger one day on their morning ride when they accidentally rode onto an area of the *Seabees* set that was earmarked to be destroyed by "heavy artillery." When director Edward Ludwig gave his signal, a series of bombs exploded just in front of them. Luckily, nobody got hurt. "Some folks went riding along the Santa Susana Pass this morning," said one wide-eyed old-timer, "and darn near got blown up there by the Japanese Army."

For the combat scenes, Republic took over Lower Iverson. In the scenes where the U.S. troops are positioned in the Upper Gorge, a portion of the Garden of the Gods is visible in the background. And **Tower Rock** makes a brief comeback after having served as a cornerstone for *Stagecoach*.

"We'll have our own barbecue"

Republic's special effects wizard Howard Lydecker, credited here as second-unit director, flooded acres of land with burning oil to create the eye-popping finale at the Iverson Gorge, including a portion of Devil's Doorway. In the old days, the Iverson family just charged a $5 fee for filming and they let the initial film companies do pretty much what they wanted. That attitude changed over the years. At the time of *The Fighting Seabees*, all contracts read that the land shall be left in the condition in which it was found. Film companies would change the landscape according to the needs of their scripts, yet after the "terrain make-up," the set-builders had to transform it right back. Generations of moviemakers admired the lifelong dedication of the Iversons to their land. So when the *Seabees* aimed to push a real tank over a cliff, Joe would not permit it. "It will crush the landscape and the rock formations below," he argued. The studio technicians built a papier-mâché replica and sent it hurtling over the **Nyoka Cliff** into the Iverson Gorge (it looked real enough).

The Lost "Garden of Gods"

In 1966, the State of California began construction on the Simi Valley Freeway, since renamed the Ronald Reagan Freeway. It literally cut the Iverson ranch in half. As a movie location, the ranch was doomed. In 1970, a wildfire destroyed the movie ranch. The Brandeis Ranch that stood in the upper part and was used as a location in the '30s (as in Wayne's *Santa Fe Stampede*) also vanished in this fire. In the '80s, the new owners began selling the property to real estate developers. The upper part is now the gated community Indian Springs (access is available to hikers) and the Lower Iverson is now California West, a private residential condominium community. The spot where John Wayne blew up the fuel tank is now filled with condos. In the middle of the two portions of Upper and Lower Iverson is Summerset Village.

A silent film director first called it "Garden of Gods." The topography has been altered a great deal, with Red Mesa Road now slicing horizontally through the center of the frame. However, the major rock features toward the top remain in place. Although the major rock formations remain intact, even movie experts will have a hard time recognizing the filming sites. Housing development hides a landscape that once was the most photographed movie location in cinema history. All that's left is a plaque mounted on a sandstone outcropping known as **Hawk Rock**: It pays homage to these "six-gun heroes and their gallant horses. They left indelible hoof prints on these trails."

<h1 style="text-align:center">22</h1>

And the Hunter
Home from the Hill

"A place to live and a place to die…"

"…that's all any man gets. No more, no less."
—The Parson (Hank Worden) to Smitty (Frankie Avalon)
as they arrive at the Alamo

John Wayne lived the life of a vagabond. He got that wanderlust early in life. The Morrison family hardly ever put down roots. In his adult life, he still had the itch to constantly move. Let's follow the trail from his birthplace to his boyhood homes on to the various homes he made as an adult, all the way to his final resting place.

The life story of John Wayne began in the small Iowa town of **Winterset**. Marion Robert Morrison was born on May 26, 1907. Maurice Zolotow, one of the few biographers who actually talked with Wayne, wrote in 1970 that the exact site of the birthplace "is still argued by Winterset old-timers." Zolotow gave 404 East Court as the address of the birthplace and used a photo of a house different from the one that fans accept today as the home on John Wayne Street. In 1961, the information booklet "Scenic Madison County, Iowa, Historical Significance" gave 404 East Court as the correct address. When Zolotow's *Shooting Star* was published, there was still no plaque or marker to indicate the place. At long last, the question has become a clear case of "If the legend becomes fact, print the legend." The John Wayne Birthplace Society opened the house for public tours in 1982. Many a John Wayne pilgrim has since journeyed to historic Madison County to tour the home of his hero. Two rooms were restored to turn-of-the-century authentic furnishings, the other two contained Wayne memorabilia. On May 26, 2007, the centennial of Wayne's birth, ground was broken for the new 6100-square-foot **John Wayne Birthplace Museum and Learning Center**. It includes a movie theater, which has the original seats from Grauman's Chinese Theater (where Wayne's first movie *The Big Trail* premiered). Whatever the original address was—it is now called John Wayne Drive.

Marion's father "Doc," as Clyde was known to most people, worked as a pharmacist on the south side of the

The John Wayne Birthplace in Winterset: since the Birthplace Society was established in 1982, more than a million visitors have journeyed to Madison County to tour the birthplace home (Carol Bassett/The John Wayne Birthplace).

historic town square (now the Village Bootery). The Morrisons lived in Winterset for almost four years before moving to **Brooklyn**, Iowa, in 1909. There Clyde found work at the Rainsburg Drug Store, located near the south end of Jackson Street. The family lived in a private home at 717 Jackson Street. A recently revealed historical marker pays homage to the movie star. Young Marion attended kindergarten at the Brooklyn Elementary School.

At the groundbreaking ceremony for the new Birthplace Museum on May 24, 2013: John Wayne's daughter Aissa, Maureen O'Hara, and her grandson Conor FitzSimons (Wayne Davis/John Wayne Birthplace).

"I've always followed my father's advice"

After just a short time, Clyde moved his family again, this time to **Earlham,** Iowa. There they switched his name from Marion Robert to Marion Michael when his brother was born in 1911 and given the name Robert. They rented a two-story home at Walnut Avenue and NW 2nd Street, the property backed-up to a railroad track. His father opened the Rexall Drugstore on Earlham's Main Street. They returned to their Brooklyn house in 1913 where Marion entered first grade. (According to different

John Wayne's return to Antelope Valley: *Somewhere in Sonora* wasn't made where the title suggested but rather somewhere close to Palmdale, his boyhood home (author's collection).

sources, before that move, they also lived in Keokuk and Des Moines.) It was in Brooklyn that Clyde was diagnosed with tuberculosis. To improve his health, they decided to move to California in 1914.

"A man's character and personality is made up by the incidents in his life"

The Morrison farm was in **Antelope Valley,** an arid basin just over the coastal range of California Mountains north of Los Angeles. Their 80-acre property was located near the Southern Pacific Railroad tracks, in the desert community of **Palmdale,** a few miles south of **Lancaster.** "To get to Los Angeles from Palmdale by horse-and-wagon was a real trip. Took a day and a half. We never left Palmdale except to go to Lancaster," Wayne told Zolotow.[1] Their nearest neighbors were a mile away.

One hundred yards from the tracks, the Morrison family built a three-room frame house, topped with a tin roof. Wayne later described it as "a glorified shack."[2] The Morrison home didn't have gas, electricity or water. "Evenings we lit kerosene lamps to read by…. We were cut off from the world. Those were the toughest times we had, but I learned a lot, too," Wayne summed it up later.[3] The Antelope Valley teemed with rabbits but the rattlesnakes were even worse. "Seems to me like there musta been millions," Wayne recalled for another biography in 1973. "The more you killed—the more they kept on comin.'" He went to school at Palmdale Public School, located on 8th Street on Palmdale Boulevard, about four miles from the Morrison farm.

In later years, he was ready to romanticize the Lancaster experience. In the companion book to the *America, Why I Love Her* record, he wrote: "Imagine a five-year-old [he was actually seven] from the flat plains of Iowa being plunked down in a land that had huge mountains looming over its

western rim that stretched for hundreds of miles eastward—the Mojave Desert."[4]

"Courage is being scared to death, but saddling up anyway"

"I've always been pretty lucky with horses, miss," young Wayne drawled in *Ride Him, Cowboy*. Yet he had an uneasy feeling about horses. This started in Lancaster and had a lot to do with Jenny, his first horse. When young Marion was enrolled as a second-grader in the **Lancaster Grammar School**, he rode the Morrison's sway-backed mare to school every day, a 12-mile round trip. "Riding a horse always came as natural to me as breathing," he told biographer George Carpozi. Marion rode into Lancaster to pick up groceries from the general store.

Yet the memory of Jenny was not a happy one. The horse got sick and people in town accused the youngster of animal cruelty. When the veterinarian found no way to save Jenny, they had to put her down. According to Wayne, "I've never gotten over that experience."[5] He even admitted to biographer Michael Munn, "I hated living in Antelope Valley."[6]

He would return to that valley, however. As the star of

Publicity still in the saddle of the white stud that belonged to "Fat" Jones, at the stables in North Hollywood (author's collection).

B-Westerns, he rode this arid strip of land again. In *Riders of Destiny*, Singin' Sandy trots to the town of **Yucca** in the Antelope Valley, just the way young Morrison did 20 years before.

"We're drivin' a herd of horses south"

In his application to join the Army, filed August 2, 1943, Wayne put horseback riding on the list of sports in which he excelled: "Horseback riding, have done falls and posse riding in pictures, not as easy as it sounds." For his first starring role in *The Big Trail*, the studio wranglers gave him a buckskin gelding to ride. When Fox sent Wayne on a publicity tour to New York, they set up a session with dozens of police officers outside the Central Park precinct station. Fox Movietone Newsreel would film the young star riding a white stallion from a stable on West 63rd Street to **Central Park West**. The reflectors of the newsreel crew hit the horse's eyes and he started bucking. The mounted police officers sneered at Wayne's discomfiture. He borrowed a club and slapped the horse across the flanks. That calmed him down. One officer criticized him not to know how to handle horses "for a westerner."[7] Wayne invited him to prove he could do better on that horse. The horse took the policeman over the hills of Central Park.

Most of the horses Wayne used in the early Westerns were rented from "picture barns." They also furnished moviemakers with horse-drawn vehicles. "Fat" Jones Stables at 11340 Sherman Way in North Hollywood was probably the best-known of the movie horse suppliers, with Hudkins Bros. Stables in Burbank a close second. Ben Johnson, who made 15 films with Wayne, married "Fat" Jones' daughter Carol in 1941.

In his Warner Westerns (1932-33), Wayne was teamed with a white stud called Duke, which was billed as either "The Devil Horse" or "The Miracle Horse." From 1940 until 1954, Wayne used a big bay named Banner that belonged to "Fat" Jones. "He was intelligent and had an instinct for this business," Wayne said.[8] When they had to put down Banner, Wayne wrote his wrangler a note: "Find me another Banner." After Banner, Wayne rode another Jones horse, Henry. He knew the importance of a good horse in the picture business. "Put a man on a horse, and right off you've got the making of something magnificent. Physical strength, speed where you can feel it, plus heroism."[9]

When Howard Hawks got ready to make *El Dorado*, he talked Wayne into using his own horse: Cochise, a beautiful but, for Wayne's size, rather short Appaloosa stallion. "You'll have to dress up a little when you ride this handsome fellow, Duke," his director advised. "Otherwise nobody'll ever notice you." Wayne used a silver band round his Stetson and quipped, "I sure don't aim to be upstaged by my own horse!"[10] He didn't necessarily care much for Cochise, as he told Zolotow, "Howard Hawks is a poor judge of horseflesh. He has bought more bad horses than anybody else that ever made Westerns." Wayne found that Hawks was always buying horses on their looks, not their quality. "He gave me a terrible horse to ride in *El Dorado*. He said it had won blue ribbons. Some dealer had put one over on him."[11]

"Lookin' back is a bad habit"

His publicist Jim Henaghan knew that, away from the camera, "[Wayne] does not act friendly with horses. A horse to Duke is what a motorcycle is to a traffic cop. Part of his work."[12] Wayne confirmed this when he gave Pilar a tour of his Encino property. It included a large pool and a cabana–guest house. When the Peruvian spotted the stables and a riding ring, she asked, "Are we going to have horses?" She assumed from all of his Westerns that the star loved to ride. "The only time I get on a horse is when I make a movie," her future husband laughed.[13]

In his first cover story in *Time* magazine, Wayne said about his riding in the early quickie Westerns, "Everything bad that can happen to you in pictures happens in those." In his memoir, production manager Robert E. Relyea described an incident that occurred when a horse named Alamo bit Wayne on the backside. "Duke loved his horse," Relyea said, "but the second interruption was more than he could stand. Wayne delivered a punch between the animal's eyes, making his point who's boss." Relyea described how Wayne then kneeled in front of his horse, put his large hands under its shoulders and helped Alamo back up, all the while staring intimidatingly into the horse's eyes.[14] As his character said in *Ride Him, Cowboy*, "Where I come from we don't shoot horses when they get ornery; we tame 'em." Still, as a Western star, he knew what he owed horses. "A man on horseback has always been the top hero. Look at the monuments— they're always a man on horseback!"[15]

"Stonehill says he can jump a four-rail fence!"

Starting with *True Grit*, Wayne rode a beautiful chestnut quarter horse named Dollor. It first appeared in the final scene on the cemetery, when Dollor was just two years old, and he rode him for the last time in *The Shootist*. The original novel did not mention a specific horse but Dollor was written into the *Shootist* script with its actual name. The quarter horse also appeared on TV's *Dynasty*. After Wayne's death, Robert Wagner rode it in a segment of his *Hart to Hart* television series. At the beginning of the '90s, the Birthplace

Society in Winterset made plans to actually buy Dollor and build a permanent stable. But the sorrel gelding lived out his years in comfort in Dallas, as a celebrity himself, and died at the age of 27 in 1995.

"Hell, the truth is, I was named after a dog!"

Back to Antelope Valley and the year of 1916 when Marion's father had to admit that the desert had him beat. That year, the Morrisons relocated once more, from Lancaster to **Glendale**. They first rented a small house at 421 South Isabel. "Doc" found work as a pharmacist at the Glendale Pharmacy on West Broadway. They still moved several times; according to some reports, they lived in five different houses during their nine years in Glendale. They temporarily moved to another rented house at 315 South Geneva Street. After that, young Morrison's address was 443 West Colorado. They got a house of their own at 404 North Isabel in 1918. In 1920, the Morrisons bought a house at 313 Garfield Avenue. After that, it was back to another rented place at 815 South Garfield. According to some sources, they also lived at 815

Increasing his horsepower: John Wayne in a publicity stunt on the *Big Jake* location. He had last performed on a motorcycle some 40 years ago, in the cliffhanger serial *Hurricane Express* (author's collection).

South Central, 129 South Kenwood and 237 South Orange. The last house Duke Morrison lived in with his family was a small cottage at 207 West Windsor.

When Marion delivered the *Los Angeles Examiner* on his paper route, his huge Airedale Duke, the family pet, accompanied him. Together, they liked to visit the local fire station, then at 315 East Broadway. It has long since become part of the John Wayne legend that the firefighters of Fire Department Station No. 1 began calling the dog Little Duke and the lanky boy Big Duke. "You can't imagine what that meant to me," Wayne told Pilar years later. "I really looked up to those guys. They were heroes in my book. When they began calling me Duke, I made up my mind to use the name from then on."

According to Zolotow, one of the volunteer firefighters was the athletic director of the Vernon Country Club in Pasadena and a professional boxer. When Duke got into some trouble with the school bully, the man showed him how to throw a punch (which reminds one of a very similar episode in the Ford classic *How Green Was My Valley*).

Young Duke got his thumb caught between the chain and sprocket wheel of his bicycle while tuning it for practice to enter a competitive race, on the boys' speedway at the corner of Hawthorne and Central Avenue. The *Glendale Evening News* reported the minor accident. This was probably the first time the future John Wayne got himself in the papers.

"I stick to simple themes"

In 1918, "Doc" managed to scrape together enough money to open his own drug store in the Jensen Building, which also housed the **Glendale Theater**, the "Palace Grand," at 124 South Grand. Young Duke spent a lot of time watching the flickers. When Rudolpho Valentino's *The*

Four Horsemen of the Apocalypse played there in 1921, he sat through it twice each day.

In Glendale, Duke also saw the filmmaking process first-hand. The demand for motion pictures was sweeping the nation, and new studios sprang up literally overnight. Location was imperative, and its rugged terrain made Glendale a center of Western movies. The city's proximity to Hollywood and its setting of the Verdugo Hills and San Gabriel Mountains made it an ideal outdoor filming site. Tom Mix made some of his serials there; and Wayne remembered seeing Douglas Fairbanks filming a woodland scene for *Robin Hood*. The railroad spur in Glendale was often used for train sequences. The studios Sierra Photoplays and the Kalem Company were even situated in Glendale at the time. The former site of Kalem was at the corner of present-day Chevy Chase Drive and Verdugo Road. As often as he could, young Duke trooped down to the sets to observe the filming. The eager boy got his first pay on a movie set when he helped hold a reflector to light a scene: a box lunch.

"Love is watching your child walk to school for the first time alone"

In Glendale, Marion was in the fourth grade at the Sixth Street Elementary School. He graduated from **Woodrow Wilson Intermediate School**, at 1221 Monterey Road, in September 1921. (He joined the Boy Scouts while at Wilson, becoming a member of Troop 4.) He attended **Glendale Union High School** between 1921 and 1925. He played football for the 1924 league champion Glendale High School Dynamiters. When an interviewer asked him years later if football really prepared a boy for life, he responded: "Do you know a better way to learn to respect someone than to have him across the line of scrimmage from you? Do you think the

During the nine years the Morrisons lived in Glendale, they inhabited more than half a dozen different houses. The one on North Isabel Street was built in 1914. Wayne's father, Clyde Morrison, purchased it in 1918 (photograph by Roland Schaefli).

In March 2021, the John Wayne Performing Arts Center at Glendale Union High School was renamed because of the recent controversy (photograph by Roland Schaefli).

color of your skin or the amount of your father's property or your social position helps you there?"[16]

Wayne returned to his high school just once, in 1949, when his half-sister graduated. According to the biography co-written by his longtime makeup artist Dave Grayson, Wayne had an arrangement with Glendale High School not to release any information about his attendance there unless it was cleared with him. The school honored this arrangement as a courtesy to Wayne until his death.

In the meantime, his parents made up their minds to move to Los Angeles and they rented a house at 812 East Fourteenth Street. After a few months, they moved to Valencia Street. Other addresses on record are 100 South Olive Street and 1513 West Pico Boulevard, probably the first places young Duke Morrison resided after he had moved out of his family home.

"When did you burn down the school?"

In 1925, the **University of Southern California (USC)** offered Duke Morrison a football scholarship and the young man became a USC Trojan, trained by Howard Jones. When he was still a Trojan, he met his future mentor John Ford on the set of *Mother Machree*. "So you're a football player," Ford teased the student who worked at the studio during his free time. "Well, playing at USC," was Duke Morrison's answer. Ford baited the young propman: "Let's see how you get down." According to Wayne, "I got down, braced on my four arms and my feet, and he just kicked my arms from under me and stuck my nose in the mud they had made for *Mother Machree* and I tell you it wasn't the sod of old Ireland. And it really hurt." So, not being interested in a motion picture career at that time, the prop boy said: "Let's try that again." Interviewed on TV by Peter Bogdanovich, Wayne demonstrated how he then kicked Ford, hitting him in the chest. "And I sat him down on the part that goes over the fence last. And he looked up with a little surprise. And there was a deadly silence. Right then it was a decisive moment in my career in motion pictures." Fortunately, not only did Ford took the incident in good humor, but also he befriended the young assistant.

"It's a fine game, football"

As a bit player, Duke got several chances to play football players. He was a Yale football player in *Brown of Harvard* in 1926, partly shot on the campus in **Cambridge**, Massachusetts. As Wayne remembered in a 1976 *Photoplay* article, "My God, they gave us ten bucks a day!" He donned

Their remarkable friendship started with a football picture: even when not involved in a movie, the friends would visit their respective locations. John Ford (on crutches) and Ward Bond (at the right) come to see their pal John Wayne in the Agoura Hills. George Waggner, director of *The Fighting Kentuckian*, is to Ford's right, with unknown Republic crewmembers (author's collection).

shoulder pads and varsity sweaters again for the 1927 silent movie *The Drop Kick*: On the campus of **Shoreham**, he is one of the USC football players in the climactic game. This probably marked Duke Morrison's first recognizable screen appearance.

Filmed at **Annapolis**, Maryland, between May and July 1929, *Salute* marked the beginning of the great friendship

Before his football career came to a sudden end, young John Wayne played a USC offensive tackle. He was arguably the most famous Trojan of the USC football team (Courtesy of the USC School of Cinematic Arts).

between Wayne, John Ford and Ward Bond. When Ford was casting this picture about the Naval Academy, he was in need of husky footballers to portray the Annapolis team. He asked Duke if he could assemble the USC team and secure permission for them to be transported to Annapolis. Wayne and the players from the 1929 USC team were each paid $50 a week for participating. He rounded up all his Sigma Chi fraternity brothers. Ward Bond, who was *not* a member, recalled, "Ford picked 14 and I was one of them. Duke didn't like this. Because he was pushing his fret brothers." Yet Ford pointed to Bond, demanding "that ugly guy." The director then made the two young men share a berth on the train and teamed them up once they had reached Annapolis. Bond recalled in a 1950 article for *Motion Picture Magazine*, "Ford, that whimsical Hibernian, saw to it that when we settled down in Annapolis, Wayne and I had the same hotel room!"[17] (The hotel was called Carvel Hall.) They were together on the field by seven in the morning, drilling under a tough Marine sergeant in that damp Maryland heat. A kinship was formed that lasted until Bond's death in 1960. In later years, whenever his frequent co-star bickered about the Hollywood system, Wayne always had a quick reply: "I did my damnedest to keep you the hell out of the picture business!"

Wayne's stay in Annapolis must have been somewhat painful for the young man as his plans to attend the Naval Academy were shattered after he finished high school. "Ever since we moved to California, I loved the sea. More than anything else, I wanted to go to Annapolis and become an officer in the Navy." He described it as "a terrible disappointment," having missed the examinations. A couple of algebra problems steered him away from an ensign's stripes and, "in a way, I guess I never got over it."[18] So he finally got to Annapolis with a movie troupe. In 1956, Wayne portrayed a Navy legend, "Spig" Wead, who went to Annapolis.

"Anybody here know how to kick a football?"

Salute was followed by *The Forward Pass*, filmed on the USC campus and at the adjacent **Coliseum** in downtown L.A. Duke was an extra. He kept appearing as a football player after he had become John Wayne. In *That's My Boy*, made by Columbia in 1932, Wayne had a small role as the star player of the Harvard team.

In 1974, Wayne came to **Harvard Square** big-style. He rode a 13-ton armored carrier, manned by members of Troop D of the Army Reservists of the 178th Infantry Brigade, Fort Devon. (They had supplied him with Hawaiians to play "VC" in *The Green Berets*.) Harvard was then the geographic nerve center of the antiwar movement, and Wayne had accepted the challenge from the Lampoon offices. He stood in the hatch, dodging snowballs tossed from Harvard dormitories. During his stay in Boston, he was at the **Ritz Carlton Hotel** in Boston Common, 10 Avery Street.

In 1931's *Maker of Men*, Columbia had him play a bit

When an injury ended his football career, John Wayne kept on playing the game in football pictures, then very popular with the movie-going public (author's collection).

This historic photograph shows the building where Duke Morrison most likely studied on the USC campus (courtesy USC School of Cinematic Arts).

part as a football player who betrays his school. In the summer of 1933, even as he was top-billed in Warners Westerns, the studio still had him to do an uncredited walk-on as a college student in *College Coach*, filmed at the studio, with some sequences shot at the Rose Bowl in Pasadena. When he was playing second banana to Tim McCoy in *Range Feud*, leading lady Susan Fleming recalled that Wayne was unhappy and drank heavily on the set; "In the shot where we had to kiss, he reeked of booze." Between scenes, Wayne confessed that his football pals "thought he was a sissy, because here he was, 'playacting in movies.'"[19]

"A man's got to have a code, a creed to live by"

Ford once called the players in *The Searchers* a "USC cast," because so many USC alumni were in it: Wayne, Bond, Jeffrey Hunter and others. An incident that occurred

Artifacts of his short but proud career as a Trojan were on display at the USC School of Cinematic Arts for 10 years (courtesy USC School of Cinematic Arts).

on the USC campus in August 1965 might have influenced Wayne's wish to do a picture about the Vietnam War. He was discussing plans for a charity benefit on behalf of burn patients at the children's hospital, and used the occasion to stroll about the campus with Mary St. John. As they stood in the grass facing the **Doheny Memorial Library**, a group of student war protesters ridiculed a young Marine. The corporal had lost an arm in battle and had decided to go back to school on the G.I. Bill. Wayne walked him to his car and thanked him for serving his country. Then he went back to the protesters, pounded his fists onto their table, and called them all sorts of names. He asked them to blame President Johnson but not a kid who had served.

In the fall of 1966, Wayne returned to USC. He had agreed to appear on a program with Bob Hope to raise money for the school's scholarship endowment. "This is a great university," he told the audience, "you owe it your best."[20] He exited to a standing ovation. In 1968, Wayne was awarded an honorary doctorate from the USC.

The **USC School of Cinematic Arts** hosted the exhibit, the Wayne Collection, for 10 years, until it was removed after the 2019 controversy. An extensive collection of personal memorabilia; the items were originally gathered and preserved by Michael Wayne: the Congressional medal, the bracelet presented by Montagnard tribesmen in Vietnam (which he never took off thereafter), even his "lucky" cavalry hat. In honor of her late husband Michael, Gretchen Wayne donated the collection for USC students and the public to enjoy.

"I don't believe in shrinking from anything"

When the USC semester ended in June 1927, Duke Morrison went back to work on the Fox lot and moved into the room above the garage of his Glendale High schoolmate, Pexy Eckles, at 328 North Orange Avenue. They had used the rooms as their "fraternity house." Duke and Pexy stayed in contact over the years; Pexy became an oil company executive in San Francisco. Whenever Wayne got up there (he usually stayed at the **St. Francis Hotel**, 335 Powell Street), Pexy joined him for a few drinks.

When Wayne was finally able to marry his sweetheart Josephine Saenz in 1933 in the garden of Loretta Young's Bel Air home, the whole USC football team acted as ushers. The wedding reception was held at the elegant Miramar Hotel in Santa Monica, now **Fairmont Miramar Hotel & Bungalows**, 101 Wilshire Boulevard.

After the marriage, the newlyweds settled into a fashionable but modestly furnished three-room garden apartment rental at **Hancock Park**, close enough to the Poverty Row studios. When their first child Michael was born in 1934, they were living at 8402 West Fourth Street. Sometimes Josie would accompany him on location. The out-of-the-way locations were not much fun for his wife. She stayed in dingy hotels while Wayne worked from dawn to dusk. One photo which got reprinted a lot shows the young couple relaxing at the then fairly new **El Mirador** in Palm Springs in January 1934, sharing the veranda with Spencer Tracy (who had a fling with Loretta Young, Josie's friend). The former Palm Springs glamour spot lives on as Desert Regional Medical Center.

"I watched you with that baby"

Their daughter Mary Antonia "Toni" Wayne was born February 25, 1936, in St. Vincent's Hospital, 2131 West 3rd

His oldest son Michael had preserved John Wayne's most personal items such as this director's chair, a gift from his mentor John Ford. After Michael Wayne's death, his widow Gretchen Wayne donated the collection to USC (courtesy USC School of Cinematic Arts).

Street, 20 minutes from the Wayne home. The young family then moved into a new home. By that time, Wayne had made enough money to buy a two-story Spanish-style mansion at 312 North Highland Avenue. As actor friend Paul Fix recalled, it was a beautiful home because Josie "had been a woman of good taste and character."[21] When they divorced on November 25, 1944, Josie got the house and everything in it.

After moving out at his home, Wayne lived for a while at Paul Fix's house. For two years, Wayne and his future wife Chata had trysts in Yuma, Arizona, and Mexico City. During the making of *In Old Oklahoma*, they slept on Fix's pullout sofa bed. In May 1943, he finally separated from Josie and shacked up with Chata in a penthouse apartment at the **Château Marmont** (see Chapter 2). When Fix was caught himself in a stormy affair with Ella Raines during the filming of *Tall in the Saddle*, his wife quickly ejected him from the premises—along with his friend Wayne and his darling Chata.

"A man deserves a second chance but keep an eye on him"

Three weeks after the divorce from Josie became final, on January 18, 1946, Wayne married Chata at his mother Molly's **Unity Presbyterian Church** in Long Beach, now a historic landmark on 600 East 5th Street. Ward Bond was best man and Olive Carey matron of honor. After the wedding, his mother Molly hosted a reception at the **California Country Club**. By this time, his mother had made a new home with her second husband in Long Beach.

After a brief honeymoon in Hawaii, Wayne and Chata returned to 4735 Tyrone Street in **Van Nuys.** He had been living there for more than a year: a one-floor bungalow, under 2000 square feet and modest by all Hollywood standards, but just a short way from his home studio Republic. The house was set back off the street, giving it a sense of privacy. When Chata's mother moved in with them, Chata nagged, "Why don't you buy me a bigger house?"[22]

They lived in the Van Nuys house until 1948. Because of Wayne's association with RKO, he was able to ask Howard Hughes for a loan so he could purchase a five-acre **Encino** estate with a 22-room farmhouse. (RKO got two percent interest. The loan was deducted monthly from his salary.) Chata wanted the house badly. When they took a second look, the For Sale signs had been taken down. "We should have bought it," she furiously insisted. Wayne finally said, "We did."[23]

The two-story home on a small hill at 4750 Louise Avenue came with a swimming pool, a guest house–cabana, a private orchard with pomegranates and oranges, and a butler named Scotty. Clark Gable was their neighbor. Wayne's

Attending the premiere of *Sands of Iwo Jima* with second wife Esperanza Baur Diaz, nicknamed Chata. She had appeared in a small number of Spanish language films (courtesy Camp Pendleton History and Museum Division).

best buddies, Yakima Canutt and Ward Bond, also lived close by.

"I'm the stuff men are made of"

After the marriage to Chata failed, Wayne moved out and rented a small house at 4031 Longridge Avenue in **Sherman Oaks**. He once quipped that the marriage license with Chata "is one autograph I wish I hadn't signed!"[24]

When Pilar came to Los Angeles to visit him, Chata had possession of the Encino estate. He moved back in after the divorce was final and took Pilar with him, assuring her, "I'll buy you anything you want if you don't like it after you've seen it."[25]

Pilar took great pride in redecorating it, replacing everything Chata had put in it. She opted for an Early American motif. She was more than pleased with the master bedroom, once described by *Photoplay* magazine: "It had been really modernized: the bed featured armrests on the sides which could be raised or lowered; a cigarette compartment for him; a pulldown book rack; a control panel for television, radio, several telephone lines—by just flicking a switch you could turn on the lights downstairs or even open the

front gate; a slide-out backgammon tray fitted into the headboard."[26]

Today, the estate still has the long macadam driveway that stretches from the front door to the electric gate at the foot of the hill. "And the street beyond the gate curves like a scythe around the land," Pilar once wrote for a magazine. "When I hear his car, I enjoy seeing him go through the comic antics it takes to get a man as big as him out of a modern car."[27]

The script *of The Searchers* listed the addresses of all personnel. In Wayne's case, however, it did not list the Encino address. They had him down at 1022 Palm Avenue, Los Angeles, and gave the phone of his secretary Miss St. John: CR-5 6178. His son Patrick was listed under the same address.

"Lay some dirt on those loose fires"

Pilar did not join Wayne on location in Japan for *The Barbarian and the Geisha*, so he was not home when, some time before dawn on January 14, 1958, she was awakened by the family dachshund, Blackie. The house was on fire. "A rush of adrenaline had propelled me into Aissa's room and then

He had made it to the top: When John Wayne became a box-office-champion, he bought the wooded Encino estate; pictured here at his barbecue place (author's collection).

My home is my castle: John Wayne strikes a relaxed pose for the photographer in 1950. The mustache was for *Rio Grande* (author's collection).

His "lucky hat" had survived the Encino fire but after he had lent it to friend Sammy Davis, Jr., for his Rat Pack movie, John Wayne had to retire his favorite headgear. The Wayne family donated it to USC (author's collection).

out of the house." The only item she grabbed before escaping was Wayne's old cavalry hat. The fire destroyed much of the second floor. She called her husband in Japan, asking, "How do you like one-story houses?"[28]

The hat Pilar saved was later borrowed by Sammy Davis, Jr., for his role in *Sergeants Three*, made in Kanab. "Any success I may have in the picture," Davis wrote in his letter of gratitude, "will be mainly due to your generosity."[29] After the Rat Pack got through with pulling the hat down over Davis' ears, Wayne had to retire his "lucky hat." It made its final guest appearance in *The Man Who Shot Liberty Valance*: The undertaker holds it in his hand as he is about to bury Tom Doniphon with it.

Wayne used the fire as an excuse to do some home

remodeling, and he installed a screening room. He had some oversized furniture, special-made. One night, Ford and Wayne were watching a movie, and Ford was smoking his usual cigar, his ashtray on the brand-new couch. When the picture was over, Ford had burned a huge hole in the middle of the sofa. He looked at Wayne and he mumbled, "We're even." Wayne knew immediately what he meant: Years in the past, Ford had bought a new shore boat with red leather–upholstered seats. Wayne flicked his ashes off the side of the boat, but still managed to set the backseat on fire. Ford never said a word about it…until the night in Wayne's projection room.[30]

Wayne buried his beloved Blackie on the grounds of the Encino estate with his own hands. He had wrapped him in a vicuna blanket that the dachshund loved. The house is still there today. The ten-foot-high brick wall with an electrically operated gate was erected by its most famous habitant.

In the November 2008 issue of *Architectural Digest*, Aissa wrote about those "tall block walls that kept us safe and apart from the world outside." Even though

The former John Wayne Estate today. The famous habitant had built the brick wall around the grounds and the electrically operated gate (author's collection).

the subsequent owners remodeled, the Encino home gives the spectator a good idea of how Wayne liked to spend his money once he became a box office champion.

"Milk for the infant and a tall beer for me"

The address 501 South Buena Vista Street in Burbank became an important one for the Wayne family. The Waynes chose the **Providence Saint Joseph Medical Center** (now between the Walt Disney Studios and Johnny Carson Park) for Aissa's birth, on March 31, 1956. "I could drive there in my sleep," Wayne had assured Pilar. Friends had suggested they should make the trip just once, but he had scoffed at the idea because St. Joseph's was just down the street from Warner Brothers. However, when his wife's water broke, Wayne seemed to fall apart. He struggled to dial the phone with shaking hands, then drove his wife to the hospital. "Duke wasn't a very good driver, but he certainly was a fast one," Pilar stated. The soon-to-be father got lost. He found the hospital by accident. Fortunately, Aissa was 11 hours late. On October 7, 1958, having just finished *Rio Bravo*, Wayne became a grandfather when Toni gave birth to a daughter at St. Joseph's. John-Ethan was born there, too, on February 22, 1962, when Wayne had just come back from France after appearing in *The Longest Day*. Exactly four years later, Marisa made her entrance. Even though the Waynes were by that time living in Newport, they still chose St. Joseph's as a birthplace. Wayne's brother Robert Morrison, 58, died on July 25, 1970, at the same hospital. In 2003, Michael Wayne, 68, died of heart failure at St. Joseph Medical Center.

"Life's been good to me, and I want some more of it"

After his cancer operation, Wayne found the house interior too dark, he felt isolated by the spacious grounds, and the smog in Encino was making him cough. "The Valley's had it," he said. On January 3, 1965, a burglar jumped the fence in Encino. Wayne chased him outside with the loaded .45-caliber revolver he kept on the headboard above his bed. After that, he decided to leave Los Angeles. Walt Disney's daughter purchased the estate and the Waynes moved down the coast to Newport Beach where the sea air would help him.[31] When they moved to Orange County, it was about to become the fastest-growing region in the United States.

Newport wasn't new to him, however. He had met Josie at the old **Balboa Inn** and went to dances at the Rendezvous Ballroom in Balboa. It was destroyed by fire in 1966 (look for the historic landmark on Newport Balboa Bike Trail). As a young man, he went bodysurfing at "The Wedge," a spot known for its powerful and unpredictable waves, off Balboa Peninsula. He injured his left shoulder there, making it impossible to continue with the Trojans. That incident cost him his football scholarship. He asked John Ford what to do next. His mentor told him to come back to the studio and "work for me next summer."[32]

"Sure I wave the American flag"

Now he was back in Balboa, 40 years later. The French provincial house found by Pilar had 11 rooms, seven bathrooms and cost $175,000 in 1967. Behind the seven-foot fence lay lovely gardens and a kidney-shaped swimming pool. The walls of his den were covered with bookshelves, rifle cases, plaques, citations and movie souvenirs (he made it a point that the den should look the same as the one in Encino). A large bronze American eagle topped the fireplace. Among the souvenirs was a rare piece of the first American barbed wire and a chunk of the wooden deck of the battleship *Arizona*. His monologue for *No Substitute for Victory*, a documentary about the Vietnam War, was shot in his trophy-filled den, in front of his "50 years of hard work" wall. Wayne made sure his Academy Award was in the shot.

As in Encino, Wayne had projection equipment installed. The screen slid electrically up into the ceiling of his den. Pilar told his biographer Tomkies, "We have a library of

Socializing with the Newport crowd: John Wayne is having a drink with unidentified friends at a place called the Balboa Warehouse (author's collection).

all Duke's films and he often laughs at himself in some of them."[33]

When Wayne was walking Peter Bogdanovich back to his car in 1967 (the young director was preparing a John Ford documentary for the American Film Institute), they took a shortcut through Wayne's sizable garage. Bogdanovich was greeted by a virtual sea of 35mm motion picture canisters—large metal cases to hold the 2000-foot reels of film. "Suddenly, here before me, were original prints of an awful lot of vintage Wayne movies, mostly brand new-looking cases, boldly marked, *Red River, Sands of Iwo Jima* and so on." A heady moment for the movie buff. "Jesus Christ, Duke, do you have 35mm prints of all your pictures?!" Wayne answered, "Just about." It had been part of his regular deal for a long time. "The studio's gotta give me a print off the original negative." Knowing that the *Stagecoach* negative had been lost, Bogdanovich was excited about the print being in reach. Wayne believed it had never been run. Golden news for film lovers because this mint copy was used to create a new negative at the AFI. According to Bogdanovich, Wayne was enthusiastic about it—especially the tax break it would bring him![34]

When the Waynes entertained guests, Pilar would call the studios about new releases, and they'd send over the 35mm film and a projectionist. Oftentimes, the Waynes didn't know beforehand what the movie was about. This led to an embarrassing moment when they showed *Rosemary's Baby* with Mia Farrow. (Farrow was supposed to appear as Mattie in Wayne's upcoming *True Grit*.) During the rape scene, Pilar reached the point where she couldn't stand it

John Wayne and TV personality Monty Hall in the garden of his Newport Beach home overlooking the harbor where the *Wild Goose* is anchored. They met to discuss "An All-Star Tribute to John Wayne." The entertainment aired on November 26, 1976, and benefited Variety Clubs International, a show business charity organization (author's collection).

any longer and ordered the showing stopped: "Get it out of here!"[35]

"Hello the house!"

Director Don Siegel described the Wayne house as being "on a peninsula surrounded by the Newport Bay. It had large, beautiful rooms, simply furnished in excellent, masculine taste. He even had a large gun room."[36] Wayne had his own ideas of what guns the shootist, J.B. Books, should use. According to Siegel, a large closet was filled with revolver holsters, stirrups and "God knows what else." Wayne revealed a derringer in the drawer of his desk. "Betcha you never figured I'd use a derringer." Wayne acted out the first scene for Siegel, how he shoots the robber "with this little sweetheart." When Siegel told him he was glad that he didn't want to wear two revolvers, one on each hip, Wayne declined, "That two-gun shit went out with William S. Hart."[37]

The house was in a gated community but still everyone wanted a John Wayne souvenir. Pat Stacy tried to keep potted plants at the end of the dock, but they were always taken. The plants in front of the house would also disappear. Even the mailbox vanished.

Wayne told *Architectural Digest* in 1977, "I find things that appeal to me and I try to blend them in here. I don't give a damn if anyone else likes them or not." When he burst in the front door, he'd always holler, "Hello the house!" and, as it was still vivid in Aissa's memory, "The air in our house crackled with his energy."[38]

When driving around Newport Beach, Wayne's car was easy to spot: his custom-made 1972 Pontiac station wagon had a distinctive bubble top. They raised the roof so that he could wear his Stetson while driving. Donated by the Wayne family to the Birthplace Museum in Winterset (Carol Bassett/The John Wayne Birthplace).

"Wild goose, flying in the night sky"

One of Wayne's main reasons to move to Newport was the 136-foot converted U.S. Navy minesweeper he had purchased in 1962. The Navy had commissioned the YMS 382 during the war and then sold it in 1948. The *Wild Goose* was Wayne's pride and joy. His private yacht was an entertainment center as well as home-away-from-home. He owned boats before. His first was the speedboat *Apache*. During the '30s, he sailed a boat named *Venus*. The slightly larger *Isthmus* came next. Wayne was fishing on board the *Isthmus*, anchored at Long Beach, when Ford's daughter came aboard. She asked him to come to see Ford after he had not spoken to him for years. Ford was now planning to put him in *Stagecoach*.

Wayne's next boat was the 76-foot *Nor'wester*. He had a favorite expression engraved on a plaque that he kept on board: "Each of us is a mixture of some good and some not so good qualities. In considering one fellow man, it's important to remember the good things and to realize his faults only prove he's a human being. We should refrain from making judgments—just because a fella' happens to be a dirty, rotten son-of-a-bitch."[39]

The *Nor'wester* was restored as a museum, anchored in **La Conner**, Washington. It showcased some items from Wayne movies. Unfortunately, on April 17, 2021, the historic yacht sank in Washington's San Juan Island after it struck submerged rocks near Stuart Island. Wayne first set foot on the *Wild Goose* in Seattle, where one of his friends had anchored it. He bought the boat for $116,000 and spent more than $1 million remodeling it to his taste. He also had all the ceilings lifted to accommodate his 6'4" frame. Berth 54 at the Lido Yacht Anchorage in **Newport Harbor** was home to the *Wild Goose*.

A short time before Wayne died, he sold his beloved boat to an attorney for $750,000. The new owner tried to sell it in the early '80s. The *Goose* spent much of that decade rotting away. Some enthusiasts found the boat in a Long Beach graveyard and decided to save it. It is now back in Newport Harbor, owned by the Hornblower Cruise Company and ready for cruises.

"Now get your divorce"

Pilar and her husband were frequent guests at the Newport tennis club, originally called the **John Wayne Tennis Club**, at 1171 Jamboree Road. It opened in 1974 and had 16 tennis courts. "I tried Duke to play but he never cared much for the game," Pilar noted.[40] Although he never took up tennis, he had backed the building of the tennis club, and he maintained an interest in it until his death. Wayne also had a business on Jamboree Road: His Deco Industries was based there.

One of Wayne's favorite hangouts was the **Big Canyon Country Club** on Big Canyon Drive. He used to go there to play backgammon or cards. At the club's groundbreaking, he turned over the first shovel of dirt. He socialized on Balboa

The skipper of the *Nor'wester,* in the mid–50s: During the short time the yacht served as a floating museum, the tour guide used to tell the story that Wayne had to buy it from his manager after damaging the 76-foot long yacht (author's collection).

The *Wild Goose* is back in Newport Harbor. Cruises including informal tours of the family's staterooms are offered. Wayne's former captain, Bert Minshall, made guest appearances (photograph by Roland Schaefli).

Island, the harborside community in Newport Beach, in a bar then called the Balboa Island Warehouse. He was also a longtime member of **the Balboa Bay Club**, 1221 West Coast Highway. The joint favored the Mexican tequila, which he called a "Who Hit John." The Yacht Club bar is now called Duke's Place. Fellow club member Joey Bishop relished telling the joke that Wayne had a Japanese gardener but no garden. "He just wanted him to come in and surrender three times a day."[41]

Wayne had acceded to the State Department's wish to meet Prince Hussein of Jordan. The Wine Cellar at the **Newporter Inn** was the place of this July 24, 1978, get-together. Another one of his favorites was a 1920s gas station converted to a steak house close to the harbor. It's now known as the **A Restaurant**, 334 West Coast Highway.

After the separation, Pilar moved into a home in Newport Beach's exclusive Big Canyon area, 14 Rue Grand Ducal. She also rented a studio inside the **Fernleaf Courtyard** in Corona Del Mar. The place was so charming that she could entertain her clients outdoors with coffee and finger sandwiches. One year later, she found herself with a full-time, elegant restaurant: She operated the Fernleaf Café for five years. Donna Reed became a regular customer. She wrote in her cookbook *Pilar Wayne's Favorite and Fabulous Recipes* (dedicated to Wayne) that he visited her occasionally and was proud of her undertaking. "Duke's Souffle" was on the menu but Wayne would always ask, "Is there any chocolate mousse left?"[42]

By 2007, his 100th birthday, most of his fingerprints had been wiped away from Newport Beach. The tennis club

After his operation at Massachusetts General Hospital John Wayne waves good-bye on Boston's Logan Airport before his flight home. He appeared in the best spirits (author's collection).

Wayne built: renamed. The affiliated Duke's team: now called the Breakers. Orange County Airport remains **John Wayne Airport**—although people recently toyed with the idea of rechristening it. His home at 2686 Bayshore Drive was sold in March 1980 for $3.48 million; it was torn down in 2002.

"What's the matter, medicine man?"

In 1964, Pilar urged him to get a checkup at Scripps, the famous clinic in **La Jolla**, at 9888 Genesee Avenue in San Diego. (Chata had been a Scripps patient with her skin problems.) "I was X-rayed at Scripps," he later told the press, "and they found a lump in my lung as big as my fist."[43] He underwent surgery for removal of a cancerous lung at **Los Angeles Good Samaritan Hospital**, 1225 Wilshire Boulevard. He was taken into surgery on September 17, 1964. When he was discharged on October 8, he had a 20-inch scar running from his left armpit down over his chest and he was told to rest for six months. On December 29, 1964, he informed the press that he had licked the Big C.

When he had to go back to La Jolla for his check-up in April 1965, he told Mary St. John that he was going there "to see if the Red Witch is waiting for me." When he returned, he said, "Well, the bitch wasn't there this time."[44] In the years to come, the cancer team looked him over on a regular basis.

"When the road looks rough ahead…"

On March 30, 1978, he checked into Boston's famed **Massachusetts General Hospital** for tests. His room was in Phillips House 8, the best accommodations available at Massachusetts General at 55 Fruit Street. (Henry Kissinger would later stay there as well.) On April 4, doctors operated to replace the mitral valve in his heart. The night before, he had gathered with his family in an exclusive restaurant called **Mason Robert,** which had been built inside the old city hall. When Wayne walked in and saw the stained glass window and the table set for 13, he joked, "'Tis the Last Supper!"[45]

In a three-hour open-heart operation, a valve in his heart was replaced with a valve from a pig. Wayne recovered faster than his doctors had expected. One physician noted, "We've seen him in plenty of movies, but I don't think many of us appreciated just how big and strong he is."[46]

After the operation, he could persuade the staff to bend their rules and let him have a dinner party with his children in his room. **Anthony's Pier 4 Restaurant** catered the steak-and-lobster fest. Before he flew out of Boston's Logan Airport, he told newspaper reporters that his next movie would be *Beau John*.

Wayne returned to Newport Beach on April 27 to

recuperate. Upon his arrival, an armada of small ships paraded by his house. His first major social outing after the heart operation was a concert by Frank Sinatra at the Universal Amphitheater on July 31, 1978. (The theater within Universal City was demolished in 2013 for the Harry Potter attraction.) When Sinatra came onstage, he looked down at Wayne and said, "Hi, Big Guy."[47]

"I know the Man upstairs will pull the plug when He wants to"

Wayne filed his last will on October 5, 1978. He gave to Michael all shares of Batjac stock and set up trusts for all his children. The sum of $10,000 went to Mary St. John and $30,000 "to my secretary, Pat Stacy."

On January 10, 1979, Wayne was admitted to the **UCLA Medical Center** on Westwood Plaza in Los Angeles. He was in Suite 948, on the ninth floor of the Wilson Pavilion. In his last TV interview just days before, he had told Barbara Walters: "They're opening me up for gall bladder, but who knows what they'll find." The UCLA Medical Center has a reputation as a medical court of last resort, a complex of specialist who deal with the gravest cases. On January 13, they operated nine hours on him. During the removal of the gall bladder, an unusual type of low-grade malignant tumor of the stomach was discovered. After three days in the eleventh floor intensive care unit, he was moved into Room 951, which looked more like a cheerful hotel suite than a hospital facility.

Escorting Pat Stacy to Frank Sinatra's opening night at the Universal Amphitheater on July 31, 1978, followed by supper at The Trader's. He picked out the fur coat for her (author's collection).

A USC fan to the end, Wayne would walk up and down the halls with his USC cap on, visiting everybody. The staff gave him some trouble about that particular cap and gave him an honorary UCLA cap. In an interview for Tim Lilley's *John Wayne Newsletter*, Aissa said that from then on, her father would go "Hi, hi, hi," then he'd tip his hat to flash his USC cap underneath.[48]

Burt Kennedy recalled that right to the end, Wayne never lost his great sense of humor. Kennedy went to see him when Wayne was down to about a hundred pounds. He brought an old friend, Al Murphy, who had worked for Batjac for years as a second assistant director. His name was really Al Silverstein, but Wayne had rechristened him Al Murphy. Kennedy and Murphy were waiting as a lot of dignitaries, including Richard Nixon, visited. When Michael Wayne finally led them in, he joked, "The reason Wayne didn't want to see you was because Al Murphy is a Jew." Wayne smiled and pointed up at the ceiling and he said, "It's the *other* Jew I don't want to see."[49]

On Sunday, February 11, 29 days after his operation, Wayne went home one last time. On May 1, he was back in Suite 948 in the Wilson Pavilion for one last operation. When Mary St. John came to say her goodbyes, he said, "Well, Mary, I guess the Red Witch finally got me."[50] John Wayne died on June 11, 1979.

The family lowered the flag outside Duke's patio to half-mast. Then the Los Angeles Country Board of Supervisors ordered the flags on all county buildings flown at half-mast. The Olympic torch atop the Los Angeles Coliseum was lighted to burn until after the funeral. (Wayne had once been the grand marshal for Gene Autry's Rodeo in the L.A. Coliseum.) For the burial, Pat Stacy chose a new black suit he had ordered at the same time he had his tuxedo made for the Academy Awards. Sy Devore's shop on 12930 Ventura Boulevard provided the tuxedo and had done the fittings at the Batjac office. The O'Connor Laguna Hills Mortuary charged $15,955.97 for funeral expenses.

"Summer's over"

The June 15, 1979, funeral was at **Our Lady Queen of Angels Parish**, 2100 Mar Vista Drive, a modern church in the Newport Beach area. Wayne was buried at dawn on June 15, 1979, ten minutes from the church. His seven children, Pilar and only a few friends were in attendance at **Pacific View Memorial Park**, 3500 Pacific View Drive, Corona Del Mar. His oldest son Michael had made all funeral arrangements. Pilar had mentioned to him that Wayne often said, "When I pass away, I would like to be cremated. Then I want all my friends to come to the house and have an Irish type of wake. Let everybody have fun and talk about the good times."

In earlier years, he had mentioned that he would like a funeral service in Ford's Chapel, the one that Ward Bond and so many other friends used. Perhaps he had changed his mind in his final days. Pat Stacy wrote that he had

John Wayne's final resting place: Pacific View Memorial Park on the Bayview Terrace (photograph by Roland Schaefli).

occasionally expressed his preference for cremation to her, with his ashes strewn from the *Wild Goose* off Catalina. But he always added, "The kids would be horrified," so his last will did not contain such a request.[51]

The family feared grave robbers; therefore, no tombstone indicates the spot where he rests. A second, fresh grave had been dug nearby and flowers placed there, to mislead any vandals. Fans were asked to place flowers at the foot of the flagpole by the entrance.

According to Pat Stacy, Wayne had decided—during the Pacific View funeral of his long-time friend Andy Devine—that he too wanted to be buried there. His view is toward Catalina Island.

The plot remained unmarked until 1999. Then, 20 years after his death, a headstone was finally placed at the site. It shows a lone rider, coming out of Monument Valley, arriving at some sort of church. On the bronze plaque is his memorable quote, "Tomorrow is the most important thing in life. Comes to us at midnight very clean. It's perfect when it arrives and puts itself in our hands. It hopes we've learned something from yesterday." Davy Crockett would probably have said, "Now, that ain't a bad stab at putting it into words."

Chapter Notes

Introduction

1. Joseph McBride, *Searching for John Ford* (New York: St. Martin's Press, 2001), 50.
2. Jack Cardiff, *Magic Hour: A Life in Movies* (Tulsa, OK: Gardners Books 1997), 116.
3. The American Film Institute, *Film Makers on Film Making* (Los Angeles: J.P. Tarcher, 1983), 23.
4. Burt Kennedy, *Hollywood Trail Boss* (Brooklyn, NY: Boulevard Books, 1997), 19.
5. Charles John Kieskalt, *The Official John Wayne Reference Book* (New York: Citadel Press, 1985), 181.
6. *Chicago Tribune*, May 11, 1947.
7. Marc Mompoint, *John Wayne: A Photographic Celebration* (New York: Skyhorse Publishing, 2014), 77.
8. Marc Mompoint, *John Wayne: A Photographic Celebration* (New York: Skyhorse Publishing, 2014), 294.
9. Lisa Langseth, "Profile: Pilar Wayne: At Home with the Duchess," *Orange Coast Magazine*, September 1984, 166–167.
10. Marc Mompoint, *John Wayne: A Photographic Celebration* (New York: Skyhorse Publishing, 2014), 141.
11. Gaylyn Studlar and Matthew Bernstein, *John Ford Made Westerns* (Bloomington: Indiana University Press, 2001), 275.
12. Pat Stacy, *Duke: A Love Story* (New York: Simon & Schuster Pocket Books, 1983), 166.
13. Public Broadcasting Service (PBS), *John Wayne, Standing Tall*, Documentary 1989.
14. Tim Lilley, *The Big Trail: A Newsletter on the Films of John Wayne* (Big Trail Publishing, 1984–1999).
15. *El Dorado* press book, Paramount, 1967.
16. Billy Liebhert and John Mitchum, *John Wayne—America, Why I Love Her* (New York: Simon and Schuster, 1977).
17. *Life Magazine*, January 28, 1972.

Chapter 1

1. Film premiere program booklet, Fox, 1930.
2. Don Siegel, *A Siegel Film* (London: Faber & Faber, 1993), 34.
3. Raoul Walsh, *Each Man in His Time* (New York: Farrar, Straus and Giroux, 1974), 239.
4. Raoul Walsh, *Each Man in His Time* (New York: Farrar, Straus and Giroux, 1974), 240.
5. Tony Mackling and Nick Pici, *Voices from the Set* (Lanham, MD: Scarecrow Press, 2000), 132.
6. Raoul Walsh, *Each Man in His Time* (New York: Farrar, Straus and Giroux, 1974), 242.
7. Sam Sherman, *Lone Pine in the Movies* (Lone Pine, CA: Museum of Western Film History, 2007).
8. Tim Lilley, *The Trail Beyond, Volume VII* (Big Trail Publishing, 2005).
9. Norm Goldstein, *John Wayne—A Tribute* (New York: Holt, Rinehart and Winston, 1979), 17.
10. Maurice Zolotow, *Shooting Star* (New York: Simon and Schuster, 1974), 81.
11. Maurice Zolotow, *Shooting Star* (New York: Simon and Schuster, 1974), 96.
12. Tim Lilley, *The Big Trail: A Newsletter on the Films of John Wayne* (Big Trail Publishing, 1984–1999).
13. Raoul Walsh, *Each Man in His Time* (New York: Farrar, Straus and Giroux, 1974), 241.
14. Brian Huberman, *John Wayne's The Alamo*, documentary, MGM, 1992.
15. Raoul Walsh, *Each Man in His Time* (New York: Farrar, Straus and Giroux, 1974), 248.
16. Kevin Brownlow, *The War, The West and The Wilderness* (New York: Knopf, 1979).
17. Raoul Walsh, *Each Man in His Time* (New York: Farrar, Straus and Giroux, 1974), 244.
18. Richard Schickel, *The Men Who Made the Movies* (Chicago: Ivan. R. Dee, 1975), 38.
19. Michael Goldman, *John Wayne: The Genuine Article* (San Rafael, CA: Insight Editions, 2013), 38.
20. Raoul Walsh, *Each Man in His Time* (New York: Farrar, Straus and Giroux, 1974), 247.
21. George Carpozi, Jr., *The John Wayne Story* (New York: Dell Publishing, 1979), 50.
22. Michael Munn, *John Wayne: The Man Behind the Myth* (New York: New American Library, 2003), 29.

Chapter 2

1. Brian Huberman, *John Wayne's The Alamo*, documentary, MGM Home Video, 1992.
2. *Life Magazine*, January 28, 1972.
3. Tag Gallagher, *John Ford—The Mand and His Films* (Berkeley: University of California Press, 1986), 242.
4. Mario DeMarco, *John Wayne—The All-American Hero* (Self Published, 1986), 65.
5. Dan Ford, *Pappy—The Life of John Ford* (Englewood Cliffs, 1979, New York: First Da Capo Press Edition, 1998), 113.
6. Maureen O'Hara TV interview, News 4, New England, 1996.
7. Maurice Zolotow, *Shooting Star* (New York: Simon and Schuster, 1974), 176.
8. E Go Collectors: *John Wayne* (Series 4, September 1976), 16.
9. Herb Fagan, *Duke, We're Glad We Knew You* (Secaucus, NJ: Carol Publishing Group, 1997), 97.
10. Aissa Wayne, *John Wayne: My Father* (London: Robert Hale, 1992), 111.
11. Marc Eliot, *American Titan: Searching for John Wayne* (New York: HarperCollins, 2014), 219.
12. Maureen O'Hara, *Tis Herself* (New York: Simon & Schuster, 2004), 286.
13. *Today Magazine*, October 29, 1969.
14. Scott Eyman, *Hank & Jim* (New York: Simon & Schuster, 2017), 70.
15. Michael Caine, *Acting in Film* (Lanham, MD: Applause Theatre & Cinema Books, 1990), 71.

16. *The Shootist*, cast and crew members interviews, Paramount Pictures DVD.

17. Mario DeMarco, *John Wayne—The All-American Hero* (Self Published, 1986), 65.

18. Burt Kennedy, *Hollywood Trail Boss* (Brooklyn, NY: Boulevard Books, 1997), 16.

19. Maurice Zolotow, *Shooting Star* (New York: Simon and Schuster, 1974), 127.

20. John Mitchum, *Them Ornery Mitchum Boys* (Pacifica, CA: Creatures at Large Press, 1989), 252.

21. Tim Lilley, *The Big Trail: A Newsletter on the Films of John Wayne* (Big Trail Publishing, 1984–1999).

22. Tim Lilley, *The Big Trail: A Newsletter on the Films of John Wayne* (Big Trail Publishing, 1984–1999).

23. Peter Bogdanovich, *Who the Hell's in It* (New York: Knopf, 2004), 281.

24. Scott Allen Nollen, *Three Bad Men* (Jefferson, NC: McFarland, 2013), 315.

25. Tim Lilley, *Campfire's Glow* (Big Trail Publishing, 1995), 152.

26. Rob Word, *Word on Westerns*, interview with Michael Blake (https://www.youtube.com/watch?v=OXYAjiYgdhs.

27. Hans C. Blumenberg, *Die Kamera in Augenhöhe—Begegnungen mit Howard Hawks* (Cologne, Germany: DuMont Buchverlag Köln, 1979), 91.

28. John Farkis, *Not Thinkin'… Just Rememberin'* (Albany, GA: BearManor Media, 2015), 797.

29. Marc Eliot, *American Titan: Searching for John Wayne* (New York: Harper Collins, 2014), 180.

30. Pat Stacy, *Duke: A Love Story* (New York: Simon & Schuster Pocket Books, 1983), 15.

31. Tony Thomas, *The West That Never Was* (New York: Citatel Press, 1989), 255.

32. Pilar Wayne, *John Wayne—My Life with the Duke* (New York: McGraw-Hill, 1987), 270.

Chapter 3

1. Editors of the official John Wayne Magazine, *Fighting for Freedom* (New York: Media Lab Books, 2016), 203.

2. Michael Munn, *John Wayne: The Man Behind the Myth* (New York: New American Library, 2003), 42.

3. Tim Lilley, *A Newsletter on the Films of John Wayne* (Big Trail Publishing, 1984–1999).

4. Tim Lilley, *Campfire Conversations* (Big Trail Publishing, 1992), 38.

5. Michael Munn, *John Wayne: The Man Behind the Myth* (New York: New American Library, 2003), 178.

6. SCV History: https://scvhistory.com/scvhistory/blancher0201.htm.

7. Yakima Canutt, *Stuntman* (Norman: University of Oklahoma Press, 1979), 92.

8. Sam Sherman, *Lone Pine in the Movies* (Lone Pine, CA: Museum Western Film History, 2007).

9. Yakima Canutt, *Stuntman* (Norman: University of Oklahoma Press, 1979), 90.

10. Sam Sherman, *Lone Pine in the Movies* (Lone Pine, CA: Museum of Western Film History, 2007), 19.

11. Yakima Canutt, *Stuntman* (Norman: University of Oklahoma Press, 1979), 108.

12. Yakima Canutt, *Stuntman* (Norman: University of Oklahoma Press, 1979), 108.

13. Tim Lilley, *Campfires Rekindled* (Big Trail Publishing, 1994), 147.

14. Randy Roberts and James S. Olson, *John Wayne: American* (New York: The Free Press, 1995), 159.

15. Herb Fagan, *Duke, We're Glad We Knew You* (Secaucus, NJ: Carol Publishing Group, 1997), 24.

16. Herb Fagan, *Duke, We're Glad We Knew You* (Secaucus, NJ: Carol Publishing Group, 1997), 24.

17. Tim Lilley, *The Trail Beyond, Volume VII* (Big Trail Publishing, 2005), 66.

18. Edward Dmytryk, *It's a Hell of a Life but Not a Bad Living* (New York: Time Books, 1978), 66.

19. Tim Lilley, *A Newsletter on the Films of John Wayne* (Big Trail Publishing, 1984–1999).

20. Scott Eyman, *John Wayne: The Life and Legend* (New York: Simon & Schuster, 2014), 87.

21. Tony Mackling and Nick Pici, *Voices from the Set* (Lanham, MD: Scarecrow Press, 2000), 127.

22. Dwayne Epstein, *Lee Marvin—Point Blank* (Tuscon, AZ: Schaffner Press, 2013), 101.

23. Dwayne Epstein, *Lee Marvin—Point Blank* (Tucson, AZ: Schaffner Press, 2013), 117.

24. Chris Enss and Howard Kazanjian, *Cowboy Creatures, and Classics—The Story of Republic Pictures* (Lanham, MD: Rowman & Littlefield, 2018), 46.

25. Scott Eyman, *John Wayne: The Life and Legend* (New York: Simon & Schuster, 2014), 233.

26. Michael Munn, *John Wayne: The Man Behind the Myth* (New York: New American Library, 2003), 76.

27. Scott Eyman, *John Wayne: The Life and Legend* (New York: Simon & Schuster, 2014), 113.

28. Tim Lilley, *The Trail Beyond, Volume VII* (Big Trail Publishing, 2005).

Chapter 4

1. Gerry McNee, *In the Footsteps of the Quiet Man* (Edinburgh, Scotland: Mainstream Publishing, 1990), 103.

2. Herb Fagan, *Duke, We're Glad We Knew You* (Secaucus, NJ: Carol Publishing Group, 1997), 106.

3. Maureen O'Hara, *Tis Herself* (New York: Simon & Schuster, 2004), 163.

4. Gerry McNee, *In the Footsteps of the Quiet Man* (Edinburgh, Scotland: Mainstream Publishing, 1990), 104.

5. Website for restoration project: http://ballyglunin.com/home-1/

6. Gerry McNee, *In the Footsteps of the Quiet Man* (Edinburgh, Scotland: Mainstream Publishing, 1990), 72.

7. Maureen O'Hara, *Tis Herself* (New York: Simon & Schuster, 2004), 164.

8. Gerry McNee, *In the Footsteps of the Quiet Man* (Edinburgh, Scotland: Mainstream Publishing, 1990), 103.

9. Peter Bogdanovich, *Who the Hell's in It* (New York: Knopf, 2004), 289.

10. Peter Bogdanovich, *Who the Hell's in It* (New York: Knopf, 2004), 294.

11. Gerry McNee, *In the Footsteps of the Quiet Man* (Edinburgh, Scotland: Mainstream Publishing, 1990), 83.

12. Maureen O'Hara, TV interview, News 4, New England, 1996.

13. Peter Bogdanovich, *Who the Hell's in It* (New York: Knopf, 2004), 289.

Chapter 5

1. Chuck Roberson, *The Fall Guy* (Surrey, British Columbia: Hancock House, 1980), 156.

2. Dan Ford, *Pappy—the Life of John Ford* (Englewood Cliffs, 1979, New York: First Da Capo Press Edition, 1998), 125.

3. Chuck Roberson, *The Fall Guy* (Surrey, British Columbia: Hancock House, 1980), 156.

4. *The Saturday Evening Post*, Memorial Issue, July/August 1979.

5. Tim Lilley, *Campfire Conversations* (Big Trail Publishing, 1992), 33.

6. *A Turning of the Earth: John Ford, John Wayne and the Searchers*, documentary, Warner Brothers, 1998.

7. George Stevens, Jr., *Conversations with the Great Moviemakers of Hollywood's Golden Age* (New York: Vintage, 2009), 243.

8. Samuel Moon, *Tall Sheep* (Norman: University of Oklahoma Press, 1992), 200.

9. Focus on Film, *Ford in Person*, Issue 6, 1971, 33.

10. Peter Cowie, *John Ford and the American West* (New York: Harry N. Abrams, 2004), 186.

11. John A. Murray *Cinema Southwest* (Santa Fe: Northland Publishing, 2000), 56.

12. Michael Munn, *John Wayne: The Man Behind the Myth* (New York: New American Library, 2003), 115.

13. Interview with the author in Monument Valley, 1992.

14. Tony Mackling and Nick Pici, *Voices From the Set* (Lanham, MD: Scarecrow Press, 2000), 128.

15. Joseph McBride and Michael Wilmington, *John Ford* (New York: Da Capo Press, 1975), 44.

16. Harry Carey, Jr., *Company of Heroes—My Life as an Actor in the John Ford Stock Company* (Lanham, MD: Scarecrow Press, 1994), 66.

17. Peter Bogdanovich, *Directed by John Ford* (Los Angeles: AFI American Film Institute, 1971).

18. Gaylyn Studlar and Matthew Bernstein, *John Ford Made Westerns* (Bloomington: Indiana University Press, 2001), 275.

19. Pilar Wayne, *John Wayne—My Life with the Duke* (New York: McGraw-Hill, 1987), 116.

20. Harry Carey, Jr., *Company of Heroes—My Life as an Actor in the John Ford Stock Company* (Lanham, MD: Scarecrow Press, 1994), 168.

21. *A Turning of the Earth: John Ford, John Wayne and the Searchers*, documentary, Warner Brothers, 1998.

22. Chuck Roberson, *The Fall Guy* (Surrey, British Columbia: Hancock House, 1980), 158.

23. Suzanne Finstad, *Natasha* (New York: Harmony Books, 2001), 171–172.

24. Harry Carey, Jr., *Company of Heroes—My Life as an Actor in the John Ford Stock Company* (Lanham, MD: Scarecrow Press, 1994), 170.

25. C. Courtney Joyner, *The Westerners* (Jefferson, NC: McFarland, 2009), 88.

26. *The American West of John Ford*, documentary, CBS TV, December 5, 1971.

27. Joseph McBride, *Searching for John Ford* (New York: St. Martin's Press, 2001), 686.

28. Pat Stacy, *Duke: A Love Story* (New York: Simon & Schuster Pocket Books, 1983), 111.

Chapter 6

1. Billy Liebert and John Mitchum, *John Wayne—America, Why I Love Her* (New York: Simon and Schuster, 1977), 138.

2. Lawrence H. Suid, *Guts & Glory* (Lexington: The University Press of Kentucky, 2002), 90.

3. Tim Lilley, *A Newsletter on the Films of John Wayne* (Big Trail Publishing, 1984–1999).

4. "John Wayne Spends Christmas in Brisbane," newspaper article, John Oxley Library.

5. Lou Sabini, *Behind the Scenes of They Were Expendable* (Jefferson, NC: McFarland, 2015), 30.

6. "John Ford on John Ford," *Films in Review*, Issue no. 6, 1964.

7. Lindsay Anderson, *About John Ford* (Medford, NJ: Plexus Publishing, 1981), 227.

8. Official Website, www.Johnwayne.com.

9. Randy Roberts and James S. Olson, *John Wayne: American* (New York: The Free Press, 1995), 272.

10. Dan Ford, *Pappy—The Life of John Ford* (Englewood Cliffs, 1979, New York: First Da Capo Press Edition, 1998), 200.

11. Peter Bogdanovich, *Who the Devil Made It?* (New York: Knopf, 1997), 140.

12. Lawrence H. Suid, *Guts & Glory* (Lexington: The University Press of Kentucky, 2002), 120.

13. *The Making of Sands of Iwo Jima*, short documentary, 1993, hosted by Leonard Maltin.

14. Lawrence H. Suid, *Guts & Glory* (Lexington: The University Press of Kentucky, 2002), 120.

15. *The Making of Sands of Iwo Jima*, short documentary, 1993, hosted by Leonard Maltin.

16. Tim Lilley, *Campfire Conversations* (Big Trail Publishing, 1992), 9.

17. Peter Bogdanovich, *Who the Devil Made It?* (New York: Knopf, 1997), 139.

18. Lawrence H. Suid, *Guts & Glory* (Lexington: The University Press of Kentucky, 2002), 121.

19. Randy Roberts James S. Olson, *John Wayne: American* (New York: The Free Press, 1995), 352.

20. Maurice Zolotow, *Shooting Star* (New York: Simon and Schuster, 1974), 276.

21. Michael Munn, *John Wayne: The Man Behind the Myth* (New York: New American Library, 2003), 131.

22. Herb Fagan, *Duke, We're Glad We Knew You* (Secaucus, NJ: Carol Publishing Group, 1997), 194.

23. John Mitchum, *Them Ornery Mitchum Boys* (Pacifica, CA: Creatures at Large Press, 1989), 135.

24. "A Candid Interview with John Wayne," *Playboy Magazine*, May 1971.

25. Chuck Roberson, *The Fall Guy* (Surrey, British Columbia: Hancock House, 1980), 179.

26. Tim Lilley, *Campfire's Glow* (Big Trail Publishing, 1995), 151.

27. Pilar Wayne, *John Wayne—My Life with the Duke* (New York: McGraw-Hill, 1987), 169.

28. John Boswell and Jay David, *Duke: The John Wayne Album* (New York: Ballantine Books, 1979), 102.

29. Scott Allen Nollen, *Three Bad Men* (Jefferson, NC: McFarland, 2013), 272.

30. "Remembering the Horse Soldiers," *True West Magazine*, January 19, 2017.

31. Lawrence H. Suid, *Guts & Glory* (Lexington: The University Press of Kentucky, 2002), 194.

32. Lawrence H. Suid, *Guts & Glory* (Lexington: The University Press of Kentucky, 2002), 248.

33. John Boswell and Jay David, *Duke: The John Wayne Album* (New York: Ballantine Books, 1979), 125.

34. Michael Munn, *John Wayne: The Man Behind the Myth* (New York: New American Library, 2003), 269.

35. Maurice Zolotow, *Shooting Star* (New York: Simon and Schuster, 1974), 365.

36. John Boswell and Jay David, *Duke: The John Wayne Album* (New York: Ballantine Books, 1979), 127.

37. Fr. Mike Ortiz, *Green Berets Chaplain* (Bloomington, IN: XLibris, 2013), 24.

38. Tim Lilley, *Campfires Rekindled* (Big Trail Publishing, 1994), 118.

39. Wikipedia, production of *The Green Berets*, https://en.wikipedia.org/wiki/The_Green_Berets_(film).

40. "Word on Westerns," Interview with Rob Word, https://www.youtube.com/watch?v=TRgeXKr3qE8.

41. Mike Tomkies, *Duke: The Story of John Wayne* (New York: Avon Books, 1971), 127.

42. *The Green Berets* press book, Warner Bros./Seven Arts, 1968.

43. Mike Tomkies, *Duke: The Story of John Wayne* (New York: Avon Books, 1971), 127.

44. Charles John Kieskalt, *The Official John Wayne Reference Book* (New York: Citadel Press, 1985), 182.

45. John Boswell and Jay David, *Duke: The John Wayne Album* (New York: Ballantine Books, 1979), 102.

46. John Wayne Enterprises website, *The Green Berets at 50*, www.johnwayne.com, Aug 6, 2018.

47. Article by the author, "Prices were High and Mighty at John Wayne Memorabilia Auction," *CinemaRetro*, October 27, 2011.

48. Richard Nixon Foundation library, https://www.nixonfoundation.org/2015/05/john-wayne-im-nixon-man/.

Chapter 7

1. Paul A. Helmick, *Cut, Print, and That's a Wrap* (Jefferson, NC: McFarland, 2001), 144–163.

2. Richard Schickel, *The Men Who Made the Movies* (Chicago: Ivan R. Dee, 1975), 122.

3. CineMonde, "Dans la brousse Africain le vieus chapeau de John Wayne sert de fétiche é Gérard Blain," *CineMonde*, February 1960.

4. Hardy Krüger, *Wanderjahre* (Cologne, Germany: Lübbe Verlagsgruppe, 1998), 28–44.

5. Joseph McBride, *Hawks on Hawks* (Berkeley: University of California Press, 1982), 144–147.

6. Press Kitt for distributors, Paramount Pictures, 1962.

7. Paul A. Helmick, *Cut, Print, and That's a Wrap* (Jefferson, NC: McFarland, 2001), 144–163.

8. "Hatari," *International Photographer*, September 1961.

9. Peter Bogdanovich, *Who the Hell's in It?* (New York: Ballantine Books, 2004), 292–293.

10. Tim Lilley, *Campfire's Glow* (Big Trail Publishing, 1995), 139–141.

11. Peter Bogdanovich, *Who the Hell's in It?* (New York: Ballantine Books, 2004), 292–293.

12. Joseph McBride, *Hawks on Hawks* (Berkeley, University of California Press, 1982), 144–147.

13. Aissa Wayne, *John Wayne: My Father* (New York: Random House, 1991), 76–82.

14. Peter Bogdanovich, *Who the Hell's in It?* (New York: Ballantine Books, 2004), 292–293.

15. Peter Bogdanovich, *Who the Devil Made It?* (New York: Ballantine Books, 1998), 444–447.

16. Elsa Martinelli, interview with the author, Locarno Film Festival, August 2, 2012.

17. Press Kit for distributors, Paramount Pictures, 1962.

18. Joseph McBride, *Hawks on Hawks* (Berkeley: University of California Press, 1982), 144–147.

19. Elsa Martinelli, interview with the author, Locarno Film Festival, August 2, 2012.

20. Paul A. Helmick, *Cut, Print, and That's a Wrap* (Jefferson, NC: McFarland, 2001), 144–163.

21. Hardy Krüger, *Wanderjahre* (Cologne, Germany: Lübbe Verlagsgruppe, 1998), 28–44.

22. *Hatari Souvenir Book*, Paramount Pictures, 1962, 9–13.

23. Aissa Wayne, *John Wayne: My Father* (New York: Random House, 1991), 76–82.

24. "John Wayne, American Legend," Interview with Red Buttons, *A&E Biography*, 20th Century Fox Film Corporation, 1998.

25. *The Personal Property of John Wayne*, Heritage Auctions catalog, 2011, 86.

26. Kisetu, interview with the author in Tanzania, October 2011.

27. Aissa Wayne, *John Wayne: My Father* (New York: Random House, 1991), 76–82.

28. Press Kit for distributors, Paramount Pictures, 1962.

29. Press Kit for distributors, Paramount Pictures, 1962.

30. Tim Lilley, *Campfire's Glow* (Big Trail Publishing, 1995), 139–141.

31. Interview with Jan Oelofse, *Sports Afield*, May/June 2012.

32. *Hatari Souvenir Book* (Paramount Pictures, 1962), 5.

33. "Hatari," *International Photographer*, September 1961.

34. "Hans C. Blumenberg, *Die Kamera in Augenhöhe—Begegnungen mit Howard Hawks* (Cologne, Germany: DuMont Buchverlag Köln, 1979).

35. Hardy Krüger, *Eine Farm in Afrika* (Cologne, Germany: Bastei Lübbe, 1999), 11–26.

36. Hardy Krüger, *Eine Farm in Afrika* (Cologne, Germany: Bastei Lübbe, 1999), 11–26.

37. Randy Roberts and James S. Olson, *John Wayne, American* (New York: The Free Press, 1995), 487.

38. Peter Bogdanovich, *Who the Devil Made It?* (Zurich, Switzerland: Haffmans Verlag, 2000), 444–447.

Chapter 8

1. Bette L. Stanton, *Where God Put the West* (Moab, UT: Canyonlands Natural History Association, 1994), 1.

2. Pilar Wayne, *John Wayne—My Life with the Duke* (New York: McGraw-Hill, 1987), 102.

3. James V. D'Arc, *When Hollywood Came to Town* (Layton, UT: Gibbs Smith, 2010), 92.

4. *Washington County News*, article on filming, July 15, 1954.

5. Letter to Howard Huges April 29, 1954 (Heritage Auctions, November 2019).

6. "John Wayne Talks with Bill Kelly," *Real West Magazine*, March 1979.

7. Michael Munn, *John Wayne: The Man Behind the Myth* (New York: New American Library, 2003), 164.

8. "New Controversy Over John Wayne's Death," *People Magazine*, November 10, 1980.

9. "New Controversy Over John Wayne's Death," *People Magazine*, November 10, 1980.

10. "New Controversy Over John Wayne's Death," *People Magazine*, November 10, 1980.

11. *Johnny, weil du Geburtstag hast* (German television documentary, ZDF, June 7, 1977).

12. Pilar Wayne, *John Wayne—My Life with the Duke* (New York: McGraw-Hill, 1987), 103.

13. *The Cowboys*, production featurette, Spy Guise Video, 1997.

14. Tim Lilley, *Campfire Conversations* (Big Trail Publishing, 1992), 116.

15. Tim Lilley, *Campfire's Glow* (Big Trail Publishing, 1995).

16. Scott Eyman, *John Wayne: The Life and Legend* (New York: Simon & Schuster, 2014), 197.

17. Bette L. Stanton, *Where God Put the West* (Moab, UT: Canyonlands Natural History Association, 1994), 46.

18. James V. D'Arc, *When Hollywood Came to Town* (Layton, UT: Gibbs Smith, 2010), 232.

19. Bette L. Stanton, *Where God Put the West* (Moab, UT: Canyonlands Natural History Association, 1994), 46.

20. Bette L. Stanton, *Where God Put the West* (Moab, UT: Canyonlands Natural History Association, 1994), 1.

21. *The Comancheros*, DVD audio commentary, 20th Century Fox.

22. Paul A. Helmick, *Cut, Print and That's a Wrap* (Jefferson, NC: McFarland, 2001), 110.

Chapter 9

1. Scott Eyman, *John Wayne: The Life and Legend* (New York: Simon & Schuster, 2014), 68.

2. Hal Wallis, *Starmaker* (New York: MacMillan, 1980), 181.

3. John Farkis, *Not Thinking' Just Rememberin'* (Albany, GA: Bear Manor Media, 2015), 2.

4. Peter Bogdanovich, *Who the Hell's in It* (New York: Knopf, 2004), 279.

5. Peter Bogdanovich, *John Ford* (Berkeley: University of Califonria Press, 1978), 50.

6. Richard W. Bann and Don Kelsen *Lone Pine and the Movies: The Lost John Wayne Film* (Newmarket, Ontario: Riverwood Press, 2018).

7. Nancy Schoenberger, *Wayne and Ford* (New York: Anchor Books, 2017), 31.

8. Tim Lilley, *The Trail Beyond*, Volume IX (Big Trail Publishing, 2007), 7.

9. *Boy's Life no. 3*, volume 67, May–June 1979.

10. Article by the author, "Prices were High and Mighty at John Wayne Memorabilia Auction," *CinemaRetro*, October 27, 2011.

11. Maurice Zolotow, *Shooting Star* (New York: Simon and Schuster, 1974), 197.

12. Rudy Behlmer, ed., *Henry Hathaway: A Director's Guild of American Oral History* (Lanham, MD: Scarecrow Press, 2001), 236.

13. Tim Lilley, *A Newsletter on the Films of John Wayne* (Big Trail Publishing, 1984–1999).

14. George Carpozi, Jr., *The John Wayne Story* (New York: Dell Publishing, 1979), 52.

15. Timothy Knight, *John Wayne in the Movies* (New York: Metro Books, 2009), 155.

16. *McQ: John Wayne in Action*, Featurette, Warner Bros. DVD release.

17. *McQ: John Wayne in Action*, Featurette, Warner Bros. DVD release.

18. "John Wayne Talks with Bill Kelly," *Real West Magazine*, March 1979.

19. *Los Angeles Evening Herald Express*, October 9, 1948.

20. Bert Minshall, *On Board with the Duke* (Santa Ana, CA: Seven Locks Press, 1992).

21. Scott Eyman, *John Wayne: The Life and Legend* (New York: Simon & Schuster, 2014), 218.

22. Chris Enss and Howard Kazanjian, *Cowboy Creatures, and Classics—The Story of Republic Pictures* (Lanham, MD: Rowman & Littlefield, 2018), 46.

23. John Boswell and Jay David, *Duke: The John Wayne Album* (New York: Ballantine Books, 1979), 92.

24. Maurice Zolotow, *Shooting Star* (New York: Simon and Schuster, 1974), 2.

25. Scott Eyman, *John Wayne: The Life and Legend* (New York: Simon & Schuster, 2014), 458.

26. "Looking at Hollywood," *Chicago Tribune*, May 11, 1947.

27. Peter Bogdanovich, *Who the Hell's in It* (New York: Knopf, 2004), 285.

28. Rob Word, *Word on Westerns*, interview with Sherry Jackson, April 21, 2019, https://www.youtube.com/watch?v=XCWmySeb4HE.

29. Melville Shavelson, *How to Make a Jewish Movie* (Upper Saddle River, NJ: Prentice-Hall, 1971), 19.

30. Nancy Schoenberger, *Wayne and Ford* (New York: Anchor Books, 2017), 189.

31. David Carradine, *Endless Highway* (North Clarendon, VT: Journey Editions, 1995), 336.

32. Pat Stacy, *Duke: A Love Story* (New York: Simon & Schuster Pocket Books, 1983), 107.

33. "John Wayne Talks with Bill Kelly," *Real West Magazine*, March 1979.

34. Michael Munn, *John Wayne: The Man Behind the Myth* (New York: New American Library, 2003), 79.

35. David Hanna, *The Life and Times of John Wayne* (Worthing, England: Littlehampton, 1979), 21.

36. Tim Lilley, *A Newsletter on the Films of John Wayne* (Big Trail Publishing, 1984–1999).

37. David Hanna, *The Life and Times of John Wayne* (Worthing, England: Littlehampton, 1979), 27.

38. Timothy Knight, *John Wayne in the Movies* (New York: Metro Books, 2009), 26.

39. Tim Lilley, *Campfires Rekindled* (Big Trail Publishing, 1994), 84.

40. Marc Mompoint, *John Wayne: A Photographic Celebration* (New York: Skyhorse Publishing, 2014), 101.

41. Phil Donahue interview with John Wayne, *The Phil Donahue Show*, 1976, https://archive.org/details/DonahueWithJohnWayne1976.

42. Scott Eyman, *John Wayne: The Life and Legend* (New York: Simon & Schuster, 2014), 483.

43. Pilar Wayne, *John Wayne—My Life with the Duke* (New York: McGraw-Hill, 1987), 41.

44. Herb Fagan, *Duke, We're Glad We Knew You* (Secaucus, NJ: Carol Publishing Group, 1997), 151.

45. "John Wayne Hawks Datril 500," Medium.com, https://medium.com/@jeremylr/john-wayne-hawks-datril-500-bristol-myers-miracle-headache-remedy-9b969c040557.

46. Maria Riva, *Marlene Dietrich by Her Daughter* (New York: Random House, 1992), 569.

Chapter 10

1. Nancy Schoenberger, *Wayne and Ford* (New York: Anchor Books, 2017), 45.

2. Joseph McBride, *Searching for John Ford* (New York: St. Martin's Press, 2001), 201.

3. Nancy Schoenberger, *Wayne and Ford* (New York: Anchor Books, 2017), 45.

4. Henry Fonda with Howard Teichmann, *Fonda—My Life* (New York: The New American Library, 1981), 190.

5. Peter Bogdanovich, *Who the Hell's in It* (New York: Knopf, 2004), 312.

6. Dan Ford, *Pappy—The Life of John Ford* (Englewood Cliffs, 1979, New York: Da Capo Press, 1998), 148–149.

7. Pilar Wayne, *John Wayne—My Life with the Duke* (New York: McGraw-Hill, 1987), 62.

8. Scott Eyman, *John Wayne: The Life and Legend* (New York: Simon & Schuster, 2014), 207.

9. Randy Roberts and James S. Olson, *John Wayne: American* (New York: The Free Press, 1995), 398.

10. Herb Fagan, *Duke, We're Glad We Knew You* (Secaucus, NJ: Carol Publishing Group, 1997), 110.

11. James Arness, *James Arness: An Autobiography* (Jefferson, NC: McFarland, 2001).

12. Chuck Roberson, *The Fall Guy* (Surrey, British Columbia: Hancock House, 1980), 123.

13. Chuck Roberson, *The Fall Guy* (Surrey, British Columbia: Hancock House, 1980), 114.

14. C. Courtney Joyner, *The Westerners* (Jefferson, NC: McFarland, 2009), 66.

15. Randy Roberts and James S. Olson, *John Wayne: American* (New York: The Free Press, 1995), 403.

16. George Carpozi, Jr., *The John Wayne Story* (New York: Dell Publishing, 1979), 161.

17. "John Wayne Supported Panama Canal Treaty," *La Prensa San Diego*, June 1, 2007.

18. Hal Wallis, *Starmaker* (New York: MacMillan, 1980), 157.

19. Aissa Wayne, *John Wayne: My Father* (London: Robert Hale, 1992), 110.

20. Burt Kennedy, *Hollywood Trail Boss* (Brooklyn, NY: Boulevard Books, 1997), 50.

21. Jean Ramer, *Duke: The Real Story of John Wayne* (New York: Award Books, 1973), 131.

22. C. Courtney Joyner, *The Westerners* (Jefferson, NC: McFarland, 2009), 92.

23. Karl Malden, *When Do I Start?* (Pompton Plains, NJ: Limelight Editions, 1997), 285.

24. Scott Eyman, *John Wayne: The Life and Legend* (New York: Simon & Schuster, 2014), 542.

25. Michael Munn, *John Wayne: The Man Behind the Myth* (New York: New American Library, 2003), 258.

26. "Viva El Wayne" *Chicago Tribune*, December 3, 1997.

27. "John Wayne After His Bout with Cancer," *Life Magazine*, May 7, 1965.

28. George Kennedy, *Trust Me—A Memoir* (New York: Applause Theatre & Cinema Books, 2011), 58.

29. Roger Ebert, *Roger Ebert's Book of Film* (New York: W.W. Norton, 1997), 142.

30. Burt Kennedy, *Hollywood Trail Boss* (Brooklyn, NY: Boulevard Books, 1997), 12.

31. Burt Kennedy, *Hollywood Trail Boss* (Brooklyn, NY: Boulevard Books, 1997), 11.

32. Burt Kennedy, *Hollywood Trail Boss* (Brooklyn, NY: Boulevard Books, 1997), 78.

33. *The War Wagon* Pressbook, Universal Pictures.

34. Hal Needham, *Stuntman! My Car-Crashing, Plane-Jumping, Bone-Breaking, Death-Defying Hollywood Life* (New York: Hachette, 2011), 99.

35. Michael Munn, *John Wayne: The Man Behind the Myth* (New York: New American Library, 2003), 291.

36. Tim Lilley, *Campfire's Glow* (Big Trail Publishing, 1995), 10.

37. Scott Eyman, *John Wayne: The Life and Legend* (New York: Simon & Schuster, 2014), 453.

38. Pilar Wayne, *John Wayne—My Life with the Duke* (New York: McGraw-Hill, 1987), 245.

39. Randy Roberts and James S. Olson, *John Wayne: American* (New York: The Free Press, 1995), 570.

40. Mike Tomkies, *Duke: The Story of John Wayne* (New York: Avon Books, 1971), 55.

41. "John Wayne After His Bout with Cancer," *Life Magazine*, May 7, 1965.

42. *Chisum*, audio commentary by Andrew V. McLaglen, Warner Brothers DVD release.

43. Tim Lilley, *Campfire's Glow* (Big Trail Publishing, 1995), 72.

44. "John Wayne Built My Career," (Chris Mitchum interview), Medium.com, December 21, 2018.

45. Tim Lilley, *The Trail Beyond, Volume II* (Big Trail Publishing, 2000), 43.

46. Yakima Canutt, *Stuntman* (Norman: University of Oklahoma Press, 1979), 224.

47. Tim Lilley, *Campfire Conversations* (Big Trail Publishing, 1992), 20.

48. C. Courtney Joyner, *The Westerners* (Jefferson, NC: McFarland, 2009), 150.

49. *Cahill, U.S. Marshal*, audio commentary by Andrew V. McLaglen, Warner Brothers DVD release.

50. Tim Lilley, *Campfires Rekindled* (Big Trail Publishing, 1994), 160.

Chapter 11

1. Billy Liebert and John Mitchum, *John Wayne—America, Why I Love Her* (New York: Simon and Schuster, 1977), 111.

2. John Farkis, *Not Thinking' Just Rememberin'* (Albany, GA: Bear Manor Media, 2015), 153.

3. Lauren Bacall, *By Myself and Then Some* (New York: Caprigo, 2005), 248.

4. Peter Bogdanovich, *Who the Hell's in It* (New York: Knopf, 2004), 298.

5. William A. Wellman, *A Short Time For Insanity* (Portland, OR: Hawthorn Books, 1974), 96.

6. Lee Server, *Robert Mitchum—Baby, I Don't Care* (New York: St. Martin's Press, 2001), 282.

7. John Mitchum, *Them Ornery Mitchum Boys* (Pacifica, CA: Creatures at Large Press, 1989), 160.

8. Lee Server, *Robert Mitchum—Baby, I Don't Care* (New York: St. Martin's Press, 2001), 284.

9. Lee Server, *Robert Mitchum—Baby, I Don't Care* (New York: St. Martin's Press, 2001), 412.

10. John Farkis, *Not Thinking' … Just Rememberin'* (Albany, GA: Bear Manor Media, 2015), 153.

11. John Boswell and Jay David, *Duke: The John Wayne Album* (New York: Ballantine Books, 1979), 105.

12. Pilar Wayne, *John Wayne—My Life with the Duke* (New York: McGraw-Hill, 1987), 128.

13. John Huston, *An Open Book* (London: Virgin Books, 1980), 266.

14. Burt Kennedy, *Hollywood Trail Boss* (Brooklyn, NY: Boulevard Books, 1997), 32.

15. Chuck Roberson, *The Fall Guy* (Surrey, British Columbia: Hancock House, 1980), 205.

16. Peter Bogdanovich, *Who the Hell's in It* (New York: Knopf, 2004), 275.

17. John Huston, *An Open Book* (London: Virgin Books, 1980), 276.

18. C. McGivern, *John Wayne: A Giant Shadow* (Bracknell, Berkshire: Sammon Publishing, 2000), 253.

19. Tim Lilley, *A Newsletter on the Films of John Wayne* (Big Trail Publishing, 1984–1999).

20. Tim Lilley, *Campfire Embers* (Big Trail Publishing, 1997), 41.

21. Hal Needham, *Stuntman! My Car-Crashing, Plane-Jumping, Bone-Breaking, Death-Defying Hollywood Life* (New York: Hachette, 2011), 102.

22. Tim Lilley, *Campfire's Glow* (Big Trail Publishing, 1995), 118.

23. "John Wayne," *Lorelei Magazine*, 50.

24. Randy Roberts James S. Olson, *John Wayne: American* (New York: The Free Press, 1995), 552.

Chapter 12

1. Leonard Mosley, *Zanuck: The Rise and Fall of Hollywood's Last Tycoon* (New York: Little Brown, 1985), 321.

2. *The Longest Day* pressbook, Twentieth Century Fox.

3. Steven J. Rubin, *Combat Films: American Realism* (Jefferson, NC: McFarland, 2011), 104.

4. Pilar Wayne, *John Wayne—My Life with the Duke* (New York: McGraw-Hill, 1987), 159.

5. Rudy Behlmer, *Memo from Darryl F. Zanuck* (New York: Grove Press, 1993), 259.

6. Pilar Wayne, *John Wayne—My Life with the Duke* (New York: McGraw-Hill, 1987), 159.

7. Charlton Heston, *In the Arena* (New York: Harper Collins, 1996), 270.

8. Pressbook, *The Longest Day*, Twentieth Century Fox.

9. Steven J. Rubin, *Combat Films: American Realism* (Jefferson, NC: McFarland, 2011), 105.

10. Tim Lilley, *The Trail Beyond, Volume VI* (Big Trail Publishing, 2004), 52.

11. Tim Lilley, *The Trail Beyond, Volume VI* (Big Trail Publishing, 2004), 54.

Chapter 13

1. "John Wayne: His Epic Off-Screen Life in Arizona," *Arizona Highways Magazine*, January 1992.

2. Documentary, *Johnny, weil du Geburtstag hast*, ZDF Zweites Deutsches Fernsehen, June 7, 1977.

3. William T. Brooks, entry on John Wayne Message Board, http://dukefanclub.weebly.com/chili-bills-26-bar-memories.

4. "John Wayne: His Epic Off-Screen

Life in Arizona," *Arizona Highways Magazine*, January 1992.

5. Randy Roberts and James S. Olson, *John Wayne: American* (New York: The Free Press, 1995), 285.

6. Herb Fagan, *Duke, We're Glad We Knew You* (Secaucus, NJ: Carol Publishing Group, 1997), 21.

7. Herb Fagan, *Duke, We're Glad We Knew You* (Secaucus, NJ: Carol Publishing Group, 1997), 67.

8. Jean Ramer, *Duke: The Real Story of John Wayne* (New York: Charter Books, 1973), 82.

9. Herb Fagan, *Duke, We're Glad We Knew You* (Secaucus, NJ: Carol Publishing Group, 1997), 95.

10. Michael Munn, *John Wayne: The Man Behind the Myth* (New York: New American Library, 2003), 156.

11. "John Wayne: His Epic Off-Screen Life in Arizona," *Arizona Highways Magazine*, January 1992.

12. "Mission, Movies and Wingfields Give Guevavi Ranch a Unique History," *Nogales International*, February 13, 2018.

Chapter 14

1. Lee Marvin interview with Ira H. Gallen, *The Director's Series*, February 10, 1986.

2. Marc Mompoint, *John Wayne: A Photographic Celebration* (New York: Skyhorse Publishing, 2014), 529.

3. Tim Lilley, *A Newsletter on the Films of John Wayne* (Big Trail Publishing, 1984–1999).

4. James Arness, *James Arness: An Autobiography* (Jefferson, NC: McFarland, 2001).

5. Tim Lilley, *Campfire's Glow* (Big Trail Publishing, 1995), 88.

6. Tim Lilley, *Campfire's Glow* (Big Trail Publishing, 1995), 96.

7. George Carpozi, Jr., *The John Wayne Story* (New York: Dell Publishing, 1979), 122.

8. George Carpozi, Jr., *The John Wayne Story* (New York: Dell Publishing, 1979), 122.

9. Pilar Wayne, *Pilar Wayne's Favorite and Fabulous Recipes* (Kansas City, MO: PAX Publishing, 1982), 170.

10. Dwayne Epstein, *Lee Marvin—Point Blank* (Tuscan, AZ: Schaffner Press, 2013), 121.

11. Peter Bogdanovich, *John Ford* (Berkeley: University of California Press, 1978), 100.

12. Dwayne Epstein, *Lee Marvin—Point Blank* (Tuscan, AZ: Schaffner Press, 2013), 131.

13. Andrew Sinclair, *John Ford—A Biography* (London: Lorrimer Publishing, 1979), 205.

14. Peter Bogdanovich, *Who the Hell's in It* (New York: Knopf, 2004), 284.

15. Dwayne Epstein, *Lee Marvin—Point Blank* (Tuscon, AZ: Schaffner Press, 2013), 132.

16. Branscombe Richmond, conversation with the author, 2004.

17. "John Wayne Talks with Bill Kelly," *Real West Magazine*, March 1979.

18. Tony Mackling and Nick Pici, *Voices From the Set* (Lanham, MD: The Scarecrow Press, 2000), 145.

19. Aissa Wayne, *John Wayne: My Father* (London: Robert Hale, 1992), 98.

20. Billy Liebhert and John Mitchum, *John Wayne—America, Why I Love Her* (New York: Simon and Schuster, 1977).

21. "John Wayne Talks with Bill Kelly," *Real West Magazine*, March 1979.

22. Pilar Wayne, *Pilar Wayne's Favorite and Fabulous Recipes* (Kansas City, MO: PAX Publishing, 1982), 172.

Chapter 15

1. Interview with the author, *Filmbulletin Magazine*, February 1991.

2. Tim Lilley, *Campfire's Glow* (Big Trail Publishing, 1995), 147.

3. Sophia Loren, *Yesterday, Today, Tomorrow* (New York: Atria Books, 2014), 118.

4. Milburn Smith, *John Wayne* (Lorelei Publishing, 1979), 52.

5. Tim Lilley, *Campfire's Glow* (Big Trail Publishing, 1995), 147.

6. Jack Cardiff, *Magic Hour: A Life in Movies* (Tusla, OK: Gardners Books, 1997), 192.

7. Sophia Loren, *Yesterday, Today, Tomorrow* (New York: Atria Books, 2014), 118.

8. Pilar Wayne, *John Wayne—My Life with the Duke* (New York: McGraw-Hill, 1987), 124.

9. Pilar Wayne, *John Wayne—My Life with the Duke* (New York: McGraw-Hill, 1987), 125.

10. Michael Munn, *John Wayne: The Man Behind the Myth* (New York: New American Library, 2003), 184.

11. Jack Cardiff, *Magic Hour: A Life in Movies* (Tulsa, OK: Gardners Books, 1997), 192.

12. Jack Cardiff, *Magic Hour: A Life in Movies* (Tulsa, OK: Gardners Books, 1997), 192.

13. Tim Lilley, *A Newsletter on the Films of John Wayne* (Big Trail Publishing, 1984–1999).

14. Sophia Loren, *Yesterday, Today, Tomorrow* (New York: Atria Books, 2014), 119.

15. Sophia Loren, *Yesterday, Today, Tomorrow* (New York: Atria Books, 2014), 119.

16. Michael Goldman, *John Wayne: The Genuine Article* (San Rafael, CA: Insight Editions, 2013), 85.

17. Pilar Wayne, *John Wayne—My Life with the Duke* (New York: McGraw-Hill, 1987), 125.

18. John Wayne Memorial Issue, *The Saturday Evening Post*, July 1979.

19. Aissa Wayne, *John Wayne: My Father* (London: Robert Hale, 1992), 84.

20. Pilar Wayne, *John Wayne—My Life with the Duke* (New York: McGraw-Hill, 1987), 169.

21. *Paris Match Archives*, June 11, 2019.

22. *The Personal Property of John Wayne* (Dallas: Heritage Auctions, 2011), 211.

23. Joseph McBride, *Frank Capra: The Catastrophe of Success* (New York: Simon & Schuster, 1992), 640.

24. Mel Martin, *The Magnificent Showman* (Albany, GA: BearManor Media, 2007), 161.

25. Maurice Zolotow, *Shooting Star* (New York: Simon and Schuster, 1974), 342.

26. Pilar Wayne, *John Wayne—My Life with the Duke* (New York: McGraw-Hill, 1987), 173.

27. Michael Munn, *John Wayne: The Man Behind the Myth* (New York: New American Library, 2003), 251.

28. Interview with the author, Film Festival Locarno, August 2011.

29. Mel Martin, *The Magnificent Showman* (Albany, GA: BearManor Media, 2007), 159.

30. Tim Lilley, *A Newsletter on the Films of John Wayne* (Big Trail Publishing, 1984–1999).

31. Tim Lilley, *Campfires Rekindled* (Big Trail Publishing, 1994), 134.

32. Melville Shavelson, *How to Make a Jewish Movie* (Upper Saddle River, NJ: Prentice-Hall, 1971), 22.

Chapter 16

1. "Scriptless in Nome, California," *New York Times*, June 19, 1960.

2. Michael Munn, *John Wayne: The Man Behind the Myth* (New York: New American Library, 2003), 118.

3. Michael Munn, *John Wayne: The Man

Behind the Myth (New York: New American Library, 2003), 118.

4. Harry Carey, Jr., *Company of Heroes—My Life as an Actor in the John Ford Stock Company* (Lanham, MD: Scarecrow Press, 1994), 21.

5. Sam Sherman, *Lone Pine in the Movies* (Lone Pine, CA: Museum of Western Film History, 2007), 7.

6. Richard W. Bann, *Lone Pine in the Movies* (Newmarket, Ontario: Riverwood Press, 2010), 36.

7. Sam Sherman, *Lone Pine in the Movies* (Lone Pine, CA: Museum of Western Film History, 2007), 19.

8. Michael Munn, *John Wayne: The Man Behind the Myth* (New York: New American Library, 2003), 114.

9. Stewart Granger, *Sparks Fly Upward* (London: Granada Publishing, 1981), 404.

10. "Scriptless in Nome, California," *New York Times,* June 19, 1960.

11. Jim Kitses and Gregg Rickman, *The Western Reader* (Pompton Plains, NJ: Limelight Editions, 1998), 246.

Chapter 17

1. Pilar Wayne, *John Wayne—My Life with the Duke* (New York: McGraw-Hill, 1987), 231.

2. Jack Cardiff, *Magic Hour: A Life in Movies* (Tulsa, OK: Gardners Books, 1997), 192.

3. Scott Eyman, *Hank & Jim* (New York: Simon & Schuster, 2017), 443.

4. Michael Goldman, *John Wayne: The Genuine Article* (San Rafael, CA: Insight Editions, 2013), 45.

5. Harry Carey, Jr., *Company of Heroes—My Life as an Actor in the John Ford Stock Company* (Langham, MD: Scarecrow Press, 1994), 11.

6. Herb Fagan, *Duke, We're Glad We Knew You* (Secaucus, NJ: Carol Publishing Group, 1997), 147.

7. Rudy Behlmer, ed., *Henry Hathaway: A Director's Guild of American Oral History* (Langham, MD: Scarecrow Press, 2001), 173.

8. Rudy Behlmer, ed., *Henry Hathaway: A Director's Guild of American Oral History* (Langham, MD: Scarecrow Press, 2001), 174.

9. Hans C. Blumenberg, *Die Kamera in Augenhöhe—Begegnungen mit Howard Hawks* (Cologne, Germany: DuMont Buchverlag Köln, 1979), 101.

10. Herb Fagan, *Duke, We're Glad We Knew You* (Secaucus, NJ: Carol Publishing Group, 1997), 148.

11. Michael Munn, *John Wayne: The Man*

Behind the Myth (New York: New American Library, 2003), 289.

12. Randy Roberts and James S. Olson, *John Wayne: American* (New York: The Free Press, 1995), 563.

13. Randy Roberts James S. Olson, *John Wayne: American* (New York: The Free Press, 1995), 563.

14. Tim Lilley, *Campfires Rekindled* (Big Trail Publishing, 1994), 16.

15. Tim Lilley, *Campfire Embers* (Big Trail Publishing, 1997), 47.

16. Rudy Behlmer, ed., *Henry Hathaway: A Director's Guild of American Oral History* (Lanham, MD: Scarecrow Press, 2001), 237.

17. Rudy Behlmer, ed., *Henry Hathaway: A Director's Guild of American Oral History* (Lanham, MD: Scarecrow Press, 2001), 237.

18. Tombstone Western Film Festival, Panel Discussion, July 7, 2002.

19. Edith Head and Paddy Calistro, *Edith Head's Hollywood* (Santa Monica, CA: Angel City Press, 2008), 239.

20. Hal Wallis, *Starmaker* (New York: MacMillan, 1980), 178.

21. John Bryson, *The Private World of Katharine Hepburn* (New York: Little, Brown, 1990), 175.

22. John Bryson, *The Private World of Katharine Hepburn* (New York: Little, Brown, 1990), 50.

23. John Bryson, *The Private World of Katharine Hepburn* (New York: Little, Brown, 1990), 58.

24. Pat Stacy, *Duke: A Love Story* (New York: Simon & Schuster Pocket Books, 1983), 71.

25. Hal Wallis, *Starmaker* (New York: MacMillan Publishing, 1980), 181.

26. John Bryson, *The Private World of Katharine Hepburn* (New York: Little, Brown, 1990), 174.

27. Bob Thomas, *Walt Disney, an American Original* (Burbank, CA: The Walt Disney Company, 1976), 351.

28. Hal Wallis, *Starmaker* (New York: MacMillan, 1980), 182.

29. Hal Wallis, *Starmaker* (New York: MacMillan, 1980), 180.

30. Pat Stacy, *Duke: A Love Story* (New York: Simon & Schuster Pocket Books, 1983), 72.

Chapter 18

1. Tim Lilley, *The Trail Beyond, Volume VII* (Big Trail Publishing, 2005).

2. Tim Lilley, *The Trail Beyond, Volume VII* (Big Trail Publishing, 2005), 47.

3. Tim Lilley, *Campfire Conversations* (Big Trail Publishing, 1992), 22.

4. Tim Lilley, *The Trail Beyond, Volume IV* (Big Trail Publishing, 2002), 20.

5. Don Siegel, *A Siegel Film* (London: Faber & Faber Limited, 1993), 7.

6. Tim Lilley, *A Newsletter on the Films of John Wayne* (Big Trail Publishing, 1984–1999).

7. C. Courtney Joyner, *The Westerners* (Jefferson, NC: McFarland, 2009), 111.

8. Hal Needham, *Stuntman! My Car-Crashing, Plane-Jumping, Bone-Breaking, Death-Defying Hollywood Life* (New York: Hachette, 2011), 95.

9. Tim Lilley, *Campfire's Glow* (Big Trail Publishing, 1995), 119.

10. *McQ: John Wayne in Action*, Featurette, Warner Bros. DVD release.

11. Chuck Roberson, *The Fall Guy* (Surrey, British Columbia: Hancock House, 1980), 268.

12. Chuck Roberson, *The Fall Guy* (Surrey, British Columbia: Hancock House, 1980), 277.

13. Tim Lilley, *The Trail Beyond, Volume II* (Big Trail Publishing, 2000), 36.

14. Glenn Lovell, *Escape Artist—The Life and Times of John Sturges* (Madison: University of Wisconsin Press, 2008), 280.

15. *The Duke in London*, Featurette, Condorde DVD release.

16. Michael Munn, *John Wayne: The Man Behind the Myth* (New York: New American Library, 2003), Foreword.

17. Hal Wallis, *Starmaker* (New York: MacMillan, 1980), 178.

18. Tony Robinson, *No Cunning Plan* (London: Sidgwick & Jackson, 2016).

19. Tim Lilley, *A Newsletter on the Films of John Wayne* (Big Trail Publishing, 1984–1999).

Chapter 19

1. Chris Enss and Howard Kazanjian, *The Young Duke: The Early Life of John Wayne* (Guilford, CT: Globe Pequot, 2009), 136.

2. Russell Birdwell, *A News Release: John Wayne's The Alamo* (pressbook, 1960), 111.

3. Tim Lilley, *The Trail Beyond*, Volume IX (Big Trail Publishing, 2007), 32.

4. Chris Enss and Howard Kazanjian, *The Young Duke: The Early Life of John Wayne* (Guilford, CT: Globe Pequot, 2009), 136.

5. Pilar Wayne, *John Wayne—My Life with the Duke* (New York: McGraw-Hill, 1987), 100.

6. Edward Dmytryk, *It's a Hell of a Life but Not a Bad Living* (New York: Time Books, 1978), 68.

7. Sam Shaw, *John Wayne in the Camera Eye* (London: Hamlyn Publishing, 1980), 21.

8. Pat Stacy, *Duke: A Love Story* (New York: Simon & Schuster Pocket Books, 1983), 62.

9. Tim Lilley, *Campfire's Glow* (Big Trail Publishing, 1995), 35.

10. Tim Lilley, *Campfire's Glow* (Big Trail Publishing, 1995), 157.

11. Jane Pattie, *John Wayne…There Rode a Legend* (Orange, TX: Western Classics, 2000), 255.

12. *Real West*, Bill Kelly interview, March 1979.

13. *Real West*, Bill Kelly interview, March 1979.

14. "Maureen O'Hara Back on Her Favorite Island," *The St. Croix Source*, March 26, 2005.

15. "Maureen O'Hara Back on Her Favorite Island," *The St. Croix Source*, March 26, 2005.

16. Herb Fagan, *Duke, We're Glad We Knew You* (Secaucus, NJ: Carol Publishing Group, 1997), 228.

Chapter 20

1. E-Go Collectors, *John Wayne Magazine*, 15.

2. Chuck Roberson, *The Fall Guy* (Surrey, British Columbia: Hancock House, 1980), Foreword.

3. Donald Shepherd, Robert Slatzer and Dave Grayson, *Duke: The Life and Times of John Wayne* (Garden City, NY: Doubleday, 1985), 504.

4. John Wayne Enterprises, *John Wayne: The Legend and the Man* (Brooklyn, NY: Powerhouse Books, 2012), 226.

5. Pat Stacy, *Duke: A Love Story* (New York: Simon & Schuster Pocket Books, 1983), 93.

6. Don Siegel, *A Siegel Film* (London: Faber & Faber, 1993), 12.

7. Don Siegel, *A Siegel Film* (London: Faber & Faber, 1993), 23.

8. Don Siegel, *A Siegel Film* (London: Faber & Faber, 1993), 23.

9. John Carpenter, audio commentary, *Rio Bravo*, Warner DVD.

10. Paul A. Helmick, *Cut, Print and That's a Wrap* (Jefferson, NC: McFarland, 2001), 122.

11. Herb Fagan, *Duke, We're Glad we Knew You* (Secaucus, NJ: Carol Publishing Group, 1997).

12. *Old Tucson Remembers John Wayne*, Old Tuscon Studios documentary, 2007.

13. "John Wayne: His Epic Off-screen Life in Arizona," *Arizona Highways* 68, January 1992.

14. Turner Classic Movies, *TCM Back at the Ranch*, commentary by Edward Faulkner, September 7, 2013.

15. Tim Lilley, *A Newsletter on the Films of John Wayne* (Big Trail Publishing, 1984–1999).

16. Maureen O'Hara, *Tis Herself* (New York: Simon & Schuster, 2004), 235.

17. Tim Lilley, *Campfires Rekindled* (Big Trail Publishing, 1994), 59.

18. Chuck Roberson, *The Fall Guy* (Surrey, British Columbia: Hancock House, 1980), 262.

19. *Word on Western*, interview with Stefanie Powers, 2015, https://www.youtube.com/watch?v=z7bssR5m-Kg&t=67s.

20. *Maureen O'Hara and Stefanie Powers Remember McLintock!* Documentary, McLintock Paramount DVD release.

21. *Word on Western*, interview with Stefanie Powers, 2018, https://www.youtube.com/watch?v=x7Su2qSCwRw.

22. Joseph McBride, *Hawks on Hawks* (Berkeley: University of California Press, 1982), 135.

23. Joseph McBride, *Hawks on Hawks* (Berkeley: University of California Press, 1982), 28.

24. Peter Bogdanovich, *Who the Hell's in It* (New York: Knopf, 2004), 272.

25. Joseph McBride, *Hawks on Hawks* (Berkeley: University of California Press, 1982), 84.

26. *Old Tucson Remembers John Wayne*, documentary, Old Tucson Studios DVD.

27. Lee Server, *Robert Mitchum—Baby, I Don't Care* (New York: St. Martin's Press, 2001), 398.

28. Paul A. Helmick, *Cut, Print and That's a Wrap* (Jefferson, NC: McFarland, 2001), 123.

29. Lee Server, *Robert Mitchum—Baby, I Don't Care* (New York: St. Martin's Press, 2001), 400.

30. Lee Server, *Robert Mitchum—Baby, I Don't Care* (New York: St. Martin's Press, 2001), 396.

31. Ed Ainsworth, *The Cowboy in Art* (New York: Bonanza Books, 1968), 8.

Chapter 21

1. Randy Roberts James S. Olson, *John Wayne: American* (New York: The Free Press, 1995), 299.

2. Tony Mackling and Nick Pici, *Voices from the Set* (Lanham, MD: Scarecrow Press, 2000), 113.

3. Patricia Bosworth, *Montgomery Clift—A Biography* (Pompton Plains, NJ: Limelight Editions, 1978), 121.

4. Gerald Mast, *Howard Hawks, Storyteller* (Oxford, England: Oxford University Press, 1982), 321.

5. Peter Bogdanovich, *Who the Devil Made It?* (New York: Knopf, 1997), 417.

6. Joseph McBride, *Hawks on Hawks* (Berkeley: University of California Press, 1982), 121.

7. Joseph McBride, *Hawks on Hawks* (Berkeley: University of California Press, 1982), 123.

8. Joseph McBride, *Hawks on Hawks* (Berkeley: University of California Press, 1982), 121.

9. Dimitri Tiomkin, *Please Don't Hate Me* (New York: Doubleday, 1959), 239.

10. Gerald Mast, *Howard Hawks, Storyteller* (Oxford, England: Oxford University Press, 1982), 298.

11. Patricia Bosworth, *Montgomery Clift—A Biography* (Pompton Plains, NJ: Limelight Editions, 1978), 122.

12. Hans C. Blumenberg, *Die Kamera in Augenhöhe—Begegnungen mit Howard Hawks* (Calogne, Germany: DuMont Buchverlag Köln, 1979), 90.

13. Joseph McBride, *Hawks on Hawks* (Berkeley: University of California Press, 1982), 85.

14. Peter Bogdanovich, *Who the Devil Made It?* (New York: Knopf, 1997), 382.

15. Joseph McBride, *Hawks on Hawks* (Berkeley: University of California Press, 1982), 29.

16. Bill Kelly interview, *Real West*, March 1979.

17. John Farkis, *Alamo Village* (Albany, GA: BearManor Media, 2005), 39.

18. Maurice Zolotow, *Shooting Star* (New York: Simon and Schuster, 1974), 310.

19. John Farkis, *Alamo Village* (Albany, GA: BearManor Media, 2005), 93.

20. Robert E. Relyea, *Not So Quiet on the Set* (Bloomington, IN: iUniverse, 2008), 121.

21. Tim Lilley, *Campfire's Glow* (Big Trail Publishing, 1995), 137.

22. Tony Mackling and Nick Pici, *Voices from the Set* (Lanham, MD: Scarecrow Press, 2000), 103.

23. Robert E. Relyea, *Not So Quiet on the Set* (Bloomington, IN: iUniverse, 2008), 119.

24. Brian Huberman, *John Wayne's The Alamo*, documentary, MGM Home Video, 1992.

25. Robert E. Relyea, *Not So Quiet on the Set* (Bloomington, IN: iUniverse, 2008), 122.

26. Tim Lilley, *Campfire's Glow* (Big Trail Publishing, 1995), 91.

27. Tim Lilley, *Campfire's Glow* (Big Trail Publishing, 1995), 92.

28. Robert E. Relyea, *Not So Quiet on the Set* (Bloomington, IN: iUniverse, 2008), 128.

29. Tim Lilley, *Campfires Rekindled* (Big Trail Publishing, 1994), 76.

30. John Farkis, *Alamo Village* (Albany, GA: BearManor Media, 2005), 93.

31. John Farkis, *Alamo Village* (Albany, GA: BearManor Media, 2005), 155.

32. John Farkis, *Alamo Village* (Albany, GA: BearManor Media, 2005), 156.

33. John Farkis, *Not Thinkin' ... Just Rememberin'* (Albany, GA: BearManor Media, 2015), 641.

34. John Farkis, *Alamo Village* (Albany, GA: BearManor Media, 2005), 39.

35. Charles John Kieskalt, *The Official John Wayne Reference Book* (New York: Citadel Press, 1985), 182.

36. Mark Rydell, audio commentary, *The Cowboys*, Warner Bros. DVD release.

37. Mark Rydell, audio commentary, *The Cowboys*, Warner Bros. DVD release.

38. Mark Rydell, audio commentary, *The Cowboys*, Warner Bros. DVD release.

39. Donald Shepherd, Robert Slatzer and Dave Grayson, *Duke: The Life and Times of John Wayne* (Garden City, NY: Doubleday, 1985), 485.

40. Corrigan's steakhouse, Tom Corrigan's website, https://corriganssteakhouse.com/about.html.

41. Shirley Temple, *Child Star* (Norwalk, CT: The Easton Press, 1988), 413.

42. Tim Lilley, *Campfires Rekindled* (Big Trail Publishing, 1994), 86.

43. Harry Carey, Jr., *Company of Heroes—My Life as an Actor in the John Ford Stock Company* (Lanham, MD: Scarecrow Press, 1994), 162.

44. Harry Carey, Jr., *Company of Heroes—My Life as an Actor in the John Ford Stock Company* (Lanham, MD: Scarecrow Press, 1994), 162.

45. Alan G. Barbour, Foreword by Louise Brooks, *John Wayne* (New York: Pyramid Publications, 1974), 9.

46. Robert G. Sherman, *Quiet on the Set!* (Chatsworth, CA: Sherway Publishing, 1984), 64.

Chapter 22

1. Maurice Zolotow, *Shooting Star* (New York: Simon and Schuster, 1974), 11.

2. Randy Roberts and James S. Olson, *John Wayne: American* (New York: The Free Press, 1995), 23.

3. Jean Ramer, *Duke: The Real Story of John Wayne* (New York: Charter Books, 1973), 9.

4. Billy Liebhert and John Mitchum, *John Wayne—America, Why I Love Her* (New York: Simon and Schuster, 1977), 101.

5. George Carpozi, Jr., *The John Wayne Story* (New York: Dell Publishing, 1979), 19.

6. Michael Munn, *John Wayne: The Man Behind the Myth* (New York: New American Library, 2003), 11.

7. Maurice Zolotow, *Shooting Star* (New York: Simon and Schuster, 1974), 85.

8. Jane Pattie, *John Wayne... There Rode a Legend* (Orange, TX: Western Classics, 2000), 151.

9. Marc Mompoint, *John Wayne: A Photographic Celebration* (New York: Skyhorse Publishing, 2014), 450.

10. Mike Tomkies, *Duke: The Story of John Wayne* (New York: Avon Books, 1971), 124.

11. Maurice Zolotow, *Shooting Star* (New York: Simon and Schuster, 1974), 361.

12. Maurice Zolotow, *Shooting Star* (New York: Simon and Schuster, 1974), 124.

13. Pilar Wayne, *John Wayne—My Life with the Duke* (New York: McGraw-Hill, 1987), 101.

14. Robert E. Relyea, *Not So Quiet on the Set* (Bloomington, IN: iUniverse, 2008), 121.

15. Jean Ramer, *Duke: The Real Story of John Wayne* (New York: Charter Books, 1973), 172.

16. Tim Lilley, *The Trail Beyond, Volume III* (Big Trail Publishing, 2001), 9.

17. Mario DeMarco, *John Wayne—The All-American Hero* (Self published, 1986), 62.

18. Jean Ramer, *Duke: The Real Story of John Wayne* (New York: Charter Books, 1973), 21.

19. Richard Bann and Don Kelsen, *Lone Pine and the Movies: The Lost John Wayne Film* (Newmarket, Ontario: Riverwood Press, 2018), 6.

20. Randy Roberts and James S. Olson, *John Wayne: American* (New York: The Free Press, 1995), 538.

21. Maurice Zolotow, *Shooting Star* (New York: Simon and Schuster, 1974), 115.

22. Marc Eliot, *American Titan: Searching for John Wayne* (New York: HarperCollins, 2014), 138.

23. Randy Roberts and James S. Olson, *John Wayne: American* (New York: The Free Press, 1995), 381.

24. *John Wayne—Duke's Own Story* (Magazine), Reliance Publications, 1979, 65.

25. Pilar Wayne, *Pilar Wayne's Favorite and Fabulous Recipes* (Kansas City, MO: PAX Publishing, 1982), 100.

26. George Bishop, *John Wayne—The Actor/The Man* (Honesdale, PA: Caroline House, 1979), 146.

27. John Wayne Enterprises, *John Wayne: The Legend and the Man* (Brooklyn, NY: Powerhouse Books, 2012), 115.

28. Pilar Wayne, *Pilar Wayne's Favorite and Fabulous Recipes* (Kansas City, MO: PAX Publishing, 1982), 130.

29. Scott Allen Nollen, *Three Bad Men* (Jefferson, NC: McFarland, 2013), 323.

30. Burt Kennedy, *Hollywood Trail Boss* (Brooklyn, NY: Boulevard Books, 1997), 21.

31. Pilar Wayne, *Pilar Wayne's Favorite and Fabulous Recipes* (Kansas City, MO: PAX Publishing, 1982), 192.

32. Maurice Zolotow, *Shooting Star* (New York: Simon and Schuster, 1974), 52.

33. Mike Tomkies, *Duke: The Story of John Wayne* (New York: Avon Books, 1971), 120.

34. Peter Bogdanovich, *Who the Hell's in It* (New York: Knopf, 2004), 276.

35. Mike Tomkies, *Duke: The Story of John Wayne* (New York: Avon Books, 1971), 121.

36. Don Siegel, *A Siegel Film* (London: Faber & Faber, 1993), 4.

37. Don Siegel, *A Siegel Film* (London: Faber & Faber, 1993), 4.

38. Aissa Wayne, *John Wayne, My Father* (London: Robert Hale, 1992), 4.

39. Pilar Wayne, *Pilar Wayne's Favorite and Fabulous Recipes* (Kansas City, MO: PAX Publishing, 1982), 113.

40. "Pilar Wayne: At Home with the Duchess," *Orange Coast Magazine*, September 1984.

41. Tim Lilley, *A Newsletter on the Films of John Wayne* (Big Trail Publishing, 1984–1999).

42. "Pilar Wayne: At Home with the Duchess," *Orange Coast Magazine*, September 1984.

43. *A Tribute to John Wayne* (Magazine), Platinum Publications, 1979.

44. Randy Roberts and James S. Olson, *John Wayne: American* (New York: The Free Press, 1995), 515.

45. John Boswell and Jay David, *Duke: The John Wayne Album* (New York: Ballantine Books, 1979), 122.

46. *A Tribute to John Wayne* (Magazine), Platinum Publications, 1979, 90.

47. Pat Stacy, *Duke: A Love Story* (New York: Simon & Schuster Pocket Books, 1983), 158.

48. Tim Lilley, *Campfire Conversations* (Big Trail Publishing, 1992), 105.

49. Burt Kennedy, *Hollywood Trail Boss* (Brooklyn, NY: Boulevard Books, 1997), 20.

50. Randy Roberts and James S. Olson, *John Wayne: American* (New York: The Free Press, 1995), 634.

51. Pat Stacy, *Duke: A Love Story* (New York: Simon & Schuster Pocket Books, 1983), 246.

Bibliography

Ainsworth, Ed. The Cowboy in Art. New York: Bonanza Books, 1968.

American Film Institute Database: https://catalog.afi.com.

Anderson, Lindsay. About John Ford. London: Plexus Publishing, 1981.

Arness, James. *James Arness, an Autobiography.* Jefferson, NC: McFarland, 2001.

Auction catalogue. *The Personal Property of John Wayne.* Dallas: Heritage Auctions Galleries, 2011.

Aylesworth, Thomas G. *The Best of Warner Bros.* Lincoln, NE: Bison Books, 1986.

Bacall, Lauren. *By Myself and Then Some.* New York: HarperCollins, 2005.

Bann, Richard W. *Lone Pine in the Movies.* Little Rock: Riverwood Press, 2010.

Bann, Richard, and Don Kelsen. *Lone Pine and the Movies: The Lost John Wayne Film.* Little Rock: Riverwood Press, 2018.

Barbour, Alan G. *John Wayne.* New York: Pyramid Publications, 1974.

Behlmer, Rudy. *A Director's Guild of American Oral History: Henry Hathaway.* Lanham, MD: Scarecrow Press, 2001.

Behlmer, Rudy. *Memo from Darryl F. Zanuck.* New York: Grove Press, 1993.

Bible, Karie, Marc Wanamaker and Harry Medved. *Location Filming in Los Angeles (Images of America).* Santa Clarita Valley, CA: Arcadia Publishing, 2010.

Bingen, Steven. *Paramount, City of Dreams.* Lanham, MD: Taylor Trade Publishing, 2017.

Bingen, Steven. *Warner Bros.: Hollywood's Ultimate Backlot.* Lanham, MD: Taylor Trade Publishing, 2014.

Bingen, Steven, Stephen X. Sylvester and Michael Troyan, *M-G-M, Hollywood's Greatest Backlot.* Santa Monica, CA: Santa Monica Press, 2011.

Birdwell, Russell. *A News Release: John Wayne's The Alamo.* New York: Pressbook, 1960.

Bishop, George. *John Wayne—The Actor/The Man.* Ottawa, IL: Caroline House Publishers, 1979.

Blake, Michael F. *Code of Honor.* Lanham, MD: Taylor Trade Publishing, 2003.

Blumenberg, Hans C. *Die Kamera in Augenhöhe—Begegnungen mit Howard Hawks.* Köln, Germany: DuMont Buchverlag, 1979.

Bogdanovich, Peter. *John Ford.* Berkeley: University of California Press, 1978.

Bogdanovich, Peter. *Who the Devil Made It?* New York: Alfred A. Knopf, 1997.

Bogdanovich, Peter. *Who the Hell's in It.* New York: Alfred A. Knopf, 2004.

Boston, John. *Santa Clarita Valley (Images of America).* Santa Clarita Valley, CA: Arcadia Publishing, 2009).

Boswell, John, and David Fisher. *Duke: The John Wayne Album.* New York: Ballantine Books, 1979.

Bosworth, Patricia. *John Wayne: The Legend and the Man.* New York: Powerhouse Books, 2012.

Bosworth, Patricia. *Montgomery Clift—A Biography.* New York: Limelight Editions, 1978.

Breivold, Scott. *Howard Hawks: Interviews.* Jackson: University Press of Mississippi, 2006.

Brownlow, Kevin. *The War, the West and the Wilderness.* London: Secker & Warburg, 1979.

Bryson, John. *The Private World of Katharine Hepburn.* Boston: Little, Brown, 1990.

Cahiers Du Cinéma, *John Ford.* Schaerbeek, Belgium: Editions de l'Etoile, 1990.

Caine, Michael. *Acting in Film.* Montclair, NJ: Applause Theatre & Cinema Books, 1990.

Canutt, Yakima. *Stuntman.* Norman: University of Oklahoma Press, 1979.

Cardiff, Jack. *Magic Hour: A Life in Movies.* London: Faber & Faber Limited, 1997.

Carey, Harry, Jr. *Company of Heroes—My Life as an Actor in the John Ford Stock Company.* Lanham, MD: Scarecrow Press, 1994.

Carpozi, George, *The John Wayne Story.* New York: Dell Publishing, 1979.

Carradine, David. *Endless Highway.* Boston: Journey Editions, 1995.

Cook, Chris. *The Kaua'i Movie Book.* Honolulu: Mutual Publishing, 2013.

Cowie, Peter. *John Ford and the American West.* New York: Harry N. Abrams, 2004.

Crowley, Roger M. *John Wayne—An American Legend.* Vienna, WV: The Old West Shop Publishing, 1999.

D'Arc, James V. *When Hollywood Came to Town: A History of Moviemaking in Utah.* Layton, UT: Gibbs Smith, 2010.

DeMarco, Mario. *John Wayne—The All-American Hero.* Self-Published, 1986.

Dmytryk, Edward. *It's a Hell of a Life but Not a Bad Living.* New York: Time Books, 1978.

Douglas, Kirk. *The Ragman's Son.* New York: Simon & Schuster, 1988.

Ebert, Roger. *Roger Ebert's Book of Film.* New York: W.W. Norton, 1997.

Eckstein, Arthur, and Peter Lehman. *The Searchers—Essays and Reflections on John Ford's Classic Western.* Detroit: Wayne State University Press, 2004.

Eliot, Marc. *American Titan: Searching for John Wayne.* New York: HarperCollins, 2014.

Enss, Chris, and Howard G. Kazanjian. *Cowboy Creatures, and Classics—The Story of Republic Pictures.* Guilford, CT: Lions Press, 2018.

Enss, Chris, and Howard G. Kazanjian. *The Young Duke: The Early Life of John Wayne.* Guilford, CT: Globe Pequot, 2009.

Epstein, Dwayne. *Lee Marvin—Point Blank.* Tucson: Schaffner Press, 2013.

Eyles, Allen. *John Wayne and the Movies.* New York: Grosset & Dunlap, A Filmways Company, 1976.

Eyman, Scott. *Hank & Jim.* New York: Simon & Schuster, 2017.

Eyman, Scott. *John Wayne, The Life and Legend.* New York: Simon & Schuster, 2014.

Fagan, Herb. *Duke, We're Glad We Knew You.* Secaucus, NJ: Carol Publishing, 1997.

Farkis, John. *Alamo Village.* Albany, GA: Bear Manor Media, 2005.

Farkis, John. *Not Thinkin'… Just Rememberin'… The Making of John Wayne's The Alamo.* Albany, GA: Bear Manor Media, 2015.

Finstad, Suzanne. *Natasha*. New York: Harmony Books, 2001.

Fonda, Henry. *Fonda—My Life*. New York: The New American Library, 1981.

Ford, Dan. *Pappy—The Life of John Ford*. Englewood Cliffs, NJ: Prentice Hall, 1979.

Ford, Peter. *Glenn Ford, A Life*. Madison: The University of Wisconsin Press, 2011.

Gallagher, Tag. *John Ford—The Man and His Films*. Berkeley: University of California Press, 1986.

Goldman, Michael. *John Wayne: The Genuine Article*. San Rafael, CA: Insight Editions, 2013.

Goldstein, Norm. *John Wayne—A Tribute*. New York: Holt, Rinehart, and Winston, 1979.

Granger, Stewart. *Sparks Fly Upward*. London: Granada Publishing, 1981.

Hanna, David. *The Life and Times of John Wayne*. London: Littlehampton Book Services, 1979.

Head, Edith, and Paddy Calistro. *Edith Head's Hollywood*. Santa Monica, CA: Angel City Press, 2008.

Helmick, Paul A. *Cut, Print and That's a Wrap*. Jefferson, NC: McFarland, 2001.

Holland, Dave. *On Location in Lone Pine*. Santa Clarita, CA: Holland House, 1990.

Huston, John. *An Open Book*. London: Virgin Books, 1980.

Instinctive Editorial. *John Wayne: From Western Hero to Hollywood Legend*. East Bridgewater, MA: JG Press, 2012.

John Wayne. Sherman Oaks, CA: E-Go Collectors Series No 4, 1976.

John Wayne Enterprises website, www.Johnwayne.com.

The John Wayne Handbook. Brisbane, Australia: Emereo Publishing, 2016.

John Wayne Magazine, *Duke in His Own Words*. New York: Media Lab Books, 2015.

John Wayne Magazine, *Fighting for Freedom*. New York: Media Lab Books, 2016.

John Wayne—Duke's Own Story. New York: Reliance Publications, 1979.

Joyner, C. Courtney. The Westerners. Jefferson, NC: McFarland, 2009.

Kennedy, Burt. *Hollywood Trail Boss*. New York: Boulevard Books, 1997.

Kennedy, George. *Trust Me—A Memoir*. Montclair, NJ: Applause Theatre & Cinema Books, 2011.

Kieskalt, Charles John. *The Official John Wayne Reference Book*. New York: Citadel Press, 1985.

Kitses, Jim, and Gregg Rickman. *The Western Reader*. New York: Limelight Editions, 1998.

Klinck, Richard E. *Land of Room Enough and Time Enough*. Heber City, UT: Parish Publishing, 1995.

Knight, Timothy. *John Wayne in the Movies*. New York: Metro Books, 2009.

Landesman, Fred. *The John Wayne Filmography*. Jefferson, NC: McFarland, 2004.

Liebhert, Billy, and John Mitchum, *John Wayne—America, Why I Love Her*. New York: Simon & Schuster, 1977.

Lilley, Tim. A Newsletter on the Films of John Wayne. Akron, OH: Big Trail Publishing, 1984–1999.

Lilley, Tim. Campfire Conversations. Akron, OH: Big Trail Publishing, 1992.

Lilley, Tim. *Campfire Embers*, Akron, OH: Big Trail Publishing, 1997.

Lilley, Tim. *Campfire's Glow*. Akron, OH: Big Trail Publishing, 1995.

Lilley, Tim. *Campfires Rekindled*. Akron, OH: Big Trail Publishing, 1994.

Lilley, Tim. *The Trail Beyond, Volume II*. Akron, OH: Big Trail Publishing, 2000.

Lilley, Tim. *The Trail Beyond, Volume III*. Akron, OH: Big Trail Publishing, 2001.

Lilley, Tim. *The Trail Beyond, Volume IV*. Akron, OH: Big Trail Publishing, 2002.

Lilley, Tim. *The Trail Beyond, Volume VI*. Akron, OH: Big Trail Publishing, 2004.

Lilley, Tim. *The Trail Beyond, Volume VII*. Akron, OH: Big Trail Publishing, 2005.

Lilley, Tim. *The Trail Beyond, Volume VIII*. Akron, OH: Big Trail Publishing, 2006.

Lilley, Tim. *The Trail Beyond, Volume IX*. Akron, OH: Big Trail Publishing, 2007.

Loren, Sophia. *Yesterday, Today, Tomorrow*. New York: Atria Books, 2014.

Loren, Sophia, and A.E. Hotchner. *Sophia: Living and Loving*. New York: Bantam Books, 1979.

Lovell, Glenn. *Escape Artist—The Life and Films of John Sturges*. Madison: University of Wisconsin Press, 2008.

MacHale, Des. *Picture the Quiet Man*. Belfast: Appletree Press, 2005.

MacHale, Des. *The Complete Guide to the Quiet Man*. Belfast: Appletree Press, 2004.

Mackling, Tony, and Nick Pici. *Voices from the Set*. Lanham, MD: Scarecrow Press, 2000.

Malden, Karl. *When Do I Start?* New York: Limelight Editions, 1997.

Martin, Mel. *The Magnificent Showman*. Albany, GA: Bear Manor Media, 2007.

Marvin, Pamela. *Lee—A Romance*. London: Faber & Faber, 1997.

Mast, Gerald. *Howard Hawks, Storyteller*. Oxford, England: Oxford University Press, 1982.

McBride, Joseph. *Frank Capra: Catastrophe of Success*. New York: Simon & Schuster, 1992.

McBride, Joseph. *Hawks on Hawks*. Berkeley: University of California Press, 1982.

McBride, Joseph. *Searching for John Ford*. New York: St. Martin's Press, 2001.

McBride, Joseph. *The American Film Institute: Film Makers on Film Making*. Los Angeles: J.P. Tarcher, 1983.

McBride, Joseph, and Michael Wilmington. John Ford. New York: Da Capo Press, 1975.

McGivern, Carolyn. *John Wayne: A Giant Shadow*. Bracknell, England: Sammon Publishing, 2000.

McNee, Gerry. *In the Footsteps of the Quiet Man*. Edinburgh: Mainstream Publishing, 1990.

Medved, Harry and Michael. *The Golden Turkey Awards*. New York: Perigee Books, 1980.

Meyer, William R. *The Making of the Great Westerns*. New York: Arlington House Publisher, 1979.

Minshall, Bert. *On Board with the Duke*. Washington, D.C.: Seven Locks Press, 1992.

Mitchum, John. *Them Ornery Mitchum Boys*. Pacifica, CA: Creatures at Large Press, 1989.

Mompoint, Marc. *John Wayne: A Photographic Celebration*. New York: Skyhorse Publishing, 2014.

Moon, Samuel. *Tall Sheep*. Norman: University of Oklahoma Press, 1992.

Mosley, Leonard. *Zanuck: The Rise and Fall of Hollywood's Last Tycoon*. New York: McGraw-Hill, 1984.

Munn, Michael. *John Wayne: The Man Behind the Myth*. New York: New American Library, 2003.

Murray, John A. *Cinema Southwest*. Moab, UT: Canyonlands, 2011.

Needham, Hal. *Stuntman! My Car-Crashing, Plane-Jumping, Bone-Breaking, Death-Defying Hollywood Life*. New York: Hachette, 2011.

Nollen, Scott Allen. *Three Bad Men*. Jefferson, NC: McFarland, 2013.

O'Hara, Maureen. *Tis Herself*. New York: Simon & Schuster, 2004.

Old Tucson Remembers John Wayne. Old Tucson, AZ: Old Tucson Studios documentary, 2007.

Ostema, Gregory James. *The Story of Harry & Mike Goulding*. Monument Valley, UT: Gouldings Monument Valley Trading Post Museum, 2017.

Pattie, Jane. *John Wayne: A Western Celebration*. Orange, TX: Wilma Russell's Western Classics, 2007.

Pattie, Jane. *John Wayne… There Rode a Legend*. Orange, TX: Western Classics, 2000.

Peary, Gerald. *John Ford: Interviews*. Jackson: University Press of Mississippi, 2001.

Ramer, Jean. *Duke: The Real Story of John Wayne*. New York: Award Books, 1973).

Rampell, Ed, and Luis I. Reyes. *The Hawai'i Movie and Television Book*. Honolulu: Mutual Publishing, 2013.

Reed, William. *Olaf Wieghorst*. Flagstaff, AZ: Northland Press, 1969.

Relyea, Robert E. *Not So Quiet on the Set*. Bloomington, IN: iUniverse, 2008.

Riva, Maria. *Marlene Dietrich by Her Daughter*. New York: Random House, 1992.

Roberson, Chuck. *The Fall Guy: 30 Years as the Duke's Double*. North Vancouver, Canada: Hancock House, 1980.

Roberts, Randy, and David Welky. *John Wayne Treasures*. New York: Metro Books, 2012.

Roberts, Randy, and James S. Olson. *John Wayne: American*. New York: The Free Press, 1995.

Robinson, Tony. *No Cunning Plan*. London: Pan Books, 2016.

Rubin, Steven J. *Combat Films: American Realism*. Jefferson, NC: McFarland, 2011.

Sabini, Lou. *Behind the Scenes of They Were Expendable*. Jefferson, NC: McFarland, 2015.

Schessler, Ken. *This is Hollywood*. Redlands, CA: Ken Schessler Publishing, 1978.

Schickel, Richard. *The Men Who Made the Movies*. Chicago: Ivan. R. Dee, 1975.

Schoenberger, Nancy. *Wayne and Ford*. New York: Anchor Books, 2017.

Server, Lee. *Robert Mitchum—Baby, I Don't Care*. New York: St. Martin's Press, 2001.

Shavelson, Melville. *How to Make a Jewish Movie*. Englewood Cliffs, NJ: Prentice Hall, 1971.

Shaw, Sam. *John Wayne in the Camera Eye*. London: The Hamlyn Publishing Group, 1980.

Shepherd, Donald, Robert Slatzer and Dave Grayson. *Duke: The Life and Times of John Wayne*. London: Sphere Books, 1985.

Sherman, Robert G. *Quiet on the Set!* Chatsworth, CA: Sherway Publishing, 1984.

Sherman, Sam. *Lone Pine in the Movies*. Lone Pine, CA: Museum of Lone Pine Film History, 2007.

Siegel, Don. *A Siegel Film*. London: Faber & Faber, 1993.

Sinclair, Andrew. *John Ford—A Biography*. New York: Dial Press, 1979.

Smith, Milburn. *John Wayne*. London: Hamlyn/Lorelei Publishing, 1979.

Stacy, Pat. *Duke: A Love Story*. New York: Simon & Schuster, 1983.

Stanton, Bette L. *Where God Put the West*. London: Four Corner Books, 1994.

Stevens, George, Jr. *Conversations with the Great Moviemakers of Hollywood's Golden Age*. New York: New Liberty Productions, 2006.

Stier, Kenny. *The First Fifty Years of Sound Western Movie Locations*. Rialto, CA: Corriganville Press, 2006.

Studlar, Gaylyn, and Matthew Bernstein. *John Ford Made Westerns*. Bloomington: Indiana University Press, 2001.

Suid, Lawrence H. *Guts & Glory*. Lexington: The University Press of Kentucky, 2002.

Temple, Shirley. *Child Star*. Norwalk, CT: The Easton Press, 1988.

Thomas, Tony. *The West That Never Was*. New York: Carol Communications, 1989.

Tiomkin, Dimitri. *Please Don't Hate Me*. Garden City, NY: Doubleday, 1959.

Tomkies, Mike. *Duke: The Story of John Wayne*. Chicago: Regnery Publishing, 1971.

Tosches, Nick. *Dino,* New York: Dell Publishing, 1992.

A Tribute to John Wayne. Roxboro, Canada: Platinum Publications, 1979.

Wallis, Hal B. *Starmaker*. London: Macmillan, 1980.

Walsh, Raoul. *Each Man in His Time*. New York: Farrar, Straus and Giroux, 1974.

Warren, Doug. *The Hollywood Reporter Movieland Guide*. Hollywood, CA: The Hollywood Reporter Incorporated, 1978.

Wayne, Aissa, and Steve Delsohn, *John Wayne: My Father*. London: Robert Hale, 1991.

Wayne, Pilar. *Pilar Wayne's Favorite and Fabulous Recipes*. Costa Mesa, CA: PAX Publishing, 1982.

Wayne, Pilar, and Alex Thorleifson. *John Wayne—My Life with the Duke*. New York: McGraw-Hill, 1987.

Wellman, William A. *A Short Time for Insanity*. New York: Hawthorn Books, 1974.

Wills, Garry. *John Wayne's America*. New York: Simon & Schuster, 1997.

Zolotow, Maurice. *Shooting Star*. New York: Simon & Schuster, 1974.

Index